Property of ↑

Please return when
finished !

Cat Hine

Home Phone: 505-823-1947
(1947)

FALL
FROM
GLORY

The Men Who Sank
the U.S. Navy

GREGORY L. VISTICA

A TOUCHSTONE BOOK
Published by Simon & Schuster

TOUCHSTONE
Rockefeller Center
1230 Avenue of the Americas
New York, NY 10020

First Touchstone Edition 1997
TOUCHSTONE and colophon are registered trademarks
of Simon & Schuster Inc.

Designed by Irving Perkins Associates

Manufactured in the United States of America

1   3   5   7   9   10   8   6   4   2

Library of Congress Cataloging-in-Publication Data
Vistica, Gregory L.
Fall from glory : the men who sank the U.S. Navy / Gregory L. Vistica.
p.   cm.
Includes index.
1. United States.   Navy—Women.
2. United States.   Navy—Officers—Attitudes.
3. United States.   Marine Corps—Officers—Attitudes.
4. Sex discrimination against women—United States.
5. United States.   Navy Dept.—Management.   6. Lehman, John F.
7. Tailhook Scandal, 1991–1993.   I. Title.
VB324.W65V57   1995
359'.00973'09048—dc20   95-39920
                                                          CIP
ISBN 0-684-81150-2
0-684-83226-7 (Pbk)

AUTHOR'S NOTE

"Books," a good friend and author told me at the inception of this project, "are never finished; they are only abandoned." I stubbornly fought that warning, trying until the very end to do one last interview, to add one last detail, and to tinker one final time. But after nearly two years of research and writing the time had come to surrender my manuscript. Fortunately for me, it was to the fine people at Simon & Schuster.

In particular, I must single out my editor Frederic W. Hills, whom I admire and respect for his patience, judgment, and dedication. Although this book initially was to be based on my journalism coverage of the Navy's Tailhook scandal, Mr. Hills had the conceptual talents to see a broader, more historical work. And he was there every step of the way offering critical advice and help. While Mr. Hills brought depth and great themes to the project, Burton Beals massaged the text with exceptional creativity and professionalism. And Hilary Black provided valuable support and encouragement throughout.

This book would never have come about had it not been for my agent, Knox Burger. There are few words that can truly describe the gratitude I feel for him. He understood the purpose of this book from the beginning and offerd his own brand of wisdom when I needed it most.

And I am indebted to the hundreds of Navy and Marine Corps officers, from the rank of ensign and lieutenant to admiral and general, who consented to interviews. In many instances these individuals risked their careers by providing key details, calendars, memorandums, or sensitive documents to me. I must also thank five former Navy secretaries and four former chiefs of naval operations who agreed to be interviewed and thus helped me to put events in perspective. And I must acknowledge the many civilian Pentagon officials who took the time to answer many difficult questions.

The bulk of these interviews were on the record and are footnoted. Scenes in which dialogue is used are based on interviews with the principal participants or on memorandums. The words "believed" or "thought," used in connection with someone's narrative, are based either on that person's account of the events or on a second source who had a direct conversation with that person. To the best of my ability, I tried to guard against selective recall or faulty memories by interviewing multiple individuals involved in a particular meeting or event.

In addition, a sizable portion of the book's narrative is based on classified and sensitive government documents. Although John Dalton, the current Secretary of the Navy, refused to be interviewed for this book (as did Admiral Jeremy Boorda, the chief of naval operations), Mr. Dalton played an instrumental part in freeing up important naval records. Early on I learned that the Naval Historical Center in Washington, D.C., was holding twenty-two boxes of former Navy Secretary John Lehman's personal files. The Historical Center at first denied that the material existed, then refused to release it. Mr. Dalton approved my Freedom of Information Request, which could have easily been denied.

The Central Intelligence Agency and the Defense Intelligence Agency were very forthcoming in providing classified documents requested under the Freedom of Information Act. In particular, I thank John Pereira at CIA and Bill Smith at DIA for their help. Also Doris Lama, the Navy's privacy act coordinator, went out of her way to identify what documents might be available. John Taylor at the National Archives helped speed up some of my requests for obscure records. And the researchers at the Reagan Library in California were especially generous of their time.

For their skills in finding the odd article or fact, I must thank Laura Miller and Ann McGill, who helped research this book. I am also grateful to many of my fellow journalists and to naval historians such as John Hattendorf at the Naval War College, David Allen Rosenberg at Temple University, Giles Smith at Rand, and individuals at the Center for Naval Analyses, all of whom provided documents or advice. Ed Offley at the *Seattle Post Intelligencer* gave me invaluable material concerning the Navy's aviation program, as did Jim Stevenson, who also read portions of the text for accuracy.

Careful readings of the manuscript were also done by several senior naval intelligence officers who must remain anonymous. And Professor Marshall Windmiller, a former teacher at San Francisco State University who became my friend, applied his intellectual rigor and broad grasp of international security issues and intelligence matters to the text. Matt Miller, an old Asia hand and colleague, provided critical input on the chapter about the Philippines. And I must thank my editor at *Newsweek,* Evan Thomas, for reading the text while on vacation and making important suggestions that improved the narrative.

Although the Navy officially did not condone the writing of this book, its public affairs officers, including Rear Admiral Kendell Pease, were always courteous and efficient in answering my many requests, even when the information was not in the Navy's best interest. They are to be commended for serving their Navy and their nation. And while this book is often critical of the Navy and its leaders, I hold in high regard the many fine men and women who serve in the fleet in order to protect this nation and uphold the Constitution so books like this can be published. They are to be saluted.

The writing and researching of this book has been a consuming effort. I could not have done it without the support of my wife, Joan, and my daughters, Rachel and Hannah. They gave up precious time so I could complete the manuscript. When times got rough, they dug down that much deeper to encourage me. Indeed, my entire family cheered me on, from my father to my ninety-year-old grandmother, who has pledged to read the entire book.

And, perhaps most important, my deepest thanks go to the ladies at W.O.W., who prayed weekly for my spiritual well-being, and for me to finish this project.

Gregory L. Vistica
Washington, D.C.

for Joan, Rachel, Hannah, and Grace,
who sacrificed their time but not their love

PREFACE

JUST BEFORE 2:00 P.M. on May 16, 1996, the nation's chief of naval operations, Admiral Jeremy "Mike" Boorda, walked into his garden at the Washington Navy Yard, placed the metal barrel of a .38-caliber pistol to his chest, and pulled the trigger. From the house, one of Boorda's aides saw the admiral collapse, and sprinted to the scene. There, he found Boorda lying on his back and gravely wounded. Blood soaked his white Navy blouse and the pistol lay by his feet. Minutes later, Boorda was rushed to Washington's General Hospital, where efforts to save his life failed. At 2:30 that afternoon, the Navy's top admiral was pronounced dead.

In the days following the suicide many asked: "What killed Mike Boorda?" There may never be a definitive answer to that question. The written notes that Boorda left behind, one for his beloved troops and one for his wife and family, were incomplete in offering a clear insight into his emotional state. It is possible, however, to empathize with the professional and personal feelings, thoughts, and attitudes that Boorda was struggling with. While this book does not delve into the state of Boorda's mind, it does take the reader into the arcane world of the Navy in which Boorda spent all of his adult life. It is a world in which Boorda thrived. A world of intrigue, political gamesmanship, and hidden agendas, one of competition among honorable and not so honorable men who plot craftily to reach the highest levels of power in the republic's oldest fighting force. It is a world where the good of the Navy often comes at the expense of honor and the truth. This is a peculiar and secretive side of the Navy, one that is carefully guarded and, by and large, off limits to the American public. Few outsiders really understand it. Not surprisingly, those running the Navy wish to keep it this way.

The story of that world, as told in this book, is one the Navy would like its troops not to read. When the hardback edition of this book was released in February 1996, the Navy went to considerable lengths to ignore it and avoid commenting on its findings. The Navy's largest exchanges, where thousands of sailors, officers, and Navy wives and dependents shop, refused to carry it. At the U.S. Naval Academy in Annapolis, Maryland, it was purged from the bookstore shelves. At the Pentagon, the brass subtly dropped hints that it would not be good for one's career to be seen reading this book. Regardless of the Navy's campaign of censorship, it has become something of an underground bible. Officers reading the book joke that they hide it in a brown paper bag. The stigma began to lift, however, after *Proceedings,* the prestigious magazine published by the U.S. Naval Institute, selected *Fall from Glory* as one of the notable naval books of the year.

One very important person, President Bill Clinton, did get a copy. Just after the book was published, James Carville brought the book to the White House as a gift for his former boss. Carville, who served in the Marine Corps, wanted the commander in chief to see just how cockeyed the Navy's world could be. Clinton had little understanding of the Navy and, though he was President, he lacked the wherewithal to truly control the brass. He is not the first President to find the Navy and its admirals a handful. Perhaps Franklin Roosevelt knew why. "The admirals are something to cope with— and I should know," FDR said. "To change anything in the Na-a-vy is like punching a feather bed. You punch it with your right, and you punch it with your left until you are finally exhausted, and then you find the damn bed just as it was before you started punching."

Certainly the Navy is more modern and powerful today, with no equal on the high seas. Bill Clinton properly called it the "finest in the world," when he eulogized Boorda. But the old traditions that Roosevelt spoke of live on. Boorda certainly understood that. And though he tried to solve the Navy's problems, in the end he failed to cope with the overwhelming pressures they placed on him. For those seeking the truth of why Boorda killed himself, Clinton had a warning. Admiral Boorda, he said, had a "deep sense of honor, which no person should ever question." The President is right in this regard. It is not Boorda who should be placed under scrutiny. Rather, the American public should take a close look at the institution that Boorda lived and died for. Only then may they fully understand the rough-and-tumble world that Boorda tried to master, a world that quite possibly killed him.

GLV
1997

≡ PROLOGUE ≡

W HEN THE DOOR to the suite at the Las Vegas Hilton opened, a prominent member of President Ronald Reagan's administration and a naked woman were clearly visible. He was lying on his back, stretched out in front of a throng of naval officers. There were probably one hundred men watching him, laughing with him and feeling there was no better place to be right then than in this room, near this man, captivated by his powerful presence.

He was the consummate Washington insider, a man who moved with shakers like Henry Kissinger and some of the most influential members of Congress from both parties on Capitol Hill. He was a young Republican conservative with impressive academic credentials, including a graduate degree from Cambridge University and a doctorate from the University of Pennsylvania. Before his fortieth birthday he had twice come before the Senate as the President's nominee for vital national security posts. He could charm the most curmudgeonly of congressmen. And outsmart the most cunning adversary. In his desk drawer he kept a chart of admirals and generals and moved them around like pawns on a chess board. "Loyalty is agreeing with me," he said so often that even such senior officers found themselves repeating it. Those who agreed found their careers buoyed by unbounded support and opportunity. Those who hesitated were stricken from his board.

He had a genius for bureaucratic infighting. He would get an angle on an adversary and strike before the victim knew what hit him. Invariably, the press rallied around him and his colorful political battles and made him a regular on the television news networks and prestigious talk shows. And his name often appeared in the news columns of *The New York Times* and other major newspapers and magazines.

The man on the floor in front of the crowd was about five feet nine inches tall and well built, athletic-looking, and fit. He was not handsome but had rugged features and diffident eyes that people found appealing and disarming. His appearance made him seem genteel, which didn't fit well with his reputation as a man who was capable of shaking your hand one day and becoming your enemy the next. His love of politics was matched by only one other addiction, flying in Navy bombers.

Several of the Navy and Marine officers now crammed into the room at the Las Vegas Hilton knew him personally and worshiped him. Many knew he was married and had three children. Almost everyone knew who he was, which made the show that much more fascinating. They were standing almost shoulder to shoulder, their necks twisting this way or that so they could take in everything. They were here for the 1986 Tailhook Association convention, the most important gathering for Navy and Marine aviators, which had been held every year in Las Vegas since the early 1960s.

Most of the officers in the room, including the man on his back, were hard-drinking renegades. Some had been partying for days, others for many hours. The carpet was spongy and damp from alcohol spilled on it by drunken military men. The room itself reeked with the odor of booze and sweat. But nobody seemed to care much. All eyes were on the man and the naked woman standing over him, wagging her bare rump in a teasing motion. The men in the room went into a throaty uproar at the sight, and their cheers and laughs got louder as the show went on.

Navy Commander Pete Stoll, an aviator who had flown some 450 combat missions in Vietnam, was standing along a wall, taking in the scene. Next to him were two younger Air Force officers from nearby Nellis Air Force Base who had come into town for the party.

"Do you know who your secretary of the Air Force is?" Stoll asked the men.

"No," the Air Force flyers said, somewhat embarrassed. "We don't know his name."

"Well, do you know who the secretary of the Navy is?" Stoll asked.

Again the Air Force men replied, "No."

Stoll curled his lips into a smile and pointed to the man whose face was beneath the woman's bare rump. "Well, there's our secretary of the Navy, right there."

It was John Francis Lehman Jr.[1] Five years earlier, President Ronald Reagan had picked him to rebuild the nation's Navy, which was all but bankrupt, its spirit broken over the last ten years by budget cuts and political leaders who saw limited uses for sea power. Reagan had dangled a dream before Lehman's eyes. He had made a bigger and bolder Navy one of the cornerstones of his defense buildup and then turned to Lehman to run it. The President and his advisers believed in Lehman, believed that under his leadership the Navy would once again rise to glory. The price tag would be high, nearly one trillion dollars. And there would be skeptics. But if anyone could pull off the gargantuan task, it was the feisty, fearless Lehman, a man with a vision for what the Navy should be.

It would have been hard for him to fail in the atmosphere of renewed nationalism that had swept Reagan to power. The country's march toward militarism was so overwhelming that its foes in the establishment press and on Capitol Hill were helpless to stop it. And at the front of the parade was John Lehman, rallying the troops and the nation with catchy slogans, running a one-man publicity campaign for more battleships, more planes and aircraft carriers "to kick their ass," as he was fond of saying about the Soviets.

For the Navy, the Reagan years were a remarkable time, a time when the decisions and leadership style of Lehman and a powerful cadre of admirals set the course the Navy would follow into the 1990s. These were years marked by great achievements, which began with the shooting down of two Libyan warplanes over the Gulf of Sidra. Navy fighter pilots captured the Palestinian terrorists who had hijacked the luxury liner *Achille Lauro*. Navy warships secretly sailed into Soviet waters, oftentimes undetected, to taunt the Russians with practice air raids near their coastline. And it was handsome naval aviators and daring submariners who thrilled millions of Americans in the movies *Top Gun* and *The Hunt for Red October*. Reagan was so enamored of the Navy that he turned to it for photo-ops when he needed a lift in the polls.

But with the successes came some of the worst disasters in military history: the Navy's most sophisticated cruiser, *Vincennes,* accidentally shot down an Iranian airliner; a mysterious explosion aboard the battleship *Iowa* killed forty-seven people; four Navy men led by John Walker sold some of America's most valuable secrets to the Soviets; and the U.S. Naval Academy at Annapolis, where the ideals of the Navy's future leaders are molded, was plagued by cheating scandals, sexual abuse of women, and cover-ups by the brass. And then there was Tailhook—which one noted sociologist[2] said was the worst catastrophe for the Navy since Pearl Harbor.

What was it that caused these and other grave miscalculations, some of which led to many unnecessary deaths and the loss of millions of dollars because of equipment failures? Was it John Lehman's fault? Or was it the failure of the most secretive and certainly the most guarded of all naval institutions—the fraternity of admirals? Why did these men, as did Lehman, deliberately and persistently mislead Congress and the American people about the nature of the Soviet threat? Why were they so quick to "circle the wagons" to cover up their mistakes and to protect their privileges from public scrutiny? Were they so drunk with power that they put their allegiance to the Navy first and the nation second?

Lehman and the admirals often engaged in open warfare as he sought to bring the Navy under civilian control. But he, too, skillfully pursued his own personal and political agenda. He made waves—big ones. And when he left

office in 1986, one persistent question trailed in his wake. Had the Navy
built a mighty maritime force that would sail on into the twenty-first century
—or a $1 trillion house of cards? Nobody really knew. Only in the years
after Lehman's departure would the answers finally emerge.

PART I
RISE TO GLORY

CHAPTER 1

ADMIRAL TOM HAYWARD WAS MAD. He sat alone in his fourth-floor Pentagon office, watching in dismay as the world he loved so dearly began to crumble. Never before had he been so humiliated. He was a quiet and diplomatic man who did not like confrontation or being challenged. The four white stars on his gold shoulder boards came from winning over the officers corps by compromise, not by bullying them. After thirty years of working within the system, his leadership approach had paid off and he had become the Navy's top admiral, the chief of naval operations. His years of military service had been difficult but rewarding. His office was adorned with the reminders of the values he had fought for. There were the pictures and memorabilia of his lengthy career. And from his desk he could see the Washington Monument, which rose like a spear into the hazy winter sky. He loved his Navy. And for the last two years he had been the undisputed king of its vast and wealthy empire.

Until now.

In Hayward's spacious office a private hallway led to a large suite where another man now sat, the new secretary of the Navy. Earlier in the day, a stunned Hayward had watched John Lehman fire the first shot in a battle that would leave the two men barely talking to each other. To Hayward, the message was clear. Lehman was trying to wrestle control of the Navy away from the king and his admirals.

Fewer than a handful of people at the upper reaches of the Navy knew in February 1981 that Hayward detested Lehman and that Lehman was not particularly fond of Hayward. Their relationship was doomed from the outset. If they had anything in common, it was that they were complete opposites. Lehman had the reputation of someone special, not for the rank and privilege he enjoyed as a youth, but because he was a whiz kid with street smarts. He grew up in a solid Philadelphia family whose ancestors had emigrated with William Penn to the City of Brotherly Love. His aunt was Princess Grace of Monaco. His great-uncle was George Kelly, the Pulitzer Prize–winning playwright. The family was Catholic, and as a boy young John had a defiant personality that dismayed the sisters at St. Luke's Elementary School, who called him a "bold and brazen article." At St. Joseph's, a Jesuit college in Philadelphia, Lehman quickly became known as a right-wing zealot and a fierce debater. He joined William Buckley's Young Americans for Freedom, the vanguard of ultraconservative youth groups.[1] And he authored a conservative political column for *The Hawk,* the college paper, in which he wrote that "Castro should have been squashed when he admitted that he was, and had always been, a communist." [2]

In 1964, his senior year, Lehman pulled a minor coup on campus by organizing the Philadelphia Collegiate Disarmament Conference, which brought some of the biggest names in arms control to the school. Most, if not all, of the participants—men like Herman Kahn, Robert Strasuz-Hupe, Admiral Arleigh Burke, and Richard Allen—were staunch conservatives and fanatically anticommunist.[3]

Four years later Richard Allen became a foreign policy adviser to Richard Nixon. And after Nixon's first presidential election, Allen arranged for Lehman to join Henry Kissinger's National Security Council staff as a legislative aide. Although he was only twenty-six and just out of graduate school, he found himself on the fringes of great power in his first government job. It was an amazing maneuver for one so young and inexperienced in the ways of Washington.

Kissinger respected his young aide's intellect and aggressiveness. But he was infuriated by his political freelancing and the alliance he struck with archrival Senator Henry "Scoop" Jackson and his chief aide, Richard Perle, known inside the Pentagon by his nom de guerre, Prince of Darkness.[4] Lehman and Perle recruited George Will, then a Senate staffer, to help write the language for a bill that would undermine Kissinger's negotiation strategy on SALT, an arms control treaty with the Soviet Union. It amazed Will that Lehman was taking part in a plot to do in his boss. "John, who was supposed to be representing Henry, sat there and helped write this language quite clearly critical of Kissinger's results," Will said. Then, when they finished, Lehman picked up the telephone and rang Kissinger to plead innocence to the whole affair. "Henry," he said, "they're just out of control up here!" [5]

Years later President Ronald Reagan chose Richard Allen as his national security adviser. Once again, Allen wanted his protégé with him and, with the help of Texas senator John Tower, who called Lehman a combination of James Madison, Horatio Hornblower, and Francis of Assisi, put pressure on Reagan to appoint Lehman secretary of the Navy.[6]

Although he was a senior official in the Reagan administration, Lehman liked to raise hell, flirt with women, and drink into the late hours of the night. At the Oceana Naval Air Station in Virginia, where he did his reserve duty as a bombardier-navigator on an A-6 Intruder, he had his own parking space. But it was not in front of the commanding officer's building. It was at the Officers Club, where he drank with his aviator friends and female groupies. When several base commanders canceled happy hour at their clubs, Lehman went through the roof.[7] He sent a flash message, a communication used for priority dispatches, to overturn the order.

His party antics appealed to the naval aviators, who viewed Lehman as one of them, an Airedale. One of his first orders was to reverse the ban on leather flight jackets. At a Tailhook convention he raised a brown shoe, once a part of the aviation uniform before being discontinued. This, Lehman said to the jubilant crowd, will now be the official shoe of the naval aviation community. Ship drivers had black shoes, submariners had tennis shoes. The Airedales now had back their own identity, brown shoes and leather flight jackets.

Tom Hayward, on the other hand, was reserved, almost aristocratic: Naval Academy graduate, test pilot, commanding officer of the aircraft carrier *America* during the Vietnam War, fleet commander. He had punched all the right tickets in his march through the ranks to become CNO in 1978. His priority was to increase readiness, not bring back shoes or jackets. He had already taken giant steps to move the Navy out of the malaise brought on by Vietnam and the neglect of the Ford and Carter administrations. He inherited a Navy that was short on everything. If the United States had gotten into a shooting match with Iran in 1980 over the hostage crisis, American aircraft carriers would have played a major role. But each ship had only enough ordnance for a three-day fight.[8] Throughout the Navy, ammunition, spare parts, and other supplies were already at their bare minimums. The supply of defensive missiles and torpedoes wasn't much better. Navy bins contained only a week's reserve. Hayward had spearheaded the drive to rebuild the Navy, and now he faced another problem. A thirty-eight-year-old reservist who passed himself off as a naval aviator was planning a hostile takeover of his Navy.

Lehman had been in office only weeks when he asked Hayward to assemble the admirals in the Washington area for the customary first meeting with the secretary. He wanted to give the troops a message. Accordingly, some fifty flag officers had filed into room 4E445, a long, skinny conference room on the fourth floor in the Pentagon. Because of the room's odd shape, there was no stage or dais. Hayward and Lehman would have to sit on two chairs at one end of the room. As they waited for the two men to appear, the admirals began to talk among themselves about Lehman, guessing what type of leader he would ultimately be. Moments after he walked into the room with Hayward, they started to wonder, "What is this thing that is taking over?"[9]

Always a polite and formal man, Hayward greeted his admirals, then began to talk about Lehman. "I really don't need to introduce to you the secretary of the Navy," he said, "but I want to tell you that he's here, he's in charge, and he's . . ." But before Hayward could finish, Lehman leapt out of his chair and firmly placed his hand on the CNO's shoulder, guiding the admiral down onto his seat. Dumbstruck, Hayward said nothing as he sat down.

After an awkward pause, Lehman turned to the long rows of admirals who were sitting straight up on their chairs, their eyes wide open. "I don't need any introduction," he said. "I'm the secretary of the Navy. This is what we are going to do. We have got to have a vision for the Navy, we have got to have a plan, we have got to have a clear sense of our purpose." Our purpose, he said, would be to sail into Soviet waters and attack the Russian motherland, "because that's what the Navy is all about." [10]

Vice Admiral Stasser Holcomb, one of Hayward's top officers, was floored. In all his years in the Navy he had never seen or heard of the CNO being summarily dismissed like that in public. He walked out of the meeting shaking his head. "It was a jarring experience," he later said. "We had an activist secretary of the Navy who was rude, who was arrogant. That put the flag community on notice that this guy was going to be involved in a lot of stuff." [11]

Lehman saw the meeting in a much different light. Ever conscious of his youth, he did not want to humiliate Hayward the veteran officer. He knew he had to throw down the gauntlet to force a showdown with the admirals. But he did not intend to use Hayward as a prop to prove that he was in charge. "Being aware as I was that I was only thirty-eight years old, I was not about to make a caricature of myself as a little Napoleon," he later recalled. "I tried to be as modest as I could be, at least in what I was saying." [12]

What he wanted to do was push the admirals to choose which leader they would follow. They could pick Hayward, whom Lehman saw as an old gentleman with ideas anchored in the past. Or they could run with him, the young politician with grand plans for the Navy's future. Lehman would leave no doubt which choice would be better for their careers.

The new secretary began to hatch his plan immediately. He summoned Commander Ted Gordon to his tradition-laden fourth-floor office known as the Secretariat. Gordon was a lawyer, and Lehman wanted to find out how much power and legal authority he really had. When Gordon walked in, Lehman rattled off a burst of instructions. "Ted, go through the laws, find out every place that talks about the secretary of the Navy, and list them for me. Tell me what is my responsibility, what are my powers.'' [13]

Lehman had been given the same briefing book that all secretaries got when they entered office, listing their powers and responsibilities. It was the traditional litany of secretarial rights. But he was certain there were others that dated perhaps to the Continental Navy of the American Revolution. He wanted all the authority he could get. He would operate within the law at first, thus the reason for asking a lawyer to review the naval statutes. But he would bend and circumvent the rules if need be and use every political means available to become the undisputed chief executive of the entire Navy. He planned to take from Hayward as much power and responsibility as the law would allow and place it under his own control.

Get back to me as soon as you can, Lehman instructed Gordon. I want to do this right.

Gordon did not think much about the request. And, at the time, Lehman didn't say what he really had in mind. He wanted to be very clear before he had any showdowns of what his powers were.[14]

Lehman was not about to underestimate Hayward and his fellow admirals, whom he knew could be ruthless, cunning, even insubordinate to the civilian leaders of the Navy. A favorite story told on the Pentagon's fourth floor by blue-suited naval officers about who was really in power, the secretary or the CNO, illustrated the contempt the officers corps sometimes had. In the story, the secretary is driving down the road in a large truck, sitting high in the cab, thrilled with the majesty and power of being in charge of such a vast institution as the Navy. But after driving a few miles with a difficult turn here and a close call there, he realizes that his steering wheel is not connected to anything. The admirals riding inside the truck are steering it and deciding which way it will go.

Lehman had his eye on an enormous prize. The naval empire stretched from the Pacific Fleet's headquarters in the hills above Pearl Harbor to the slums surrounding the Philippine shipyards in Subic Bay to the rich and ancient port cities of Europe. More than a million sailors, Marines and civilian workers, stationed at hundreds of naval installations throughout the world reported to the Department of the Navy.

The CNO and his admirals commanded a world-girding blue-water fleet with no equal on the high seas, one designed to show the flag or wreak havoc on any nation at a moment's notice. In a crisis, Henry Kissinger and the national security advisers who succeeded him would always ask the Navy, ''Where are the carriers?'' While the Air Force and the Army were enjoying a nine-to-five lifestyle back home in the United States, the Navy had been dispatched nearly 280 times since World War II to international hot spots.[15] An $18 billion aircraft carrier battle group was the most visible sign of American resolve. Of the Navy's twelve groups, five or more were steaming at one time in the Atlantic and Mediterranean, the Pacific and the Indian Ocean, or some other world waterway.

But it was not just manpower and ships that made the Navy powerful. It was an enormous corporation with assets equal to those of the first seven *Fortune* 500 corporations.[16] Its money flow in the early 1980s was triple that of AT&T and nearly double that of Texaco, IBM, and Ford. During the Reagan buildup and beyond, the Navy did billions of dollars' worth of business each year with shipbuilders, high-tech electronic companies, aircraft manufacturers, architects, plumbers, and just about every other American profession and tradecraft. The ripple of dollars from the construction of just one $4 billion aircraft carrier often flowed to all fifty states.[17] Every billion dollars in the shipbuilding account created twenty-seven thousand direct jobs for a year and fifteen thousand indirect jobs. The equipment that went into a new carrier, from heavy pumps and valves to everyday essentials such as beds and toilets, was built in every state of the Union.

Then there were the immense economic benefits that came after an aircraft carrier was completed. One flattop alone meant more than $120 million yearly for the economy of the city where the ship was stationed.[18] And the amount of money increased dramatically if the Navy also decided to station the carrier's battle group, which could mean ten additional ships, in the same city. The leaders of the Navy decided which naval or Marine installation should be closed or where a new base should be built, a power that gave them considerable influence over the fate of a metropolitan area dependent on the defense budget. The economic clout that the Navy brought to bear was as efficient as a weapon, a weapon that was used as political leverage over a congressional delegation to force it to toe the Navy line.

Lehman knew that the chief of naval operations and his minions would go to great lengths to keep their empire intact. He shared Harry Truman's attitude that the admirals were Fancy Dans, members of a hidebound institution who thought they were beyond reproach. And in their defiance of anyone who opposed their authority or their policies, they could be ruthless. Those who spoke out against the system often found themselves in psychiatric wards or the victims of a trumped-up psychological evaluation.[19] The admirals could remove an officer at any time for any reason simply by saying that they had lost faith in his leadership ability. And the flag officers had their own police agency, the Naval Investigative Service (NIS), which Lehman called the Admiral's Gestapo.[20] And as an added bit of protection for the senior officers, the director's rank at the NIS was elevated from captain to rear admiral. Ironically, it was Lehman himself who had penciled the order on the back of an envelope.[21]

The admirals saw themselves as the guardians of a service in which six presidents had served, a pride that fueled not only their élan but also, as Lehman knew, their elitist attitude. Winning their allegiance would perhaps be his greatest challenge as secretary. In fact, the fraternity of admirals, about 250 strong, was one of the most exclusive and selective in the world. Those vying for entry faced a promotion process that the most cynical officers described as a variant of the time when political bosses in Boston and New York cut deals in smoke-filled back rooms. Even officers with unyielding faith in the Navy's ability to do things the right way have compared the process to the way the Catholic Church picks the pope.

Once a year the admirals convened a promotion board and met in secret to select about twenty-five men they wanted to join their fraternity.[22] The Marine Corps also met and picked less than a handful of generals. Federal law prohibited even the slightest hint of cronyism throughout the entire process. But in the months, weeks, and days prior to the board meeting, the men who ran the sea service and the Marines took part in a great trading game of flesh and careers. Unofficial lists of favorites were compiled. Names were swapped. IOUs were called due. Promises were made. And in the end they congregated in a back room to do their bidding like horse traders. They came with their candidates and cajoled, bantered, and politicked to get them into the fraternity.[23]

Once in, the admirals, especially the most senior ones, have lived off the U.S. Treasury as if they were tycoons with personal airplanes, cars and drivers, and some of the best golf courses in the nation.[24] They have lived in beautiful homes, frequently in private retreats called "Admirals Row," an area traditionally off limits to the public, although the homes with their carefully manicured grounds are paid for by taxpayers. In one year alone, the price tag for cutting the lawns at the homes of the admirals in Hawaii was $61,000.[25] The Navy had been told to do away with that costly service by Defense Secretary Caspar Weinberger's office but never did so.

Their offices were lavishly furnished, with expensive cut glass, rich wood, and plush furniture. One officer who reached flag rank had a $50,000 couch built. Another Navy office bought a forty-eight-piece service of china and crystal wineglasses, even though the purchase of such items had been discouraged by Weinberger's office.[26] The admirals also kept a flock of servants, maids, cooks, and gardeners, all paid for by tax dollars. Then there were the large expense accounts to entertain guests. For the top admirals, each was given several hundred thousand dollars a year to spend as he saw fit.

The Navy has spent millions of dollars each year to furnish the admirals with their perks. One of the most extravagant costs, which the brass goes to great lengths to camouflage, is for their personal airplanes. Hundreds of thousands of dollars are spent on fuel, maintenance, and the salaries of their support crews.[27] The top admirals and generals fly in their jets all over the country, all over the world, all the time. One admiral flew his mistress with him during business trips throughout Europe. Another used his personal plane to bring a stash of alcohol into the country, setting off a tiff with U.S. Customs. Often they descend on the same meeting or conference within minutes of each other.[28] And Admiral Robert Kelly, who retired as the commander of the Pacific Fleet in 1994, was notorious for flying his personal P-3 around Asia to, among other things, play golf. After arriving in Thailand, he commandeered the U.S. embassy aircraft in Bangkok on February 29, 1994, to fly to Utapao for a round of golf.[29] According to members of his staff, he was such a fanatical golfer that he fired a young sailor who misplaced his golf clubs (a charge Kelly denies). Kelly had asked him to polish his clubs for a tournament, and when the sailor finished he mistakenly put the admiral's clubs in Mrs. Kelly's car. When Kelly got to the golf course, he opened up his trunk and flew into a rage because his clubs were not there.[30]

The admirals have zealously guarded their perks and protected each other from those prying into the fraternity. When one admiral faced inquiries about his misbehavior from the press in the late 1970s, the Navy's chief of information, Rear Admiral Bruce Newell, reminded the public affairs officer handling the story about one simple fact. ''Just remember, he's a member of the fraternity.'' The implication, said the public affairs officer, was ''Don't sell this guy down the river if you know what is good for you, because he's special.'' Newell later left the service, became a Protestant minister, and was defrocked after being exposed for having sexual liaisons with his parishioners.[31]

When an admiral had to be fired, the Navy routinely did it in secret, letting the officer quietly leave the service, with full benefits and a retirement pension, regardless of the nature of his misconduct. But in several cases the Navy swept the abuses under the rug, allowing the admiral to be promoted. Some of their violations bordered on the humorous and petty.[32] Overweight admirals ordered their records changed to show that they met the Navy's weight requirements. Others had their medical records altered. One admiral wanted five bicycles at a reduced price from a Navy exchange, just because he was an admiral. Other abuses were more serious, such as adultery, misuse of government funds, and alleged manslaughter.

Although the admirals and the CNO are subservient to the secretary of the Navy, Lehman could not have fired Hayward outright if he had wished to do so. Lehman was well aware that since World War II, CNOs have, in most cases, deftly brushed aside their civilian bosses as transient political appointees who must be listened to but not seriously followed.[33] And in seeking to wrest control of the Navy from Hayward, Lehman was taking on a formidable opponent. Hayward had already positioned himself well in his first two years in office. He had immense powers and had carved out a wide base of support on Capitol Hill, in the Pentagon, and, more important, in the White House under Jimmy Carter. He was responsible for buying almost everything the Navy needed, preparing budgets, recruitment, and picking officers for top spots, selections that were usually rubber-stamped by the secretary. That gave Hayward a direct line to the war-fighting commanders in chief of the various fleets and forces around the world, a power that the secretary did not formally have. And as a member of the Joint Chiefs of Staff, Hayward also had considerable influence in shaping the orders that the secretary of defense issued, recommending which battle groups should go where in a show of force or an actual conflict. As a member of the Joint Chiefs, he reported to the defense secretary, not the Navy secretary, which gave him additional clout over Lehman.

It was not always such a tilted arrangement in favor of the admirals. The CNO's job was created by a rider to the naval appropriations bill passed by Congress on March 3, 1915. The secretary's position dated much farther back to the creation of the Navy Department in 1798, when Benjamin Stoddart became its first civilian leader.

The CNO's powers were limited at first, with the top admirals having to defer all major decisions to the secretary. But gradually, over the course of many years, the office grew in power, responsibility, and size. In 1916 Congress mandated that all orders issued by the chief of naval operations should be considered as if they came from the secretary of the Navy. In 1924 Congress gave the CNO control over all ship repairs, personnel, and supplies. But it was during World War II that the office came into its own. Admiral Ernest J. King consolidated his control over the Navy, a grip that the chief of naval operations has never really relinquished since.[34]

Admiral Chester Nimitz, who won fame for the Navy during World War II as a daring commander, also won respect inside the Navy when he was the chief of naval operations from 1945 to 1947. Ironically, it was the success of Nimitz and the Navy during the world war that almost did in the sea service. Instead of reaping public acclaim for their victory in the Pacific, Nimitz and his admirals found themselves fighting for the Navy's very existence. Their main adversary was not only the Air Force, which ended the war with Japan by dropping the atom bomb, but the drive to consolidate all of the services under one mantle: the Department of Defense.

The Navy battled the idea with a vengeance, fearing it would lose its autonomy and end up playing second fiddle to the Air Force and Army. Opponents were already pointing out that the Navy no longer had a mission. It had destroyed the Japanese navy, and there were no other fleets to challenge American sea power. Why pay for an expensive aircraft carrier when one Air Force bomber could drop an atomic bomb anywhere in the world?

Nimitz won a short-lived battle, maintaining a certain amount of independence for the Navy in the new Defense Department. And realizing that the Air Force had a monopoly on the atom bomb, Nimitz pushed for the Navy's own nuclear weapons and propulsion systems. In 1947 he approved early plans for nuclear-propelled submarines equipped with atomic missiles. But the battle with the Air Force was far from over. Nimitz's successor, Admiral Louis E. Denfield, found in 1947 an even more determined Air Force. Denfield fought the Air Force's lock on strategic nuclear bombing with plans for a supercarrier that could handle Navy planes capable of carrying an atom bomb.

The interservice rivalry came to a head when Defense Secretary Louis A. Johnson ordered the new carrier *United States* broken up on the building ways at Newport News. This and Johnson's move to shift Navy funds to the Air Force for its B-36 bomber set off the "revolt of the admirals," a political rebellion that would be repeated in similar fashion some thirty years later over the Tailhook affair. When it was all over, Johnson fired Denfield, two other admirals, and a Navy captain.

Lehman was determined to rule with the same kind of iron fist. He had no intention of letting the admirals turn him into a ceremonial figurehead like past secretaries. Lehman had studied how each of his predecessors handled the admirals. Traditionally, Navy secretaries were happy to christen ships and watch parades, allowing the CNO and his admirals to run the Navy. There have been exceptions. During the Truman era, James Forrestal was extremely powerful, as was Paul Nitze in the Johnson administration. And Graham Claytor was far from a pushover but had his hands tied by President Jimmy Carter. Now that he was Navy secretary, Lehman wanted to reinstate the concept that it was the political leaders, not the sovereigns with stars on their shoulders, who should reign supreme over the Navy.

In his run for the job, Lehman had used his past political connections to Nixon and Kissinger to carefully garner the support of four former CNOs, a move that would place Hayward in the awkward position of taking sides against his predecessors. One of the former chiefs, Arleigh Burke, had been retired for twenty years but was still revered by the officer corps. The three other former chiefs were equally impressive men in naval history: Thomas Moorer, the hard-nosed Southerner; Elmo Zumwalt, one of the youngest CNOs ever; and James Holloway. It was Holloway who had called Lehman after Reagan's 1980 election victory to inquire: "Who do I have to speak with to help get you appointed secretary of the Navy?" [35]

Hayward had his own impressive track record. When he took over from Holloway, the Navy had not been able to maintain top-notch sailors and officers. The majority of sailors were high school dropouts. Many had criminal records. And drug and alcohol abuse was rampant throughout the fleet. Forty-seven percent of the Navy's personnel was smoking marijuana. Another 11 percent was snorting cocaine. Manpower shortages became so acute that several ships could not leave port. Hayward did not believe the statistics at first. He relented only when the numbers were confirmed by his personal aide and then took steps to clean up the mess. In a videotape that every sailor and officer in the fleet was ordered to view, Hayward gave a stern warning: "We're out to help you or hammer you; take your choice."

Lehman paid little attention to Hayward's accomplishments and believed that he and his tong of officers had an unhealthy lock on the leadership positions. He had to impose his own authority over the Navy if he was to help fulfill Ronald Reagan's pledge to rebuild American military might. But Tom Hayward was not about to let his ship be sunk from beneath him—at least not without firing a few shots. And if there was one thing Hayward could be proud of, it was the win-loss record he had accumulated in the many political battles he had fought as an admiral, especially his cunning victory in Hawaii. He had won that fight against all odds. And he would do his damnedest to win this one, too.

CHAPTER 2

IT WAS THE COLDEST it had been in Hawaii for twenty years when Tom Hayward awoke on the morning of January 19, 1978. That week the local newspapers had told residents of Honolulu to bundle up during the night but said the island's pleasant tropical weather and gentle trade winds would soon return. As Hayward climbed out of bed, the rising sun was already streaming through the windows in his spacious home on Admirals Row in the Makalapa section of Honolulu. The weather forecasters were right. Today would be quite warm, warm enough for Hayward to wear traditional Navy whites.

Hayward showered, then dressed in a freshly pressed uniform. Rows of multicolored awards were pinned just below his gold aviator wings—one of his proudest accomplishments. Even at his age, he was still an impressive sight in a naval uniform. Daily rounds of tennis kept him in shape, and at fifty-three he could still play three sets in the sticky Pacific heat.

Downstairs in the kitchen, Navy stewards had laid out his breakfast and morning newspapers as they did every day. Next to the local paper was the *Early Bird,* one of Washington's most widely read and influential daily newspapers. It rolled off an Air Force press by six A.M. in Washington and was rushed to the White House, the Central Intelligence Agency, the State Department, and the top Pentagon brass. Inside its magazine-size pages was the hottest news compiled from the major dailies and networks about the goings-on in the world of national defense and foreign affairs. The sixteen-page newspaper was faxed each day to Pearl Harbor, then hand-delivered to Hayward's home, where the stewards had it ready for their boss, the commander in chief of the Pacific Fleet.

Hayward had been in the job for a little more than a year now. He figured that the prestigious post, which is responsible for providing U.S. naval forces to cover 103 million square miles of ocean, from Cape Horn to the Bering Sea to the Persian Gulf, would be his last major assignment. After that he was planning to retire in Hawaii. He did not expect that one day soon he would become the chief of naval operations.

There was a short blurb in the *Honolulu Advertiser* that day about a visit to Hawaii by Senator Sam Nunn, the Georgia Democrat who was working his way up the political seniority chain to become the chairman of the Armed Services Committee. It wasn't unusual for an important senator to be in Hawaii during the winter, so the paper gave Nunn's visit short shrift. Three paragraphs reported that he could not get a feel for naval operations in the Pacific by staying in Washington. That was all. There was no mention of Nunn's meeting with Hayward scheduled for that morning.

Hayward had to laugh at the press. He had no sympathy for pesky reporters missing what would have been a big, page one story for the Washington and New York newspapers. But there was no way that even the best investigative sleuths could have uncovered the controversial war plans he had been working on since his arrival in Hawaii. Few people outside the most upper reaches of the Navy even knew. Nunn had no idea what he was about to hear. Not even President Carter was aware of the top secret plan Hayward had codenamed Sea Strike.

Sam Nunn was not a run-of-the-mill politician, and he had more than a passing interest in the military. In fact, he was a keen observer of the armed forces. Nunn, who wore heavy-rimmed glasses with thick lenses and had the appearance of a harmless bookworm, had made a name for himself by taking on the U.S. military and debunking its preparations for World War III in Europe. Now he was turning his attention to Asia and the Pacific and to the U.S. military commanders responsible for fighting a war in the largest ocean in the world. He had asked President Carter's secretary of the Navy, Graham Claytor, for permission to interview Hayward and any other senior officer who might wish to provide briefings. Hayward had little choice but to agree. That wasn't a problem. His dilemma was whether to unveil Sea Strike. It would be a major risk to divulge prematurely a plan that opposed the White House's existing naval policy in the region. A few months earlier Hayward had watched President Carter first humiliate, then fire Army general Jack Singlaub for publicly criticizing his plans to withdraw U.S. troops from South Korea. Singlaub had committed political suicide by speaking out publicly. Hayward was not about to make such a foolish mistake. He was more politically astute than that.

But it was no secret that Hayward disliked Carter's defense priorities. Under Carter, the Navy was obligated to carry out the Swing Strategy, a plan for shifting most naval warships from the Pacific to the Atlantic to carry out sea control and transport missions in a European war with the Soviet Union. The Swing Strategy, which was instituted after World War II and became national defense policy after Korea, had always been something of a nightmare for Hayward. Now, as the head of the Pacific Fleet, he was in a real quandary if he was tasked to carry it out. He believed the Soviets would have a field day with the Navy absent from the Pacific. He saw the Swing

Strategy as an insane, mindless plan that lacked strategic foresight and could do irreparable harm to the nation's security. But the Swing Strategy was so ingrained in the national military psyche that the Pacific Fleet's entire stock of ammunition was stored east of the Mississippi, making it closer to Europe.[1]

Something had to be done, but it had to be done carefully and with the utmost secrecy. So in July 1977 Hayward began working on Sea Strike, a complete revamping of the Navy's strategy for the Pacific and therefore the entire national defense plan. To help him, Hayward wanted someone he could trust implicitly, an officer who understood the role that military power played in international relations and one who would look out for the best interests of the Navy when Sea Strike came under scrutiny. But the man he put in charge would also have to have an unorthodox view of the Navy—he had to be willing to take on the institutional biases that supported the Swing Strategy.

After mulling over various candidates with his top aide, Captain Bill Cockell, Hayward chose Captain Jim Patton, a diesel submarine officer with a Ph.D. from the Fletcher School of Law and Diplomacy, who had just finished up a stint on Secretary of State Henry Kissinger's staff. Cockell made the call on behalf of Hayward, asking if Patton would be interested in joining the staff. Sure, Patton said. And when he arrived in Pearl Harbor, Hayward wasted no time in laying out the dismal conditions. "Jim, the defense plan is a shambles," he said. "I want you here to inspire me as to how to fix it. Calculate what it would take to make an offensive thrust against the Russians. We're not talking about trench warfare kinds of things. Use the mobility inherent in naval forces to hit and run, strike and withdraw into the breaches of the Pacific."[2]

It was a challenge that might prove impossible to meet. Having worked at the highest levels of government, Patton knew that every president and every secretary of defense for the last thirty years had endorsed the Swing Strategy. The allies depended on it so much that missions were assigned to the Pacific Fleet's carriers, Marine forces, and other assets once they arrived in Europe. Patton looked at Hayward, took a breath, and responded matter-of-factly. "Aye, aye, Admiral. I'd be happy to try to do that."

Hayward sat back on his admiral's chair, momentarily quiet. "We should keep our powder dry," he said, until we know what we're talking about. "It doesn't do any good to rant and rave about an inept plan unless you have a much more intelligent plan immediately available."

Patton agreed, then left to find his office.

The first chore would be to recruit the best minds in the Navy. Hawaii had been a dumping ground for naval officers who were past their prime. Patton needed new blood. He would have to go outside the Pacific to find the talent that Hayward's new thinking required. Several people were pulled from the Center for Naval Analyses, a civilian Navy think tank, and from intellectual postings in the defense community around Washington. Within weeks Patton had assembled a brain trust that he called the Wise Man's Team. And for the next five months the team worked almost seven days a week, often from morning to midnight, drafting a new battle plan that went counter to almost everything the U.S. military had been training for since World War II.

Patton placed a large map on the wall of his office and used a big, black chalk board to sketch out the team's thoughts about how to fight the Russians. "We would sit there and look at this map, and we would argue," he later recalled, sometimes so loudly that "the Marine shore patrol came up one night to see what the hell was going on." [3]

By January 1978 the Wise Man's Team had come up with Sea Strike. Hayward endorsed it, but while doing so, he brought to the surface what was on everybody's minds. "Suppose we are successful," he said. "Suppose we succeed in having the government, the Joint Chiefs of Staff, the national command authority, reverse thirty years of the Swing Strategy and sign up to an offensive fight in the Pacific." Then what? Without saying it directly, Hayward was subtly reminding them that they were on the verge of bucking the establishment. Boat rocking in the Navy often led to ostracism and was something few officers took part in. But everyone was eager to put the new plan to the test. And Hayward decided that Sam Nunn would be the first guinea pig.

After breakfast Hayward headed out the door for the five-minute walk down the hill to the Pacific Fleet headquarters. He was going to let Patton brief Nunn. Better him than anyone else, Hayward figured. But when he saw Patton, he had second thoughts. His chief of war plans was poring over the written text he would use to brief Nunn. "No, no, no," Hayward said, his voice rising with each "no." He told Patton that this was a vital message that needed to be conveyed with confidence, not line by line. You have to inspire Nunn, make him believe in it, he said. "You understand this. You created a lot of this. We have dialogued it for two or three nights a week for months. If you can't stand on your feet and explain it to somebody, then I have the wrong guy."

The room was silent for a long moment as the two men looked at each other. "Aye, aye, admiral," Patton said. The text was out. He would use the plastic view graphs on the overhead projector as a guide and talk from memory.

Nunn arrived a short time later, accompanied by Carter's undersecretary of the Navy, James Woolsey, who would later become, for a brief period, President Bill Clinton's director of central intelligence,[4] and Jeff Record, an intellectual gadfly known for asking questions like "Who needs the Marine Corps?" The entourage, which included various other aides, filed into Hayward's windowless office, which had changed little since World War II, where for a few moments they exchanged pleasantries. Then they walked across the passageway to a small conference room that Admiral Chester Nimitz had used to hash out the battle plans for the war in the Pacific against the Japanese.

Patton, a man of history, could not help but feel the presence of Nimitz, an admiral known for his innovative ideas. Oddly enough, Sea Strike would use some of the same principles employed by Nimitz as he island hopped across the Pacific. The enemy might have changed, but the foundations of offensive naval warfare in the 1970s were not much different from those of the 1940s or, for that matter, from naval strategist Alfred Mahan's views at the turn of the century.

Inside the conference room, the men shuffled around a small table, picking their seats. Hayward sat near the large wall map posted six months earlier by Patton, since he planned to use it as a geographical guide to Soviet naval power in the Pacific. Sitting around him were some of the best minds in the defense world. All had one goal: to ensure victory should war with the Soviet Union erupt. Whether or not Sea Strike would become the accepted doctrine to help guarantee that victory depended in large measure on the outcome of the day's briefing.

Hayward began in a slow, smooth, almost soothing voice that filled the room. He was a man of stature who exuded confidence when he spoke. Without getting out of his chair, he pointed to the map, identifying key areas where the Soviet navy had strongholds in Asia and the Pacific. There was the former U.S. naval base in Vietnam, Cam Ranh Bay, a modern installation America had used during the war that was now occupied by the Soviets. The Red Banner Pacific Fleet could stop at strategically important bases in India and Yemen, at the mouth of the Red Sea. In the Middle East, the Soviets could use the ports of its allies Syria and Egypt.

It was obvious, Hayward said, that the Soviet navy had become a blue-water fleet for the first time in its history. And he believed the Soviets had the capability to deprive the United States of the free use of the seas, thereby creating political, economic, and military disaster. Soviet attack submarines trailed U.S. Navy battle groups and submarines the minute the carriers and their escort ships left San Diego, Alameda, or Puget Sound. The Soviets had developed two new submarines, the *Yankee* and *Victor* classes, which were quieter and faster. And they were developing long-range reconnaissance and bomber aircraft and cruise missiles that could be fired from the air and below and above the sea.

After watching Soviet naval exercises, U.S. naval intelligence officers and the experts in OP-96, the plans, programs, and evaluation division, concluded that the Russians were practicing surge attacks against a U.S. carrier battle group. Wherever the Soviets had bases, the American analysts predicted, they could launch more than one hundred cruise missiles at an American naval armada in less than sixty minutes.[5] Hayward believed that the Navy was incapable of stopping the flurry of missiles that would skim above the ocean waves at hundreds of miles per hour. And when he finished talking, the general impression was that any Soviet move into the Pacific was a challenge to American dominance in the region that dated back to Teddy Roosevelt.

Then Patton took the floor, placed a plastic view graph on the screen, and confidently began his presentation. "If the Russians see us leave the Pacific," he pointed out, "see that we're not going to do anything, they must feel very confident that with very minor forces they can not only hold the Pacific and bedevil the hell out of us in Hawaii and California and Alaska, they can take the Aleutians." He told Nunn that they could then shift from the Far East more than two hundred thousand troops, twenty-four divisions in all, to Europe in under thirty days—faster than the United States could bring forces across the Atlantic to counter them. At that, Patton looked at Nunn to see if the point had sunk in.[6]

If Nunn was surprised by the revelation, he wasn't showing it. He sat like a schoolboy on a wooden bench, looking at Patton with a blank stare. But it was definitely a new wrinkle that Nunn and his staff were unaware of. Naval intelligence, the CIA, and the Defense Intelligence Agency had never considered that the Soviets could shift such a large number of fresh forces so quickly to the front. Nobody had paid any attention to the two hundred thousand–plus troops in the Soviet Far East—except the Wise Man's Team. It was an intelligence failure of the first order. "Imagine that," Patton said years later. "Here are all these NATO planners, all these years counting how many Russians they are going to see on day number one, and [they] never considered for a moment that the Russians could almost double their forces in a very short period of time."

The Wise Man's Team had figured it out after Hayward arranged for a U.S. spy satellite to take pictures of the Great Siberian Railroad, which stretched across six thousand miles and nine time zones. The railroad was considered such a low priority in the intelligence community that there were few if any recent photographs of it. As a result, the CIA and the other intelligence agencies still believed the Great Siberian was a single-track railway with no supporting infrastructure that could be used only for transporting small numbers of people into and out of Siberia.

When the classified photographs came back, Patton's team was astounded. The Soviets had very quietly built up a vital troop lift system, in which large numbers of military units could be shifted over internal transportation lines. It was clear from the photographs that not one, but two sets of rails were running from European Russia to Siberia. After examining a series of daily photographs from outer space, Patton's team was able to calculate that one hundred trains traveled each way each day. What also stood out in the pictures were the major repair centers positioned about every one hundred miles along the route. Near each center the Russians had piled wood ties, steel rails, and enough heavy equipment to clear both tracks of their trains.

Patton told Nunn that the Soviets had refurbished the tracks to carry the Far East divisions to Europe, and there was nothing the United States could do to stop them. "We had no long-range bombers that could get to the railway system," he said. "We had no saboteurs. The only way we could affect that railway system was at a time of thermonuclear exchange, and then it and all the rest was irrelevant." But Sea Strike, he told Nunn, provided another way to stop the movement. If the U.S. Navy stayed in the Pacific and forced the Soviets into a fight there, the divisions would stay put.

The idea was to lure Soviet ships into open waters, away from their land-based bombers, and attack and destroy them in a series of naval battles using the offensive punch of several aircraft carriers. The Wise Man's Team had devised new communications techniques and tactics that would allow several carrier battle groups to operate together as one fighting force. It was a concept new to the Navy, whose admirals were trained to operate only a single battle group. "We could bring massive forces together in such a way as to really damage the hell out of their major facilities," Patton said in describing how an attack would be staged. "We're not going to stay out there and tough it out with them for a week and let them figure out smarter ways to fight. We would be there for maybe twenty-four hours or thirty-six hours, then we would disappear again," he said, which would allow the American forces to regroup and repeat Sea Strike.

Nunn finally had a question. What about the carriers? he asked. What were their capabilities? How many would you lose?

That was *the* question, and one Hayward had struggled with since the Wise Man's Team first began toying with the idea of an offensive strategy. At one point early on, he had posed the underlying dilemma to Patton. "Well, Jim, I see what you want to do. What am I going to lose? If I lose too much, then clearly I can't go back again."

"How much are you willing to tolerate?" Patton asked.

"I'll take whatever Nimitz took in the first year of World War Two."

In the four major engagements of 1942, Nimitz had put everything down on the line in every battle. "Risked it all," Patton told Hayward, "and never lost less than 25 percent of the ships engaged and 50 percent of the airplanes."

In other words, Hayward could expect to lose one aircraft carrier, with five thousand men and some eighty aircraft, as well as an assortment of destroyers and cruisers, in each Sea Strike battle. He didn't like it, but war was not a pretty business. If that was all the Navy would lose, he told Patton, then go ahead and write it into the plan.

When Patton answered Nunn's question, the senator didn't even flinch. Nunn was smart enough to know that war was messy and American fighting men would die, despite the best-laid plans.

The briefing lasted two hours. Nunn was "impressed," he told Hayward, that this kind of work had been going on out here. Then he left.

It was hard for the Wise Man's Team to get a good sense of how Nunn really felt. They wanted to believe that he was sincere in his remarks about Sea Strike. But with the exception of his question about the carriers, he had never tipped his hand one way or the other.

Patton also had a nagging thought that Nunn was more impressed with Hayward than he was with the briefing. And if that was true, then he had to be looking at Hayward now as a potential candidate to replace Admiral Jim Holloway as the next chief of naval operations. Although Nunn could not tell the Navy whom to choose, as a key senator on the Armed Services Committee, which confirmed nominees for top military spots, he had a lot of clout, enough to derail any potential candidate.

Hayward himself was unsure about Nunn's reactions to the brief. After lunch the two men spent several hours together on a tour of Pearl Harbor. Hayward later said good-bye and dropped the senator off at his quarters, then went home. If he had lingering doubts about Nunn's impression of him or the Sea Strike brief, they ended a short while later with a knock on his front door. There stood Sam Nunn, holding a tennis racket. "I notice you have some tennis courts out here," he said. "How would you like a game?"[7]

After a couple of sets, the two men retreated to Hayward's home on Admirals Row. They ate dinner in the backyard and talked for hours about Sea Strike, politics, life in Washington, and where the Navy should be heading. Each man enjoyed the other's intellect and broad knowledge about national security issues. It was the beginning of a long friendship.

• • •

Hayward's gamble to brief Nunn paid off. In the following months he received a steady stream of top-level visitors from Washington. They came for the Sea Strike briefing and to get a look at the admiral who had the courage, or was just crazy enough, to defy the Pentagon's conventional war-fighting wisdom. Harold Brown, Carter's secretary of defense, was the first to call on Hayward about six weeks after Nunn's visit. Like Nunn, Brown came away impressed with Hayward.

The next official to be ushered into Chester Nimitz's old conference room was Secretary of the Navy Graham Claytor, a railroad executive before joining the Carter administration. Claytor picked out a chair in the middle row and made himself comfortable as Patton began rattling off his by now very polished presentation. A few minutes later Claytor fell asleep. Still, it turned out that he was persuaded enough by what he did hear to set in motion a study to find creative new ways to fight the Russians in the North Atlantic.[8] And when he returned to Washington he ordered a civilian academic named Francis "Bing" West from the Naval War College in Newport, Rhode Island, to go see Patton.

West promptly made the ten-hour trip to Pearl Harbor, scooped up all of the Wise Man Team's data—which until then had been kept under lock and key because Hayward refused to let anyone copy the material—and headed back to the East Coast.

If Jim Patton thought he could stop the Soviet juggernaut from six thousand miles away in Siberia, Bing West believed he could kill it in the North Atlantic, thus preventing hundreds of thousands of troops stationed on the Kola Peninsula above the Arctic Circle from descending south to a war in Europe. West's study, which would eventually become known as Sea Plan 2000, called for the American carrier fleet to attack the vital military bases on the Kola and industrial centers deep in the interior. That, West believed, would force the Russians to stay put.

The idea to attack the Kola had been part of NATO's strike plans for war with the Soviet Union since the 1950s, with England and Norway providing the naval power, not the United States. But well before the 1980s, the plan was discarded as unrealistic. The geography alone made the mission exceedingly dangerous. From mid-November to mid-January the sun does not rise above the horizon on the Kola. And rough seas toss a ninety-thousand-ton carrier around like a cork, making aircraft launches and landings dangerous and at times impossible. If a pilot could not land and had to eject, or was shot down, he would die within minutes in the frigid water, even with his cold-water survival gear on.

If there was one plus to the wintry weather, it was for the Russians. A vagrant current of the Gulf Stream leaves seventy miles of waterways along the Kola free of ice, allowing ships to transit out to the Atlantic. Three major ports lie along the Kola coast, and approximately forty military airfields dot the peninsula. Two army motorized divisions and a marine regiment were located on the Kola. And approximately 135 of the Soviet navy's 278 general-purpose submarines, 46 of its 85 "boomers"—ballistic missile subs—75 surface ships, and 224 helicopters, jets, and long-range aircraft were attached to the Northern Fleet.[9] Their location in the Arctic waters at the top of the world offered a natural protection from their enemies, who would have to sail through hundreds of miles of Soviet waterways and homeland defenses before they would be in position to attack.

To reach the Kola, the American Navy would have to breach the G.I.U.K. Gap, a maritime Maginot Line that stretched from Greenland to Iceland to the United Kingdom and marked the entry to the Soviet Union's backyard waters. Once through the gap, the fleet would then round the North Cape at the northernmost tip of Norway and enter the Barents Sea. It was a perilous journey that would leave the American Navy open to attack. Nevertheless, West's plan claimed a casualty rate that was almost identical to that of Sea Strike—the loss of one aircraft carrier for each engagement.[10] That, Patton grumbled when he saw the plan, was impossible, given the differences in geography, weather, and the simple fact that the Russians had three to four times the number of resources on the Kola. For years they had salted the coastal waterways above the G.I.U.K. Gap leading to Murmansk with hard-to-find diesel submarines and minefields. And they had land-based bombers that could pound away at the U.S. fleet for two days before American carriers could get close enough to launch their own bombers.[11] The prevailing view among Patton and his colleagues was that there would be little left of the fleet.

This is intellectual dishonesty, Patton said to himself when he was briefed months later on Bing West's study. "How the hell can they anticipate such low attrition in that environment?" he groused to Hayward. And oh, by the way, what the hell are they doing it for, anyway? he wanted to say.

Hayward didn't like it any more than Patton. But he knew his hands were tied. "Jim," he replied, "we're not going to fight this."

On Capitol Hill, the chairman of the Senate Armed Services Committee called his fellow senators to order. Sam Nunn had been back from Hawaii for about five months and was now strongly backing Hayward for the job of chief of naval operations. In a few minutes the committee would begin passing judgment on the various officers who had been nominated by the President for key leadership posts in the military—including Tom Hayward. When his name came up, the committee approved his appointment as the top uniformed officer in the Navy.

CHAPTER 3

As millions of americans prepared to cast their votes for Ronald Reagan in the 1980 presidential election, a supersecret U.S. intelligence satellite was whirling over the Black Sea, taking photographs of the Soviet Union's vital shipbuilding center known as Nikolayev. The KH-11 Keyhole satellite, a billion-dollar technological marvel, passed over Nikolayev about every three days, adjusting its photographic lenses and mirrors to capture objects as small as a football that lay miles below. The last pass over the giant yard yielded little new intelligence, which surprised few Navy analysts. Shipbuilding was measured over months, even years. Spotting change on a day-to-day basis was an almost impossible feat. And the Soviets were masters at deception. They even gave their skill a name: *maskirovka*.

One of their cleverest tricks was to construct a warship's hull in two pieces, usually in a large warehouse or other covered area to shield it from satellite photography. The shipyard workers would wait until the last welds were in place, then roll the steel hulls out to the dock on rails. Overhead photographs would show an empty dock one day. And three days later the makings of a large cruiser would appear.

As the Keyhole satellite glided through the darkness of outer space, it took less than a second to snap its pictures of Nikolayev while simultaneously beaming them down in digital code to a ground station at Fort Belvoir, Virginia, a windowless, two-story concrete structure. Technicians there converted the images into high-resolution pictures. And with the help of computers, the analysts manipulated the photographs, looking for the slightest changes from prints of earlier shots taken of Nikolayev.[1]

The first noticeable difference was a large mound of steel stockpiled near a long graving dock.[2] The Soviets had used the dock to build the *Kiev*-class warships, small flattops that carried vertical takeoff and landing jets called Yak-38 Forgers, and Hormone helicopters. Besides the steel, there was another oddity the photo interpreters picked out. The Soviets had also enlarged the graving dock. With this new intelligence the analysts reached a safe conclusion: the Soviets were preparing to build one very big ship. Would it be a new class of warship or a giant cargo vessel? Perhaps a big aircraft carrier? At that point no one knew the answer for sure.

The analysts at Fort Belvoir immediately beamed a flash message to officials at the Naval Intelligence Support Center, a bland-looking government building just over the Washington border in Suitland, Maryland, alerting them that something hot had been found. Similar messages went to the CIA, the Defense Intelligence Agency, and whoever was on the photo center's "gimme list," a roster of intelligence agencies that demanded every scrap of information that resulted from overhead surveillance.[3]

Twenty-four hours later, several photographs landed on the desk of Rear Admiral Sumner Shapiro, the director of naval intelligence. Nicknamed "Shap," the short, plump admiral with a deep voice and a shiny pate had spent a lifetime studying the Russian navy. On his way to becoming the Navy's top spymaster, he had pulled duty in the 1960s as the assistant naval attaché in Moscow, where he met Admiral Sergei Gorshkov, a legendary naval officer who ran the Soviet navy for nearly thirty years. "I was not impressed with him socially," Shapiro would later say, "but professionally I was, and I have been watching him very closely for twenty-five years now."[4] Shapiro never wavered in his belief that it would be a fatal mistake for the West to underestimate the crafty old Russian, who at seventy-one was still breathing new life into the Soviet navy. "He has really turned it around," the intelligence chief had once said admiringly to a congressional committee.

Shapiro reviewed the intelligence report that accompanied the satellite photographs, as he always did when new information came in, then bundled up the file and hustled over to see Hayward. The daily 8:30 A.M. intelligence meeting was about to begin. It would be the perfect venue in which to explain what was going on in Nikolayev.

At 7:30 A.M. Tom Hayward returned the salutes of the two Marine sentries guarding the Navy Command Center, as he did every morning when he entered the secure room down the hallway from the CNO's office. Naval officers in the Pentagon referred to the room as the Flag Plot because it was built to resemble an admiral's command center on a warship that carried the same queer name.

Walking into the Flag Plot was like stepping back in time. The large bank of phones and communications gear was, in some cases, twenty-five years old. If Hayward wanted to eavesdrop on his battle fleet commanders deployed at sea, technicians had to painstakingly alter the radio equipment to tap into the proper frequencies. The Flag Plot was manned twenty-four hours a day by officers who kept track of hundreds of Navy messages and telephone calls for the CNO. It was the nerve center of his naval empire.

The most prominent feature in the room was the main tactical display, a large board on which naval officers plotted the whereabouts of the U.S. and Soviet fleets. There was also a secure briefing theater where Hayward held court each morning, starting with a "shape up" brief from his key staff members, usually Holcomb, Cockell, and Patton, who went through the message traffic that had come in overnight. A short summary on the readiness of each deployed battle fleet followed. Then the chiefs of legislative and public affairs reported what was happening on Capitol Hill and in the press.

By 8:30 a gaggle of admirals filed into the theater for the daily intelligence brief. The most interesting topic on today's agenda was the new find in Nikolayev. Hayward understood the value of intelligence and how it could drive the shaping of policy—particularly when it concerned the Soviets. For much of his career he had been preoccupied with the Soviet threat, first as a young aviator, later as a fleet commander, and now as the CNO. Just when he thought the Navy had figured out Soviet intentions, some new bit of intelligence trickled in to change the equation. The photos laid out in front of him were proof of that.

And it just wasn't what he saw in the photographs that troubled him. While the American Navy was building seven new classes of warships, the Soviets had more than a dozen classes under construction. Of particular concern was the battle cruiser *Kirov,* a powerful new warship that the U.S. Navy felt carried a punch similar to its old World War II *Iowa*-class battleships, whose sixteen-inch guns could shoot a shell the weight of a Volkswagen Beetle twenty-three miles.

In the last year the Soviets had also built two new classes of submarines, including one gigantic, twenty-five-thousand-ton "boomer boat" that was going through its sea trials before deploying to the fleet in 1984. At 557 feet long, it carried a new missile armed with a nuclear warhead that U.S. naval intelligence officers claimed could reach the United States from 4,600 miles away. Soviet premier Leonid Brezhnev named this underwater monster *Typhoon.* And just beginning sea trials was the *Alpha,* with a nuclear reactor twice as powerful as earlier models. It was a fast-attack, deep-diving submarine with a new titanium hull that the U.S. Navy said was capable of forty-three knots while submerged.[5] No U.S. submarine could match it, and no aircraft carrier could outrun it. Six of these *Akula*-class submarines were due to enter the Northern Fleet in the early 1980s.

Hayward had always believed the Soviets would build a large blue-water fleet. But he was surprised nonetheless by the speed at which the new ships were now sailing out of the yards. At any given time some thirty boats were under construction in the Soviet empire. In the bigger scheme of things, the Soviet naval buildup made no sense. The Soviet Union was a great land power that controlled much of the Eurasian continent. It had a massive army, which consumed the majority of the Soviet defense budget; the Navy's share was 20 percent.[6] Of all three branches of the military, the Soviet navy fell at the bottom of the pecking order and had the least political backing. Yet Gorshkov was building ships as fast as his production yards would allow. What added to the puzzle was that although the Soviets now had more warships, deployments to distant waters, which were exceedingly rare, had not changed since 1974. The vessels, for the most part, were staying in local waters.

What in the hell are the Russians up to? Hayward wondered out loud. Satellite photos were fine for the bean counters to determine the number of ships, but they couldn't tell him what the Russians were thinking.

He wanted answers.

At the intelligence brief that day, Shapiro offered his opinions. He believed the Soviets were embarking on a new and dangerous phase in the development of the Red navy that sought control of the high seas.[7] Everything Shap knew about Gorshkov told him one thing: the Soviets were building a carrier at Nikolayev. And judging by the new size of the graving dock and the large amount of stockpiled steel, it would be a big one, perhaps equal in tonnage to America's supercarriers.

In the last several years Shapiro's intelligence network had put enough pieces of the puzzle together to make a WAG, better known in the Navy as a wild-ass guess, about Gorshkov's interest in aircraft carriers. The Kremlin's leaders had originally shunned the behemoths. But later intelligence reports began popping up about the Soviets' interest in projecting power abroad with carriers. The Office of Naval Intelligence had also learned in 1977 that the Soviets were building an airplane catapult and arresting gear test facility at the Saki naval air base in the Crimea that was due for completion in 1983. Only big U.S. carriers used catapults. All the telltale signs indicated that one day the Kremlin would build a supercarrier. And that, Shapiro believed, would be a major threat to the United States. On this, he sounded like a broken record. "I've been screaming for twenty-five years, 'The Russians are coming, the Russians are coming,' " he said one time in exasperation to a congressional committee. "The people on this committee have listened to me, but not everybody else in this town."

As Shap spoke about the new carrier—first called *Tbilisi,* then later *Admiral Kuznetsov*—Hayward listened intently. Although the new photographs did not yet show a ship in the water, they went a long way toward confirming the WAG—and Shapiro's worst fears. But when the morning brief ended, Hayward sensed that Shapiro was not getting the whole picture. There was a gaping hole in the U.S. Navy's knowledge about the Soviets' motives and intentions for their fleet. And members of Hayward's staff said Hayward felt that Shapiro and his analysts were not looking in the right places to uncover that vital information.

Naval intelligence had done a fairly good, but overly conservative, analysis of the Soviet navy's capabilities, counting ships, missiles, aircraft, and other assets. Almost every day vast amounts of new intelligence came into the Navy from satellites and agents all over the world who were spying on the Soviet fleet. Little-known covert groups like Task Forces 157 and 168 had gathered over the years a tremendous amount of hard-to-get information. The agents carefully watched Soviet ships in most major seaports in Europe, Asia, and the Middle East, sneaking as close as possible to a vessel, attempting to detect nuclear weapons, take photographs, or log unusual features on the ship.

Back in Washington, every tidbit was funneled into the Navy's intelligence database on the Soviet fleet. The files contained information on the Soviet's sixty-three ballistic subs, an underwater fleet with a combined total of 950 tubes for launching nuclear missiles.[8] The Navy knew in precise detail what types of satellites the Soviets had, how they functioned, how to jam them, and when they were rocketed into space. Miles and miles of microphones strewn across the ocean floor tracked Soviet subs coming and going from their ports in the Far East and the North Atlantic. On any given day, the American Navy was confident that it knew which Soviet subs were at sea and, with almost 100 percent accuracy, believed it could pinpoint their whereabouts.[9]

America's own subs lurked just outside Soviet harbors, tapping underwater telephone lines and snapping photographs of warships. Intelligence-gathering surface ships eavesdropped on secure and unsecured conversations, storing the data for experts at the National Security Agency to decipher. The saying was that the U.S. Navy even knew when the commander of the Red Banner Pacific Fleet was on the toilet. All of this when pieced together played a vital role in assessing Soviet intentions. But it was only one part of the intelligence puzzle. It showed that the Soviets had a lot of ships, with a lot of missiles. But it didn't reveal if, when, and how the Kremlin would use its Navy in a war.

That gnawed at Hayward. He wasn't getting the answers he wanted. As he often did, he turned to Cockell for advice. Cockell understood Hayward's most intimate concerns and ideas and could help him sort things out when the world didn't seem to make sense. A brainy, soft-spoken intellectual from

San Diego, Cockell was one of the best strategists in the Pentagon. He grew up a Navy brat under the tutelage of his admiral father. The elder Cockell was a blimp pilot. His son Bill, a lifetime bachelor married to the Navy, was a ship driver, better known as a surface warfare officer.

The younger Cockell kept a collection of rare books on naval history in a special humidified room. Besides his interest in obscure books, he had a talent that was unique among naval officers. He was fluent in Russian and had a passion for Russian history. For Cockell, reading the latest version of a Soviet military tome was preferable to a night of socializing. If anyone could think like a Russian naval officer, it was Cockell, a man widely respected in the Navy for his brilliance and honesty.

When Hayward became chief of naval operations, Cockell was one of the three advisers he brought with him from Pearl Harbor. And shortly after Cockell arrived in Washington, Hayward asked him to organize the various competing and conflicting strategies, from Sea Strike to Sea Plan 2000, that were emerging within the Navy on how to fight a naval war with the Soviet Union. Cockell spent three months drafting a top secret global war plan called the Naval Forces National Strategy.

The fifteen-page narrative, so highly classified that only a few people could read it, outlined a series of objectives and alternative naval strategies to force the Soviets to fight a war on a multitude of fronts simultaneously.[10] The underlying message in the document stressed taking the fight to the Soviets, instead of guarding the Atlantic and waiting for them to attack. Among the options was striking the Kola, which neither Hayward nor many of his fellow admirals were particularly fond of. Cockell included it anyway, primarily because he felt that if the President asked for such an attack, the Navy had better be prepared to carry it out.

But the Naval Forces National Strategy had its limitations. For one thing, Cockell had prepared it two years before the Keyhole spotted the new carrier at Nikolayev. But its biggest flaw was that Cockell drafted it from an American point of view. Although he believed the Soviet Union planned to use nuclear weapons at sea from day one of a conflict, his study offered limited insight into the values, aims, and objectives of its leaders. The reason was simple. There just wasn't enough intelligence to draw from.

Now, two years later, Hayward was still grumbling about Shapiro and the lack of good intelligence. He knew the Reagan administration would be pressing for the latest assessment of the Soviet fleet, and all he could do was to point to the rapid increase in the number of ships. Was it an early sign that the Soviets were preparing for a naval war? Were they building ships just to keep the communist state's workers employed? What were the Russians up to?

Three weeks after the election, Hayward decided to force the issue. He told Cockell he wanted to see Shapiro again. And when the two men met, the atmosphere in the CNO's office was tense. "You're not giving me the bottom line, Shap," Hayward said with a slight tone of intolerance in his voice. "You've sent all of this intelligence. What does it mean?" [11] Shapiro and one of the Navy's brightest young intelligence analysts, Rich Haver, sat quietly as the CNO rattled off a number of questions that neither man could answer confidently. Haver grew up in the New Jersey suburbs of New York City wanting to be a naval officer. When the Naval Academy turned him down because of vision problems, he went to Johns Hopkins University, where he played lacrosse, baseball, and basketball. In 1968, with the Vietnam War in full swing, he was given a commission and ended up flying missions over the north for two years as an electronics intelligence officer. After the war, Admiral Bobby R. Inman talked him out of leaving the Navy for law school and convinced him to join naval intelligence as a civilian.[12]

I know they are building a *Kirov*-class cruiser and it's 754 feet long and 91 feet wide, and it's got these weapons systems on it, Hayward continued. "But why are they building it? What are they going to do with it? What's the purpose for it? Where does it fit into their strategy? Is this a problem for the Navy, or is this something we should ignore? I want you to put together a group that looks into this question that will not only come down here and tell me how many ships they are building and how many submarines," Hayward said, "but why!" There has to be another way of sizing up the Soviet fleet than just counting tonnage, bullets, and butter. Think like the Russians, Hayward and Cockell instructed. Only then can we understand what questions to ask. Then we can reach proper answers and develop a new war-fighting plan to deal with the threat accordingly.

After Hayward dismissed the group he called Cockell into his office. Write a tasking order, he said, directing Shapiro to set up a team of analysts to study the problem. Haver was put in charge. Commanders Tom Brooks and Mike Cramer, who would later become Bill Clinton's chief of naval intelligence, joined the team. Shapiro, soon to retire, would oversee the effort. Cramer had just returned from Moscow, where he had served as naval attaché. Haver picked him for his analytical abilities and because of his firsthand experience with the Russians. The third key person on the team was Commander John "Mike" McConnell, who, ten years later, would be seen on CNN around the world during the Persian Gulf War, conducting daily briefings as an admiral for the Pentagon press corps. Later still he would run the National Security Agency in the Clinton administration.

The group's final member was Commander William O. Studeman, a respected officer who would rise to the rank of admiral, become a chief of naval intelligence, and then become deputy director of the CIA. Studeman was writing his top secret thesis at the Naval War College when he got the nod. Coincidentally, his thesis was on how the Navy could deny the Soviets their objectives in a war.

Inside the most secretive channels of the Navy, the Haver group became known as Team Charlie. Over the next fourteen years its members would dominate the naval intelligence community and the Navy's war-planning efforts like no other group of officers.

On Thursday morning, February 26, 1980, Sumner Shapiro appeared before the important House Armed Services Seapower Subcommittee chaired by Representative Charles E. Bennett, an influential member from Florida who was a big Navy supporter. The admiral came equipped with charts, pictures of Soviet naval vessels, and a promise. "What I will be briefing you on this morning is an all-source briefing," he told the congressmen, "derived from various sensitive sources, to give you the best appreciation possible of what it is we face."

As the congressmen stared down from their dais at the bald little admiral sitting at the table in front of them, Shapiro raised the proverbial red flag. "It's been a banner year for the Soviet navy," he said. "Somehow Gorshkov convinced the Soviet leadership that they need to put the resources, the scarce resources, of the Soviet Union into building a navy that gives them an offensive capability. We've seen a complete turnaround in the Soviet navy, particularly in the last couple of years, a shift from a purely defensive force, one that was an extension of the land armies, if you will, to one that can project power, strike the enemy, the United States."

Several members looked surprised, curious about what new type of advances the Soviet navy might have made. As he held their attention, Shapiro unleashed the Navy's favorite doomsday scenario. "I'm talking about the ships," he said, "that carry the ballistic missiles, submarine-launched ballistic missiles, that are on station right now off of both our coasts and are otherwise targeted against the United States."

Shapiro then ran the congressmen through the Soviets' inventory of warships. Speaking in his deep voice, he described as succinctly as he could each of the ship's most threatening capabilities, as well as the Soviets' shipbuilding program, which he called a "a monstrous effort on their part." He also dropped a few hints about the new carrier which stimulated the lawmakers' curiosity. "We think it's going to have catapults and arresting gear. It's going to be, we feel, like about sixty thousand tons, carrying, depending upon the mix of aircraft, about sixty, let's say, high-performance aircraft. We believe it will be nuclear powered, but we really don't know that at this point.''

Several committee members pressed for more information, but Shapiro resisted. The Navy could use the carrier later, perhaps at a critical time when more news about such a threat would sway a vote or two on an important budget issue. ''If I could give you one bottom line to all of this, sir,'' Shapiro said to Bennett at the end of his testimony, ''it's really no big surprise. We've seen it coming, and I think the important thing is that it's the momentum that they've got, the tremendous momentum, and I think a far greater technological capability than anybody ever gave them credit for.''

The United States Navy, Shapiro warned the committee, ''can't sit placidly by, complacent.'' The message he wanted to get across to the men who held the Navy's purse strings was clear: The Soviet navy was an offensive fighting force on the verge of surpassing the American fleet in capabilities; if nothing was done to stop this trend, the U.S. Navy could be destroyed at sea.

It was an ominous message indeed. But was it true? Or was it merely the same old story that had been told to Congress and the American public for nearly twenty years? Almost every senior admiral and intelligence officer knew the truth about the capabilities of the Soviet navy and had done their best to bury it. For twenty years, cloaking its warnings in Cold War rhetoric, the Navy had chosen to perpetuate a lie.

The leaves were turning their traditional reds and golds and yellows in the fall of 1964 when the chief of naval intelligence traveled up to the scenic East Coast town of Newport, Rhode Island. Vice Admiral Rufus Taylor was on an unusual mission to the Naval War College to visit a quiet but determined professor. It was unheard of for a three-star admiral to come calling on an academic, let alone one who held the rank of commander, three steep steps below Taylor's pay grade. Taylor was a legend in the intelligence community and would shortly become deputy director at the CIA, which made him all the more important. Most admirals would have summoned Commander Robert Herrick down to the Pentagon, sending an order early enough before a meeting to make the junior officer sweat a bit. But Taylor wanted to talk with Herrick on Herrick's turf, man to man, naval officer to naval officer. That was the courteous thing to do. Too much was riding on his mission to let protocol get in the way. Bob Herrick was threatening to expose the Navy's hypocrisy about the Soviet threat.[13]

Herrick was a graduate of the Naval Academy, which automatically made him a member of an elite and secretive club known as the ''ring knockers,'' a euphemism for the heavy class ring each received upon graduation. The higher-ranking ring knockers were at the top of the naval food chain and literally controlled who got what jobs, who would become an admiral, who would pass and who would fail in their careers. Herrick had entered the fleet as an ensign in 1944, the very bottom of the chain. When the Pacific war ended with Japan's surrender in Tokyo Bay, he'd asked for the unheard of —a discharge. The Navy grumbled over an academy graduate committing such a faux pas and refused. Herrick was obligated to pay back the cost of his education. Period. And that meant fulfilling the then mandatory seven-year commitment. If he had to stay, Herrick decided, then he was going to find himself a niche, something that would make his seven years bearable.[14]

It didn't take long before he discovered his calling: analyzing the Soviet navy. His first step was to attend the Intelligence Postgraduate School for training. Next was Russian Language School. Then came his first real job. From 1950 to 1953 he served as a Soviet analyst in the Office of Naval Intelligence, where he excelled. The ring knockers saw him as one of their best and brightest, an officer who could make admiral if he followed the rules. They sent Herrick to the Russian Institute at Columbia University, where he earned a master's in international relations and completed course requirements for a doctorate. He became fluent in Russian and could read the Cyrillic alphabet, which allowed him to see for himself what the Soviets were saying in their military journals. That gave him a rare independence. He could make up his own mind, without the information being filtered or censored by institutional prejudices.

After Columbia, Herrick wound up as an assistant naval attaché at the American embassy in Moscow. He traveled extensively for two years in the Soviet Union, participating in cruises with the Russians aboard a mine-sweeper of the Northern Fleet and aboard a destroyer in the Pacific Fleet. In 1956 the Navy transferred him back to Washington, where he became the Soviet intelligence desk officer in the Office of Naval Intelligence. He went on to attend the Naval War College in 1962 for a year of study in Newport. He graduated a year later. And because of his substantial knowledge of the Soviet fleet, the college asked him to stay on as the staff intelligence officer.

In 1963 Herrick volunteered to give the War College's annual lecture on the Soviet navy. Top admirals and other important dignitaries from Washington routinely attended the widely touted event. And the Navy sent officers from around the fleet to hear what the college's best brains had to say about the Soviet threat. Herrick had a wealth of information he wanted to share. For the last thirteen years he had been watching, listening, writing, learning all he could about the Soviets, how they thought, what they believed in, how they would fight a naval war, what were their strengths, what were their weaknesses. He had read and collected many hundreds of valuable books and journals on the Soviet navy and had conducted many personal interviews with communist officers. He had compiled it all into a personal library valued at a half-million dollars, which he would later will to the Office of Naval Intelligence.

All the while Herrick had been sizing up the Soviet threat. And he didn't like what he found. Finally, in 1963 he reached a point in his career where he had to act. He felt that if he didn't speak out, he would compromise his intellectual integrity. Thus, after the naval officers had filed into the auditorium to hear him speak, Herrick began a lecture he knew might end his career. "The Soviet navy is unquestionably defensive in its strategic orientation," he told a stunned audience. He believed that the Soviet fleet was not an offensive, blue-water Navy out to get the United States. It was simply not the threat that the U.S. Navy claimed it was. The Soviets' main priority was not to come out and fight, but to defend the homeland from an aggressive American Navy.

His words fell like bombs. It was heresy.

After the lecture, the admiral who was president of the Naval War College summoned Herrick to his office. Herrick had often visited the senior officer, stopping by to discuss the latest intelligence. Their conversations were usually over a cup of coffee and always informal. Today there was no coffee and no niceties.

Stand at attention, the admiral ordered.

"Yes, sir," Herrick said.

The visibly angered admiral reached into his desk drawer and pulled out a manuscript of his own that he had submitted to the journal *Foreign Affairs,* "which they had the good sense not to publish," Herrick said years later. "He handed it to me and he said, 'This is what we believe.' I glanced at it enough to see that it was the same old thing."

That's not what I believe, Herrick said. My research has borne out my conclusions. The Soviet navy is not a threat. It's purely a defensive fighting force. "He stood up and looked at me for a long second and said, 'Go.' "

A year later in 1964, Herrick stood before the podium again, delivering the annual lecture on the Soviet navy. It was the same message, only stronger. He had just finished writing his doctorate, an exhaustive study titled "Soviet Naval Strategy," which examined fifty years of theory and practice. It was meticulously researched and well documented, with literally hundreds of footnotes listing communist publications.[15] Herrick asked the Naval Institute, a quasi-official organization presided over by the CNO, to publish his dissertation in a book. But the chief of naval operations refused, Herrick recalled, saying such a book was not in the Navy's best interest.

Although disappointed, Herrick was not surprised. His work went against everything the Navy had been saying and would continue to say for the next twenty-five years.

After Herrick's second lecture, Rufus Taylor knew he had to do something to rein in a man who was fast earning a reputation as a rogue. He and the other admirals believed that if Congress knew the full extent of Herrick's studies and called him down to Washington to testify, the Navy would be in deep trouble. The U.S. Navy's argument that the Soviet navy was a growing offensive power would be picked apart. And without the threat, the Navy's budget would undoubtedly shrink. Taylor had had enough of Bob Herrick. He telephoned and arranged to meet with his defiant intelligence officer. And when he arrived at the War College, Taylor unleashed a whirlwind in Commander Herrick's office. "If you behave yourself," he warned Herrick, "you will be promoted to captain." He didn't have to say what he really meant: If you don't shut up, your career is over.

Herrick already knew that his days in the Navy were numbered. He had taken the unholy position of criticizing official Navy policy. Perhaps the only thing that had protected him this far was being a ring knocker. But to Herrick, his academy ring and his oath to the Navy mattered little now. He had already decided to resign his commission. After twenty-four years of loyal service to his country, years he had enjoyed despite the dispute over the Soviet threat, he quit.

"The die is cast," Herrick told Taylor calmly. "I've already accepted a position at Radio Free Europe."

Four years later, in 1968, the Navy finally published Herrick's book but took the unusual step of attaching a disclaimer, which said the conclusion that the Soviets operated a defensive navy was controversial and not supported by all naval thinkers. The Navy also called for comments and articles expressing alternative views to be published in the Naval Institute's journal, *Proceedings*. The mainstream Navy easily discredited Herrick and his work as quackery, which guaranteed that his book would not be widely circulated. In 1995 *Soviet Naval Strategy* was so hard to find that it was considered almost a collector's item.

Rufus Taylor returned to Washington content that the Navy's secret estimates, which grossly pumped up the dangers of an offensive-oriented Soviet fleet, were secure. He had known all along that the Navy possessed thousands of pages of top secret code word documents that supported many, if not the majority, of Herrick's findings. The documents came from a highly placed American spy and would remain classified for another thirty years.[16]

They were so sensitive that the CIA even classified the code word given to them: Ironbark. Between 1961 and 1962, an agent named Oleg Penkovskiy, a colonel in the GRU, the intelligence directorate of the Red Army, had provided volumes of Ironbark material, classified information of the highest importance to the West on the Red Navy and the other branches of the military. The information poured into CIA headquarters, which shared the material with the Office of Naval Intelligence and its sister spy agencies in the Pentagon.

The documents on the Red Navy gave the West a detailed inside view of the problems plaguing the Soviet fleet. Russian admirals had written a series of long-running articles in the Soviets' top secret defense journal called *Military Thought,* outlining their strengths, weaknesses, and fears. A major concern was that the U.S. Navy would launch a Normandy-style invasion of their country, using its powerful aircraft carriers and its Marines. The only way the Soviets figured they could defeat the American fleet was to use tactical nuclear weapons, from antisubmarine depth charges to antiship missiles. There was little doubt that from day one a naval war would go nuclear,[17] and that the Soviets planned to strike at naval ports in Hawaii, Europe, and if possible in the continental United States.[18]

The Soviets would have to resort to nuclear weapons because their naval forces were so weak. The documents exposed extensive problems in command, control, and communication. Even their reconnaissance planes did not have the range to reach out and find an American battle group, a fatal flaw in preparing for a combat. And if they happened to get lucky and find the U.S. fleet in the open ocean, the Soviets would have tremendous problems marshaling forces to carry out what was called a surge attack, a coordinated strike from the air, from beneath the sea, and from ships firing from over the horizon.[19] There were bound to be "leakers," missiles that penetrated the Navy's defensive perimeter, but Russian naval forces had never been able to coordinate with any efficiency the arrival of submarines with surface ships and land-based aircraft.[20] Invariably a bomber would arrive first on the scene, well before a submarine or a surface ship. That cut the striking force by a third and increased the odds that the U.S. Navy could easily repulse the attack. One of the primary weaknesses of the submarine fleet was lack of communications while submerged.

Even more troubling, the Soviets had not figured out how to target their cruise missiles with any accuracy, a problem that would plague them well into the 1980s.[21] This was no secret to the U.S. Navy. Shapiro had seen evidence of it during fleet operations and quietly informed Admiral James Holloway in a private meeting. He'd also told Holloway that overhead reconnaissance gave the United States the advantage of being able to see the

Soviets move their bomber forces from internal bases to staging areas near the ocean to increase their range.[22] And these were second-tier bombers. The front-line Backfire rarely operated in ocean areas. The early warning would give the U.S. Navy time to prepare for a potential attack by dispersing its battle fleet, spreading a dozen or more warships out on the ocean into an area the size of Texas.

By the time Penkovskiy was exposed and executed, the U.S. Navy knew that their communist foes were not ten feet tall, but closer to dwarf size in terms of naval power.

Five years before Ronald Reagan was elected to the presidency on a promise to strengthen American defenses in response to Soviet expansionism, William Colby, the director of central intelligence from 1973 to 1976, reached his own conclusion on the Russian fleet: "We could take the Soviet navy out in a busy afternoon," he remarked.[23] It may have been a glib statement, but Colby had seen the increasing number of intelligence reports that came into the spy agency and the Navy after the Ironbark revelations a decade earlier. To the conservative and longtime covert operator with the CIA and its predecessor, the OSS, the information left little doubt. The Soviet navy was a paper tiger—despite what the admirals were still telling Congress and the American public.

After some twenty years of Gorshkov's modernization efforts, the CIA's intelligence, as well as reports from the U.S. Navy, clearly showed the dismal shape of the Soviet fleet.[24] Among other shortcomings, the Russians towed their ships around to save gas and wear and tear on poorly designed propulsion systems. And their ships spent 85 percent of their time at anchor in the Mediterranean and other seas.[25] "I'm not going to worry about them," Colby replied after being told about the figures.

And Colby was not the only government official aware of the reports. Throughout the 1970s and up to the time Lehman took charge of the Navy and beyond, the U.S. intelligence community had accumulated a vast amount of information that undermined the admirals' official position on the Soviet naval threat. Naval attachés based in American embassies around the world had provided some of the best reports. Trained as intelligence operatives, they maintained diplomatic status, which allowed them to mingle with Soviet officers and visit their ships when they pulled into port. The attachés would go below decks and see cramped sleeping quarters, filthy toilets and showers; they looked in the galley to see what the menu was; and they mentally recorded the slim number of safety features that would save a sailor's life if the ship was on fire or sinking.

Compared to American vessels, the quality control, for both Soviet ships and crews, was nearly nonexistent. Morale, which can mean the difference between victory and defeat at sea, was extremely low. Alcohol abuse was rampant, and while the navy was predominantly Russian in makeup, ethnic strife among rival sailors was often vicious.[26] And the Soviet fleet suffered from desertions due to poor and dangerous working conditions, low pay, and, in general, the daily dread of life aboard a Russian warship.[27]

When naval attachés visited the Soviets' front-line ships that routinely pulled into Yugoslavia, they were shocked. From a distance the vessels bristled with heavy weapons, a hallmark of Soviet ship design. But on closer inspection, the attachés could see that the tops of the surface-to-air and surface-to-surface missile launchers for nuclear and conventional weapons were rusted shut. They reported back to Washington that some of the launchers were dinged up so badly that they doubted missiles could be fired at all.[28] One U.S. naval officer reported that "when we got aboard to scrape the paint and touch the missile launchers, and talk to the captains, we saw what a terrible job they had done putting those ships together."[29] Naval attachés in Moscow filed similar reports on missile launchers, saying, "We doubt very much that this thing is going to work; it's crappy. Their missile launchers, they have a down time of more than 33 percent."

When the Soviet navy made an unprecedented visit in Boston harbor, naval intelligence officers covertly mingled among the tourists who came aboard for a novel tour of the vessels. They scraped the paint to determine how resistant it was to salt water. Small samples of steel were gouged out of a bulkhead to determine the metallurgy of the ships. "We came back with fragmentary reports," said Stasser Holcomb, "that said, 'Gee, the skin of these ships is rough, the corrosion control isn't good, they don't have the redundancy, the people aboard the ships have limited tasks, none of these commissioned officers or warrant officers have broad responsibility."[30]

Even submarines, which were a top budget priority for the Soviets and were considered the greatest threat to the U.S. Navy, were so loud when they did put to sea that "we could hear them halfway across the Pacific," said one admiral. Not only were they inferior in terms of quietness, the submarines were prone to radiation leaks and nuclear meltdowns, which had happened on several occasions at sea and in port.[31] The U.S. Navy's Office of Naval Intelligence kept a detailed list of Soviet submarine disasters but never discussed them in detail in public.[32] All told, from 1956 to 1993, 126 Russian submarine incidents were recorded, including 8 sinkings and 22 radiation accidents. Over 500 sailors lost their lives in Soviet submarine disasters.[33]

The first Soviet sub disaster happened in the late 1960s in a prototype-class nuclear-powered submarine, K-19. In 1970 a *November*-class attack submarine sank in the Bay of Biscay. In February 1972 the Navy knew that a Soviet *Hotel*-class nuclear submarine was hovering just below the surface for three weeks during a terrible Atlantic storm.[34] And they knew that the ship had a major radiation leak, which had contaminated most of the vessel. A short while later the Navy learned that twelve Russian sailors were locked for three weeks in the contaminated portion of the ship before they were rescued. Eventually the Navy learned that twenty-eight men died.[35]

In July 1979 a reactor on an *Echo I*–class nuclear-powered attack submarine suffered a meltdown in the Pacific. And in 1985, near the Far Eastern Soviet city of Vladivostok, the headquarters of the Red Banner Pacific Fleet, an *Echo II*–class nuclear-powered attack submarine's reactor exploded during refueling, sending a plume into the sky that showered the area with radiation that is still detectable today.[36] Although the radiation leakage was smaller than Chernobyl's, it was extremely lethal and could have been worse if the ship had been up and running for several weeks. At the time of the explosion, a group of Japanese schoolchildren visiting Vladivostok were rushed home to a nation that knew firsthand the true horrors of nuclear radiation.[37]

Few if any of the reports on the shortcomings of the Soviet fleet made it into the mainstream briefs provided to the members of Congress because they contradicted the official U.S. Navy position. Although the Navy would not admit it publicly, privately its leaders knew they were sitting on a vault of information that showed the Soviets were not a threat. But it was also obvious that to speak out would end a career. "You just did not stand up and call a spade a spade," said one senior intelligence officer who had filed scores of classified reports on Soviet shortcomings.

The Navy was so eager to preserve its budget and protect itself in the Pentagon turf wars that it concealed the true story about the Soviet fleet and purposefully embellished its size. Although the U.S. Navy reached some estimates as high as 3,000 Soviet ships,[38] it used a smaller but still grossly misleading figure of 1,700 for testimonies before Congress and in other public statements to the press. It was about three times the actual number of warships dispersed among the Soviets' four fleets.

In reality the Soviet fleet averaged around 562 ships, including 284 general-purpose submarines and 284 large surface combatants. In addition, it had 85 "boomers," ballistic missile submarines.[39] Soviet naval air forces numbered about 1,200 aircraft, from helos to jets. The Soviets rarely if ever discarded old ships or aircraft, which had created a fleet of first-line, second-line, third-line, and fourth-line equipment. The gap in readiness and capabilities between the first line and the fourth line was so extensive that some U.S. Navy analysts concluded that less than 10 percent of the Soviet navy could steam outside of its home waters.[40]

The attitude within the CIA, shared by Colby and others, that the Soviet navy was not a major threat, changed substantially when Admiral Stansfield Turner took over the agency in 1977. A Rhodes scholar, Turner found the CIA's analysis lacking. There had always been an uneasy alliance between the CIA and the Navy, especially on the subject of rating Soviet naval power. The CIA's small Soviet navy analysis division reviewed the same intelligence as the Navy but often reached opposite, or less inflated, conclusions.[41] "I don't want to run them down," Turner said of his new CIA analysts. "They are basically good people, but they didn't have the expertise." [42]

While Turner tended to take the worst-case scenario, his boss, President Jimmy Carter, knew better. Carter, a Naval Academy graduate and former submariner, was well aware of the secret that the Navy had managed to conceal. "Yes, we were aware of it," Defense Secretary Harold Brown recalled. "I discussed on more than one occasion with President Carter that the Soviets kept their fleet at sea a small fraction of the time. It was true of their submarines, it was true of the surface navy as well. We knew this was associated with limitations in maintenance and readiness, and we saw a big difference between the U.S. fleet and the Soviet fleet, in this regard." [43]

As Carter's chief of naval operations, Hayward, as well as his staff, had read the intelligence reports and often discussed Soviet naval deficiencies. "You could paint a picture that these guys aren't as tough as we thought they are," Holcomb recalled. "On the other hand, you look at the huge numbers of everything they had and what could be done sensibly with those things and you would say you have to err on the side of assuming they are better than worse. And we didn't like what we saw."

Shapiro's February 26 appearance before Bennett's committee only added to the confusion that was growing within the naval intelligence community. Many had watched in dismay as he came close to outright deception. The chief of intelligence continued to push the party line that the Navy was falling behind the Soviets.

Shapiro knew better. Three weeks earlier, Team Charlie had told Hayward and several other admirals that many of Bob Herrick's conclusions were right on the money. For ninety minutes Rich Haver ran through Team Charlie's findings and laid out what they believed were the Soviets' real naval war plans that would not change for the next fifteen to twenty years. As he spoke, Hayward, Cockell, Admiral James Watkins (the vice chief of naval operations), and Rear Admiral Ken McKee, a man known to flash wide grins and smoke big cigars, sat around a table in a tiny conference room on the fifth floor of the Pentagon. The Soviet navy, Team Charlie concluded, was a defensive force whose chief mission was to protect the homeland and its missile-bearing submarines. "It was nothing like they had imagined it to be," said one participant in the meeting.

Perhaps the team's most startling conclusion concerned the mission of the Soviets' nuclear-missile submarines. Shapiro had juiced up the congressmen that Thursday morning by saying Soviet submarines were patrolling off the U.S. coasts, prepared to shower American cities with nuclear warheads. It was a white lie. A number of top secret studies at the Center for Naval Analyses, a quasi-official government-supported think tank that did work for the Navy, clearly showed that since the late 1970s the Soviets had kept their boomers submerged in bastions, protected areas in the Barents Sea and the Sea of Okhotsk, guarded by their attack subs.[44] And rarely did they sail into the open oceans past naval choke points like the G.I.U.K. Gap or the Kurile Islands in the Pacific, where they would be vulnerable to U.S. naval forces that would track them relentlessly like bloodhounds. And because the Soviets knew their missile boats were vulnerable, only fourteen boomers were at sea in their bastions at any given time.

CNA analysts also found that the Soviet Union would not use the submarines in a first-strike intercontinental nuclear attack on the United States. The missiles, which could not destroy hardened U.S. nuclear silos, would be withheld for potentially protracted nuclear operations against soft targets like military bases. Other missiles would be withheld as a long-term reserve.[45] And some analysts even questioned whether Soviet missiles could adequately function, as the SS-N-17s and SS-N-20s had targeting problems and a tendency to explode in flight.[46]

It was hard for many of the admirals to believe what Haver was telling them. Most had grown up with the memories of Germany's submarine victories in World War II. In a six-month period during 1942, fourteen German U-boats had sunk 450 allied ships. The majority of the U.S. Navy's admirals believed that the Soviets, with the largest underwater fleet in the world, had copied German naval strategies and would go after U.S. transports in the Atlantic. But intelligence officers in the Navy and at the CIA showed that this view was wrong. The Soviets did not plan to send their attack subs or their surface ships into the Atlantic if a war broke out. They were to be held back to guard the bastions.[47] It was the exact opposite of what the admirals had been saying in public.

And Team Charlie didn't put much credence in the new carrier spotted at Nikolayev. Nine years earlier, in 1971, an American spy satellite had passed over Nikolayev and taken pictures of *Kiev*. Alarm bells rang throughout the Navy when the admirals said that the 37,000-ton vessel was the Soviet Union's first *real* carrier. The intelligence, they said, provided unmistakable proof that the warship posed a significant threat to the U.S. Navy.

In their own eyes, the admirals saw what they wanted to see: an aircraft carrier with jump jets and helicopters that also bristled with missiles and could take part in an amphibious landing. In reality, the three *Kiev*-class carriers that rolled off the assembly line and took to sea beginning in 1976 turned out to be nothing more than antisubmarine, anti–aircraft carrier warships.[48] The Yak-38 Forgers aboard the *Kiev* were so inferior, they could stay aloft only for some twenty minutes. And when the jets took to the air, they always stayed within visual sight of their ship.[49]

When Haver completed his presentation, Hayward asked the admirals in the room for their input. He was uneasy with some of the findings, but he was intent on drafting a new maritime strategy for the Navy. Haver's Team Charlie may have been too overzealous in trying to complete its charge to answer Hayward's persistent questions about Soviet naval intentions. This was only the first brief. If need be, Team Charlie could be reined in. "Does anybody see that there is something violently wrong with any of this?" Hayward asked. "Does it make sense?"[50]

A general debate followed, with each of the officers pitching in, until Hayward halted the discussion with a question for Haver. "What do we need to do next? If this is all right, what do we need to do?"

"I need an audience," Haver said. "This is so highly classified that only the four of you can hear it. Even if you believe it, most of the people inside this structure have no idea how to deal with this problem. So we need an audience."

"I have a solution to that," Watkins said. He pointed to McKee, a submariner, and told him, Get the bright young lieutenant commanders and commanders in this building, take about a dozen of them and clear them, make them a special team, and tell them we want a strategy derived out of all this intelligence.

Hayward agreed. But his initiative would come with a high price. A bitter split among the intelligence community and the analysts at the Center for Naval Analyses was polarizing the upper reaches of the Navy. Hard-liners who sided with Sumner Shapiro still clung to their personal and institutional prejudices that painted the Soviet navy as a growing offensive threat, while claiming that the American fleet had lost maritime superiority. The anti–Bob Herrick cabal of officers who for years had lied to Congress refused to bend.

Their bitter foes were a new breed of spooks who supported Team Charlie's charter and were willing to admit that the U.S. Navy had consistently overrated its archival. Damn the old guard secret, they argued. Stop the charade, and let's exploit the Soviets' weaknesses, not exaggerate them. "With the right strategy, we would have destroyed them in about ten days," said one Team Charlie member. "We would have blown their socks off. They would not have known what was coming at them."

≡ CHAPTER 4 ≡

WHEN JOHN LEHMAN came into office on February 5, 1981, he figured that time would be his biggest enemy, not the bruising debate over the Soviet threat. He knew he had two, maybe three years at the most, to rebuild *his* Navy to *his* design. After that, he was certain that Congress would slow to a trickle the money promised for the Reagan military buildup.[1] He had no doubts that the Navy would even face cuts or a budget that offered no real growth.

Lehman was preparing to ask Congress for nearly a trillion dollars over the next seven years to fund the largest peacetime buildup of the Navy in the nation's history.[2] But he knew he wouldn't get support on Capitol Hill or public backing if the squabble within the intelligence community was out in the open to be debated. For twenty years the Navy had misled Congress about the Soviet fleet. If the admirals came clean now, opened the vault to the intelligence files on the Russians, Congress would be aghast and might cut billions off his budget request.[3]

Lehman had to keep the lid on while pushing the party line. He embraced Shapiro's position that the Soviet navy was a worldwide threat, challenging the American fleet in every body of water on the globe. At times his rhetoric got so extreme that even his advisers joked that he had seen Russian submarines under sportfishermen off the South Carolina coast. While some of his advisers saw the propaganda campaign as just a budget driver, others were alarmed over the distortions in truth provided to Congress. Peter Swartz, a Lehman confidant, finally said to him, "You know what you can do, John. You can tell the truth."[4]

But Lehman replied that he couldn't sell the buildup without a major threat. The old Swing Strategy would never win the big budgets he wanted for the Navy. He had to have a bold new battle plan, and the Soviet Union was the bogeyman who would make it work. Lehman envisioned carrier task forces attacking the Soviet mainland, striking the Kola, or Kamchatka and Vladivostok in the Pacific. It was controversial, which would ensure that it would be debated on the Hill and draw attention to the needs of the Navy. A perfect budget driver.

If the Navy's critics accused him of grandstanding, Lehman would have a solid fallback position. A maritime strike against the Kola, he said, would protect Norway from Russian occupation. If they took Norway, Lehman claimed, Soviet air forces could threaten northern Great Britain. Finally, a U.S. Navy attack would prevent the Kremlin from shifting the thousands of troops and masses of war matériel based in the north to the central front in Europe. In the Pacific, an attack there would tie down the two hundred thousand Soviet troops stationed in Siberia.

Political leaders in Bonn and Paris and London, who had once supported strikes against Murmansk, were now openly hostile to the idea, calling it in private radical and out of touch. But as Lehman saw it, the political battle was not in the capitals of Europe, it was on Capitol Hill. Therefore his plan had to be foolproof, one that played up the Soviet threat while simultaneously winning over Congress and the American people with its daring. He knew the other services would fight him for every last penny of the defense budget, but Lehman figured he could handle their secretaries, Verne Orr at Air Force and Jack Marsh at Army, who didn't have his connections on the Hill.

Both men would ratchet up the Soviet threat in typical Cold War rhetoric. But Lehman took the hype one step farther. Not only were the Russians coming, they had a target: Alaska and its vital oil fields. "People forget that Anchorage is only about two thousand miles from the major Soviet naval base," he said in interviews with the press.[5] "Alaska is an extremely lucrative strategic target for the Soviets because of our increasing dependence, particularly in a time of war, on the oil supplies from that state."

If anyone doubted that Sergei Gorshkov's fleet had the power to strike at the United States, Lehman and the admirals pointed to the *Admiral Kuznetsov* and her sister *Kiev*-class flattops. And they invoked the bloated and misleading number of 1,700 Soviet ships, while the Americans had a paltry 460, which would be hard-pressed to turn back a massive Russian naval advance. "Such a condition is not acceptable if peace is to survive," Lehman said before Congress, adding ominously that the U.S. Navy's superiority over the Soviets was gone.[6] There was no guarantee that America would prevail in a battle at sea. It was time to build ships, and *fast, fast, fast!*

For the lawmakers kept in the dark about the Soviets' inferior fleet, it was easy to invoke the Red Menace as a reason to support the U.S. Navy's costly rearmament. And once hooked, Lehman would reel in the legislators with a simple yet controversial scheme. He would front load the 1982 and 1983 Navy budgets, requesting billions more dollars early on and taking less money in the years past 1984. If he could get enough ships under construction now, there was no way anyone could stop the Navy's buildup. And once he had the ships, Congress would be forced to buy airplanes and pay for men to operate them.

It was a gamble, but Lehman was a gambler. His hero, Teddy Roosevelt, had taken a similar risk when he sent the Great White Fleet on a world tour with only enough money to get it halfway. Roosevelt's gamble paid off. Backed into a corner, Congress doled out more money to bring the ships home. Lehman knew if his plan was airtight, had enough pork in it, and had specific rewards for a congressman's district, then he too could back the Hill into a corner.

From the first day Lehman set foot in his fourth-floor office, there was no doubt among the secretarial staff that he was marching to the beat of Roosevelt's drum. He idolized the former President, calling him "my hero." The first aircraft carrier he could name, which had been funded under Jimmy Carter but commissioned on Lehman's watch, was affectionately called *Theodore Roosevelt*. Over his desk in the Secretariat hung a photograph of Roosevelt as an assistant secretary of the Navy, sitting at a desk carved like a submarine, with a spittoon in the corner.[7] Lehman would often prattle on about what a dynamic leader Roosevelt was. He would drop not-so-subtle hints that they were both thirty-eight years old when they were appointed to their Navy jobs. And although the oil portrait of a secretary was traditionally not hung in the Pentagon until after his retirement, Lehman had his picture placed between paintings of Teddy Roosevelt and Franklin D. Roosevelt on the wall leading up to his office.

Ted Gordon and a handful of officers who watched Lehman operate early on soon had the feeling that their youthful new boss had the same ambitions "T.R." did for the White House. They figured the Navy job was just a stepping-stone. And it didn't take long before the naval community started describing Lehman as a modern-day Roosevelt. "I tell you, when he came in we thought he was Teddy Roosevelt," observed Gordon. "I think he thought he was Teddy Roosevelt."[8] Stories among the staff likening the brash new secretary to the bullish Roosevelt easily found their way to the defense correspondents eager for news about the rising stars in the Pentagon.[9] Invariably they lionized Lehman and compared his goals for the Navy to Roosevelt's fleet of battleships that had vied for command of the seas in the early 1900s.

Many, but not all, of the comparisons were accurate. Roosevelt was an outspoken reformer, a naturalist, a man of letters, a soldier, and a statesman. Lehman was an outspoken reformer, too. He immediately began streamlining the Navy bureaucracy. He too was an outdoorsman, an avid hunter and fisherman. And he was a prolific writer. But he was not a soldier. And he had yet to reach the lofty position of statesman. Physically the two men were approximately the same height, and both had a firm build. Both men found challenge stimulating and frequently rooted for the underdog. And both loathed the press (Roosevelt coined the term "muckraker") but would cleverly use the media to advance their personal agendas.

Neither man could keep his hands off the Navy. In 1905 Roosevelt descended in the *Plunger,* one of the Navy's first submarines, and insisted to the skipper that he be allowed to operate the submerged vessel. A year later he took command of the battleship *Louisiana* for a trip to Panama to see how the builders of the canal were doing.[10] Lehman, during his six-year tenure, would attempt to pilot every type of aircraft in the fleet, although he was not always qualified to do so. He sailed on submarines beneath the polar ice caps. And in an act that would have impressed Roosevelt, Lehman unmothballed four World War II battleships for duty in the 1980s. He was so fond of the battleships that he placed a scale model of the *Missouri,* the dreadnought on which Japan had surrendered in World War II, in the hallway near his office. When visitors strolled through the Navy floor on guided tours of the Pentagon, Lehman would jump out to greet them. "Did you see my battleship?" he would ask excitedly.[11]

History had indeed recognized Roosevelt and his Navy. History would also record a spot for Lehman simply because, at thirty-eight, he had become the youngest secretary of the Navy in the twentieth century. But Lehman would need more than his youth to be remembered in the same light as Roosevelt. He needed a Great White Fleet, too. He was determined to build "the Six Hundred Ship Navy." The idea had been around for a long time, first popping up under Donald Rumsfeld, secretary of defense in the Ford administration. Rumsfeld commissioned a study that recommended in 1975 that the Navy needed six hundred ships to counter the Soviet fleet.[12]

Lehman seized the idea and began his campaign to make the Six Hundred Ship Navy a household phrase and the hallmark of his buildup. It would dovetail nicely with Hayward's work to create a new offensive strategy for the Navy, from starting Team Charlie to pulling together the sundry war-fighting plans like Sea Strike and Sea Plan 2000 into one coherent document. Lehman began building on Hayward's work, calling it the Maritime Strategy.

He knew if the public was going to put up with huge Navy budgets, it had to understand the complexities of naval warfare, which could be mindboggling even to the experts. The solution was to coin phrases that conjured up images of big ships on a big mission. Both the Maritime Strategy and the Six Hundred Ship Navy were catchy names easy for Congress and the public to identify with and support. "Of course I had to oversimplify things," Lehman later said, "because that's what you have to do in Congress. It's no good to have a brilliant strategy if it cannot be articulated to congressmen so they can understand it. It's got to be in simple declarative sentences and simple syllogisms. If it's too complex, it won't work." [13]

Although the strategy was simple, Lehman's aims were extravagant. He wanted fifteen carrier battle groups, not twelve, at a price of $54 billion. One hundred–plus nuclear-powered attack submarines, not eighty-eight. Forty new Trident submarines at nearly $1 billion a pop, each equipped with the new D-5 missile. A 50 percent increase in amphibious ships to ferry the Marines. Twenty-seven Aegis-equipped cruisers at nearly $1 billion each. Dozens more cargo ships. Thirty-one mine-warfare ships. And topping off the list was the renovation of four World War II–era battleships at approximately $2 billion.[14]

It was the most expensive and ambitious plan ever for a Navy not at war. And the pricey numbers didn't go unnoticed. A small cadre of analysts at the nonpartisan Congressional Budget Office was studying whether there were enough dollars in the U.S. Treasury to match the high price tag.

On Capitol Hill, Peter T. Tarpgaard, a retired naval officer, caucused with some fellow CBO analysts. And as they crunched the shipbuilding numbers, an entirely different picture from that given by the Navy was starting to emerge.

The budget experts believed that Lehman's plan would be difficult to support—in fact, almost impossible to support in the latter years of the 1980s and the 1990s. In short, as it was now presented, the Six Hundred Ship Navy simply was not affordable. "It is quite likely," Tarpgaard argued, "that we will have a Navy ill suited to the tasks it is most likely to face." [15] He and his colleagues wanted to force an honest debate about the numbers and raise questions about whether it would be possible to replace the most expensive ships by smaller and cheaper vessels and still maintain a large fleet.

Tarpgaard believed if the Navy followed Lehman's unusual formula, it would have to build 230 ships over ten years to reach the Six Hundred Ship Navy by 1996. The high number of new ships was needed to offset older ones being retired. He tallied up the price tag at more than $170 billion. A final report that would land on the desks of the vitally important Senate and House Armed Services Committees was many months away. But already alternatives were being drafted by the CBO, including an option for 540 ships built around 12 aircraft carriers. The report, if it got a good bounce in the press, could sink Lehman's dream Navy.

There was a similar concern in the secretary of defense's office.

In public, Caspar Weinberger backed his outspoken Navy secretary's plan, never wavering in his support. His convictions concerning a bigger military were as hard as the steel on the bow of a battleship. The party line was for six hundred ships, and Weinberger and his Pentagon associates would stand behind it. And with them stood their biggest ally, Ronald Reagan, who had routinely used the buzz words "the Six Hundred Ship Navy" and was calling for "maritime superiority," another Lehman coinage, in his speeches. But in private, a heated debate among Weinberger's top lieutenants about Lehman's plan had been gearing up ever since the election. Was it possible? What would happen if the shipyards ran into trouble? What would happen when the money pledged by lawmakers like John C. Stennis, the powerful Democratic senator from Mississippi, ran out? The $170 billion CBO figure was only for building new ships and overhauling old ones. The Navy would need as many as one hundred thousand more sailors and officers to man the new vessels.[16] That meant recruiting more people, paying more salaries, finding more housing, and providing medical and retirement benefits for active duty and civilian workers. Up to $10 billion more would be needed.[17]

Then there was the aviation plan. Under President Carter the Navy had lost as many planes to attrition, from age, crashes, and other factors, as it had bought.[18] As a reserve aviator, Lehman felt duty bound to reverse this. He would personally craft an aviation plan, and it would cost an additional $128 billion.[19] About $57 billion of this was to buy a fleet of 620 A-12 Avengers, a new stealth bomber that would replace the Navy's aging A-6 Intruders. The A-12 was a "black" program, so highly classified that its budget numbers were not revealed to Congress.

All Congress really knew about the aviation plan was that Lehman said the Navy needed 1,917 new aircraft to fly off the new carriers he wanted to buy. He saved and expanded the F/A-18 Hornet. And he called for a whole line of other new airplanes and upgrades for older aircraft like the venerable F-14 Tomcat fighter. Research and development would run into the billions. And once built and bought, the aircraft would cost many hundreds of millions of dollars into the late 1990s to maintain and operate. Training one new pilot alone ran more than $2 million.

Although the new plan to rebuild the Navy would be spread over several years, it would come on top of the Navy's day-to-day costs of operating and maintaining its existing fleet. The Navy would need 8 percent real growth in its budget each year to pull off Lehman's plan. That type of growth was unprecedented, even during the Vietnam War years. "I felt it was warranted, but I didn't feel it was achievable," Richard Armitage, a top Weinberger strategist, would say at the regular budget meetings to slice up the defense budget.[20] Larry Korb, an outspoken aide with a bald head and heavy-rimmed glasses, fretted to Weinberger that there was not enough money to support the Six Hundred Ship Navy and modernize the other services, too. The Army and Air Force would suffer at the expense of John Lehman, Korb told Weinberger. Lehman closely monitored the debate and who was taking sides against him. He tucked away in the back of his mind Korb's articulate and persuasive opposition. When the moment was right, he would get even.

For the time being, Weinberger and his colleagues kept their concerns secret and put the best face on the Navy's buildup. Korb, a former naval aviator, and Armitage, a burly, tough-talking SEAL with several tours in Vietnam, sat tight. "We were all a big happy family," Armitage would say. "It takes a while before you draw daggers and go for each other's throats."

Several weeks after Shapiro appeared before Congressman Bennett's Seapower subcommittee, Hayward took his seat in front of the panel on a Thursday morning in the Rayburn House Office Building. The congressmen assembled to hear his testimony admired Hayward. He was not a man who rattled easy. As the skipper of the carrier *America* during the Vietnam War, he had seen enough death and destruction to cripple the spirit of even the strongest man, but not Hayward. The lawmakers respected that, which gave the admiral a special rapport with the committee members.

Hayward was a persuasive witness. But one of his favorite and most effective means of selling the Navy to Congress took place at the 6 P.M. private dinners he held sporadically in the CNO's private dining room for various members. There Hayward would be as frank as he could be about the Soviet threat. Although the lawmakers knew Hayward's words in public were chosen for political impact, how they might play on the Hill, at the private dinners they had tremendous swaying power.

Whether Hayward liked it or not, as the CNO he was now a politician, the uniformed Navy's chief lobbyist on Capitol Hill. It was his job not only to support the party line for more ships, more airplanes, and more men to keep up with the Russians, but to sell the Navy's position, regardless of whether its customer, the American people, needed it. Hayward's two predecessors, Elmo Zumwalt and James Holloway, had established such an inflexible policy toward the Soviets that he had little choice but to follow their lead. Both admirals had been strong advocates for the U.S. Navy but had made a number of dramatic public statements about the dangers of the Soviet fleet that boxed Hayward in.

Zumwalt had been particularly dire. If the two navies went to war, he had said, there was no guarantee that the United States would win. Holloway during his tenure had said that holding the Mediterranean in wartime, a

long-standing obligation to NATO, would be "uncertain at best." On the
day Hayward took over, Holloway remarked at the elaborate change of
command ceremony that the United States Navy retained only "a slim
margin of superiority" over the Soviets.

Hayward had at first followed Holloway's line. But now, testifying before
Bennett's subcommittee, he took an even more ominous tone. "This year I
have very carefully reassessed the state of the naval balance in consultation
with my senior operational commanders," he informed the congressmen.[21]
"The judgments that emerged from that process have led me to conclude
that it would be misleading to continue speaking of a 'narrow margin' when,
in fact, we have entered a period in which any reasonable estimate of the
balance falls within the range of uncertainty.

"In other words, the situation today is so murky, one cannot with confidence state that the U.S. possesses a margin of superiority. If we do, it is so
cloudy and tenuous as to be unreliable—both as a deterrent and as assurance
of our ability to prevail at sea in a conflict with the Soviets. So I have
concluded that continued focus on the 'thin margin' serves little practical
purpose, and risks misleading by suggesting that we are indeed capable of
measuring the balance with fine-tuned precision when, in fact, experience
tells us that is not the case."

Hayward didn't waffle in his message. If the United States Navy went to
war, it might lose. But whether he truly believed that was another matter
entirely. He was still trying to make sense out of Team Charlie's intelligence
assessments. In fact, he was not sure what to believe.

With Hayward on board, most lawmakers were willing to go along with
Lehman's dream to build six hundred ships, at least for now. Many still
cringed over the Soviet invasion of Afghanistan, which produced daily headlines in *The Washington Post* and *The New York Times*. And who could
forget the failed Desert One raid to free the American hostages in Iran, a
military failure that Ronald Reagan had so artfully exploited during his
campaign? Few congressmen wanted to be seen as weak on defense or the
Russians.

Still, some felt it was their duty to warn the Navy that so much money in
the hands of the admirals was like giving them a license to steal. "Money is
going to be plentiful, no doubt for a while," Stennis had told Lehman during
his Senate confirmation hearings. "But that is not a license to carelessly use
it, or use it in any way except a frugal way, as I see it."[22]

Lehman had assured Stennis he would not waste a penny. "Senator, you
have my pledge," he said.

CHAPTER 5

ON FRIDAY, MARCH 6, at 9:15 A.M., Ronald Reagan sat at the head of a conference table that seemed to fill the entire wood-paneled Situation Room in the West Wing of the White House. Dick Allen, the new national security adviser, introduced the subject about to be discussed—the Navy's spy network.[1] "Mr. President," he began, "these people have something very important to tell you, sir."

Next to Reagan was Vice President George Bush, a veteran of hundreds of intelligence briefings while CIA director four years earlier. Admiral James Watkins, the Navy's number two officer, Ed Meese, and Allen had pulled up chairs next to Bush. Across the table sat White House chief of staff Jim Baker, Secretary of Defense Caspar Weinberger, and his deputy, former CIA official Frank Carlucci.

John Lehman had yet to arrive. He was in a nearby White House office on the telephone, getting the latest information on his first major public relations gaffe. He had named a new attack submarine *Corpus Christi,* which in Latin means "body of Christ." The Catholic Church took offense, as did several peace activists, including one man who began a water-only fast.[2] The peaceniks had turned a simple ship naming into a PR bonanza, pitting the Navy against the Catholic Church. Lehman had held firm, refusing to change the name. Finally Reagan ordered his defiant secretary to accept a compromise and a new name: the *City of Corpus Christi.* The Jesuit-trained Lehman relented but had built up a mighty grudge against the church.

Lehman's frustrations continued when he walked into the Situation Room and found that his chair at the big table had been swiped by another administration official. "What the fuck is this?" he demanded of Rich Haver, the head of Team Charlie who was scheduled to give the briefing.[3]

"Mr. Carlucci came in here and moved your name tag," Haver responded. "He also took your place and your chair."

"Well, dammit, I need a chair!" Lehman said, looking up at the six-foot-three-inch Haver.

At that, Haver went off to find a chair for the new secretary of the Navy. When he returned, and Lehman sat down with the President and his top advisers, the lights in the Situation Room darkened and the brief began.

Rich Haver had earned the nickname "the talking dog of the Potomac" for a good reason. Speaking to presidents for Haver was as easy as barking was to a dog. He was a gifted analyst, politically astute, and he spoke with a vocabulary that commanded attention. He knew just how far to push, when and when not to massage a point, and he was smart enough to keep his mouth shut when the occasion called for it. He would end up at the CIA, but not before he played a major role in the Persian Gulf War as an assistant secretary of defense for intelligence policy to Dick Cheney.

Haver had given a similar presentation to Jimmy Carter when he moved into the White House. It was an overview of the Navy's hush-hush submarine operations that took place in Soviet territorial waters, electronic eavesdropping by surface ships, and human intelligence-gathering activities. But the Carter brief had been years ago—an eternity in the intelligence world in which the latest and most crucial information can be only hours old. In the last five months alone, since Tom Hayward had ordered Haver to create Team Charlie, the secretive group had broken new ground in figuring out Soviet naval intentions. However, none of Team Charlie's cutting-edge work in defining the Soviet threat was officially on the day's docket for the President. Haver was supposed to brief Reagan about the Navy's dicey spy missions. As commander in chief he had to know about them so he could approve their continuation. They were "delicate matters of the intelligence process," one official told the group, "that the president might be involved in and needed to be aware of." [4]

But Haver and Rear Admiral John L. Butts, who had served as the naval assistant to President Dwight Eisenhower, would broaden the brief to explain the rough outlines of the Maritime Strategy. It was too good a chance to pass up. The Navy was trying to articulate a controversial new philosophy for how it would conduct a war with the Soviets. Reagan understood the politics behind the Six Hundred Ship Navy. Now it was important for him to understand why that Navy was being built and what it could do. Haver was sandbagging Reagan, taking advantage of ninety minutes with the President to plead the Navy's case. But it was essential to get his backing for the Maritime Strategy if it was to succeed. It was worth taking the risk.

Dick Allen, who was no stranger to the secretive world of covert operations, opened the meeting with a few brief introductions, then turned it over to Weinberger. Although the defense secretary was pushing for a big military, he was sensitive to the trauma of Vietnam and preferred diplomacy over militarism. Weinberger and the Joint Chiefs of Staff had argued repeatedly that the administration needed the consent of Congress and American public opinion before troops could be deployed.

A lawyer by training and a pianist by devotion, Weinberger was a short man with a full head of dark hair. Because he liked a good joke as much as anyone, colleagues who sat regularly with him in the President's secure briefing room frequently pulled pranks on him or had a good laugh at his expense. Being short, Weinberger raised his adjustable seat in the Situation Room almost to the limit, which let him sit comfortably at the big conference table. This, of course, did not go unnoticed at one meeting by Secretary of State George Shultz. When Weinberger excused himself from the table for a brief moment, Shultz lowered his seat. "Then Weinberger came back in and sat down and his chin almost hit the top of the table," said one observer with a hearty laugh.[5]

Now Weinberger was all business as he began telling the President how the Navy obtained its information and what some of its intelligence successes were. He spoke for about two minutes and recommended to Reagan that it would be beneficial for the nation to allow the Navy to continue its efforts. Then he introduced Watkins, a Naval Academy graduate who was vice chief of naval operations, the admiral who ran the Navy's day-to-day affairs. Watkins was from a prominent Southern California family wired into Republican circles. His mother was a power broker in the California Republican Party. And his baptismal godfather, Earl Jorgensen, who owned a large Southern California steel company, belonged to Reagan's kitchen cabinet.[6]

Watkins had shunned the riches of the business world, choosing instead the underwater world of Navy submarines, itself a powerful institution with rewards equal to if not beyond those found in civilian life.[7] As he moved through his career, "the Wat," as he was known at Annapolis, set his sights on one day becoming CNO. Now, with his political connections to Reagan, he was almost assured the post.

As would be expected, Watkins saw the immense benefits in stealth that the submarines offered, especially in collecting hard-to-get intelligence inside Soviet waters. This intelligence was a boon for the Navy, he told Reagan, adding that the information was critical to the Navy's mission. Then he turned the meeting over to Rich Haver and Admiral Butts, who would speak about the nature of naval intelligence.

Haver had been polishing his brief for several weeks, adding a video and a slide show, at the recommendation of Lehman, to cater to the President's skills as a visual learner. Lehman knew then what would later become a regular criticism of Reagan, that the President could not easily grasp complicated written material. Haver made certain that his briefing was stocked with easily comprehensible facts, figures, and vignettes, and halfway through it was obvious that Team Charlie's careful planning had paid off. Reagan sat ramrod straight on his chair, his eyes glued to the screen, mesmerized by what he saw. At one point he leaned over to George Bush and asked the former director of central intelligence a question: "Did you have something to do with this, George?" Bush grinned at Reagan, then gave the President a little background on how some of the programs that Haver was talking about began or were supported under his tenure at the CIA.

Reagan was fascinated by the Navy's dangerous submarine exploits, code-named Special Navy Control Program, which had been taking place since the late 1970s. Navy submarine crews and frogmen had devised a way to plant sophisticated electronic recording "pods" on underwater communication lines used by Soviet military officials. About every month a submarine and its frogmen would return to retrieve the tapes and place new ones inside the pods. To get instant access to that information, the Navy was experimenting with an undersea plow at Port Hueneme in Southern California that would lay a cable from Greenland directly to the pods on the north coast of the Soviet Union, thus eliminating the submarine's work.[8] Pushed by Admiral Butts, the project included similar plans for the Pacific and would have cost an estimated $1 billion. The idea was apparently abandoned in the late 1980s.

On rare occasions U.S. subs even operated inside Soviet harbors, collecting electronic and photographic intelligence. Exposure would likely have led to death for the crew of 120-plus officers and enlisted personnel. It was a dangerous mission, Reagan could easily see, both politically and militarily. "Where do you get guys like this?" he asked Haver.

"Sir, they're just Americans," Haver said.

Everything was going smoothly, just as the Navy planned. The trick was to make a complex story simple. And from Reagan's reaction, Team Charlie's leader had done just that. About thirty minutes later Haver clicked off the projector and the lights went back on in the Situation Room. "These are the problems we're wrestling with, and these are the issues we're trying to deal with," he said to the President, then waited for questions from those assembled.

Reagan was the first one in the room to speak. The Navy's daring operations, he said with a broad smile, reminded him of the famous World War II movie *Hellcats of the Navy,* which he and Nancy Reagan had both starred in. At the mention of Hollywood, some people in the room became uncomfortable. For fifteen minutes Reagan rattled off colorful anecdotes about how the movie had been filmed and how impressive the naval officers were who had taken part in it.

Then the President began to ask some fairly astute questions. Had the Soviets changed their opinion on nuclear war now that they were facing him in the White House?

It was a loaded question that required a truthful but tactful answer. Although Reagan had publicly blistered the Soviets during the campaign, Haver said, "It isn't what they think of you in the last six weeks, sir. We're talking about how they were behaving over the last five to ten years."

Reagan nodded his head in agreement and continued to ask questions that pertained to nuclear weapons, weapons of mass destruction that many Americans feared the hawkish President didn't fully understand and might be compelled to use.[9] How do they plan for nuclear war? he asked. How do the Soviets train for nuclear war, and how do they intend to fight it? How do they select their targets?

Reagan understood the Navy might be the tip of the U.S. sword in a skirmish at sea with the Soviets that could quickly lead to an all-out hot war. His fiery young Navy secretary had been threatening to steam American warships across the Atlantic and into Russian waters to sink the Soviet fleet. Would such a naval war, Reagan wanted to know, go nuclear from day one? And if it did, could it be contained at sea, or would it spread to a nuclear exchange on land, where population centers would be threatened?

Early Soviet policy, Haver said, had relied on almost immediate use of tactical nuclear weapons at sea. Ironbark had clearly spelled that out and said it was likely a nuclear battle at sea would evolve into strategic nuclear war. But now the emerging consensus within naval intelligence was that the Soviet admirals seemed to be stepping back from the brink, relying first on conventional weapons to guard the fleet and the homeland. The strategy was, first and foremost, to protect the submarine bastions so Soviet ballistic missiles could be used as a reserve force. The Soviets had drawn a six-hundred-mile defensive perimeter around the bastions located on the Kola and in certain areas of the Pacific. Every major Soviet surface warship and combat aircraft and 75 percent of the Russian submarine force would remain in local waters to defend the bastions.[10]

Under the Maritime Strategy, Haver said, the Navy would take the fight right to the Soviet Union, search out its nuclear missile boats, and sink them. It would force the Soviet navy to fight on several fronts instead of concentrating on a set engagement in Europe. The Navy had to take the initiative in the first ten days, Haver explained, establish fronts on the Kola, in the south with the help of Turkey, and in the Pacific. If it did so, the probability of success nearly tripled. If we allow the Russians to set all of the pieces on the chess board, he said, American losses will go up significantly trying to bring naval power to bear.

If war did break out, Haver went on, nobody was completely sure how the Soviets would react. If they saw the tide turning against them, saw the Americans sinking their missile-bearing submarines, they might pull the nuclear trigger rather than face the prospect of loosing their boomers. What might seem irrational to the admirals of the U.S. Navy might be completely logical to the admirals of the Red Navy. On the other hand, an overwhelming U.S. naval force might deter them from war in the first place.

"We are working on that problem," Haver told the President. "The real idea is to get it solved before it explodes. To convince the other side that we know what they are going to do and if they are looking for success, they will not find it."

It was guesswork at best.

When the brief was over Reagan was gracious in his praise of the Navy. He thanked Haver, and then he and his advisers, with the exception of Weinberger, trooped back up to the Oval Office.

"You have a lot more work to do now, sonny," a smiling Weinberger said to Haver as they walked out of the Situation Room.

"Yes, sir, I know."

Although Admiral H. D. Train II was stationed down the coast from the Washington elite, his Norfolk headquarters was the undisputed capital of American sea power. That alone gave Harry Train enormous clout within the Navy.

The six-foot-two Train, whose pitch black hair had turned white when he reached the age of thirty, was considered by many to be perhaps the classiest officer the Navy had had in a long, long time: son of an admiral, Annapolis class of '49, accomplished submariner, mentor to scores of officers, and now commander in chief of the Atlantic theater, in which he wore three distinct hats.

As CinC-Lant, Train wore the "purple" uniform of a unified commander, responsible for all U.S. forces in the region. Wearing his Lant-Fleet hat, he supported the Sixth Fleet and presided over the Second, both of which patrolled forty-five million square miles of ocean—from the shores of New York to the Mediterranean to the frigid waters lapping the Soviet Union's northern coast. And last, as Sac-Lant, all nuclear forces assigned to the region fell under his bailiwick.

Train understood the value of intelligence no matter how off the wall it was. His father had been a battleship commander on the *California* on December 7, 1941, when Japanese bombs sank the dreadnought in Pearl Harbor. Within a year, the senior Admiral H. D. Train was director of naval intelligence, serving in that position until 1944. "I lived my life with the overlay of intelligence on my consciousness," Train said about his father's influence.

Rich Haver knew that Train would listen with an open mind to the intelligence that Team Charlie was compiling. And he knew that Train's vote of confidence in what the team was doing was critical. All the efforts to tear down the institutional walls that guarded the Navy's darkest secrets about the Soviets would be futile unless the operational commanders like Train embraced the new concepts. Team Charlie boasted the Navy's best and brightest intelligence officers, but it had little power to force these admirals, who would send their ships and men into harm's way, to accept their findings.

Shortly after the Reagan brief, Haver traveled down the Atlantic seaboard to Norfolk to present Team Charlie's findings to Train. In Train's headquarters' building, he gave a similar but more detailed brief than he had laid out for Reagan. He spoke about the submarine bastions and how the Soviets planned to keep the majority of their Navy in local waters to defend against advancing American ships. When the full concept of the Soviets' naval war strategy hit Train, he literally jumped out of his seat. "By God!" he said with a look of amazement on his face, as if a lightbulb had just clicked on. "Why didn't I realize it? This is naval strategy devised by a field marshal. Damn, it all makes more sense now. These people haven't left their infantry trench or tank turret."

The Soviets, Train realized, had simply extended the basic logic of land warfare to the sea. "That could be their biggest weakness," he said matter-of-factly, "because it's not the same." He could see how the Soviet naval defenses could be defeated. But he was not sure the U.S. Navy had the wherewithal to do it. There would be constant sniping among the surface, submarine, and Air Force barons, each guarding their turf, each with their own agendas not necessarily in synch with the overall good of the Navy. Only the submariners, with Watkins ringing the Klaxon, wholeheartedly accepted the idea of surging past the G.I.U.K. Gap into the Norwegian Sea to operate in hostile but familiar waters.

The admirals who had a violent reaction to the new offensive strategies that Reagan found so appealing had been egged on by Stansfield Turner, who had retired as Carter's director of central intelligence. "Cockeyed theories," Turner protested, "that are nothing more than a budget ploy." Stoic Harold Brown, who was once so enamored with Sea Strike's offensive thrust, had turned against the idea of conducting naval operations in Soviet waters. "I thought and think that is absurd," he said. "In my judgment," Soviet land-based aircraft with cruise missiles would "have devastated the carrier fleet." And Patton, who had briefed Brown on Sea Strike and now sat on Hayward's executive panel, pooh-poohed the whole strategy as useless mumbo jumbo.

Even Hayward, who had originally choreographed Team Charlie's effort, was uncomfortable with some of its results. The institutional biases that shaded the Shapiro clan still played on him. Although he wanted to be progressive about sizing up the Soviet threat and find the best way to defeat the Russians, he found it hard to accept some of the new but controversial thinking.

But Train realized that under the new strategy being shaped by Team Charlie and the Strategic Studies Group, which Hayward had established at the Naval War College, the Second Fleet would play a major role in confronting the Soviet fleet—in peace or war. There was also a more subtle prejudice at work. He and Watkins were the top two candidates to replace Hayward in the CNO's job, and leading the charge on a new strategy would be beneficial.

The idea was to use the Second Fleet as a test laboratory to wed the new intelligence with new battle tactics and strategy. One of the panels that would oversee this test was the Advanced Technology Advisory Board, which kept track of Team Charlie's intelligence analysis. During mock battles fought in U.S. coastal waters, the Second Fleet's commanders would mix new technologies with the various intelligence and tactics under study, perfect those that showed promise, and discard those that proved unreliable. And under Lehman's expensive rebuilding plan, up to five aircraft carrier battle groups, one battleship surface action group, and three replenishment groups of supply ships would make up the Second Fleet. The armada would have the equivalent firepower of forty World War II carriers.

Many of the battle fleet commanders briefed by Team Charlie dismissed the new strategy of sailing past the G.I.U.K. Gap as pure fallacy. But gradually, over the next several years, they would come to appreciate the offensive thrust the Navy was taking. As more and more of the intelligence puzzle on the Soviets began to piece itself together, the battle fleet commanders started to believe that the new strategy could work. And in real-life exercises along the coast, and countless war games at Newport, in which Team Charlie and the SSG locked themselves inside a gaming room protected by armed Marine guards, Rich Haver's team concluded that the air defense network guarding the Soviet Union was more bark than bite. It could not only be penetrated, it could be crippled. And the weakest link in the system was along the vitally important Kola Peninsula. The Navy found that it could park its aircraft carriers inside a Norwegian fjord, seal it off with an attack submarine, and launch air strikes with near impunity. The sheer cliffs would shield the carriers from cruise missiles and Soviet radar. In simulated raids on Murmansk, Navy fighters and attack jets avoided U.S. Air Force radar planes by flying low through the mountainous region all the way to the Kola. In a war, the Americans would pound away at the air defenses, punching holes through the network for Air Force bombers carrying mines, missiles, and nuclear weapons.

Another startling fact that Haver had not mentioned to Reagan in the Situation Room was that the Navy could carry out its task in the Atlantic and the Pacific with twelve aircraft carriers if a war with the Soviet Union lasted less than six weeks. That raised an important question: Did the Navy need to spend $54 billion for three more aircraft carrier battle groups?

Over the next thirty-six months, three classified strategies would be written and debated. Team Charlie members spent more than one hundred days each year on the road, presenting their view graphs and top secret documents to the Canadians and the British, who were at first cool to the idea. In Halifax, Team Charlie briefed the Canadian admirals in a closed-door meeting "that didn't require them to sign five hundred clearance papers," said one participant.[11] The admiral in charge of the Canadian navy had so many questions that he kept team members locked up in the room for fourteen hours. The Navy brought British admirals to the United States and cleared them for the most sensitive war games at the Naval War College. "We really put a full court press on, that we knew what we were talking about and it would work and there was a significant position here for the Royal Navy," said a Team Charlie member.

In the United States, the Navy ran its supersecret black war games at the major CinC's conferences at Maxwell Air Force Base, Fort Leavenworth, Kansas, and Newport to educate the nation's top military officers about where the Navy was going with its new strategy. And Watkins took the budding naval strategy into the tank, the Pentagon's secure briefing room, where the members of the Joint Chiefs of Staff gnawed it over. At first it was seen as Navy grandstanding, but gradually the Army and Air Force came to see the benefit in opening up additional fronts to distract the Soviets' high command.

By spring, as the November election faded, the Navy was well on its way to a new chapter in its history. The whole service was going through a transformation, a new jingoism that Navy leaders from Teddy Roosevelt to Bull Halsey would have saluted smartly. "We just all believed that we could sink the Soviet fleet," Lehman said.[12] "The carriers could survive and could attack the periphery of the Soviet Union in a way that the Soviets could not tolerate."

CHAPTER 6

LEHMAN WENT TO PENSACOLA, FLORIDA, on one of his first tours of the fleet as secretary of the Navy. Up in Washington he was isolated, held captive by the daily grind, the budget battles, and the constant struggle to keep the admirals in line. Getting outside the beltway to a Navy town, especially one like Pensacola, which had a long tradition of being an aviator's paradise, recharged his sense of purpose. Every naval aviator began his flight training in the sleepy Gulf Coast town. The Naval Aviation Museum was there. And another historic site called Pensacola home—Trader Jon's, a bar with a rich reputation that catered to the Airedales' peccadilloes.

One of Lehman's favorite ways of getting the scoop on what was really going on in the Navy was to sit around a table with a pitcher of beer and chew the fat with the troops. In Pensacola he ended up in the bar at the Officers Club, drinking with a crowd of aviators. Alcohol was flowing steadily, and Lehman made a promise to bring back leather jackets, the trademark of World War II– and Korea-era pilots. He got the fliers so worked up over the jackets that they hoisted him on their shoulders and marched around the club, chanting "SecNav! SecNav! SecNav!" to the beaming secretary of the Navy.[1]

Lehman enjoyed swapping war stories with the fliers, and he himself took great relish in recounting his experiences in the Vietnam War. He claimed he had gone on active duty four times to fulfill his annual requirements as a military reservist. It was an odd story for those who knew the real one. Although tens of thousands of Americans had died in the bloody conflict, Vietnam was not a place of hardship for Lehman. Each of his trips to Vietnam had lasted only a matter of days. And his visits were as a government official, not as a fighting man. He was safe from the war because his 1964 enlistment in the Pennsylvania National Guard had protected him and the sons of other middle- and upper-class families, like Dan Quayle, the Indiana senator who later became vice president, from the draft.

It was a convenient means that many eligible men used to shield themselves from conscription and the possibility of being sent to Vietnam. Each year after 1964, more and more soldiers, sailors, and Marines were required to meet the U.S. military commitment to the war. The Army in particular, which occupied Vietnam with more than a half-million troops, constantly needed more young men to replace those killed or maimed in the bloody war. Although approximately six million Americans served in Vietnam, National Guard units were activated only once in 1968, during the Pueblo crisis.[2] Military reservists in the Army and Navy also played a minor role. Few if any reservists did their annual two-week training in Vietnam.[3]

In 1966 Lehman transferred to the Air Force Reserve. And in 1968, with the aid of Arleigh Burke, he switched to the Naval Reserve, receiving the rank of ensign. There were other bureaucrats who held positions similar to Lehman's in the Reagan administration or who had brilliant careers ahead of them, men like Jim Webb, Richard Armitage, and Daniel Ellsberg, whose conservative convictions and sense of duty had led them to volunteer for the war. Even Lehman's old boss, Henry Kissinger, had his education and career delayed by Army service during World War II.[4]

Several people in the Reagan camp bristled over Lehman's draft history. To them he may have been a political hawk, but he was a political hawk of the worst kind: one who hadn't had the courage to tough it out in Vietnam. Jim Webb's anger grew measurably when he saw a photograph that showed Lehman wearing on his Navy uniform a Vietnam campaign ribbon, an award that required that a recipient spend at least thirty days inside the war zone on active duty.[5] But it was not his draft evasion that became an issue when Ronald Reagan's transition team began selecting people for various jobs in the new administration. Reagan's "kitchen cabinet," the small brain trust that had been with the president-elect since his days as governor of California, was screening potential candidates for everything from secretary of state to postmaster general.

Three of the brain trust's most influential men, Michael Deaver, Ed Meese, and Lyn Nofziger, all opposed giving the secretary of the Navy job to Lehman. Deaver had promised the job to an old California hand, Bob Nesen, as a reward for his loyalty to and support of the Reagan cause. Nesen had long been a member of the inner circle and had served in a previous Republican administration as an assistant secretary of the Navy. To Deaver, the match fit. More important, Nesen could be counted on as a Reagan loyalist. He was a proven friend, a Californian, and a man Reagan knew.

But Dick Allen, Lehman's longtime mentor, had little use for Nesen and thought the former car dealer incompetent for a post that would play a vital role in Reagan's military buildup. Without hesitation he threw a monkey wrench into Deaver's plan to pass over John Lehman. As the campaign's national security adviser, Allen had Reagan's ear on military matters, an area that the incoming President, even though he had once served in the

Army, knew little about. During the campaign, under Allen's guidance, Lehman had become a trusted member of the cloak-and-dagger "October Surprise Group," which not only prepared briefing materials for the candidate, but also collected a vast amount of political and military intelligence, some of it classified, from the Carter administration. It was not hard for Allen, a persuasive force, to make a case for Lehman while at the same time convincing the President that Nesen would be better suited for another posting unrelated to national security issues, perhaps as ambassador to Australia. Reagan agreed.

A few days later Reagan was on the telephone in his California home, talking to Pendleton James, the transition team's personnel chief. Reagan's call had come in to James's Washington office at the transition team's headquarters on M Street around 9 P.M. on a nippy December night, and as the conversation neared an end, Reagan said casually, "Oh, by the way, Pen, I've made a decision on the Navy secretary."[6]

"Who is that?" James asked.

"John Lehman," Reagan answered.

"Okay, thank you, Governor."

Not knowing of Reagan's decision, Deaver and Meese called James later that evening on some other personnel issues, and James unknowingly dropped a bombshell. "I got a call from the governor," he said. "He wants to go with John Lehman at Navy."[7]

Meese and Deaver were shocked. "Pen, hold that until we get back. We need to talk to the governor about this situation."[8]

In Washington, a town where people make lasting enemies, not friends, Deaver had heard talk that Lehman got his gold aviator's wings in a cushy deal that appeared to be unethical and possibly against Navy regulations. If there was wrongdoing on Lehman's part, it might be enough to derail his nomination.[9] Some Lehman supporters believe that Deaver made sure that the incoming Reagan team studied Lehman's military record for anything that might disqualify him for the Navy job, although Deaver denies this happened.[10]

Lehman had long advertised himself as a member of the elite and macho community of naval aviators. And he perpetuated the yarn that he had been a naval aviator during the war, which was not true.[11] But his romance with naval aviation was real enough. It began in July 1972 when he arrived on board the aircraft carrier *Saratoga*.

The carrier was lumbering back and forth at fifteen knots in the Tonkin Gulf, a body of water that rims the southern shore of China and North

Vietnam. The mammoth warship created a forty-foot-wide wake of bubbling white foam that stretched like a tail for hundreds of yards. Sara, as the ship was affectionately nicknamed, was not the biggest of America's carriers, but if stood on end, the one-thousand-foot-long ship would be almost twice as high as William Penn's hat on Philadelphia's City Hall. Thousands of feet of gray passageways meandered throughout the giant carrier. Miles of telephone and electric wires and metal piping lined the bulkheads, twisting in every direction. The *Saratoga* was a small city. It had a bank, a barber shop, a hospital, a dentist, a shrink, and a police force. And it was home to five thousand war-weary men.

But operating conditions had become so bad on the *Saratoga* that the ship was called the "Sorry Sara." The engineering crew had a major chore just to keep the carrier afloat. In 1971, in fact, it had nearly sunk in Piraeus, the Greek port near Athens, when a rubber gasket thirty feet below the waterline used in the conversion of salt water to fresh water failed. To refloat the 79,000-ton carrier, the flight deck had to be cleared of planes, and, in quick succession, fifty-three jets hurtled off the ship. Disobeying orders, one pilot, Lieutenant Commander Vince Lesh, whose call sign was Gin Head because he drank heavily on ship, accelerated straight toward hundreds of sunbathers on a beach at more than several hundred miles per hour and fifty feet above the water. At the last second, as the sunbathers scattered in all directions, he made a seven-G turn parallel to the beach, pulled the nose up slightly, and put his F-4 Phantom into a tight aileron roll. Lesh yanked back on the stick and climbed sharply to gain altitude before peeling off.[12]

When Lehman arrived on board *Saratoga,* he told Rear Admiral Jack Christiansen that his boss, Henry Kissinger, had sent him to Vietnam because of the fierce debate the admiral had triggered about a cluster of islands off the coast of Haiphong, the north's main port.[13] Jack Christiansen had been warned through an internal Navy message from Admiral James Holloway, then the commander of the Seventh Fleet, that a member of Kissinger's staff was coming.[14] Shortly before Lehman's visit, Christiansen (one of the carrier battle group commanders who carried out Nixon's orders to mine Haiphong harbor) had dropped some unauthorized mines around the islands. He wanted to drop more because the North Vietnamese were getting around the mines by floating ashore war matériel from ships that anchored at night in protective bays. Christiansen didn't realize that the message traffic concerning his plans was being monitored by the National Security Council. It became obvious to him only when Lehman showed up on *Saratoga* to see what all the fuss was about.

"What the hell is going on out here?" Lehman inquired.[15]

Christiansen, who was known as "the Big Cooley," was about as mean and big as they come. A man with a strong, protruding jaw, he spoke with years of experience and a vocabulary that would make a longshoreman wince. One of his better phrases was "If you don't play ball with me, I'll stuff the bat up your ass."

Christiansen recounted his plans to a skeptical Lehman. "The problem with you, Jack," Lehman said, "is you don't understand Washington." [16]

The Big Cooley looked down on the five-foot-nine-inch Lehman for a moment, then said, "John, you are full of shit. I was in Washington when you were still in high school. I've had five tours in Washington! No, I understand Washington. You," he said, pointing at Lehman, "don't understand what a real war is!"

Figuring that he would back down, Christiansen challenged Lehman, a man he would grow to respect but describe as a smart-ass, cocky little bastard. "How would you like to have a ride over the beach and get shot at?"

Much to his surprise, Lehman said yes. Christiansen cleared the flight with Holloway, then picked his best pilot to fly Lehman in an A-6 Intruder that belonged to VA-75, a bomber squadron based at the Oceania Naval Air Station in Virginia. Commander Charles M. Earnest, a man who was known as a deep thinker and an intellectual rather than a macho attack pilot, was the squadron's skipper. He had a master's degree in physics and was on his third tour in Vietnam aboard the *Saratoga*.

Lehman was taken down to the ready room to be outfitted in the approximately twenty-five pounds of equipment. Lehman stepped into a G-suit, which would help to reduce the crushing G-forces that could cause blood to rush so quickly from his brain that he would black out. Over the G-suit he put each foot through the straps of a torso harness to which a parachute and lap fittings were attached. Hooked to this was a survival vest that had an inflatable life preserver, a knife, shark repellent, a mirror, and other lifesavers. Earnest and the other aviators suiting up holstered pistols. Then they headed up several decks to the well-worn flight deck.

When Lehman and Earnest walked onto the flight line, Christiansen pulled Earnest aside for a private word. "Take him over the beach and scare the shit out of him," he told Earnest. "But don't kill him, for chrissakes!" [17]

Earnest and Lehman ascended the thin ladder into the Grumman-built aircraft and began a preflight inspection. Earnest had flown the Intruder thousands of hours and felt that he could pilot the plane blindfolded. Still, he knew that anything could go wrong on a catapult shot. He would have only seconds to check all of his gauges and react if an engine failed or if the cat stroke gave way. If something did malfunction, he would have to decide whether to fight the Intruder into the sky or eject. If he waited a second too long, he and Lehman would ride the aircraft to the bottom of the ocean. And if the two men didn't drown in the cockpit, they might be run over by 79,000 tons of steel and chewed up in the aircraft carrier's twenty-foot-tall propellers.

On the deck, the booming voice of the air boss came over the loudspeakers, giving the order to start engines. The plane captain immediately twirled his fingers, a wordless sign that told Earnest to fire up the Intruder's two engines. The bomber suddenly came alive. And Earnest began to put it through a series of checks to ensure his flaps and other flight controls worked properly. On the outside of the cockpit, the plane captain gave a thumbs-up as Earnest moved each piece of external metal. Then he taxied the Intruder to the catapult slot, which ran from about the middle of the ship to a point near the bow. A young sailor kneeled down below the throbbing engines and placed the plane's tow bar into the catapult shuttle. Earnest could feel the steel bar lock into place.

Saratoga had completed its turn into the wind and was ready to shoot the Intruder into the bright sky. The huge blast shield rose from the deck behind the jet to deflect the 37,000 pounds of thrust roaring from the aircraft's engines. Earnest saluted the catapult officer, and the Intruder's engines exploded into full military power. The plane was shot forward like a rocket at 160 knots, and there was a loud thump when the plane's wheels left the greasy asphalt of the flight deck. Deck crews watched the glow coming from the jet's engines as it slowly lifted into the sky.

Within a few minutes the A-6 was over Cat Ba Island near the entrance to Haiphong harbor, and North Vietnamese gunners began filling the sky with antiaircraft projectiles. Earnest veered the Intruder away from the fire. The aircraft's instrument panel registered four G's as the Intruder banked to the right, at the same time rolling upside down.[18] On the ground there was a bright flash, followed by a small object that was growing larger in size as it headed for the A-6.

"What the hell was that? A SAM?" Lehman asked.

"No, look right there above you," Earnest instructed him.

"What's that?" Lehman asked, his eyes fixed on a projectile that had been shot out of an eighty-five-millimeter cannon. The North Vietnamese had gotten to be pretty good shots as the war went on, and American jets, the ones lucky enough to survive, often returned with holes the size of a baseball in their tails and wings.

"Don't worry, we're out of range," Earnest reassured his white-knuckled passenger.

Heading back to the ship, Lehman was exuberant. It was as if he had found a calling. As a kid living outside Philadelphia, he'd pedaled his bicycle to the Willow Grove Naval Air Station to watch planes land. On occasion his father had taken him to the Officers Club for lunch, and Lehman would see the pilots in their leather flight jackets and fantasize about being a flier.

After the Intruder returned to *Saratoga* and popped up its canopy, Christiansen noticed that Lehman was "like a kid who discovered his foot." [19]

"God damn, this is the best thing since free grits," Lehman said to Christiansen.[20] "How can I get my wings?"

Lehman's flight with Earnest had been arranged by Christiansen and Holloway for no other reason than his VIP status as an aide to Kissinger.[21] He would not become officially qualified as a bombardier-navigator until about five years later.[22] But it was an irregular deal outside normal operating procedures, if not outside regulations. In 1974 he had approached the staff of Admiral Holloway, who was chief of naval operations, inquiring what had to be done for his acceptance into the aviation program.[23]

Holloway was initially reticent, telling one aide that it was against the law to let a reservist receive training as an aviator. And Lehman was already in his thirties, whereas most candidates were ten years his junior. As a reservist he wouldn't add to the active duty pool of pilots, which was another negative. Why should the Navy, Holloway wanted to know, relax the rules for Lehman?

The issue was dropped by the Navy, but not by Lehman. Once he had set his mind on something, he did whatever it took to achieve it. Lehman sought out Christiansen, who was back in Washington. The Big Cooley was sympathetic but told Lehman, "John, you can't get a set of Navy wings just because you want them."[24] When he first saw Lehman, Christiansen thought he was like "all the Ivy League guys who get reserve commissions in the Navy because they have a dinner jacket that looks pretty good and it's nice for summer parties."[25] But he would come to see Lehman as an important Washington player who could do the Navy some good. Eventually Holloway agreed and opened the door for him to officially get flight training.

Lehman was allowed to become a naval flight officer at his own convenience.[26] He never went straight through the official flight training program required of all aviation candidates that can take up to two years for pilots and twelve months for naval flight officers.[27] Under normal circumstances, a reservist would have to go on active duty to complete the program. Lehman completed the aviation syllabus piecemeal, by convincing pilots to take him up on training flights so he could accumulate flight hours.

Holloway was aware of this and saw nothing wrong with it. "I assured myself that he was not breaking that fundamental rule as a naval reserve

officer who was getting pilot training. That could have put us all in jail."[28]
Over the years Lehman gradually accumulated enough flight time to qualify
as a naval flight officer, and according to Holloway, he was a very fine
aviator. But now his enemies seized on this irregularity, hoping it would be
enough to disqualify him for the job as secretary of the Navy. His supporters,
including Senator John Warner, an old friend of Lehman's who served on
the Armed Services Committee, took the offensive. Finally all sides agreed
to have Tom Moorer, the former chairman of the Joint Chiefs of Staff and
also a Lehman friend, review the flight records.

Within a few days of Reagan's December call to Pen James, he and his
trio of advisers were in Washington. They had convinced Reagan to back
off on the Lehman nomination, at least temporarily. Now they were meeting
in transition headquarters and the issue had come up again. It was imperative
that the Reagan team soon reach a consensus not only about who got the
Navy job, but about who would get the nod for Army and Air Force. So far it
looked as though Jack Marsh was in line for Army and Verne Orr, Reagan's
campaign comptroller, would become secretary of the Air Force.[29]

Deaver, Meese, and Weinberger were all sitting around Reagan, arguing
the merits of each candidate. "George Bush and I sat over on the other side
of the room and we didn't say one word," James recalled. "We sat there
and it was a very heated, very frank conversation. It was my first real
exposure to watching these three close advisers. They were not intimidated
in the least. They were talking to a peer, the governor."[30]

James was watching Reagan, who was listening to his advisers hammer
away on each other's candidates. "He let those three guys say whatever they
want and spill it out, and spill it out they did," James said.

When the discussion ended, Reagan stood up. "Okay, let me think about
this and I'll get back to you."

The meeting ended without closure. Lehman was still very much in the
running.

While Moorer was sifting through his flight logs and other personnel data,
Lehman had grown increasingly worried that he would lose out on the Navy
job. Once again he turned to his mentor, Dick Allen. "This is it," he said.
"It's time to pull out all the stops."[31]

Allen knew how much his protégé wanted the job and knew how effective
Lehman would be at the helm of the Navy ship. He called a number of
people who were Lehman partisans to crank them up and urge them on to
further action. But in the end it was George Bush, the former naval aviator
and friend of Lehman's, who had a private talk with Reagan and quietly
convinced him that Lehman would be the best man for the job.[32]

On January 22 Lehman answered his ringing telephone. He could barely control his excitement when he realized who was calling. "Could you please hold the line for President Reagan?" A few seconds later Lehman could hear Reagan's voice. "John, I'd like you to be the secretary of the Navy. Welcome aboard." [33]

But when he assumed the post he had so diligently campaigned for, it soon became clear to Lehman that not everyone at Navy welcomed him aboard.

≣ CHAPTER 7 ≣

TED GORDON SAT at his government-issue desk on the fourth floor of the Pentagon and slipped the last of the legal briefs and memoranda into a folder marked "SecNav Powers." Lehman would be pleased. Gordon and a team of lawyers had done their homework and found some unusual secretarial powers that had long been forgotten. It would be up to Lehman to decide how to act on the information. Yet Gordon could not help but think that his file was going to tick off a lot of people.[1]

He grabbed the folder and headed out of his corner office toward Lehman's suite. His presentation would have to be quick and precise. Lehman was already becoming famous for his short attention span. If he got fifteen minutes with the new secretary, he was lucky. Briefers who made mistakes or came unprepared paid the price with unending and hostile questions. Some were even cut off and not-so-politely dismissed within a few minutes. But Gordon knew his material was important, so he prepared himself. He always did. He figured he would get at least fifteen minutes.

If there was one thing that set Gordon apart from the rest of the officers who crowded the fourth floor, it was his not-so-striking presence. In his Navy whites he looked soft and somewhat frail, appearing more like a scholar than a warrior. Poor eyesight had almost kept him from a military career altogether. His dream had been to attend West Point. His father was an Army man, and he wanted to follow suit. His dreams were dashed when his local congressman appointed him to the Merchant Marine Academy. But when he showed up for his physical, the doctors rejected him for poor vision. He had a bad eye.

Gordon enrolled in a small Pennsylvania school called Wilkes College. Although he weighed only about 150 pounds, he made the college football team and started as a running back, a position he had played in high school. One day out of the blue, he got a call from a scout for the Naval Academy who had seen him play. "How would you like to go to the Naval Academy?" he asked. Gordon jumped at the chance.

Annapolis gave him a medical waiver for his poor eyesight and put him in a company with John Dalton, a slow-talking Texan who would work in the Carter administration and later go on to become President Bill Clinton's secretary of the Navy during the end of the Tailhook affair. At the academy, where students had to play sports, pass rigorous courses, and take part in military training, Gordon fell in the middle of his class. But years later he would shoot to the top in terms of career advancement. He was the first of his peers to make admiral.

After graduating from the academy, Midshipman Gordon pinned on his ensign bars and spent the next six years of duty assigned to the supply corps. He did several tours at sea, one off the coast of Vietnam during the war, then ended up as a contracting officer at the Philadelphia Naval Shipyard, where he noticed that many of the problems he faced concerned legal matters. The law, he found, intrigued him. So he applied to law school and was accepted by Temple University in Philadelphia. But the Navy would not allow him to attend as an active duty officer. He would have to take a three-year leave from the service and pay for his schooling out of his own pocket. Without a steady income, it would be tough. He thought about it, then left for Temple.

In 1973, with a law degree under his belt, Gordon returned to the Philadelphia shipyard. A short while later he was dispatched to the Pentagon and assigned as an attorney for the admiralty, a job that put him in the inner sanctum of that select fraternity. Within two years he moved over to the Navy's Office of Legislative Affairs, which dealt with Capitol Hill. He would soon win a reputation for his political astuteness and for understanding how to work around the bureaucracy and find loopholes in naval regulations. There was no doubt that he had a keen legal mind and a genius for advising his bosses on thorny questions involving the Uniform Code of Military Justice.

From the Hill, Gordon found himself back on the fourth floor, working for an assistant secretary of the Navy in the Carter administration named Joe Doyle, who had won a Silver Star during World War II. Doyle was also an attorney, having worked for Shearman & Sterling, one of the larger and more prestigious New York law firms. The two men got along well, despite Gordon's bitter diatribes against President Carter's policies. Gordon seethed over Carter's orders to be more frugal during the nation's energy crunch. Under direction from the White House, janitors in the Pentagon turned off the hot water and removed all the knobs. Another Carter order that irked Gordon was the new charge to park in the Pentagon's parking lot. Petty, Gordon thought.

Gordon didn't know if his work for a Carter appointee had landed him on John Lehman's shortlist for expulsion to the fleet. The loyalties of military officers are supposed to lie not with a political party or an individual, but

with the institution. In reality Lehman knew that the uniformed leaders of
the Navy were just as politically motivated as their civilian counterparts.
He had seen it many times during the transitions of the Nixon and Ford
administrations. Although some officers were able to make the switch to
new leadership, many were so loyal to one boss that they couldn't support
new men with different views. There was no place for men like that on the
Lehman team. He wanted his own people.

As Gordon announced himself at Lehman's office, his fate was still far
from clear. He took a deep breath and walked in.

"Get your ass in gear, you're moving," Lehman ordered.

"Fine, I'll be glad to," said Rear Admiral James "Ace" Lyons.[2] He hung
up the phone in his Pearl Harbor office and smiled. He wants me to come
back to Washington and set up the secretariat, Lyons repeated to himself.

Ace Lyons was the kind of officer almost every good combat commander
wished for in a war. He was a creative tactician with endless energy, and a
man who lived by the words "Take no prisoners." As a captain assigned to
the staff of an aircraft carrier in the 1970s, Lyons had made a name for
himself as a promising planner and strategist. His reputation among the
officers corps was spreading as a man who avoided timeworn solutions to
new war-fighting problems. Why fight a war with old-fashioned strategies
and battle plans? he would say. Think ahead. Look for new and uncanny
ways to defeat your opponent. His untraditional views won him an impressive following, including John Lehman, who met him during the Ford administration. It wasn't long before the two men became close friends and started
collaborating on a variety of projects, one of which was to defeat Jimmy
Carter.

For all his gusto, Lyons had one big problem. He was an officer who
found it hard to operate in peacetime. The rub against him was nearly
universal among the admirals: *If we could only put him in a cage and
unleash him in war, he would be okay.* Lyons was always looking for a fight.
He constantly badgered his colleagues, telling them to get off their butts and
become war fighters, not cowering bureaucrats. He did not have the polish
of a Hayward or Holcomb. Nor did he have the patience and worldly manner
of Cockell, who many thought was the Navy's smartest man.

In fact, Lyons was a brute. A balding, heavyset officer, he played tackle
at the academy and had a reputation as a man who could drink a fifth of
whiskey in one sitting. And he had no problem saying a few fuck-yous in
every other sentence. When two Coast Guard admirals showed up at his
office, one of whom had won a Silver Star during the Vietnam War, Lyons

kept them waiting for twenty-five minutes before poking his head out the door and asking, "What the hell are these fucking pussies doing here?"[3] But he had one thing going for him that his fellow admirals did not. The rank and file loved him and his gung ho attitude. They shared his disdain for officers who made a career sitting behind a desk and not at sea. In reaction to that kind of support, all the admirals could do was roll their eyes and shake their heads when Lyons's name was mentioned. Hayward was one of them. After Lyons was promoted to rear admiral, he was banished to the Pacific and a dead-end job with no future. "You have to recognize that being sent out there," Stasser Holcomb said, "was not a kind job for a surface warfare guy. It was an indicator that the community did not have great hopes or admiration for him."[4]

Some considered it a miracle that Lyons even made flag rank. For that he owed Admiral Bill Crowe, who would later become chairman of the Joint Chiefs of Staff and then Bill Clinton's ambassador in London. At the time, Hayward was commander of the Pacific Fleet and had been tabbed by Holloway to head the promotion board to pick twenty-five or so captains for the rank of rear admiral. As the list narrowed, there were more names than openings. And Lyons was one of the last hopefuls. Although it was against regulations, Hayward called Crowe for advice on the remaining candidates.

"If you could pick one captain, who would it be?" he asked Crowe.

"Without hesitation," Crowe responded, "it would be Ace Lyons."

Years later Hayward was still kicking himself for listening to Crowe. Now Lyons was coming back to Washington to be Lehman's talent scout, picking officers and civilians to fill the posts in the Secretariat. Hayward felt that was not only his job, but his right. "Of course Hayward was all pissed off when the first name out of John's mouth was mine," Lyons later recalled. "I wasn't in the building thirty minutes when Hayward sent for me."[5]

Before reporting to Hayward, Lyons stopped to see Lehman. "John, I'm going in to see the CNO. You got any messages for him?"

Lehman thought for a moment. "Well, please convey to him," he said, "that my door is always open." Lehman said that he wanted to do what was right and best for the Navy. "I want a cooperative relationship with him."

Lyons nodded and left.

Down the hall, Hayward waited for Lehman's new right-hand man. Whether or not he wanted to admit it, he was slowly losing control of the kingdom. By the time he had assumed command on June 30, 1978, the Navy had taken huge cuts under Nixon and Ford. In 1968, at the peak of the Vietnam War, the Navy had nearly 1,000 ships. Less than six years later, there were about 500 ships. By 1981 the number had dropped to 479. Deep cuts were made across the board but fell like a hatchet on the Navy's beloved carrier fleet. Before Vietnam there were thirty-three carriers. By the time Jimmy Carter took office there were thirteen, and he had no plans to build any more. In fact, Carter talked openly about only eight carriers. That sent chills up the admirals' spines.

The cuts were nothing like those after World War II. From its fleet of 1,200 ships, the Navy fell to 237 vessels by 1950. Aircraft were cut from 40,000 to 4,300. Ninety percent of the Navy's more than three million troops were sent home. The ships that survived World War II sailed on to take part in the Korean and Vietnam conflicts. But these vessels had now reached the end of their life span and required more maintenance. *Saratoga,* which had nearly sunk not once but twice in Grecian waters, clearly showed that ships built in the 1940s and 1950s were wearing out. During Vietnam, the Navy had deferred maintenance on the majority of its ships, in part because the money needed to refurbish and overhaul its destroyers, cruisers, and carriers went to pay for its share of the war. This financial burden left the Navy with a fleet of aging, poorly maintained warships.

With a shrinking fleet, most of the Navy's senior leadership focused on building the Navy back up in terms of numbers of ships. Zumwalt's Project 60 study to revamp the Navy after Vietnam had recommended six hundred ships. Holloway had done a study that said the Navy, depending on its commitments, needed between six hundred and eight hundred ships. The Joint Chiefs of Staff settled on the larger number and added that twenty-three aircraft carriers would be needed to carry out the Maritime Strategy if the United States got into a long war with the Soviet Union. Hayward knew otherwise. Team Charlie's war gaming showed that if a superpower conflict was short, six weeks or less, the Navy could get by with twelve carriers. After six weeks fifteen carriers would be needed because of the way the Navy rotated its warships—six months at sea, six months at home. This would be altered in a war, but in a way that would not impair maintenance, as had happened during Vietnam.

Hayward knew he would never see a fleet of twenty-three carriers in his lifetime. That was unrealistic. Still, he was concerned about numbers, too, and wanted to increase the firepower of the fleet, but he had taken a slightly different approach from that of his predecessors. The budget tended to drive everything, from the way the admirals looked at the size of the fleet to how they would fight a war. Previous CNOs had always tried to convince Congress that they needed as big a Navy as possible to placate the three barons: aviation, submarine, and surface. Then they would develop a strategy, based primarily on the Navy's size, for how to use the fleet in warfare.

Hayward had tried to flip-flop the thinking process. Under his tutelage, the admirals had agreed not to ask for particular force levels, leaving that political battle solely for Congress to fight.[6] Rather, Hayward was pushing for higher readiness, spare parts, ammunition, pay, and benefits. As he had done with Sea Strike, he wanted to size up the threat, then build a Navy accordingly.

Although Hayward disliked Lyons and cringed at the thought that he now had so much power, in reality the two men were dedicated to the same goal Lehman was: to rebuild the Navy. Now Lyons was sitting before him and Hayward began to burrow in. Why was it, he asked Lyons, that Lehman sent for you? Why didn't he ask me to help him set up the Secretariat? I was available. I have my staff ready to go. What's going on here?[7]

Lyons passed on Lehman's message for cooperation. But, Lyons recalled, he put little effort into delivering it, and the words fell on deaf ears. Hayward was clearly irritated that he was being squeezed out of the picture by a rear admiral he should have gotten rid of a long time ago. Lyons remained relatively quiet as Hayward ticked off all the reasons the CNO should be picking the most qualified people for important jobs, officers he knew better than anybody.

"Look," Lyons finally said, "you ought to understand that better than anybody else. People send for people they trust and value their judgment, and who they are comfortable with." Hayward had little more to say. He dismissed Lyons.

Ace Lyons had come back to the Pentagon like a conquering hero. A man shunned by many of his colleagues would now have a major say in picking its leaders. He set himself up in an office right across from Lehman's. And from day one he could walk in to see Lehman whenever he wanted. He had better access to the boss than Hayward did. But it seemed probable that the less Hayward saw of Lehman, the better. At least it delayed the confrontation that was sure to come.

Lehman, on the other hand, was pushing Hayward's buttons. He would frequently walk down the private hallway that linked his office to Hayward's. The hallway allowed the secretary and the CNO direct access to each other without having publicly to stroll down the fourth floor. Lehman knew it drove Hayward crazy if he showed up without a warning. But he did it anyway.

As Lyons went about his job of filling top spots, he couldn't have cared less that Hayward was being cut out of the loop. In fact, picking people for the CNO's own staff without first asking Hayward gave him a certain sense of joy. Hayward tried in vain to push his own people but was rejected by Lehman and Lyons.

Holcomb watched the daily slights and the purges of Hayward's staff with growing anxiety. Here comes Ace Lyons from the western Pacific, Holcomb would say, and "thereafter they began bypassing the CNO with respect to who ought to be on his own staff and who ought to be promoted to the Navy staff. What came out of that was a systematic purging. It must have been frustrating for Tom Hayward to go into the secretary with a slate of people he thought should be in the jobs, particularly with respect to aviation, and find he couldn't get any of them through."

Neither Hayward nor any of the senior admirals knew what to expect next from Lehman and Lyons. So far the first weeks of the new administration had been nothing short of pandemonium for the blue-suiters, and they waited in anticipation, wondering what would come next. Armed with Ted Gordon's file, Lehman was about to hit them with the shock of their lives.

Lehman had been holding staff meetings every day with one or two of Hayward's admirals, usually Stasser Holcomb, who systematically described what the Navy's priorities were. Holcomb, who was generally considered to have a razor-sharp, analytical mind, was the Navy's top planner. He headed OP-90, which included OP-96, OP-96N, and several other divisions involved with programming, budget, systems analysis, and information systems. On the Navy's organizational chart, they all fell under the control of the CNO, Tom Hayward. On Lehman's priority list, OP-90 didn't even rank. He hated the whole idea of OP-90 and its people, who still practiced a type of numbers-driven analysis that Defense Secretary Robert McNamara and his whiz kids had made famous during the Vietnam War.

Now, as the daily meetings and briefs dragged on, Lehman became increasingly impatient. Finally he could take no more. At one of the sessions he told Holcomb and the others, "This is not doing me any good. I don't want all that stuff. I know what we're going to do and I'm going to do it. So let's not have any more of these. I'm going to tell you what I want." [8]

But every time he exerted his authority over a particular issue, he would hear the same response from Hayward and the admirals: But you can't do that! We do that!

"No, you don't!" Lehman would shoot back. "I do that." It's right here in my powers, he would say, and would recite chapter and verse the information in Gordon's "SecNav Powers" file. [9]

Gordon watched the exchanges with a certain sense of amusement. "I knew what he was doing because he had asked for specifics. He wanted to know where his strong points were and where his weak points were on a statutory basis. What he wanted was to know what he could do clearly," Gordon said, "what arguments he could give people who questioned him." [10]

Lehman had prepared himself well before he took on the admirals. Gordon and Rear Admiral John Jenkins, the Navy's judge advocate general, had briefed him and the soon-to-be civilian counsel, Walter Skallerup, on just what he could legally get away with. Their meeting, in Lehman's office, lasted beyond the normal fifteen minutes that Gordon thought he would get. Lehman listened attentively as Jenkins and Gordon opened up with an overview of the U.S. Code as it applied to the secretary of the Navy. In the early days, they told Lehman, the secretary's authority was sweeping, even more powerful than the secretary of war's. The Navy secretary's strength came from his independence and from being an overseer of a fighting force that dated back to the beginning of the Republic.[11]

Before the creation of the Department of Defense in the Truman administration, there were two war-fighting departments that competed with each other for control of the nation's military might. One was the War Department, the other was the Department of the Navy. And there were two separate bodies of law, one dealing with the Navy and the Marine Corps and one dealing with the Army. "The statutory powers of the secretary of the Navy, historically, were much broader than the statutory powers of the secretary of war," Jenkins explained. "And the reason they were much broader . . . was a very broad sweeping provision." [12]

Lehman inched forward on his seat as Gordon and Jenkins told him about this provision, a statute that had been long forgotten but was never scratched from the legal books. "The secretary of the Navy shall run the Department of the Navy." Not the CNO and his admirals. Not the secretary of defense. The secretary of the Navy was king of the empire. There it was, in black and white. It was the club Lehman had been looking for, a catchall phrase that gave him complete legal authority to run the Navy the way he wanted to.

Mr. Secretary, Gordon and Jenkins continued, you have the right to hire and fire officers, set up promotion boards, pick the men sitting on the boards, and send any board back should you believe the board did not follow your precepts. The secretary, Gordon said, has the authority to appoint whomever he wishes to the various naval committees that advise the chief of naval operations and the admirals, such as the influential Research Advisory Committee. He can even pick who sits on the CNO's executive panel, long the purview of the top admiral. As Lehman saw it, he could assign any officer he wanted to whatever job he wished. That would certainly cause a lot of heartburn among the admirals.

He could wipe out whole divisions or create new ones. He could change procedures for buying ships, airplanes, and other essentials to make them more competitive, which would force defense contractors to cut their profit margins. He could decide what types of ships would be built and what type of war-fighting gear they would be equipped with. He could restructure aviation, his pet peeve. He could even divide up the fleets if he wanted.

Lehman believed he also had total control over the Naval Academy, home of the ring knockers who had a stranglehold over the Navy. The bulk of the Navy's top admirals who filled all the important positions were academy grads. Lehman couldn't resist striking at something the admirals considered sacred. "None of the CNOs could bear the thought of my tampering with the holy of holies," Lehman said after he set up a blue ribbon panel to review the academy's curriculum. "There was the existing academic advisory board. I put a lot of people on that who had a different perspective." [13]

Gordon also told Lehman that the secretary of the Navy used to be the President's sole adviser on naval affairs and once held a cabinet seat. Those two powers had become moot after the creation of the Defense Department, which made the service secretaries subservient to the secretary of defense. But Lehman believed he could operate as if they were in effect.

Soon after their meeting it became clear very quickly to Gordon that Lehman's liberal interpretation of his powers "was not routine, that it was in fact going to have an enormous effect on the Navy." [14]

One of the first challenges to Lehman's authority occurred early and unexpectedly over the plan to take the giant battleship *New Jersey* out of mothballs. The idea to reactivate the forty-year-old ship had originated under Jimmy Carter as a ploy to win congressional support for the second round of talks on the SALT treaty concerning nuclear weapons. Carter and his defense secretary, Harold Brown, were besieged by a good many members of Congress who insisted that the administration would have to show an intention to beef up American conventional capabilities if they wanted support for SALT.

So Carter asked Brown what big-ticket items each service could quickly put into operation. "Since I thought we should beef up our conventional capabilities, too, I was happy to negotiate something like that," Brown recalled. [15] It was an interesting switch for Carter, who had come to Washington wanting to cut $5 to $7 billion in defense spending. He left the White House pushing a bigger defense budget, up to $200 billion per year.

When Brown turned to the Navy, Hayward produced a plan that he and Holcomb had been working on for some time to reactivate *New Jersey* and some older aircraft carriers and cruisers. Brown was dubious about reactivation of the battleships. Although President Carter's last defense budget grew 5 percent in real terms and included substantial increases for the Navy, Hayward's elaborate plans for *New Jersey* died on the vine. Brown had nipped the idea, partly because the cost was considered extreme.

Hayward had rekindled the plan in early 1981. As soon as he took over, Lehman began preparing a supplemental to Carter's last defense budget, in effect asking Congress to provide more money for the Navy. Each of the services was doing it. Hayward reasoned that *New Jersey* could be the first jewel in the crown of the Navy's rebuilding effort. He broached the idea to Lehman, who invited the CNO into his office to discuss the scheme. Hayward unfolded some blueprints on a small table that illustrated what *New Jersey* would look like and what it could do when refitted with the latest technology.

Lehman cringed when he glanced at the drawings The ship was almost unrecognizable. Of the three large gun turrets that the battleship was famous for, the one on the stern of the ship had been eliminated. In its place was a flight deck for aircraft called Harriers, or jump jets, which could take off vertically. And under the flight deck were more than one hundred vertical box launchers for the Tomahawk cruise missiles that could be tipped with nuclear warheads.

This is a "fucking gold-plated" plan, Lehman said to himself, and he told Hayward that it could cost as much as $2 billion. "I really put my foot down," he later said.[16] Lehman was determined to reactivate not just *New Jersey,* but its three sister ships, *Iowa, Wisconsin,* and *Missouri.* And there was no way that he could bring them all back at $8 billion. He knew that if he wanted to build a lot of new ships for the Navy, he had to drive down the cost of ship construction. *New Jersey* would be the litmus test. Get rid of the flight deck, Lehman told Hayward. We don't need to put jets on a battleship.

Both men wanted what they thought was best for the Navy. They just couldn't agree on who would lead the charge. "It's the old story of two kids wanting the same piece of candy," Gordon would say. "Lehman comes in and he's a little bit bigger than the other kid and he took it away. In the end game it was better because he had more influence, more power, and more friends." [17] Still, it would take months before the battleship issue was resolved, and even Lehman's backers on Capitol Hill found the whole concept hard to swallow.

When airplanes depart National Airport in Washington, D.C., they frequently fly over the Pentagon in a low and slow pattern. It looked to Ted Gordon, who often sat in his corner office watching the jets, as if they were going to slam into the five-sided building. On occasion the jets' roaring engines would even drown out the telephones ringing in the outer offices of the fourth floor. In early March there were no airplanes about to crash into Gordon's office, but his telephone was ringing loudly.

"Commander Gordon," he said, picking up the telephone.

"You're a counsel down in the assistant secretary's office, aren't you?" asked the voice on the other end.

"Yes," Gordon answered.

"We've put together this organizational chart, and we think we need a legal review," said John Pieno, who was working with Ace Lyons to place civilians and officers in top Navy spots. "We heard you know a little about this. Would you mind taking a look at this and telling me what you think?" [18]

No problem, Gordon said. I'll be right down. He left his office and walked down the hall to a room Lyons had commandeered. There he met Pieno, a Navy commander who was an old friend of Lehman's. Lyons always ignored Gordon, which infuriated him and often led to bitter arguments between the two men. Lehman enjoyed their bantering and would sit back and laugh when the two of them got into it.

Pieno pulled out an organizational chart that listed each of the positions he and Lyons wanted to fill, then explained to Gordon what types of individuals they were looking for.

"What do you think?" he asked.

"It's illegal," Gordon said.

"What do you mean?"

"Look," Gordon explained, "you have too many assistant secretaries. And you have left out some important duties that assistant secretaries are supposed to perform. Also, there is nobody slated to do reserve affairs, which is required by law. Let me take it back to my office," he said, "and rework it."

In three hours he was back in Pieno's office with a redesigned chart that conformed with the law. From then on Gordon worked with Pieno on vetting the officers and civilians being brought on board the Lehman team.

By the end of April Lyons had returned to Hawaii, content that before he left Washington, most of the top spots had been offered to the best candidates. They were men who would follow Lehman's orders to the very end. Although the law didn't allow Lehman to control fleet operations, he would do it through his own people. If the admirals resisted, Lehman would replace them with officers he would promote to the admiralty. It was simple management mathematics.

Among the most important posts was shipbuilding. That went to George Sawyer, who was the president of J. J. McMullen, a respected naval architecture and engineering firm. A former executive at Bechtel Corporation, Sawyer was at the top of his business career when Lyons and Lehman began courting him. He was making a comfortable salary that would be cut dramatically to about $55,000 a year if he took the Navy job. Worse, he would also lose a huge amount of money in stock options and other compensation. The financial loss in itself was a good enough reason to say no.

Sawyer was a deep-voiced, gentle man who seemed never to lose his temper. His organizational capabilities were supreme, and he had a mind that could think big without losing sight of the little details. Some called him visionary in shipbuilding circles. He was excited about the huge Reagan budgets, which would mean the Navy could build a massive fleet of warships. And Sawyer could be the captain of the construction program. That was tempting. He was a former nuclear submariner who had spent ten years in the Navy after graduating from Yale on an NROTC scholarship. He could come back as a real leader and make real changes. That was incentive enough to accept Lehman's offer.

The downside, Sawyer knew, was that the job would require fourteen-hour days. What about his two teenage children? And what about his wife, who was terminally ill? How could he devote time to both the Navy and his family? In the end the pros outnumbered the cons, and he joined the Lehman team.

Another vital position was head of research and development. Lehman wanted a man who could cut through the red tape and get new technologies into the fleet quickly. For that he picked Melvyn Paisley. The two men first met when Lehman owned Abington Corporation, a defense consulting firm that he, his brother Joseph, and several friends, including Richard Perle, began after Jimmy Carter was elected. The business became a lucrative occupation for Lehman. Abington paid him a salary of $180,000 and had contracts with major firms, including the giant aircraft company Boeing. It was Paisley, then a vice president at Seattle-based Boeing, who gave Lehman and Abington a contract worth as much as $350,000 a year between 1977 and 1981.[19]

Lehman was taken by Paisley's slap-'em-on-the-back style, his off-color stories, and his successes as a World War II fighter pilot and businessman. And Lehman, who owned a Corvette, liked the fact that Paisley drove a Jaguar XKE sports car. Paisley was a ladies' man, three times married and twice divorced. He also had a habit of embellishing his accomplishments. He claimed to have a master of science degree from the Massachusetts Institute of Technology, but he had attended the university for only a single semester. As for his war record, Paisley's performance in recounting how he shot down nine enemy aircraft was dramatic and heroic but not true. He was credited by the Pentagon with four kills and two "half kills."[20] Many on the staff thought of him as slimy. But Lehman was gripped by Paisley's charm and found in him a man who had the personality and qualities he valued. They became close friends, were seen on the Washington social circuit, and soon began to hunt and fish together.

There would also be positions for old friends like Roger Duter, a former

Navy pilot who had taught Lehman how to fly using only instruments, and
Don Price, a Marine officer Lehman first met while on assignment for Henry
Kissinger in Stuttgart, Germany. Lehman had introduced himself to Price as
Ensign John Lehman. Price took one look at him and didn't like what he saw.
He was not in uniform. He had on a Navy peacoat without any insignias. He
was carrying a tape recorder that was playing songs by the Bee Gees. And
Price, a spit-and-polish Marine, thought that Lehman's hair was too long for
an officer on active duty. What is an ensign doing going in to call on a four
star? he said somewhat angrily to himself.[21] But Price soon found that he
and Lehman had more in common than he'd once thought. And whenever
Lehman came to Germany, he made it a point to go bar hopping with Price.

Price went back to Vietnam in 1972 and distinguished himself on his next
tour advising the South Vietnamese troops along the DMZ. In April he was
sitting on a hilltop when he spotted three helicopters in the distance heading
toward him. The war was again heating up, as North Vietnam had just
launched the Easter Offensive. The military incursion triggered a massive
U.S. response. Haiphong harbor was mined, and U.S. Navy and Air Force
aircraft had once again started bombing the north.

Price watched the helicopters approach, their blades churning through the
air, making the familiar *whomp, whomp, whomp, whomp* sound as they
swooped over the green countryside. He saw that two of the helicopters were
Army gunships, and that they were flying on each side of the third, larger
aircraft. Probably bringing in some senior generals or other VIPs, Price
thought.[22]

After the aircraft landed and the dying rotors wound down, the pilot of
the VIP chopper pulled off his radio headset, jumped out, and walked over
to Price with his hand extended. It was John Lehman, who had got himself
on active duty. He gave Price a hearty handshake and told him that he was
there for Kissinger to see how Vietnamization was working. Price was
delighted to see his friend. But he couldn't help thinking, What the heck is
he flying that for? He's not qualified to fly that![23]

Over the next several days during Lehman's stay in the DMZ, the two
men found time to sit on top of a bunker, drink Christian Brothers brandy,
and watch B-52 bombers lumber overhead en route to drop thousands of
tons of explosives on the cities and towns of North Vietnam. In the years
that followed, Price rose to the rank of lieutenant colonel and the two men
remained friends. Now he had been picked to become Lehman's private
fix-it man. He was loyal, friendly, and, like a good Marine, always willing
to carry out whatever mission Lehman sent him on.

The other officers on the Lehman team varied in personality and ranged
in rank from commander to admiral and general. There was John Pieno,

whom Lehman had met on one of his trips to Vietnam. Commander Paul David Miller became Lehman's personal executive assistant. Commander Tom Lynch, a big, happy-go-lucky football jock who had starred at the Naval Academy, was an administrative aide Lehman picked for the job of Senate liaison. Brigadier General Mike Mulqueen was Lehman's Marine aide. According to members of Lehman's staff, he eventually would have to talk Lehman out of using a Navy aircraft and truck to transport fish he had caught on a fishing expedition in Florida.[24] Captain Jimmy Finklestein would become Lehman's public affairs officer. He would devise a media strategy that heaped so much positive press on Lehman that Weinberger regularly had his military assistant, General Colin Powell, call with orders for Lehman to tone down his public image.[25]

In the fleet, Lehman would come to rely on men like Captain Frank Kelso and Commanders Joe Prueher and Mac Williams to fill various jobs in the Secretariat. Prueher was a handsome attack pilot with the reputation of a leader who would not ask his men to do something he would not do first. Williams, a Southerner, had a sharp tongue and, like Lehman, a biting wit. He was a lawyer who had no problem putting loyalty to his boss first and foremost.

Kelso, who was on the verge of becoming a rear admiral, was the one man who didn't seem to fit in. He was a submariner, which made him an outsider in the aviation world that Lehman was so enamored with. But Lehman was impressed with his creative mind concerning naval operations and capabilities. More important, Kelso was a passive man, willing to put himself above the petty differences the admirals had with Lehman and wholeheartedly support the concept of civilian leadership. He was also willing to turn a blind eye to officers who broke the rules. Hayward had once asked Kelso to investigate a submarine captain who was retaliating against several crew members for complaining about his violations of safety procedures. Kelso downplayed the probe, which incensed Hayward, who ended up having his personal staff investigate the case.[26]

The one person Lehman couldn't replace was Hayward. His four-year term, mandated by law, would last for another eighteen months. The other top military officer whom Lehman did not dare challenge was Marine Corps Commandant General Robert Barrow, a tough-as-nails Southerner from Louisiana. But Barrow posed no problem. He genuinely liked Lehman and, in any case, was due for retirement in two years.

By April everybody whom Lehman and Lyons had approached either had a job or had accepted offers to join the team—everybody, that is, but Ted Gordon. In the first two months of Lehman's tenure, Gordon had done yeoman's work. He was instrumental in preparing the "SecNav Powers" file, and he had reorganized the list of assistant secretaries that would have been an embarrassment if released publicly. He had grown close to Lehman during the last few months, seeing him as many as six and seven times a day. Lehman was comfortable with Gordon and his advice, and Gordon felt at ease with the new secretary, who was about his age.

Still, Lehman had yet to ask him to come aboard. So Gordon decided to see Lehman and inquire about his future. He took the one-minute jaunt down the fourth-floor corridor, and after being escorted into Lehman's office, he made his move.

"Mr. Secretary, I have a problem," Gordon said.

"What's that?" Lehman asked.

"I'm finishing up here and I don't have a job."

Lehman looked at Gordon for a brief moment, not realizing he was unsure of his future. "What would you like to do?" he asked.

"I want to stay working for you," Gordon answered.

"Good idea, that's a good idea," Lehman replied immediately. He told Gordon that he would create a special job for him to handle his personnel affairs on Capitol Hill.[27]

≡ CHAPTER 8 ≡

"WHAT THE FUCK IS GOING ON? What in the hell are you doing?"

John Lehman was almost foaming at the mouth, screaming into the telephone at Tom Hayward, who was five thousand miles away in Washington. It was April 13 and Lehman had just arrived in Pearl Harbor after a long flight on his personal airplane.

During the trip, Frank Carlucci had called him on the plane's secure telephone with a puzzling question. "John, what's going on?" Carlucci said.[1] He had heard that Lehman was pulling back on the nomination of Ace Lyons to take over the Second Fleet. Was it true?

What do you mean? Lehman asked, his voice rising in exasperation. Under the new Maritime Strategy the Second Fleet would be the heart of the Atlantic strike force. Who better to handle one of the best jobs in the Navy than Lehman's bullish sidekick, Ace Lyons? Lehman wanted Lyons to sail right up to the Soviet Union's doorstep. All the new intelligence being developed by Team Charlie showed that was what the Soviets feared most. So why not provoke them? Why not send the Second Fleet into the Kremlin's own Arctic waters, where the U.S. Navy could train and test battle plans in actual conditions? Why not let the Soviets see firsthand what the U.S. Navy was capable of? If training operations were successful in such a harsh environment, it would signal that the Navy was prepared to take the fight right to the Russian motherland.

But now something seemed terribly wrong with Lyons's nomination.

"Tom Hayward says that he won't support this nomination for Second Fleet," Carlucci said. He told Lehman that after he had left, Hayward came down to Cap Weinberger's office and was steadfast in his opposition. He said Lyons was simply not qualified for the job, and that he had somebody else in mind.[2] Carlucci said the secretary of defense wanted to know what was going on.

As Carlucci spoke, Lehman was growing more irate by the minute. He assured Carlucci that he was 100 percent behind Lyons and that he was the most qualified admiral to take command of the fleet. Then he hung up the phone and placed a call to the chief of naval operations.[3] He was mad, mad as can be, at Tom Hayward.

• • •

The dispute over Lyons was only the latest squabble between Hayward and Lehman. Ever since he'd become secretary in February, Lehman had repeatedly hammered away at the admirals, accusing them of lacking the initiative to set the Navy on a new course.

Hayward and his trusted aide Bill Cockell felt Lehman was way out of line and out of touch with what was really going on in the fleet. They watched in amazement as repeated press leaks about the lack of a grand strategy, stories that originated in the Secretariat, gave the Navy and its CNO a bum rap. Lehman knew all too well that Hayward had put the Navy on track toward the new Maritime Strategy. Before the 1980 presidential election, Hayward had established Team Charlie and the Strategic Studies Group at the War College. Rich Haver had even briefed Lehman personally on what Team Charlie was doing. Yet in public, Lehman continued his soapbox speeches declaring that the Navy lacked direction.

On April 6, the week before he left for Hawaii, Lehman had blasted the admirals at the War College in Newport. He traveled up the coast to deliver a speech he called "Hail the Return of Strategy." That was followed by a steady stream of interviews with the media in which Lehman complained about the rudderless Navy that he had inherited. "Month after month I submitted requests," he said, "to be briefed on the overall naval strategy. It wasn't until May 1981 that it became clear why it was never put on my schedule: it did not exist!"[4]

Peter Swartz, who was one of the key naval officers involved with the development of the Maritime Strategy, tried to explain to Lehman that he was wrong. But when he brought up Hayward's accomplishments, Lehman dismissed them with a wave of his hand. "It suited him tactically to allege that the admirals were all stupid and he was smart," Swartz said. "It was part of John's whole shtick for everybody to believe that he got on a white horse and rode in and cleaned up the town. The fact that we didn't like that aspect of it, he didn't give a shit. He used to say, 'You owe six hundred ships to me. You owe the Maritime Strategy to me. All you guys owe all this shit to me. If it wasn't for me, you would be acting like quavering admirals.' "[5]

Hayward, who was anything but a quavering admiral, finally decided he had to set Lehman straight. "Bill," Hayward said to Cockell, "we have to do something about bringing the secretary up to speed." The mild-mannered Cockell, who had also been perturbed at Lehman's almost daily attacks, readily agreed.

If the shoe were on the other foot, Lehman would have galloped down the private hallway that linked his office to Hayward's and popped in unannounced. But Hayward had been reared on protocol. After some thirty years in the Navy, the aristocratic admiral had grown accustomed to proper etiquette. It went against his demeanor to barge in on the secretary of the Navy. He might even have preferred being piped aboard by a bosun's mate to announce his presence. But that was a tradition for ships, not inside the Pentagon. The telephone would have to do. He called and asked to see the secretary.[6] Lehman invited him over.

Hayward made himself as comfortable as he could in the secretary's office, then opened up the file he had brought. Lehman was about to see something that few people outside the most upper reaches of the admiralty even knew existed: Cockell's top secret "Naval Forces National Strategy," a fifteen-page blueprint for a global naval war with the Soviet Union.

Lehman was impressed and thought Hayward had something of value here. Years later he would acknowledge that Hayward's work "certainly had an influence on fleshing out the strategy. He provided most of the options to get force out there quickly. I didn't agree with [some of] the specifics, but they were all along the lines of 'Let's build a Six Hundred Ship Navy.' "[7]

The call from Pearl Harbor to the Pentagon took a few moments to get through to the CNO's office. But Hayward was not immediately available. He would have to call Lehman back.

A short while later Hayward's call rang in Lehman's Pearl Harbor room. "What the hell are you doing?" Lehman demanded. "You signed off on this. I sent it down there with your signature on it."

"Well, you know," Hayward said, "I want to talk to you when you get back."[8]

That wasn't good enough for Lehman, who was not about to be put off. He wanted answers, and he wanted them now. Before he left for Hawaii, Lehman had had a bitter fight with Hayward over the nomination, but the CNO begrudgingly agreed to support Lyons. Against his better judgment, he signed the promotion chit that would give Lyons three stars and command of a major fleet. Now he was trying to go behind Lehman's back and sabotage the nomination. He was deliberately disobeying orders. And Lehman was not about to let the issue lie until his return to the Pentagon.

Although Hayward had grown used to Lehman's often condescending tone, he still resented being bullied and treated as if he knew nothing about the Navy or its people. The enlisted sailors and officers were *his* people. He knew them, knew their fears and their needs, and knew most of them were dedicated career people. Lehman, on the other hand, was a politician. His kind came and went at the whim of the voters. Hayward had dealt with many men of the same ilk. They were to be tolerated. They were mere blips on the radar screen of a career naval officer who spent twenty or more years in the service. In most instances, the Navy men simply outlasted their civilian taskmasters.

"I'm getting very bad vibes from the admirals," Hayward told Lehman. After Lehman chose Lyons for the Second Fleet, Hayward secretly began polling the three- and four-star admirals, the Navy's most senior officers, about the nomination. Cockell, who was keeping tabs on the polling, noted that "virtually every response was negative."

Nobody wanted Lyons, Hayward told Lehman, adding that the majority of the top admirals sided with him and not the secretary of the Navy on this issue. Lyons was considered an outcast. He was dangerous. There was no way he should have control of a fleet, especially one that would sail into Soviet waters and might cause an international incident. After several minutes Hayward tried to end the conversation by pushing another officer for the job of Second Fleet, but Lehman cut him off. "No!" he said in his most authoritative voice. "I'm not interested in him." Ace Lyons, he said, had all the right attributes. He was willing to go out on a limb, even risk his career if things backfired with the naval operations in Soviet waters.

Lehman and Lyons had had long discussions about operating above the G.I.U.K. Gap and east of the North Cape on the tip of Norway. It had been years since the Navy had held a major exercise in the northernmost regions of the Norwegian Sea. During the Ford administration, sixty-five warships, including one U.S. aircraft carrier and two British flattops, had practiced sea control operations 120 miles from the Soviet Norwegian border above the North Cape.[9] But they did not round the cape into the Barents Sea. The North Cape had long served as a kind of trip wire for both superpowers.[10] If the Soviets had rounded it en masse, the U.S. Navy would have put its forces on heightened alert, concerned that Moscow might be preparing for a war.[11] If the Americans had done the same, the Soviets would have gone to battle stations.

Sailing beyond the North Cape was an unacceptable provocation to the Soviets as well as to the Norwegians, who treated the waters at the top of the world exclusively as their own. The Soviets also had their own nationalistic claims to the seaways. If the Americans steamed into the Barents Sea, they would undoubtedly send out hundreds of aircraft and warships to bully and drive off the U.S. invaders. And if something went wrong, such as a collision between an American and a Soviet warship, or an aggressive aerial dogfight ending up in a shooting match, World War III could be under way. Both sides understood that and treated the North Cape with a healthy respect.

Although Team Charlie had developed a small mountain of data suggesting the Navy could survive above the Gap, conventional wisdom inside the Pentagon concluded that if the Navy sailed into the teeth of the Soviet bear, it was risking a major defeat. But Lehman needed a mission for his Six Hundred Ship Navy. So he taunted the Kremlin at every opportunity and warned the Soviets what was in store for the Red Banner Navy. "We cannot accept compromise as to who is going to come out second best. We cannot accept parity. We must be prepared to put them on the bottom if we are challenged. We must be able to go in harm's way and prevail." [12]

It was a time for boldness, for taking the offensive, he and Lyons believed, not for hiding in the dark. Since his days at St. Joseph's, Lehman had preached an extremist anti-Soviet line. In the new Reagan administration, he was as bullish as any among the ultraconservatives wanting to intimidate the Kremlin whenever the chance arose. If the 1980 presidential elections meant anything, Lehman often said, it was that the American public wanted a strong military it could be proud of and one that would stand up to communist aggression around the world.

Ace Lyons could carry out that mission. He was outspoken, gruff, at times crude, but most important, he was the type of officer who would be unpredictable in a war. "He was a guy with an instinct for offensive strategy who had a practical feel for it," Lehman said in Lyons's defense. "He wasn't just sitting back in an armchair."

Hayward wasn't at all convinced that Lyons was up to the job. But Lehman persisted. "My nominee is Lyons," he said, cutting off the CNO. "I've heard you. Now do what I said."

It was over that quickly. Lehman had beaten Hayward again.

Hayward had lost another round in the bureaucratic war to control the naval empire. He had done his best to defeat Lyons, even to the point of being insubordinate to the secretary of the Navy. He tried to put it out of his mind. He had more important things to worry about, and there would be other battles to fight. Still, it was hard to swallow. But instead of brooding about it, Hayward put on his Joint Chiefs of Staff hat and began planning a naval operation that Lehman would salivate over, but one in which the secretary legally had no operational control. Tom Hayward thought it was time to beat up on Muammar el-Qaddafi.

In 1973 Qaddafi had declared the Gulf of Sidra to be part of Libya's territorial waters. Punishment would be swift, the Libyan dictator warned, for those who trespassed across his "line of death" that marked the entry into the gulf. Richard Nixon had refused to send the Sixth Fleet past the line. And Carter rejected Hayward's pleas to challenge Libya for fear it might jeopardize the American hostages held in Iran. The Reagan administration reversed course and said the United States would match every Libyan provocation with an escalated response.

During one of the regular meetings in the Tank, the Joint Chiefs' secure conference room, Hayward broached the subject of humiliating Qaddafi. The gulf is an international waterway, he said. The easiest and most effective way to undermine Qaddafi and demonstrate American resolve was to conduct a Freedom of Navigation exercise in the Gulf of Sidra. There was little, if anything, Qaddafi could do to stop the Navy from operating there.

The Joint Chiefs liked the idea.

Although twenty-five thousand people worked in the Pentagon, only a handful were in on the planning for the Reagan administration's first military show of force. On the surface, its intention was peaceful. But lying just below the legalese about this being a freedom of the seas issue was a secret plan for war. If Qaddafi did something stupid like pull the trigger, the Navy had a series of planned combat responses ready to go. With the Joint Chiefs' approval, the rules of engagement were also softened. Pilots could finally shoot if they were threatened.

Hayward and the Joint Chiefs ordered Rear Admiral James Service and his Sixth Fleet battle group to the gulf. In the predawn hours of August 18, eleven warships, a submarine screen, and the aircraft carriers *Forrestal* and *Nimitz* would steam past the "line of death." At first light, Qaddafi would wake to find the Great Satan in his front yard.

One hundred seventy-five miles down the eastern seaboard from Washington, the Second Fleet's command ship, *Mt. Whitney,* slowly cut through choppy Atlantic waters. On board, Vice Admiral Ace Lyons was preparing to take the Navy on a historic voyage. He felt Qaddafi was a sideshow, a harmless camel jockey with a third-rate military. The real sparks would fly not in the desert, but in the frigid waters of the Barents Sea, where Lyons planned to sail his Second Fleet.

His change of command ceremony aboard the ship, at which Lehman and Harry Train spoke, was only days old when Lyons did what he was best at: being unpredictable. While *Mt. Whitney* steamed peacefully off the Virginia coast, he unleashed a hurricane of change inside the 620-foot-long ship. Get the staff together, he told his executive assistant. I want to be briefed on the upcoming Ocean Safari exercise. The naval exercise in the North Atlantic, which would involve eighty-three warships from the United States, Great Britain, Canada, and Norway, was just a matter of weeks away. As his officers crowded around him, Lyons sensed the nervousness of many of the men. My reputation precedes me, he thought.

"Okay," Lyons began. "Tell me what's going on." [13]

His staff gave him a quick rundown about which ships were involved and what navigational tracts they would be assigned as they sailed into the Atlantic. The operational order spelling out the entire exercise had already been sent over Navy communications to all the commanding officers and the allied task force commanders who would take part. His allied counterparts, Lyons learned, were due aboard the *Mt. Whitney* for a final briefing before departing for the North Atlantic.

"That's fine," he said, "but that's not what we are going to do. I'm canceling the operational orders." [14] After a moment of silence, Lyons said they were going to change the exercise. And this was what they were going to do. There was only one way to see if the Navy's new Maritime Strategy worked. Team Charlie planners could talk until they were blue in the face. And the war gamers could play with their little ships and aircraft in their nice, cozy, safe war rooms. Lyons planned to do the real thing. We're going to take the fleet not just into the North Atlantic, he told his staff. We're going into the Norwegian Sea, east of the North Cape, and into the Barents.

Then he gave one final order. When the new navigational tracts were assigned and the plan was complete, he wanted it hand-delivered. He did not want the order to go out over the Navy's communications system.

It was an odd directive. But Lyons had a gut feeling that somehow the Soviets had managed the impossible. They were reading U.S. military communications. And he was not alone in his fears that a mole lurked somewhere in the military, perhaps even in the Navy. Admiral Bobby Inman, a longtime spook who ran the National Security Agency, also sensed that all was not well. Whenever the Navy conducted a large exercise, Soviet ships were always waiting in the operational area. And when U.S. missile subs sortied from their bases, Soviet submarines were in position to trail them. Even during the Vietnam War the enemy had seemed to have forewarning of when and where U.S. air strikes would occur. If the missions were changed at the last minute because of bad weather, the North Vietnamese were still ready.

It was uncanny. There were just too many coincidences for Inman. In the late 1970s he had ordered Rich Haver to visit the Navy's top admirals to inquire about how they handled their secure communications. Haver reported back to Inman that he was thrown out of more offices then he cared to talk about. "I got a lot of 'You must be crazy, get out of here's," he told Inman. Nobody was willing to believe that U.S. communications, the most sophisticated in the world, might have been compromised. It was impossible, the admirals said.

Lyons and a handful of other officers thought it wasn't and were receptive to Bobby Inman's emissary. Lyons too had seen the coincidences. Something was wrong. What he didn't know was that years earlier John Walker, a Navy warrant officer, had supplied the keys to the nation's secure communications system to Moscow. The FBI would not catch Walker for three more years.

Lyons was not about to take any chances. There was no way the Soviets could know what his plan was if it was hand-delivered. He knew where he wanted to go and what he wanted to do. And nobody—not the Russians, not even his timid fellow admirals, the few who knew what he had in store—could do anything about it. He planned to surprise the hell out of the Soviets.

In the most secure offices of the CIA, the Navy, and the Defense Intelligence Agency, an order was given to begin a wholesale look at the capabilities, intent, and technological prowess of the Soviet navy. The National Intelligence Estimate (NIE), which was a by-product of the entire intelligence community, would be called NIE 11-15-82/D, a secret study that would remain classified until December of 1994.[15] Its drafters hoped that it would settle once and for all the issue of whether the Soviet fleet was a growing offensive threat or a defensive navy charged with protecting its homeland.

Although the naval intelligence officers assigned to Team Charlie would be key players in helping to write the new NIE, the most senior Navy official with the heaviest pen would be John Lehman. And if there was one thing Lehman and his staff were sure of, it was that a defensive Soviet navy would not sell well on Capitol Hill. He was not about to let the intelligence pukes sink his fleet.

▰ CHAPTER 9 ▰

At first light on July 27, Commander Sy Manning pulled a blue Navy ball cap tight over his head, stuffed a wadded-up palmful of chewing tobacco into his right cheek, and then bit down on a large unlit cigar. The damp morning chill hung over Puget Sound, leaving a thin layer of moisture on the rails of the battleship *New Jersey*. There was just enough wind coming off Vancouver Island in the northwest to add a bite to the morning air. The cold would send most people scurrying below decks. But not Sy Manning. He was a weatherbeaten sea dog from the old days when the pride of the Navy was battleships, not aircraft carriers. He would stand this watch as he had hundreds of others.

The dreadnought was moving silently in the narrow Strait of Juan de Fuca, its long, pointed bow cutting through the murky shipping channel at about five knots. On the bridge, Manning scanned the normally busy waterway for other ships, his eyes stopping on the oceangoing tug dead ahead at fifteen hundred feet. The tug's diesel engines purred, barely strained by the two-inch-thick cables attached from its stern to the prow of the 45,000-ton battleship. It was *New Jersey*'s lifeline.

Having such a magnificent warship under tow was certainly not the proudest day in Manning's life. But then again, it had been twelve years since *New Jersey* had been at sea and fired her sixteen-inch guns in anger during the Vietnam War. After she had served in three wars, the Navy had mothballed her in 1969 to its Bremerton graveyard, where the behemoth lay moored adjacent to the legendary *Missouri,* the battleship that Japan had surrendered on. "Rest well, yet sleep lightly and hear the call, if again sounded to provide firepower for freedom" were the words of the *New Jersey*'s last captain when her colors were hauled down.[1]

Now under orders from John Lehman, *New Jersey* was once again coming to life. Over the years, the famed ship had become a nesting grounds for seagulls and pigeons. Its teak decks had been spoiled. Brass fittings had gone unpolished. Engines had lain idle. But the general condition of the steel hull, which in some places was eighteen inches thick, was good. It would be a daunting task to transform a platform designed to fight in World War II into a modern missile-firing warship. Some of the new missiles would be tipped with nuclear warheads. A battery of new electronic and communications systems would be added. And a helicopter landing pad would be installed. But the additions would not alter *New Jersey*'s sleek profile. It would be a fitting face lift.

Manning and his skeleton crew of twenty-two men had come aboard to oversee the towing operation after the Navy pronounced the ship seaworthy. So far, the operation had proceeded without a hitch. In thirty minutes the battle wagon and her tug would round Cape Flattery and then sail west for fifty miles into the Pacific before turning south for the Long Beach Naval Shipyard some fifteen hundred miles away. As the 888-foot-long *New Jersey* began its turn into the Pacific, it looked like a giant, gray ghost from the pages of naval history. Silent. Nothing but dead iron. The only noise came from a passing Washington State ferry that gave the ship one final toot.

The symbolic beginning of the Six Hundred Ship Navy was under way.

Eleven days later, George Sawyer, assistant secretary of the Navy for shipbuilding, sat in his office and thumbed through the news stories about *New Jersey*'s August 6 arrival in Long Beach. Press coverage had been favorable since the ship began its journey south. The stories on the ship's arrival were even better. Sawyer knew that would make his boss, John Lehman, happy. Positive media meant everything to the Navy secretary. He even kept a manila folder marked "SecNav Blasts" in his file cabinet to keep track of reporters who criticized him and the Navy. If we're going to sell our product, Lehman told his public affairs officers, we have to aggressively market it to the press. In this case, at least, the flaks, as the press called the PAOs, had done a good job of getting the reporters to put a pro-Navy spin on their stories about *New Jersey*.

It was a welcome relief. There had been an avalanche of criticism from the pundits, driven by active duty and retired naval officers, about renovating *New Jersey* and her three sister ships, *Iowa, Wisconsin,* and *Missouri.* Even a pro-Reagan Congress, which would have to dole out nearly $2 billion to modernize the World War II warships, was skeptical.[2] Plans for refitting the old ships had become so expensive and so time-consuming, the lawmakers told Lehman, that it was unclear whether they met the initial goal of providing an interim increase in naval power relatively quickly and at a relatively low cost.[3] And Lehman's close friend John Tower, chairman of the important Armed Services Committee, told him the cost estimates for *New Jersey* alone, which had jumped from $247 million to $325 million in less than two weeks, were too fickle and would be hard to support on the Senate floor.

Lehman stood his ground and flexed all his political muscle. "The battle-ships are one of the most cost-effective initiatives I have seen in my experi-ence in government," he said before Congress on May 5. "It is a ship we could not afford to build today. It is a ship that would probably cost us $3 billion to duplicate. It is a ship that goes as fast and can steam as long as any of the most modern ships in the fleet today." [4] Teddy Roosevelt would have sat up in his grave and applauded. Still, the renovation proposal was touch and go until Sawyer was able to firm up the numbers. Congress finally relented and funded enough money in three separate years to pull all four battleships out of mothballs.

When *New Jersey*'s overhaul was completed within budget and ahead of schedule twenty-one months later, Sawyer could have crowed a little if he had wanted to. But he would leave that to the President, who traveled to Long Beach for *New Jersey*'s December 28, 1982, recommissioning cere-mony. "We have been questioned for bringing back the battleship," Reagan said, standing in front of the red, white, and blue bunting that hung from the ship's rails. "It seems odd and a little ironic to me that some of the same critics who accuse us of chasing technology and gold-plating our weapons systems have led the charge against the superbly cost-effective and maintain-able *New Jersey*."

Lehman smiled as Reagan spoke. The President's words had a familiar ring to them. In preparation for the speech, Lehman had provided his favorite buzz words to Reagan's staff. "We are . . . building a six-hundred-ship fleet, including fifteen carrier battle groups," Reagan said.

Lehman could not have said it better himself.

The refitting of *New Jersey* and her sister ships was an important victory, and while it may have received the lion's share of attention from the media and on Capitol Hill, its cost was only a small portion of the $120 billion–plus shipbuilding strategy that Sawyer had been jiggering and rejiggering over the last several months.[5] Congress had granted the Navy two big supple-mental requests to the 1981 and 1982 defense budgets. Now Lehman and Sawyer were working on the Navy's share—$82 billion (the equivalent of nearly $120 billion in 1995 dollars)—of Reagan's first real budget for 1983.[6] The big push would be for aircraft carriers and their escort battle groups. The Navy had twelve battle groups, and Lehman wanted fifteen—at a price of $54 billion.[7]

The costs and how quickly the Navy could build up its carrier force had been key elements addressed in a summer meeting in 1981 among Lehman, Sawyer, and Hayward. The three men and several aides crowded into a fourth-floor conference room in the Pentagon. Hayward was feeling good about Lehman for adopting his suggestion to bring back the battleships and was ready to tackle the carrier issue.

"Do you like the *Nimitz?*" Sawyer asked Hayward.[8]

Some eyes in the room rolled upward at the question. *Nimitz,* a supercarrier, was the biggest warship in the world, the envy of every navy from Moscow to Peking. Since the demise of the battleships, it was the queen of the sea. But the question was, in reality, a missile aimed at Hayward. In the Carter administration, Hayward had backed smaller, conventionally powered carriers that would be cheaper and easier to build. But in Lehman's mind there was no question that the future of the Navy would lie on the big decks of the *Nimitz* class. Sawyer knew they would be expensive. And he knew from experience that the price would only go up if the admirals began gold-plating future ships in the class. "The key to doing anything rapidly is you are going to have to like what you have got," Sawyer explained to the group. "If we have to develop a new carrier, forget it, it won't happen in our administration. We will never see another carrier. But if you like the *Nimitz,* I think I can deliver you a program where we will build more."[9] It might just be possible, he added, to get Congress to fund two supercarriers in the 1983 fiscal year budget.

"We like the *Nimitz,*" Hayward answered. But he thought it was unlikely that the other services would sit by placidly while the Navy took home an extra $8 billion next year for two new carriers.

Everybody in the room knew that Hayward was right, that the Air Force and the Army would go ape. But Sawyer was confident that Lehman could handle the politics. Hayward wasn't so sure. "Good luck," he said with half a smile as Lehman left for the Pentagon's third floor to talk with Frank Carlucci about front loading the budget.

Lehman had yet to win over Carlucci. Weinberger could be manipulated and so far had stood behind Lehman, even when he was unsure about where his Navy secretary was going. Although Lehman eventually would broach with Weinberger the subject of buying two new carriers, he needed to get Carlucci on board. "Give me a big jump this year and I will give it back to you next year," he told Carlucci.[10] "I made a deal with Frank," Lehman later recalled, that would give Sawyer more leverage when he haggled price with Newport News, the shipbuilding giant. Carlucci liked the idea and promised to press the issue with Weinberger. The secretary of defense blessed the plan, too. Lehman's Six Hundred Ship Navy had just sailed around another big hurdle.

With Carlucci and Weinberger on board, the next task was to cut a deal with Ed Campbell, the president of Newport News, which was the only yard in the country capable of putting 3.5 million man-hours into building the 91,000-ton *Nimitz* carriers. Sawyer's friendship with Campbell went back years to the time when he was president of the naval architecture and engineering firm of J. J. McMullen. He telephoned to pass on the news that the Navy was going to build two new carriers. We need a commitment from Newport to build them quickly, he said. Newport had just begun construction on *Theodore Roosevelt* under a contract negotiated by the Carter administration that Sawyer knew allowed for "a nice long leisurely schedule." That had to be changed, Sawyer said.[11]

How would you feel about a suitable bonus-penalty contract? he asked Campbell. If Newport came in ahead of schedule, the shipyard could make millions more in profit. If not, the Navy made money. Either way, Sawyer figured, the Navy came out ahead. But to make the package work, he told Campbell, you have to move the completion date for the *Roosevelt* up eighteen months. That would let Lehman commission the *Roosevelt* on his watch. If he couldn't do that, no deal.

Campbell agreed.

So far, so good. Three important pieces of bureaucratic stone had fallen into place. Only one more hurdle, but perhaps the biggest one, lay ahead—Congress.

On the surface, the Senate, where the Republicans held a majority, would be an easier sell than the Democrat-controlled House. Senator Gary Hart, the Colorado Democrat, would be a worthy foe, Lehman knew, and his bipartisan Military Reform Caucus was becoming a burdensome anchor on the Six Hundred Ship Navy. Lehman and Hart had already squared off at several hearings over the size and needs of the Navy.

"He used to stand up," Hart said, "and hold his thumb and first finger about three inches apart and say, 'Here are the kinds of ships Gary Hart wants to build.' And then he would spread his arms wide and say, 'Here are the kinds of ships we want to build.' And of course everybody would laugh and think it was a big joke."

Lehman would laugh the hardest. But if there was one thing he knew about Congress, it was that each member put his personal agenda above party affiliation. Although his party may have had a majority in the upper body, that did not guarantee crucial votes for Lehman's Six Hundred Ship Navy. A good example of unpredictability, Lehman soon realized, was Ted Stevens, the Republican whip from Alaska who had opposed renovating the battleships. Lehman's legislative team had followed Stevens's voting record closely. In fact, they were keeping track of a number of key members of

Congress to determine who was likely to vote with or against the Navy in the big 1983 budget.

Under Lehman's watchful eye, the officers kept a political box score on the lawmakers' defense votes, and the Navy gave each member a national security index rating. Stevens, who had a reputation as pro-defense, received a paltry 57 percent Navy rating because he tried to scuttle the battleships.[12] He was furious when the scheme was exposed. Although Lehman fired Rear Admiral A. K. Knoizen over the tiff, the real mastermind was Captain Brent Baker, who would later become an unpopular chief of public affairs for his errors in handling press coverage of the Tailhook scandal.

The national security index was one of many political tricks Lehman had learned while studying under Henry Kissinger, a master at political gamesmanship. Being Kissinger's legislative gofer had helped Lehman establish himself on the Hill. But his support came more from the conservative Republicans and their right-wing network, who saw Lehman as a golden boy and Kissinger as soft on communism.

Among the network's more notable members were Richard Viguerie, Irving Kristol, and businessman Joseph Coors, the brewery tycoon. They helped to identify, support, or steer promising young conservatives like Lehman to fellowship opportunities, research grants, publishers, or staff positions in the executive and legislative branches of government. One of the conservative group's more important talent-spotting agencies, the Intercollegiate Studies Institute, had seen Lehman as an up-and-comer and helped meet his financial needs with a $1,500 Weaver fellowship during graduate school. Lehman also was an editor of the *Intercollegiate Review,* the organization's publication.

Another cornerstone of the right-wing network was the Foreign Policy Research Institute, once affiliated with the University of Pennsylvania, where Lehman had completed his doctorate. It was part and parcel of the U.S. government's military and intelligence apparatus involved with the Cold War. Unknown to many scholars at the university, the Foreign Policy Research Institute had close ties to the CIA, which provided funding for its publication, *Orbis.*[13] Over the years *Orbis* contained numerous articles favorable to the intelligence community and the positions of the spymasters who covertly influenced the foreign relations of the United States.[14] The institute had a long history of cooperation with the CIA and military intelligence agencies. And a former CIA officer and retired Army colonel, William Kintner, who would go on to be Richard Nixon's ambassador to Thailand during the Vietnam War—from which the CIA launched numerous covert operations in Southeast Asia—was the institute's deputy director.[15]

Kintner had offered Lehman a job in 1967 at the institute as a staff member. That same year, a number of universities and research centers had come under attack by scholars and the media for their secret links to the CIA. Exposés in *Ramparts* magazine and *The New York Times* uncovered a nest of financial arrangements like the one afforded the Foreign Policy Research Institute at Penn that ignited an uproar of anger and soul-searching among academics.[16] Despite the controversy, which lingered for several years, Lehman accepted Kintner's offer.

As Navy secretary, Lehman enjoyed the spooky world of intelligence operations and occasionally dabbled in various covert plans. Earlier in the year he had plucked Marine Lieutenant Colonel Oliver North from obscurity at the Naval War College after reading a paper he wrote on the uses of the battleship. Lehman asked Richard Allen to hire North for a job on the National Security Council, which Allen did. And Lehman would stay in touch with North during his Iran-contra dealings, which ultimately ended in failure and undermined Ronald Reagan's second term as President.

Even with all his conservative connections and friends in Congress, Lehman still decided to stage a lobbying blitz to rally support for his Six Hundred Ship Navy. He had Ted Gordon and others prepare a briefing book describing all of the advantages of big aircraft carriers. "It was a classified book," Gordon said, "and Lehman and I would go over to the Senate lobby and we would just grab senators as they would come by, and we would brief them. We would just hang around down there." [17]

It seemed to Lehman and Sawyer that all the necessary political steps had been taken. But there was one thing that neither they nor anybody in the Navy had any real control over, and that was Peter Tarpgaard's CBO study.[18] If it was taken seriously by Gary Hart's reform caucus and got a good bounce in the media, it could send the Navy's shipbuilding plans into a tailspin.

Ace Lyons peered over the weather reports on his flagship, the *Mt. Whitney*. "Dammit, we'll have to delay," he said. The weather in Norfolk had turned sour and would get a whole lot worse. There was a hurricane brewing in the South Atlantic that, if it kept to its present meteorological patterns, would move up the eastern seaboard, then head into open ocean before turning north toward the Norwegian Sea—precisely the route that the Second Fleet planned to take into Soviet territorial waters. A large number of European ships were in Norfolk already, prepared to sail on Lyons's orders. The British flattop *Invincible* and the flagship *Fearless* were moored near the U.S. carrier *Eisenhower,* which would be the centerpiece of the armada. *Eisenhower* was under the command of Rear Admiral Jerry Tuttle, who called himself S.L.U.F.—short little ugly fucker.

The storm on the outer edge of the hurricane now hitting Norfolk had already wreaked havoc on *Eisenhower,* knocking out much of its communications system. Under most conditions, having no communications would be a big negative. But as part of the exercise, Tuttle and Lyons had decided to run the task force in the dark. All the ships would shut down their radar and electronic gear. The process was called EMCON, and it made a ship virtually silent and almost impossible to detect. Any electronic noise might alert the Soviets to their whereabouts. So every allied ship knew before it left Norfolk when and where it was supposed to show up for its part of the mission in Soviet waters. There would be no need to communicate.

Like Lyons, Tuttle was a maverick prone to taking on the system. And there were those in command positions above him who didn't like some of his innovative ideas. One was his administrative boss, Vice Admiral Thomas Kilcline, whose son had died in a 1979 crash of an F-14 Tomcat because of engine failure. Tuttle had spent the last month putting the *Eisenhower* battle group through its work-up cycle for deployment to the Barents Sea. When Kilcline realized what he and Ace Lyons were planning to do with the carrier, he gave Tuttle a stern warning. "Jerry," he said in a deadly serious tone, sticking his finger in Tuttle's chest, "if you lose one aircraft, I'm court-martialing you." [19]

Tuttle had enjoyed too many successes over the last thirty days to worry about Kilcline's threats. He was still smiling about the recent training op off the North Carolina coast, in which he had proved that even the best radar couldn't find a carrier if it didn't want to be found. Two B-52s, simulating Soviet Bear reconnaissance planes, had flown east on a clear day over the Atlantic, looking for *Eisenhower.* Four different times the giant aircraft went on search missions. And each time the carrier used various electronic warfare techniques to confuse the B-52s' radars. When the jets were within radar range, Tuttle ordered the crew to fire the carrier's close-in weapons system, a rapid-firing weapon designed to shoot down low-flying missiles. Tuttle realized that the uranium in the spent shells could also confuse the fire control radar on a reconnaissance airplane. From the air, "it looked like blips of ships," Tuttle said. "We saturated the radar scopes to make it look like they had measles. And we were jamming and everything else. They couldn't discriminate which was the ship and which was the round." [20]

If he could fool the American radars, Tuttle damn well knew he could fool the Russians. "We studied how to beat their satellite ocean surveillance system," he later said. "We found out how to defeat the Bears. We used all kinds of cover and deception, all kinds of electronic warfare."

After poring over the weather charts, Lyons decided to follow the hurricane right into Soviet territorial waters. It was important to get the exercise done well in advance of the upcoming budget vote. Lyons was already planning to brief members of Congress on the expected success of Ocean Safari and how the Navy could carry out its new mission to take the fight right to the Russian homeland. But there was another reason for riding the hurricane's tail than just political necessity. The weather would further shield the eighty-three ships from Soviet reconnaissance. Lyons figured the task force could sneak into the Soviet den without Mother Bear even noticing.

The seas were calm in the Mediterranean as Jim Service's Sixth Fleet battle group steamed for Libya. In the Flag Plot on the fourth floor of the Pentagon, Tom Hayward could see each ship's location as it was plotted on the main tactical display. Navy personnel used grease pencils to mark the Sixth Fleet's distance, speed, and expected arrival off the coast of Libya. The battle group was moving south at about fifteen knots. By tomorrow, August 18, the carriers *Nimitz* and *Forrestal* would be in place and increase their speed to begin near round-the-clock flight operations. Hayward felt once the flight ops began, there was a better than even chance that fighting would break out. If it did, Service would follow the measured responses worked out earlier with Hayward and the Joint Chiefs. Hayward was so sure that there would be hostile action with Libya that he planned to sleep in the Flag Plot.

He enjoyed the hustle and bustle inside the room. He routinely walked the one hundred feet from his CNO's office to the Flag Plot to see how and where the Navy's fleets were dispersed around the globe. For the Libyan operation he was able to punch into the Navy's communications circuits and listen in as his commanders communicated among themselves. Hayward liked the fact that he could do it without the officers knowing it. He planned to do it throughout the exercise.

The Flag Plot had changed little since Admiral George Anderson, a former CNO, paced the room during the Cuban missile crisis. Navy personnel kept track of where the U.S. ships were then in much the same way they were now doing for the Libya operation. In another twenty-four hours, Hayward could see, things would get tense, but nowhere near the anxiety levels that Anderson had faced in the Cuban crisis. Anderson had a reputation as an irascible old son of a bitch and had no qualms about invading Cuba. Fearing the Navy might touch off World War III, Defense Secretary Robert McNamara visited the Flag Plot to supervise Anderson and the naval operations. After a few questions from McNamara and his Whiz Kids, Anderson not-too-politely showed them the door. McNamara was appalled. Don't you realize I'm the secretary of defense? he said. Anderson answered by saying that wouldn't mean anything to the Marine sentry outside.

Unlike Anderson, Hayward respected the civilian leadership, although he thought Cap Weinberger could have been a stronger leader, especially in supervising John Lehman. The nice thing for Hayward was that Lehman had little to do with the Libyan exercise. This was an operational matter, run by the admirals, not the secretary of the Navy. And the admirals were keeping Hayward informed of every detail.

Service had been called back to Washington to brief Hayward and his colleagues on the Joint Chiefs of Staff. And Hayward was getting regular back-door briefings from Admiral Ron Hays in London, the CinC of naval forces in Europe. "Admiral Hayward," Hays recalled, "he's a hands-on guy, and he was continually asking questions about what was going on, what our plan was, and that sort of thing. So I kept him informed."[21] Hays did it out of loyalty and as a courtesy because his boss was a U.S. Air Force general in Germany, not Hayward.

Between the briefings and his tapping into the Navy's communication circuits, Hayward knew just about everything that was taking place. Libya was sure to know that the Navy was coming. Notifications to airmen and mariners had been made on August 12 and 14, advising the nations in the region that the United States planned to conduct naval operations in the international waters of the Gulf of Sidra. Now those operations were under way, and as he headed back to his office, Hayward was confident that the Qaddafi's "line of death" would become a line of misery.

CHAPTER 10

JUST AFTER DAWN on Wednesday, August 19, 1981, the *Nimitz* began a slow, wide turn into a gentle summer breeze sixty miles off the coast of Libya. As the four giant screws beneath the fantail pushed the gray bow around into the wind, five thousand men were already running through their paces for another day of flight operations in the Gulf of Sidra.

Above the placid Mediterranean, *Nimitz*'s 4.5-acre flight deck was a sea of activity. In aviation lore it was called the "dance of the deck," although less astute observers describe the power and grace of carrier operations as organized chaos. Everywhere, sailors in color-coded jerseys scrambled across the floating airstrip, their eyes tearing from caustic fumes, their ears protected from the deafening roar of jet engines. Men in purple were fueling airplanes. Safety teams in white stood nearby. Crash crews in red waited for the jets to begin flying. Utility men wore blue, plane captains wore brown, and flight directors were in yellow. Each man played a small but vital part in the carrier's mission: to launch aircraft.

By 6 A.M. weapons had been checked and rechecked. Aviators had been briefed in their ready rooms and were now manning their aircraft. On cue from the air boss, whose voice boomed over the loudspeakers, the pilots started their engines. Two F-14 Tomcats inched forward, their Pratt & Whitney TF-30 engines throbbing as they taxied toward the ship's four catapults. The 01 code number painted on the lead Tomcat marked the aircraft as the squadron commander's personal plane. The black ace of spades on the aircrafts' tails identified the squadron as Fighting 41, the "Black Aces," out of Oceana Naval Air Station in Virginia. The pilot in 01 was Commander Henry M. "Hank" Kleeman, a veteran of the Vietnam War.[1] Kleeman was a big farmboy with five sisters, who fought a constant battle to keep his weight down. He was a tad under five ten, but he had massive legs the size of a pulling guard. Although he hadn't played football at the Naval Academy, where he had scored all A's (with the exception of a D in physical education), he had roomed with Roger Staubach, the famous quarterback who starred for the Dallas Cowboys.

In the last twenty-four hours the Black Aces and their fellow aviators on

Nimitz and *Forrestal* had had dozens of hassles with Libyan pilots. The two carrier battle groups had arrived August 18 on schedule and immediately begun flight operations that came within twenty-five miles of Libya's coast. Fearing the naval presence was a plot by Washington to topple Qaddafi, the government-controlled news agency stated that Libya "will fight by all means for its territorial waters." Before the exercise ended, Qaddafi's air force would challenge the Americans forty-five times. Each time the Libyan jets streaked toward the battle groups, U.S. Navy fighters escorted them away.

The previous day, the first of the exercise, had been particularly busy. Several of the intercepts had turned into routine dogfights, as the jets twisted and turned, trying to get on each other's "six o'clock," or tail, position, which would mean a kill in real combat. Photographs were taken. A few middle fingers were extended. But nothing out of the ordinary took place.

Today Kleeman would lead a two-plane section with his wingman, Lieutenant Larry "Music" Musczynski. They would fly the southern CAP, or combat air patrol. Just after 6 A.M. Kleeman climbed into his jet, buckled his Koch fittings, and pulled down on his straps as tight as he could to keep negative G-forces from lifting him out of his seat. In a matter of minutes his jet sat near the bow of the carrier, where a young sailor kneeled beneath the cockpit and placed the plane's tow bar into the catapult shuttle. The *Nimitz* had completed its turn into the wind. The huge blast shield rose from the deck. Kleeman saluted the catapult officer, and the Tomcat's engines exploded into afterburner. The plane was shot forward like a rocket at 160 knots. When it hit the end of the bow, there was the characteristic loud thump as the plane's wheels left the carrier. Deck crews watched the flames shooting like jagged spikes from the jets' two engines as it slowly climbed upward.

Kleeman pulled back on his stick to increase altitude. At just over six thousand feet, he rendezvoused with an A-6 airborne tanker and topped off the Tomcat's fuel tanks. After breaking away, he increased altitude and leveled off at twenty thousand feet. The F-14 Tomcat was capable of doing Mach 2 in all types of weather. But weather would not be a problem today. The sun was starting to come up, and the sky would soon turn a deep blue. Kleeman would be able to see for miles.

Already aloft and directing the jets were a pair of E-2C Hawkeyes, radar planes that kept track of hostile bogeys. The Hawkeyes' electronic gear could see for hundreds of miles and picked up every Libyan aircraft as they lifted off from their land bases. In the backseat of 01, Lieutenant David Venlet, the radar intercept officer, kept in radio contact with the Hawkeyes and studied his own scope for hostile aircraft. Right now the radar scope in the $40 million fighter was all clear. The F-14's radar was so powerful that Venlet could track twenty-two targets simultaneously. The aircraft's fire control system was designed to lock onto and fire an assortment of missiles at six targets. Each Tomcat carried the long-range Phoenix, a supersonic air-to-air missile that could strike a bogey from 150 miles. On each wingtip hung the deadly AIM-9L heat-seeking Sidewinder. There was nothing quite like the Tomcat in the world, Kleeman knew. Maybe the U.S. Air Force F-15 Eagle came close. But that was it. There was no way, Kleeman figured, that the Libyan pilots would be crazy enough to pull their triggers.

At 7:15 A.M. the radio in Kleeman's aircraft crackled. To the west, U.S. and Libyan jets had gotten into a hassle. The two aviators in 01 listened to sounds of grunts and strained voices as the American crews fought for advantage over the Libyans. A few seconds later Kleeman and Venlet's radar suddenly picked up two Russian-made Sukhoi Su-22 Fitters about forty miles away. The jets had launched out of Ghurbadiyah air field and were zooming north toward the *Nimitz*.

Kleeman roared ahead. At seven miles he eyeballed the two bogeys and, with Musczynski behind him, screeched toward the jets for a head-on intercept. At just under three miles Kleeman positively identified the jets as Libyan, each carrying Soviet-made heat-seeking Atoll missiles. Kleeman attempted to change course to get behind the jets. But each maneuver was matched by the Libyans, who changed course with him. All four jets were now closing head on at twelve miles per minute. Their combined air speed was over one thousand knots. And as the lead Libyan jet closed within one thousand feet, he radioed his wingman. Speaking in Arabic, he said, "I am preparing to fire." The Libyan pilot then squeezed off a missile. "I have fired."

For the briefest moment, Kleeman was astonished. There was no mistaking what was bearing down on his Tomcat. The Libyan had fired a missile. It was a crazy shot. The Atoll was designed to be fired at the rear of an airplane so it could home in on the heat being generated by the jet's engines. A head-on shot was a waste of a missile. Kleeman banked his jet to the right, and the Atoll passed below the aircraft's fuselage.

The lead Libyan pilot pulled back hard on his stick while rolling the aircraft into a left-hand turn. Musczynski, who was still amazed that a shot had been fired, did a crossover maneuver and gave chase. Kleeman changed course in a high-G turn and pursued the second Fitter, which was running as fast and as hard as its pilot could push it for the safe haven of his desert homeland. Kleeman spotted the jet as it flew across the low morning sun. He waited for the Libyan to pass the sun, then radioed to Musczynski: "I'm going to shoot." Seconds later a nine-foot-long Sidewinder streaked through the air at Mach 2.5 and struck paydirt. Kleeman eyed his kill and saw the pilot eject with a full chute.

Musczynski's powerful Tomcat easily caught up with the lead Fitter. As he checked his missile selection, he began to question whether he should attack the Libyan jet. For a frightful second, thoughts about starting World War III crossed his mind. He could hear Kleeman yelling in his headset to shoot, shoot, shoot. But he still hesitated. Then, at a half mile away, Musczynski squeezed off one Sidewinder. The missile and the Libyan jet exploded with such intensity that Musczynski had to pitch up violently to avoid a sky filled with debris. The second Libyan pilot was not so lucky. He ejected, but his chute was on fire.[2]

In sixty seconds the dogfight was over and the Tomcats paired up en route back to the carrier. Musczynski was pumped up and shaking uncontrollably. Kleeman radioed *Nimitz*. Two Libyans splashed, he said. At least one observable chute. The response was not unexpected. "The admiral wants to talk to you when you get back."

As he approached the carrier for a landing, Kleeman was still thinking about the shoot-down, hoping they had done the right thing.[3] The normally unshakable Kleeman was nonplussed. It took him two tries to get aboard.

Admiral Ron Hays's mind was going at warp speed. *Nimitz* had just radioed up to his headquarters in London that less than two minutes ago two F-14 Tomcats had downed a pair of Libyan jets. As the information dribbled in, Hays felt proud about what had happened. But at the same time he was worried. Kleeman and Musczynski had done what they had been told to do and had "taken action that is justifiable," he said to himself. But, "Will there be second-guessing in Washington that is going to damage the Navy?"[4]

Hays picked up his telephone to find out.

In Stuttgart, Air Force General Willy Y. Smith's telephone was ringing. Having just arrived in June, Smith was the new deputy to Army General Bernard Rogers, head of the European command. He had yet to have his first cup of coffee when he heard Hays's voice on the other end of the telephone. We just shot down two Libyan jets over the Gulf of Sidra, Hays informed him. Both American jets returned safely to the carrier.

There was a moment of silence as Smith thought about the shoot-down and who would have to be informed. "I got his attention," Hays said years later. "He wasn't upset, but he was certainly anxious because it was very significant."

The two senior officers knew that the chain of command had to be notified, and quickly. That meant the Joint Chiefs of Staff and Cap Weinberger. Hays figured they would need a situation report to help write a diplomatic note of protest. Before he called Smith he had already ordered his deputy to draft a message "accusing the Libyans of hostile action against the force that was operating legally." Both Hays and Smith figured that Bernie Rogers would support the language. And the State Department would have to be notified, too. If it was up to retired Army General Al Haig, the hawkish new secretary of state, the protest note would not mince words. It would have to be sent to the Libyan government via the Belgians. The United States had broken diplomatic relations with Qaddafi in 1979 when a mob burned down the American embassy during an anti-American demonstration.

Approximately an hour later, a protest note was delivered to the Libyans. The final paragraph had Haig's signature toughness all over it. "The government of the United States views this unprovoked attack with grave concern. Any further attacks against U.S. forces operating in international water and air space will also be resisted with force if necessary."

When Hays hung up, Smith did not place his telephone back in its cradle. His boss, General Rogers, the top U.S. officer in Europe, had to be informed. The duty officer on the Joint Chiefs had to be notified, too. And somebody had to wake up Cap Weinberger. It would be a long day.

In the Flag Plot, Tom Hayward was awake at 1:20 A.M. when the shoot-down took place. He knew about it even before Hays because he had been eavesdropping on the Sixth Fleet's communications networks. He was somber but not concerned about the political ramifications. "The pilots were just doing their job," he told Bill Cockell, who arrived in the Flag Plot at 5 A.M. Then he went back to monitor the exercise.

Get my plane ready, I want to fly down to the *Nimitz*, Hays said to his aide. I'm going to shake some hands. "Those pilots were showing some backbone."[5]

The admiral was feeling a bit more at ease about the shoot-down, but he still had reservations about what Washington's reaction might be. By traveling down to the *Nimitz*, he could ease his concerns and get firsthand information about the incident. If he was nervous, undoubtedly the crews of the two F-14s were, too—perhaps even more so. Hays knew he could do something about that.

Nimitz was due to conclude its exercise late that afternoon. On board, the aircrews and enlisted personnel were ecstatic over the shoot-down. After the two F-14s landed on the carrier, a horde of people surrounded the jets, slapping the fuselage as if to say "That a boy." All four pilots got the same support. Still, a pall hung over the celebration. Had they done the right thing?

As Hays's jet lifted off the tarmac in London, only a handful of people in the world knew that the United States had just flexed its muscles. There would be a lot of second-guessing, even by America's allies. Italy, after all, had a substantial number of nationals living in Libya. And Rome was a lot closer to Tripoli than Washington. The Italians had to live with Qaddafi in their backyard. And a lot of Americans, Hays began to realize, also worked in Libya's oil fields. Libya produced about 10 percent of American oil imports. Two months earlier, in May, the United States had expelled all Libyan diplomats and urged the 2,500 American oil workers in Libya to come home. The administration would have to repeat the request again today. Was Qaddafi crazy enough to make a move on the Americans in retaliation? Both *Forrestal* and *Nimitz* were prepared for the worst. They had contingency plans already drawn up for striking more forcefully at Libya should the need arise. Everyone knew that things could get nasty real quick.

As Hays flew south over the Mediterranean, the nation's top military officers from Stuttgart to London to Washington were holding their breath to see how Ronald Reagan and the Pentagon's civilian leaders would respond. Reagan had been tough during the campaign, promising to punish two-bit dictators like Qaddafi if they threatened the United States. But that was campaign rhetoric. This was the real thing. If anyone doubted that, all they had to do was look at the score card: U.S. 2, Libya 0.

In Virginia Beach, Carol Kleeman was still asleep when her telephone rang well before sunrise. She picked up the phone and said hello.[6] A Navy duty officer was calling to inform her that her husband had been involved in a combat incident but was fine. She was told that a public affairs officer would help her with the media, and although the Navy couldn't order her not to speak to the press, it was best not to.

It didn't take long before reporters and television crews started showing up in droves. One of the first networks to arrive was NBC, which sent a camera team and a correspondent down from Washington, hoping for an exclusive interview. The media had also found out that Kleeman's parents lived on a farm in southern Illinois and promptly knocked on their door.

Carol Kleeman had already decided not to do any interviews. Not because of the Navy's request to keep the media at arm's length. And not because she wasn't proud of her husband. She was damned proud of him. But she was a little scared. Libya meant Qaddafi, and Qaddafi meant terrorism. The

Kleemans had four children, and the last thing she wanted was to broadcast to the world where they lived.

"Can we take a picture of the outside of your house?" an NBC cameraman asked. Not wanting to be combative, Carol just shrugged. I don't think I can stop them, she figured. Later on, her telephone rang again for what seemed like the hundredth time. A telegram from the *Nimitz* had come in, and the Western Union employee wanted to read it to her. A copy of the telegram would arrive later, she was told. It was from Hank.

> PLAYERS WERE HANK, DAVE, MUSIC AND LUCA. ONE WIN EACH.
> VERY GOOD DAY. ALL ARE HAPPY AND SAFE. AM VERY PLEASED
> WITH PERFORMANCE OF WHOLE SQUADRON. WOULD STILL RATHER
> BE WITH YOU. LOVE HANK.

When the printed message came, Carol framed it and hung it on a wall in her Virginia Beach home.

The Pentagon pressroom was jammed with TV cameras and defense correspondents eager to sink their teeth into the first big military story of the Reagan administration. Cap Weinberger was standing at the podium. Although he had been notified of the shoot-down around 1:30 A.M., he did not look as if he had spent a sleepless night. He was immaculately groomed, every strand of his thick black hair combed neatly into place. It was still early in the morning, and not all of the facts about the shoot-down were known. The Navy was in the process of debriefing Kleeman and the other pilots. And the flight recorders in their jets were still being analyzed.

The reporters jockeyed for position as Weinberger and Lieutenant General Philip J. Gast, director of operations of the Joint Chiefs of Staff, began the press conference. Few of the questions that were asked had any meat to them. But one of Weinberger's last answers, although guarded, was a clear indicator of the pride he felt about the shoot-down. It was in response to a reporter who remarked: "You said that they carried out their mission extremely well. It seemed as though you are almost proud of the way—"

"I don't think it's necessary to try to do any amateur psychoanalysis at this time," Weinberger interjected. "It seems to me that the mission of the planes was to fly patrol and, if attacked, if fired upon, to respond. That's exactly what they did, and I would say again without leaving myself open to any other interpretations that I think they carried out their mission extremely well."

Right after the shoot-down, the defense secretary dispatched a message to the *Nimitz* that said much the same thing: "Congratulations on a most professional performance under very demanding circumstances. Please express my admiration and appreciation to all those associated with the conduct of the Open Ocean Missile Exercise. The pilots of the two F-14s who were forced into an engagement carried out their responsibilities with particular courage and skill. Well done.''

Sixty-five miles off the California coast, the President of the United States donned a blue Navy ball cap emblazoned with ''USS *Constellation*'' and pulled a jacket over his white shirt with the carrier's logo on it. He looked every bit the distinguished admiral paying tribute to his troops.

Since the Libyan incident a day earlier, Ronald Reagan had yet to say anything publicly about the military action. Privately he was so pleased with the Navy that he told Michael Deaver it would be nice if his aides could paint two little jets on the side of the presidential limousine, symbolic of the two air kills.[7]

Reagan had interrupted his California vacation on August 20 to come out to the ship, which was cruising in gentle Pacific swells west of Los Angeles. It was a brilliant, sunny day, and he was sitting on an armchair on the flight deck as Navy F-14s flying at near supersonic speeds shot by at wave-top level. In their wake A-6 Intruders dropped bombs into the blue ocean that sent columns of foamy white water high into the air. At one point during the demonstration, Reagan stood and saluted as each of the warships in the *Constellation*'s battle group steamed past in the President's honor.

Then he strolled through the massive man-of-war, greeting officers and sailors with a smile and praising them for the job they were doing for their country. In the ship's giant hangar bay below the flight deck, he stood in front of a parked F-14 Tomcat and addressed a large group of men. Giving one of his most aggressive speeches, he vowed retaliation for those who would attack Americans. ''Let friend and foe alike know America has muscle to back up its words, and ships like this and men like you are the muscle.'' The crew erupted into cheers as the President went on. ''But what is most important,'' he said to the still cheering crowd, ''it is also impressive to the enemies of freedom in the world, and we had an example of that just night before last on the carrier *Nimitz*.''

Before he left, Reagan addressed the entire five-thousand-man crew on the ship's intercom. ''We'll all sleep a little better at night knowing you're on duty.''

Back in London, Ron Hays breathed a sigh of relief at Reagan's remarks. In the last ten years he had seen his beloved Navy and its sister services defeated in Vietnam and fail miserably during the *Pueblo* incident, the *Mayaguez* rescue attempt, and the disastrous Desert One fiasco in Iran.

Vietnam, the nation's longest and most divisive war, had been particularly hard on naval aviation. The Navy had only one ACE, Randy Cunningham, and he wouldn't shoot down five jets until the war's last stages, long after such feats could have any impact on the outcome of the conflict. Nearly eight hundred naval aviators had been shot down. Three hundred seventy-seven men had been killed, sixty-four were missing in action, and one hundred seventy-nine had been taken prisoner. In the last year of the war, *Saratoga* lost seventeen of its planes. Between 1963 and August 15, 1973, when the war ended, 859 Navy aircraft were lost in combat or operational accidents.

The losses in matériel and human life alone were staggering. Just as troubling were the feelings of isolation among the fliers. By and large rejected by the American public, naval aviators turned inward, finding solace in their camaraderie. They drank hard and played hard to keep up their morale. And yearly events like the Tailhook gatherings in Las Vegas, where they could really cut loose, became a holy pilgrimage.

Feelings of anger and rejection were not confined to the naval aviators. The entire Navy was in a deep malaise. It didn't help that the nation's two other celebrated military fiascoes, the *Pueblo* and the *Mayaguez,* were Navy and Marine operations. And lest anyone forget, the helicopters that failed during Desert One belonged to the Department of the Navy. All those misadventures had, of course, been magnified by the media, which painted Uncle Sam's military as a helpless Gulliver defeated by the world's tiny Lilliputians.

But now, a sixty-second dogfight had washed away the sins of the past. Here was the President of the United States standing tall on a Navy vessel, sending a signal to the world that American naval forces would be the primary instrument for projecting U.S. power abroad. "Boy, that made a tremendous impression," Hays recalled. "There wasn't any second-guessing from the administration that said, 'Well, why didn't you do this or do that and maybe this incident wouldn't have occurred.' He didn't waver, and that's the kind of thing the military understands and supports."

The nation also seemed to sense that the Navy was undergoing a spiritual rebirth. In the last twenty-four hours, pictures of the four Navy pilots who had shot down the Libyan jets were on the front pages of practically every newspaper in the country. Americans were applauding the sixty-second duel over the Gulf of Sidra. In the small towns and big cities across the nation, everyone relished Reagan's new nationalism and the redemption of the military. Finally, after so many painful years of neglect and failures, the Navy had scored a hit.

CHAPTER 11

As DUSK FELL over the Soviet republic of Kazakhstan on August 24, 1981, a fiery blast turned the twilight sky into an inferno of bright light. The ground rumbled, and from within the plumes of smoke and brilliant glow a ballistic missile lifted off from its launch pad at the Baikonur Cosmodrome, one of the Soviet Union's most secretive military centers.[1]

On the other side of the world, inside a Colorado mountain, U.S. military personnel at the NORAD command center monitored the missile's trajectory to determine where it was aimed. The rocket now heading for the atmosphere was based on the SS-9, an early-model intercontinental ballistic missile, the kind that carried nuclear warheads. In a matter of minutes the American technicians watched Cosmos 1299 drop its boosters and head into the dark vastness of space. NORAD then began disseminating intelligence reports to U.S. military space commands scattered across the world that the Soviets had launched another surveillance satellite.

Riding atop the liquid-fueled rocket was a nine-ton, nuclear-powered RORSAT that would glide for ninety days in a low orbit above the earth. Its sole mission was to track Ace Lyons's task force, which had put to sea four days earlier.[2] Inside the Russian space center located in a Moscow suburb, technicians had been monitoring the armada with two other satellites already aloft that circled the globe each day. But these two birds had their limitations. Their biggest flaw, unknown to the Soviets, was that they were tracking the wrong fleet.

The reason was simple: Jerry Tuttle was hiding eighty-three warships.

Several thousand miles northeast of Washington, D.C., information about the new Soviet launch was beamed down by satellite to *Mt. Whitney,* which was riding on the tails of the hurricane straight for the G.I.U.K. Gap. The high seas and near gale force winds made the passage miserable. Even the most hardy sailors were getting seasick. And pilots on *Eisenhower* wondered out loud whether they should be flying in such dangerous conditions. Although they would not admit it, they were scared to death about ending up in the Norwegian Sea's frigid waters. Despite the gripes, Lyons pressed on.

Inside the *Mt. Whitney*'s command center, a darkened room that looked like the bridge on the fictitious starship *Enterprise,* the Navy's electronic warfare officers plotted the new Soviet satellite's course to determine when it would fly over the piece of ocean that Lyons's task force now occupied. They had already entered the coordinates of the two other Soviet satellites that had now been aloft for several days, carefully calculating each time the birds would make an overhead pass. The two EORSATs sent out a passive radar beam from horizon to horizon, like a giant fishing net trying to catch myriad electronic frequencies pulsating from a fleet of ships. For the past several days the EORSATs had been transmitting back to Moscow the signals of a carrier battle group heading out to the open ocean, away from the Soviet Union. And beneath the churning sea, several Soviet attack submarines had been following the same emissions.

But Ace Lyons was heading in the opposite direction, or due north toward the Kola Peninsula. The battle group moving away from the Soviet Union was a fake. Lyons pulled an old trick and copied the radar signals of a carrier and its escorts onto a tape, put it on a destroyer, and sent the warship emitting its false sounds and frequencies thousands of miles in the other direction. Meanwhile he steamed north with every ship in the armada sailing under EMCON conditions, their electronics and radars shut off.

Deceiving the new satellite would not be as easy. The bulky RORSAT, which was thirty feet long and nine feet wide, used active radar. Its nuclear reactor shot down to earth a powerful beam hundreds of kilometers wide that looked randomly for ships on the water. If a ship was *ping*ed, radar beams then bounced off it and back to the satellite. But the RORSAT was crude in its design and had a difficult time differentiating among sizes of objects on the water and the number of ships. Lyons exploited this weakness by dividing the allied task force into sections, dispersing each over a fifty-thousand-square-mile grid in the Norwegian Sea.

At the center of the grid was *Eisenhower.*[3] Affectionately called "Ike," the massive carrier was, of course, the easiest platform to pick out. But Tuttle and his crew jammed and confused the RORSAT by zapping the satellite with a radar beam that contained dumb data. There was a downside to this, however, in that Soviet technicians knew the Americans were somewhere near the RORSAT's last fly-over. And to jam the satellites, Ike had to momentarily turn on its own radars, which emitted signals that could be picked up by the two EORSATs. The Soviets could then triangulate the three satellites to pinpoint the whereabouts of the allied task force.

So far, they had not been able to do so.

The task force was well past the G.I.U.K. Gap, and the Soviets had yet to find it. "We drove them absolutely insane, absolutely insane," Tuttle would later tell naval analysts writing the after-action reports on the mission. "We never got overflown by the Bears until we got up off their coast. But even then they had difficulty keeping track of us because we would move. They never ever got into a position where they could conduct a mock strike on us." [4]

Now deep inside Soviet territorial waters, Lyons decided it was time to send a wake-up call to the Soviet navy. He ordered a squadron of F-14 Tomcats, some tankers, and attack jets to prepare for a mission that would push the outer edge of the aircrafts' envelope—and U.S.-Soviet relations.

The headquarters of the Red Banner Northern Fleet in Severomorsk was a frenzy of activity. The U.S. Navy's sojourn into the Soviet Union's backyard waters had caught the Russians by surprise. They knew the Americans were out there, somewhere above the Gap. But that was about all they knew.

Bear reconnaissance planes had been trying to locate the armada for several days, but because of the bad weather and Tuttle's electronic warfare antics, they had been unable to do so. Several Bears were now refueling above the clouds, not far from the coast of Murmansk, before returning to the search. Transferring fuel was not a pilot's favorite chore. The large fuel baskets that dangled from the end of a tanker had been known to crash through a cockpit and injure pilots. What was more disconcerting, however, was that when two airplanes were linked together, each was extremely vulnerable. But in their home waters, close to Murmansk, the Russians were not worried about a surprise attack inside the Barents Sea.

And that was when the Navy jets hit.

From out of nowhere, the squadron of jets roared past the large, four-engine Bears at near supersonic speeds in a surprise flyby.[5] As quickly as they arrived, they were gone. The message that Lyons and Tuttle wanted to send was made clear to the rattled Soviet pilots: We can strike you anywhere, even off your most remote coast.

Before the fighters and the accompaniment of radar-jamming EA-6s and KA-6 air tankers had streaked off *Eisenhower,* Tuttle knew in advance where and when the Bears would be refueling. He had installed aboard the carrier a secure fax machine that received photographs from a KH-11 Keyhole satellite as it passed over the Kola Peninsula.[6] It was real-time intelligence that allowed him and Lyons to prepare the mock attack run against the Soviets. The Navy jets were careful to stay below five thousand feet, beneath the beams of the Soviets' shore-based radar. The Navy knew that the Soviet land-based radar system was vulnerable. They knew when the Russians activated it and how they searched for hostile aircraft. They knew its weak points and its strengths. With all of this data, coupled with the weather, the jets were almost impossible to spot.

When the Navy jets struck, they were nearly a thousand miles from *Eisenhower,* which was well beyond the 468-mile range[7] considered safe to operate at. The carrier's bubble, or protective zone, normally extended for five hundred miles around the ship. F-14s operated at the edge of the bubble, intercepting enemy airplanes long before they could threaten a carrier. But a thousand miles was unheard of, and flying such distances from a carrier was shunned by Kilcline and his fellow admirals. "They told me it was impossible," Tuttle said later. "They had so many damn restrictions, you couldn't intercept outside of two hundred miles. I was intercepting at one thousand miles."

In a matter of minutes a horde of Soviet fighters and attack aircraft chased after the American raiders. Angered and humiliated by the U.S. Navy's show of force, the Soviets launched hundreds of sorties in the following days at the allied task force. If the Russians couldn't find them at first, now they were at least trying to drive the invaders out of their territorial waters. On the *Mt. Whitney* Lyons turned to his staff and said, "Good God, yeah! Look at all the free training we're getting. We're getting to run our intercepts against the real McCoy."[8]

For the bullish Lyons, the fun was only beginning. The clincher in the whole operation was when he sent a U.S. Navy cruiser and several other warships around the North Cape trip wire and deep into the Barents Sea.[9] It was the first time the Navy had breached the sensitive boundary in nearly twenty years.

The entire exercise above the G.I.U.K. Gap was vintage Ace Lyons, an offensive show of force that fell well within the guidelines that John Lehman gave to him orally before the task force sailed. The two men knew the mission could be dangerous and that it would be controversial. And they most certainly enjoyed the fact that it would infuriate the Soviets, who would undoubtedly file a diplomatic protest. But if the Navy wanted to test its new offensive Maritime Strategy, it had to do so boldly. Lyons knew many of his peers in the admiralty would criticize him for needlessly provoking the Soviets. Although they were men of war, they feared war and believed that Lyons would touch off a superpower confrontation. Their criticism mattered little to Lyons and served only to further separate them from John Lehman, who shielded his favorite admiral from any retribution. Lyons took the heat in stride, telling members of Team Charlie, who were anxious to see how the Soviets would deal with the Navy's tactics, that it was like taking advantage of getting raped. "Why not enjoy it? If we have already been tried, convicted, and sentenced, why the fuck not do it? Look, there is nothing to lose here, we're not going to scare anybody, we're not going to upset them." [10]

That was one thing Lyons turned out to be wrong about. The Soviets viewed the exercise in the harshest terms and complained for years about it to American naval attachés. At the time, *Pravda,* the communist state's chief press organ, wrote a stream of critical articles, including one that Lehman enjoyed and remembered years later. "They denounce me," Lehman recalled, "saying in effect another maniac like Jim Forrestal has taken over the Navy. And if he keeps on this way, he will end up just like Forrestal. Which I thought was great."

Forrestal, a former secretary of the Navy and defense who was commonly referred to as the Driven Patriot, had committed suicide by jumping out of a window in a hospital where he was being treated for mental illness.[11]

After nine days of exercising at the top of the world, Lyons ordered his battle group to turn south on September 18 and sail for the G.I.U.K. Gap and the open waters of the Atlantic. But before the *Eisenhower* and its escorts left the Norwegian Sea, the Navy had to complete one final mission.

Just off the west coast of Lofoten, Norway, *Eisenhower* turned into the wind and cleared its flight line. Approaching the ship was a boxy transport plane that delivered personnel and equipment to the fleet. Navy flight crews called the carrier on-board delivery plane the ugliest aircraft in the fleet. The passengers inside sat facing the rear of the plane, a weird sensation made even more uncomfortable when the aircraft snagged the arresting cable. The two-engine turboprop grabbed the wire with a jolt, then taxied over to the carrier's island. There the crew lowered the plane's tail ramp so the secretary of the Navy could walk out.

Wearing his flight suit and brown leather aviator's jacket adorned with colorful squadron patches, Lehman addressed the ship's personnel in the large hangar bay below the flight deck. "We're up here proving that we can and we will win if the Soviets choose to attack in NATO," he told the exuberant crew. "We're going to kick their ass. And you guys are here proving it." [12]

When *Mt. Whitney* and its battle group returned to Norfolk, Lehman and Lyons's first step was to attempt to turn the Second Fleet's sojourn to their advantage in the budget process on Capitol Hill. They held up the success of the mission into the Barents Sea as proof that the new Maritime Strategy could work. The after-action reports about the exercise now being drafted by the Navy and the Center for Naval Analyses were breathtaking, revealing just how convincing the Navy's electronic warfare capabilities were. But the Navy's success said more about the poor shape of the Red Navy and its dismal air defenses, as Haver had pointed out to President Reagan seven months earlier, than it did about the U.S. Navy's own capabilities.

Still, Lehman declared victory in the press by announcing publicly that the Navy's new strategy would be to attack the Kola Peninsula with aircraft carriers. Secretly, without Hayward's knowledge, Lehman's staff arranged for Lyons to brief the Senate Armed Services Committee about his mission into Soviet territorial waters.

On the day of the hearing in October, Hayward found out about the plot and decided enough was enough. He telephoned Norfolk and told Lyons to stay put.[13] On the surface, Hayward believed it was inappropriate for the Second Fleet commander to usurp the responsibility of his boss, Harry Train, the CinC in charge of the Atlantic. Privately he recoiled at the thought of Lyons standing before Congress, beating his and John Lehman's drum. Hayward decided that the white-haired and diplomatic Train would carry the Navy's water up to Washington. But Train had no idea what was going on behind the scenes between Hayward and Lyons.[14] And although Train was Lyons's supervisor, Lyons's special relationship with Lehman allowed him the unusual arrangement of reporting to the secretary's office. In fact, Train had little knowledge about the planning for the U.S. naval actions east of the North Cape or the provocative strikes on the Bear reconnaissance planes. "Harry Train resided in a different galaxy from us," Tuttle said. "He thought we were just hot-dogging it."

On Capitol Hill, Train sensed something was not right when committee members wanted to know if he really would send two carriers up to the North Cape to bomb the Soviet navy's Northern Fleet into the stone age at the outset of a war. He did a lot of tap dancing as he tried to come up with a good answer. "Yes, we could do it, we would take enormous losses," he said finally. "It wouldn't be what I would opt to do."[15]

His testimony was less than convincing and sowed seeds of doubt about the effectiveness of the Maritime Strategy, which Lehman was using as justification for his Six Hundred Ship Navy. Lehman was livid at Train. He told his aide P. D. Miller to get the admiral on the telephone.

Train was back in his Norfolk headquarters only a few minutes when his telephone rang. It was his executive assistant. The secNAV was on the line. Train picked up the telephone, not entirely sure what Lehman would say. "You dumb shit!" Lehman screamed. "You're jeopardizing my whole plan!"[16]

• • •

Harry Train's star dimmed substantially after his testimony. If there were hopes that he was still in the running to become the next chief of naval operations, they were dashed by his appearance in front of the congressional committee. He was already being outshone by the glowing reports arriving in Washington from the Pacific Fleet, now under the command of Jim Watkins.[17] Watkins and Train each kept a carrier in the Indian Ocean. Every day the readiness level of the two carriers was posted on the main tactical display in the Flag Plot. Green meant the carrier was prepared to fight a war. Yellow meant it would take twenty-four hours to replenish weapons lockers, train all pilots, and complete other necessary steps required for combat. Red meant the carrier had a problem that was out of hand.

For the past three weeks Hayward had been staring at the display and growing more angry each day. "Every morning at eight o'clock the CNO would look up there," Patton recalled, "and the battle group in the Pacific Fleet would be in green and the battle group from the Atlantic would be in yellow or red." Finally Hayward had had enough. He stormed past the two Marine sentries guarding the entrance to the Flag Plot and strode into the foyer of his office where Cockell and Jim Patton were sitting. "Goddammit!" he yelled. "They're red again. Get Admiral Train on the telephone." Then he walked back into his private office.[18]

A few moments later Cockell stuck his head into Hayward's office. "Admiral Sandy Sanderson is on the line, sir. Admiral Train is in a meeting in Brussels. Would you like to talk to Sandy?"

Sanderson, who had had the misfortune of commanding *Saratoga* when it sank in the Greek port of Piraeus, now had the bad luck of being Train's deputy. But Hayward shook his head no. He did not want to speak with Sanderson. "I want to talk to the commander in chief of the Atlantic Fleet, if there is one!"

Before the end of the year, the Wat would be picked as Hayward's replacement.

It was, strangely enough, an odd choice. Lehman and Watkins may have been Catholics and conservative Republicans, but they could not have been more different in their personalities and beliefs in how the Navy should be run. And while Lehman enjoyed his yearly jaunts to the Tailhook Association conventions in Las Vegas, Watkins tried to distance himself from the debauchery.

He did, however, find himself attending Tailhook one year with John Lehman. And that sent almost everyone in the Navy's aviation leadership circles into a chronic state of anxiety. The new CNO was a devout Catholic and not much of a drinker. That year Captain Gary Hakanson was president of the Tailhook Association. Watkins's aides told Hakanson that the CNO not only wanted to attend the convention, he also wanted to visit the hospitality suites, where, unknown to him, much of the misbehavior took place, so he could meet face-to-face with naval aviators in a social setting.

"Shit, what am I going to do?" Hakanson asked a friend and fellow pilot.[19] He decided that the best time to take the Navy's top uniformed officer through the suites was at noon on Saturday. "Nobody will be there then," he said. When Watkins and Hakanson got off the elevators on the third floor, the long hallway connecting the suites as well as the party deck on the hotel's third floor were virtually deserted. As luck would have it, most of the aviators were still sleeping or nursing their hangovers.

The Watkins entourage went into a suite. It was practically empty, with few officers in the room. The CNO, with Hakanson closely in tow, walked up to an area where Lieutenant Robert Yakeley stood. "This is Admiral James Watkins, the chief of naval operations," said Hakanson, who by now realized that the officers had probably been up all night.

Yakeley then gave a roundhouse slap on Watkins's back and asked, "How are yah, yah old bubble head?"[20]

For the most part, Watkins ignored such behavior, especially Lehman's peccadilloes. But it wasn't long before he was down in the Tank, bitching and moaning about the way Lehman was running the Navy.

With the selection of Watkins as the next CNO, Tom Hayward had moved to protect his two key aides, Bill Cockell and Stasser Holcomb. He arranged for both admirals to get important commands out in the fleet, as far from Washington and John Lehman as possible. It was routine for the CNO—in fact, for any senior admiral—to watch out for his underlings and to pave the way for their ascension to four stars. Hayward had no qualms about championing the careers of Cockell and Holcomb. Both men had served him and the Navy loyally and would continue to be an asset to the sea service.

Lehman, however, thought otherwise. He never forgave Cockell and Holcomb for not supporting his own effort to become secretary of the Navy. In his revenge, he blocked promotions for both admirals and eventually forced them to retire prematurely. If he had done otherwise, Lehman believed, it would have been a sign of weakness on his part.

Holcomb, who would enter the private business world, also infuriated Lehman because he opposed the Maritime Strategy, particularly attacks on the Kola Peninsula. "Shit, I've been around town awhile, and you can't keep secrets long in Washington," Lehman said. "Here he was up on the Hill talking behind my back and feeding information behind my back, undermining the forward strategy."[21]

The mild-mannered Cockell would end up working as a civilian for Colin Powell on the National Security Council, where he would prosper. He was finally out from under the secretary's thumb. Now Cockell was in the enviable position of being able to report on Lehman to the most senior defense officials in the Reagan administration.

Hayward made plans to retire in Hawaii and become an international business consultant. On the one hand, he left the Navy proud of his accomplishments, especially in laying the groundwork for the new Maritime Strategy. He had thrown his support behind Watkins instead of Train because he felt that Watkins would best be able to stand up to Lehman. At his retirement at the U.S. Naval Academy in Annapolis, Hayward held his head high while passing on the keys to the empire to Watkins. Inside, however, he was a bitter, angry man, who was scornful of Lehman. Since Lehman had arrived on the scene in February 1981, Hayward, for all intents and purposes, had lost control of the Navy. And he knew it.

≣ CHAPTER 12 ≣

For MORE THAN A YEAR NOW, John Lehman had secretly been putting together a dossier on Admiral Hyman Rickover, the father of the Navy's nuclear submarine program, for the sole purpose of building a case to get him fired.[1] The file contained information about Rickover's supporters, his appearances on Capitol Hill, programs he opposed, and embarrassing revelations about illegal gratuities he had received from the shipbuilding industry. Ultimately the file would grow and read like a charge sheet for a court-martial. Lehman guarded it closely and labeled it with the designator RICKOVER—EYES ONLY—JL, to keep others from seeing its contents.

Admiral Rickover was a small, frail man whose uniforms hung so loosely that he looked like a scarecrow. But he was a legend in naval history, and with that fame came tremendous power and influence. No one in the Navy or, for that matter, in the entire Department of Defense could get a handle on him. Even past presidents of the United States had been intimidated by the Polish Jew who was born on January 27, 1900, in Makow, a village then part of tsarist Russia.

Certain factions in the Navy had tried to get rid of Rickover before but failed. There were too many obstacles, including Congress, which would have had to okay the retirement package. Congress saw Rickover as a dedicated national servant fighting the greed of the corporate defense barons. He was the guru of the Navy's submarine service, having designed the reactor that propelled America's first nuclear sub, *Nautilus*. His designs, which relied primarily on manual operations with little automation, as well as his orders were not to be questioned. And they weren't—even when he committed a monumental blunder.

Rickover had dumped the nuclear reactor from *Seawolf* into the North Atlantic in the 1970s, an environmental nightmare that is still kept secret today. Few objected openly, but privately many submariners had troubled consciences about a hot reactor sitting on the seabed.[2] The reactor gave off so much radiation when it was in service on a prototype submarine that the Navy allowed *Seawolf* to be stationed in only two ports, New London and

Key West. *Seawolf* had to wait up to forty hours before it could pull into port so its reactor could cool down.

Rickover's clout on Capitol Hill was tied to the most influential members of Congress. There was so much respect for him among the lawmakers that when the Navy failed to promote him past captain, Congress stepped in and made him an admiral. Even Jimmy Carter, who had been trained as a nuclear submariner in Rickover's Navy, had a special affinity for the old admiral who was nearing eighty but still taking submarines to sea for their shakedown cruises.

When a move was made during Carter's tenure to retire Rickover, the President called Navy Secretary Ed Hidalgo into the Oval Office to discuss the matter. "You've been able to put up with him for two years, Eddy," he said. "Can you put up with him for another two years?"[3]

"Sure, Mr. President," Hidalgo replied, not telling Carter he sided with the forces who wanted to get rid of Rickover. "I can tolerate him for two more years."

Now it was Lehman's turn, and he was not about to tolerate the old admiral whose power rivaled his own. Nor could he afford Rickover's heavy-handed tactics with the defense industry. Rickover had been merciless on the contractors building the Navy's submarine fleet—so much so that the Navy and some firms like General Dynamics were in open warfare, fighting it out publicly in congressional hearings and the press.

General Dynamics and its subsidiary, Electric Boat Division, was one of only two shipbuilding companies in the nation capable of turning out the sophisticated nuclear-powered warships that the Navy had come to rely on. Electric Boat had built more than half of the Navy's submarine fleet, which gave it a near monopoly on submarine construction that dated back to World War I. Since 1977 the company had won every contract for a new version of an attack sub known as the 688, or *Los Angeles* class. And it was the only shipyard in the country that built the gigantic Trident, a submarine nearly as long as two football fields that moved stealthily in the ocean, carrying some two dozen D-5 nuclear missiles capable of striking the Soviet Union from six thousand miles away with pinpoint accuracy.

Without the yard, with its experienced designers, its production lines already pumping at near capacity, and its work force trained in the fine art of piecing together America's underwater sub force, Lehman knew his grandiose plans for the Six Hundred Ship Navy were doomed. General Dynamics was already having trouble meeting its commitments to the Navy, blaming the delays in construction primarily on Rickover's change orders and his obsession with quality control.

Twenty-one subs under construction were a total of twenty-one years behind schedule when Lehman became secretary. And work had been so shoddy that thousands of welds were flawed or missing. In some instances steel that did not meet Navy standards had already been welded into place beneath some of the vessels' nuclear reactors—the heart of an attack sub. Whole sections of several submarines had to be ripped apart to repair the defective welds and replace the steel. Even worse, General Dynamics expected the Navy to pay $100 million for the company's screw-ups. The new claims turned on an esoteric clause that the Navy used to insure the yards against "all risks" of accidents, fires, floods, and other calamities. Under the "all risk" clause, General Dynamics charged that the Navy, as the insurance underwriter, was legally beholden to foot the bill.

It was an intolerable situation for the new administration. The lax time schedule cut into Reagan's plans to up the nuclear ante against the Soviets because the lead ship of the Trident class, the *Ohio*—which was the key leg of the nation's nuclear triad of B-52 bombers, land-based missiles, and seaborne subs—was nearly three years behind schedule.

The entire naval buildup was jeopardized by the standoff between the Navy and Electric Boat. It was poisoning the well. Both Lehman and Sawyer knew the General Dynamics debacle was a bigger disaster than most people realized. They were staking their reputations on trying to launch an unproven, unorthodox, and risky shipbuilding strategy. And unless Lehman could solve "the E.B. mess," it would be the political blow that might sink him and the Six Hundred Ship Navy that had become Reagan's most visible symbol of rearmament. If he failed, the President failed.

On March 17, 1981, Lehman and Sawyer were in the secretary's office preparing for battle. Sawyer sat on a couch by a window with a view of the Washington Monument. Lehman sat nearby, mentally rehearsing the closely guarded plan they had concocted over the last several weeks for David S. Lewis, the powerful board chairman and chief executive officer of General Dynamics. The silver-haired Lewis, who was a near legend in the defense industry, had already entered the Pentagon and was making his way up to the fourth-floor Secretariat. Any minute he would appear. Although anxious, Lehman and Sawyer were ready for the Southern gentleman who had a temper like a volcano. The trap had been carefully set.[4]

A few days earlier, Defense Secretary Cap Weinberger and his top aides had signed off on the plot. They were fully aware of how much was riding on this meeting, not least of all Ronald Reagan's promised military buildup. Something had to be done about Lewis and the E.B. mess. And that was exactly what Lehman and Sawyer were planning to do. "We were going to hit him with a two-by-four to make him know we were serious,'' Lehman recalled. He would be the bad cop and do the walloping. The even-tempered Sawyer, they agreed, would play the role of the good cop and pick up the pieces.

Once Lewis realized the two men were playing for keeps and understood that their hardball tactics could do his company great financial harm, Lehman and Sawyer would take the first steps toward reconciliation. They really had no other choice but to eventually offer a carrot. The future of the Navy's new $120 billion–plus shipbuilding strategy hinged on whether Lehman and Lewis could eventually strike a deal.

Under Lehman's plan, the Navy would have to more than double its present shipbuilding schedules to nearly thirty boats a year, a monumental task because ships normally take years to build. Lehman and Sawyer needed every yard that was available to take part in the program. Competition, they believed, was the answer. They had to get the yards to wage a bidding war against each other that would lower prices and increase productivity. If Lehman could get men like Lewis to change the way they ran their companies, force them to tighten their belts, then the Navy and the nation would reap sizable benefits. It was a big if.

"Mr. Secretary, David Lewis is here,'' came the voice over Lehman's intercom.

"Hello, David,'' Lehman said as the chairman and his political lobbyist, Ted LeFevre, walked in. The air in the room was electric as the four men shook hands, then sat down around a small table near the couch.

Lehman wasted no time zeroing in on Lewis. "Look, David,'' he began, using the tone of a parent scolding a child, "putting in claims for your own mistakes, putting in the wrong steel and expecting us to pay for that, tearing it out and then wanting us to pay for that, then charging us to make it all right, bespeaks a contempt for the customer that is just beyond my understanding.''[5]

Lehman was visibly worked up and getting madder as he continued. He told Lewis that by the end of the day he was going to announce that he was halting Electric Boat's contract with the Navy to build four new 688 submarines and giving the work to Newport News on a sole-source contract. Lewis knew that was millions of dollars in work going to a competitor. Just like that. No bid. Nothing.

Although he was not the kind of corporate chieftain who could be easily intimidated, Lehman's diatribe caught Lewis by surprise. He was expecting to have a compromise settlement offered to him on the insurance claims.

The tough-talking boss of General Dynamics was momentarily speechless. But then he lost it. "You wet-behind-the-ears young whippersnapper!" he exploded. Yelling now, he told Lehman that he didn't have to take this, that General Dynamics had been honest and forthright in its dealings with the Navy. It was the Navy, not his company, that had mismanaged the submarine program. Lewis blamed one admiral in particular for his travails: the elderly and tempestuous Hyman Rickover.

The meeting ended with the two men shouting at each other and without closure. Lewis would not budge on the insurance claims, even though Lehman was threatening to put Electric Boat out of the subbuilding business. But in the weeks and months ahead, Sawyer would keep a secret channel open to the company, even as Lewis filed an $18.9 million claim and suggested more would follow. Publicly the Navy and General Dynamics were at loggerheads. But privately both sides were working on a deal that would later get rid of Rickover and P. Takis Veliotis, the hot-blooded Greek who managed Electric Boat. These were the two protagonists who stood in the way of improved relations.[6] Veliotis had at first tried to pamper Rickover. When that failed, he took a new tack: he stood up to the little admiral. He wanted to teach him a rough lesson, that he, Takis Veliotis, was a master shipbuilder and a man not to be toyed with. But that strategy failed, too. Rickover and Veliotis became mortal enemies. Rickover continued to run the entire submarine program with an iron fist. And Veliotis fought him nearly every step of the way. It was a blood feud with no end in sight.

Lehman and Sawyer knew that Rickover had to go. But if he went, they wanted assurances from Lewis that Veliotis would go, too.

Much of the information Lehman had compiled to use against Rickover had been collected by the Naval Investigative Service in a secret probe conducted with his full support. Other information came to Lehman via Paul David Miller, his executive assistant. When combined, it documented the incestuous relationship between Rickover and the shipbuilding industry, which had long acquiesced to his demands for personal favors and expensive handouts.

It was common knowledge within the submarine community that Rickover had sought hundreds of trinkets from the shipbuilders in exchange for favorable treatment. For years senior officers in the Navy had heard rumors about gifts of gold and diamonds. But they had become numb to the abuses, and because of Rickover's volatile temper and near dictatorial powers, they did not wish to jeopardize their own positions by revealing the improprieties. Even Lehman's two predecessors, Graham Claytor and Edward Hidalgo, had had an inkling as early as 1977 that Rickover might have been breaking federal law. When P. D. Miller found out about this, he wrote an internal memorandum to Lehman underlining Rickover's name four times and saying: "Sometime in the Mid-77 came to SecNav's attention rather lavish gifts."[7]

Apart from the violations, Rickover was indeed past his prime. Although the eighty-year-old admiral ran in place every day, flapping his arms like a bird for aerobic exercise, he could not stop the aging process. He was plagued by incontinence. At times he became incoherent and bizarre in his behavior. If he liked an oil painting hanging on a Pentagon wall, he would take it down and carry it back to his office. And he refused to admit that he had lost the sharp edge that had made him such a famous figure in the underwater world of submarines. During his ritual of taking new submarines out to sea for their initial shakedown cruises, Rickover had lost control of the La Jolla, nearly sinking the vessel in the Atlantic. Even George Sawyer, who had once studied under the master, felt it was time for Rickover to go and pitched in in the effort to topple him.[8]

Rickover had known since November that Lehman wanted to get rid of him, but he considered the young new secretary as nothing more than a nuisance and certainly not a threat. He paid little attention to Lehman's request in 1981 that he retire. After all, it was not the first time that the civilian leadership had moved against the father of the nuclear Navy. He had then relied on his influential friends, who included three former presidents and the powerful incumbents who supported him on Capitol Hill.

Rickover was sure that they would again rally to his side in this, the final battle of his sixty-year naval career. Two important Republican senators on the Armed Services Committee, Strom Thurmond of South Carolina and John Warner, a former secretary of the Navy from Virginia, had written letters requesting that Rickover be renominated for another two-year tour. In the House, Joseph Addabbo, chairman of a key congressional committee, had personally written to Reagan, urging him to extend Rickover's commission. And Addabbo's colleague, Charles Bennett, wanted to name an aircraft carrier after the admiral.[9]

Lehman seethed over the congressional flattery. But now he had built a watertight case, much of it compiled without Rickover's knowledge, that would convince the admiral's supporters on Capitol Hill that he was a political liability. He had also received support from Weinberger, who had explained to Rickover it was time for him to go, and he had Jim Watkins, a former Rickover disciple, smoothing the way into retirement. And not only did Lehman plan to get him fired, he would add the ultimate insult to injury by putting a letter of censure in Rickover's personnel file. He would also ultimately fine General Dynamics $676,000 for giving Rickover the trinkets.[10]

After months of careful scheming with the assistance of Watkins and Sawyer, Lehman arranged for Rickover to meet with President Reagan to receive a personal "that a boy" from the commander in chief. To help soothe Rickover's ego, Reagan planned to offer him a position as a science adviser to the President. The meeting was set for January 8, 1982.

On Thursday, the day before the Oval Office meeting, Lehman and Sawyer had officially ended the E.B. mess by reaching an agreement with General Dynamics. The company dropped its insurance claims and won more lucrative contracts for Tridents and *Los Angeles*–class submarines. Sawyer came up with the idea of offering a bonus-penalty contract that awarded Electric Boat more money if its subs rolled off the docks ahead of schedule. If they were late, the company paid the penalty. The arrangement allowed both Lewis and Lehman to save face. General Dynamics would reap $300 million in profit and a fat contract to build a series of Navy warehouse ships. For Lehman, the deal would permit Sawyer to restart the engines on the Six Hundred Ship Navy.

There would also be another long-range benefit for David Lewis. George Sawyer would jump ship for a $200,000-a-year job with General Dynamics. His defection was made shortly after his wife died and solely for financial reasons to help make up for the losses he had incurred while working as a public servant.

Lehman, dressed in a dark suit, arrived at the White House on Friday shortly after 11 A.M. There, sitting on a couch in the Oval Office reception area, was Rickover. The Navy secretary walked up to the admiral and extended his hand.[11]

"What the hell are you doing here?" Rickover said in a raised voice. "You have a hell of a nerve after you fired me!"

Lehman, keeping his emotions in check, explained that he had been asked by the White House to sit in on the meeting of officials in the administration.

"You know what everybody in the Navy is saying about you, that they know what you're up to," Rickover said. "Everybody in the Navy is talking about you, and I intend to tell the President all about it."

"You are welcome to tell the President whatever you like," Lehman shot back. "But I would suggest that you bear in mind the best interests of the Navy—"

"What do you know about the best interests of the Navy?" Rickover interrupted angrily.

"—and the best interests of the President," Lehman finished.

"What the hell do you know about the President?" Rickover said in a voice loud enough to cause heads to turn. Lehman looked around the room and could see that the receptionist and three other guests were watching the exchange. Embarrassed by the argument, he tried politely to advise Rickover that it would be better if he took the high road in his retirement. "Bear in mind, Admiral," Lehman said, "that you have an obligation to do what you can to use your time to help the President in his responsibilities in whatever you say, and not to use the time to vent your spleen."

"You have a hell of a goddamn nerve!" Rickover fired back.

A few minutes later the two men were led into the Oval Office. Reagan, who was a courteous man, greeted Rickover warmly. After photographs and several minutes of pleasantries, he led Rickover toward a pair of chairs near the fireplace. From his seat on the couch near Reagan's chair, Lehman could eye Rickover in his baggy suit. He felt like pouncing on the old man but knew that was out of the question. And he knew he had to be respectful of Reagan and the presidential office, which limited his words and tone. Cap Weinberger sat next to Lehman on the couch. Chief of Staff Jim Baker and the President's longtime California friend, William Clark, sat on another couch opposite them.

With the flames crackling in the fireplace and the historic portraits hanging on the room's walls, it was a peaceful and cozy setting—but not for long once Rickover launched into his tirade. "Mr. President," he began, "that pissant knows nothing about the Navy." Rickover turned to Lehman and continued, "You just want to get rid of me. You want me out of the program because you want to dismantle it." He turned back to Reagan, who had not known all the details in the plot to get rid of Rickover. Reagan looked puzzled but remained calm as the other men, especially Weinberger, squirmed uncomfortably on their seats. Weinberger shot a look at Lehman as if he wanted to wring his neck. "He's a goddamn liar," Rickover said, now looking at Reagan. "He knows he is just doing the work of the contractors. The contractors want me fired because of the claims and because I am the only one in the government who keeps them from robbing the taxpayers."

Reagan handled the elderly Rickover with charm, never raising his voice in anger at the admiral or in defense of Lehman or Weinberger, who had brought this unseemly debate into the Oval Office. After a short while he agreed to Rickover's request to discuss his retirement in private. Lehman and the three others left the room, not knowing what would be the final outcome.

Three weeks later Rickover retired officially. Gracefully.

• • •

The men who went to work in the Secretariat on February 5, 1982, were an excited, happy bunch. Lehman had been in office one year now. If there was any doubt about who had taken control of the naval empire, the youthful secretary's victory over Rickover ended it. Two previous Navy secretaries had tried but failed to fire the admiral. The coup that toppled Rickover was indeed a major accomplishment. Whether or not the process was fair mattered little. All that counted was that Rickover was gone.

In Lehman's eyes another king had fallen, too. Although Tom Hayward had yet to retire, as far as Lehman was concerned he was now little more than a powerless, ceremonial figurehead. The Navy's top admiral would be gone in July, replaced by Jim Watkins. And the beleaguered CNO's two comrades, Stasser Holcomb and Bill Cockell, had already departed. Their positions were being filled by men like Ace Lyons, who thought like Lehman and believed in his management philosophies, men who would buck the system, bend the rules, and step over the line if the situation required it.

There were many in the officers corps who hung their heads in shame and felt like fools for not standing up to Lehman. They resented his meddling, his cronyism, and his arrogant attitude that his decisions were the only ones that mattered. Now it was too late. After one year in office, Lehman and his confederates had all but closed their grip on the reins of power. Although they were despised by many, there was no doubt that they were having a remarkable run. The Lehman team had begun a rebuilding process that would firmly plot the Navy's course for the next fifteen years. The centerpiece of their efforts, the Six Hundred Ship Navy, was steaming ahead with apparent ease through the political hoops in the administration and on Capitol Hill. The Maritime Strategy had given the Navy a new lease on life. Morale was soaring. Recruitment was up and personnel were reenlisting by the droves. Away from the power struggles in Washington, naval officers in the fleet began to feel proud once again, as if they were in a Navy filled with the spirit of Bull Halsey.

Even the political appointees in the Reagan administration who sat on the all-important Defense Resources Board, the panel that met once a week to divvy up the budget pie, could not help but notice the Navy's aggressiveness, epitomized by Lehman. "Johnny was a wild man in those budget hearings," recalled Verne Orr, who was Reagan's first Air Force secretary.[12] Orr, who had served in World War II as a naval officer, viewed his rival as a bantam interested in furthering his own career. "We crossed swords, but I didn't make a career of crossing swords with Johnny. There was no profit in it."

But before Orr left at the end of Reagan's first term, he and the Navy secretary had a knock-down over Lehman's flight credentials. One day, out of the blue, Lehman called the Air Force secretary. Verne, he asked, could the Air Force provide him a helicopter to fly to New York so he could land on top of a building for a Navy PR stunt?

"Sure, Johnny, we'd be glad to do it," Orr answered. "But you're not the pilot. You're the co-pilot." Angry over the rejection, Orr recalled that Lehman upbraided him for questioning his skills and said he had qualified as a helicopter pilot, which entitled him to wear gold pilot's wings. He would even send a memo to Orr listing his flight hours in a variety of airplanes, including helicopters.[13] "Our feeling was they weren't genuine wings," Orr said. "They were conferred by Johnny on Johnny."

Lehman had indeed gone through the Navy's helicopter flight training program, but it was an arrangement similar to the deal provided for his A-6 Intruder training. According to knowledgeable sources, Navy helicopter instructors allowed Lehman to complete only 20 percent of the training syllabus and in some cases changed grades so that he appeared to be more qualified than he actually was, although both Lehman and his attorney claim he completed the course.[14] The Naval Investigative Service launched a probe and found that Lehman's performance evaluations had been inflated, a violation of naval regulations punishable by court-martial. The results, however, proved politically cumbersome for the uniformed leadership. How was the Navy going to discipline its civilian head?

The investigation never surfaced in public. But Orr was well aware that Lehman did not meet the Air Force's standards to fly helicopters. "We weren't about to let Johnny take it," he said. "We weren't about to risk one of our helicopters."

After Orr's departure, Lehman's relations with the Air Force did not improve when Pete Aldridge took over. As the past head of the Pentagon's Plans, Analysis, and Evaluation, Aldridge was one of the key strategists who had drafted the classified plans for the Six Hundred Ship Navy in 1975 under then Secretary of Defense Donald Rumsfeld. The fact that Lehman was taking credit for participating in the study then, and now claimed to be its father in the Reagan administration, irked Aldridge. "John Lehman wasn't even involved with the damn thing," he said.[15]

Although the two men were not enemies, they were not close friends, either. If anything, they shared a relationship driven by the competitive nature of the Pentagon's budget wars. And at times the competition extended even to petty things, such as a wager over a football game.

Aldridge and Lehman had made a bet over an upcoming Navy–Air Force football game to be played in Colorado Springs. The losing team would give one of its helmets to the winning team. The two service secretaries had also made a side bet. The loser would have to give a sweater from his academy to the winner. Both trophies, Lehman and Aldridge agreed, would be exchanged immediately after the game on the fifty-yard line.

At the start of the game, which was televised nationally, Lehman approached Aldridge, gloating that "the Naval Academy is going to beat the Air Force Academy by sixteen points. Not two touchdowns, sixteen points!" He was wrong. With five minutes to go, the score was Air Force 40, Navy 6. Aldridge was congratulating his players on the Air Force sidelines when a Navy public affairs officer approached him to report that Lehman would not meet him at center field. "You tell John," Aldridge said to the officer, "that I'm going to be in the field on the fifty-yard line and I'm going to have a microphone in my hand and explain to this entire crowd why it is I'm sitting here by myself." [16]

The public affairs officer beat a hasty retreat back to Lehman. A few minutes later Lehman showed up with a Navy football helmet. He is pissed off beyond belief, Aldridge thought happily to himself. Then Lehman took off his jacket, pulled off his Naval Academy sweater, and threw it at Aldridge. "I am so fucking tired of losing to the Air Force Academy!"

"I thought he was going to fire the coach at the Naval Academy that day," said Aldridge, who took the Navy football helmet back to his Pentagon office and had "40 to 6" painted on the side. "I had this trophy case outside the door, so I put that helmet in it with the score painted on it." Aldridge took immense delight in knowing that Lehman routinely had to walk past the helmet when he attended staff meetings with the secretary of defense.

Although the Navy's athletic teams found victory elusive, on Lehman's first anniversary in office he personally had lost only one political fight. It was the bitter defeat at the hands of the Catholic Church over the naming of the nuclear-powered submarine *City of Corpus Christi*. Lehman was preparing to even the score.

In March two personal notes handwritten on the stationery of a three-star lieutenant general arrived in Lehman's office. They were dated March 3 and 4 and had come from the state of Washington, where the first Trident submarine was slated to be based in Bangor in June.

> John—
>
> Just finished speaking with your Captain Dewey.
> The information I gave to him . . . will be in the letter I am having typed up today—but I missed one thing. The Archbishop said that he plans to be in the group who, in their small boats will

try to prevent the first Trident sub to sail up the Hood Canal to
Bangor next summer.
  Good luck on the speech.—
  Hi to Barbara—

  Bill

The general also included an addendum to the note that left no doubt about
how he felt about the target of his surveillance:

  A couple of thoughts for the Archbishop to ponder
  The Berlin Wall
  Poland—
  Where would he choose to live other than the U.S.—In Russia
  he could not speak like this. He criticized the U.S. continually—
  never the other side.

  Best,

  Bill[17]

  Lehman was delighted by the information. Lieutenant General Bill Le
Bailly was a retired Air Force officer who had worked for Lehman at Abington, the consulting firm he established when he left the Nixon administration.
Le Bailly was one of the spies quietly reporting to him about Raymond
Hunthausen, the Roman Catholic archbishop in Seattle. A peace-loving man
who wore Nike tennis shoes, Hunthausen was an outspoken opponent of the
Navy's new Trident base and the stealthy submarines that carried enough
nuclear weapons to destroy the Soviet Union many times over. Nine months
before, in a speech at a Lutheran gathering, Hunthausen had called the
Trident base the "Auschwitz of the Puget Sound," a comparison to the Nazi
concentration camp in Poland that Lehman found insulting to the Navy.
  In January, as Lehman celebrated his first year in office and the massive
buildup the Navy had begun under his guidance, Archbishop Hunthausen
announced that he could not support the arms race and would withhold
one-half of his federal income taxes in protest. The archbishop made the
pledge because of a "deep conviction inside myself that nuclear weapons
are wrong and I could not be a part of their production."
  The FBI and the Naval Investigative Service had placed Hunthausen under
surveillance, each maintaining a file on him and others who protested at the
Bangor base. There was also another, equally powerful organization that was
monitoring Hunthausen's speeches and appearances at protest rallies, even

during church functions. It was the Knights of Malta, the Catholic organization with historic ties to the CIA and the Vatican. A network of rich and successful men and women who exerted considerable influence throughout the world, the Knights represented power and prestige.

In the United States, many of Lehman's conservative friends belonged to the Knights, as did Lehman's new CNO, Jim Watkins.[18] The Reagan administration's ambassador to the Vatican, William Wilson, and Al Haig were also members. So were Richard Allen and Bill Casey, both of whom had teamed up with Lehman to run the political intelligence network against President Carter during the 1980 campaign.[19] The American Knights disagreed not only with Hunthausen's antidefense positions, but also with his stance on homosexuals and his liberal interpretations of church doctrine. They wanted him fired, and they were a formidable alliance. Michael Schwartz, a conservative Catholic close to many prominent Republicans, helped coordinate the effort in the United States and noted with some pride that much of the Reagan administration's national security apparatus was composed of conservative Catholics.[20]

It came as no surprise to many in the church when Lehman decided in March to take public the fight against Hunthausen. A comment made by the Navy secretary to a friendly bishop then located in Montana—that he was out to get Hunthausen and that he would do it before a certain date—had circulated widely within church circles. It would be a calculated risk on Lehman's part, but the odds were not all that bad when the conservatives weighed in on the side of the Navy. There were also certain factions in the church who opposed Hunthausen, including Cardinal O'Connor of New York, a former Navy chaplain and archbishop of the military, who often visited the Pentagon office of his good friend Jim Watkins.

Several of the conservative bishops feared that Hunthausen was becoming the symbolic head of a peace movement within the church that actively opposed not only the Navy's Trident sub program, but Reagan's plans to modernize the nation's nuclear arsenal. A similar alarm struck Lehman and other conservative Republicans, who were concerned that under Hunthausen's leadership the church's rank and file could become a formidable foe of the administration.

In a file he kept on the bishops, Lehman had a summary of the church's viewpoints on nuclear war that dated back to Pope Paul VI. Lehman, who believed the United States could fight a nuclear war and win it, was troubled over the growing opposition to nuclear deterrence that various church leaders had adopted in past years. "[N]ot only is it wrong to attack civilian populations, but it is also wrong to threaten to attack them as part of a strategy of deterrence," the bishops had said in 1976.[21]

By 1981, when Hunthausen began his nonviolence crusade, his language on nuclear war was growing even stronger. And Hunthausen was not only the most strident in his denunciations, he was the most sought after by the media, which described him as a crusader to save the world from nuclear Armageddon. Among his suitors was TV talk show host Phil Donahue, who planned to take his show to Seattle to report on the growing debate over the archbishop.

Lehman lashed out at the archbishop and the Catholic Church in a provocative speech that did not mince words.[22] On Sunday, March 8, the Jesuit-trained Lehman spoke to an audience of two hundred at the Chapel of the Four Chaplains, a nondenominational church at Temple University in his hometown of Philadelphia. "We have stood by silently while vocal advocates of unilateral disarmament on the part of the United States and of free men have sought to capture public attention, and been lionized by the media as if they spoke for the consensus of the religious leadership in this country," Lehman told the Sunday churchgoers.

"In a particularly tasteless example of this unfortunate trend," Lehman continued, his voice rising in anger, "the Catholic bishop of Seattle last year publicly called our new naval submarine base at Bangor, Washington, the American Auschwitz. Such an ignorant and repugnant statement illustrates how far the abuse of clerical office has gone in some instances. There is, I believe, something deeply immoral in the use, or should I say misuse, of sacred religious office to promulgate extreme political views."

The next day a banner headline ran across the front page of the *Seattle Post-Intelligencer:* CHIEF OF NAVY RIPS BISHOP FOR NUCLEAR STAND.

Although Seattle and its environs in the Pacific Northwest were home to several naval bases and air stations and had a pro-Navy bent, the local population was divided over Lehman's harsh words for a man with whom many in the area may not have agreed, but saw as sincere about world peace. For his part, Hunthausen shrugged off Lehman's personal attack and vowed that he would not remain silent.

Lehman's spies, the Knights of Malta, and conservative Republicans continued to shadow Hunthausen until the controversy reached a climax. This coalition funneled information to Wilson at the Vatican, and Wilson in turn rang the administration's bells that something had to be done about the American bishops—and Hunthausen. Finally the Vatican moved to silence Hunthausen. The Holy See ordered an investigation that focused on Hunthausen's liberal interpretations of the scriptures, primarily his push for more freedoms for women and homosexuals in the church. Although the Vatican did not acknowledge Hunthausen's antiwar protests, privately Pope John Paul, who had a reputation as a staunch anticommunist, was trying to establish strong ties with the Reagan administration. The Vatican felt it had no other choice but to strip Hunthausen of his powers. That set off another bitter confrontation between the liberal and conservative factions in the church, which led to the Vatican later reinstating the archbishop's authorities.

By taking on Hunthausen and the Catholic Church, Lehman sent the message that he and the Navy were not going to back down from any institution. It had a chilling effect not only on Lehman's political opponents, but on the senior officers corps in general. Anyone working on a project who questioned even the remotest directives from the secretary's office felt as if he were walking on eggshells.

PART II
FALL FROM GLORY

CHAPTER 13

BILL MANTHORPE CLUTCHED the secret view graphs under his arm and hustled around the corner to the E-Ring corridor in the Pentagon. Just ahead was the secretary of the Navy's private conference room, where he was scheduled to brief John Lehman on how many types of ships, aircraft, and weapons were needed to carry out the Navy's mission against the Soviet fleet. It was February 1982, and Manthorpe's "net assessment brief" was the first in a long series of classified presentations that the CNO's staff would give the secretary to help him prepare for the fiscal year 1983 defense budget—the big one, as Lehman liked to call it—which was coming up for a series of votes through the spring and into late September.

Manthorpe had already given his brief to the Navy's top admirals at the October 1981 CinC's conference in Annapolis. But Lehman had yet to see it or to ask how the net assessment was shaping up. In fact, he had not shown the slightest interest about what any of the systems analysts in OP-96, the Navy's programming, planning, and assessment shop, were doing. It was no secret on the fourth floor that Lehman viewed the work Manthorpe and his colleagues did as about as useful as a pot to piss in. He routinely called them "Gosplanners," a barb meant to compare the analysts to Russian planners in the Soviet Union. He particularly disliked Carlisle Trost, an admiral who had graduated first in his Naval Academy class and now headed up OP-96, which oversaw Bill Manthorpe's division.

Manthorpe paid little attention to Lehman's personal prejudices. And he was far from a shrinking violet, viewing himself as a tough salesman who would stand his ground when checked. He was a trained intelligence officer and had spent years spooking around the Soviet Union as a naval attaché, confronting some pretty tough KGB folks not so eager for him to learn their secrets. In 1978 he left the Navy with the rank of captain but stayed on as a civilian intelligence officer. By the time he finally retired in 1994, he had risen to become deputy director of naval intelligence.[1]

Manthorpe's years behind the Iron Curtain gave him some fairly crystal-clear insights about the makeup of the Soviet navy, insights that were evident in the briefing materials he brought for Lehman. Much of the data that went into the net assessment brief had come from Team Charlie, which had figured out how the Soviets planned to use their warships in a naval war. Manthorpe had used that intelligence to draft a net assessment heavy on submarine warfare to exploit weaknesses in the Russian navy.

When the briefing got under way in the conference room, Manthorpe clicked on the projector and placed the first view graph on the screen. It showed the size of the U.S. Navy and the Red Navy and compared types of warships, such as cruisers, destroyers, and submarines. He replaced this with a graph comparing the numbers of submarines. Here are ours, Manthorpe said, pointing to a small spike on the graph, and here is the number the Soviets have. The Soviet spike seemed to jump off the view graph. The next graph was more detailed yet. It compared the Soviets' antisubmarine warfare (ASW) capabilities, which included killer-hunting subs and surface ships outfitted specifically for that mission, to the U.S. Navy's ASW resources. The message on this graph was clear: the Soviets were putting the majority of their efforts into defensive submarine warfare.

Ten minutes into the brief, Manthorpe placed the fourth view graph on the overhead projector and could see that Lehman was practically coming out of his seat. The secretary was perched on the edge of his chair, his elbows planted on the table and his eyes burning holes through the screen. There was a glaring distinction on this graph that was immediately noticeable: the two navies, Manthorpe commented, did not look as if they were designed to fight each other. The Soviets' primary focus was on their home-water submarine bastions. The Americans' was on aircraft carriers. If the Navy wanted to deal effectively with the Soviet threat to the United States —the boomer boats—the Maritime Strategy should be a submarine-driven effort. The Navy should be developing more ASW capabilities and building many more submarines than were planned to go into the bastions and sink the Soviet underwater fleet.

Lehman disagreed. He was pushing for more carriers to strike land bases in the Soviet Union. But Manthorpe saw the carrier as subservient to the submarine. A submarine had more stealth, was not as vulnerable as a carrier or as costly, and, if sunk, lost only 125 men. A carrier, on the other hand, would lose five thousand men and eighty-five airplanes and take years to replace—an investment in hardware alone that neared $5 billion. And a carrier was a lousy platform for fighting a submarine war.

There was growing awareness outside the Navy in the early 1980s that large flattops were not the indestructible behemoths that the carrier admirals liked to believe. Cruise missiles, such as the French-built Exocet that had had devastating effects in the Falklands War, might not sink a carrier, but they could put it out of action. Why spend billions of dollars on big, easy-to-hit targets? became the question of the day. Why not build smaller, less expensive ships? Lehman's archrival Gary Hart and his Military Reform Caucus had come down on the side of small in the "big versus small" debate. The Colorado senator and his key aide, Bill Lind, had drafted an amendment to the 1983 Defense Appropriations Bill to kill Lehman's plans to front load the budget in order to buy two new *Nimitz*-class carriers. In a letter to his colleagues on the Senate Armed Services Committee, Hart said that "surface ships have proven more vulnerable than many expected." He was pressing to defer the construction of one of the carriers and replace the other with two smaller, forty-thousand-ton flattops propelled by conventional power.

At every opportunity Lehman sought to discredit Hart, either in his congressional testimony, in private meetings, or in correspondence to members of the administration. In a letter to Vice President George Bush, he would write that a major Hart speech on military reform reminded him "that among the calamities of war, none was greater than soldiers accustomed to plunder and garrets filled with scribblers accustomed to lie." [2] He would also write to Bush that "there is a place for Gary Hart's cheaper navy of small, lightly armed ships. They belong in the Libyan Navy, the Soviet Navy, the Cuban Navy, etc." [3]

The Navy knew all too well that Hart's position certainly had merit. Back in the 1970s a collision between the light cruiser *Belknap* and the aircraft carrier *Kennedy* had proved it. As reports about the accident filtered in to the Flag Plot, it became clear that the Navy was facing a major debacle. James Holloway, the CNO at the time, was terrified that the press would find out that a cruiser had left *Kennedy* dead in the water for four hours—an eternity for a ship of war.[4] Holloway and his admirals had been telling Congress that carriers were invulnerable to anything but a direct hit from a nuclear warhead. And now a fender-bender had turned *Kennedy* into a sitting duck.

Lehman and the carrier admirals were also arguing that bigger meant not only better, it meant invincibility to every weapon but a nuke, the same inane position taken by Holloway. Moreover, Lehman and his admirals kept secret the Navy's intelligence reports that revealed the Soviets' probable weapons in a war against the carriers were nuclear. One of the primary vessels built expressly for this purpose was the Soviets' *Oscar*-class submarine, which could fire its twenty-four nuclear-tipped cruise missiles at a carrier from three hundred miles away. Although the Soviets had targeting problems, a nuke only had to be close to achieve catastrophic results. That's why he believed, Manthorpe said, concluding his brief, that the Maritime Strategy should be built around stealthy submarines and antisub warfare ships rather than carriers.

Lehman was stunned by Manthorpe's presentation. Although Manthorpe hadn't actually said it, the last few graphs displayed on the screen spoke it loud and clear: John Lehman was building the wrong type of Navy to fight the Soviet Union.

It appeared to those in the room that the secretary of the Navy was in a state of shock. He and the President and Cap Weinberger had spent the last year pushing the Six Hundred Ship Navy, built around fifteen carrier battle groups, to Congress and the American public. It was the carriers that had put Qaddafi back into his box. It was carrier-launched aircraft that had jumped the Bears off the coast of Murmansk. Now the Gosplanners were telling him that he had it all wrong.

Lehman had had no idea that this kind of analysis was going on in a spartan office less than three hundred yards from his own suite in the Secretariat. Manthorpe had caught him totally by surprise. "Wait a minute. What are you doing this for?" Lehman asked in a voice that reverberated through his private conference room. "If this kind of stuff ever got out of the Navy, it would be a disaster! Don't you recognize that there are things in there that our enemies could use against us?"[5]

"Yes, of course I do," Manthorpe said. "But this is an internal Navy document. It is not intended to get out of the Navy."

"Well, yeah," Lehman seemed to agree, "but they are going to get a hold of it." If the congressional committees—or worse yet, the press—uncovered the assessment, it could undermine his Six Hundred Ship Navy. If Hart and the Reform Caucus got it, they would drive a wedge between the two competing points of view and most certainly bury Lehman's plans for the two new carriers, plus their twenty-four-odd escorts and the 170 planes that would go along with the armada. Hart recognized what Manthorpe did: that the Soviets were a submarine navy, and to fight it the United States needed more subs and ASW capabilities. Already the Reform Caucus was questioning the Aegis radar systems on *Ticonderoga* cruisers, accusing Lehman's admirals of fudging test results. The billion-dollar cruisers were designed to protect the carriers. Fewer carriers meant fewer cruisers. The net assessment brief in Hart's hands would be another nail, if not the last one, in the coffin.

Manthorpe tried to rationalize the need for his analysis. "If you're manufacturing toothpaste," he said, "and you want to sell this product, you have also got to know in your own mind all of the deficiencies in the product you're selling. If this net assessment highlights deficiencies, then I'm not telling you to do anything about them. I'm just saying you ought to know about them."

Manthorpe's visit to the conference room lasted for forty-five minutes. But only ten minutes were devoted to the net assessment. Thirty-five minutes went into a heated exchange between him and the secretary, with Lehman trying to undermine Manthorpe's arguments. "Lehman did not listen to good advice," Manthorpe later said. "And he did not listen to objective advice in the net assessment. He didn't want any part of it. It didn't fit with where he was going."

Lehman went back to his office and decided to keep a close eye on the goings-on inside OP-96. It was time, he finally concluded, to get the Navy to speak with one voice. He knew the officers who remained loyal to the system Hayward had established still resented him. Lehman had to somehow settle them down, to keep them from interfering with his grand plans. In some areas Lehman's team had few, if any, problems. George Sawyer was getting along famously in his office with the admirals under his charge assigned to designing a shipbuilding strategy. On Capitol Hill, the likable Tom Lynch and Ted Gordon were paving the way for congressional approval of myriad Navy programs and the 1983 budget. Gordon was a natural politician, Lehman could see. Within the Secretariat, Lehman's staff did not take a step without his approval. Walking out of line meant walking out the door and not coming back. And relations between Lehman and his new CNO, Jim Watkins, were still warm as they enjoyed a honeymoon period. P. D. Miller saw to that. He had established a back-door channel to Watkins and made sure that the admiral knew Lehman's most private plans.

If there was a weak link, it was Mel Paisley, the former Boeing executive to whom Lehman had given free rein to cut through the procurement red tape. Many people felt uneasy around him, as if they always had to check to see if their pockets had been picked. Paisley was too laid back, too much the good old boy. People began talking about him and complaining. The Naval Investigative Service even had reports that Paisley was goading female employees to perform oral copulation under his desk.[6]

John Nieroski, the head of OP-96D, another branch under Carlisle Trost, was having nothing but trouble working with Paisley. Nieroski was the adviser to the secretary and the CNO for resource analysis. He was responsible for putting together an independent cost analysis for major Navy programs going through the acquisition process. And on more than one occasion he was so fed up with what he called Lehman's flaky numbers that he threw his Pentagon pass on the desk and threatened to quit. When there were discrepancies between Lehman's costs and those prepared by Nieroski, the secretary's people always said, "Don't worry, we'll make the numbers work." When his aides told Lehman that Nieroski had repeatedly warned that his cost estimates didn't stand up to a good scrubbing, Lehman finally shouted, "Who the hell is Nieroski?"[7]

As for Paisley, Nieroski didn't like or trust him. "You know what a big bag of wind is?'' he would say about Paisley. ''Well, you haven't seen one until you see this bag.'' Paisley, Nieroski believed, was playing fast and loose with cost estimates for various programs. But Nieroski couldn't pin him down because he was having a difficult time getting access to the original estimates provided by defense contractors. The multimillion-dollar Trident II missile program in particular, which Lehman was trying to accelerate, had become a bone of contention. For months Nieroski had been asking for the classified budget figures on the program, but he kept getting the brush-off. Finally he made a personal visit to Paisley's office.

''Look, you have to give me some numbers,'' he demanded of Paisley. ''We're doing an independent cost estimate, and I'm not getting the data. How are we going to do our estimate? Give me some performance data, give me something!'' [8]

Paisley interrupted him and picked up his telephone. He called the admiral in charge of the Trident program, spoke for a few minutes, then hung up. Then, turning his attention back to Nieroski, he said, ''You'll get all the data you want.''

As Nieroski walked out the door, he whispered to Paisley's aide, ''I'm not going to get a damn thing and you know it.''

''You're probably right,'' the aide whispered back.

The file did come. And when Nieroski got his first good look at the numbers being used to support the Trident II program, he was incredulous. All of the figures were rounded off in the millions of dollars, with very little, if any, substantiation for the various items in the program. Nieroski couldn't believe it. How had they come up with this nonsense?

''John's going to have a marvelous time with this.'' Commander Harlan Ullman was laughing at the thought. Lehman's horror at the Manthorpe brief was nothing compared to the jolt that the classified document lying on Ullman's 1950s-vintage desk was about to deliver to the secretary.

To the uninformed civilian, the document was nothing more than Navy gobbledygook, column after column of random numbers labeled with meaningless acronyms.[9] To Ullman, the Extended Planning Annex, an obscure, long-range budget study, was the most controversial report he had been involved with in a long, long time. It was so explosive, in fact, that Jim Watkins and his deputy, the vice chief of naval operations, conveniently left town after the EPA was completed on July 19, 1982, so they didn't have to be around when Lehman was briefed on it.[10]

Everyone knew that Lehman was going to blow his top.

Ullman leaned back at his desk to think about the difficult road that lay ahead with Lehman. Just about everything in his little cubbyhole four hundred yards from the secretary's office was surplus material. If it wasn't metal and painted Navy gray, it was solid wood and built like a battleship. Ullman and his chief assistant, Commander Steve Woodall, had been working on the EPA for the last eight months, a time of high hopes for the Navy. If there was one undisputed message coming out of the Secretariat and the White House, it was that hundreds of billions of dollars would be pumped into the Navy throughout Reagan's term. The mental vision conjured up by Lehman's constant drum beating was of an endless money pipeline that flowed from the national treasury to the secretary of the Navy's office.

Ullman and Woodall knew it wasn't true. Convincing others that it was pure hyperbole, however, would be a near impossible task. At one point Ullman had turned to Woodall, a man many thought was abrasive but an officer who could be silly enough to pen in a happy face below his signature. "Steve, look," Ullman said in their tiny office, "we're rushing down a path toward six hundred ships. We all want to get there, but our history has been that there have always been a lot of financial land mines along the way." The problem was, he continued, "in the heady rush to get things turned around, the land mines are conveniently overlooked." [11]

This time, however, the two naval officers had made sure that the EPA did not overlook the "financial land mines." Ullman and Woodall dotted every *i* and crossed every *t* as they reviewed the Navy's $942 billion, long-range budget plan.[12] They crunched numbers on ships, personnel, and aircraft procurement. They calculated the service life of each ship in the fleet and determined when various types of ship and airplane classes would have to be retired. The two questions they kept asking each other as they went along were "Do we have an affordability problem?" and "If so, how do we correct it?"

The answer to the first question, they saw, was without a doubt "Yes." When they pulled together the data, hashed it over, and rehashed it, the answer always came out the same. "[T]he upper limit on what we can afford," Ullman wrote, was twelve carriers and between 450 and 500 ships. That was about the size Navy that Jimmy Carter had planned for. "There was a terrific amount of excitement, and there was a lot of money initially in the budget," Ullman later recalled, "and my view was that the excitement and the amount of money was clouding some good judgment." [13]

The second question would never be answered. Nobody in the Navy wanted to admit that there was no way the nation could afford the Six Hundred Ship Navy.[14]

Ullman was right on another matter, too. Lehman had flipped his lid when he was briefed on the EPA. And the unfortunate recipient of his wrath was

Carlisle Trost. Bill Manthorpe's net assessment was bad enough. But this report, more than any other internal Navy document, was the most dangerous threat to Lehman's plans. If it somehow leaked outside the Pentagon, it would be more grist for Gary Hart's Military Reform Caucus, and it would be a bonanza for the press corps. The CBO report, written by Peter Tarpgaard, which said the Navy could not afford the buildup, had flopped, partially because it had been done by outsiders. But now Lehman's own people were saying in a classified report that the Navy would face hardship and run out of money in the late 1980s and into the 1990s if the secretary went ahead with a massive rebuilding effort.

There was only one thing Lehman could do. He had to discredit the report. And fast.

It took only a matter of days before the EPA began to circulate within the Pentagon bureaucracy. Whenever Lehman went to a staff meeting on the third floor, where the defense secretary's offices were located, he would be asked about the EPA and how he planned to reconcile his numbers with those of Woodall and Ullman. "It was a constant battle," Lehman would later say. "They would throw the Navy Extended Planning Annex at me and say, 'You can't afford these.' "[15] One of Lehman's biggest fears was that David Chu, the Pentagon's director of program analysis and evaluation, would join forces with the admirals and use the EPA to undermine him.[16] "That is pure Lehman," Cap Weinberger later said. "John always used to conclude every argument, no matter which side he was on, with the statement that he knew the brass were against him."[17]

When Lehman showed up in Weinberger's office to make a full-scale assault on the EPA, the defense secretary listened like a patient father, as he always did when Lehman was in hot water. Although Weinberger had supported Lehman for the secretary's job, at times he wondered if he had made the right decision. More than once he had taken Lehman out to the woodshed for a private scolding—which in itself was rare, considering Weinberger was not a man built for confrontation.[18] He had come into office with a management style that allowed his service secretaries great leeway. But too often Lehman took advantage of Weinberger's passiveness. He never seemed to get the message that the defense secretary was trying to put his foot down for the final time. Lehman would routinely run off the reservation again and have to be reined in yet another time.

When Weinberger and his staff had ordered Lehman not to use his favorite expression, "maritime superiority," in public speeches or to the press, Lehman simply picked up the telephone behind his desk that rang in the White House. He asked his brother Chris, a White House aide, to get Reagan's speech writers to insert the phrase into the President's speeches on national defense. When Lehman was reprimanded for using the phrase, he simply declared: "I'm just quoting the President." Lehman kept in close contact with Admiral John Poindexter and Marine Lieutenant Colonel Bud McFarlane, two high administration officials—without Weinberger's approval. Fed up, Weinberger exploded when he unexpectedly ran into Lehman at the White House. What the fuck are you doing here? he demanded.[19]

Weinberger also hit the roof over an interview Lehman had with Ed Prina, a former Navy captain turned journalist for the conservative Copley News Service, in which he said the Pentagon would be more efficient "if we could get rid of these six thousand bureaucrats . . . who are accountable essentially to nobody." The Prina piece was followed by articles from other news organizations and caused a stir inside the Pentagon.

Usually such episodes were followed by a letter from Lehman to Weinberger, apologizing for his mistakes. To soothe his boss over the Prina piece, Lehman sent a handwritten note on his personal stationery, adorned with a four-star flag.[20]

> Cap
>
> I very much regret the embarrassment by the . . . article, which was a replay of last week's Prina article. The permanent bureaucrats like Spinney do take power away from the Secretary of Defense. I was simply too unguarded with Prina, whom I consider a friend.
>
> It is unfortunate that a by-product of an active public affairs strategy is an occasional blunder like this.
>
> I need to be more careful, and I shall.
>
> John

Weinberger's staff, particularly Larry Korb, had watched Lehman pull the wool over Weinberger's eyes with growing alarm. Korb was convinced that the Navy could not afford the massive buildup it was embarking on. In a Defense Resources Board meeting that spring, he cut into Lehman and said the Navy was going to leave a huge debt to future generations of naval leaders and the nation.

"Who cares?" Lehman responded callously. "We're not going to be here."[21]

The remark hung in the air for a while, until Carlucci broke the silence. Although Carlucci was a hands-on bureaucrat with lots of government experience, he had no more control over Lehman than Weinberger did. He looked at the Navy secretary for a few moments, then said in a sarcastic voice, "That was very statesmanlike, John." [22]

If there was one thing Korb knew, despite what Lehman was telling Weinberger and the Congress, it was that the Navy's numbers didn't add up. The EPA was additional proof. Korb had crunched his own set of numbers, not just on the Navy, but on Reagan's entire defense buildup. In a secret briefing for Weinberger, Korb said the administration would need hundreds of billions of dollars more than it was asking Congress for to sustain the buildup. The contents of the meeting were leaked to George Wilson of *The Washington Post,* which caused not only embarrassment but anger among Reagan's cabinet, and the administration made those who attended the briefing take a polygraph test in the hope of exposing the leaker. The true source was never identified.

Korb knew he was on solid ground concerning Lehman's numbers, which were the most suspect of those of the three services. He knew Lehman would have to do some fast talking to convince Weinberger otherwise and defuse the growing momentum of Ullman and Woodall's Extended Planning Annex.

When Lehman finally got a one-on-one with Weinberger, who didn't understand all the nuances in shipbuilding, he made his case. The EPA, he said, was "based on the faulty premise that we would continue to procure ships in the way we always had. Look, don't hold me to the way the admirals have been buying ships in the past because we're just not going to do it that way." Competition, he said, would drive the unit price of ships and airplanes down, not up, making the whole program affordable. "We believe in competition."

Weinberger went along with Lehman, believing the Navy was not off on a money-spending spree with no future payoff. That could not have been farther from the truth. As Lehman left Weinberger's office, he had already been putting together one of the most grandiose spending schemes in the Navy's history. It was called Strategic Homeporting, which critics of the Navy quickly dubbed "homeporking."

The day that Gary Hart's amendment to kill the two *Nimitz*-class carriers came up for a vote on the Senate floor, John Lehman was strapped into the bomber-navigator's seat of an A-6 Intruder flying on a reserve training mission over the Mediterranean. That Lehman was on active duty was a source of agitation to some White House staffers, who saw it as a publicity stunt. Before he left, Lehman had sent a two-and-a-half-page press release over to the White House, alerting the administration to what he was up to.

Bob Garrick, a retired admiral and former public affairs officer now working for Meese, thought it was a bad idea for a member of the administration to go on active duty. He cut down the press release to one paragraph, sent it back, and telephoned Lehman to offer some advice.

"John, it's enough of a problem that the secretary of the Navy is going on active duty," Garrick said. "But do you know what it does to a commander when the secretary of the Navy shows up as a lieutenant commander and the poor bastard has to write a fitness report on you?"[23]

Garrick could tell that Lehman wasn't listening. Still, he thought it was important that Lehman understand the full ramifications of what he was doing. "Why don't you say you're going to go on a familiarization tour and take your twelve days' active duty on that basis? In the best interest of the Navy and the presidency, I don't think you should go on active duty."

He hung up feeling that Lehman didn't give a damn about what the White House had to say. A short while later Garrick was scanning the newsmagazines and saw a picture of Lehman in full flight gear climbing into a Navy aircraft. "That dirty son of a bitch," Garrick said to himself. "He went down there just to get flight time and put the CO in an embarrassing position."

Lehman had flown out to the aircraft carrier *Kennedy* with Ted Gordon and some other members of his staff. He was aloft in an A-6 now, peering into his scope to get a fix on the target being towed by a Navy ship. His concentration was broken by a voice in his headphones. It was Ted Gordon, who was on the *Kennedy,* from which Lehman had just taken off. I've been in touch with Washington to find out how the Hart vote was going, Gordon said with a big smile on his face. We won.

On hearing the news, Lehman dropped his bombs and said, "So much for Gary Hart," as if he had just bombed the senator's Capitol Hill office.[24]

Shortly after the Hart vote, the Senate passed the defense appropriations bill, which awarded $239,474 billion to the Pentagon, a $61 billion increase over Carter's 1980 defense budget.[25] The Navy received nearly $81 billion, followed by $74 billion for the Air Force and $57 billion for the Army.[26] The biggest chunk of the Navy's appropriation, more than 30 percent above inflation, went to procurement and research and development. Lehman got his two carriers, plus $3 billion for three Aegis-equipped cruisers and about a half billion to recommission the battleship *Iowa.*

After the budget passed, Lehman appeared on December 1, 1982, at an all-day seminar on military spending held by a landmark think tank in Washington, the Brookings Institution. He had been saying all along, publicly, that the Navy would get its money. Privately there had been doubts, which were exacerbated by Bill Manthorpe's net assessment and the EPA.

And although nobody outside the Navy knew it, the debate over whether the Soviet navy was defensive or offensive was still raging within the intelligence community. Lehman had kept that from spilling out to the public, knowing that a defensive Soviet navy could undermine his buildup on Capitol Hill.[27] Somehow, through political cunning and good luck, he had managed to keep the lid on these diversions and make good on his promises.

Now, at Brookings, Lehman decided to gloat a bit about his success. "Sorry," he said to the critics who were still lambasting his buildup. "It's too late to stop it. . . . We've got the Six Hundred Ship Navy."

He was so confident that nothing could turn around the fleet buildup that he considered leaving his post. Frank Carlucci was resigning as deputy secretary of defense, and Lehman let it be known that he wanted the Pentagon's second most important slot. Some in the Navy were amazed that he would give up a job he had fought so hard to get and was so successful at. He was credited for rekindling the Navy's esprit de corps. He had done more in the last twenty-two months to build up the Navy than any past secretary with the exception of Forrestal. The accomplishments of Verne Orr at Air Force and Jack Marsh at Army were impressive but fell far short of Lehman's.

There were some, Korb among them, who saw the job switch as vintage Lehman; he was a man who craved power. The media had painted Lehman as a golden boy, a man destined to go on to bigger and better things in the administration. Secretary of defense, national security adviser, even a vice presidential candidate someday, were not out of the question. Korb knew that Lehman would leave the Navy in a heartbeat and not look back if he got Carlucci's job.

Later that December Dave Kassing, president of the Center for Naval Analyses, answered the ringing telephone in his home. He picked up the receiver and heard the familiar but sedate voice of Robert Sproull on the line. Sproull was president of Rochester University in New York, which managed the contract between the CNA and the Navy. After the two men exchanged pleasantries, Sproull started in. I've been talking with John Lehman, he said slowly. He wants to fire you. He wants to replace you with Bing West.[28]

Kassing was astounded at the thought of being fired. And he was angry that West would be a party to such a plan. When West was out of work years ago and down on his luck because no one would hire him, Kassing had come to his rescue and given him a job. Now West, who was being eased out of his current job as assistant defense secretary for international security affairs, had joined forces with Lehman.

Kassing didn't understand why Lehman had decided to pick on him. A conservative economist trained at the University of Chicago, Kassing was a quiet intellectual who tried to keep himself and the CNA out of the public limelight. But Lehman didn't see it that way. Although some called CNA analysts the Navy's scholarly prostitutes, the institution had become a thorn in Lehman's side. Shortly after Ullman had finished the EPA, one of Kassing's analysts, Robert Pirie, now an assistant secretary of the Navy in the Clinton administration, decided to take a more in-depth look at the long-term budget. Pirie, a former Defense Department official in the Carter administration, came up with results similar to Ullman's. No matter how you looked at the buildup, jiggered and rejiggered the numbers, the Navy could not afford the fleet it wanted to build. Disaster loomed ahead if the Navy continued on its present course.

The CNA had also done some revolutionary work on the Soviet navy that undercut Lehman's arguments for a buildup. It was a CNA analyst, Jamie McConnell, who had first concluded in the mid-1970s that the Soviets were keeping their submarines in bastions and would not use them in a first strike. Many at the CNA who were working with Team Charlie were also uncomfortable with Lehman's and Shapiro's distortions of the Soviet threat. The prevailing view at the think tank was that the Soviets had a defensive fleet. And several staffers were helping to build NIE 11-15-82/D, the national intelligence estimate on the Soviet navy that was due to be released next year, in March 1983.

All of these reports when combined were among Lehman's biggest worries. The Navy may have won its first major budget victory, but there were five more years to fight over money. If Kassing was gone, replaced by someone like West who was more amenable to Lehman's ideas, he would have one less threat to his programs. But Sproull stood up for Kassing and told Lehman that he did not have the authority to hire or fire the president of the CNA.

On December 29 the university's board of overseers passed a resolution expressing confidence in Kassing. Lehman backed off and told Mel Paisley to examine the problem and look for some means to replace Kassing and, if need be, Rochester as well. Paisley knew there was more than one way to skin a cat and the best way to get rid of Kassing was to put the CNA contract out for bid.

On Capitol Hill, several congressional staffers on the Armed Services Committee watched Lehman's handling of the CNA affair with growing alarm. They persuaded Sam Nunn to call the Navy secretary on the carpet to explain himself. Nunn summoned Lehman to appear before the committee and burrowed in on him about Kassing. The exchange soured both men's view of the other to the point where they refused to deal with each other personally. Professionally their relationship wasn't much better. The two men differed over the Maritime Strategy and one time got into a public shouting match at a congressional hearing.

Lehman sensed he had stepped over the line with Nunn and tried to make peace. Although the Georgia politician was a Democrat, he was a conservative one and prodefense to boot. It would be better to have Nunn in the Navy's corner rather than opposed to it. But Nunn wasn't buying, and Lehman finally sent a handwritten note on his personal stationery, adorned with a four-star flag, pleading with Nunn to talk to him.[29]

Dear Sam

I am told you flattered me by mention in dispatch's again last week. As you know I have tried to see you to talk about reorganization for the last two years. Always I get a nice call from Arnold, which I appreciate, but no meeting. I would like to discuss the issue with you over lunch alone if you have a free day before Christmas.

Best regards

John

While Lehman extended an olive branch to Nunn, he secretly went after his top aide, Arnold Punaro, a power broker on the Armed Services Committee. Punaro was a reserve Marine officer who would rise to the rank of brigadier general. Through the grapevine Lehman had learned that Punaro was missing a fitness report in his military record. That meant one of two things: a bad evaluation had somehow been expunged from his record or a reporting senior had simply slipped up and forgotten to write a report, which happened quite frequently in the reserves. Lehman intended to find out. According to someone with firsthand information, he sent a Marine lieutenant colonel on his staff over to Marine Corps headquarters to steal a copy of Punaro's records, which he did. But there was nothing to the missing fitness report, and Nunn and Punaro remained as hostile as ever to Lehman.

As the affair rolled on, Weinberger became uncomfortable. He did not know that Lehman was trying to get rid of Kassing in order to make room for West. Weinberger appointed Richard D. DeLauer, defense undersecretary for research and engineering, to arbitrate the whole mess. That meant trouble for Lehman. He had had his spies out for DeLauer for some time and kept a thick file on his public statements, deeds, even gossip. One report about a reception DeLauer attended said: "Dr. R. DeLauer, in a loud voice, was overheard to be personally critical of the Secretary of the Navy, John Lehman. Dr. DeLauer, in addressing several gentlemen, was heard to make statements such as: 'John Lehman is an unprincipled SOB.' 'Lehman tells us in the Pentagon one thing and then he goes and makes his own deals on the Hill.' " [30]

DeLauer had less luck in dealing with Lehman than Weinberger and Carlucci and was unable to mediate the CNA debacle. Finally Sproull wrote a letter to the deputy secretary of defense, saying, "The university is not willing to continue if the leadership of [the center] is to be designated by the Navy." A short while later the Navy awarded the contract to the Hudson Institute, a conservative research center in New York. Under the arrangement Kassing had to leave his post.

Kassing was not the only official to lose his job. In a much quieter debate, one that did not garner headlines, Lehman shut down two other Navy institutions that had questioned his plans. Gone from the Navy's roles were Bill Manthorpe's OP-96N and Harlan Ullman's office, which had done the EPA. A short while later Lehman also got rid of John Nieroski, the cost expert and head of OP-96D. From now on Lehman and his team would do their own analysis.

That was how many people thought it should be. It was Lehman's genius behind the buildup. If he said it could be done, why doubt him?

Not only did Lehman not get Carlucci's job, but Paul Thayer, the man who was sworn in as deputy secretary of defense on January 12, 1983, vowed to cut the Navy's budget by as much as $18 billion over five years. The first target on his hit list was the Navy's new two-carrier deal with Newport News. Although Congress had appropriated the money, Thayer had the authority to redirect the money to another service.

If the rug on the floor of his Pentagon office represented Thayer's personality, then John Lehman would have his hands full. It was a bearskin complete with a stuffed head and big white fangs.[31] Thayer was not anti-Navy, nor was he against a strong defense. Originally from Texas, he had been a Navy fighter pilot who rose to head the LTV corporation, a large defense contractor. Lehman and others in the Navy believed that Thayer was out to get the Navy because LTV had lost the contract to build the F/A-18 Hornet to rivals McDonnell Douglas and Northrop. To Thayer that simply was not true. He was not out for revenge for a lost business deal. His cause was to ensure that each of the military branches received the same treatment.

In just under two years Thayer could see that Lehman had cleverly manip-

ulated Weinberger and the Reagan White House to win the lion's share of
the 1983 budget. Although Thayer's friend Verne Orr was no match for
Lehman, the Air Force had still managed to hold its own in the budget wars.
It was the Army, Thayer realized, that was getting shortchanged—at the
expense of Lehman's Navy. That would have to stop. It was the Army that
won wars and held territory. The Navy and its carriers, Thayer believed,
were not at all what they were cracked up to be by Lehman and the admirals.
His rule of thumb was simple. Almost two-thirds of every dollar that went
into an aircraft carrier, its air wing, and its escort ships was spent on defending the battle group. Thayer told Lehman that spending $1 billion on an
Aegis-equipped cruiser didn't make any sense at all. He said an aircraft
carrier had very little offensive punch. Out of the eighty-five aircraft aboard,
less than two dozen were A-6 bombers. And some of those could not even
drop bombs—they were tankers. Sending carriers and their escort ships to
win a war was lunacy. "I went on record several times," Thayer recalled,
"that to consider that an aircraft carrier was anything but a liability in a
major all-out war was silly. It was really a head-in-the-sand dogmatic attitude that could not survive in the cold hard facts of life." [32]

Thayer took his concerns about the Navy to Weinberger. He wanted to
have an open door to Weinberger's office. So they met every morning around
8 A.M. In his role as the number two man in the Defense Department, he saw
himself as the chief operating officer of a company and thought that he
should have more authority over the service secretaries, including Lehman.
Thayer wanted to be up front with his boss and give him an educated view
of the issues based on years of toiling in the defense world, an experience
that Weinberger didn't have. "Cap, the Navy and the White House keep
harping on this six-hundred-ship Navy, and they cannot tell you what the six
hundred ships are that they want. It is absolutely absurd for us to be pointing
toward a goal," he told Weinberger, "unless we have concrete details on
everything they plan to build." [33] Weinberger agreed but did not act on the
advice.

Something had to be done, and Thayer told Weinberger that he had to get
a modicum of fiscal responsibility in the Pentagon. He knew in early 1983,
when Reagan's defense buildup was still in its infancy, that Congress would
not tolerate the huge budget requests the Pentagon was making. As preparations for the 1984 budget got under way, Thayer and Weinberger attended a
breakfast in Tennessee senator Howard H. Baker's conference room. Baker,
the Senate Republican majority leader, had invited over some key committee
members from Armed Services to try to strike a deal over how big the
budget should be before it went to the floor for debate. Weinberger was
pushing for a 15 percent increase, and Baker wanted something around 10

percent. Thayer could see that Weinberger wouldn't budge. "Screw both of you," Baker finally said. "We'll let you stew in your own juices. I'm not going to do anything to help you if you're going to take that attitude."[34] The defense budget shrank every year after that.

On January 12, the same day that Paul Thayer was sworn in, the fight over Strategic Homeporting had begun. George Sawyer wrote a letter to Claiborne Pell, the Democratic senator from Rhode Island. Sawyer was responding to an October 28, 1982, letter from Pell that had questioned Lehman's Strategic Homeporting plan to disperse the ships he was building in new and costly ports. Lehman figured he could spread them out in the districts of key lawmakers on the House and Senate military authorization committees who supervised defense spending. It would be a back-door way to ensure funding for the Six Hundred Ship Navy over the next several years. No politician would turn down millions of dollars in income for his district. Defense dollars, Lehman knew even in early 1983, would soon start to dwindle. But he was betting that lawmakers who had been promised new ships would come down on the side of the Navy in future budget battles.

Pell was particularly upset that no local, state, or federal officials had been consulted about bringing additional ships to Rhode Island. For the white-haired senator, it rekindled painful memories about the Navy's sudden decision to pull ships out of Rhode Island in 1973. That unexpected move, Pell told Lehman, "created unemployment and hardship from which the state has never fully recovered. The abruptness of the Navy's decision also produced a sense of distrust and bitterness."

"It is clear," Pell continued, "that the return of a significant number of ships to Rhode Island would have a major economic impact, and whether the true, long-term overall impact on our state would be positive or negative is yet to be assessed. I know that I have very real concerns of my own on this point." He went on to say that the cities of his state would face significant new challenges and problems if the Navy homeported more ships in Rhode Island. He was not saying no. He just wanted more study and consultation with officials from his state.

Sawyer's letter in response was carefully crafted to use Pell's own words to punish him. "I understand your concerns over additional Navy ships being brought into Newport and the possible economic and environmental impact on the local area," he wrote. "Therefore, the secretary of the Navy has reevaluated plans for increasing the Navy presence in Newport and decided not to base two additional Naval Reserve Force frigates there."

When Lehman saw a copy of the letter, he scribbled across the top: "George

Bravo!'' He loathed Pell. In 1975, during his confirmation hearings for the deputy's job at the Arms Control and Disarmament Agency, Pell had ribbed him hard about his honesty and integrity. Four years earlier, on January 27, 1971, Lehman had called Senator William Fulbright shameless and mischievous and denounced the staffers of the Foreign Relations Committee for divulging classified information to the media.[35] Although it was common knowledge that Lehman had made the remarks, he denied it publicly.

When Lehman sat down before Pell in room 4221 of the Dirksen Senate Office Building on Tuesday, February 11, 1975, the senator was still irritated over his remarks about Fulbright. The litmus test that the committee would use to judge Lehman was not his experience or his position on nuclear arms, Pell said. The litmus test for confirmation was his honesty. ''The important thing is, is the nominee lying or telling the truth? This is the fundamental point.[36] I have inquired into your candidacy,'' Pell scolded, ''. . . and I have made calls within the government to the ACDA and to the State Department and also to the people who have left both these organizations. I have received one reply supportive of it. All I received, except one neutral, were negative.''[37]

Lehman had tried to reassure Pell and his Senate colleagues. Under oath, with the accompanying threat of perjury, he spoke calmly and without the slightest hesitation. ''I did not, I repeat, accuse anyone on the Foreign Service Committee or the staff of leaking information.''[38]

''I think it is good you lay it on the table that you did not,'' Pell replied.[39] Although the Senate confirmed Lehman, his answers to Pell's questions had been less than honest.[40]

Lehman never forgot that hearing. In his world of politics, Pell was an enemy. And enemies, especially Democratic ones, had to be punished. Now it was payback time. By not putting ships in Pell's state, he was depriving Rhode Island's citizens of millions of dollars in economic benefits. It was a crafty move, and Lehman knew it would pay off. It wasn't long before the boom was lowered on Pell. Within weeks of the announcement to cut off Rhode Island, scores of letters poured in from state and federal legislators and community and business leaders, urging the Navy to reconsider its decision. Rhode Island's other senator, Republican John Chafee, told Lehman that ''our state slogan will soon be changed to 'Have you hugged a sailor today?' ''

It was not a big Navy victory. But small victories added up. More important, it illustrated how politically significant the Strategic Homeporting plan could be. Rhode Island's political leaders were fighting over just a few ships. Imagine what could have been done with the 140 new and refurbished ships that would need homeports. At one point Lehman took out a legal pad and drew three lines down the page. In the first column he listed half a dozen cities that would get ships and others that would get new multimillion-dollar ports. In the second column he wrote a date when each city would get its ships. And in the third he penned in the costs.[41]

On a page titled "Gulf Coast," he wrote in nine cities, several of which would get new ports. On another concerning the West Coast, he listed San Francisco, Pearl Harbor, and Long Beach, the hometown of Republican California governor George Deukmejian. In the Pacific Northwest, Lehman had already decided—a month before the Navy officially began the plan[42] —that his longtime friend Senator Scoop Jackson would get the aircraft carrier *Nimitz* and its entire twelve-ship battle group. Along with the hundred million dollars the ships would bring to Washington, Jackson would get another bonus: a new homeport in Everett. It was one of nine new homeports Lehman wanted to build in key congressional districts across the nation.

Initially the Navy considered some two dozen cities, including New York, which was being looked at for a new homeport on Staten Island. New York's Senator Alfonse D'Amato pressed Larry Korb in the summer of 1983, saying, "Listen, you don't want to go to Boston. You buy nothing up there. It's all Democrats. Who gives a damn about Rhode Island? Hempstead, New York, where I come from, is bigger than the whole state. You gotta go to New York. It just makes good political sense."[43]

New York's politicians were not the only ones lobbying hard for ships. On September 21, 1983, ten U.S. senators and eight congressmen from the Gulf states met with Lehman to present their case for homeporting a battleship group in their area. What the Navy didn't say, however, was that Congress had yet to appropriate the $478 million to overhaul the *Wisconsin*. The Navy was dangling the prospect of a port before it had a ship to put into it.

The Navy was coy about its financial estimates, too. Publicly Navy officials predicted that Strategic Homeporting would cost between $217 million and $800 million in its entirety. Even numbers as low as $100 million were tossed around by some. The idea was to keep the actual amount ambiguous so nobody could pin the Navy down on how much the Strategic Homeporting plan would actually cost. But Navy officials were more precise on the positive estimates for local cities. Corpus Christi, for example, would be on the receiving end of a $100 million Navy payroll, and ship repair companies could win up to $60 million in new work.[44]

The General Accounting Office, which began an investigation into the plan, accused the Navy of "hiding the true costs of homeporting." In an internal memorandum, an admiral complained that the GAO investigators "had a short fuse . . . because they were unable to meet the deadline, we are becoming whipping boys."[45] The true costs were, in fact, kept hidden. Chapman Cox, an assistant secretary in charge of logistics, had told Lehman in a 1982 memo that military construction outlays alone would be between $1.6 billion and $2.2 billion.[46] But that didn't take into account the daily maintenance and operational costs. Hospitals and dental clinics would be needed. Bowling alleys, softball fields, naval exchanges, all the things required on a Navy base, would have to be built. For the more budget-conscious officers like Ullman and Woodall, it was a nightmare that would only add to the tremendous long-term costs down the road that they had predicted in the EPA.

Because the plan was so fluid and politically explosive, Lehman made the new CNO, Admiral James Watkins, the point man to protect himself from criticism. When Watkins sent out an "ALNAV" message, which went throughout the Navy, updating the Strategic Homeporting concept, he did so knowing that it was written in such a way as to shield Lehman from any political fallout. "The introductory words are heavily couched to allow you to disclaim its contents," Chase Untermeyer, an assistant secretary, wrote in a memo for Lehman. All the CNO asks is that you "interpose no objection" to the message.[47]

To counter the critics who said his plan was nothing more than pork barrel politics, Lehman had a fallback position: the Soviet threat. But he still couldn't shake the pork label that Honolulu mayor Frank Fasi emphasized in a speech to a group of retired federal employees. John Lehman, Fasi said, was trying "to sell a military force to any city interested in buying. The secretary of the Navy needs to rethink his priorities."[48]

In March the CIA released its sixty-one-page national intelligence estimate on the Soviet navy. In the two-page preface the NIE drafters endorsed Lehman's hard line toward the Soviet Union. It said the Soviets had

- developed a long-range ballistic missile;
- deployed their first sea-based, fixed-wing tactical aircraft and begun a new carrier for high-performance jets;
- achieved significant developments in the application of nuclear propulsion to warships;
- continued modernization of their fleet through the deployment of nine new classes of ships;
- begun testing a long-range land attack cruise missile capable of being launched from the sea or air.[49]

But in the document's "key judgments" section, the NIE reaffirmed Team Charlie's findings that the Soviet navy was a defensive fighting force, and that "this wartime strategy will remain essentially unchanged over the next 15 to 20 years." The underlying message of the NIE was that the Soviet navy was not a major threat. In fact, it said the Soviet navy would take part in a Third World crisis only if it did not risk an escalation with the United States.

Lehman and Ace Lyons, who was now assigned to the Joint Chiefs of Staff, immediately went to work rewriting the findings. The verdict would have to be changed. As it stood now, the NIE begged one question: Why do we need six hundred ships and the Maritime Strategy, which risks nuclear war, if the Soviets are not going to come out and fight? The one saving grace for Lehman was that the 1983 NIE was marked "Secret," which meant it would not be distributed outside the CIA, the Pentagon, and the National Security Council.

By the summer of 1983 Paul Thayer's feud with John Lehman was making headlines in *The Washington Post*. The two bureaucrats had been sniping at each other for eight months, and Thayer was growing weary. "This place isn't big enough for both of us," he finally said to Weinberger.

On August 11 Thayer was running the weekly meeting of the Defense Resources Board. Because Howard Baker was insisting on tighter budgets, Thayer had asked each of the services to clamp down. He instructed the Navy to cut ships, thus putting the brakes on Lehman's Six Hundred Ship Navy. Before the meeting, Paul David Miller had lifted a copy of Thayer's questions concerning Navy shipbuilding. When Thayer called on Lehman to explain what the Navy had done to come into compliance with his earlier order to cut money from its budget, Lehman did an end run. He simply lowered the cost of each ship to meet Thayer's request.

When Thayer heard the costs he boomed, "I don't believe those cost figures any more than I believe in the tooth fairy!"[50]

Weinberger happened to come in during the meeting and began talking to Thayer about numbers of ships. When Lehman tried to interject, Thayer yelled, "Shut up!"

"Mercy," Lehman said in a sarcastic tone. Weinberger listened, then said that he supported Lehman's numbers, overruling Thayer and shocking Verne Orr.

Forty minutes after the meeting broke up, Orr telephoned Thayer, whom he considered a friend. "Paul, there's a time a guy needs a friend," Orr said. "Will you go have lunch with me?" Orr waited what seemed like several minutes for Thayer to respond. Finally the Texan said, "Yep."

They met a short while later on Capitol Hill and Orr said, "Let's have a couple of drinks, because we need them." Orr then told Thayer that he thought Weinberger had made a big mistake in overruling him in front of the service secretaries and the rest of the officials present at the morning board meeting. It was unlike Cap, Orr said. It was very unfortunate.

As the two men ate lunch, back at the Pentagon Weinberger was hearing the same message from one of his aides. "Cap, if you do that one more time to Paul Thayer, you will probably have to get a new deputy secretary," Will Taft said.

"Do what?" Weinberger said, not realizing his mistake.

Taft explained that overruling Thayer in favor of Lehman was the wrong thing to do in front of everybody because it undercut his authority. Weinberger took the tip graciously.

At lunch a steward came up to Thayer and told him there was a telephone call for him. Orr noticed that his lunch mate was gone for quite some time. When he returned he was smiling. "Cap called and apologized. He said he meant no harm and was not trying to usurp my authority, and whatever I wanted to do was fine." [51]

Bolstered by Weinberger's support, Thayer went back to his office and dictated instructions for Lehman to get rid of one of the new *Nimitz*-class carriers. And once again Lehman got on his White House phone to tell his brother Chris what was going on. His solution to this new problem was to ask Reagan to name the carriers before Thayer could get rid of them. Lehman suggested *George Washington* and *Abraham Lincoln,* two names he knew Reagan would embrace. Not knowing about the squabble, Reagan signed off on a press release naming the two warships.

Four months later Thayer resigned. [52]

Senator Barry Goldwater, the conscience of the Republican Party, was furious on almost a daily basis over Lehman's handling of the Navy. He was not one to hold back his criticism of the Reagan administration. When he thought someone on the Reagan team was mucking up, he said so. And Goldwater believed Lehman had been way out of line for months. At one point he castigated Weinberger for not reining in his Navy secretary over a budget issue involving airplane tankers. "I can't believe it," Goldwater wrote, "but again I have to write you to find out if you are still in charge of the Pentagon. Cap, what is going on here? Are you in charge of the Department of Defense or is John Lehman? When is the Secretary of the Navy going to abide by U.S. law and your explicit guidance?" [53]

Goldwater was equally harsh on the Navy's new homeporting plan. As a former military officer and now a sitting member of the U.S. Senate, there was one thing Goldwater knew well—pork. And Lehman's sell-a-ship campaign to the highest bidder, he told Weinberger, was "pure unadulterated politics" and a waste of money. Further, one of Goldwater's main interests was in reorganizing the military's command structure to make it more responsive. The various layers between the CinCs in the field and the decision makers in the White House and Congress made the command structure cumbersome and often unruly. It was an example of the old cliché about one hand not knowing what the other was doing.

Lehman watched Goldwater's interest in the subject with some skepticism. As a by-product of his ideas on restructuring, the power of the service secretaries would be taken away and given to the Joint Chiefs of Staff, which Lehman was intent on stopping. He hired a retired Marine general, J. D. Hittle, who had been around in the late 1940s and early 1950s when the Defense Department was established, to advise him on the subject. Hittle took the assignment as any Marine would: head on. He wrote a series of insightful memorandums for Lehman marked "Very Personal" on how the secretary could use the CNO and the commandant of the Marine Corps to sabotage any efforts by their colleagues on the Joint Chiefs who were pushing for military reform.[54]

Lehman had already squashed one report on military reorganization drafted by a retired Army officer at the Heritage Foundation, the ultraconservative Washington think tank run by Ed Feulner, Lehman's old roommate. And his staff critiqued another reform package sponsored by Missouri congressman Ike Skeleton as "beneath reasonable analysis. To sum up, most of this is garbage."[55] Lehman wanted reform, but he wanted it done in a way that kept the status quo or gave the service secretaries more power, not less.

On October 23, 1983, at 6:22 A.M. in Beirut, a suicide bomber drove a yellow Mercedes truck into the Marine compound in Lebanon, killing 241 Americans. The nation grieved over the loss of life, human beings blown to bits by a bomb the equivalent of twelve thousand pounds of TNT. Reagan grieved. General P. X. Kelly, the new Marine Corps commandant, a Jesuit-trained Irishman like Lehman, went into a deep funk for three months.

But in the nation's pain and the military's misfortunes, Lehman saw a silver cloud. He asked Ted Gordon and some other staff officers to piece together an organizational chart of every CinC and their headquarters in the military.[56] When they finished, the chart was three feet wide and thirty-five feet long. Gordon rolled it up, and he and Lehman went over to see Goldwater.

In the senator's office Lehman began his pitch. "Barry, we've got to revise the whole war-fighting command structure. We had this fiasco in Beirut, and we don't know who made the decision," he said, to bivouac the

Marines at the Beirut airport, a location that exposed them to daily danger. "We think it is some major, way down here." At that Gordon and another officer unfurled the chart around Goldwater's office, taking up three walls. Lehman pointed at some obscure guy. "This is probably the guy. But we can't prove it. We have to change this."

When Goldwater later became chairman of the Senate Armed Services Committee, he did change it. But it was in exactly the opposite direction from that which Lehman had recommended. "My thinking on reorganization of the Pentagon was not influenced by John Lehman," he said.[57] "In fact, most people felt that Lehman was the Pentagon's biggest opponent of defense reorganization."

It would soon become clear why. If Lehman had so far managed to outsmart his enemies, the restructuring of the military leadership would eventually lead him down the road to ruin.

CHAPTER 14

IN OCTOBER 1984 a small publishing house affiliated with the Navy printed a technothriller about a Soviet submarine crew trying to defect to the West. By February Tom Clancy's *The Hunt for Red October* was a smashing success and would eventually sell over four million copies worldwide before becoming a major motion picture. In the space of a few months it seemed as if everybody was reading about the Navy.[1] At the White House, Reagan said that *The Hunt* was "the perfect yarn." In the Pentagon, admirals were opening doors for Clancy. On the submarine *Rickover,* crewmen would wear the name tags of the heroes in the book. And Lehman chided that the book was so realistic that if Clancy were an officer, he would be court-martialed for revealing classified information. Privately Lehman was giddy over the publicity. Almost overnight, Tom Clancy had made the Navy a service of American heroes. Navy men were brave and true, their weapons always worked, and the good guys always won.

It was a great tonic for what seemed to Lehman and his staff like an endless number of foul-ups and disasters that began with the October 1983 bombing of the Marine barracks. "I think we should admit to ourselves that the public impressions thus far of the administration's military achievement are not very favorable," Harvey Sicherman, a top Lehman strategist, wrote in a confidential memorandum. "Instead of a season of good news, we have had months of bad news."[2]

Sicherman was a close friend of Lehman's and a man who loved history.[3] He was an idea man, a big-picture guy who was able to see through the morass. "In short," he wrote Lehman, "the critics are saying that the Navy gets the biggest share, is very inefficient, follows the wrong strategy, builds the wrong ships, and is still unready for serious business." He designed a strategy for Lehman to knock down the drivel of negative criticism in a series of public speeches. "Over the past year or so," he wrote, "you have defended the Navy's record on most of these issues but usually one at a time. This made sense when the critics were one at a time. It seems to me, however, that there is ample need and great opportunity for you to deliver a standard speech that deals with the entire opposition. The main theme should be obvious: good news about the Navy. Above all, you must be very certain that the good news is hard—that it will withstand intense scrutiny.''

Lehman liked Sicherman's memorandums, which were sprinkled with historical quotes from famous figures and warnings that if he sought national attention in his speeches, he would be the subject of jealousies and nitpicking. Lehman read all of them thoroughly, often underlining several key points, and in the future he would put Sicherman's strategies to good use.

To strike back at the terrorists after the Beirut bombing, Ace Lyons, who was now Lehman's top military planner, and Jerry Tuttle, who commanded a two-carrier battle group off Lebanon's coast, were pushing hard for a Navy-only option to bomb Iranian and Hezbollah fighters responsible for the attack on the barracks. After weeks of delay Washington acquiesced, but the Joint Chiefs gave Tuttle little time to prepare. His plans to attack at midday, so Syrian antiaircraft gunners would be looking into the sun, were rejected in favor of an early morning launch.

At 7:20 A.M. Navy jets streaked off the carriers *Independence* and *Kennedy* with the wrong bombs and little preparation on a mission that would end in disaster. The jets came in low across the Lebanese horizon, illuminated by the rising sun behind them. Syrian gunners had a field day: two Navy planes were shot down, one aviator was killed, and Lieutenant Robert Goodman was captured. The Navy damaged a radar site and knocked out two gun emplacements. But two days later the radar was up and running. Lehman saw a letter that Goodman wrote from Syria to his father saying he was okay. But despite that good news, the secretary blew up over the poor showing. The Navy tactics were outdated, ill planned, and lacking in imagination. He decided to create a school for attack pilots, similar to the fighter jocks' Top Gun Fighter Weapons School at Miramar, to develop new bombing strategies. It was called Strike University, and Joe Prueher, the handsome and macho attack pilot befriended by Lehman, would be its first commanding officer.

The Navy's other big-ticket weapon steaming in Lebanese waters, the battleship *New Jersey,* had not fared much better. Lehman had pushed Weinberger hard to get the warship deployed to the region. He knew having the old battlewagon off Lebanon's coast offered a very effective military option and a signal of U.S. willingness to escalate if need be. The ship, which cost $2.2 million a month to operate off Lebanon's coast, had seen no action since its arrival on September 26.[4] And the longer it sat idle, Lehman knew, the greater its risk of becoming analogous to the Marines who had been sent to Beirut, targets that were not willing to fight back. After nearly a month of hand-wringing, the administration finally authorized *New Jersey* to fire its sixteen-inch guns. In December, 288 shells weighing two thousand pounds landed indiscriminately in the Lebanese countryside, killing "the odd shepherd," as Lehman put it. Although the Navy had spent about $64 million to maintain its forces in Lebanon, there were no artillery spotters on the ground or in the air to direct the bombardment. Inside the Pentagon, officers were repulsed at the mindless shelling and finally convinced Weinberger to turn it off. Beirut was a humbling defeat for the nation. For the Navy, whose forces bore the brunt of the failures, Lebanon illustrated that even a huge, six-hundred-ship Navy could do little against a small, determined foe.

Two days after the Marine barracks was demolished, the United States invaded Grenada, a tiny island in the Caribbean known for its spice production and cheap medical schools. The overall objective, to drive off the Marxist forces in control of Grenada and free American students, was achieved. And the administration gleefully pushed the story that its October 25 assault was a sign of new toughness, a symbol of American power and resolve. But there was another side to the story the Pentagon tried to keep under wraps. Despite the massive arms buildup handed to the Defense Department, the military had carried out its task clumsily. As many things went wrong in the operation as went right. One of the unexplained gaffes was how some six hundred Cubans on the island were able to hold off six thousand U.S. troops in a number of battles.

The Navy, which spent about $47 million[5] for its share of the invasion, experienced problems on almost every front. One costly mission had four members of SEAL Team Six, an ultrasecret commando squad, rendezvousing with a warship off Grenada's coast. High wind whipped across twelve-foot seas when the SEALs, each carrying more than one hundred pounds of equipment, parachuted into the rough water. But there was no boat in sight because no one had told the pilot he was not over the target when he signaled the drop. All four SEALs perished, and their bodies were never recovered.[6]

When American troops did get ashore, they were plagued by poor communications and no unified command. Army officers had to fly out to Navy ships to arrange ship-to-shore bombardments. One Army officer in Grenada was so frustrated in trying to communicate with the Navy that he used his AT&T calling card on a pay telephone to contact his command at Fort Bragg, asking them to relay his plea for fire support to the Navy ships just a few miles away from him.[7] To add to the embarrassments, when the Navy's top commander in the Grenada operation, Vice Admiral Joseph Metcalf, returned to Norfolk, the U.S. Customs Service found twenty-four Soviet-made assault rifles on his personal airplane. Metcalf took responsibility for the incident, trying to protect the people on his staff whose names were taped to the guns. But still the story steamrolled in the press, putting the Navy into the middle of a bothersome scandal.

Lehman admired Metcalf, a feisty little admiral who was a war fighter in the mold of Ace Lyons. Rumor had it that the Russians used a picture of Metcalf wearing a Navy ball cap and sunglasses while biting a big cigar as propaganda to show that the Yankees were renegade cowboys, not professional soldiers. Lehman liked that image. But with it came the impression that no one was controlling the warriors and the admirals were somehow immune to the rules. And the Metcalf case seemed to underscore that. While Admiral Metcalf got a mild reprimand, several soldiers and Marines faced courts-martial for trying to bring home war trophies.

On the day the story initially broke, Lehman and Ted Gordon were driving over to Capitol Hill. As they approached the Rayburn House Office Building, they saw a pack of journalists and TV crews that had staked out the front entrance on a tip that Lehman was coming to testify. "Oh, God," Lehman said, "they're after me. What do we do?"[8] Gordon had watched Lehman interact with the press before and knew that he could handle himself for about five minutes, staying to an official Navy line. After that he strayed and would make a wisecrack or take a potshot at somebody. This was not the time to risk that. Gordon drove around the congressional building to another, private entrance.

The Metcalf case was playing big in Congress. Les Aspin of Wisconsin, a former professor and now senior member of the House Armed Services Committee, took to the floor on Tuesday, April 16, 1985, to raise questions about how well flag officers were investigated. "Was Metcalf shown favoritism because he was an admiral?" Aspin asked.[9] "Was his offense fully investigated?" Aspin believed it was not, but he fell short of saying Metcalf was guilty.

He pointed out that Metcalf's superior, another admiral, had short-circuited the investigation by shutting down a probe by the Naval Investigative Service. "NIS was not free to make its own decision whether or not to pursue the case further," Aspin told his colleagues. "NIS never had the opportunity to establish just what Metcalf was responsible for. Was he bringing the weapons into the country for resale? Was he bringing them in for personal souvenirs?"

Les Aspin may not have convicted Metcalf on the House floor, but the story bounced around in the media for days. In the last fifteen months it seemed as if every time Lehman opened up the newspaper there was another Navy screw-up.

Within weeks of Aspin's speech, Congress was up in arms over reports in

San Diego that aviators at Miramar's Top Gun air station were paying $900 apiece for airplane ashtrays that should cost $28.94. And that wasn't all. That April Navy auditors turned up other questionable purchases.[10] An $18.94 socket for the F-14 Tomcat cost $404.23. And the Navy was paying $2,444.54 for aircraft ground locks that should have cost $179.15. One of the worst examples was a $.04 diode, a common electrical device that allows a current to flow in one direction. The Navy paid $110.00 for it. It was also footing bills for $600 toilet seats and $436 for $15 hammers.

It was price gouging in the extreme. Grumman Corporation paid back $150,434 for its share of the overcharges. But that didn't solve the problem. The ashtray, hammer, and toilet seat became symbols for what was wrong with the costly Navy buildup. And the flap was undermining Lehman's goal to lower prices. He had repeatedly said that competition among defense contractors would make the Six Hundred Ship Navy affordable.

To that end, he had taken a number of steps to streamline how the Navy bought its equipment. The previous December he had decided that at least one hundred admirals would have to attend either Harvard Business School, Wharton School of Business, or the Naval Postgraduate School to become "material professionals." In February he abolished the Naval Material Command, which oversaw the procurement bureaucracy. And he forced the head of the command, Admiral Steve White, a close associate of Rickover's, into retirement after thirty-three years in the Navy. In a March 1985 memorandum, White suggested the new system wouldn't work, primarily because Lehman was running it. "I could not reconcile the basic difference between myself and the Secretary of the Navy, John Lehman, over a principle of management," he wrote in his resignation letter.[11]

Even Lehman's staff was queasy over the move. Ted Gordon had warned that getting rid of the command would lead to more trouble than it was worth.[12] And Paul Nitze, a former secretary of the Navy and longtime adviser to presidents, took the unusual step of criticizing Lehman: "I believe his decision was ill advised and will be reversed in time." Lehman went ahead anyway and installed direct phone lines from his office to each of the Navy managers involved with various programs like the F-14 or the Aegis radar system. Under the new system of procurement, he had become the policy czar. He wrote a good-news letter to Barry Goldwater in April, saying he had eliminated "one entire layer of bureaucracy," [13] and ended by telling the senator these changes "will strengthen and improve our material acquisition process." Now, less than six months after he began his reforms, a toilet seat, ashtray, and hammer were dramatizing what was wrong with Lehman's new system, not what was right.

Members of Congress saw the issue as good politics, a chance to lambaste the defense contractors while threatening to cut billions out of the Navy's budget. The General Accounting Office, which had already kicked up its heels over Strategic Homeporting, had shown up at Miramar to do yet another investigation of the Navy. The press followed the story eagerly, and as the momentum mounted, Lehman knew he had to do something to appease his critics. He decided it was time to sacrifice an admiral. He fired Rear Admiral Thomas Cassidy as well as Miramar's base commander, Gary Hakanson, who earlier had guided Watkins on his tour of the Tailhook convention.

As the commander of the Pacific Fleet's fighters and E-2 Hawkeyes, Cassidy had nothing to do with the base procurement system. He was a renowned pilot, which made him something of a folk hero to the older aviators. But some of the younger pilots resented him. There had been a rash of accidents at Miramar that involved airplane parts falling from jets while airborne. Cassidy lectured each squadron: If you lose any more fucking pieces from your aircraft, you're all history. A short while later he was streaking down the runway in an F-14 when he hit the wrong button, sending the jet's external gas tanks and fuel spewing through the base. After the incident the aviators at Miramar nicknamed him ''Hop Along'' Cassidy.

Of course Cassidy did not fire himself for violating his own orders. But when Lehman fired him in early May over the procurement scandal, the younger aviators were the first ones to applaud. Cassidy's removal did not last long. Because he was not responsible for the costly and embarrassing blunders, the admiralty felt he was being made a scapegoat. In an unusual if not unheard-of move, Cassidy went public on May 31, declaring that he had been wronged. Lehman finally relented and reinstated him two months later. Privately he said he wished he had never fired him in the first place.

The ashtray tiff at Miramar only added to the drumbeat of negative publicity. It seemed as if the Navy were sliding down a slippery slope. And no one knew how to stop it.

John Lehman rose early on May 20, 1985, and jumped into his chauffeured government sedan. His driver and personal aide had brought the usual morning stack of reading material, the *Early Bird, The Washington Post,* and *The New York Times,* as well as an assortment of other paperwork that had to be scanned. The one story that mattered most to Lehman had yet to break. But he knew that when it hit the nightly news shows and the front pages, the Navy would be dragged into one of its worst crises in years, perhaps in its history.

As Lehman's car made its way to the Pentagon, FBI agents had already swooped down early that morning on a Ramada Inn in nearby Rockville, Maryland, to arrest John Walker, a retired warrant officer. The charge was treason, spying for the Soviet Union. The FBI would round up three other accomplices in the spy ring: Walker's son Michael, an enlisted sailor serving aboard *Nimitz;* John Walker's brother Arthur, who had retired from the Navy with the rank of lieutenant commander in 1973; and radioman first class Jerry Whitworth, who had left the sea service in 1983. The story made banner headlines for weeks.

On Tuesday, the day after John Walker's arrest, Lehman met with his lawyers and key people from naval intelligence and the Naval Investigative Service. They gathered in his Pentagon office, with its large windows that looked out toward the Washington Monument and, ironically, the Soviet embassy. The speakers that hung near the windows played soft music to counter Soviet electronic eavesdropping efforts. That safeguard seemed almost laughable today considering John Walker had given Moscow the Navy's most precious secrets for at least seventeen years.

The mood was dour, if not incredulous. The Naval Investigative Service had already done a quick damage assessment. Before Walker retired, he'd had a top secret crypto clearance. He and his brother Arthur had served on ballistic missile submarines and were cleared for some of the most sensitive information about U.S. and Soviet underwater activities. At one point in his espionage career, Walker had been in charge of the communications spaces for the Atlantic Fleet Submarine Force. Whitworth had been the classified material systems custodian on several ships, including two carriers, which meant he was in charge of key lists, technical manuals, and all other crypto-graphic material. It was an extremely sensitive position. Michael Walker had had the least access and had to steal classified documents on *Nimitz.*

It was an unprecedented security breach. But what was perhaps the most damning, and certainly the most politically harmful to the Navy, was that the spy ring had been able to operate for so long without attracting suspicion. Had it not been for a family squabble that led John Walker's wife to go to the FBI, the spies would still be selling secrets to the Soviets.

As Lehman listened to his inner circle deliberate about what to do, he decided that the Navy had to take the initiative not only to determine how much damage had been done, but to make sure that justice was swift and harsh. Was it possible, he wanted to know, to bring the two Walkers and Whitworth back on active duty so they could be prosecuted in the Navy's strict judicial system? He had little confidence in the Justice Department and believed that its lawyers would treat the spy case like a white-collar crime. That would be intolerable. And he was not sure that Weinberger could guarantee a harsh sentence, either.

The Navy, on the other hand, was famous for its hanging judges. It had even switched judges in one espionage case to help ensure that a guilty verdict would be reached. The answer to Lehman's question was yes, but why do it? If the three retirees were brought back on active duty, the government would have to pay them their active duty wages. Why compensate traitors?

What Lehman really wanted to do was have them all shot or hung. And he had no bones about saying it publicly. He thought the sentence for treason should be like the ones given in the nineteenth century: "That you . . . be hanged by the neck, but not until you are dead, but that you be taken down again, and whilst you are yet alive, your bowels be taken out and burnt before your face; and that afterwards your head be severed from your body and your body divided into four quarters." [14]

It may have been satisfying for Lehman to imagine such a fate for the Navy spies, but that was out of the question in the twentieth century. The best he could do was push for the death penalty, which now did not exist in peacetime for espionage. [15] He turned to the Navy's general counsel, Walter Skallerup, to see if there was a way to circumvent the Justice Department that would ensure a draconian sentence for the spies. Skallerup responded in a private memo that was not reassuring.

> I had my staff research the possibility of prosecuting espionage under the criminal code of Virginia. While there is no espionage statute *per se,* there is the crime of treason which includes giving aid and comfort to an enemy of the state. Treason is punishable as a Class 2 felony for which imprisonment for life or for any term not less than 20 years is authorized.
>
> Aside from the sentencing considerations, I see some real problems with satisfying the definition of "enemy." [16]

Captain Mac Williams, the uniformed legal adviser to Lehman, was uncomfortable with the talk about trying control the Walker case. He shared the same feelings of anger as Lehman did over the harm done to the Navy. And he was repulsed that the information supplied to Moscow may have put U.S. sailors and officers in jeopardy in a war. But Williams knew the law and the Navy's penchant to dabble with it to force certain outcomes. He warned Lehman that it would be inappropriate to interfere with the legal process. The Navy called such tampering "command influence," undue pressure from senior officials that could undermine a case.

In his heavy Southern accent, Williams stressed caution. We don't want to screw the case up, he said. We have to be careful of what we say. But before he could go farther, the secretary cut him off. "If I want your opinion, Mac, I'll ask for it. This is a political problem. The issue here is not whether John Walker is guilty or what did he give away. The issue is whether the Navy is prepared to take this medicine like men and prepared to do something about it, or whether the Navy resists change."

Lehman needed a quick response to fend off the critics in Congress and elsewhere who would zero in on the Naval Investigative Service's abysmal counterintelligence record. He had to get out in front, take action, before his critics could seize the initiative. He ordered random polygraph tests for personnel with security clearances, and he expanded the counterintelligence efforts of the Naval Investigative Service. He also decided to cut the number of security clearances within the system. There would be an immediate reduction of 10 percent with a goal of 50 percent. Curtailing access to classified information might not solve the problem, but it would send the right message that the Navy was taking action to guard its secrets. In the long run, however, it would prove ineffective. Those who had clearances were still careless in the way they handled classified information.[17]

Before the meeting broke up, Lehman agreed to have Rich Haver, the head of Team Charlie, do a complete damage assessment and interview all Navy personnel from admirals to seamen, if need be. It would be difficult, Lehman knew. In fact, it would be almost impossible. Between 1965 and 1985 the Navy had transmitted 97.4 million messages.[18] One aircraft carrier alone transmitted and received up to 2,500 messages a day. Ninety-nine percent of them were encrypted, which mattered little now. How many of these messages did the Russians have?

Almost immediately Haver found that the Navy's records that logged who passed what information over which communications circuits were inadequate or incomplete. In some cases they didn't exist. One of his biggest problems, one that he would not be able to overcome, was that there were no records at all about who used secure telephones. There were record logs about who sent what classified or unclassified messages over the Teletypes and when. But there was nothing about who picked up secure telephones and chatted away. The general opinion among the officers who used them was that they were safe and impossible to compromise. If they knew the person on the other end, they would talk freely about anything, and a lot of them did.

After speaking with several officers, Haver found it impossible to accurately reconstruct who had said what to whom. And not all the officers interviewed in the damage control process wanted to cooperate. At one point Haver reported back to Rear Admiral William O. Studeman, who was now director of naval intelligence, that "people immediately got faulty memories, either deliberately, or they just didn't remember." Haver finally completed a classified damage assessment report as well as an unclassified talking paper for if and when Lehman or Watkins testified before Congress. "We are assuming the worst with regard to loss," the report concluded. "Will require changes that may be expensive and certainly will require changes we would not have otherwise made, but we *must* take this approach." [19]

The Navy had to spend about $100 million to repair damage done by the Walkers and seal off its secret communications from interception. By October Watkins was saying publicly that serious damage had been done to the Navy, but it was not catastrophic.[20] He said that, at most, submarine, ship, and airplane warfare tactics might have to be modified to offset the presumed loss of secrets. But the full extent of the damage was never known because of the lack of records.

When it came time to announce how John and Michael Walker would be prosecuted, Lehman, Williams, Haver, and some others met with Weinberger in the defense secretary's third-floor Pentagon suite. Although none of them liked it, they all agreed to a plea bargain in which the senior Walker received life in prison and his son twenty-five years. As part of the arrangement, Walker agreed to testify against Whitworth.

Lehman left the meeting angry, feeling as if the country had been betrayed by the lawyers and bureaucrats. On October 29, the day after the agreement was announced in a Baltimore federal courtroom, he lashed out at the deal. "We in the Navy are disappointed at the plea bargain. It continues a tradition in the Justice Department of treating espionage as just another white-collar crime, and we think that it should be in a very different category." Lehman ended his remarks, which were like a missile aimed at Weinberger, by saying: "The acts were traitorous acts and ought to be treated differently from insider trading."

When Weinberger heard the news he was incredulous. Lehman had signed off on the plea bargain. What in the hell was he doing? He had gone off the reservation before, but this time he was not-so-subtly accusing Weinberger of supporting a stinky deal. Two days later Lehman ate crow when Weinberger's office released a two-page statement rebuking the secretary of the Navy.

> Secretary Lehman and I have reviewed completely the facts and circumstances which resulted in the plea-bargain in the Walker case. Secretary Lehman now understands that he did not have all the facts concerning the matter before he made several injudicious and incorrect statements with respect to the plea-bargain. Secretary Lehman now has all the facts and is in complete agreement with the Government's decision.

Although Weinberger punished Lehman publicly, inside the Navy his willingness to stand up to a deal that he thought was wrong, one many viewed as wrong, was looked upon with pride. Lehman was able to get out in front of the Walker problem and stay out in front. It was a show of decisive leadership. If he had to take a few punches on the chin, so be it. He made his stand and took his lumps.

By August of 1985 it appeared as if Ace Lyons was washed up. Since the heady days when he took the Second Fleet up past the North Cape, his career had stalled. He had had a remarkable run during Lehman's rise to power, going from a one-star rear admiral to a three-star vice admiral. But now not even the powerful Navy secretary had been able to get him to the top of the food chain—four stars.

The year before, Lehman had wanted Lyons to be the assistant to General John Vessey Jr., chairman of the Joint Chiefs of Staff, the nation's highest military body. Unknown to Lehman, Tom Hayward had privately made arrangements before he retired for Cockell, who was still kicking around as a two-star admiral in San Diego, to get the post when it came open. Lehman was dead set against Cockell ever setting foot in the Pentagon again, believing it would be a sign of weakness to let a Hayward man return to Washington. After months of back-room squabbling, Vessey intervened and picked Vice Admiral Arthur S. Moreau Jr. as an alternate candidate. Cockell retired and went to the NSC as a civilian. Lyons stayed put on Lehman's staff.

Several months later the Navy put together a long overdue plan to break up the Atlantic command.[21] Since the 1960s the Navy had known it was too much work for one admiral to take responsibility for the region's nuclear forces, oversee the Atlantic Fleet, and be in charge of Army, Air Force, and Navy troops assigned to the theater. Lehman proposed making the Atlantic Fleet its own command, with a four-star admiral in charge: Ace Lyons. This time Weinberger balked, rejecting the scheme on Vessey's advice.

That August Lehman sought to elevate Lyons to four stars as the commander in chief for southern Europe, with headquarters in Naples, Italy. Now Army General Bernard Rogers, the supreme allied commander in Europe, nixed the promotion. On Weinberger's recommendation Moreau moved from his Pentagon job to that post. Lehman was disgusted that he could not overcome the resistance of the senior military brass. Inside the Navy he had near total control over whom he chose for which positions. Although the Senate and Weinberger had to sign off on the top admirals' jobs, it was usually a rubber stamp. But when his admirals were in the running for joint billets involving other services, they were subject to a number of political checks that Lehman could do little to influence. He had used up most of his political capital over the last four years. Even Weinberger was not listening as he had before.

Still, Lehman was undeterred. He was known for not giving up in a fight, even if he was beaten and bloodied. There were always other ways to circumvent the bureaucratic barriers. He was a master at going around the rules to get what he wanted. And if there was one prize he wanted most, it was to reward his people with top jobs and admirals' stars. No one deserved that more than Ace Lyons. He may have been a bull in a china cabinet, but he was a Lehman bull. He was loyal and deserved better.

The break for Lyons came in late August 1985 when Lehman sent over to the White House a promotion slate dubbed the "twenty-four-star switch." Summer was traditionally the time when most of the assignment changes for admirals took place. This year, coincidentally, Vessey had to be replaced as chairman of the Joint Chiefs, and Weinberger selected a Navy man, Admiral William J. Crowe, the grandfatherly officer who had befriended Ace Lyons years before. Crowe was CinCPac, commander in chief Pacific, and his departure began what the admirals called the "daisy chain"; if one spot was empty, filling it would create a slate of other openings.

This year the daisy chain was in rapid motion. Besides Crowe's vacancy, two other admirals were retiring, the head of the Pacific Fleet and the four-star officer who ran the Atlantic command. At the same time Weinberger had finally approved breaking up the Atlantic command, making room for another four-star admiral to be in charge of the fleet. Four of the very best operational jobs in the Navy had to be filled, which increased the odds for Lyons. Privately Lehman was grooming him to become chief of naval operations. But Lyons would need a major four-star command if he ever hoped to become the Navy's top officer. Now, in August, Lehman inched his friend one step closer to that goal. Lyons, with Weinberger's blessing, became commander in chief of the Pacific Fleet. Under him were two fleets, the Seventh and the Third, hundreds of ships, thousands of airplanes, and 103 million square miles of ocean to play in.

He also had to play diplomat. In Asia and the Pacific, the Navy was considered an honest broker and a peacekeeper among the sometimes fractions nation-states of the area. The Reagan administration also sought to use China as a counterweight to perceived Russian encroachment in Asia and the Pacific. Weinberger and Al Haig had visited Beijing in 1981 and 1982. And Lehman, seeking to improve relations between the two navies, arrived in China in 1984. His talks with Chinese defense officials covered a variety of topics. At one point he even lobbied on behalf of a personal friend, Charles H. Kamen, who was trying to sell some SH-2 helicopters to

Beijing.[22] His major accomplishment, however, was in laying the ground-work for a historic visit to China by the Pacific Fleet in 1986.

Ace Lyons would lead the mission. He would also have to lead the charge against New Zealand. In February 1985 the New Zealand government had adopted a nuclear-free policy, telling the United States that it would not allow nuclear-propelled ships or weapons of mass destruction into its territorial waters. It was a diplomatic nightmare in that New Zealand was a member of the ANZUS treaty with Australia and the United States. There was a way out, but it was never seriously considered. Under New Zealand's new policy, only ships with nuclear weapons and reactors were excluded. But the U.S. Navy's staunch position was never to acknowledge that its ships carried nuclear weapons. It was not about to change that position or identify non-nuclear-equipped ships by allowing them to make a port call.

Lehman took a hard line. He called for relocating American defense facilities and insisted to Weinberger that economic sanctions be imposed against New Zealand. Weinberger was reluctant. But Lehman persisted and ordered his staff to write a formal recommendation for trade sanctions. A memorandum to Lehman on the subject started out strong: "Following up on the issues raised about New Zealand's trade relationship with the U.S. in view of their intransigent and naive port visit policy . . ." But it ended in a whimper and a warning that harsh treatment against an ally and friend could backfire.[23] Lehman was beside himself with anger. In a handwritten note about the New Zealanders to Weinberger, he said:

Cap

Look at these bastards, bragging that their trade with us increases even as they kick us in the teeth. How about moving my memo to you on trade and Hobart.

John[24]

Weinberger remained opposed. And even with Lyons now firmly ensconced in Pearl Harbor, Lehman could not change U.S. policy toward New Zealand.

That summer Lehman and the Navy's carrier admirals were concerned that the Airedales were not getting their fair share of the best jobs at sea, which ultimately led to flag rank. To correct the problem, Lehman ordered a comprehensive review of the Navy's promotion process for major sea commands, such as aircraft carriers and other deep-draft warships like large amphibious vessels.

Command of deep-draft vessels was traditionally divided up among the Navy's three branches, ship drivers, submariners, and aviators. Each community had its own pool of front-runners for the senior jobs, and each had its own peculiar way of ensuring its candidates were promoted in rank up the pyramid until they became eligible for a major sea command. To be promoted in rank, an officer needed to have command preferably beginning at an early stage in a career. But to have command, you needed be promoted ahead of your peers. It was a catch-22 promotion system rife with cronyism that began at the lowest levels of the officers corps. And the aviators were the worst offenders.

Federal law guaranteed that every officer up for advancement in rank be reviewed by an impartial selection board. To get around the law and make sure the right people were promoted, the heads of the aviation community would meet in private and discuss who should get command of a squadron, who should become a department head, and who were the hotshots best suited to commanding a nuclear aircraft carrier. What mattered most was one's "community reputation," not managerial skills or whether a person was a good officer. In some instances the senior aviation leaders even identified junior officers to be picked for admiral ten years before they were eligible. The system was stacked against women and minorities. Even white males who were competent but not accepted by the community were shunned.[25]

The aviators' duplicity may have been extreme, but they were not alone in rigging the promotion process. The submarine community, the silent service, was an old boy network still suffering from Rickover's patronage system. The ship drivers, although not innocent of the practice, historically put more weight on merit than politics. But that was changing with the advent of the Aegis-equipped cruisers, warships many saw as equal in prestige to a carrier. The new warships spawned a cabal of officers called the Aegis Mafia, who decided which men would get command of these high-tech vessels.

The Major Sea Command Review that Lehman ordered was aimed at the most senior officers, those men who had made it through the selection process as lieutenants and commanders and were now captains on the fast track vying for the top jobs and flag rank. One officer identified in the review was Captain William Terry, a helicopter pilot who was bound for admiral's stars.[26] He had gone from executive officer on *Okinawa*, a giant Marine amphibious assault ship, to the commanding officer of the main helicopter training squadron in San Diego, then back again to *Okinawa* as the vessel's captain. That summer of 1985 the ship was at sea on a tour of Asia and the Pacific, which included a stop in western Australia.

In September Terry stood on the bridge as the mammoth ship slowly came to a halt and tied up in the port city of Freemantle. Freemantle and nearby Perth were favorite stopping points for American ships patrolling the busy waters of the Indian Ocean, which lead to the Persian Gulf and the Arabian peninsula. Now, with New Zealand off limits, liberty calls in Australia became even more important.

The two cities were considered the "outback" of western Australia. And besides proximity to the seaways of the Indian Ocean, Perth, which had begun as a penal colony in the 1800s, was a favorite Navy port for another reason: Australian women. When U.S. ships pulled into local waters and were greeted by either protesters or others in small boats, the American sailors would shout down from the rails: "We're here! to fuck! your women!"[27]

Senior officers would warn their crew members on the ship's internal communications system about drinking too much, rowdiness, or breaking Australian law. In one warning about rape, an officer reminded the ship's crew that fourteen-year-old girls were legal.[28] Topless women routinely turned out in droves to greet the crews and attend the parties sponsored by various ships. The Americans took out advertisements in local newspapers, inviting only women to their parties. "Ladies—the U.S. Navy and Marine Corps invites you to a complimentary private dinner dance. Come enjoy yourselves with the sailors and Marines." During one port call, some enterprising naval aviators publicized a party by scattering invitations over Perth from an F-14 Tomcat that passed over the city.

The senior officers enjoyed partying, too, but they generally stayed away from the gatherings at the Perth Hilton or other hotels. Terry planned to celebrate on his captain's gig, or motor launch, with some friends on a cruise up the Swan River, which runs between Perth and Freemantle. Taking the launch out for a day was a favorite pastime of most senior American officers who visited Perth or any other port city. It gave the skippers a chance to relax after the pressures of being in command of a ship. The off-duty boat trips were notorious within the Navy for partying and heavy drinking. And the boats were often outfitted with various luxuries. One Navy captain asked that a $5,098 wine and stereo cabinet be installed on his gig.[29]

On September 30 Terry had his gig lowered overboard. The end of September brings to a close the rainy season in western Australia, and the river is a favorite recreational spot to enjoy the change of season. A large number of boaters meander lazily through the lowlands, trolling some fourteen miles between Perth and Fremantle.

About 1:15 in the afternoon, two Australians, Richard Graham and James McKendrick, launched their own small boat and had been on the water for about fifteen minutes when they spotted Terry's launch heading toward them, not an unusual sight considering the number of Navy port calls in the area. They exchanged waves with Terry and some of his friends who were on the launch. Seconds later, as Terry sped off, the wake from the American launch began breaking over the small boat. According to McKendrick, full of water, the dinghy rocked back and forth, throwing the two men into the icy river. Bobbing up and down, they could see the naval officers on the launch looking back at them. McKendrick was waving his arms frantically and yelling ''Help! Help!'' in a desperate attempt to get the American boat to turn around.[30] Graham meanwhile was floundering in the cold water. I can't swim to the shore, he told McKendrick. Float on your back, McKendrick said, trying to get him to relax. But Graham began slipping into unconsciousness, and McKendrick grabbed his collar, trying to keep his head above water. When he realized that the launch was not going to turn around, he paddled as hard as he could toward shore, dragging Graham with him. His arms ached and his fingers were cramping from the cold water. All he wanted to do was keep Graham from drowning. With his strength diminishing rapidly, McKendrick lost his grip on Graham's collar and his friend sank to the bottom of the river. He reported the accident and what had caused it to authorities. Two days later Australian divers found the body.

The day after the accident, October 2, *Okinawa* weighed anchor and left Freemantle. A day later the U.S. consulate in Perth released a statement from Terry blaming the two Australian men for the accident. He said McKendrick and Graham had intentionally rocked their boat and dived into the river. Then they swam to shore, the statement said, so there had been no need to turn around and offer assistance. Local eyewitnesses came forward to dispute Terry and the Navy's version of the story, which appeared in the local press for the next several days. But *Okinawa* and Terry were already gone. And the case was closed.

The Navy, whose image had taken a beating that year, was not about to push for a formal investigation. There was no interest in seeking the truth. The Naval Investigative Service did not get involved.[31] And to the best of everyone's memory, there was no internal judge advocate general inquiry. Moral courage was sacrificed in order to keep an explosive story from further tarnishing the Navy's reputation. Years later senior JAG Corps lawyers were incredulous that nothing had been done. To them, if McKendrick's version of the story were true, it was a case that bordered on manslaughter, yet no one held Terry accountable or told him privately to retire.

Rather, Terry was promoted to the rank of rear admiral.

• • •

That year, 1985, ended on another sour note. On November 21 Jonathan Jay Pollard, a civilian intelligence analyst with the Naval Investigative Service, was arrested for espionage. He had been spying not for an enemy, but for an ally—Israel. There were four major espionage cases in 1985, called the Year of the Spy. Two of them, two of the most embarrassing for the nation, were Navy related. And they had occurred on Lehman's watch.

CHAPTER 15

HANK KLEEMAN TOOK SEVERAL STEPS toward the landing gear of the F/A-18 Hornet, stopped, stared for a few moments, then proceeded on to the engines, where he repeated his brief, studied gaze. He walked briskly around the jet, his eyes darting from one end of the plane to the other as if he were undressing it, looking for any hidden problems before he took the Hornet aloft that morning of December 3, 1985, into the rain-soaked clouds hanging over Southern California.

The Hornet was the Navy's newest warplane. Billions of dollars had already been pumped into the single-seat aircraft designed to be both a fighter and a bomber. Since the jet had begun its full-fledged test flights around 1980, it had gotten mixed reviews. The word among the aviators was that it was unruly, even dangerous. Just off the drawing board and still under design modifications, the Hornet was full of glitches. Already five jets had crashed because of a faulty landing gear system. And pilots had had to bail out of several others for a variety of troubling reasons. At nearly $23 million a copy, each plane was an expensive loss, not only for the Navy, but for the reputation of the aircraft's builder, McDonnell Douglas.

One of the jet's earliest, most unexpected riddles was exploding engines.[1] No sooner was that problem solved than test pilots realized the Hornet had a slow roll rate, which could be fatal in combat. The jet was supposed to be able to complete a 360-degree turn in two seconds. It took the Hornet four and a half seconds. In a costly and difficult fix-it, several hundred pounds were added to the wings to stiffen them. Then, during one test flight at Patuxent River, the jet did something it was not supposed to: it went into a flat spin and ended up at the bottom of the Chesapeake Bay. A relatively cheap adjustment of the computer's software solved the spin problem. But what proved almost fatal to the program were structural cracks found in the tail section after only four hundred hours of flight time, instead of the required six thousand. This problem, too, was eventually solved, but not before millions of dollars were spent on repairs. And there were myriad other complaints about the jet, from its weak radar to its inability to strafe targets. By 1985 the Hornet was shaping up to be a billion-dollar lemon.

Although the engineers said they had ironed out the worst bugs, they couldn't seem to fix the landing gear snafu with 100 percent certainty. The one thing that crash investigators did know for sure was that a wet runway increased the chances of a gear malfunction. The Navy issued orders to pilots, advising them to be careful if they encountered wet landing conditions. Beyond that, it could be a computer problem or a score of other undetected flaws.

It was three weeks before Christmas, and Kleeman was in a hurry as he inspected the jet. His walk-arounds always seemed to bring good luck. He had done one before he flew all of his 128 combat missions in Vietnam. And he had done one the day he and his wingman shot down two Libyan jets over the Gulf of Sidra four years and four months ago. The walk-arounds also revealed something else about Kleeman. It showed that after twenty years of flying in the Navy, after more than one thousand day and night landings on aircraft carriers, he was still a serious aviator who took nothing for granted. He knew that the smallest problems could kill an unsuspecting pilot.

The sixty-second duel over the Gulf of Sidra and the few months of fleeting fame as an American hero had had little effect on Kleeman's ego. If anything, the recognition had mellowed him. He had always been a tender man, a flier so quiet that those who flew with him sometimes wondered if he had fallen asleep while airborne. Although he sometimes found it difficult to express himself in words, he was known to well up and cry over a sad story or a touching scene in a movie.[2] After the Libyan engagement, which had shaken him up, he and his wife, Carol, began talking more about life after the Navy. Kleeman was just forty-two, but he looked forward to the day when he could say good-bye to the dangers of flying high-performance jets. The Navy had always been good to him, and it rewarded him for his role in the shoot-down. He got a promotion to captain. And in May the Bureau of Personnel issued orders for him to take command of VX-4, a prestigious test squadron at Point Mugu, an air base close to Los Angeles. He even had a better than half chance to make admiral. Still, the idea of spending quality time with his wife and their two girls and two boys had more appeal.

The Kleeman family had moved from Virginia to California earlier that year, settling down in Camarillo, a quiet bedroom community in Ventura County, one of the Golden State's nicer areas. It was a twenty-minute commute to Point Mugu, which Kleeman made most days in his Datsun 300-ZX. On this winter day he had risen before dawn. The early morning hours didn't bother him. Neither did the glass of Scotch he had had the night before while he watched the Miami Dolphins defeat the Chicago Bears 38–24 on *Monday Night Football*. Tuesday morning was gloomy and damp, not a good day for flying the Hornet. While his family slept, he showered, shaved, and put on his uniform. Carol would be up soon. She had an appointment later that day for a mammogram at the Navy hospital in Long Beach. If the breast exam had not not been a routine checkup, Kleeman would never have thought twice about canceling his planned flight to Miramar in San Diego. His weekly meeting with Captain Jack Snyder, a lanky fighter pilot who commanded the West Coast training squadron, could easily have been rescheduled. Snyder, a popular officer, also happened to be president of the Tailhook Association that year.

After dressing, Kleeman went downstairs, had his usual Coke and breakfast roll, then headed out the door. Around 6:30 A.M. he slipped behind the wheel of his sports car and drove down the hill to the nearly deserted streets of Camarillo. Across town, the rising Southern California sun was peeking through patches of coastal fog and clouds, casting a jagged shadow on the pavement as it danced along Kleeman's jet and another Hornet parked on the tarmac. Mechanics were scurrying around the aircraft, looking for any last-minute "down gripes" that might ground the jets when Kleeman arrived for his usual walk-around. The airmen found no serious problems. The plane captain signed a form indicating the jets were clear to fly, then handed it to Kleeman. He signed his name under the category "I have inspected all discrepancy reports . . . and accept this aircraft for flight."[3]

Shortly after 8 A.M. Kleeman climbed up a ladder and into his jet. An airman helped him get strapped in, making sure he was secure and hooked up to the radio and that his ejection seat was armed. "Thanks for everything," Kleeman said.

The young airman smiled and said, "Have a nice flight, and see you when you get back."

At 8:30 A.M. the two Hornets streaked down the runway together at Point Mugu and into the overcast sky. Inside his cockpit, Kleeman hit the switch to retract the jet's landing gear. And as the spinning tires came inside the plane's belly, the planing link, a short piece of metal attached to one wheel, accidentally bent. When he banked his jet south for San Diego, Kleeman didn't have a clue about the foul-up. Had he known there were problems, he would have radioed his wingman and then Miramar, to advise the base that he would have to use the short runway with the arresting cable stretched across it. All Navy bases offered the device, which would catch a plane's tail hook for an emergency landing. That had been the standing order for the last two years for Hornets experiencing landing gear problems.

Although Kleeman had nearly four thousand hours in Navy warplanes and had graduated at the top of his test pilot class, he did not know the Hornet well. As he sat strapped in at twenty thousand feet, he had less than fifty hours of flight time in the quirky little jet. And because his new command job at VX-4 was so time-consuming, he had cut short by approximately 75 percent the training package required to fly the Hornet. Of the sixty-seven training requirements listed in the syllabus, Kleeman had completed only fourteen. But the safety officer who tested Kleeman, Lt. Robert McLean, also flew with him and "observed no weaknesses" in his knowledge of the aircraft's flight systems.[4] It was not as if Kleeman were an inexperienced pilot who had not been in a bind before. McLean felt Kleeman could handle any emergency.

About forty miles from Miramar, the two Hornets barreling south at several hundred miles per hour were ordered into a holding pattern over Oceanside, home to the sprawling Camp Pendleton Marine Base. The runways at Miramar were temporarily closed. It had been raining off and on for two days in San Diego, and the air field was soaked and strewn with debris called "FOD" that might get sucked up into an engine, causing a catastrophe.

Finally, one of the runways was swept clean and reopened, and the two jets were cleared to begin their approach. Kleeman waited for the first Hornet to land, then began his own descent about a minute later. As he broke out of the clouds, he could see the ten-thousand-foot-long runway with its puddles of water and a dirt perimeter that had turned into thick muck from the heavy rains. At nine miles out, his radio crackled. "X-ray fox two zero," the air traffic controller said, reading the designator XF-20 given to Kleeman's Hornet.[5] "Miramar final controller, radar contact, nine miles from touchdown, how do you read me?"

"Loud and clear," Kleeman responded.

"X-ray fox two zero, runways are wet, standing water at the intersection."

Kleeman acknowledged by saying simply, "Two zero."

At six miles from touchdown, his radio crackled again. "Begin descent. Short field arresting gear runway . . . is derigged. Three miles to touchdown. Slightly off course. Wind calm. Cleared to land runway two four right. Recheck gear."

"Gear is down," Kleeman said. If there were problems with the jet's landing system, they weren't apparent or Kleeman wasn't aware of them. So far, his approach was routine. He would be down in a few seconds.

"You're now on course. One mile from touchdown," the controller said.

At 9:11 A.M. Kleeman crossed over the approach lights at about 160 miles per hour, white vapor trails streaming from each wingtip. He put the Hornet down on the runway, and within a few seconds the aircraft's speed had dropped nearly in half as it traveled forward, kicking up rooster tails of water behind it. In the air traffic control tower at the west end of the field, a supervisor was eyeing the jet's approach after it broke out of the clouds. He watched the aircraft hit the halfway mark where water had pooled on the runway. There was a big splash, partially obscuring the jet as it passed through the water. A moment later his eyes opened wide with alarm. Kleeman's Hornet was drifting to the right. "Watch the F-18!" he ordered. Before his voice trailed off, he was yelling for somebody to hit the crash horn, which began blaring over the tower's loudspeaker.

Inside the jet, there was little Kleeman could do. He was a helpless passenger strapped on top of forty thousand pounds of spinning metal that was sliding out of control. First the aircraft fishtailed, throwing up more water. Then it did a 180-degree turn, hurtling backward down the runway. Then it spun around and began skidding sideways off the pavement toward the brown muck. At the edge of the field, one wingtip sank twelve inches into the soft ground, forcing the jet to stand up on end. It hung there for a long moment, with the wing bending like the pole of a pole vaulter, cocking itself for a great heave into the air. As the jet lurched skyward, the canopy bolts exploded, shooting the cockpit's Plexiglas canopy seventy-five feet away. Then the jet came down with a *whomp* on its back, driving the top of the pilot's seat ten inches into the mud.

The crash horn was blaring and sirens screamed throughout the base as rescue trucks raced toward the wreckage. One of the aircraft's engines was still running, and jet fuel was spewing out toward the cockpit, puddling around Kleeman's head, which was resting inches from the mud. Incredibly, he was still alive. His eyes were wide open, his oxygen mask had been knocked off, and a thick film of blood, fuel, and muck was caked on his face. Kleeman was waving his arms as Debra Simpson and another firefighter approached the crash with caution, fearing an explosion or fire. The fireman took his hand, trying to calm him. There's no fire, he said. We'll get you out as soon as we can. Simpson took the other arm and found a good, strong, steady pulse.

Meanwhile the ambulances finally showed up. The crash alarm at the Top Gun base was out of order in the medical center, and the tower had to call for help on a telephone. But when they arrived, there was no doctor. And "Tilly," the crane rushed over from public works to raise the aircraft, was not functioning properly. Even if it had been fully operational, no one was sure if Kleeman had fired the ejection seat in an effort to get free of the out-of-control aircraft. The canopy had been shot off, which indicated he had begun the ejection process. And if he had, and the rescue workers raised the Hornet, Kleeman would be shot like a cannonball into the ground and killed instantly. No one at the crash scene, however, was familiar with the Hornet's ejection seat, and therefore no one could disarm it. A call went out to find someone qualified for the task. Thirty minutes later a sailor arrived from a carrier parked at the pier about fifteen miles away at North Island.

During the confusion, rescue workers continued to dig furiously with shovels around the cockpit, trying to make more room to get oxygen to Kleeman. He was hanging upside down, partially restrained in his harness. One of the harness straps was cut away so Simpson could get to Kleeman's body. She could see that his lips were turning blue. She checked his pulse, which was still stable, and she could feel a steady heartbeat. That was good. Time was her worst enemy. Kleeman was severely injured. And the longer he stayed pinned in the plane, away from proper medical care, the less likely it was he would live. He began to move and started flailing his arms uncontrollably. His pulse shot up to over ninety beats a minute before it began to slow. Thirty seconds later his pounding heart stopped.[6]

Forty-five minutes after Kleeman touched down, his aircraft was finally raised and his body extracted from the twisted fuselage. Surgeons later determined that he had died after about fifteen minutes from a severed spinal cord. Still, there was a feeling among the members of the rescue team that if not for a comedy of errors, they might have saved him.

Later that day Carol Kleeman was returning home from the Long Beach Naval Hospital. She turned the corner onto her street and from halfway down the block could see someone standing in front of her house.[7] As she got closer, she realized it was Captain Moon Vance, Point Mugu's commanding officer. She stopped the car in the middle of the street, paralyzed with fear, sensing deep inside that something was terribly wrong with Hank. Vance hurried over.

"But he's okay, isn't he?" she pleaded.

"No, Carol, he's not," Vance said softly.

The whole episode was a jolt. The Navy was five years into a trillion-dollar buildup, yet Miramar, the top jet station in the country, had been ill prepared to deal with a crash. The Navy's judge advocate general investigation was long and detailed.[8] It attempted to find answers to why the crash horn in the medical center was broken and not repaired. It tried to determine why no doctor had appeared immediately at the scene. Why was the crane broken? And perhaps the most puzzling question, why did one of the Navy's most experienced pilots not realize he was flying in a death machine?

The biggest unknown, one the Navy did not address, was why were the trouble-plagued Hornets still flying?

The Hornet crash at Miramar revived some rotten memories for John Lehman. He had long suspected McDonnell Douglas's ability to build a new high-tech warplane within budget and had wanted on several occasions to cancel the program.[9] Each time some new mechanical glitch had popped up, he'd threatened to pull the plug, but each time he'd backed off. Although the quirks often seemed unmanageable, they were to be expected in a new jet just off the design boards. By the time Kleeman died, the Navy and McDonnell Douglas believed they had fixed—with the exception of the landing gear—most of the apparent problems.[10] At that point the best that could be done with the gear was to install inside the cockpit a "bitching Betty," a computerized female voice that warned the pilot of a planing link failure.[11]

In fact, the Hornet would eventually end up with perhaps the best flight control system and avionics of any combat jet flying in the world's air forces.[12] It would need less maintenance than other jets in the Navy's inventory. In some cases, repairs to major components took only minutes, although it would be more costly to work on the jet as it got older.[13] And it would prove to be a remarkably simple airplane to work on, to fly, and to store in the limited spaces of an aircraft carrier.[14]

But there was one malignancy that all the repairs and engineers could not cure: the Hornet had plenty of bark, but very little bite. It couldn't fly far enough to carry out deep strikes, and it couldn't carry a lot of bombs. Navy pilots at VX-4, Kleeman's old squadron, and VX-5 on the East Coast called it the "one-man, one-way, one-bomb plane." Test pilots found that if the jet carried two one-thousand-pound MK-83 bombs with no external fuel tanks, it had a combat radius of 220 nautical miles.[15] For the Hornet to fly 320 nautical miles with two bombs, three external fuel tanks were needed to supplement the plane's internal tank.[16] If more bombs were added, then the fuel tanks had to be taken off, further reducing the aircraft's range. And with all of the excess metal hanging on the jet, it couldn't fly at high speeds to perform its fighter mission. The aircraft may have been fun and easy to fly, and one of the best dogfighters in the world, but it had questionable military value in its dual role as a fighter-bomber. Even in its short-range mission to provide close air support for Marines conducting amphibious landings, the Hornet was lacking.[17]

All this posed a dilemma for Lehman. On the one hand, he saw the value of keeping the jet, but on the other, an aircraft with little bite was not worth the $30 billion the Navy planned to spend buying it. The Navy was now at a pivotal time in the modernization of its aviation program. Many of its aircraft were based on designs and technologies from the late 1950s and early 1960s. They were old, prone to accidents, and took more and more maintenance to keep them running. As an aviator himself, Lehman saw the strain this put on pilots. As a strategic thinker, he knew a dilapidated naval air force could undermine the Maritime Strategy, which was based primarily on carrier-launched warplanes being able to strike deep within the Soviet Union. To that end, Lehman and the carrier admirals predicted the Navy needed nearly two thousand new aircraft for its fleet of fifteen carriers.[18] Lehman knew the aircraft they decided to build now—from helicopters to fighters and stealth bombers—would carry the Navy into the twenty-first century until new, more creative technologies came on line. The price tag, however, would be staggering, running as much as $80 billion and potentially more if the A-12 Avenger went into production.

From the outset, Lehman had been in a buying mode. His attitude, one that many admirals shared, was buy now and worry about the bills later, because sooner rather than later the money was going to run out. But at the moment it was plentiful and doled out without a great deal of consideration for the returns it might produce.

The Navy began work on new airplanes, like the multibillion-dollar A-12 stealth bomber, the T-45 trainer, the advanced tactical fighter, and the V-22 Osprey, which took off like a helicopter but flew like an airplane. Designs began on a common air frame called the ''advanced tactical support aircraft'' for surveillance and transport planes and for a new sub chaser called the P-7. A new line of helicopters was conceived. The Navy was looking at future aircraft as well, including new versions of vertical takeoff and landing jets that could revolutionize carrier operations. And Mel Paisley's old company, Boeing, began to build new composite wings for an improved Intruder, called the A-6F, even though the firm had no prior experience for the task and its price was high.[19] As an A-6 bombardier-navigator, Lehman had an inordinate interest in the A-6F program and demanded that it be adequately funded.

But questions about the accident-prone Hornet remained. Despite his own doubts, Lehman was partial to the concept of having a lightweight fighter that could be produced quickly in large numbers to complement the F-14 Tomcat. Originally the Hornet was conceived to do just that, and on the cheap. But because the Navy desperately needed a replacement for its A-7 Corsair, a single-engine light bomber, the admirals had decided early on that the Hornet should be both a fighter and a bomber. And a short while later the Navy began touting the Hornet as an interim replacement for the A-6 Intruder, a long-range, all-weather heavy bomber. Although it was now the do-everything plane, both the A-7 Corsair and the A-6 Intruder could carry heavier loads and fly double or more the distance of the Hornet without spare tanks. But as the Navy kept piling new roles and missions on the little jet, the admirals did relatively little to rebut criticism about its poor fuel specifications.

Although Lehman had the ammunition he needed to kill the program, he still vacillated. The aviator side of Lehman, the one plugged into the squadrons around the fleet, told him the Hornet was not the pilots' first choice and, if kept, could actually do more harm than good. Morale would suffer, and so would other aircraft programs like the F-14. His secretary side, however—the one responsible for putting aircraft onto the fifteen carriers, no small task by any means—had to look at the negatives of cutting a program in which the Navy had already invested more than $1 billion in research and development. Either way he could have an open revolt on his hands. If he didn't handle this right, the aviation program could be set back years, damaging the nation's national security.

For months Lehman fought his demons about what to do. It was no use turning to the admirals for advice. The aviation community was polarized over the Hornet. The admirals who were light-attack pilots stood behind the Hornet with both feet in the ring, ready to take on any and all opponents. The fighter pilots obliged willingly, citing several failed operational tests, the long string of fixes, and the overall question of its military value.

At times it got ugly. Debates ended in screaming matches and on occasion spilled into the mainstream press. Everybody was blaming everybody else for the logjam over the Hornet. The admirals took the easy way out and blamed Congress. They were quick to point out that several components of the Hornet were built in Massachusetts—the Democratic home of House Speaker Tip O'Neill and Senator Ted Kennedy. It was a political plane, they said, forced down the Navy's throat by Capitol Hill. "That's bullshit," Lehman chided. The Navy was just as culpable. Lehman laid the blame on Tom Hayward and the systems analysts in OP-96 and on the staff in the office of the secretary of defense. "The deal was brokered with OP-96," he said. "It was their airplane as much as the OSD's airplane. The one thing that it wasn't was the aviator's airplane."

Although Lehman had developed a fearsome reputation for steamrolling people who got in his way, this time he chose the middle ground. There was good political reason for not being decisive. McDonnell Douglas and its co-contractor on the airplane, Northrop, had too much clout in Washington. Tom Jones of Northrop, which built the tail section of the Hornet, was a close friend of Ronald Reagan's and enjoyed considerable influence in the White House. "There are only so many fights that you can fight at a time, and I was prepared to fight that fight," Lehman said. "It could have undone me because Tom Jones was very powerful in the White House at the time. He was almost a de facto member of the kitchen cabinet. He was a big contributor to Reagan from the earliest years, and Reagan liked him." [20]

Rather than take McDonnell Douglas head on, Lehman made an end run.

He would challenge the company on price. The Hornet's initial unit price in 1975 was $9.6 million.[21] By December 1980 it had shot up to $11.4 million apiece. And by the summer of 1981 the jet cost $15.8 million. When Lehman finally decided to clamp down on the price, the cost to fly one Hornet out of McDonnell Douglas's plant had soared to $26 million.[22] The Navy intended to buy 1,355 Hornets to help keep the unit price down. But that strategy didn't work, and the price continued to escalate.

Although Lehman got McDonnell Douglas to lower the Hornet's fly-away price to $22.5 million, he later regretted not killing the program. "I'm sorry I didn't," he said. So were a lot of aviators, who saw the Hornet become the Navy's golden program at the expense of other, well-established but extremely costly aircraft like the F-14. Despite the deal with McDonnell, the Hornet's price would continue to escalate, costing almost two and a half times as much as it was originally supposed to.[23] And Hank Kleeman was not the only victim. In dozens of cases, the Navy's blind support of the F/A-18 Hornet would prove to be downright deadly.

The aircraft carrier *Constellation* turned into the wind in preparation to launch the F-14A Tomcat now gunning its engines on the greasy flight deck. Lieutenant Pat "Killer" Kilcline, son of Vice Admiral Tom Kilcline, was at the controls of the jet, which was on an Alert-5 status. That meant a pilot and his radar intercept officer had to sit in the Tomcat—for hours, if necessary—and be ready to go in five minutes to defend the ship against any and all threats.

At midmorning Kilcline got the order to go, and to go fast. He was to intercept two F-14s that had been launched earlier, which were simulating a supersonic Soviet missile attack on *Constellation*. The Russian missiles, which could fly at supersonic speeds, were the Navy's biggest fear. Even with Aegis, and the close-in weapons system designed to guard a battle group, the Navy had yet to devise a foolproof way to defend against the fast-flying weapons. The most that could be hoped for was that the Soviets' notorious targeting problems would send the missile astray or that it would malfunction and explode in flight or fail to release properly. One of the Navy's defensive strategies was to use the F-14 to either shoot down the missile or, better yet, pick off the attacking bomber before it could fire its weapons. The Navy liked to describe that strategy as hitting the archer before he could shoot his arrows.

Kilcline's practice mission to shoot down the plane simulating a missile attack was to be the last of the day. After the intercept he was scheduled to fly to Miramar for some time off before *Constellation* departed on a six-month tour of the West Pacific. The "Connie," as the ship was called, was steaming several hundred miles off the Southern California coast in calm seas. The warm summer sun that pierced through high clouds was heating Kilcline's cockpit, making him feel as if he were in an oven. The canopy was up, which allowed an ocean breeze to cool him off. But still he was sweating in his flight suit and the twenty-five pounds of gear strapped to his body.

When the order came to launch, he lowered the canopy and fired up his engines. Then he saluted the catapult officer and the jet was shot forward at 160 miles per hour, a sensation that the Airedales described as a lifetime E-ticket at Disneyland. Two and a half seconds later the jet jumped off the bow with the characteristic loud thump and rose into the air, twin spikes of bright orange flames shooting from its two engines. Kilcline kept the jet in afterburner as it continued its climb in full military power to thirty-four thousand feet. He opened the ship up to Mach 1, and within seconds the Tomcat broke through the marine layer at a forty-five-degree angle into a bright blue sky. Dead ahead were the two F-14s simulating the missile attack.

Kilcline's first practice shot was at the nose of one of the opposing jets. Then he put his Tomcat into a high-G, high-angle-of-attack maneuver to come around for another strike. But as he pulled hard on the stick, something unexpected happened—one of the Tomcat's two TF30 engines stalled.[24] The jet began to spin around and around and around. In a little more than five seconds it was in a fully departed flat spin. Kilcline and his radar officer were in two seats way up in the nose of the very large Tomcat. It was as if they were a pinwheel on a stick that was spinning out of control and getting faster and faster. As the Tomcat twirled and dropped toward the ocean thirty-four thousand feet below, the G-forces began to build until they had reached more than twelve, a force so powerful that it threw Kilcline's body forward, pinning him against the airplane's instrument panel. Frozen against the cold metal, he was helpless.

"Eeeee-j-e-c-t! Eeeee-j-e-c-t!" Kilcline screamed in a strained voice to the radar officer behind him.[25]

"I can't! I can't!" yelled the backseater, who was experiencing similar but slightly less powerful G-forces.

The thirty-five-ton jet continued to spin and drop, with each new twirl unleashing unbearable forces on the two men. Behind their oxygen masks their eyes began to swell and bulge out of their sockets. Blood vessels started to burst in their faces so rapidly that their skin color turned purplish black. The whites of their eyes were now blood red.

Kilcline pleaded for the backseater to pull the ejection handle. Each time came the same response: "I can't! I can't!"

The two men knew that bailing out at supersonic speed would be extremely dangerous. If the wall of air they hit coming out didn't kill them, a number of unknowns might very well do the job. If the seats didn't fire straight up and far away from the airplane, they might hit their heads on the fuselage. And ejection seats often went out crooked or would tumble upside down. Pilots who ejected under the best of conditions took a beating regardless of whether they followed all the safety procedures. Torn limbs, cracked skulls, and broken necks were not uncommon. One young backseater who mistakenly bailed out at Mach 1 left a trail of black rubber from his boots along the top of the airplane as he was dragged to his death.

Still, all Kilcline wanted to do was get the hell out of the Tomcat, which was now getting closer and closer to hitting the water. With each tick of the altimeter, they knew their fate was sealed. "We're going to die! We're going to die!" screamed one of the aviators.

Seconds later the Tomcat exploded into the deep blue Pacific, sinking to the bottom like a rock.

To the public, the crash and deaths of the two aviators in July 1979 seemed like just another accident, the price military pilots were willing to pay to fly the fast jets. But it was more, much more than a simple crash of a $35 million aircraft, although the Navy could never readily admit it. What killed the two men, and would kill aviators all the way up to the end of 1994 and lead to the crashes of nearly forty F-14A Tomcats, became known as the "engine/flight control problem"—a problem the Navy knew about but decided was too expensive to correct.[26]

The Navy secretly calculated how many F-14s it could financially afford to lose before it had to replace the jets' Pratt & Whitney TF30 engines and install a new flight control system.[27] The admirals decided it was cheaper to lose a few jets than to spend more than $2.5 billion on new equipment.[28] Although they formulated the acceptable loss rate for the jets, what was never written into the equation was the human toll. Many aviators in the fleet assigned to fly in the F-14 knew about the Navy's ghoulish figures and shared one cheapening thought: "We just don't matter much to the admirals in Washington."[29]

The Navy had known since it bought its first Tomcats that the TF30 engines would not work well on a high-performance fighter like the F-14. The engines were originally built for the Douglas F6D Missileer, an aircraft designed in the 1950s to stay on station for long periods of time, loitering back and forth at slow speeds so it could shoot off its missiles.[30] The Missileer and its TF30 engines were not crafted for the rapid acceleration or deceleration of a fighter. Nor would the aircraft use afterburners or initiate high-G turns or a high angle of attack, all the things that the TF30 had problems with. The F6 idea died a quick death, but the TF30 lived on and eventually was used in the Air Force's F-111. That was where the engine first encountered failures due to compressor stalls. The Navy tried the engine in its A-7 Corsairs, where it enjoyed less than marginal success. Ultimately, however, the carrier admirals abandoned the TF30 in favor of the Rolls-Royce Spey engine for the A-7s.

In 1969 the Navy began contemplating a replacement for the F-4 Phantom and settled on an early version of the Tomcat, a Grumman design called 303. This jet was to be outfitted with the TF30 for a short period of time, so the Navy could field the Tomcat quickly to the fleet. The carrier admirals wanted to get the jets on line to counter the Soviet fighters they felt posed a threat to the Navy. In January 1969 a contract was let to Grumman, and three years later the first Tomcats arrived in the fleet. Thirty-two of these fighters were to serve on an interim basis with the TF30, replaced by the next Tomcat upgrade, which would be equipped with the advanced technology engine (ATE), a powerful beast that offered more thrust.

It was never to be. The ATE was canceled, leaving the Tomcat, which was built around requirements for an engine that produced upward of fifty-eight thousand pounds of thrust, with a less than acceptable power plant. Millions of dollars were spent trying to turn the TF30 into a reliable fighter engine.[31] But it still had compressor stall problems and difficulty operating at high angles of attack and going in and out of afterburner. It also blew up on occasion, throwing sizzling metal blades through the fuselage. One of the fixes made the engine smoke so much that it acted like a lighthouse at night for any fighter searching for the U.S. jets. Finally the Navy was forced to tune down the engines and cut the thrust so they wouldn't go into a compressor stall. It also issued a number of instructions, among them an order not to fly the jet at a high angle of attack. Pilots began complaining they had to fly the engines rather than the airplane. In public, Lehman was one of the most vocal critics of Pratt & Whitney, saying before Congress that the engine was "probably the worst engine-airplane mismatch in many years. The TF30 is just a terrible engine. The sooner we are out of it, the happier I will be."

But there was another, equally troubling quandary: the flight control system. When the F-14 had a compressor stall, the system went haywire, throwing the jet into a flat spin in under ten seconds that was next to impossible to pull out of. Grumman and NASA each developed new systems that when combined helped reduce the spin problem. A pilot now had up to thirty seconds to control the aircraft before it went into a fully departed flat spin rather than the normal five to ten seconds. It was a major breakthrough, but the Navy chose not to incorporate it on its fleet of F-14s.

The F-14 aviators who watched the Navy's lackadaisical approach to upgrade the Tomcat believed the Hornet and the admirals who supported it were entirely to blame. The Navy had puffed up the F/A-18 before Congress and in public, pledging unrealistic performance standards. The light-attack admirals could not let the F-14 overshadow the Hornet, which in reality was having trouble meeting its expectations. Both the Tomcat and the Hornet had good qualities as well as deficiencies that in the worst extreme killed pilots. But each airplane was undermining the other by competing for money, political backing on Capitol Hill, and support within the naval aviation community. It was a schism that was more than a friendly rivalry. Careers and lives were at stake. So too were billions of dollars. One of the programs had to give. And much to the dismay of the Tomcat community, the Navy decided the F/A-18 Hornet was to be the plane of the future.

Hundreds of millions of dollars that could have been used to buy new engines and install the NASA-designed flight control system were diverted in the late 1970s and early 1980s from the Tomcat to the Hornet.[32] The F-14 was a cash cow. Theoretically such diversions were against the law. Congress appropriated funds for specific programs, but the Navy paid little attention to the monetary constraints and cleverly found loopholes to shift the funds around. Besides, there was so much popular support for the Hornet on Capitol Hill that no one bothered to ask for a proper accounting.[33]

But the Tomcat was far from grounded. Lehman scraped together enough goodwill and money to begin a new effort to upgrade the F-14s. The program had a twofold aim. First, the Navy would remanufacture old F-14A Tomcats, adding only new General Electric engines; these would be called the A-plus version. Later a new digital flight control system would be added to the old air frames, a piecemeal approach that would help keep down the costs. At the same time, a complete new airplane would be built by Grumman with a $65 million price tag for each jet.[34] The plane's new designator was F-14D. Its pet name was Super Tomcat. And the new program manager was Captain Jack Snyder, the commander of the West Coast training squadron. For the next five years Jack Snyder would fly by the seat of his pants to save both the airplane and his career. In each case he would lose.

Senator Lowell Weicker had been around Washington long enough to know when someone in the government was "polishing a turd."

On October 28, 1985, the Navy, with John Lehman's approval, released a "Good News" memorandum to the Connecticut Republican and other members of Congress, boasting that it had saved $1.6 billion in the development of six types of naval aircraft.[35] Lehman attributed the savings to the vigorous management style he had instilled in the Navy, one that emphasized competition among defense firms. He had taken the same principles he'd used to get the shipbuilding industry to lower its prices and applied them to aircraft manufactures with resounding success, Lehman believed. "Every Navy aircraft today is less expensive in constant dollars than it was four years ago— every Navy aircraft. Lee Iacocca can't say that about Chrysler. We can say that about Navy aircraft," Lehman bragged in a speech at the Naval War College.[36]

Most lawmakers accepted the "Good News" memo at its face value as a sign of frugal management and left it at that. It was refreshing to know that Lehman was watching over his budget, which was more than many in the government were doing. But Weicker, a member of the powerful Senate Appropriations Committee, sensed Lehman was playing fast and loose with the numbers. He had other information from his staff and Pentagon insiders that contradicted the Navy's claim and showed that Lehman had it all wrong.[37]

For Weicker, this was an integrity issue. The secretary of the Navy was making statements that did not appear to be true. On November 4 Weicker sat back in his plush Senate office and dashed off a letter to Joseph H. Sherick, the Pentagon's inspector general, in which he asked him "to verify the accuracy of the unit cost data provided by the Navy. If you find that it is inaccurate, then I would like the name of the person responsible for providing the Congress with this information."[38]

Sherick's office put several agents on the case, including his youthful, blow-dried deputy Derek Vander Schaaf, who was gaining a reputation as an enemy of the Navy. Vander Schaaf and his colleagues believed the barb was sour grapes on the Navy's part; all he was doing was holding Lehman and the admirals accountable. If he had to put their feet to the fire in the process, that was his job. And after months of work, the inspector general's report concluded that Weicker's concerns were indeed valid. Lehman and the Navy overstated aircraft prices from 1976 to 1980, while the same costs were understated for the last five years.

The Department of Defense was not alone in its conclusion. Rolf Clark, an independent civilian analyst under contract to the Navy, found similar cost discrepancies in the unit price of airplanes. There were no dips in pricing to support Lehman's claims. In fact, according to Clark, aircraft prices had gone up considerably. Clark's study was never released, and his contract was not renewed.

The forces in the Pentagon who now lined up behind the inspector general were attacking the secretary of the Navy with the same bureaucratic knife that Lehman often used on his own targets. As he pondered how to respond, he was being cut to pieces. He decided to take the offensive and call into question the Pentagon's own numbers. If he could sow enough seeds of doubt, the inspector general's report would wither on the vine. Lehman had always had a keen ability to get out in front of a bad story, which he tried to do on this one at a Pentagon news conference. "We stand behind the $1.6 billion and are very proud of it," he said. Then he decided to stick his finger in the inspector general's eye and cement the impression that the Navy was unquestionably correct. "We squeezed out another $60 million in savings" on top of the $1.6 billion, Lehman said after his accountants reviewed the Pentagon report.[39]

Little did Vander Schaaf and his colleagues know, nor could they have known, that they were seeing only the tip of a very big iceberg. Lehman's much ballyhooed fixed-price contracts, in which he forced defense contractors to stick with one firm price regardless of cost overruns, were eating away at several new aviation programs. Almost from conception, the A-12 Avenger, which was being designed and built on a fixed-price contract, was plagued with problems. Because the A-12 was trying to incorporate so many unknowns into the plane, such as stealth, composite materials, and ways to increase range, it was impossible to determine an accurate development price. It was so highly classified that only a few individuals with access to the black program had an inkling the bomber was on the road to ruin and a $1 billion cost overrun in its development phase. Moreover, the need for a new stealth bomber to match the Air Force's B-1 overshadowed any misgivings.

Lehman had been uneasy at first about the Avenger. He had pledged that before he left office he would provide the A-6 community, his fellow bomber aviators, with a state-of-the-art aircraft. His initial choice to fulfill that promise was the A-6F. But as the Air Force pushed ahead on its own stealth planes, the Navy realized that if it did not have its own long-range, modern bomber, it faced the prospect of losing the deep-strike mission. That threat in itself was reason enough for the Navy to batten down the hatches and move full steam ahead on the A-12.

There were other serious signs, besides the TF30 quagmire, that the Navy's aviation plan was running out of money and under tremendous pressure to juggle so many programs at once. The carrier admirals had started with a big piggy bank full of money. But it was spread thin, with each program getting a little something rather than one getting a lot. When the money began running out, Lehman shifted funds from the spare parts and weapons accounts into the acquisitions side of the aviation plan. It was the "rob Peter to pay Paul" syndrome, but it was keeping the various programs above water. It wouldn't become obvious until the Persian Gulf War some five years later that the aviation program was in serious disarray, so much so that the Navy's very existence as a force capable of exerting air power seemed very much in question.

CHAPTER 16

WITHIN WEEKS OF ARRIVING at his Pearl Harbor headquarters to take command of the Pacific Fleet, Ace Lyons was quite prepared for a showdown with the Soviet Union.

The Navy was unequaled in the region for the force and influence it could bring to bear in diplomatic and military affairs. That made Lyons one of the most powerful admirals in the Pacific Rim. It was a stroke of luck that he had come this far in his career. As a young ensign he had injured his arm so severely in an automobile accident that the Navy had wanted to discharge him. That was the first bump on his road to flag rank, which at times had reached a dead end. But with perseverance and ambition he'd pressed on. Now he was at the top of the pyramid, looking down on all those who had wanted him to fall years ago. It was enough to make his head swim.

With his rise in stature came the perks afforded to Lyons's predecessors. Each morning he rose in Tom Hayward's old home on Admirals Row in Makalapa. The light from the rising Hawaiian sun still spilled through the large windows, warming the spacious house. Stewards fixed coffee in the downstairs kitchen and laid out the morning papers and the all-important *Early Bird*. By 6:15 Lyons was out the door for the short walk down the hill to Pacific Fleet headquarters. Once there, he would grab a cup of coffee and a stack of overnight messages to read, then plop himself down at his desk, which had once been used by the great Chester Nimitz. The admiral who had galloped his way to victory across the Pacific in World War II was a war fighter, a man most naval officers felt had brass balls the size of grapefruits. And when it came right down to it, many thought Lyons was cut from the Nimitz cloth.[1] Nimitz's glory had come from defeating Japanese imperialism. Lyons had his sights on no less grand a scheme: to crush Soviet expansionism. He now had the mighty Pacific Fleet to do it and the political backing from Lehman to try to pull it off. In fact, if ever the time was ripe to prove just how powerful the Navy believed it could be, it was now. And if ever there was an admiral tough enough to lead the charge, it was Ace Lyons.

In January 1986, the Navy publicly unveiled the Maritime Strategy in the

Naval Institute's journal, *Proceedings*. It had been five years in the making and had gone through several evolutions since Team Charlie began the effort with a secret order from Tom Hayward. Small portions of it had previously been leaked to the press, especially the idea of sinking Soviet nuclear-missile submarines hiding in their protective bastions. The media reports, which speculated that Moscow would "use them rather than lose them," caused a furor, with many in the Navy and on Capitol Hill complaining that the new plan was unnecessary, reckless, and a sure way to erode the firebreak separating conventional from nuclear war.[2]

In an effort to quell the damning press coverage, the Navy in 1983 had announced key elements of the Maritime Strategy. Now, in 1986, the brass was laying the whole thing out for all to see. One reason for the disclosure was to correct the "misinterpretations or exaggerations" floating around. The other reason, of course, was to make the now routine pitch to Congress and the public justifying a very large, aggressive Navy built around fifteen aircraft carriers and six hundred ships. It was also a way to keep the momentum, and the money, of the early 1980s flowing into the last few years of the Reagan administration.

To give it credibility, Lehman, Jim Watkins, and P. X. Kelly, the square-jawed Marine commandant, each wrote a lengthy article describing different aspects of the global war-fighting plan. A fourth contribution, prepared by Peter Swartz, was an exhaustive bibliography. Swartz, who had been instrumental in pulling together several versions of the strategy, began his section with a reference to Tom Hayward, as a tribute for beginning the drive toward a new offensive strategy.[3]

The backbone of the three articles was an anti-Soviet rhetoric that maintained the Red Banner Fleet was now more than ever a major threat to the U.S. Navy. Lehman stuck with the inflated number that the Soviets had 1,700 ships. And he portrayed in dark terms the Soviet's few aircraft carriers and naval air forces. In Lehman's words, "the Soviet Navy's postwar expansion has created an offensive-oriented blue water force, a major element in the Soviet Union's global military reach. No planner, civilian or military, can ignore the growing dimensions of Soviet maritime power."[4]

The *Proceedings* supplement, which was being called an official White Paper, was a throwback to the days when the admirals misled Congress about the dangers of the Soviet navy. There were no references to the attaché reports about the dismal state of the Soviet fleet. Nor was there a mention of the CIA's secret national intelligence estimate, which stated clearly that the Soviet navy was a defensive force intent on protecting the homeland—not on coming out to sink the American fleet, as the Navy still maintained.

In the years leading up to the Maritime Strategy's public unveiling, members of Team Charlie, who had now moved into the upper ranks of the naval intelligence community, had consistently written secret reports that the Soviet navy was in decline and faced major maintenance, operational, and personnel problems. Open ocean sorties and exercises off both U.S. coasts had already peaked or were in the process of winding down. Even at their height, they were only a fraction of the size of American naval operations in Soviet waters. And often they were done in response to the Navy's new Maritime Strategy. Some Soviet exercises were indeed belligerent, including practice cruise missile attacks by Soviet Bear bombers on Alaska, the Aleutians, and the West Coast of the United States. But overall, because of a multitude of problems, plus shortages of gas and spare parts, the great bulk of the Soviet fleet now lay at anchor or was restricted to training operations in coastal waters. The Joint Chiefs were certainly aware that the Soviet threat had diminished. At Admiral Bill Crowe's request, Lyons traveled back to the Pentagon in July 1986 to brief the Joint Chiefs of Staff, Caspar Weinberger, and his deputy Will Taft on how he had shut down Soviet submarine operations in the Pacific. It was obvious to all but the most extreme naval hard-liners like Lehman that Admiral Gorshkov's navy was in the throes of a full-fledged retreat.

As the Soviets pulled back, the U.S. Navy, in an effort to prove that the Maritime Strategy could work and that it was the spearhead of Reagan's new militarism, stepped up its naval warfare activities on almost every Soviet front. The exercises were more aggressive and closer to Soviet territory than Lyons's foray in October 1981. Warships steamed in the Baltic and Black Seas. They routinely sailed past the North Cape in the Barents Sea, and aircraft carriers were parked in the Norwegian fjords. The intelligence-gathering ship *Caron* and the Aegis cruiser *Yorktown* sailed to within six nautical miles of the Crimean coast. On another mission, the two ships operated nine miles from the Black Sea fleet headquarters at Sevastopol.

Submarines hunted down the Soviet boomer boats beneath the polar ice cap and performed mock sinkings. In one exercise the Navy sent forty-four of its fifty-four East Coast attack submarines with full weapons load on a twenty-four-hour notice rushing toward the North Atlantic.[5] U.S. Marines carried out amphibious landings with British and Dutch troops in northern Norway to prove allied ground forces could attack and occupy turf in the Arctic Circle. The Marine assaults were not lost on the Russians, who always feared a Normandy-style invasion.[6] And P. X. Kelly made sure Moscow had no doubts his Leathernecks were coming. His Marines, he said, "could land on the North Cape, the eastern Baltic or Black Sea coast, in the Kuriles, or on Sakhalin Island."[7]

In the Pacific, before Lyons took over, the Navy began its first large-scale

carrier operations in the Sea of Japan since 1968. The Marines carried out
the first amphibious landings in the Aleutians since World War II. And in
July 1984 two aircraft carrier battle groups, led by *Vinson* and *Midway,*
entered the Sea of Japan and sailed within fifty miles of Vladivostok, the
headquarters of the Red Banner Pacific Fleet. Admiral William Crowe, who
left his job as the CinC in charge of all forces in the Pacific to become
chairman of the Joint Chiefs of Staff, had been instrumental in pushing the
new exercises.[8]

Crowe had a flair for secrecy and had no problems using the Navy in an
aggressive manner to provoke a confrontation or demonstrate the awesome
military might of the United States. One of his favorite targets was Iran. As
chairman he increased his attention on Tehran, searching for ways to poke a
stick in the ayatollah's eye. And in his quest for new ideas, he often called
privately on Ace Lyons for advice.[9] Crowe had been a mentor to Lyons and
had noticed early on that he could be a brilliant tactician and war fighter.
Lyons was tough, smart, and willing to risk his career if he thought he was
doing the right thing. Crowe liked that in an officer and convinced Tom
Hayward that Lyons would make a good admiral. And it was Crowe, Lyons
recalls, who as chairman circumvented the Navy's chain of command to
arrange secret warship movements in the Persian Gulf to intimidate Iran.[10]
After a while it had become almost routine for Lyons to provide ships and
matériel to carry out the Joint Chiefs' secret missions in the gulf.

Lyons had worked for Crowe once before. He trusted him and saw him as
a fine naval officer. Crowe's exercises in the Pacific were unprecedented for
their bravado. But Ace Lyons would outdo them all.

On August 21, 1986, Lyons rose early, as he always did, and headed down
to his office. He grabbed a mug of coffee, then sat down to read the overnight
message traffic. Much of it was about an exercise that was just starting to
get under way.[11] Two of the Navy's most potent warships, *Vinson* and
Vincennes, which a week ago had sailed with their escorts from California,
were about to enter Russian waters in the North Pacific. The *Vinson,* a
ninety-thousand-ton *Nimitz*-class carrier, was the Navy's newest flattop.
Chained down on its decks were dozens of F-14 Tomcats, their tails protruding overboard some six feet to compensate for limited space. Below decks
were the A-6 Intruders, each capable of long-range heavy bombing, and an
assortment of other aircraft. Weapons lockers were also filled to the brim,
and air crews were briefed and told to be prepared for a lot of activity.

Vincennes, the high-tech cruiser Lehman was so enamored of, could track
more than two hundred targets at one time with its sophisticated Aegis radar

system. That much was known. What was unknown was whether the men operating the machines could handle the data load, especially in the fog of war. Even a practice exercise in which Soviet warplanes were targeting the carriers had its stresses. If a crewman misinterpreted critical data about an airplane's flight pattern and passed on bogus information, the captain might push the missile-launch button and end up with a catastrophe.

The two ships and their battle groups were taking part in one of the first of a dozen major missions Lyons had on the drawing board. Some would be highly public, such as FLEETEX and Team Spirit, and be advertised as routine. Others would be secret, initiated with no official records so no blame could be laid on any one person if they failed.[12] The Soviets would go ape shit over some of them, Lyons knew, but there was little they could do to stop him. They would protest to the State Department. There would be hundreds of Soviet fighters and bombers zooming and booming past the ships, if they could find them. And there would be some close calls. But that was what Lyons wanted. He wanted to see the enemy in action up close. That's what war was all about.

Lyons and his staff began planning exercises almost immediately after he arrived in Pearl Harbor in the fall of 1985. He had called his new staff together to spell out what lay ahead for the Pacific Fleet, the challenges, dangers, and rewards. "My charge to everybody is Don't compromise, and keep charging," Lyons began. "That will be our battle cry."[13] It was similar to the pep talk he had given on *Mt. Whitney* when he took over the Second Fleet in 1981. Then, and now, Lyons wanted to kick a little Russian ass. As he spoke he was excited, in a confident way, about his new post. The Pacific Fleet had more responsibilities and a massive ocean in which to show the flag. It could be done, Lyons knew, because he had nearly twice the number of assets as he'd had in Norfolk. It would be double the work, but he would also have double the fun. With Crowe pushing for more offensive-oriented missions and John Lehman's anti-Soviet rhetoric, the training maneuvers had to be bold. And they would be.

For this exercise now under way, the Navy was about to sail into the most sensitive Soviet waters—the bastions where the Russians kept their boomer boats. Lyons's war planners had laid out the navigational grids for the Sea of Okhotsk and the Bering Sea, waters not visited by the Navy since World War II. Separating the two seas was the Kamchatka Peninsula, a sliver of land packed with major Soviet military bases, including the homeports for its boomer boats. Lyons was determined to teach the Soviets a lesson and stop their mock Bear strikes on U.S. territory. It was the Air Force's responsibility to intercept the Bears, but nothing was being done about it. Finally, to stop the Soviet flights, Lyons stationed F-14 fighters and A-6 attack aircraft in Alaska that would take part in the exercise now under way. And because he couldn't keep the fighters there indefinitely, he spent $24,000 to have plywood replicas of F/A-18 Hornets constructed and placed on the runway. After every pass of a Soviet satellite, the Navy would move them to make it appear as if they had flown a mission.

By August 24 the two battle groups had separated, and *Vincennes* and four other warships sailed through the Kurile Island chain and into the Sea of Okhotsk under the watchful eye of the Soviets. At about the same time, *Vinson* and its escorts headed north, then disappeared from the Russians' radar screens. The battle group had turned off its electronics and radars and was operating under EMCON conditions. They continually fooled the Soviets' satellite surveillance system, which was scanning the area with active and passive radar beams hundreds of kilometers wide, looking for the U.S. armada. For nine days *Vinson* remained undetected while the ship conducted the first carrier operations in the Bering Sea since the Second World War.[14]

As the Soviets searched in vain for the *Vinson* battle group, there was another, equally threatening exercise under way in the Norwegian Sea. A massive U.S. and allied force of 150 warships and three carriers had sailed past the G.I.U.K. Gap and landed twelve thousand Marines near Narvik, Norway. The Americans were now conducting major war maneuvers simultaneously on both sides of the Soviet continent. Lehman and his admirals were confident Moscow would see these only as training drills, not preparations for a preemptive strike. But Moscow had become testy about the Navy's constant violations of its territorial waters. To the Kremlin it was not just an infringement of its sovereignty, it was a constant embarrassment. In response, Soviet naval forces had become more aggressive in their tactics to drive off the Americans and their allies. Relations between the two superpowers had improved somewhat in Reagan's second term but were still marred by his March 8, 1983, speech, in which he had described the Soviet Union as "the focus of evil in the modern world." Six months after the "Evil Empire" speech on September 1, a Soviet fighter pilot shot down a Korean Air Lines jumbo jet with 269 people aboard that had strayed over the Kamchatka Peninsula. Reagan called it a "crime against humanity." In the following days, the two navies sparred in the crash zone, looking for remains, sometimes coming close to blows.

Now the Navy had ships all over the Kamchatka region and near other bases on the Soviet mainland. Even as the Kremlin's leaders concentrated on the two military actions in the Pacific and the Norwegian Sea, Lyons ordered the dreadnought *New Jersey* and the carrier *Ranger* and their battle groups to cross the Pacific and meet up with *Vinson*, which was now heading toward the Sea of Japan. Both groups surged across the ocean under EMCON conditions and remained undetected.

Then, suddenly, on September 16, 1986, the *New Jersey, Ranger,* and *Vinson* battle groups popped up in the Sea of Japan within striking distance of every Soviet naval base in the region. Once there, the two carriers began launching mock bombing runs on the Soviet bases. In some cases A-6 bombers would hug the water, then pop up and head straight for the enemy installations, only to break off just before entering Soviet air space. The attacks would be equivalent to Backfire bombers practicing attack runs on San Diego or Norfolk. The Soviets came out en masse to meet the Americans, and there were several close calls when aerial dogfights broke out between opposing aircraft. At one point a F-14 pilot had four MiGs on his tail and believed he was a dead man.[15]

On September 26 the battle groups dispersed and *New Jersey, Vinson,*[16] *Vincennes,* and several other ships sailed through La Pérouse Strait into the Sea of Okhotsk, where they did a high-speed run north, as if they were preparing to attack the Siberian coast. Four days later they broke off their mission and sailed into the North Pacific, where they joined forces with *Ranger* to take part in FLEETEX 86, a large gathering of ships off Petropavlovsk.

Petropavlovsk was a main target for Lyons. Earlier he had stationed the nuclear-powered cruiser *Long Beach* about two hundred miles northwest of Attu. Then, for the first time, he had the ship fire a Tomahawk cruise missile toward Adak Island some seven hundred miles away. The Soviets watched the missile launch with keen interest. With a slight change in navigation, the missile would fall on Petropavlovsk.[17]

Much of what Lyons was doing was classified and therefore not known back in the United States. Although the general public was in the dark about the Navy's secret operations in Soviet waters, the Russians knew all too well what was going on and, strangely enough, respected Lyons for outsmarting them. "They knew it was he who did it, and they admired him for that," recalled Kevin Healy, a retired Navy captain who was a key aide to Lyons.[18] Before Healy left the Navy he attended the War College, where he met a number of Soviet officers.[19] "They would have my bio and know that I had worked for Ace Lyons," he said. "They respected him for his abilities. They just liked the guy; he was one of theirs in many ways, in terms of he was a tough, hard guy who knew what the hell he was doing."

Although Lyons was becoming a folk hero within some circles of the military, in public he was an unknown commodity, overshadowed by another of John Lehman's favorite admirals. On the other side of the world, in a small seaport on the west coast of Italy, Vice Admiral Frank Kelso was making a name for himself as a dynamic leader. He commanded the Sixth Fleet, headquartered in Gaeta, near Naples, which traditionally dealt with flare-ups in the Middle East involving U.S. interests.

Because of the Navy's continual focus there, where tensions always bubbled just below the surface, an ambitious admiral could use the job as a catapult to stardom. Some admirals did everything they could to ensure that the Sixth Fleet would always be in the right place at the right time. Kelso was not one of them. He was neither overly ambitious nor the type of officer who craved personal acclaim. One of his great strengths was just being himself, a country bumpkin from Tennessee. Good fortune, it seemed, just fell into his lap. Lehman had picked Kelso for the job of commanding the Sixth Fleet, and President Reagan made sure he had plenty of work. In short order, Kelso became a key figure in a series of controversial and highly public military actions led by the Navy as part of the administration's fight against terrorism.

The most noteworthy had been the October 1985 seizure of an Egyptian airliner, spiriting to safety a group of terrorists who had murdered a crippled New Yorker after hijacking the *Achille Lauro* cruise liner.[20] A Navy captain assigned to the National Security Council came up with the idea of "pulling a Yamamoto" on the terrorists, referring to the World War II Japanese admiral whose plane had been shot down by U.S. fighters over the Pacific. As it turned out, *Saratoga,* one of Kelso's Sixth Fleet carriers, was in the area en route to a port call in Yugoslavia after having just finished an exercise. It could provide the F-14s needed for the job.

Marine Lieutenant Colonel Oliver North picked up the idea and pushed it through the highest levels of the administration, which included three of North's fellow Naval Academy graduates: Bill Crowe, who had been chairman of the Joint Chiefs of Staff for less than a month; Bud McFarlane, a Marine lieutenant colonel; and John Poindexter, a vice admiral. All four officers shared similar core values instilled in them at Annapolis. And all believed secrecy and covert operations were needed to conduct foreign affairs. By the end of 1986 all but Crowe would leave under less than honorable circumstances because of the Iran-contra scandal.

Crowe liked the concept of grabbing the EgyptAir jet but wondered if it was doable. He consulted his joint commander in Stuttgart to see if it was physically possible. Both men agreed the Navy could pull it off. President Reagan approved it, and a message was sent to Kelso, instructing him to put a plan into action. Kelso then spoke over a secure voice circuit with Rear Admiral David Jeremiah on *Saratoga,* advising him to turn around and launch two F-14s and an E-2C Hawkeye radar plane but saying nothing else.

Reagan was determined to catch the terrorists. In the early moments of the crisis, he had dispatched SEAL Team Six to storm the ship, but *Achille Lauro* sailed for Port Said, Egypt, before the commandos arrived. There the hijackers surrendered to Egyptian authorities. Reagan pressed Egyptian president Hosni Mubarak to extradite the terrorists to the United States or Italy for prosecution. But Mubarak lied, telling Reagan they had already been released to representatives of the PLO, who had taken them out of Egypt.

The United States was in a difficult situation. Mubarak was a friend, and the Reagan administration didn't want to embarrass him or cause him problems with the volatile Islamic forces threatening pro-Western governments in the turbulent Middle East. But Reagan wanted the hijackers brought to justice, with or without Mubarak's help. The only problem was that the U.S. intelligence community didn't know where the hijackers were, nor were there good intelligence assets in Egypt to find them.

A break came late one evening during the crisis when Italian intelligence officers provided a critical asset. They had an electronic bug on Mubarak's phone and knew that a plane was being readied to take the terrorists to safety in Tunisia.[21] With the help of the Italians, the National Security Agency was able to monitor Mubarak's telephone conversations and learn the time, route, and flight number of the EgyptAir 737.

At 7:10 local time on October 10, two F-14 Tomcats leapt off *Saratoga*'s deck. Six minutes later the E-2C was catapulted into the night sky. Within a minute after that, Jeremiah received another secure call from Kelso, laying out the plan. Jeremiah decided to launch more Tomcats and load the jets' twenty-millimeter cannons with tracer bullets. The rules of engagement allowed the Tomcats to fire across the plane's nose but not shoot it down. The tracers would light up the sky and most likely scare the Egyptian pilot into cooperating.

Precisely as planned, six Navy F-14 Tomcats surrounded the EgyptAir 737 over the Mediterranean. It had been a difficult job to find the jet in the first place. No fewer than sixty commercial planes were flying in the area. To make sure the pilots had the right airliner, one Tomcat flew within feet behind each likely target and shined a flashlight on the tail numbers. When they identified number 2843, they knew they had the 737 and radioed back to *Saratoga*.

On *Saratoga* voice circuits were open so Jeremiah could talk with Kelso, the joint commander in Europe, the Flag Plot, and the National Military Command Center in the basement of the Pentagon. Everybody could hear the Navy pilots. The F-14s, flying with their lights out, moved in close, taking positions on each of the plane's wingtips. Peering out of their Plexiglas canopies, they could see inside the EgyptAir 737 as the terrorists relaxed while a stewardess served them drinks. No one aboard had a clue what lay just feet from them—until the Hawkeye broke radio silence.

"EgyptAir 2843. This is Tigertail 603, over." It was the Hawkeye, trying to make contact with the Egyptian pilots, who failed four times to respond. Finally the 737 answered.

"Tigertail 603. EgyptAir 2843. Go ahead."

"EgyptAir 2843, Tigertail 603. Be advised you're being escorted by two F-14s. You are to land immediately—immediately—Sigonella, Sicily. Over."

"Say again," the confused Egyptian pilot asked. "Who is calling?"

The F-14s turned on their lights and startled the pilots, and the passengers in the 737 could see the menacing Tomcats. After a few more exchanges, the airliner agreed and headed toward Italy, where it would land and the terrorists could be taken into custody by Italian forces. As it complied with the F-14s, the EgyptAir pilot asked another airliner in the vicinity to relay the news to Cairo. "I'm telling you, two fighters, two fighters intercepting, demanding me to steer heading for Italy."

Reagan was ecstatic over the Navy coup. For the terrorists, he let loose one of his famous one-liners: "You can run, but you can't hide."

The *Achille Lauro* incident was a feather in Lehman's cap, and he praised Frank Kelso for running such a smooth operation. Kelso was still in command of the fleet during the attacks on Libya a year later in March and April, when the Navy sank a number of enemy boats and took out some radar sites. Both military operations won Kelso accolades from the highest levels of the national security apparatus, especially Lehman, who believed all along that Kelso was "one of the very best men on active duty."

By the end of March 1986 Lehman had to make a decision about who would replace James Watkins as chief of naval operations. It would be a difficult choice. In Lehman's eyes, Kelso possessed the qualities he thought a naval officer should have to be CNO. But so did Ace Lyons. Unfortunately Lehman could pick only one man for the post. It was agonizing for him to decide between the two men, a choice akin to picking who might live or die; the man who lost out would have to retire from his beloved Navy.

In the end it was easier than Lehman might have imagined. Ace Lyons had a list of enemies as long as the wake of a battleship. Four times in 1985 Lehman had tried to promote him to a top job, and four times he had been blocked by Cap Weinberger or his deputies. Lehman had stood up for Lyons, telling Weinberger that he reminded him of Lord Nelson, Britain's most famous admiral and the hero of the Battle of Trafalgar. But the defense secretary was not impressed.

There was no gray area with Lyons. Either you loved him or you hated him. He had more experience than Kelso, had a better war-fighting mind, but he was abrupt and often crude. That sort of behavior was anathema to Kelso. His slow, soft-spoken Tennessee accent gave him a Southern charm. He had a kindly manner and listened first before he lost his temper. Despite his gentlemanly qualities, he could be ruthless when required, although it was rare. Kelso chose instead to see the frailty of the human spirit, knowing his officers made mistakes, just as he had done on occasion when he was making his way through the ranks. Everybody deserved a second chance, Kelso believed. It was a genuine quality, but he exercised it almost to a fault by being excessively lenient.

Perhaps his best quality, one Lehman certainly cherished, was that Kelso was not a boat rocker like the more independent Lyons. Although Lehman would always remain loyal to Lyons, he needed someone who would not fight him the way past chiefs of naval operations had. Lyons might not start out opposed to Lehman, but he was headstrong enough to tell the secretary when to go jump in a lake.

When Lehman had become secretary, he'd had to accept Tom Hayward for eighteen months. Then Watkins had been forced on him, which was not all that bad a choice in Lehman's eyes. Watkins was every bit a match, both intellectually and politically. For a good portion of his tenure as CNO, Watkins had pulled his hair out over Lehman's leadership style. One of their biggest battles was over who would select officers to flag rank. Each man considered it his prerogative.[22] And neither would back down. The result was gridlock and a six-month backlog in promoting the Navy's admirals. Now Watkins was on the way out, and true to Lehman's personal goals, he wanted somebody subservient to him and to the concept of civilian control of the Navy. That meant Frank Kelso.

"Are there other good candidates?" Reagan asked Vice Admiral John Poindexter, who was now his national security adviser. The President sat at his desk in the Oval Office, listening intently as Poindexter explained that by picking Kelso, Lehman had excluded other, more qualified officers. Kelso had a good public image as the result of Libya and *Achille Lauro,* but he was junior to the majority of the three- and four-star flags. If Reagan signed off on the deal, he would be leapfrogging Kelso over twenty-five other, more senior admirals, which would cause a lot of heartburn. The last time it was done was in 1970, when President Nixon picked Vice Admiral Elmo Zumwalt for the post. "By picking Kelso," Poindexter told Reagan, "the country is losing a lot of good experience. I don't have any problem with Kelso being a CNO at some point in the future. In picking him at this point, we're going to jump over a lot of qualified officers and lose a lot of experience. There will be plenty of time for Kelso to be CNO."[23]

Reagan was puzzled by what he was hearing. The nomination had come from Lehman via Cap Weinberger, who in signing off on it must have supported the choice. Yet now Poindexter was saying that the whole thing was unusual and that perhaps the President should think about other admirals for the job.

"Like who?" Reagan asked.

"Admiral Carl Trost," Poindexter said, not telling Reagan that he had been a longtime friend of Trost's.

"The next time Cap comes over, let's talk about this," Reagan said to Poindexter.[24]

A few days later Reagan, Weinberger, and Poindexter were sitting in the Oval Office, discussing Lehman's selection of Kelso. Weinberger told the President that he was not committed one way or the other to Kelso and was deferring on the nomination to Lehman. In fact, Weinberger had been angered about how Kelso's name came to him. When it was time to pick a new CNO, the military aide to Weinberger, Vice Admiral Don Jones, called P. D. Miller, asking for a list of candidates.

"The secretary has already picked his guy," said Miller, who was winding up his tour as Lehman's personal aide.[25]

"That's fine," Jones said, "but I really think you ought to put together a menu of candidates, because the secretary of defense likes to have a choice."

"There is no choice. Kelso is the man," Miller said.

When Kelso's nomination file did arrive, Jones took it to Weinberger and explained what was going on. After several days Weinberger had not moved the file from the place where Jones had laid it on his desk. "It's quite obvious to me that you have trouble here," Jones said, "and probably because you don't feel you have been asked to make a choice. You've been asked to rubber stamp a selection."

"Is there anybody else you can think of?" Weinberger asked.

"Well, Admiral Trost is down in Norfolk, and he is eminently qualified."

"Ask him to come up and talk to me," Weinberger said.

Jones got Trost on the line and told him to get up to Washington, that the secretary of defense wanted to interview him for the job of chief of naval operations. Carlisle A. H. Trost was a large, broad-chested man who now commanded the Atlantic Fleet. He was a submariner by training, a man with tremendous intellectual powers who had graduated first in his Naval Academy class. The class yearbook said, "Dutch 'Don't ask what the initials mean' Trost academically had no worries. He was well versed in the law of survival of the fittest. His major ambition was to develop a 'twin-screwed, single-stroke, double-acting, quick-return, right-answer slide rule.' Vice president of the class and a top man academically, Carl had the stuff of which leaders are made." Trost exceeded the expectations of his fellow midshipmen. But his strong personality was his main weakness. He detested Congress and the media and the idea that he would have to carry on a working relationship with both institutions. Despite that, he had the essential attributes required for the job of CNO.

Even so, he told Jones, "I'm not interested." [26]

"Right. Get yourself up here," Jones said.

"I'm busy."

"You don't seem to understand . . ."

When Trost finally arrived for his 8:15 A.M. appointment, Weinberger escorted him into his office and the two men talked about what type of leader was needed to run the Navy. Finally Weinberger looked at him intently and said, "You might end up as a candidate." But after the meeting was over, he walked into Jones's office, perplexed about Trost. "Don, he doesn't want the job."

Jones looked at Weinberger and smiled. "Mr. Secretary, he had on a clean shirt, a fresh haircut, and a nice-looking suit. Yes, he wants the job." At that, Weinberger started laughing.

When Trost left Weinberger, he walked up a flight of stairs to the fourth floor of the Pentagon. Lehman had called Trost in Norfolk and ordered him to appear in his office the minute he finished with the secretary of defense. Trost was now standing before Lehman, who wasted no time in getting to the point. "I'm not supporting you," he said. "You're insufficiently compliant." Lehman didn't like Trost. He thought he was one of the original Gosplanners, a Hayward man. He was the admiral who had brought Lehman the bad news about the EPA in 1982. Trost would be a throwback to the old days, when the fraternity of admirals ran the Navy. That would never do. At one point he told Trost, "You're just another fucking Boy Scout." [27]

Later at the White House, Reagan asked Weinberger, "What do you think of Admiral Trost?" [28]

"He's a very fine officer," Weinberger said. "I have no problem with that."

"By this time the President was fully aware that Lehman wanted to jump over a lot of qualified officers," Poindexter recalled, "and that Cap didn't have strong feelings about it, and that Cap readily acknowledged that Admiral Trost would be a good candidate." [29]

To try to stave off defeat, Lehman played his trump card. During one of his frequent breakfast meetings with George Bush, he relayed his frustration about not having his first choice approved by the President. "This makes it impossible for me to do my job," he told Bush. "It's not a threat, it's a fact of life." [30] He said that if Kelso did not become CNO, he would resign. Bush promised to discuss Lehman's concerns with Reagan.

Secretary of the Navy John Lehman, a Ronald Reagan appointee in 1981. A macho, hard-drinking party man enamored of naval aviation, Lehman was also a tenacious and skilled political infighter who orchestrated the largest peacetime naval buildup in the nation's history.

Admiral Tom Hayward, the chief of naval operations, depicted below shaking hands with Reagan, detested John Lehman. A by-the-book Naval Academy graduate and former fleet commander, Hayward was the father of the Maritime Strategy, a brilliant but controversial plan for fighting the Soviets, which Lehman enhanced and appropriated as his own.

3

Secretary of Defense Caspar Weinberger often had to rein in the charismatic but unpredictable Lehman. Here, the two men are on board the newly commissioned *Theodore Roosevelt*, one of four supercarriers that were the crown jewels of Lehman's near trillion-dollar naval buildup.

4

To preserve the rationale for his massive naval buildup, Lehman moved to divert evidence that the Soviet navy—with lumbering helicopter carriers like this—was vastly inferior to the American fleet.

Ronald Reagan gets a "high five" at a naval academy graduation. Reagan was all for secret naval operations in Soviet waters, even though he was aware that the provocative raids might touch off a full-scale nuclear confrontation.

Richard Allen, Reagan's first national security advisor (center), and Vice President George Bush (left), a former naval aviator himself, strongly supported Lehman and his Six Hundred Ship Navy. Al Haig (right), who served briefly as Secretary of State, was also a big fan and a proponent of the Navy's aggressive Maritime Strategy.

Lehman's plan to overhaul four retired World War II battleships, like the *Missouri* pictured here, would cost the nation approximately $2 billion. Critics argued that such ships, as well as Lehman's supercarriers, were only marginally useful in an age of missiles.

7

8

Commander Hank Kleeman and three other Black Aces became national heroes for shooting down two Libyan jets over the Gulf of Sidra in August 1981. The sixty-second dogfight seemed to signal that the Navy, demoralized by a series of major blunders after the Vietnam War, was back on the path to glory.

Where two of his predecessors had failed, Lehman succeeded in forcing into retirement the cantankerous but powerful Admiral Hyman Rickover (right), the father of America's nuclear Navy. Meeting with Reagan and Lehman in the Oval Office, Rickover exploded with anger and called Lehman a "pissant" who knew nothing about the Navy.

9

John Walker (left), a former navy warrant officer, and three cohorts, including his own son, stole naval secrets for the Soviets for more than seventeen years. Walker's arrest revealed the shockingly sloppy way the Navy handled secret communications. The full extent of the damage done to U.S. national security by Walker's treachery is still not known.

10

Admiral James Watkins (left), Hayward's successor as chief of naval operations, and John Lehman cheer lustily at an Army-Navy football game. Watkins, once an ally but still an admiral of the old school, grew increasingly frustrated by Lehman's interference in matters traditionally reserved for the Navy's admirals.

11

12

The engines and flight-control system on the F-14 Tomcat (above) were so trouble-plagued that scores of the costly high-performance jets crashed, killing many naval aviators. As much as $5 billion that could have been used to improve both the Hornet and the Tomcat were diverted to develop the A-12 Avenger (below), which was never built and was finally canceled because of cost overruns and mismanagement.

13

14

Hank Kleeman, the hero of the Gulf of Sidra dogfight, was killed when his F/A-18 Hornet flipped upside down at the Miramar Naval Air Station because of faulty landing-gear design.

15

John Lehman with Tom Cruise, star of the hit movie, *Top Gun*. Cruise's portrayal of a hard-drinking, womanizing naval aviator merely suggested the way these hot-shot pilots really behaved. By the end of "ladies night" at the Miramar officers' club, the drunken Navy men were engaged in public sex in cars, behind bushes, and in the bathrooms of the club.

16

17

Angered by Lehman's threat to resign if his crony Admiral Frank Kelso (shown above talking with Lehman) was not appointed chief of naval operations, Ronald Reagan backed another admiral, Carlisle A. H. Trost (left) for the job. Trost tried in vain to end Lehman's stranglehold on the Navy.

Two Navy men making friends at Subic Bay in the Philippines, a "rest-and-recreation" stopover for naval personnel. Elsewhere, the Navy hired prostitutes, commonly referred to as "hostitutes," to work in some of the bars and clubs.

18

19

Lehman reviews the troops with Weinberger on the last day of his job as Navy Secretary, April 10, 1987. Finally fed up with his abrasive style, Weinberger replaced Lehman with James Webb. Although Lehman was gone, the course he had set for the Navy would bring that once proud service to the brink of financial and moral bankruptcy.

20

Melvyn Paisley, another Lehman legacy, headed up the Navy's research and procurement programs. Paisley and several others would become the targets of an FBI and Navy investigation called Ill Wind, the largest procurement scandal in Pentagon history.

21

Jim Webb (left) thought that Admiral "Ace" Lyons, Lehman's alter ego, was ill-suited for high command. Soon after he was made Pacific Fleet commander, Lyons began to engage in questionable and provocative naval operations that eventually led to his dismissal.

22

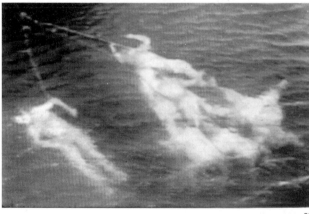

23

The Navy's aggressive operating style finally ended in tragedy in the Middle East when the high-tech state-of-the-art cruiser *Vincennes* mistakenly shot down an IranAir commercial airline, killing all 290 passengers and crew onboard. (Left) Retrieval of bodies.

Admiral William Crowe, chairman of the Joint Chiefs of Staff, attempts to explain the *Vincennes* tragedy at a Pentagon press conference. He was later accused of covering up key details about the shoot-down that implicated the Navy.

President George Bush picked H. Lawrence Garrett III as his Secretary of the Navy. Garrett inherited a Navy buckling under the weight of Lehman's massive buildup, and an admiralty preoccupied with regaining its prerogatives and privileges. Although he attended two rowdy Tailhook conventions, Garrett denied knowing about any debauchery, a half-truth that would lead to his dismissal.

An explosion in a gun turret on the battleship *Iowa* killed 47 crewmen. The Navy got another black eye when it botched the investigation and claimed that Seaman Clayton Hartwig was responsible, a position it was later forced to abandon for lack of evidence.

27

Admiral Joe Prueher (above), one of
Lehman's favorite aviators, got into hot
water as Commandant of the U.S.
Naval Academy when midshipmen
chained Gwen Dreyer, a female student
at Annapolis, to a latrine. When Dreyer
and her father, a naval academy graduate (shown together at right), went public with the incident, Dreyer's father
said that Prueher tried to intimidate
them by threatening to release photographs that would prove Dreyer had
been a willing participant.

28

Even with its cruise missiles, shown here during a spectacular launch from the battleship *Wisconsin*, the Navy played second fiddle to the Air Force during the
Persian Gulf War. Demoralized by their poor showing in the war and openly hostile
to their leadership, the naval aviators who attended the 1991 Tailhook convention
were in a mood to party.

29

30

31

The Navy's admirals had long known about the licentious behavior at Tailhook conventions, where naval aviators paraded around with their genitals exposed and participated in lewd acts with prostitutes and female entertainers. Lieutenant Paula Coughlin (right), was the most well known of 83 women assaulted at the party. During the investigations that followed, the Navy's top brass scurried for cover while Captain Frederick "Wigs" Ludwig (below), who had written a letter that led to the exposure of the scandal in the newspapers, faced a court-martial and eventually had a nervous breakdown.

32

33

Rear Admiral Duvall "Mac" Williams, who had been one of Lehman's closest aides, headed the Naval Investigative Service and was accused of withholding information about Tailhook to protect Admiral Frank Kelso, another Lehman intimate, who was now chief of Naval Operations.

34

Rear Admiral Ted Gordon, a lawyer who had researched the legal precedents that had enabled Lehman to seize virtually unprecedented power over the Navy, and now the Navy's Judge Advocate General, was also accused of mishandling the Tailhook investigation. Both Williams and Gordon retired under a cloud.

35

After Garrett was fired, Sean O'Keefe (left), a protégé of Defense Secretary Dick Cheney, was appointed Secretary of the Navy by President Bush to clean up the Navy. During O'Keefe's brief tenure, the Pentagon Inspector General's report revealed the truly shocking extent of the Tailhook scandal and the Navy's inept handling of the investigation, which bordered on a cover-up.

36

President Bill Clinton appointed John Dalton, a former Naval Academy graduate, Secretary of the Navy as the Tailhook scandal still spiraled out of control. Dalton's efforts to hold senior naval officers accountable were undermined after his role in the failure of a Texas Savings and Loan came under federal investigation.

37

Admiral Jeremy "Mike" Boorda succeeded Frank Kelso as chief of naval operations. The skeletons in his closet rattled around earlier attempts to protect Lawrence Garrett's troubled sailor son and claims that his own son had received preferential treatment.

38

When a female American sailor was raped by Soviet sailors during a visit of Soviet ships to San Diego, Admiral Charles Larson tried to frustrate the Naval Investigative Service's pursuit of the case. Later, Larson was Navy Secretary Dalton's unlikely choice to be the Superintendent of the Naval Academy who would clean up the mess after a cheating scandal erupted into another major embarrassment for the Navy.

39

40

Lieutenant Kara Hultgreen and the wreckage of her jet, which crashed while she tried to land on an aircraft carrier. Sensitive to its treatment of women in the wake of Tailhook, the Navy claimed that engine failure, not pilot error, was at fault. But a further investigation, and still secret report, revealed that Hultgreen, who had been rushed through training, was, in fact, responsible.

42

41

Rear Admiral (select) Everett L. Greene, who headed up the Navy's division to fight sexual harassment, was brought up on court-martial for harassing two female officers. Despite his being acquitted of all charges, the Navy demoted him.

The CNO selection was still up in the air when Reagan, Bush, Poindexter, and Don Regan, the chief of staff, met in the Oval Office for the morning national security briefing. As the meeting came to an end, Bush told the President, "John Lehman said that if Kelso wasn't approved, he would resign." [31]

"That's it," Reagan said, somewhat angry that he was being pushed around by Lehman. "I'm not going to pick Kelso."

On June 30, 1986, at 11 A.M., John Lehman walked onto the front steps of Bancroft Hall at the Naval Academy. The sun was shinning brightly in historic Annapolis as he looked out on the large crowd, which sat anxiously before him to witness one of the Navy's most important and cherished traditions. Standing on one side of Lehman was Caspar Weinberger, who had come out the thirty miles from Washington for the change of command ceremony. Next to the two secretaries stood James Watkins and the admiral who would become the new king of the naval empire: Carlisle Trost. "As you can well imagine, today is for me a day of rather considerable excitement and a day of many emotions," Trost said. "A deep sense of humility, together with more adrenaline pumping into my system than I ever thought possible. I have a feeling of 'Let's go.' " [32]

Lehman's loss over the Trost fight with Weinberger was a bitter blow. He had been in office for five years, begun every reform imaginable, and filled all the key jobs with his people without ever picking the Navy's most important uniformed leader. He told Weinberger that he could not work with Trost, and that he would step down sometime the following year. [33] In the meantime, a peace offering would have to be made. In one of his earliest meetings with Trost, Lehman pledged his support, then added in all seriousness, I don't like you, but I will work with you.

Hope for a good relationship dwindled fast. After just a few weeks the honeymoon was over. Trost was beside himself with Lehman's effort to dominate the flag selections. It was the same logjam that he had created for Watkins. And Trost could now see what was holding up the process—the promotion of Lehman's longtime aide P. D. Miller from a junior rear admiral to a three-star vice admiral. Miller was dear to Lehman's heart, the classic story of the little guy making good. As a child, he never really knew his father. Later, his stepfather, a former boatswain's mate, pushed him toward the Navy. The young man thrived in the Navy, rising quickly in rank from an ensign to a lieutenant commander. He made even the difficult jobs look easy. As a junior lieutenant commander, he won acclaim as an aide to the vice chief of naval operations, Admiral Robert Long, who was Hayward's number two man. Lehman recognized his abilities and asked him to join his staff.

Miller became the door keeper, guarding his boss from both real and perceived enemies, a filter man who knew all but said little. He knew the secrets and what really went on in the inner sanctum of the Secretariat—the deals, the political fights, the vendettas that had to be settled. Lehman and Miller had become so close that some people referred to them as blood brothers. When Miller was up for promotion from captain to flag rank, Lehman asked Missouri congressman Ike Skeleton to do away with the position of commodore (then equal to a one-star rear admiral) because Miller wanted to be an admiral, not a commodore.[34] Miller had spent five years guarding Lehman's door. Even old stalwarts like Ted Gordon and Mac Williams, who once had carte blanche access to Lehman, had to go through Miller to see the secretary.

When it came time to pay Miller back for his loyalty, Lehman was generous—too generous, in the opinion of Watkins. He gave command of the Seventh Fleet, where Ace Lyons could watch over him, to his forty-five-year-old aide. Watkins balked at that, arguing that Miller needed more time in grade as a rear admiral. Now Trost was mucking things up, vehemently opposing the nomination. Trost thought Miller was a good officer who would mature into a first-rate admiral if he spent more time in his current job as commander of a cruiser-destroyer squadron in San Diego. He had been in that job for only four months, and Trost felt he could use the sea time. The last time Miller deployed to sea with a ship was in 1979. In fact, he spent his entire time as a captain working in staff jobs at the Pentagon. If Lehman could break Miller free, his youthful aide would advance from a rear admiral to a vice admiral in only seventeen months. That was so rare, few could remember the last time it was done.

The Miller deal was too much for Edward L. Fike, the conservative journalist who ran the editorial page of the *San Diego Union.* "The last thing the Navy needs in a time of emergency is a bunch of fawning, inexperienced, unqualified bureaucrats in command," he wrote in a commentary piece. Lehman, who saw a conspiracy in every fight, blamed Ed Prina, the former Navy captain and journalist, for the drumbeat against Miller. Prina had tapped his Navy contacts opposed to Miller and written a number of key articles throughout the summer that questioned the wisdom of putting him in command of the Seventh Fleet. Because it was in a big Navy town, the newspaper played heavy with the secretary of defense. On July 25 Lehman tried to discredit Prina in a note to Weinberger. "Prina is a shill for Hayward and Turner. This is the classic pattern they used to sink Kelso and Ace— delay it in the tank, then leak to Prina."[35]

To justify the nomination, Lehman had Ted Gordon research similar promotions going back to the Civil War with Generals George McClellan and Ulysses S. Grant. In a lengthy memo Gordon reported that McClellan was thirty-five and Grant forty-two when Abraham Lincoln put them in command of the Union Armies. In World War I General John Pershing went from a captain to a brigadier general, passing over 862 other Army officers. And George Marshall, the famous World War II general, never commanded troops in combat. But perhaps the most grandiose comparison was between Miller and Dwight Eisenhower, who went from a lieutenant colonel in 1941 to the full rank of general in 1944. And Eisenhower promoted Arleigh Burke, the famous CNO, over ninety-two other admirals because the Navy needed "younger, more vigorous officers in positions of responsibility." [36]

If these famous men of war with little experience could advance so quickly, Lehman asked, then why should anyone be opposed to P. D. Miller? He won the battle. After two months Trost saw that his opposition was futile and backed Miller "for the good of the Navy."

While Miller's career soared, Ted Gordon's stalled. He had served Lehman for four years now and was still a captain. Miller had come into the Navy about nine months before Gordon yet had become an admiral a year before him. Now he was a three-star and Gordon was not even on the flag selection list for 1986.

Gordon could not have been happier for Miller. Both men were united in their campaign to serve Lehman and had become good friends in the process. For the last several years Gordon was Lehman's go-between on sensitive political issues with key lawmakers who had to be courted in order to win votes and other favors. Whenever Lehman went to the Hill, Gordon went too and sat close enough to Lehman to answer a question or respond with a quick fact. And he helped prepare the issue books used for Lehman's testimonies. "I did an awful lot of stuff for him, most of it left unsaid. Nothing illegal, nothing improper. But I followed every order." [37]

It was a difficult assignment for Gordon in that military regulations restricted him from overtly lobbying elected officials. Worse from a career perspective, he was often at odds with senior admirals, who resented that a young officer would be cutting deals in the halls of Congress. Rear Admiral Bruce Newell, who had gone on to head up the Navy's Office of Legislative Affairs, went to Lehman to complain about Gordon's political activities on Capitol Hill.

"Mr. Secretary, your man Gordon here has made a statement on the Hill that is not Navy policy," Newell told Lehman.[38]

Lehman listened to what the admiral had to say. Without responding, he turned to Gordon. "Ted, did you say that?"

"Yes, I did, Mr. Secretary."

Lehman turned back to the admiral, who was expecting Gordon to be keelhauled for speaking out of line on the Hill. Nodding at Gordon, Lehman told Newell, "Anytime he speaks, he speaks for me."

On October 6, 1986, Gordon finally put on his first star as a rear admiral. But the promotion was not without controversy. A panel of Navy lawyers picking the next admirals for the Judge Advocate General Corps did not select Gordon for promotion to flag rank. Lehman was incensed and ordered the board to remove one name and place Gordon on the list.[39] In short order Gordon would be in charge of the Naval Investigative Service, which was the stepping-stone for judge advocate general of the Navy.

On November 25 a glum Ronald Reagan walked into the White House briefing room at 12:05 to announce that he had fired Oliver North and that John Poindexter had resigned over the Iran-contra scandal.

Although Lehman was not a central figure in Iran-contra, he had been close to the players and was mentioned in several top secret memoranda for helping the covert operation. In 1984 he had introduced David Walker, a British SAS officer who attended Cambridge with him, to North. Walker ran Keenie Meenie Services, an outfit whose expertise was skullduggery and sabotage and one that assisted North with covert operations inside Nicaragua. One top secret memo prepared by the National Security Council on December 4, 1984, for McFarlane said, "David Walker will assist in Military training for Nicaraguan Democratic Force (FDN) to destroy Nicaragua."[40]

Lehman watched the momentum against the contra operation build in Congress as bits and pieces about it dribbled out in the press. When it exploded into the Iran-contra scandal, he knew there would be personnel shake-ups in the White House. In adversity there was always opportunity. Rumors coming out the National Security Council had been predicting for some time now that Poindexter was in trouble and would eventually have to be replaced. Lehman had his eye on the job.

One conservative who wanted Lehman to be the next national security adviser to the President was Ed Feulner, head of the influential Heritage Foundation. Feulner and Lehman had been roommates during college and had stayed close ever since. Although Lehman was a long shot, Feulner and others managed to get his name placed on a short list of candidates that included Admiral Bobby Ray Inman; William Hyland, the respected editor of *Foreign Affairs* magazine; and David Abshire, one of the founders of the Center for Strategic and International Studies. Being among these candidates elevated Lehman's status in Washington circles. He was no longer just a service secretary: he was a candidate for one of the most important jobs in the government.

On May 23, 1986, Feulner wrote a letter to Lehman, encouraging him not to give up hope on the prospect of a higher job in the administration.

> Dear John,
>
> Hang in there. You've got one helluva fan club out here in the real world who want to be helpful.
>
> Cheers!
>
> Ed

Later, months after Lehman lost the job, he wrote a personal note on his four-star stationery back to Feulner to thank him for his support.

> Dear Ed
>
> I am deeply grateful for the confidence you showed in sticking your neck out picking me for the NSC. (I am also deeply grateful I didn't get the job.) I look forward to seeing you to catch up.
>
> Cheers
>
> John

It may have seemed a personal setback not to have been picked. But Lehman had no hard feelings and was sincere when he said he was grateful for not getting the job. There were bigger things on the horizon. His regular luncheon partner, George Bush, whom Lehman had originally endorsed for President in 1980, had started to make rumblings about another presidential run in 1988. If he won, Lehman would have a choice of a number of key jobs, including national security adviser. He had already begun laying the groundwork. He had the Navy begin an exhaustive search to compile Bush's military record. It was an impressive packet when completed and contained aircraft action reports, citations, chronologies, and articles. "Details vary," the naval historian Dave Baker wrote in a memo about the Bush material, "but his exploits make for exciting reading." [41]

Perhaps just as exciting, for Lehman, was the prospect of moving from the Pentagon to the White House.

≡ CHAPTER 17 ≡

ON OCTOBER 2, 1986, John Lehman's personal DC-9 descended over the Las Vegas desert and touched down at Nellis Air Force Base. He always enjoyed flying out west this time of year to attend one of the Navy's most infamous rituals.[1] Officially it was called the Tailhook Association convention. And it was authorized by the highest levels of the Navy, so fliers from around the world could benefit from professional seminars on aviation issues. Unofficially it was called a group grope, bacchanalia, drinking bout, or any other cliché synonymous with sex, booze, drugs, and rock and roll.

Lehman liked being with the Airedales at Tailhook as much as they enjoyed the fact that he was willing to shed his title and blend in as one of the boys. Since coming into office in 1981, he had tried as often as his schedule allowed to attend the annual event. It was here, among the men who risked their lives daily plying the dangerous trade of flying combat jets, that Lehman felt most comfortable. His world in Washington was becoming more complex almost daily. Even his closest confidants could see that he now had as many enemies as friends in the Pentagon and the administration. Carlisle Trost and most of his fellow admirals thought Lehman was unbalanced. Jim Webb, a top Weinberger aide and onetime Lehman supporter, believed he was paranoid. And his congressional backers no longer embraced his politicking.

There were more critical stories about the Navy from a press corps that had once gushed over him. Lehman would simmer for years over a piece about him in *The New Republic* called "Fool of Ships: How One of Washington's Slickest Operators Keeps the Navy Abloat." Even by Washington standards, the article's tone was razor sharp. "Lehman's ambitions are not unusual; his tactics are," wrote author Tina Rosenberg. "He has wrecked careers, snookered Congress, and lied to his bosses. He has used a dazzling array of creative tricks to get what he wants. He is famous for knifing his enemies." One quote from an unnamed source said Lehman "is one of the two or three slimiest men in Washington."

But outside of Washington, where the fleet lay moored and the war fighters concentrated on doing battle with the Russians, he was seen as a savior, a modern-day Teddy Roosevelt who carried a big stick and still considered gunboat diplomacy a proper way to conduct foreign affairs. With the massive buildup of the Navy, with his brashness and can-do attitude, Lehman had touched off a renaissance of pride and confidence, a renewed sense of purpose for the sailors and officers corps.

He had promised more ships and airplanes, better pay and benefits—and he had delivered. The Navy, thanks to Lehman, had become the tip of Reagan's sword. For Reagan, the battleships and carriers and Top Gun pilots were a symbol of everything that was right and good about America and its military power. The Navy had shot down Libyan warplanes, captured dangerous terrorists, and defiantly sailed into the home waters of America's archenemy. Although the general public shared in the rebound of patriotism, there was no way for it to experience the true emotions of being one of Reagan's warriors.

Together, Reagan and Lehman had unleashed a powerful psychological fever in the Navy. Esprit de corps was booming among the submariners, among the ship drivers, and especially among the Airedales, who had a "don't fuck with me, I'm bulletproof" attitude. The fliers had come to be Lehman's superstars, the champions of the Maritime Strategy. That strategy was perhaps the most important, certainly the most controversial, innovation in naval warfare since the Second World War—and carrier air power was at the center of it.

If anything could adequately gauge the morale of the aviators, it was Tailhook, which was like a knot meter that recorded their blustery élan. And by 1986, as the aviators began arriving in September for this year's 'Hook, the needle was about to jump off the gauge. In May, Paramount studios released Top Gun, which featured Tom Cruise as an F-14 fighter jock.[2] Lehman, who posed in black-tie attire in front of an F-14 with Cruise at a preview screening, generously donated the Navy's assistance. The secretary boasted that the Navy's help and the accurate depiction of naval aviation contributed greatly to the movie's box office success, which was significant: gross sales from its domestic showing alone topped $175 million.[3] For the Navy, Top Gun was the best recruiting poster in its history. Almost overnight, recruiters were besieged with young kids who wanted to fly Navy fighters.

But there was another kind of realism in the movie as well, one that the carrier admirals would later say did immeasurable harm.[4] It was the flying and drinking and sex side of the aviators' lives that was so prevalent during the high times of the Lehman years. In one of the early scenes Tom Cruise shows up at the Miramar Officers Club, where he spots Kelly McGillis, who shuns his macho overtures. Cruise, decked out in Navy whites, then follows her into the ladies' bathroom.

"What do you want to do, just drop down on the tile and go for it?" McGillis asks.[5]

"Actually, I had this counter in mind," Cruise replies, pushing on the sink top while flashing his Hollywood smile.

"That would be real comfortable, yeah," she says in a sarcastic tone.

"It could be," he responds.

In the movie, the woman pursued by the fighter pilot walks out, leaving him to "crash and burn." In real life women were not only having sex with the aviators in Miramar's bathrooms, they were doing it in back rooms, in the bushes, and in the parking lot. Every Wednesday night at the Officers Club was ladies' night, and guards were ordered to let on base any woman who showed up at the gate. Women came in droves, eager and willing to engage in a night of sex and drinking with the handsome flyboys. And Miramar's police were unofficially told not to patrol near the Officers Club, where the fliers were having public sex or leaving the parking lot intoxicated. Wednesday nights at Miramar became almost as infamous as the Tailhook gatherings.[6]

As Lehman's DC-9 came to a stop on the tarmac at Nellis, the air field was already filled with military jets, a display of hardware that made the base look as if it were preparing for a war. Many aviators personally flew their own F-14s or A-6s to the party. At $3,000 per hour for gas, maintenance, and wear and tear, it was an expensive ticket from the East Coast or upstate Washington.[7] Other officers drove to Las Vegas across the hot and barren Mojave from the many military bases scattered across Southern California. They wound their way through Lenwood, Barstow, and Goodsprings, little hamlets along Highway 15 that led to the bright lights and vice of Las Vegas, which rose like Oz out of the desert. Still others took one of the many C-9 Navy transport planes that were shuttling the Tailhookers, at a cost of several hundred thousand dollars, from air bases around the nation. The military planes, which were reconfigured passenger jets like Lehman's, stopped in El Toro, and Washington, Texas, Virginia, Tennessee, and Florida —wherever there was an air base with fliers in need of a lift to Tailhook. Besides the free flight, many of the officers in attendance were receiving a per diem. They were getting paid to party—just as John Lehman was.

Randy "Duke" Cunningham, who today is a conservative Republican member of Congress from San Diego, had been to several Tailhooks during his years as a Navy fighter pilot. But nothing, nothing he had seen at past 'Hooks rivaled the sexual gymnastics and drunkenness at the 1985 gathering. The party, Cunningham complained, was out of control. Something had to be done to rein in the aviators. If not, somebody might drink himself to death or, worse, an accident might kill an innocent bystander. If it went on this way, the Navy would pull its official support and send the Tailhook Association packing from its free office space at Miramar.

In its infancy, Tailhook was a loose-knit association of pilots who took their name from the tail hook, which allows Navy jets to catch the landing wire on an aircraft carrier. The organization began in 1956 when a group of Navy and Marine pilots met for a party in a sleepy Mexican village called Rosarito, a small town about twenty-five miles south of San Diego on the Pacific Ocean. The margaritas were good and cheap, and the beer was plentiful. Those who came in the first two years did so to drink a little bit and tell war stories. If somebody who had driven into Mexico drank too much, the aviators took his keys away to keep him from driving.

After two years the party moved to San Diego, where most of the aviators were stationed. In four years, as the party's reputation grew within naval aviation circles, the organization had been thrown out of most local hotels. So, in 1963 it migrated to nearby Las Vegas, where nobody seemed to mind the men launching couches and other items from hotel windows. Even the ill-fated attempt at waitress throwing was overlooked, despite the fact that one woman catapulted by the men missed a swimming pool and landed with a thud on the concrete. Fortunately she received only a few minor scrapes and a broken leg.[8]

One year, however, the Sands Hotel said enough after the Tailhookers threw a piano from a room near the top of the fifteen-story building.[9] And that wasn't the only thing the fliers threw out of the hotel's windows. In one suite, which was rented by a defense contractor, the company closed the bar and ordered the naval officers out so everyone could attend an official function downstairs. That didn't sit well with some of the fliers. As an evening cocktail party got under way outside on a patio some fifteen floors below, a group of men broke down the door of the suite. After consuming most of the liquor in the room, they began to throw all of the furniture out the window and onto the patio below. Guards from the Sands sent up to stop the rampage were kept at bay by aviators who doused them with high-pressure firehoses.[10] After that the convention moved to the Las Vegas Hilton, where Barron Hilton received the naval aviators with open arms.

Early on, the Navy and Tailhook knew they had to tone down the party side and play up the benefits of the convention. The Navy began sponsoring informal seminars in the morning on aviation issues, which became a big hit, both for the free beer served and because young pilots could have a frank conversation with senior officers on a wide range of issues from airplane design to safety. The lines among ranks had intentionally been blurred to encourage straight talk. It wasn't uncommon for a pilot to stick his finger in an admiral's chest and say, Listen up, sir, if you don't fix this airplane, it's going to kill a lot of people.

The admirals were not opposed to the tough questions or, for that matter, pulling a prank or two. One year at an earlier convention, an admiral landed his jet at Nellis, folded up its wings, and drove with a police escort to the Hilton several miles away. Another admiral, Bear Taylor, dressed up as a Civil War general and rode a white horse into the Hilton Hotel. And Vice Admiral Jack Ready was well known for being able to drink a beer while standing on his head. Ready called it his inverted pitch hangup. Another admiral liked to party so much that his call sign was Bar Fly. The junior officers appreciated the pranks and laughed at the idea of what hell-raisers the admirals must have been as lieutenants.

But by 1985, at almost the exact time when naval aviators were capturing the *Achille Lauro* terrorists, a noticeable change had taken place among the younger officers. The Airedales had become insubordinate, even threatening, to many admirals who attended the convention. Some attributed it to alcohol. Others felt it was a mixture of alcohol, testosterone, and the ''don't fuck with me, I'm bulletproof'' attitude that Lehman seemed to inspire among the fliers.

At the 1985 'Hook, the Top Gun suite had sponsored a drinking contest. Whoever could knock back the most kamikazes would win a Japanese-style headband. It wasn't long before the drunken men wearing their kamikaze headbands ventured downstairs to the Hilton's lobby and started jogging in unison among the guests, pulling the slot machines and throwing dice on the craps table.

Meanwhile, upstairs on the party floor, booze and sex were omnipresent in the hospitality suites that individual squadrons rented for the weekend. Women, most of whom were prostitutes, were busy working, engaging either in sex acts, stripping, or tending bar. In one suite a female Navy lawyer, who is now a naval judge, was serving drinks in a suite while topless.[11] An aviator walked into another suite where a prostitute was having sex with five officers at once while their friends watched. In still other rooms, men were sitting around drinking and watching X-rated movies on television like *Blonde Bombshell* or *Erotic City*.

The admirals who attended the 1985 party were worried. When the convention was over, many of them clambered aboard a military transport plane for a change of command ceremony in Hawaii. During the six-hour flight each recounted in some detail the abuses they had either experienced, seen, or heard about. By no means were these admirals altar boys. All were aviators, most of whom had seen duty in Vietnam. And they had come up through the ranks of flying and drinking. But they sensed that the younger generation of officers was losing respect for the chain of command. And the lewd acts, which had always been a part of the aviation community, seemed to be getting more raunchy. Most of the admirals shook their heads at the latest fad: ball walking. A male officer would unzip his fly, pull out only his testicles, zip his pants back up so his scrotum was left hanging out, then walk around the party. "It didn't hurt if you did it right," said one flier. Ball walking was considered a manly thing to do. As the act became more widespread, a T-shirt that read "HANG 'EM IF YOU GOT 'EM" was sold at the convention.

The admirals on the plane bound for Hawaii agreed that a special meeting of the Tailhook Association board would have to address these problems. Duke Cunningham concurred. A board member himself, he wrote a memorandum to his colleagues, expressing his "disdain for the conduct or, better put, the misconduct of several officers and a lack of command attention which resulted in damage and imprudent action. . . . Dancing girls performing lurid sexual acts on Naval aviators in public would make prime conversation for the media." [12]

There was no doubt that change was needed. Many naval officers were in agreement with that. But Cunningham, a majority of aviators felt, was the wrong guy to do it. For him to raise a fuss was like the pot calling the kettle black. Publicly Cunningham was a war hero, the first U.S. pilot and the only naval aviator to become an ACE in Vietnam by shooting down five enemy planes. But there was another, darker side to him. Those who were on cruises with him claimed he was a womanizer and had been picked up by the shore patrol on several occasions for drunkenness. [13] And few outside of the fighter community and the upper reaches of the Navy knew that he had almost been court-martialed for illegal and unethical behavior at Top Gun.

Like many aviators serving during the war, Cunningham had a reserve commission. And like most of his fellow pilots, he hoped to get a regular commission in the Navy. He had applied for one before he'd shot down his first plane but had been rejected because he had such a poor record as an officer. Then he shot down a second plane and reapplied. Again he was rejected. He kept trying but was always denied. Finally, after he shot down five enemy warplanes, the Navy realized it had a public relations problem. It had a bona fide national hero who wasn't being permitted to join the regular Navy. Admiral Elmo Zumwalt's office prepared the paperwork, and just months before he was to be discharged, Cunningham was given a regular commission. [14] Even so, his standing among his peers did not improve. Two commanding officers at Top Gun, where Cunningham was an instructor pilot after the war, had rated him at the bottom of his squadron, saying he was a subpar naval officer. Top Gun's first commanding officer, Ron "Mugs" McKeown, a war veteran with a MiG kill, said Cunningham "couldn't write a simple declarative sentence. I had a hard time with that." [15]

Cunningham, who declined to comment on his record, believed he was a notch above the others at Top Gun and insisted he was going to receive the Medal of Honor for his heroics in the sky over Vietnam. He even had hundreds of photographs of himself printed and would hand them out in public. "Hi, I'm Randy Cunningham," he would say, "the first Vietnam MiG ACE." [16] The Navy had decided instead to award him and his radar officer, Bill Driscoll, the Navy Cross. But a day before the secretary of the Navy was to arrive for the ceremony, Cunningham protested to McKeown. "I'm not going to accept it," he said. "I've been promised a Medal of Honor."

"Randy, come in the office," McKeown ordered. Inside, McKeown tried to get through to him. He had done some background checking on Cunningham's claims about the Medal of Honor and found they didn't hold up. "Let's get something straight," McKeown said. "You are not going to get the Medal of Honor. You are going to get the Navy Cross. And let me tell you, you and Bill are both going to go get haircuts and you are going to be splendid in your blues tomorrow and you are going to be as American as apple pie. And you are going to thank a grateful nation for heaping its praise on you and be humble. And if you are not, I'm going to rip your tits off." [17]

Shortly after McKeown left Top Gun, his replacement, Jack Ready, ran into a more serious problem with Cunningham. Still deeply wounded about his rating among the instructor pilots at Top Gun, Cunningham broke into Ready's office after hours and rifled through the personnel files on the other fliers in the squadron. He read the fitness reports on each officer and saw who was rated first, second, third, and so on. According to the ratings, he was at the bottom of the pack. Steaming mad, he replaced the files and was determined to confront Jack Ready about his low standing. [18] During the week he came back and demanded to know why he was rated so poorly. To Ready he counted off the standings of the other officers contained in their evaluations.

"How do you know that?" Ready asked, puzzled by Cunningham's intimate knowledge about the private data of each officer. There were only two ways for him to be privy to such information, Ready knew. Either he had gotten together with the other instructors and they all compared fitness reports, which was unlikely, or he had somehow gotten access to the officers' records, which was illegal and unethical.

Cunningham solved the riddle. "Because I came in here and went through your files and compared them," he said.

Ready ordered him out of his office and decided, hero or no hero, that Cunningham should be court-martialed. He met with the officers in Cunningham's chain of command, who all agreed the breaking and entering incident was grounds for serious discipline. But before they could go much farther, reality set in. The Navy was not about to kick out its only Vietnam ACE. That would be a public relations disaster.

Not only was the incident covered up, Cunningham was promoted. Despite being passed over three times before by a screening board, he was given command of VF-126, an adversary squadron at Top Gun that painted its planes in the colors and markings of the Soviet Union and mimicked their dogfighting techniques against American pilots.

Now Cunningham was questioning his fellow aviators' integrity for their behavior at Tailhook. And they resented it. Alone, he had little chance of getting the association's members to abide by higher standards of conduct in Las Vegas. But the admirals, particularly Vice Admiral Edward H. Martin, the chief of naval aviation, and Rear Admiral Jim Service, who had run the first Libyan operation in the Gulf of Sidra and was now the head of the Pacific Fleet's air forces, were threatening to cut off Navy support and the free flights to Las Vegas. The board, realizing that disaster loomed ahead unless something was done, agreed to a special meeting on September 26, 1985. Among its solutions were limits on the number of hospitality suites, blacklisting bad suites, issuing warnings to commanding officers of squadrons causing problems, and eliminating the suites for one year.

Jack Snyder, who found himself in the unenviable position of being the president of Tailhook, was directed to respond to Martin's complaints. On October 9 Snyder's six-page letter was sent back to Martin's office in the Pentagon. "We must make some meaningful changes now," he wrote, "while our intensity is clearly focused on the issue." He ended the letter by pledging to put "the word 'professionalism' back into the centerpoint of 'Hook '86'" and listed several reforms for Martin to choose from.[19] Snyder recommended adult leadership and guidance in the suites, the elimination of drinking contests, and no lewd conduct. Content that the association was taking action, Martin cooled off.

He could, in reality, do little else.

How could he and his fellow admirals implement a strict regime when the secretary of the Navy was taking part in the debauchery? It was Lehman who had sent out the flash message rescinding the order by base commanders to cancel happy hour at their Officers Clubs. It was Lehman the party animal whom intoxicated fliers had hoisted above their heads in Pensacola, when he'd promised to bring back leather flight jackets. And it was Lehman who had raised a brown shoe at an earlier Tailhook, saying the aviators would have their own distinct footwear, their own special identity. And it was Lehman who spent many a late night at the Officers Club at Oceana. Lehman wasn't about to stop all the fun.

When he was on Kissinger's staff, one of Lehman's parties caused such a stir that it made Maxine Cheshire's gossip column in *The Washington Post*. Lehman and two friends had co-hosted a party at which male guests had to check their trousers with a maid at the door. The guest list was given to Cheshire, who printed a column that ran in the *Post* with the amusing headline BLACK TIE, BUT NO PANTS. Cheshire's column ignited a flurry of negative letters to the White House, complaining about the lack of morality among members of the administration. After the story ran, Kissinger warned his young assistant, "Lehman, you are going to have to make a hard choice. You are going to have to either keep your mouth shut or your pants on. You don't have to do both." [20]

One of Lehman's girlfriends at the time, Bonnie Burbidge, recalled his crazy antics. "I don't know if he was just not astute or aware enough to know the consequences of what he was doing or if he was just Irish enough to test it." [21]

One night, a close friend of Burbidge's was in town, so she asked Lehman to find a male friend for the woman so the couples could go out on a double date. When the two men showed up to greet the women, they were both stone-cold drunk. Later in the evening, as Burbidge and her friend were leaving Lehman's town house in Washington, he was so drunk that he tripped Burbidge and they both fell down the stairs. Once outside the house, Lehman saw that his friend had hoisted the other woman on his shoulders and was walking down the sidewalk. He caught up with them and started biting the woman on her buttocks.

Lehman may have been the spiritual leader of the licentious customs in the Navy in the 1980s, but he was far from the inventor. Those who bore responsibility were many of the admirals and the captains now being groomed for flag rank who were junior officers during the Vietnam War. If the admirals tried to clamp down now, they would be accused of a double standard.

Ever since military pilots first flew in World War I, they have tended to prefer the wild side of life. But it was during Vietnam, an unpopular war at home and a grim and terrible one on the front lines, that the drinking and sex side of the aviators flourished. Going off the line in Vietnam, American aircraft carriers sailed from the Gulf of Tonkin for a liberty call in the Philippines. It was an occasion the aviators took great relish in celebrating. In December 1972 the aircraft carrier *Kitty Hawk* had been on the line for nearly forty-five days before breaking off for its final voyage home. On its way back to the United States, it too would stop for a much needed break in the Philippines. Most of the fliers were below decks now, relaxing in their squadron ready rooms with a drink. They would pull out a bottle of Chivas, or Johnnie Walker Red Label, or a six-pack or two of beer. Because ice was in short supply on a ship, to chill a six-pack the officers put it in a garbage can and sprayed the can with a fire extinguisher. Other fliers just lay around catching some much needed sleep in their staterooms.

The off-the-line parties began as soon as the carrier lost sight of Vietnam's coast, sometimes earlier. They had been going on for as long as the war had, and they would continue until the last U.S. ship left Vietnam for good. Nick Criss, a graduate of Princeton, was the Alert-5 pilot on *Kitty Hawk* during its last cruise out of the gulf. While his friends yucked it up below decks, Criss passed the time by dozing off in the cockpit of his plane.

It seemed unfair to the fliers down below that Criss would have to miss such a momentous party, so some of them decided to place a dummy in the cockpit to make it appear as if a pilot were sitting there ready to go. The fliers carried a stuffed flight suit out to the Alert-5 aircraft and sat it in the pilot's seat. They hunched the dummy over and laid the helmeted head in the crook of an arm that was placed along the rim of the cockpit. Anyone looking at the jet would have thought the pilot had just dozed off. The navigators who sat in the back of the Phantom and were scheduled to fly the Alert-5 were not told by the fliers that a dummy was in the front slot. When they climbed up the fuselage, they would pat the dummy, believing it was a sleeping pilot, and get into the plane's backseat. Meanwhile Criss and the other pilots partied in their squadron ready rooms.

It took the carrier approximately thirty-six hours to cross the South China Sea. Approaching the Philippine coastline from the sea offers a spectacular view. The P.I., as it was known, is a nation of seven thousand islands that are peaks of a partly submerged mountain chain. The two largest islands are Mindanao in the south and Luzon in the north, where Subic Bay and the capital city of Manila are located. From the sea, the cities rimming Subic Bay look disarmingly tranquil. The lush green forest extends down to white sandy beaches that ring turquoise water. Beautiful white thunderheads reach for miles into the sky above the hills surrounding the bay. It looks like a postcard of paradise until you get an up-close and personal view.

When *Kitty Hawk* entered Subic Bay, it slowed to ten knots as it rounded the peninsula that marked the entry to the shipping channel. It would be almost two hours before the giant man-of-war rested at its pier at the Cubi Point Naval Air Station, several miles inside the bay. *Kitty Hawk* came within one hundred yards of its pier, then several tugboats appeared on the scene and began the slow process of easing the carrier's massive hull into place. One wrong move, too much power here or not enough there, and the eighty-thousand-ton carrier would crush the pier. It took almost an hour just to dock the boat at Cubi Point. Shortly afterward the crew descended on the Navy clubs, bars, and brothels of Subic Bay.

The Cubi Point Officers Club sat on top of a hill that offered a magnificent view of the carriers parked below and the entire bay. The hill was occasionally used as a launch platform for daredevil pilots who drove their cars from the peak to see if they could get a very unaerodynamic automobile airborne. Nobody was killed in these stunts, but several cars were wrecked.

If the aviators were not trying to fly their cars, they were crashing them into buildings. One day Mel Munsinger, who would later become the skipper of the aircraft carrier *Constellation* in 1985, and some other officers had gone up to the Navy club at Balikitan for a night of dinner and drinks. When it came time to leave, Munsinger and his friends tried to get a taxi back to Cubi, but to no avail. After several unsuccessful attempts, one of the aviators called the shore patrol and said, "All hell is breaking loose up here. Get the hell up here!" The police raced up to Balikitan, and when they went running inside the club, Munsinger and crew stole the shore patrol van to get back to Cubi. The driver revved up the engine, but instead of putting it in reverse, he drove forward, straight through the club's doors.

Other government clubs had similar catastrophes. The Cubi Point Officers Club was nearly destroyed on numerous occasions as a result of drunken melees. Aviators would routinely end up in fights with Marines or beat up on themselves. As soon as one punch went flying, the whole place would erupt into a brawl. It was common for the commander of an air wing to lead his men into the club and throw one to two thousand dollars on the bar to cover damages. One young lieutenant on *Kitty Hawk,* Tom O'Connor, had a penchant for throwing bar stools through plate-glass windows at the Cubi Officers Club. The display was as much an act of crazy machismo as it was an emotional outlet, a release from the daily dangers of flying over Vietnam, then coming back and trying to land on the flattop.

One rather destructive rough-and-tumble port call during the Vietnam War involved a previous visit by *Kitty Hawk.* After the carrier left the Philippines to return to the line in Vietnam, it received a message from the commanding officer of Cubi Point, itemizing $1,500 in damages to club property. The crew on *Kitty Hawk* responded by remitting a check in the amount of $3,000 and sending a message stating that $1,500 was for the last visit and $1,500 was for the next stopover.

The port calls got to be so rambunctious and destructive during the war that a special cinder-block annex to the Cubi Point Officers Club was built to accommodate the wild young warriors. It was virtually indestructible. Lights were protected by steel mesh, and the bar was made from solid wood. The annex was first called the "Red Horse" in honor of the Cubi Point commanding officer who ordered it built. In later years the fliers called it "the ready room," and some called it "the Tailhook Bar."

A small-scale catapult was built along the floor. The Navy men took a center-line gas tank from an F-4 Phantom and cut the top off of it so a cockpit seat could be placed inside. Compressed air propelled the unit down about forty feet of tracks that went through swinging barroom doors and into a small pond outside the cinder-block walls. The object of the ride was for the person sitting in the cockpit to drop a small tail hook and catch a wire before the tank blasted through the doors and splashed into the pond.

A couple of days after the carrier arrived in December 1972, the *Kitty Hawk*'s air wing was having a party in the Red Horse and giving the catapult a good workout. There were several hundred officers and about ten American schoolteachers and nurses, which made the women the center of attention. As the evening wore on, one attractive woman had managed to anger most of the Airedales by repeatedly asking to ride the catapult. So finally they strapped her in and sent her on her way down the rails. When she crashed through the swinging doors, most of the men in the air wing were standing around the pool urinating in the water that the woman was now falling head over heels into.

By 1986 the catapult was gone, but the P.I. was about as raunchy as it would ever get.[22]

The two Filipinas were swaying to the music as they moved toward a round table where a half-dozen naval officers were drinking San Miguel beer. The girls could not have been more than sixteen years old, if that. They wore spaghetti-thin G-strings that were wedged between their buttocks. A scanty tank top hemmed just below their bare breasts covered the upper portion of their bodies. The girlie-girls worked as hostesses at Marilyn's Super Inn, one of the many bars ringing the Subic Bay and Cubi Point Naval Bases that employed teenage females to entertain American military men. Navy men had a special title for the girls: "L.B.F.M.s—little brown fucking machines."

When the two young girls reached the table, they did not sit with the officers. Instead they got down on their hands and knees and crawled under the table. The officers, of course, knew what the girls were doing. That's how the game was played. One of the men at the table yelled, "Let's play smiles," and the officers placed their hands palm down on top of the wooden table, careful not to knock over the bottles of San Miguel.

Below the table, the two teenage Filipinas pulled the men's pants down to their ankles and stroked their genitals. As the girls went from one man to another, rubbing his penis and testicles, the men tried not to smile. That was the object of the game. After a few more minutes of fondling, the young girls each selected one man and performed oral copulation. Above the table, the two men tried to pretend as if nothing were happening. When it became obvious who was getting the blow job, one of the officers would yell and point and the table of men would explode in laughter.

Marilyn's was famous for this game of "smiles" from the Vietnam War up to the 1990s, when the U.S. military was forced out of its bases by the Philippine government. Marilyn's business cards were sort of a collector's item, popping up even in 1994 in the headquarters of the admiral in charge of the Navy's air forces in the Pacific. On the front side, the card read

Marilyn's Super Inn
And the original No. 1
home of the No. 1 cocksucker
in the Philippines
With some new super cocksuckers
just out of boot camp

On the backside of the card was the word "details." And below this were graphic descriptions of what kinds of sexual services the Navy men could buy: "titty chewing, inverted positions, dog fashion with barking and yelping," and so on.

About fifteen minutes from Marilyn's was New Jolo, another seedy establishment dubbed the "Peso Palace of the Far East." As the girlie-girls danced above them on a table, the Navy men would stack a handful of Philippine pesos on the rim of a beer bottle. Then one of the dancing girls, moving her hips to the beat of some pop tune that was blaring over the boom box, her legs opening and closing, would come toward the bottle of beer with pesos stacked ten deep. Positioned over the bottle, she did deep knee bends to the beat of the music, up, down, up, down. And with each pelvic thrust the coins began to disappear, one at a time, into her vagina.

At another table another group of Navy men drinking San Miguel were yelling at a young woman performing another vagina trick. White puffs of smoke drifted upward past her navel, each puff more pronounced as she flexed her labia, which held a lit cigarette. And if it wasn't a cigarette or coins stacked on a beer bottle that the Navy men came to see, it was a fish.

There was little sexual gratification in watching a dancing woman wrap a condom around a live fish, then insert it into her vagina and dance to the beat of the music, the tailfin flapping up and down as if the fish were hooked on a fisherman's line. It was more a matter of seeing firsthand something so freakish that most people when told about it couldn't believe it. And if the men got tired of sex shows, they would go to Pauline's and feed baby chicks to the three-foot-long alligators that were kept in a moat just inside the bar's entrance.

Subic Bay was the Navy's best kept secret. Although the admirals knew about the goings-on in town, few if anyone among the general public back in the United States were aware of what the sailors and officers of the Navy were doing on their liberty calls there. Certainly members of Congress, who funded the bases, did not know it was a rite of passage for young naval officers and enlisted personnel to be indoctrinated to the Philippines in places like Marilyn's or New Jolo.

The skipper of a squadron or ship would usually assign one or two officers to take a green officer out on the town for his baptism. The only Navy policy they had to follow was called the P.C.O.D., an acronym for "pussy cut-off date." Commanding officers used a simple formula to order their troops when to stop having sex with the local whores on a liberty call. Because it took on average thirty days to treat a case of venereal disease, the men had to stop screwing the whores in the Philippines thirty-one days before they would arrive home.

If the green officer and his sponsors didn't go to Marilyn's or the Peso Palace, they would drive to seamy Angeles, a town near Clark Air Force Base. By chopper it would take roughly ten minutes as the crow flies. Although the United States dumped between $150 and $200 million each year into Subic Bay's economy, the infrastructure, especially the roads, was typically Third World. The drive from Cubi Point to Clark took about one hour on a lousy road that twisted through areas that once had been nearly impassable jungle. There were one thousand such joints in Angeles, Subic City, and Olongapo, or PO City, as it was called, where a sailor would either get laid, get his pocket picked, or get hustled by some con man—that is if he was still walking after a night of drinking San Miguels or an evil concoction called a *mojo*, which turned timid men into "bulletproof" drunks. And intoxicated men fell prey to a host of evils, including the "Benny boys," teenage transvestites who prowled the streets offering sex on the cheap.

Also common were drinking contests in which teams of men had to drink so many pitchers of beer in a certain amount of time. The rules of the contest allowed participants to go to the bathroom, but only to urinate. If one person vomited, the whole team lost. It happened on several occasions that a flier would grab a pitcher of beer, drink it in one or two belts, then vomit back into the pitcher. Rather than lose the contest, the flier would drink his vomit, which was usually a mixture of beer and bile.

All that separated PO City from the Subic Bay Naval Base was a slow-running, shallow creek that served as a canal for the city's raw sewage to pass into the bay. The Americans called it "Shit River." And it was, perhaps, the most glaring symbol of the relationship between the affluent Americans and their impoverished Filipino hosts in Subic Bay. Every day children as young as ten years old loitered in boats below the bridge that spanned the feculent river, begging the rich Yankees for petty change. The beggars were nicknamed "Hey Joe boys" because they called all the Navy men Joe.

"Come on, Joe, throw me a peso, Joe."

"Don't be cheap, Joe, throw me a peso."

"Come on, Joe, don't be cheap bastard."

Two or three "Hey Joe boys" sat in canoelike Bonka boats some fifteen feet below the bridge, begging for change. Sometimes a teenage Filipina, in traditional dress, would stand in the boat and plead for money, too. "Hey, Joe. I love you, Joe. No shit. Throw me a peso, Joe, and I show you my tits."

The girl or a boy stood on the bow of the boat with a long-handled fishnet fashioned out of chicken wire that was used to snare the pesos. If they missed the coin, a little boy would be in the water in a second, searching through the filthy brown muck for this paltry bit of American charity.

It was a sobering experience for even the most hardened military personnel. A good many of the officers and sailors who crossed the bridge into Olongapo stared long and hard at the children. There was nothing like this back in the States, nothing like the "Hey Joe boys." Navy personnel often threw the children money and hoped like hell they caught it. If their limited generosity didn't assuage the Navy men's guilt, it served at least as a toll for entering the vile city of Olongapo, which the children called home.

When the Navy finally pulled out of the Philippines in the 1990s, the military men left behind thousands of Amerasian children. A good many were fathered on a rambunctious port call by a sailor who then sailed for home, never to return. During a return trip to the United States, a Navy ship's medical department would announce a "conscience call," so any last-minute cases of venereal disease picked up during liberty in the Philippines could be treated. Husbands and boyfriends lined up by the score in the gray catacombs of the ship.

On the trip home, commanding officers reminded their crews that "what you see over here, stays over here." The fact that their men might have gotten some teenage Filipina bar girl pregnant didn't enter into the equation. By and large, the children left behind by U.S. servicemen faced a miserable life of racism and ostracism because many were fathered by African Americans. The best an offspring of a Filipina and a Navy man had to look forward to, which was exceedingly rare, was a job as an entertainer. Although the Amerasians were cursed as illegitimate misfits in the conservative Filipino culture, they were usually blessed with beautiful features that served them well in the entertainment business. As fate would have it, however, their striking features also made them wanted commodities as prostitutes working in the bars or on the streets. That was the destiny of the majority of the bastard children. And over the years a rather unique class of people developed: prostitutes giving birth to children who would follow in their mothers' footsteps and would be, in turn, impregnated by American sailors and give birth to even more bastard children. By the time the Americans finally left in 1992, there were at least three generations of street kids who had grown up as male and female prostitutes working the bars around Subic Bay.

Not only did the Navy approve of the activity, it knowingly hired prostitutes to work in some of the Officers Clubs in the Philippines. Officially they were called hostesses. But the Navy men had another, more accurate term for the women: "hostitutes." They worked in the bars and clubs of the different bases, offering intercourse and a range of other sexual acts. At Cubi Point the women also worked as masseuses, where the Navy men would routinely ask for "a steam and a cream," a sauna or steambath and a massage, which included a hand job from the hostitute. At the bachelor officers quarters, a sign-up sheet for the women was provided to the men while on a layover in the Philippines.[23] And in 1991 a Navy commander handling a raffle to raise money for Navy police around Subic Bay made plans to provide a prostitute as one of the prizes.[24] Prostitutes also operated out of the Chief's Club, a bar for the noncommissioned officers.[25]

The Navy's unwillingness to discipline its troops in the Philippines led to serious social problems and enhanced stereotypical attitudes among the men that women were mere sex toys. The lack of discipline could also be deadly. In the mid-1980s two aviators showed up at the Cubi Point Air Station early one morning for a 7:30 flight. The officers had been up drinking and carousing all night and were still intoxicated when they climbed into their F-14 Tomcat. The takeoff went smoothly enough. But once airborne the aviators became disoriented, and, believing they were going to crash into a high mountain near the base, they both ejected. One man died almost instantly. The second officer was injured but alive when he came down in the dense jungle surrounding Cubi Point. There he soon bled to death. Ironically, one aviator's call sign was Masher.[26]

• • •

That Friday night in September 1986, John Lehman stepped off the elevator and onto the party floor of the Las Vegas Hilton. The inside of the X-shaped Hilton is a maze of dimly lit corridors about ten feet wide with low ceilings. They were more like tunnels than hallways in a fancy resort hotel. On the third floor a row of hospitality suites lined the long, dark corridor and faced out to a large patio deck with a nearby pool. Various aviation squadrons from Miramar to Whidbey Island and Norfolk to Cecil Field had rented the suites on the third floor and set up bars and other entertainment for the four-day Tailhook party.

Lehman was there to join the party, and, turning a corner, he walked head on into a tunnel filled with sweaty, smelly men spilling alcohol everywhere and on everybody. The hallway was the best way to get to the third-deck party, but at times it became so impassable that the Airedales dubbed the walk down the tunnel "running the gauntlet." As Lehman approached, the men made enough room for him to squeeze through toward the hospitality suites. A hooker was performing a strip-tease act in one of the suites to the whoops and hollers of the men inside. Lehman popped in, and it wasn't long before he was taking part in the show. He lay down on the floor beneath the naked dancer and placed a rolled-up dollar bill in his mouth. The women slowly gyrated her hips in a downward motion, with each thrust rewarded by a loud cheer from the men. Finally, her vagina resting on Lehman's face, she snatched the bill with her labia.

"That's what I call leadership," said Bob Lawson, a Tailhook official who witnessed the act. "It's just the wrong kind."

That same Friday night Lieutenant Roxanne Baxter, an attractive naval aviator, walked off the third-floor elevator and into the tunnel of sweaty, smelly men. Baxter was known as anything but a shrinking violet. She was a weight lifter and kept in top physical shape. And she had a reputation as a good aviator who could handle herself in the toughest situations. As she approached the hallway, the men standing along the walls made way for her. But when she started down the corridor, she felt a hand reach up her leg and grab her crotch.[27] She took a few more steps and then stopped as the gravity of what had just happened to her sank in. Then she turned sharply and eyed two officers whom she thought looked guilty. One of them smiled and pointed to the other officer. Baxter quickly walked up to the man and slammed him against the wall. At the same time she grabbed his balls as hard as she could. With her face inches from his, she stared at him and said, "How do you like it?"

≡ CHAPTER 18 ≡

"**I** SHOULD HAVE LISTENED TO YOU ABOUT LEHMAN," Cap Weinberger said, raising his eyebrows and wrinkling the lines across his forehead. He often made that face when he was saying something serious. And now, as he spoke with Michael Deaver, Weinberger was almost apologetic for picking Lehman as Navy secretary back in 1981. "I should have gone with Bob Nesen like you wanted to." [1]

Lehman had repeatedly pushed Weinberger's buttons, at times driving the usually passive secretary of defense to fits of anger. He would be the first to admit that Lehman's tenure had brought some high highs to the Navy and the nation. But there had also been some low lows that undermined the loftiest successes. Lehman's handling of the Walker spy case had been particularly hard on Weinberger. That was the last straw, and he had decided not to tolerate another of his affronts.

On Monday morning, February 16, 1987, Weinberger was sitting in his Pentagon office, again stewing over Lehman. This time the Navy secretary was meddling in the promotion process. Furious over the results of a selection board that chose commanders for advancement to the rank of captain, Lehman felt the board's chairman, Vice Admiral Bruce DeMars, the Navy's top submarine officer, had hand-picked too many nuclear submariners at the expense of aviators and ship drivers. [2] Unless DeMars backed down and added four officers favorable to Lehman in place of four submariners, he was going to dissolve the board and its findings. Lehman believed he had the right to do it under his secretarial powers, which he had, in fact, used to send back the results of six previous selection boards whose findings he did not like. And Mac Williams, Lehman's military lawyer, was firmly in his corner, offering a broad interpretation of the law to support him.

In the past, Hayward and Watkins had been unable to stop Lehman's domination of the promotion process. They had watched as the secretary used his powers to reward friends with good jobs or increases in rank. But now Carlisle Trost was determined to draw the line. [3] This was more than just a fight over a captains' selection board. It was a duel over who would control the Navy, Lehman or the CNO. For the last six years Lehman had

had his way, running roughshod over the admirals. Trost saw the careers of men he believed to be first-rate officers cut short for no other reason than politics. Lehman's dictatorial style, Trost believed, was to the detriment of the Navy, and this was a showdown he knew he had to wage. Lehman was vulnerable to charges that he had violated the law, and if Trost struck now, he might deal the secretary a fatal blow and win back the power usurped from the admirals. To DeMars Trost gave one important order: Do not back down. And above all else, don't compromise your principles. There were to be no deals.[4]

The final arbitrator in the bureaucratic war would be Weinberger. He was already peeved about Lehman dabbling in another, more important selection process in October, that of choosing Marine brigadier generals for the rank of major general (according to officers who worked with Weinberger and Lehman). A selection board picked eight generals but passed over two officers whom Lehman and P. X. Kelly thought should have been promoted. Lehman asked the board's chairman to add James Mead, an aviator, and Michael Sheridan, an infantry officer, to the list. The Senate had taken the matter under investigation, and the outcome did not look good. The Senate, in fact, would block the nominations.[5]

Weinberger had always shied away from confrontation, but he decided it was time to draw the line and find another secretary of the Navy. He telephoned Jim Webb, who was one of his favorite assistant secretaries of defense, and asked him over for a talk.

Webb walked into Weinberger's office a few minutes later and sat down. He was not a large man, but he had a commanding presence that almost everyone in a room could feel. As a Marine platoon leader in Vietnam, he had won the Navy Cross and the Silver Star (the second and third highest combat decorations), two Bronze Stars, and a Purple Heart. He had graduated from the Naval Academy in the class of 1968 with Ollie North. The two men had faced off in the finals of an intramural boxing tournament, and North had narrowly won the three-round match. After Vietnam Webb settled down to write novels, then strayed into journalism and became a success, winning an Emmy for television reporting from Beirut. In 1984 he joined Weinberger's staff as an assistant secretary for reserve affairs.

He was always tough, sometimes uncompromising, in his Pentagon post, which gave him a reputation as a hard-ass unwilling to listen to opposing views. It was not that he was stubborn, although he could be. Webb just abhorred decisions made solely for political reasons. But under the stern personality was an emotional man. He was a true believer in the nation he served and was passionate about the concept of duty, honor, country. He had grown to dislike Lehman for lacking two qualities he held most high: honesty and integrity. He was also irritated by Lehman's military record. Webb had put his life on the line several times in the Vietnam War and had been wounded. Lehman had popped in and popped out, never gutting it out in the trenches.

Webb at first had admired Lehman's zeal to rebuild the Navy. At one point he wrote a secret "Eyes Only" report for him titled "Future Use of Reserve Forces." "This is what I was doing while you were at the Army game," Webb said in his cover note to Lehman. "It was not much fun, but I think the Navy made out better here than they did in Philadelphia. Please hold this pretty close." [6] The report was controversial in that Webb recommended the "active Army and Air Force to be smaller, with a consequent rise in reserve forces, that the Marine Corps should essentially remain the same, with some focus on reserve missions, and that the Navy should continue to grow, both in active and reserve components." Webb also advocated that the United States wean itself from NATO. If the report leaked, he would have come under fire for taking sides with the Navy. Lehman read it and scribbled across the front page, "Good paper."

Slowly, however, Webb began to believe that Lehman's leadership style was doing more harm than good to the Navy. And finally Weinberger had come around to the same conclusion: Lehman had to go. Webb had known for some time that Weinberger was frustrated with Lehman. On several occasions Weinberger had told him the same thing he told Deaver.[7] Now he was turning to Webb and offering him the post of secretary of the Navy. You're the best man for the job, he said. Will you do it? Webb had planned to leave his assistant secretary's position to return to writing novels. But he could not refuse Weinberger's personal request.

That same day Weinberger called Reagan in the White House, informing him that he wanted Webb to replace Lehman. The President had no qualms about cutting Lehman loose or about Webb. If that's what you think is best, that is fine with me, Reagan told Weinberger. Publicly Reagan would offer the usual regrets about Lehman's departure. But privately he had grown tired of Lehman and the constant fights that the Navy secretary seemed always to be in.[8] Lehman said that Reagan had asked him to rescind his resignation threat over Trost's appointment as CNO, which he had.[9] But he had still made up his mind to leave and told Will Taft, one of Weinberger's top aides, that he would probably resign in the spring of 1987.

But that Monday, February 16, Lehman was watching the morning news while on a skiing vacation with his family in Sun Valley when he practically fell out of his seat.[10] A newscaster was saying that he had announced plans to leave the Pentagon. Weinberger, Lehman later said, had decided it was time for him to go and chose the date. At the same time, Weinberger's office leaked Webb's name as the administration's choice to be the next secretary of the Navy.

At a press conference the following day, Lehman said nothing about being shoved several months early from a post he described as "the best job in the world." Instead he took the high road, praising Weinberger. "We have essentially put in place the Six Hundred Ship Navy and restored the readiness of the fleet," he said, "and the training, and the morale, and the personnel, and the spare parts. The Navy is in very good shape. The Marine Corps is in very good shape, and so I think it's time to move on."

Although his personal relationship with Weinberger had remained friendly, his professional dealings with him had soured considerably. "I don't think Cap shed a lot of tears when I left," Lehman later recalled.[11] Even so, he said he would stay on a short while to help ease the transition to new leadership. Some saw the offer to help as more of a hindrance than a benefit and blamed Lehman for a host of roadblocks. Webb's paperwork was misplaced several times in the White House, which slowed down his nomination in the Senate. Trost's staff believed that Lehman was behind the snafu, that somehow he had gotten his allies in the administration to muck up the process. What troubled Webb more was Lehman's last-ditch efforts to leave his imprint on the Navy. P. X. Kelly's tour as Marine commandant was close to expiring, and Lehman wanted to pick his successor.

"Hey, I've got good news for you," he said to Webb. "You're going to help me name the next commandant. And you can name the next CNO."[12]

Webb was not about to acquiesce on such an important nomination. He wanted to shape his new team to his liking, not to his predecessor's. Webb knew that Lehman and Kelly wanted a Marine A-4 pilot whom Webb felt had a less than stellar record. "Wrong," Webb responded. "I'm going to name the next commandant." He wanted and got General Al Gray, a tobacco-chewing, crusty, old-style Leatherneck.

Lehman was not deterred. Dozens of new ships were slated to come off the building ways and had to be commissioned. Although many of the vessels would enter service under Webb, Lehman chose names for some and wrote several dozen letters to people promising to make them sponsors on commissioning day. And one of his final triumphs concerning new ships came as an unexpected surprise. Congress was so impressed with Lehman and George Sawyer's two-carrier deal with Newport News in 1982 that it appropriated enough money for two more carriers in the fiscal year 1988 budget. Before the congressional decision, Lehman would not have reached his magic number of fifteen carriers, which he had described as a litmus test for the success of his buildup.

No sooner had Webb blocked the Marine Corps power grab than Lehman set off on another spree. One infamous ploy became known as the "midnight massacre." Just days before he was to leave office, Lehman issued twelve far-reaching instructions to either reorganize or do away with whole departments of the Navy. The move caught Trost and Webb by surprise and caused general chaos in the commands on the chopping block.

At his last press conference, Lehman could not resist one parting shot at his old nemesis from Georgia, Sam Nunn, who was now the chairman of the Senate Armed Services Committee. A reporter, who knew that Lehman had sculled for Cambridge University, asked in jest who he thought would win this year's traditional race between Oxford and Cambridge. "Oxford," Lehman replied, "has as much chance of defeating Cambridge as Sam Nunn has of stopping my two new carriers." [13]

Trost heard the remark and was livid. He knew Nunn would rise above the fray, but it wouldn't help the Navy's cause on Capitol Hill to have the outgoing secretary challenge the lawmakers over an $8 billion contract. He couldn't wait for Lehman to be gone. Every day seemed to bring a new surprise and, to Trost, new embarrassment.

On April 10, after six years and two months, Lehman passed the Navy's helm to Webb. As he walked out of the Pentagon on his final day, he left behind a mixed legacy. He had come into office warning that the Soviets had surpassed the United States in naval power. For the Navy's downturn he had heaped blame on Jimmy Carter and his predecessors for building too few ships. The only way to correct that dangerous situation, he'd said, was to launch *his* multibillion-dollar Six Hundred Ship Navy. But he was never to reach that magical number. By using a clever counting strategy that included reserve forces and putting off the retirement of older vessels, Lehman would claim he had fallen just a few ships shy of six hundred when he retired.[14] In actuality, he fell about ninety vessels short. In fact, a Rand study later found that more ships were constructed in the mid-1970s than during Lehman's six years in office.[15] Still, he was able to get the Navy four new *Nimitz*-class carriers, which, at a cost of some $18 billion, was no minor feat.

But his biggest imprint was on the officers corps. Some saw him as the strongest secretary since James Forrestal, the "Driven Patriot" who had ruled over the naval empire in the 1940s. Others, like Trost, saw him as inherently evil, a complicated man on a constant drive for power. A good portion of the officers corps had a schizophrenic view of Lehman, seeing him as both a villain and a hero. Even those officers who fared poorly under him, like Tom Hayward, conceded the Navy reached a zenith in the 1980s under Lehman's leadership comparable to the high times at the turn of the century and during and after World War II. But the best indicator of how the brass felt about him came at Lehman's final secretarial function, a farewell dinner hosted by P. X. Kelly and the Marines. The Navy's admirals declined their invitations.

• • •

On Monday, April 27, Carlisle Trost sat down with a reporter from Cox News Service, the owner of the Southern newspaper the *Atlanta Journal Constitution*. It was not coincidental that he chose Georgia's leading paper for one of the few interviews he granted the press.[16] He planned to set the record straight about Lehman's comments concerning Sam Nunn.

The Navy's public affairs office usually trained the admirals in how to deal with the media before an interview. They would bring in an admiral and pepper him with the most innocuous questions. Always, the public affairs people took an "us versus them" attitude and warned the admirals that reporters were dishonest sleuths trying to score a big story at the Navy's expense. It was better to avoid interviews than risk the embarrassment of saying something stupid. But Trost, angry over the shots at Nunn, was not about to mince his words. He had no problem with telling the reporter that Lehman's departure was "like a fresh breeze."

There was more to come. Not a few minutes had gone by before Trost dropped a "holy shit" line. "John Lehman," he said, "was not a balanced human being. The things that annoyed people about John Lehman were his disdain of senior military personnel, his tendency to override anyone who had a disagreement with him or contrary thought, and his habit of playing favorites. 'Play ball with me and you'll do well. Don't play ball with me and you're out.' There was a saying he had: 'Loyalty is agreeing with me.' Well, that's not the military definition of loyalty. Loyalty is not to the individual, but to the service." [17]

As for Lehman's dig at Nunn, the CNO was equally caustic. "Comments like that do damage because it appears he is the spokesman for guys like me. Well, he is not. Nor was he the spokesman for his successor. For a man to do that just a few days before he leaves office is like tossing down the gauntlet and not sticking around for the fight."

Lehman could never understand why Trost, a man he once called "just another fucking Boy Scout," was so bitterly hostile to him. He held no personal animosities against Trost or his fellow admirals. Lehman's attitude was that Navy politics was a rough-and-tumble business. Feelings might get bruised, but at the end of the day everyone should get together for a beer and laugh over their daily battles. It was an odd perception, and few of the admirals really understood it. By the time Lehman left, the majority of admirals, with the exception of those he heaped praise on, wanted nothing more to do with him.

After Lehman heard about Trost's remarks, he practiced one of his own commandments: When attacked, attack back. "I felt like the retiring marshal of the Old West, backing out of the saloon with guns blazing because every punk wants to take a shot at him on the way out. Sad to say, Carl Trost was among them, as we have seen." [18]

• • •

On a warm fall day in 1987, Jim Webb left the Pentagon and traveled east
to Annapolis. It was September 30, and Webb was to deliver a speech as
part of the Forrestal lectures on leadership at the Naval Academy. Webb was
as frank in his public speeches as he was in private conversations. He made
no secret of his opposition to broadening the role of women in the military
and was adamantly against putting female troops in combat units. And he
was adamantly against mixing men and women at his alma mater, the Naval
Academy on the banks of the glassy Severn River. He felt women did not
belong in the service academies because their presence softened the training
necessary to condition men for leadership in combat. Webb was still of the
mind that the academy trained iron men for wooden ships.

In the weeks leading up to his visit, word had circled among the female
midshipmen that the new secretary was coming to speak. The women wanted
to protest but knew a public march or demonstration would not be tolerated.
So they decided on something a little more subtle that was sure to make their
point. Early in the morning, just before Webb was due to arrive at the
academy, the women littered the grounds with bras and panties and other
lingerie.[19] The Public Works Department was still picking up the underwear
as Webb drove to Bancroft Hall.

Webb's opposition to women was embraced by an informal group of male
midshipmen who called themselves "Webbites."[20] For them, Webb was
right on the money when he referred to female midshipmen as "thunder
thighs" during his remarks about women at the academy. The Webbites
grew into a secret organization called the WUBA Klux Klan, whose goal
was to rid the Naval Academy of women. WUBA was an acronym for the
uniforms of the first female midshipmen: women's uniform blue alpha. The
male midshipmen had another interpretation of WUBA: women used by all.
Other WUBA jokes also circulated among the groups of midshipmen.

How are a WUBA and a bowling ball similar?
You pick them up, put three fingers in them, and throw them in
the gutter.

What do you call a mid who fucks a WUBA?
Too lazy to beat off.

Several men in the class of '79, who graduated before women became
integrated at the academy, were going to inscribe on their class rings LCWB
—last class with balls. At the last minute they changed it to *Omnes Viri*,
Latin for "All Male." And the majority of the men at the academy took part

in abusive and vulgar "cadence calls," commonly referred to as marching chants in the Navy and "jodies" in the Army. The songs glorified violence toward women and, although outlawed by the Navy, were never far from the male midshipmen's lips. Members of the Male Glee Club, for example, a group of goodwill ambassadors for the Naval Academy, used to sing a lurid variation of "The Candy Man" on bus trips:

THE S&M MAN

Who can take a chain saw,
Cut the bitch in two,
Fuck the bottom half
and give the upper half to you. . . .

The S&M Man, the S&M Man
The S&M Man 'cause he mixes it with love
and makes the hurt feel good!

Who can take a bicycle,
Then take off the seat,
Set his girlfriend on it
Ride her down a bumpy street. . . .

Who can take an ice pick
Ram it through her ear
Ride her like a Harley,
As you fuck her from the rear. . . .

By the time Webb became secretary, the Navy had ample evidence that the assimilation of women at the academy had yet to achieve any true level of success. Under Lehman the Navy had commissioned a study that examined the adaptation of female midshipmen to academy life since eighty-one women arrived on July 6, 1976, as the first plebes in the history of Annapolis. The findings, which were based on a ten-year period, were to be released in 1986. But when the data were pulled together, the information was not exactly what the Navy considered good public relations. Instead of women being integrated into the system, the report found that they were more isolated than at any time since they first entered the male-run institution. According to Carol Burke, a professor at the Naval Academy, rather than release it, the Navy squashed the report.[21]

It was not just at the academy, or once a year at the Tailhook convention, that an antifemale attitude flourished in the Navy. Although there has been a long history attached to the legend about a sailor having a girl in every port, before Vietnam Navy men by and large still treated women with old-school charm and respect. Vietnam, with all of the emotional baggage it carried for the men fighting there, was a turning point for how naval personnel treated women. In the years following the war, male attitudes toward women in the Navy became more and more hostile. That women broke through the gender gap at the Naval Academy was seen in 1976 as a setback that had to be revenged. Academy graduates carried their beliefs into the fleet, where women sailors and officers were treated as second-rate individuals. Books like *The Hunt for Red October* and the movie *Top Gun* only bolstered their belief that the Navy was a service for supermen.

Women were often the target of petty pranks. Male pilots drenched sanitary napkins in ketchup, then taped them to the controls of the helicopter to be flown later that day by the Navy's first two female pilots. On another occasion male officers hoisted a woman's bra up the mast. One of the first female fighter pilots, Mary Lou Jorgensen, was given the call sign "Jugs" by the Airedales at Miramar, where she was stationed in the mid-1980s. On one mission Jorgensen was assigned to fly a tanker that gassed up the fighters. During an in-flight refueling practice, when the jet's male nozzle made contact with the female basket, a pilot from the *Constellation* on the receiving end radioed over to Jorgensen. "I'm having a hard time getting it in," he said. "Oh, it's in now. I'm going to push it in farther and farther. Oh, it's in all the way now. Is it as good for you as it is for me?" [22] On another occasion Jorgensen was flying the aircraft that pulled a target for aviators to practice shooting at. One aviator missed the target and nearly struck Jorgensen's aircraft, which won him a strong rebuke. "Geez, Jugs," the pilot quipped, "you're supposed to pull the rag, not wear it."

Jorgensen dealt with the male machismo and sexism like many other female officers: it was better to act like the men than fight them. Roxanne Baxter, who had been assaulted earlier at Tailhook, ended up one summer as the only woman on *Constellation* for a cruise in the North Pacific. On board she heard through the grapevine that the male officers planned to lampoon her during a skit to be performed as part of the *Fo'c's'le Follies,* a traditional ceremony on board attended by the carrier's captain and the admiral in charge of the battle group.

The first skit was the "butt brothers." The bare rear ends of two officers protruded through a sheet and spoke to each other as if they were talking heads. One of the butt brothers was an angel, the other was a devil. Sitting beneath the two rear ends was a male officer wearing a mop for a blond wig. He was supposed to be Baxter, who was imagining the conversation between the two butt brothers.

"Oh, that wing commander, he's so cute," the angel butt said.

"Fuck him, fuck him, fuck him," the devil butt said, encouraging Baxter to have sex with the wing commander.

Then Baxter herself took the stage. She was dressed in her green flight suit and stuffed the arms to mimic one of the muscular pilots with the call sign "Flex." "Are there any A-6 pilots out here?" she asked. When the aviators roared back, Baxter grabbed her crotch. "Oh, yeah! Oh, yeah! I need a package check," she said, which was slang for having a woman grab a man's penis and testicles.[23] Then she unzipped the bottom portion of her flight suit and pulled out a squadron drinking flag that she had stolen earlier and gave it back to the cheering fliers.

"I got lewd just to give it back to them," she later recalled. "I wasn't going to let these bastards think that they were going to knock me down and make me cry. In some ways I won a lot of respect. But I lost some respect with myself for doing that. But that's what they want."[24]

Early in his first year on the job, Webb got a call from the Naval Investigative Service, the sleuthing agency that Lehman liked to call the Admiral's Gestapo. The NIS wanted to know if he could clear a sizable block of time on his calendar for a briefing about Mel Paisley and an investigation codenamed Operation Ill Wind. Sure, Webb said, come on up.

Paisley had left office several weeks prior to Lehman's departure. But before he retired from government service to head his own defense consulting firm, Lehman had allowed him to keep his top secret security clearances. He still had access to information concerning the most supersecret black programs and to procurement decisions being made that affected scores of industry contractors. The deal, which gave him valuable inside data, ensured he would have a considerable leg up on his competitors.

One of the NIS's leading fraud experts, Byron Taylor, who walked into Webb's office with other investigators, stressed one thing: secrecy. The agents swore the secretary of the Navy to silence. It had to be that way if Ill Wind was to succeed. Weinberger did not know about it. Attorney General Ed Meese was clueless, despite the fact that the FBI was extensively involved. Even Lehman had been kept in the dark. Nobody but those with an absolute need to know had been told.

Taylor said more than seventy-eight FBI agents and fifteen NIS agents were involved in the case. They had wiretaps on the telephones of high-ranking Pentagon officials, big-money consultants, and employees of some twenty defense contractors, including the nation's largest firms. They had cast a wide net over twelve states to determine if Paisley and other former Pentagon officials, who were now private consultants, were bribing Defense Department procurement officials to help clients obtain government contracts. The investigators, working with the U.S. Attorney's Office in Virginia, were preparing 275 subpoenas. It was shaping up to be the largest white-collar crime case in history. Some investigators even began saying it would dwarf the Wall Street insider trading scandal that had netted Michael Milken and Ivan Boesky. The man at the center of this scandal, Taylor said, was Mel Paisley. The government had bugged his consulting office and tapped his telephone. There was no doubt that he was in it up to his ears. So too were other Navy officials.

When the meeting concluded, Webb was seething. How could this have happened? How could Lehman have set up such an arrangement for Paisley to retain his security clearances? The cushy deal might not have been illegal, but it certainly was unethical. Webb immediately canceled Paisley's security clearances, using the excuse that it was an out-of-the-ordinary arrangement not afforded to other former Pentagon employees. Webb kept his promise and didn't tell anyone.

The following year, on June 14, FBI and NIS agents searched thirty-eight offices and homes of defense contractors, consultants, and Pentagon employees in the twelve states under scrutiny. Even Pentagon offices were included in the dragnet. And a handful of members of Congress became suspects as well. Before charges were filed against anyone, James Exon, the conservative Democratic senator from Nebraska, said, "I want to see somebody go to jail." [25]

Within a week of the raids, Lehman's name surfaced as a target of the investigation. *The Washington Post* reported that he might have tipped Paisley off that he was the subject of a federal investigation. Lehman himself had grown suspicious that his telephone was being tapped. He even suspected that he was being followed by government gumshoes.

The *Post* story was only the first shot. In the following months Lehman's name stayed on the front pages as the scandal continued to unfold. The media homed in on the procurement changes that he had installed to make it easier to build the Six Hundred Ship Navy. His reforms of the system, which included eliminating the Naval Material Command, increased competition among defense contractors and gave more power to a handful of Lehman aides like Paisley. It was such a move, the pundits claimed, that had opened the door for the corruption now being investigated by the Justice Department. Mel Paisley and sixty-seven others were convicted on various counts of bribery and conspiracy to commit theft. Paisley was sentenced to forty-eight months and sent to the federal prison camp at Nellis Air Force Base in the Nevada desert. In the end, despite all the adverse publicity, Lehman was never charged with any wrongdoing. But the procurement scandal was just the first of his "legacies."

CHAPTER 19

A<small>T</small> 3 P.M. on June 18, 1987, Ace Lyons closed his office door and wheeled around to face the secretary of defense, who was sitting by the old Nimitz desk. Weinberger had arrived earlier that day in Hawaii and had been chauffeured over to the Pacific Fleet headquarters for a private meeting with Lyons. It wasn't long before their conversation turned to a top secret plan to attack Iran that Lyons called "Window of Opportunity."[1]

Lyons, with Admiral Bill Crowe's approval, had begun building the plan nine months earlier. And along the way he routinely passed on updates to Crowe without telling others in his chain of command about the plan's contents.[2] At the low end of the war-fighting threshold, Crowe wanted the Navy to run a series of secret naval operations to intimidate Iran, similar to the in-your-face exercises used against the Soviet Union and Libya. At the high end of the spectrum, which Lyons favored, was a full-fledged, massive attack. He even picked a date for the war to begin: August 26.[3]

With the decline of the Soviet navy, Iran had become a top priority to Lyons and other admirals like Crowe, who believed in aggressive, forward-deployed naval operations. Iran was where the action was, and Lyons and the others wanted a piece of it. Iran and Iraq had been fighting a bloody land war since September 1980. In 1983 the battle moved to the sea, with Iran blockading Iraqi ports in the vital Persian Gulf. Iraq retaliated by attacking merchant vessels and issuing a warning for neutral ships to stay clear of the war zone. Both sides had strewn the northern gulf with antiship mines, which made navigation treacherous. And Iran had upped the ante by placing Chinese-made Silkworm missiles around the narrow Strait of Hormuz at the mouth of the gulf. The religious mullahs in Tehran now had the ability to close down the strait and cut off a sizable percentage of the world's oil flow.

From his command post in the hills above Pearl Harbor, Lyons had followed the fighting with alarm. Aggression was building, and the war was spreading. He warned whoever would listen that American security interests, spelled out in the Carter Doctrine, would soon be threatened and that the United States was slowly being dragged into the Persian Gulf quagmire. War, Lyons strongly believed, was inevitable. And if that was the case, the

United States should wage it on its own terms. Over the last year he and Crowe had exchanged numerous telephone calls between the Pentagon and Pearl Harbor to discuss what should be done in regard to Iran.

Crowe was in a tough spot. Publicly the United States was taking a neutral position on the war, describing it as a regional conflict between two nations that had no diplomatic relations with Washington. But privately the mood in the Pentagon and the administration had turned jingoistic toward Tehran. With the Iran-contra scandal beginning to spiral out of control, the administration had shifted toward Iraq, even providing it with targeting data and other military intelligence. Although no one would say so publicly, what many in the administration wanted was to pick a fight with the Shiite state. A lot of people, including Lyons, still grumbled about the overthrow of the shah, American citizens being taken hostage, and the humiliation of the failed raid to rescue them. Lyons and many of his fellow officers stationed in the Pentagon wanted to settle the score. All sorts of ideas were floating around about how to do it. But Lyons's was one of the boldest. He was a pro at preparing for a war and how to fight it. This much Crowe knew. It wouldn't hurt to get something down on paper.[4] So he gave Lyons the go-ahead.

Now Weinberger was in Lyons's office, waiting for the commander in chief of the Pacific Fleet to begin his brief. Lyons dropped his large frame onto a nearby chair. In the back of the room, Kevin Healy also sat down and prepared to quietly take notes on the conversation. In 1982, before going to work with Lyons, he had served as an assistant to the chairman of the Joint Chiefs of Staff. He had heard all the stories that Lyons was a bull in a china shop who left a trail of broken glass wherever he went. Healy knew that Lyons may have been out of control at times, but he got the job done, and in a war that's what mattered. Healy only shrugged his shoulders as Lyons systematically alienated the Pentagon's brass, especially the CNO, Carlisle Trost.

Weinberger knew the stories, too. And on more than one occasion he had been left to pick up the pieces. To Weinberger, Lyons was a loose cannon. To Lyons, Weinberger was a peacenik. He disliked his penchant for wanting to resolve a conflict with diplomacy rather than military force. He thought Weinberger was the wrong man for the defense secretary's job, and that he and the bullish secretary of state, George Shultz, should switch cabinet posts. Shultz was due to arrive in Pearl Harbor in five days and was scheduled for an hour-long visit with Lyons.[5] A former Marine, Shultz was tough and understood the value of military power as an instrument of foreign policy.

But Weinberger had surprised many of his critics in April by agreeing to let Navy ships protect Kuwaiti oil tankers sailing in and out of the Persian

Gulf. Lyons thought the idea, dubbed Earnest Will, was fraught with problems and railed against it to the press, which angered Weinberger. Lyons
said it would be better for the oil tankers to dock in Saudi Arabia and stay
away from Kuwait and the northern gulf, which was being mined constantly
by the Iranians. Another danger, although minor, was that the Iranians were
using speedboats armed with an assortment of mortars, rocket-propelled
grenades, and small machine guns to harass merchant ships. But the escort
mission did offer some benefits that could dovetail nicely with Lyons's battle
plan. If Iran attacked a Navy-escorted tanker, it could serve as an excuse to
hit back with overwhelming force. Lyons knew that using an excuse made
good political sense. But in his heart he felt the United States already had
enough reason to flatten Iran. He still fumed over the 241 Marines killed in
the bombing of their barracks in Beirut. As far as he was concerned, the
Iranians should have to pay for that. And he had just the plan to do it.

Lyons began drafting Window of Opportunity after U.S. intelligence inter-
cepted an Iranian message reporting that Tehran could tolerate a tit-for-tat
fight with the United States, a low-intensity struggle that was nothing more
than a series of minor skirmishes.[6] But Lyons seized on another part of the
intercept that reported that the Iranians could not afford to get into a long,
protracted war with the United States. "They were not prepared for what I
was doing," he said later.

"We could shut off 70 percent of their import and export in three days,"
Lyons told Weinberger.[7] The best time to strike was in sixty-nine days,
between August 26 and 28. At least two carriers, Constellation and Ranger,
and their battle groups, as well as a battleship task force, would then be on
station in the northern Arabian Sea. The French, he said, would be there,
too, and were offering a carrier and its aircraft in support of the operation.
The Navy, under Lyons's direction, was already providing targeting data to
the French. Although more firepower was not needed, Lyons was hoping to
augment that force by two additional carriers and would choose Kitty Hawk,
Enterprise, or Midway.

"We weren't screwing around," he said years later. "We were going
after them. We were going to mine their ports, go after their power grids.
We were going to march up the gulf." Of Iran's only, inoperable nuclear
power plant, Lyons said, "I was going to take it out for good measure. It
was the whole shebang. I was going to shut down Iran."[8]

Even before he briefed Weinberger, Navy pilots had already been in
action over Iran. One of the Navy's two covert P-3 reconnaissance squadrons
had been taking photographs of the Silkworm sites, which were deployed in
a horseshoe pattern around Bandar Abbas. The missions were dangerous. The
P-3s had to fly along Iran's coastline, and they were unarmed and terribly slow.
To protect them, Lyons ordered three F-14 fighters to ride shotgun on each

photo mission. The fighters were also probing Iranian air defenses to determine how quickly Iran could scramble its warplanes to intercept the F-14s.[9] As it turned out, the response time was not very good, primarily because most of their assets were in the north for the war with Iraq.

The photographs of the Silkworm sites were used to construct exact replicas of the missile launchers. And Navy pilots were carrying out practice strikes on the mock Silkworm batteries, preparing for the real thing. The Navy, Lyons told Weinberger, was ready to go. "We're going to strike a blow for freedom," he said. "It may even bring down the Khomeini regime."

Weinberger's reaction was perplexing. He just sat there, not taking notes, saying little, and looking at Lyons. When he left, one thing was clear: Lyons and the Navy were itching to start a war with the Iranians. And in the weeks after Weinberger's visit, Lyons grew impatient. He had yet to get the go-ahead from the Pentagon. Even Crowe, for all his earlier gusto, was hesitant. "I'm not sure how far he wanted to go," Lyons later recalled. "Crowe thought we were asking a lot of the President because of Iran-contra." [10]

Despite no formal approval from Washington for an all-out slugfest, Crowe and Lyons continued their back-channel dialogue about conducting some secret naval operations in the Persian Gulf. And although Lyons was dismayed about Weinberger and Crowe dragging their feet, he forged ahead anyway with his plans to bomb Iran into the stone age.

A month after Weinberger left Pearl Harbor, Jim Webb made the ten-hour trip out to Hawaii to meet with Lyons for a one-on-one talk. Lyons and his staff were not enamored with Webb; they believed that he had turned on Lehman and was not up to being secretary of the Navy. When Webb came through the Pacific, Lyons's staff referred to the jaunts as "amateur hour," complaining that he spent more time going to World War II battle sites than he did meeting with heads of state, some of whom felt snubbed.

Lyons briefed Webb on his plan to shut down the Persian Gulf. Impressed, Webb offered him an open door: If you ever have to speak with me directly *on anything,* call me. Lyons interpreted the message as a clear sign not to worry about the chain of command. And he quickly took Webb up on his offer. He drafted a lengthy report on his views about how the Navy should run its operations in the Persian Gulf. It was a thought-provoking analysis, which Lyons shared with some close friends, primarily for critical input. When he felt comfortable with it, he sent it off to Washington.

• • •

At 1:45 on August 4, Kevin Healy put the telephone caller on hold, then quickly walked the few steps from his office over to see Lyons. "Chairman's on the line," he said.

As Healy headed back to his office, he could hear Lyons's loud voice boom, "Bill, how are you?" when Crowe came on the line. A few seconds later Healy was at his desk. He picked up the telephone receiver and began taking copious notes on the conversation between Crowe and Lyons now under way. It was not an uncommon practice for the admirals to have their aides monitor communications and keep an almost word-for-word log. It was done as an insurance policy to protect themselves if some decision blew up and the Navy was looking for a scapegoat. Many of the Navy's most critical decisions made by the top admirals were reached during private telephone conversations or through personal correspondence to each other, known as P-Fors. These rarely were seen by anyone but the sender and the recipient. And after being read, they were sent to irretrievable archives or destroyed. Like the verbal communications, they left a shadowy trail.

Healy had monitored many of the telephone conversations between Crowe and Lyons. Most of them, which were kept secret from the chairman's staff,[11] had to do with the deployment of naval forces. Lately Crowe had been calling about ship movements to Iran. Today, in early August, he wanted to ask Lyons a favor. "I need the *Guadalcanal* up in the gulf," Crowe said, referring to the Navy's amphibious assault ship, which could carry a battalion of Marines and thirty-one minesweeping helicopters.[12] But Lyons was dead set against sending the giant ship into a hostile environment, fearing it would be a sitting duck without support. He argued for several minutes about why it made no sense to put one amphib, which had little offensive punch and even less defensive capability, inside the gulf.[13]

"I got to have it," Crowe said. He told Lyons that Marine General George Crist of the Florida-based central command, which was responsible for the Middle East, desperately wanted the vessel. "Crist is giving me all sorts of fits," Crowe said. That July, one of the Kuwaiti oil tankers, now flying the Stars and Stripes as part of the tanker escort mission, had hit a mine. Crist needed some antimine equipment right away, and *Guadalcanal,* with its fleet of helicopters, was the best solution. But he wanted to take the Marine battalion off and just use the ship for a helicopter platform. Lyons argued that the Marines were needed aboard to protect the ship, and Crist would finally agree to that.

"Okay, I'll do it," Lyons told Crowe. "But I do not want any messages, because if you send me a message, we will read about it in the press, and that will complicate and compromise this transit. You can't tell anybody. I'm not telling Hays."[14]

Lyons had been having problems with Ron Hays, who was now commander in chief of all U.S. forces in Asia and the Pacific and therefore Lyons's operational boss. Lyons thought Hays, who had fretted over the Libyan shoot-down six years earlier when he'd commanded U.S. naval forces in Europe, was unwilling to take chances. And Lyons and Crowe had already cut Hays out of several operations because they were concerned about leaks from his staff that would muck up the secret missions they were planning. "You have to cover me on this," Lyons finally said. "If I told CinCPac, the headquarters would leak everything." Crowe agreed.[15]

Then Lyons devised a plan to keep *Guadalcanal*'s transit secret and sail the ship through the Strait of Hormuz at night. He had his staff put out bogus reports that the ship had broken down with engineering problems and was stuck in Diego Garcia, the Navy and Air Force base in the middle of the Indian Ocean. Then he had the ship rigged with running lights to make it look like an oil tanker. "The long and short of it is," Lyons later said, "I snuck the goddamn thing in there before anybody knew what happened, including the Iranians."[16] *Guadalcanal*'s main mission would not be just to sweep for mines. It was to serve as a platform for a secret Army helicopter squadron that was sent to the Persian Gulf to covertly hunt Iranian mine-laying ships at night.

That was not the only highly classified adventure under way that summer to deal with the Iranian threat in the Persian Gulf. Crowe, Lyons, and several other Pentagon officials had also put together an even more elaborate, hush-hush scheme. In June 1986 Crowe had called Lyons, asking if he could ship some SEAL patrol boats that had been used in Vietnam's rivers during the war, up to Travis Air Force Base in Northern California. There, a giant C-5 cargo plane would fly them to the Persian Gulf. Lyons warned that the small vessels, called PBRs, were too slow to keep up with the Iranian speedboats. But Crowe persisted, and Lyons shipped the boats north from San Diego. Also sent on the C-5 were five Stinger teams.[17] While the SEALs would hunt down the Iranian speedboats, the Stinger teams, trained to fire the handheld antiaircraft Stinger missile, would guard against any low-flying enemy aircraft. The special units would operate from both *Guadalcanal*'s decks and a giant barge that the Kuwaitis had paid for. The whole mission was top secret, and only a handful of Pentagon and administration officials were on a "need to know" list. Crowe, who had sanctioned the secret naval operations, ordered Lyons not to tell anyone.[18]

That summer another sensitive issue came up. The Navy ships in the gulf were carrying nuclear weapons; what would happen if one of those ships was struck by a hostile missile? Nobody really wanted to find out how big the kaboom would be. A nuclear explosion in the small Persian Gulf could be a nightmare, potentially killing large numbers of people. The Navy immediately dispatched a series of top secret messages ordering all ships in the gulf to unload their weapons of mass destruction.

While the Navy ships were unloading the nukes, Lyons sent orders to have 50-caliber machine guns mounted on each vessel. It was yet another effort to compensate for the Navy's lack of equipment to deal with the fast-moving Iranian speedboats. He also had the ships that were outfitted with the Vulcan antiaircraft gun, which shot four thousand rounds a minute, reconfigure the close-in weapons so they could strafe objects on the water. If the gun made contact with a speedboat, it would cut it, and its occupants, into tiny little pieces.

When Hays was finally informed of the secret back-channel communications between Crowe and Lyons, he was stunned. He had known and respected Lyons for much of his naval career. The same went for Crowe. But he also knew that Crowe's flair for secrecy and Lyons's reputation as a loose cannon were a combination that could easily lead to his being excluded from some of the more controversial operations in the gulf. "What Admiral Lyons was doing," Hays recalled, "was cutting out his operational commander. There was a clear pattern of that. Onetime oversight would have been understandable, but a clear pattern that was established is unacceptable." [19] And yes, Hays said, the chairman of the Joint Chiefs of Staff was also to blame. "You see, CinCPac is the immediate superior to CincPacFlt. Not Bill Crowe."

On August 8, a little more than two weeks before Lyons's Window of Opportunity would open, *Constellation* was steaming in the north Arabian Sea, just off the Iranian coastline. Phil Anselmo, the carrier's skipper, sat on his captain's chair on the bridge, watching his men below prepare for another day of flight operations. Ace Lyons was soon due to arrive on board. He planned to personally hand-carry his battle plan to Anselmo and Rear Admiral Lyle Bull, the commander of the task force. Anselmo was a former New York schoolteacher who gave up the education field to fly as a radar intercept officer in an F-14. A dead ringer for New York senator Alfonse D'Amato and with a Bronx accent to boot, Anselmo would soon enter the fraternity of admirals. Lyons liked him and viewed him as one of the few true war fighters in the Navy. Anselmo was not afraid to make a decision, even if it meant sending his pilots into a war.

Lyle Bull ran the battle group from below decks in *Constellation*'s Flag Plot. He was something of a legend within the aviation community. As an attack pilot in Vietnam, he had won fame and the Distinguished Flying Cross for a daring raid on downtown Hanoi. He was hard-nosed, brutally up front, and a man who had little fear of death or the politically correct in Washington. He had recently left the Pentagon, where he was as frustrated with the bureaucracy as Ace Lyons was. But the two men had much more in common than their distaste for Washington politics. Both were old-school warriors who felt many of the Navy's admirals were "desk jockeys" winning their stars as staff officers inside the Washington Beltway. Both men had the foul mouths and abrasive personalities of longshoremen. And both were not beyond sharing in a hard night of partying with their men.

Bull's troops worshiped him. He was the kind of officer who would not ask his men to do something that he had not done first. The junior officers saw him as a true leader, an admiral who led from the front, not from the rear. As a tribute to him, the Airedales on *Constellation* put together a racy little publication they called *Bull's Brigade Song Book*. When the book came off *Constellation*'s printing presses, it contained forty songs collected over the years by both Navy and Air Force aviators. Many of the tunes were sung by Bull and the officers when they pulled into port or at other gatherings like Tailhook.[20] Lyle Bull liked one ballad called "I Love My Wife":[21]

> I love my wife, yes I do, yes I do.
> I love her truly.
> I love the hole that she pisses through,
> I love her ruby red lips
>   and her lily white tits
>   And the hair around her ass hole.
> I'd eat her shit
>   gobble, gobble, gobble, chomp.
> With a rusty spoon . . . with a rusty spoon.

Another favorite among many of the fliers was "Nellie Darling":

> Oh, your ass is like a stovepipe, Nellie darling, And the nipples on
>   your tits are turning green.
> There's a yard of lint protruding from your navel, you're the ugliest
>   fucking bitch I've ever seen.
> There's a million crabs abounding 'round your pussy, when you piss,
>   you piss a stream [as] green as grass.
> There's enough wax in your ears to make a candle, so kindly make
>   one, dear, and shove it up your ass.

The songbook may not have been issued as part of every sailor's ditty bag, but it made its way through the officers corps and became something of a collector's item four years later at the height of the Tailhook scandal. Naval aviators thought the title, *Bull's Brigade,* was fitting. They believed Bull truly understood what made them tick and why they had such an attraction to heavy drinking and unusual sexual fantasies. They felt that each time they went aloft, they were cheating death. And they were proud of the fact that they lived dangerously. It was the glue of their camaraderie and the main reason for their lust. Bull was one of them and understood how real their fears could be and how difficult it was for male aviators to express them. Navy psychiatrists had even tried to explain the emotional makeup of a flier in an internal study titled "Sex and the Naval Aviator." It was so provocative that the Navy decided not to release it.

Phil Anselmo, *Constellation*'s skipper, certainly knew the dangers of naval aviation. As the commander of a floating city with five thousand sailors and officers, every day in the unpredictable Middle East was fraught with new problems and uncertainties. Recent intelligence reports warned that Navy ships might be the target of small private planes packed with explosives. Terrorists had detonated a Mercedes-Benz full of TNT at an American target more than once on the ground in Beirut and gotten away with it. Why not try the same strategy in the air? For the Navy, the threat was troubling. The Navy had to have clear-cut proof that a Cessna or Piper Seneca flying near one of its ships was on a suicide mission before it could even contemplate taking some action to shoot it down. But if it waited too long, and the small plane was indeed packed with explosives, it might be too late to avoid a catastrophe. Intelligence reports also suggested that Iranian F-4 Phantoms often hid behind a commercial airliner to mask them from radar. Then they would suddenly break out, trying to take advantage of the element of surprise. The Navy's rules of engagement put into place as part of Earnest Will allowed fighter pilots to shoot down an aircraft they deemed hostile. But if the plane turned for home, U.S. pilots had to break off the attack. American aviators were hoping they could squeeze off a shot before the Iranian pilots could turn and run.

Another problem that Anselmo faced was simple logistics. His airplanes were flying the majority of their missions inside the Persian Gulf while *Constellation* steamed outside in the Gulf of Oman. A long-standing Navy policy restricted its carriers from operating inside the narrow and shallow Persian Gulf. Besides the navigation problems, the Navy feared that the narrow waterway would hinder a carrier's mobility, thus making it vulnerable to enemy aircraft and missiles. The steadfast rule meant the ship's crew had to work that much harder to keep the airplanes flying for extended periods of time.

The sun was still high on August 8 as Anselmo sat in his captain's chair on the bridge. He squinted through the thick glass to the dark asphalt flight deck below, where a pair of F-14s had taxied over to numbers one and two catapults near the bow of the carrier. In a matter of seconds the blast shield rose, the pilots saluted, and the jets streaked off the carrier with a loud thump, their engines pumping the Tomcats into the blue sky.

The F-14s linked up with a tanker, took a full load of gas, then went looking for the P-3 reconnaissance plane, which was on another look-and-see mission of the Silkworm sites around the Strait of Hormuz. For several weeks now the P-3s and the F-14s had been keeping a vigil over tankers moving in and out of the Strait of Hormuz. As part of the reconnaissance mission, they were also keeping careful watch on the Silkworm batteries. If the Iranians locked and loaded a missile on the rails, that would be considered a threat, possibly even a provocation.[22]

On several occasions the Iranians had sent their own long-range P-3 reconnaissance planes, which Iran had bought from the United States before the revolution, to see what the American fleet was doing. The Iranians also launched F-4 fighters to try to drive away U.S. Navy aircraft that had strayed intentionally into Iranian air space to collect intelligence on air fields. It was not the first time Navy jets had violated the air space of a Middle East nation. In 1983, when the United States was caught up in the Lebanon debacle, Navy jets had overflown Syria and collected valuable photographs on scores of surface-to-air missile sites.[23] French jets flying from the carrier that was to take part in Lyons's war on Iran were also conducting similar but even deeper flights inside Iranian territory.

As the F-14s protected the air space behind the P-3 reconnaissance plane, Navy radar aircraft picked up a pair of Iranian jets that had just launched out of Bandar Abbas and were heading south. In all, the Iranians would send six Phantoms into the air that day, apparently after the P-3. The two F-14s were directed to close on the hostile jets. The four aircraft sped toward each other at well over nine hundred knots. At approximately eight miles, one of the F-14 pilots fired a Sparrow missile, but it malfunctioned and missed its targets. The lead pilot, Lieutenant Commander Robert Clement, then shot his own Sparrow at the Iranians. Seconds later he could see a bright orange ball ringed in black smoke. By this time the other pilot, Lieutenant Bill Ferran, had fired yet a third missile. Right after the engagement, the radio in the two F-14s cracked, "Weapons tight," which was an order not to shoot, that the Iranians were not on a hostile mission. But it was obviously too late. The two pilots accelerated and pushed their sticks forward to fly close to the water, a maneuver used to get out of a combat area in a hurry. Because they had bugged out so fast, they were not even sure if their missiles had downed any Iranian jets.[24]

Later that day Bill Crowe called Ace Lyons. "What am I going to tell the press?" Crowe asked. Neither Crowe nor Lyons could be sure if Clement had downed the Iranian jet. Still, they were concerned about public reaction in the United States.

"Tell them we fired warning shots to drive the Iranians away," Lyons responded.[25]

A few days later Lyons was aboard *Constellation,* praising the pilots, along with Lyle Bull. This was a day to rejoice, he said. Later he would caucus with Bull, the French admiral, and several other officers to go over the battle plan for Iran. The only thing he was waiting for was three words: "It's a go."

On August 22 Lyons left *Constellation* and boarded his personal airplane, a reconfigured P-3 sub chaser, for a flight to Guam. He was due to touch down on the tiny island at 6 P.M. Pacific time. The P-3 was not the fastest plane around and certainly not the most luxurious. But what it lacked in status, the crew made up for in amenities. It had a nice private cabin with a large bed, a superb galley, and a first-rate bar. It was also set up with the best communications gear, which allowed Lyons to be in contact with *Constellation* floating in the Gulf of Oman or with Carlisle Trost in the Pentagon. Healy remembered one "Eyes Only" message from Trost that arrived on the airplane as they were flying from Hong Kong to Subic Bay. "It was one of the nastiest, meanest, most vicious messages I have ever seen," he said. Lyons had taken it upon himself to change a Navy regulation that required officers over a certain age to meet stringent physical fitness standards. He had done so after a friend of his, Rear Admiral Jack Darby, died of a heart attack while jogging. Although Lyons thought he was doing the right thing, he didn't have the authority to change a regulation. And Trost blasted him.[26]

After his P-3 landed on schedule and he settled into his VIP quarters, Lyons told Healy to get the CNO on the line. When the call went through to Washington, Healy signaled to Lyons, then dutifully recorded in his notebook what the two men talked about during their thirty-four-minute conversation:

"Giving CNO a rundown on the trip out to *Constellation.* On the subject of *Guadalcanal,* he says, based on a call from CJCS [chairman of the Joint Chiefs of Staff, Bill Crowe] himself, we developed an OPDEP [operational deception] plan to get *Guadalcanal* into the gulf. We did not tell anyone, did not tell Hays and did not want to tell his deputy. He's totally pissed off but it worked. We also stuffed four PBRs and five stinger teams into a C-5, and flew them to Jabal. Also at CJCS's direction did not tell anyone. Lots of good OPDEP working." [27]

The following morning Lyons climbed aboard his P-3 for the 3,318-mile flight over the Pacific to Hawaii. As he flew home he was content that the well-oiled Navy force now floating near the Strait of Hormuz could indeed deliver a blow for freedom. He had laid the groundwork, put the assets into place. It was now up to the White House to decide just how far it was willing to go in its fight against terrorism.

But approval would never come. Trost went ballistic when he understood the full magnitude of what Lyons had in the works for Iran. "That son of a bitch has done it again," he said to one of his personal aides. He ordered Lyons to stand down the carriers.[28] Then he placed a private call to Ron Hays in Pearl Harbor. It was time to put an end to Ace Lyons's shenanigans once and for all.

The final week of August did not come easy for Hays. He had not known about the secret ship movements, the SEALs, and the Stinger teams sent to the Persian Gulf until after the fact.[29] Now Trost was telling him another secret he hadn't known: Ace Lyons had a huge naval armada poised to strike Iran. Hays did know that for years Lyons had gotten away with pushing things right to the edge because of his close relationship with Lehman. But now Lehman was gone, and Hays decided to put his foot down. He would go to Weinberger directly. He knew the defense secretary would listen to him. At an earlier meeting in Weinberger's third-floor Pentagon office, when Hays was going through the appointment process to be commander of all U.S. forces in Asia, Weinberger had made an unusual overture.

"I am contemplating approval of a recommendation from Lehman that Admiral Lyons be your naval component commander," he told Hays.[30]

"I think that would be great," Hays replied. "Admiral Lyons and I go back a long way. I know how he operates."

Weinberger glanced at Hays. He knew that few people had been able to control Lyons. "If you ever get to a point where this becomes too hard for you," he said, "let me know and I will do something about it."

Hays decided he had reached that point. He sat down and wrote a letter to Weinberger, saying that he could no longer tolerate a subordinate commander circumventing him or the chain of command. But as he wrote the words that would damn Lyons, he found himself becoming almost nostalgic. The last several years supervising Ace Lyons had been as frustrating as any experience of his career. Yet he had great respect for Lyons as an innovator. "He's an action-oriented guy, he gets things done," Hays would say. "He's not perfect by any means, and certainly his propensity to exclude his bosses was a major distraction." Hays wrote to Weinberger that he had endured this pattern to the extent he could. But now his and Lyons's staffs were at loggerheads, and the relationship between Washington and the Pacific was jumbled. "I just couldn't stand it anymore, the disruption being caused by his modus operandi."[31] He wanted Lyons to go. Now.

The letter arrived on Weinberger's desk on September 3 and produced the whirlwind of activity that Hays hoped it would. Weinberger wasted no time in laying the groundwork for Lyons's removal. He called the White House and cleared it with the President. Then he struck a deal with Sam Nunn and John Warner of the Senate Armed Services Committee, which had the final vote on what grade an admiral would retire at. Everyone agreed that Lyons could end his career as a four-star admiral if he would go quietly. If he decided to fight it, which many feared he would because of his bombastic personality, the Senate would demote him to two stars. The deal was to be strictly confidential. Besides the humiliation the Senate and the media could heap on him, Lyons would take a sizable cut in his retirement pay. Trost was also holding something else over Lyons's head. He believed Lyons was illegally using his P-3 airplane to transport furniture for his wife's antique business and that the government was footing the bill for the care of Lyons's dogs.[32]

That day three letters were drafted. One from Webb to Weinberger explained why Lyons had to be removed as commander in chief of the Pacific Fleet. One was from Webb to Trost, advising the CNO about the action to fire Lyons. And the third, from Webb to Lyons, said, "I hereby order you relieved of duty." All three letters would be sealed in a pouch and sent by courier as soon as Trost telephoned Lyons in Hawaii to break the news. It was a call that Trost was not looking forward to.

All that day, as word of Lyons's departure slowly leached throughout the corridors of the Pentagon, neither Webb nor Crowe, both of whom had encouraged Lyons to do an end run on the chain of command, pitched in to stop the bloodletting. Webb mattered little to Lyons. But with Crowe, Lyons the cowboy had lost his best horse.

"This is a private phone call; is your aide on the line?" Trost asked Lyons. There was a audible click as Kevin Healy cradled his receiver. The call had come through on September 4, shortly before noon in Washington, to compensate for the difference in time with Hawaii. As Trost began, his aide, Rear Admiral Tom Paulsen, stayed on the line, taking notes on what was sure to be a contentious conversation.

Trost and Lyons had never gotten along. Even at the Naval Academy, where Trost was a brigade commander and Lyons a year his senior, they had had their differences. Trost was a spit-and-polish midshipman who found Lyons's antics for pushing the rules at Annapolis unbearable. Both men had climbed through the ranks to reach the pinnacle of their careers, Trost by adhering to the rules, almost to a fault, Lyons by bending them, almost daring to be caught. Only one man could win this showdown. And Trost had all the cards. But Lyons was not about to go down without a fight.

"You can't do it," Lyons told Trost when he was informed that he was being forced to retire. It was as much a challenge as a threat. But Trost was not deterred. It's a done deal, he said. As soon as he hung up with Lyons, a Navy commander would get on an airplane and hand-carry the three letters from the Pentagon to the headquarters of the Pacific Fleet. "I'm telling you this, Ace," Trost said in a stern voice. "You need to understand that you can either go quietly as a four-star, or put up a fight and retire in the rank of rear admiral." He said that Weinberger, the President, Nunn, and Warner were all on board, supporting his departure as a full admiral. "The choice is yours."

Lyons hung up on Trost, murmuring "Fuck you" under his breath.

The next day Tom Paulsen was sitting in the Pentagon office of Admiral Hunnington Hardisty, the vice chief of naval operations. As they were talking, the telephone rang. It was John Lehman, calling to protest the firing of Lyons. Paulsen got up to leave, motioning that he did not want to eavesdrop on the conversation. "Don't you dare leave," Hardisty said.[33]

After hearing Lehman out about how unfair it was to treat Lyons in this fashion, Hardisty said there was nothing he could do. It pained him to watch Lyons's career end this way. He had been Lyons's deputy in Hawaii before taking over the second most important job in the Navy; it was primarily because of Lyons that he'd gotten the vice chief's slot. Lehman liked Hardisty and had concurred with Lyons when he picked him for the post. But now all that was in the past. There was little Hardisty could do but pass on what Trost and Weinberger had in store for Lyons. "John, they have Ace's balls in one hand, and a rusty razor blade in the other, and they are going to cut," he said. There was no way for Lyons to fight it. Weinberger had cleared it through the White House and gotten two of the most influential senators in Washington to agree to the deal. "I'm a good friend," he said, "but there is nothing anyone can do. Ace doesn't have a leg to stand on. I'm not bullshitting you."[34]

Lehman knew he could do little to turn the decision around. It was indeed a hopeless battle. He could see that Trost was going after his people, one by one. "It was the revenge of the nerds," he later said of Trost's efforts to clean house. Lyons agreed and felt as if he had been set up. During all of the controversial naval operations, both in the Sea of Okhotsk and the Persian Gulf, Lyons said that he had kept his superiors informed, either by telephone or by message. Now, Lyons realized, they all had conveniently forgotten.

On October 1, 1987, Ace Lyons officially retired during a change of command ceremony in Pearl Harbor. At his side was John Lehman, the man who believed in him and who had given him the opportunity to prove that he could be one of the Navy's most unorthodox war fighters. Both men had challenged the autocratic authority of the admirals with varying degrees of success. But in the end, it was the admirals who had won out. And never again would they relinquish their power. Ironically, the admirals were now practicing the lessons they had learned from Lehman—how to survive by waging political war in any format that would destroy their opponents.

So far, four key members of Lehman's dream team had left the Navy under less than stellar circumstances. Mel Paisley was serving time in jail because of Ill Wind. George Sawyer, who had left government service in 1983 to join General Dynamics, had been indicted on criminal charges in 1985. He had failed to disclose his private job talks with the defense firm and the travel expenses paid by the company during his last months as a Navy official. He was acquitted after Lehman took the stand as a character witness, saying how Sawyer was tough on the contractors, especially General Dynamics. Sawyer, Lehman said, had also saved taxpayers millions of dollars.[35] And P. X. Kelly, the Marine commandant, was tainted by the generals' promotion board and unable to rebound from the finger pointing that the Beirut bombing was somehow his fault.

Lehman himself was still under a cloud as a result of Ill Wind and would never be able to clear his name from the innuendo and negative stigma attached to the scandal. Gradually, as the media began to lose interest in the story, Lehman's face dropped off the front pages of the nation's newspapers. But the damage had been done, and his aspirations for any other post in Washington were dashed when presidential candidate George Bush dropped him from a short list of advisers likely to get top jobs in the new administration.[36] Of Ill Wind, Bush said he was "offended and shocked, like all Americans, at the abuse of public trust that these allegations represent."

In the months following his departure, Ace Lyons watched the Navy head down a slippery slope as it continued its secret operations in the Persian Gulf. He fretted that another disaster like Beirut loomed on the horizon. There didn't seem to be any clear mission. For this Lyons blamed Crist, Crowe, and others running the military's operations in the Middle East. "Crist was like a kid in the toy shop of Macy's department store," Lyons said of the equipment he had sent piecemeal to Crist at Crowe's request. "He wanted anything and everything that was ever available. He had no concept."

On the one hand, there was an effort under way to intimidate Iran in the same way the Navy had provoked Libya and the Soviet Union. The covert operations were aggressive and to a certain degree successful. Navy SEALs and the Army helicopter gun ships had, on several occasions, caught the Iranians seeding the gulf with mines. On the other hand, Crowe was hesitant to unleash a major attack, "to shut down the gulf," as Lyons put it, even though U.S. intelligence intercepts revealed that this was what Iran feared most. The Navy had to navigate between pushing right to the edge, then backing off to avoid a war that might enflame the Middle East. To Lyons, the policy was confusing at best and reckless at worst. There were numerous times when Iran gave the United States ample reason to dust off the Lyons battle plan. But in each instance the President backed off and ordered a measured response.

On April 14, 1988, *Samuel B. Roberts,* a Navy frigate involved in the escort operation, struck a mine. The explosion blew a twenty-five-foot hole in the left side of the ship and catapulted the *Roberts* some ten feet out of the water. Fuel spewed throughout the engine room, fumes went up the stack, and a 150-foot-tall fireball shot into the air. Had it not been for the heroic efforts of the crew, the ship would have sunk. In response, the Navy destroyed two oil platforms and, later, two Iranian naval vessels that engaged U.S. ships. To Lyons, who was watching the events unfold as a civilian, it was a weak-kneed response. "Shut the goddamn gulf down," he said. "Then we wouldn't have to worry about anything."

Lyons's prediction that disaster lay ahead was about to come true. *Vincennes,* the billion-dollar warship Lyons used during the daring naval operations in the Seas of Japan and Okhotsk, had arrived in Bahrain on May 29, 1988. Within a matter of days other U.S. warships in the Persian Gulf had given the cruiser, now under the command of Captain Will Rogers, an ominous moniker: "Robocruiser."

Just two hours after sunrise on July 3, the temperature in the Persian Gulf was already one hundred degrees as the *Vincennes* trolled slowly in the Strait of Hormuz. Sailors moving around the deck were bemoaning the beating sun and the yellowish haze that blanketed the gulf as fine-grained sand whipped across the water from the Arabian Desert. Before long it would be so hot that metal objects on the ship would be untouchable. By midday the sand, which had the consistency of talcum powder, would coat the decks, railings, and gun mounts. Before the sun set, even the ship's air-conditioning unit would bog down under the baking heat.

At 6:33 that morning, Will Rogers was shaving in his captain's quarters when his phone buzzed. "Skipper, you better come down," said the duty officer in the combat information center, a space age war room two decks below. "It sounds like the *Montgomery* has her nose in a beehive." [37] Rogers was more than eager to get to the scene forty miles away, ordering "all ahead flank." He was not about to be left out of a fight.

Will Rogers had come late to the Navy, winning a commission in December 1965 at the age of twenty-seven. But he made up for his late start by embracing the Navy's gung ho agenda, especially under John Lehman, when officers were encouraged to be combative and risk takers. Those who did were identified as warriors and rewarded handsomely with the best jobs that led to flag rank. Early on, Rogers was considered someone to watch.

One of his first good breaks came in 1981, when he was assigned to the SSG, the Strategic Studies Group, at the Naval War College, which accepted only the most promising officers. At the time, the SSG was working side by side with Team Charlie on the secret war games being used to develop the Maritime Strategy. Tom Hayward had established both groups to help him convert the Navy into an offensive powerhouse. When Lehman came aboard, he took Hayward's ideas one step farther and insisted that the SSG develop creative, unpredictable, and aggressive war-fighting strategies.

Most of the naval officers assigned to the SSG were rabid about changing Navy doctrine. Slowly their enthusiasm filtered into the other courses being taught at the War College and eventually into the fleet, where it was reinforced by officers like Ace Lyons, who took their war-fighting job seriously. If there was one story that summed up how naval officers felt about their trade in the 1980s, it was an old tale about Admiral Isaac Kidd, the Atlantic Fleet commander, standing down a Soviet man-of-war. During a naval exercise in the 1960s, a Soviet ship steamed through the formation and pointed its guns at Kidd's ship. Kidd sounded the Klaxon and ordered battle stations. In a matter of moments he had every gun trained on the Soviet vessel.

"Do you want to start World War Three?" the startled Soviet captain signaled to Kidd.

"If I do," the admiral replied, "you will be the first to know." [38]

As *Vincennes* raced north to support *Montgomery,* this war-fighting esprit was still very much alive and well in Will Rogers. He was aggressive, intensely combative, and willing to push the edge of the envelope. Even before the ship left San Diego, Rogers had been in the habit of violating the rules of engagement during war-gaming exercises. At a Subic Bay briefing on the rules of engagement for the Persian Gulf, the most senior officer present from *Vincennes* was a lieutenant. By early July Rogers was regarded as trigger happy.[39] He reminded some people of the renegade skipper played by Richard Widmark in the movie *The Bedford Incident,* a man who somehow slipped through the cracks in the system to command one of the Navy's most lethal weapons of war. Widmark had been on a fictional hunt of a Soviet submarine that ended with the accidental firing of a nuclear missile. As *Vincennes* crashed through the gulf waters at thirty knots, Rogers was on the real thing.[40]

As *Vincennes* closed on *Montgomery,* the frigate reported there were now some thirteen Boghammers, a type of Iranian speedboat, in the area and that a series of five to seven explosions could be heard coming from a nearby tanker. Richard McKenna, a captain assigned to the staff of Rear Admiral Tony Less, the officer in charge of operations in the gulf, ordered Rogers to dispatch his helicopter to investigate but to keep his ship out of the immediate area. Moments later *Oceanlord 25* lifted off the cruiser's stern and into the air. Then Rogers charged north while his crew went to battle stations and manned the small arms stations on the ship's rails.

At 8:40 McKenna was startled to find *Vincennes* well north of where he had ordered Rogers to remain. Irritated, he radioed the ship to find out what was going on. Rogers offered several excuses that failed to impress McKenna. He instructed the skipper of *Vincennes* to head south away from the action. Rogers was nonplussed at the order. "You want me to do *what?*"[41] McKenna, who was in Bahrain, could hear laughter in the background coming from the men in the combat information center on *Vincennes.* Now angry, he ordered Rogers out of the area. "Aegis arrogance," he muttered at the end of the conversation, a reference to the elitist attitude among the officers who commanded the high-tech warship.

Rogers complied but left his helicopter to patrol the situation. The pilot, Lieutenant Mark Collier, followed the speedboats as they headed back toward Iranian territorial waters. Although the Navy's rules prohibited Collier from flying closer than four miles to the boats, he approached within two miles and was greeted by a burst of weapons fire.

"Did you see that?" Collier yelled out.

"Yeah," said a petty officer aboard the aircraft. "Let's get out of here. That was an airburst—antiaircraft fire."

Collier pushed the chopper down to the water and away from the boats. His co-pilot got on the radio back to *Vincennes.* "Trinity Sword, this is Oceanlord two five. We're taking fire. Executing evasion."[42]

In the combat information center, Rogers listened to the message, then barked out several commands. "General quarters," he demanded. "Full power!" The four gas-turbine engines kicked in, and the ship was once again speeding north at thirty knots. At 9:40 the chief quartermaster advised Rogers that he had just crossed the twelve-mile limit and was in Iranian waters, a violation of international law. Rogers paid no attention. He was in hot pursuit. Two minutes later the fleeing Iranian gunboats turned around and headed back toward *Vincennes*. Rogers now had ample reason to open fire on the boats. He radioed back to Less and asked for permission. Less was at a disadvantage. Although he was in one of the Navy's most sensitive commands in the world, he did not have a Link-11 communications circuit, which would have given him real-time access to tactical intelligence. Had he been equipped with it, he could have watched each step of the pursuit as it unfolded. Operating in the blind, he issued an order. "Take Boghammer groups with guns. I say again, take Boghammer groups with guns."

Nearby, the commanding officer of the frigate *Sides*, Captain David Carlson, was monitoring the radio circuits and cringed at the order to fire. He glanced at his executive assistant Lieutenant Commander Gary Erickson and they both turned their thumbs down. It was a bad decision. Another officer on the frigate said, "Why doesn't he just push his rudder over and get his ass out of there?" Carlson ordered Erickson to the bridge to sound general quarters.

"What's your worst concern?" he asked Carlson as he was leaving.

"We might have to massacre some boats here," came the reply.[43]

At 9:45 Captain Mohsen Rezaian went through his final checklist in the cockpit of his Iranian Airbus before leaving Bandar Abbas for a short flight to Dubai on the other side of the gulf. Then he radioed the tower that he was ready for lift-off. Two minutes later the American-educated Rezaian pushed the throttles forward, and Iran Air Flight 655 with its full load of passengers rolled down the runway and into the morning sky.

"Captain, we have a contact," the tactical action officer on *Sides* said to Carlson. "*Vincennes* designated this contact as an F-14 coming out of Bandar Abbas."

"Do we have it?" Carlson asked.

"Yes, sir, we've got skin. It's a good contact," the action officer said. The *Sides'* air search radar was bouncing off the Airbus. Carlson glanced at the readings and saw that the aircraft was at about three thousand feet and traveling at 350 knots. He asked if the aircraft was emitting any military radar.

"No, sir. She's cold nose. Nothin' on her."

"Okay, are we talking to him?" Carlson asked.

"We are trying every net with this guy, and so far we have no response," came the reply. Both *Sides* and *Vincennes* were trying to raise the Airbus on the International Air Distress and the Military Air Distress frequencies.

"Okay, light him up," Carlson instructed. The *Sides'* powerful fire control radar painted the aircraft. In past engagements, Iranian warplanes would turn and run if a U.S. warship locked its missiles on them. Carlson saw that the contact on the radar scope didn't move. It was still climbing and gaining speed.

"Got any ESM [electronic support measures]?" he asked.

"Nothing."

"And he's still not talking?"

"No, sir, we're getting nothing out of him."

Carlson thought about the information for a moment. It's not a threat, he said. "He's climbing. He's slow. I don't see any radar emissions. He's in the middle of our missile envelope, and there is no precedent for any kind of an attack by an F-14 against surface ships. So, nonthreat." [44]

Inside the darkened combat information center on *Vincennes,* the sailors operating the Aegis system had labeled the Airbus "unknown, assumed enemy." Although this was a regular scheduled flight, the Navy, as a matter of routine, considered anything coming out of Bandar Abbas hostile because the airport doubled as a military base.

On this Sunday morning, thirteen thousand feet in the air above *Vincennes,* Captain Mohsen Rezaian was oblivious of the battle shaping up below and the frenzied efforts to contact him by radio. Rezaian was paying more attention to the climb-out phase of his flight. He was likely monitoring the approach control frequency at Bandar Abbas and air traffic control at Tehran Center. He had no idea he was heading on a path that would take his commercial airliner over *Vincennes.*

On the cruiser, Lieutenant Commander Scott Lustig, the tactical commander for air warfare, caucused with several of the radar operators who were concerned about the approaching target. One of the officers had the Aegis system query the commercial airliner's transponder to determine if it was friend or foe. The return signal indicated that it was a commercial airliner. But when he scanned a printed listing of scheduled commercial flights, he somehow missed Iran Air Flight 655. Could it be an F-14 masquerading as a civilian airliner? U.S. intelligence had warned of this. And the Navy knew that Iranian warplanes hid behind commercial jets to guard them from radar. Lustig issued an order to warn the incoming aircraft.

"Unidentified aircraft . . . you are approaching a United States naval warship in international waters." There was no response.

As the battle with the speedboats raged on and the bogey neared the *Vincennes*, Rogers and several other officers could not help but think about another Navy ship, the frigate *Stark*. A year earlier an Iraqi jet had accidentally fired two missiles as the frigate was conducting an engineering exercise eighty-five miles northeast of Bahrain. *Stark*'s radar had picked up the approaching jet but labeled it a friendly aircraft. Moments later the two missiles had struck the ship and turned it into an inferno. From then on, "Don't take the first round" became a battle cry for Rogers and other surface warfare officers on duty in the gulf.[45] Rogers announced to the crew that he was going to have the ship's fire control radar lock onto any hostile plane that came within thirty miles. If it continued on and breached twenty miles, he was going to shoot it down.

In the combat information center, Lieutenant William Montford was standing behind Rogers, monitoring the circuits and writing down the timeline of events. He looked over Lustig's shoulder and saw that the aircraft approaching overhead was climbing slowly and squawking the code of a commercial airliner. At 9:51 he chimed in with a warning: "Possible commair." Rogers raised his arm to acknowledge him. *Vincennes* then sent out three more warnings to the aircraft. "Iranian fighter . . . you are steering into danger and are subject to United States naval defensive measures."

Rogers felt he could wait no longer. He was sure the jet was hostile and was coming to the aid of the Iranian speedboats. Then came information that convinced him he was right. The computer operators manning the sophisticated Aegis system, which was supposed to track up to two hundred targets simultaneously, erroneously reported that the aircraft was indeed an F-14 and was no longer climbing. It was descending and picking up speed.

With the aircraft eleven miles away, Rogers reached over his head and turned a firing key that allowed the ship to launch its Standard missiles. A light flashed on the console of the missile systems officer, indicating he was clear to fire when ready. He asked for a verbal clarification. "Yes, take," came the response. At 9:54 he hit the fire authority button. Seconds later two missiles were airborne, searching for Iran Air Flight 655.

Ten miles away Rezaian was on the radio to Bandar Abbas. The airliner had reached the first checkpoint on its flight across the gulf to Dubai, and Rezaian was calling in to report that he was on course. So far it had been an uneventful flight.

"Have a nice day," the tower radioed.

"Thank you, good day," the pilot replied.

Thirty seconds later a burst of shrapnel ripped off the left wing of his jet and tore through the aft fuselage. Iran Air Flight 655 and its 290 passengers plummeted to the waters below.

The naval operations that Crowe had launched in the Persian Gulf more than a year ago had now ended in disaster, as Ace Lyons had predicted. Crowe, however, was having nothing to do with taking the blame. He would say If mistakes were made, they were "below my pay grade." [46]

In the eleven hours that followed the accident, a time of great anguish for Rogers and his shipmates, Crowe had tried to piece together what happened. Tony Less had awakened him at 3:18 A.M. in Washington to inform him about the skirmish with the Iranian speedboats. At 4:00 A.M. he had gotten a call from the Middle East, saying an F-14 had been shot down. An hour later another call reported that it might have been a commercial airliner. That morning information from *Vincennes* poured in to the Navy and the Joint Chiefs of Staff, reconstructing the battle with the small speedboats, Collier's flight, and the path of Iran Air 655. By that afternoon Crowe felt he had enough information to go public. The details were sketchy, but good public relations mandated that the Pentagon try to get out front on the story, to interpret the events that had taken place several thousand miles away in the gulf. Crowe knew that if he did not take the initiative, the sole source for news on the crisis would come from the Iranians.[47] The press corps was alerted that the chairman of the Joint Chiefs would give a brief on the shoot-down at 1:30 P.M.

Dressed in his summer whites, Crowe stood behind the podium and told the reporters that there had been a terrible accident. Turning to a map that depicted the accident, he used a pointer to take the press through the event, which had begun three-plus hours before the shoot-down, when Rogers steered his ship against the small boats. He said that based on information from Rogers, the Iranian Airbus was flying outside the commercial air corridor and failed to respond to repeated warnings. He told the press that the aircraft was descending and picking up speed and that Rogers was only defending his ship. On the map, *Vincennes* was shown to be in international waters at the time of the shoot-down. But nobody in the press corps knew that the ship had ventured into Iranian territory. Not then, nor in the following days, did the Navy attempt publicly to correct the error. It later told Congress that the ship had been in territorial waters.

The day of the shoot-down, General Crist, with Crowe's approval, chose Rear Admiral William Fogarty, a senior officer on the command responsible for the Middle East, to investigate the downing. The report has never been fully declassified. But when the unclassified version was released, it supported the ship's version of the entire event. And Crowe, in his five-page endorsement of the report, blamed Iran for letting its airliner "fly directly into the midst of a gunfight." He didn't explain how Captain Mohsen Rezaian would have known that *Vincennes* was chasing down thirteen small boats thirteen thousand feet below.

In its haste to put the best picture on the shoot-down, the Navy found itself in a difficult political situation. Clearly Rogers had fouled up and shot down a commercial airliner. But how could the Navy punish him for shooting at a target he thought was hostile, when it wanted to court-martial the skipper of *Stark*, Glenn Brindel, who had been forced out of the service, for *not* firing at an Iraqi jet more than a year ago? It couldn't. So the Navy rewarded Rogers and the crew of *Vincennes* with combat action ribbons. Rogers retired honorably, although with the shoot-down forever on his conscience. Lustig, the air warfare coordinator, was awarded the Commendation Medal for "heroic achievement" and his "ability to quickly and precisely complete the firing procedure."

When Sam Nunn saw the commendation letters, he decided the Navy had gone too far. Why should a crew be rewarded for killing 290 innocent civilians? And how, others would ask, could Lehman's trillion-dollar, state-of-the-art Navy have made such a tragic miscalculation?

PART III
THE GLORY IS GONE

CHAPTER 20

THE PRIVATE CEREMONY in the spartan Pentagon office was simple and quiet, typical of the man who was being sworn in as the sixty-fifth secretary of the Navy. There were no celebrities, no heavyweight politicians, and no long-winded speeches. Missing too was a phalanx of reporters and photographers knocking themselves out for the "first day on the job" story about a new administration official. Few in the media even knew, or cared really, that H. Lawrence Garrett III was taking his oath of office this warm spring day, May 15, 1989.[1]

That Garrett stood there now, promising to lead the Navy to the best of his ability, was a surprise to many in the Washington constellation. He had neither the commanding presence of Jim Webb nor the bravado and cunning of John Lehman. Larry, as he was known, was small in stature, wore glasses that hung over a plain nose, and had thin lips that turned almost white on the very few occasions when he got angry. Everything about Garrett was measured, from his careful speech to the way he signed his name; he always used a small ruler to make his signature precise and straight along the bottom edge.

He had been Jim Webb's undersecretary of the Navy and had chosen his old office, rather than the big secretary's suite next door, for today's official swearing-in. "He's a good number two man," Webb had said of his deputy, whose greatest fault was that his lawyer's training made him too rigid. Although Webb considered him a first-rate administrator, he could see that Garrett lacked the charisma and decisiveness of a solid leader. If he had to discipline someone, he would agonize for days on end, seeking a way to avoid that unpleasant task. He always looked for the good in people, even when they were guilty.

Garrett had never been the top man before, in any organization, and Richard Cheney, the new secretary of defense, was wary of his ability to steer the Navy on a straight course in the years ahead. At every mark the admirals would be there, ensuring that Garrett never assumed the power that John Lehman had. Cheney knew the admirals could be a problem. When he'd been sworn in two months earlier, he had asked Steve Herbits, a former

Pentagon official, to identify what type of leader was needed to run each branch of the armed forces. Herbits prepared a one-page memo on the Army, Air Force, and Navy that described what obstacles lay ahead for each civilian service secretary. For the Navy he advised appointing a person who understood the tradition-bound admirals, but a man with enough independence and strength not to be coopted by them. The admirals, Herbits emphasized, were defiant of civilian authority.[2]

Whether the brass would capture Garrett was a question no one could really answer that spring as Cheney went through the process of deciding who should get what political appointments. Garrett's track record so far gave no indication either way. He did have a well-known weakness of being in awe of the brass. But his backers felt he could keep his emotions in check if he had to call an admiral on the carpet. Still, Cheney was uneasy. All he really knew about Garrett came from Richard Armitage, the burly ex-SEAL and Naval Academy graduate whose good name carried considerable weight inside the Pentagon. Armitage felt that Garrett had paid his dues as the undersecretary and now deserved a shot at the top job. He too had his doubts, but he figured he could help his friend along if he got into a jam.

No one, not even Armitage, really knew what made Garrett run. Those who worked for him said he was such an intensely private man that he could count on one hand the people he called close friends. On occasion he would loosen up and reveal some facet of his personal life that usually left the listener with his jaw on the ground. Some of the most difficult memories for him were of his childhood years.

Garrett grew up poor in Miami, in a working-class household. His father was barely able to put enough food on the table despite toiling at three jobs, including one as a night watchman. His mother was often sick and never seemed to have enough time for Garrett and the rest of the family. In later years when Garrett recalled his youth, he would say that his mother had treated her children like chattel. There was scant love and little of the nurturing a child needs to develop self-esteem and confidence. It would have a long-lasting effect on Garrett. His closest advisers said this lack of love made it difficult for him to be compassionate, even to his son and grandchildren. And it had made him an insecure person as an adult.

When he was in third grade, Garrett would tag along with his father to his night watchman's job. He knew his father was tired from his day jobs, and he wanted to keep him from falling asleep. Despite his vigilance, his father would drift off, and rather than wake him up, Garrett would pick up his dad's large flashlight, with its beacon shining brightly, and make the night watchman's rounds, checking empty buildings and dark alleyways for burglars and transients. He was scarred to the bone. His dad had always wanted the best for young Larry and had hoped to send him to college. But when he was a teenager, his father said there was just not enough money.

As a teenager, Garrett ran afoul of the law on a minor charge.[3] The incident served as a wake-up call, and the boy began to plan a future that would somehow include college. His brother was not as fortunate and would serve a considerable length of time in jail.

After his father died, Garrett enlisted in the Navy in 1961. He did not join for the adventure of seeing the world. Rather, the pay was good and he could get a college education out of it. Although he earned a decent wage as a sailor, Garrett worked other jobs outside the Navy, too, sending home whatever extra money he could. He spent the first years in submarines. Then he applied for the officers corps and was accepted. Three years later, in 1964, he received a commission and became a naval flight officer. He was assigned to a maritime patrol squadron and dispatched to the Vietnam War.

After the war he got a law degree and in 1972 was assigned to the Judge Advocate General Corps, where he was ultimately promoted to the rank of commander. He was detailed to the White House as part of a legal team that helped draft the federal regulations pertaining to the Ethics in Government Act of 1978. It was unforgiving and dull, but Garrett worked much harder than the others on the staff. And before long he became well known as a sharp lawyer who was willing to toil late into the night to get the job done. The Navy was not entirely pleased that Garrett had found success working in the executive branch. The judge advocate general told him that staying at the White House was not good for his career and he should return to the Navy. But the administration offered him the civilian post of assistant counsel to the President. He had twenty years in service, enough time to collect a pension when he retired, so he left the Navy without much regret and joined the White House staff. That led to his later being named the Pentagon's general counsel, where he served under Cap Weinberger and found himself caught up in, among other things, the Iran-contra scandal. Garrett helped Weinberger produce notes and diaries that were being requested by the government's independent counsel, Lawrence Walsh. Garrett has never said if he was aware of the illegal dealings, and those close to him doubt that he did anything wrong.

When Webb replaced Lehman in 1987, he asked Garrett to become his deputy. Few thought he would accept because it was a demotion in political seniority. But Garrett joined up with Webb with little hesitation. He told friends that it was what he truly wanted, to be back with the sea service. One friend said you could take Garrett away from the sea but could not take the sea out of Garrett. "The Navy was truly Larry's family," said one former associate, "the big bosom mother with her arms wide open, saying, 'Come here, I'll give you a big hug.' "

When Bush was elected in November, Garrett was eager to stay on in the new administration and hoped that he might be chosen Navy secretary. But he did not have the rapport with Bush that he had with Reagan. For the most part, Bush knew even less about Garrett than Cheney did. But it made sense to keep the continuity of the past administration, and Garrett was given the job. As an insurance policy, Cheney made Dan Howard, a former spokesman on the National Security Council who had helped him on his confirmation through the Senate, Garrett's deputy. Among other things, Howard would be Cheney's spy.[4] Cheney, in fact, picked most of Garrett's staff, which dumbfounded Webb, who said the new secretary had sold his soul to get the job.[5]

No matter who had taken the helm that year, the challenge of governing a service as complex as the Navy had become in the past eight years was indeed daunting. In almost every measurable category it was sinking under the weight of John Lehman's massive buildup. Warnings made in 1981 and 1982 that the Navy could not afford six hundred ships, that there would be severe manpower shortages, and that the aviation plan was too ambitious and stretched too thin had come home to roost. Faced with the first wave of ship retirements, Jim Webb resigned in 1988 rather than fight Defense Secretary Frank Carlucci. Webb and Carlucci, who had replaced Weinberger, were bitter foes. He had even complained to his staff that the new defense secretary had more time for his ashtray then he did for him.

Even Trost and his personnel experts revealed publicly that the Navy had been unable to recruit and retain the one hundred thousand new people required to man the fleet Lehman tried to build.[6] There was a shortage of qualified petty officers. And sailors were having to spend more time at sea than in past years. Defense budgets had declined steadily, making it impossible to pay for the myriad new programs that Lehman had begun. Since he had front loaded the 1983 budget, real growth had stayed in the minus column in every year but 1985, when the Navy took control of a $6 billion retirement fund managed by the Pentagon, and 1988, when Congress appropriated about $8 billion for two new carriers.[7]

But as the budgets shrank, costs associated with the Strategic Homeporting plan and the Navy's worldwide infrastructure, which was expanded to accommodate more ships, kept skyrocketing. Even though new homeports had been cut from thirteen to six, the plan was still consuming hundreds of millions of dollars in maintenance and construction costs.[8] There would be sparkling new naval stations in the Pacific Northwest, in metropolitan New York, and in three states along the Gulf of Mexico. But there would be too few ships to put into the new facilities.

As the Navy built new piers and dredged channels, Cheney was drawing up plans to cut the fleet even more than Carlucci had. He wanted 450 ships, which was about the same number recommended by the classified Extended Planning Annex study that Lehman had quashed in 1982. Because the Navy had so overextended itself, some internal budget drills predicted the fleet would have to shrink to about three hundred ships if it was to survive in the future. It was clear to Cheney, a pragmatic politician from Wyoming who favored cowboy boots with his business suits, that there was no real need for Lehman's Six Hundred Ship Navy.

Although the rationale behind the drive for a big Navy—the Soviet threat —had been weak all along, now it no longer existed. It was obvious to everyone that the Soviet navy had indeed collapsed. The few out-of-area deployments that the Red Fleet had conducted had stopped. Ships were rusting at anchor. And the Bear flights near the Aleutians that demonstrated that Soviet cruise missiles could threaten Seattle or San Francisco were a thing of the past.

Trost had seen the fall of Gorshkov's navy firsthand on an autumn 1989 trip to the Soviet Union. On board *Slava,* one of the Soviet's newest warships, he spotted the poor conditions that naval intelligence officers had been reporting for nearly two decades about the Red Banner Fleet. There was a quarter inch of paint everywhere—on operating rods in the engine spaces and on hatches that were painted shut. Although Trost still viewed the Russians as potential adversaries, he knew Mikhail Gorbachev's glasnost and perestroika had forever changed the Soviet navy and its sister military services. The Cold War was ending, the Berlin Wall was coming down, and the Navy would soon find itself without a mission.

There was now no reason to sail carrier battle groups aggressively past the G.I.U.K. Gap to threaten Murmansk or parade them defiantly into the Sea of Okhotsk. Fortunately, the Maritime Strategy was never tested in war. But the downside of this for the Navy was that nobody knew if it would have worked. Would the opening of additional fronts in the Kola or in the Pacific have kept the Soviets from moving troops and resources to a war in Europe? Ace Lyons and Jerry Tuttle had proved that the Navy could sail its big-deck carriers and their escort ships into positions to strike at the Soviet Union without being spotted. But that was only half the battle. How well the fleet could have survived after that during a war was another matter altogether.

The harshest critics of the Maritime Strategy saw the idea of sending a mere six carriers to attack the Soviet mainland as nothing more than a pinprick on the Russian Bear's behind. If the war had remained conventional, that was certainly true. For all the billions of dollars spent on carrier air power, the Navy still did not have a good heavy bomber. The futuristic A-12 Avenger was running into tremendous design problems and was years away from entering the fleet. The A-7 was being retired. The A-6 was so old that the Navy restricted its flight operations to three G's, half the force the plane was originally designed for. The F/A-18 did not have the legs to reach its targets. And even if it did, the warplane did not carry a great payload of bombs. Although the F-14 was designed as a stand-off fighter, if it got into a dogfight with large numbers of Soviet aircraft, nobody knew how well the engines would hold up. If the war went nuclear, however, the Navy did have the capability to penetrate Soviet air defenses with aircraft and missiles and destroy many coastal cities and military bases.

But perhaps the weakest rationale for the Maritime Strategy was exposed in the CIA's national intelligence estimate, which said the Soviet navy was a defensive force that did not intend to, and did not have the assets to, attack the U.S. Navy's convoy lines if a war broke out. The CIA report, which proved to be correct, had damning political consequences. If the Soviets were not the threat that the Navy was making them out to be, why did the nation need the Six Hundred Ship Navy, the Maritime Strategy, and Strategic Homeporting? Why did it have to spend hundreds of billions of dollars?

Lehman, the admirals, and many conservative politicians and bureaucrats said it was all part of Ronald Reagan's rearmament effort to outspend the Soviet Union and therefore drive it to its knees. Lehman claimed the CIA didn't know what it was doing, that its NIEs were frequently wrong. But the Navy's own intelligence officers revealed the folly of that argument. Rich Haver's Team Charlie had shown as early as 1982 that the Soviet navy had never been a match for the U.S. fleet. And this assessment was bolstered by the Navy's own intelligence reports from agents (which were purposefully ignored by the admirals in Washington) who had seen firsthand the dismal shape of the Soviet navy.

One thing was clear: John Lehman's grandiose plans left a walloping bill for Dick Cheney. And as he began looking for things to cut, he questioned the need for the admirals' beloved carrier fleet. He planned to mothball four conventionally powered flattops. And the battleships, brought back by Lehman at a cost of nearly $2 billion, had become too costly to operate. As the debate went back and forth about what to do with the behemoths, a freak accident on *Iowa* was to become the beginning of the end for the program.

• • •

When *Iowa* was reactivated, Lehman's public affairs officers had ratcheted up the fanfare just as they did for the other battleship commissionings. The party line was proud and rich in history: the magnificent dreadnoughts had served honorably since the time of Teddy Roosevelt's Great White Fleet and would continue to do so into the twenty-first century. But as the massive buildup began to collapse and the Navy became stretched too thin, many warships, including *Iowa,* began to suffer.

When Captain Fred Moosally took command in 1988, the ship was something of a rogue fated for catastrophe.[9] In one of *Iowa*'s three gun turrets, "Moose," as he was known, found a hatch that had been lying on its side and leaking hydraulic fluid for two years. The crew was using twenty-five-watt lightbulbs because they were afraid they would blow fuses at the fifty-watt level. Sailors complained about the ship's gun-loading system and had seen bags of propellant torn open and the leakage of black powder. The ship was short 37 of the 118 sailors needed to fire the massive sixteen-inch guns. And 40 percent of the crew turned over each year, leaving *Iowa* with inexperienced seamen and a shortage of petty officers, the backbone of any warship. Training records were missing, and, worse, Moosally realized many of the men he inherited were dopers or had marginal performance evaluations. Moose took it upon himself to improve a very bad situation. Although he made some advancements, the ship's operations were far from perfect.

On April 19, less than a month before Garrett was sworn in, the battle-wagon was steaming on a calm day in the South Atlantic. Inside the number two turret, an ill-trained crew who had never worked together before was preparing to fire one of *Iowa*'s Volkswagen-size shells. Only one sailor, Clayton Hartwig, the gun captain, had any considerable experience. When the orders came down to prepare the ship to fire a salvo, a 2,700-pound projectile was rammed into the gun barrel. Four decks below, sailors loaded bags of propellant onto a hoist car in the ship's magazine and sent it up to the turret. A rammerman rolled the bags onto the loading tray. After several other steps he pushed five bags of propellant into the gun's breech, retracted the loading tray, and readied the gun to fire. It took forty-four seconds to prepare the left gun, which was followed by "Left gun ready." Seventeen seconds later came "Right gun ready." But the center gun was still not ready. After eighty-three seconds a sailor was yelling, "I have a problem here. I'm not ready yet. I have a problem here. I'm not ready yet."

What came next was a thunderous, ship-shaking explosion. The propellant detonated and burst walls and blew open hatches. Smoke and fire swept through the turret. Above deck, the front of the turret was blown out as sailors looked on in horror. When the concussion ended, forty-seven crew-men had been killed instantly.

The accident and the investigation that began on April 20 were to be Garrett's nightmare. Valuable clues needed to determine what set off the propellant had been swept overboard when firefighters washed down the gun room. The investigation itself began amidst controversy. The Navy rejected a board of inquiry in favor of a single investigating officer, Rear Admiral Richard D. Milligan. But Milligan, who had commanded *New Jersey,* had never before headed an inquiry of this magnitude. One of his first orders, which everyone came to regret, was to authorize a complete cleanup of the turret, which further hindered investigators looking for evidence.

Garrett and the Navy were under tremendous pressure to conduct a thorough investigation that would explain the cause of the explosion. The Navy had fought a bitter political fight to bring the battleships back, and the brass knew opponents of the program would seize on the deadly accident at sea as an excuse to get rid of the ships.[10] The Navy put together an investigative team of some fifty experts from seven military labs. They checked for mechanical malfunction of the guns and put the propellant and black powder to every conceivable test that might replicate the explosion. They dropped it from one-hundred-foot towers and they burned it with cigarette lighters. The propellant or black powder would ignite, but not under conditions that might exist on *Iowa.*

Then a team of investigators concluded that the propellant had blown up while it was being rammed. Technicians reconstructed the shattered rammer and found that it had pushed the propellant twenty-one inches too far into the gun. But the only way they could get the same results as the blast on *Iowa* was to ignite the propellant between the two bags closest to the projectile, deep inside the breech. That it could ignite so far into the gun made no sense. Again they were stymied.

Just when they were at their wits' end, Hartwig's sister, Kathy Kubicina, sent a letter on May 8 to the Navy, raising questions about her brother's $101,000 Navy insurance policy. Hartwig had left it to a friend on the ship, Kendall Truitt. She thought her family was entitled to it. Suddenly the case changed overnight. Now it seemed to Ted Gordon, the head of the Naval Investigative Service, that the Navy had a potential criminal case on its hands.[11]

Naval investigators showed up at the Hartwig home in Cleveland at 11:30 one evening and stayed until 2:00 A.M. When they left they had unearthed six large military knives, a scrapbook of clippings of naval accidents, and, from Hartwig's new typewriter, a list of his gunnery mates' names. These items helped to convince the Navy that Hartwig was fascinated with destruction, bent on suicide, and capable of mass murder.[12]

Armed with the new lead, the NIS began conducting scores of interviews with naval personnel. Then one day the NIS sat Seaman David Smith down for several rounds of questioning. Hours turned into days and days into weeks. When the NIS finished with Smith, he had finally told the agents what the Navy brass had longed to hear: the missing clue that had caused the explosion was Hartwig. On May 25 Smith claimed that Hartwig said he could make a pipe bomb with an electronic detonator. Under relentless pressure, Smith said he had seen an electronic timer in Hartwig's locker.[13] The NIS found no timer but confiscated a book entitled *Getting Even: The Complete Book of Dirty Tricks.* After more testing using a timer, and after an FBI psychological profile that concluded Hartwig had been rehearsing all his life for violence and death, the Navy was convinced by mid-June that it had its man—and thus an easy explanation for the blast: sabotage. By July 15 the Navy had completed a sixty-six-page report that blamed Hartwig and an electronic detonator—even though the evidence remained weak. In fact, Seaman David Smith had retracted his statements.

Armitage and Cheney had watched the investigation and the press leaks unfold and were concerned that there might be a rush to judgment on the Navy's part. When Armitage heard that the Navy was going to blame Hartwig, he telephoned Garrett to warn him off. He knew that the first instinct in the Navy was to protect the Navy rather than protect the truth. He could see that the brass was circling the wagons. It would not go over well with the American public to lay the blame for a mysterious accident on a dead sailor. He had to convince him to back off. "Look," Armitage said to Garrett, "have a very gracious statement. You ought to come out and say that if there is one chance in a thousand that the kid is innocent, you would rather make the error and come down on the side of innocence."[14]

Garrett sat at his desk on the fourth floor of the Pentagon and listened patiently. Hanging on the wall behind him was the mesmerizing picture of Marines raising the Stars and Stripes on Mount Suribachi on Iwo Jima. Thousands of Americans had died on that Pacific island. "Uncommon valor was a common virtue," Chester Nimitz said of the bloody campaign. Could a Navy that spurred such bravery and integrity in its people be wrong about *Iowa*? Garrett wanted to believe that the admirals would not knowingly blame an innocent sailor. The investigation had been thorough. He had seen the findings himself. The case seemed airtight, he told Armitage. He was going to back up Milligan's report. After Armitage hung up the telephone, he sensed that Garrett was afraid to hurt the Navy.

On September 7, 1989, Milligan released the report of the *Iowa* investigation, blaming the explosion on Clayton Hartwig. The Navy claimed that Hartwig had been spurned by another sailor on the ship, Kendall Truit. It was this rejection, Navy officials said, that most likely caused Hartwig to blow up the ship. Garrett and the admirals hoped it would put an end to the debacle. But, in fact, Armitage's words would come back to haunt them all.

CHAPTER 21

IN EARLY 1990 Joe Prueher's once promising career was no longer a Cinderella story—and he was angry about it. If the brewing scandal involving his new job at the Naval Academy became public and blew up, he might have to retire prematurely. Too much was on the line. It was time to use the bruising, hardball tactics that he had learned as an aide to John Lehman.

The handsome attack pilot had come a long way in the Navy since he'd graduated from the academy in 1964 with a bachelor's degree in science. A year after leaving Annapolis, on December 29, he pinned gold aviator's wings on his chest. The war in Southeast Asia beckoned, and Prueher distinguished himself for bravery in the air. After Vietnam it was test pilot school, followed by George Washington University and a master's in international relations. Then Lehman picked him as the first commander of Strike University, where Prueher and his staff taught attack pilots new bombing tactics in the Nevada desert. From there he became Lehman's executive assistant.[1]

Now he was the commandant of midshipmen at the Naval Academy and was responsible for instilling honesty, integrity, and honor into the Navy's future leaders. It was a job many considered the first step on the path to more important positions at the top of the Navy. Prueher was just forty-eight, had recently been voted into the fraternity of admirals, and was considered a promising candidate who one day might even have a shot at being chief of naval operations.[2]

Although he was seen as a golden boy, right now it did not seem as if he had the Midas touch. After the humiliation of the *Iowa* explosion just months earlier, Prueher and the young midshipmen he commanded were caught up in a scandal that was on its way to becoming another national embarrassment. On December 8, 1989, the pervasive antiwoman attitude at the academy—the finger pointing, the insults, the name calling, and the dirty tricks—blew up. That evening Gwen Dreyer, a second-year student from California, was lying on her bed before calling it a night.[3] As usual, it had been a grueling day for her of academics and sports. Added to that was the excitement of the Army-Navy game to be played in Philadelphia that week-end. Everybody was pumped up.

Dreyer had mixed feelings about the male-dominated institution she had wanted to attend since she was fourteen. The Navy was in her blood and always on her mind. Her father and grandfather had graduated from Annapolis. She devoured Tom Clancy's books and longed for the day that she might serve her country like Clancy's fictitious hero Jack Ryan. At first she was so happy to be there that she used to pinch herself to see if it all wasn't a dream. But with the good came the bad. Plebe year, the most difficult year for any midshipman, had been particularly hard on her. Women were still not accepted by the male students at the school, and Dreyer did everything she could to shed her femininity. But the more she tried to fit in, the more she felt like an outcast. By the end of her first year she started thinking that as a woman in the Navy she would never be respected as an officer.

It was not just because of the repeated pranks—although they were bad enough. At night when Dreyer and her roommates were sleeping, men would sneak into their room and place plastic frogs in their underwear drawer or leave a piece of meat on the floor. One time they left a used condom on her roommate's pillow. In full view of their female classmates, they would play tag by tapping their exposed penises on each other's shoulders. And they would watch pornographic movies in their rooms. One time a group of women decided to walk in and watch a skin flick along with them, a caper the men found amusing. When they weren't laughing at the women, they were cursing them. As Dreyer walked down the halls, the men would shout: "Dreyer, you're fucking ugly." [4]

Around 8 P.M. that night, while she was lying on her bed, two male midshipmen burst into Dreyer's room. One of the men was the officer responsible for handling personnel complaints on her floor. Although he was supposed to serve as a type of ombudsman, Dreyer claims he had a reputation for violence.[5] He carried a piece of rope and ringed it around his fingers to keep his hands occupied so he would not hit people with his fists. For months, Dreyer recalled, he had been chiding her with angry taunts. Earlier that day she had hit him in the face with a snowball. He had wrestled her to the ground with such force that Dreyer felt as if she were being mauled.

Now he and another man were standing over her. One grabbed her arms while the other took her legs. They carried her out of the room and headed for the men's lavatory. "This is not right, don't do this," Dreyer pleaded as she struggled to free herself.[6] Then she saw a pair of handcuffs and began struggling more and yelling for them to stop. Inside the bathroom were more men who watched as Dreyer was chained to a urinal. Some men exposed themselves and laughed as they pretended to urinate. One midshipman broke out a camera and started taking photographs. When it was all over, Dreyer went back to her room, lay on her bed, and cried.[7]

Soon after, her father, Gregory Dreyer, a naval reservist, academy graduate, and civilian scientist employed by the Navy, stormed down to the academy to demand that the men who had physically and emotionally abused his daughter be punished. While academy officials promised the Dreyers swift action to investigate the incident and told Gwen that they needed dedicated women like her to stay in the institution, privately the Navy was taking a different tack. With input from academy officials, the office of the secretary of the Navy began to build a case against Gwen Dreyer. By perusing her record, Larry Garrett's staff concluded that she had made overtures to other colleges as a freshman, which to them was an indication that she planned to leave. They also believed that her father had pushed her into attending the academy, and now she was rebelling by using this incident as an excuse to drop out. There was an even more damaging story brewing in Garrett's office that winter, one that claimed Gwen Dreyer had been a willing accomplice in the handcuffing.

Dreyer was not aware of the high-level case and the attempts to discredit her. She decided to remain at Annapolis, telling her family that if things improved for her in the following semester, she would stay. If not, she would go.[8] But almost immediately the atmosphere began to turn sour. Prueher's deputy called her into his office with a warning. "We have the photographs of the incident," she would remember him saying. "You don't look like you were upset. Don't get angry and make a big issue of this. We will take care of it."

Soon Dreyer started to feel as if the best way to end the turmoil was to put her faith in the academy's leaders. She was tormented by nightmares and male midshipmen who continued to harass her. When she walked into a room full of men, they all laughed at her. She felt so humiliated that when her fellow students passed, she would quickly place her hand over her name tag. Maybe the school was right, she thought to herself. Maybe she and her family were making too much out of it.[9]

Then punishment was doled out. And it was not what the Dreyers expected. Two midshipmen received demerits and loss of leave time. Six others received written warnings. That only enraged Gregory Dreyer, who continued to press the issue with the Navy. Prueher had had enough of the senior Dreyer. So far the case had not leaked to the media and was still being handled internally as a good-natured prank that got out of hand. That it was not in the press was the good news. But Prueher and academy superintendent Rear Admiral Virgil Hill were still on Garrett's hot seat. The last thing Garrett wanted after *Iowa* was more bad news—especially at the prestigious institution that was supposed to be a cut above society. If the Dreyer incident was not handled right, both their careers could be over. Prueher called Dreyer into his office and said that "my parents were out of control," she would recall, "that I should calm them down." [10]

But he didn't stop with her. A few days later Gregory Dreyer answered the ringing telephone in his Alexandria home. To his surprise it was Joe Prueher, who was at first condescending, then threatening, Dreyer said. "If you continue to press this," Prueher told him, "we will be forced into a defensive crouch."

"When Gwen was chained to the urinal, there were a lot of pictures taken, a lot of pictures," Dreyer would recall Prueher saying. He had reviewed the photographs and told her father that "your daughter did not seem unduly stressed." He warned Dreyer that if he did not back off, if he continued to make an issue of the case, he would be forced to use the pictures. "Don't start a witch-hunt," he said.[11]

Dreyer hung up the phone and was bursting with anger. To him, Prueher was one of the most despicable human beings he had ever met. He was not about to drop the matter. And in May, when Scott Harper, a reporter for the local paper in Annapolis, got onto the story and called Dreyer, he was more than ready to talk. His daughter had now resigned from the academy and he felt it was important to tell her story. He had kept detailed notes of the whole affair, from telephone conversations to records of the disciplinary hearings. It was a reporter's dream for Harper—and a nightmare for the Navy.[12]

Within days of Harper's story in the *Annapolis Capital,* the news that midshipmen at the prestigious Naval Academy had chained a woman to a urinal made the front pages and nightly broadcasts of media outlets across the nation. And once again Garrett had a difficult choice to make.

On Wednesday, May 23, Garrett summoned Prueher and Hill to his fourth-floor office in the Pentagon. The two admirals made the thirty-two-mile trip from Annapolis to Washington in the afternoon and were ushered into the secretary's suite, where Garrett demanded an explanation about what was going on at the academy. First the national embarrassment over Dreyer. And within weeks of that incident, a midshipman had raped a civilian girl on academy grounds. Then some students had broken into faculty offices to copy the "double E," an electrical engineering examination, which was notoriously difficult to pass. Who was running the school, Garrett wanted to know, the midshipmen or Prueher and Hill?

Hill assured Garrett that they had things under control. He had ordered a change in the academy's system for dealing with hazing and harassment, reconvened the Women Midshipmen's Study Group, and asked the academy's official Board of Visitors to appoint a special panel to examine the

Dreyer incident. But Hill had very little credibility at this point. His recommendations were seen by some as the fox guarding the henhouse because no non-academy-affiliated organizations were called in to conduct an independent probe. Some faculty members wondered if Hill even understood the plight of women at the academy and in society at large. At the first faculty meeting after the Dreyer debacle, Hill had told a joke about breasts to a group of instructors that included women.[13]

And Prueher's reputation on Capitol Hill was not faring much better. The Senate Armed Services Committee asked the Dreyers to attend a private meeting to lay out their side of the story, which they gladly did, including a detailed accounting of Prueher's threats.[14] After the meeting the committee told the Dreyers that Prueher would have a hard time advancing in rank past one star. The message for the Navy was clear: As long as the sexual harassment issue loomed in the public's mind, Prueher might find it difficult to win Senate confirmation to a higher rank.

Garrett was not pleased with the rash of blunders at the academy that were showing up in the press and giving Congress reason to conduct investigations into the Navy. Already several committees had launched their own inquiries. And several members were lashing out at the institution. Maryland's Democratic senator Barbara Mikulski demanded action. "What we need to work on at the United States Naval Academy," she said, "is an attitude change."[15]

Garrett told Prueher and Hill that these incidents had to stop. He would not tolerate the mistreatment of women or any midshipmen. He decided that they had to let the nation know the Navy was serious about fixing things at the academy. So before the two men returned to Annapolis, a statement was drafted for release that night. In it, Garrett expressed his personal concern about Dreyer's plight and ordered the Navy's inspector general to investigate the case and other events that raised questions about how well the academy was being run under Prueher and Hill. "We will not condone and will not tolerate hazing, sexual harassment, or any other mistreatment of individuals in the naval service," Garrett's statement read. "Appropriate disciplinary action will be taken against anyone involved in such actions."[16]

A week later, on June 1, as part of an effort to placate the academy's foes concerning its treatment of women, Hill wrote a letter to all incoming female midshipmen "to extend his personal commitment to the protection of their civil rights here."[17] But Garrett's hopes that the academy's problems would be kept under wraps until new reforms took hold were dashed when the inspector general's report was released along with three others, one of which found "a breakdown in civility and discipline, which contributes to an environment conducive to sexual harassment and discrimination."[18] After fourteen years of women attending the academy, their fate had changed little, the report said.

Another of the reports issued that day criticized the Navy for keeping the public in the dark about the Dreyer affair. Only after it broke in the press six months afterward did the Navy take the matter seriously. But the shenanigans at the academy were not the only thing that Garrett and the Navy were keeping from the public.

That Garrett didn't fire Hill and Prueher, or sternly discipline them for a failure of leadership, only reinforced the fears that he was being coopted by the brass. Garrett's staff had even recommended that Hill be retired, and at times Garrett entertained the idea. But in the end Hill was allowed to finish his tour and move on to another job.[19] His reprieve came as a result of pressure from the CNO and the top admirals who lobbied Garrett hard for him and Prueher. According to staff members close to the affair, they did this knowing that Hill was apparently in violation of several standards of conduct regulations and potentially federal law for accepting gratuities from the Naval Institute, which was located on the academy's grounds and considered a defense contractor under Pentagon rules. There were also two hot-line calls on Hill for misusing government funds on a lavish remodeling of his office and for building a gym in his superintendent's home.[20]

Garrett's decision to verbally reprimand Hill and Prueher, which was never explained fully in public, was a slap on the wrists, if that. But it was his decision to make, and he felt deeply that when the President signed the paperwork making him secretary, he did so putting his trust in Garrett's integrity to run the Navy the way he saw fit. If that meant going overboard in protecting an individual, so be it. At first his staff was alarmed about his jurisprudence. But soon they came to see their new boss as a complex man. One side of him wanted to be the stern disciplinarian to prove that he, and he alone, was in charge. The other side, however, was not tough enough to hammer people. It was not that he lacked wisdom. What he lacked was mean-spiritedness.

When he came aboard, Garrett was handed a case by Mac Williams that concerned an enlisted female who was on the promotion list for warrant officer. Williams explained that the woman should be removed from the list because she had had public sex in the back of a pickup truck and had performed oral copulation on a van full of sailors—all violations of the Uniform Code of Military Justice. Garrett told Williams he was not so sure that her entire career should be ruined because of two foolish deeds. Williams, Garrett said, would have to talk him out of his position not to penalize her. "Mr. Secretary," he jokingly said in his heavy Southern lilt, "if you decide to keep her, I want you to transfer her to my command." In the end the sailor was punished.

Whenever a sailor or officer died, regardless of how, Garrett would personally sign a letter to the family. As was his habit, he would ask how the person had died, and in one case his staff was reticent in its explanation. When Garrett persisted, the story he heard did not put the Navy in a good light. A police officer had shot and killed a sailor after a robbery. Garrett still signed the letter out of compassion for the sailor's family.

When Sam Nunn's letter came in questioning why the Navy had awarded the Commendation Medal to Scott Lustig for his role in the downing of Iran Air Flight 655, Garrett had his staff investigate. They asked Commander Ron Swanson, who had helped write the language for Lustig's medal, for an explanation. Swanson also defended Lustig before the Fogarty commission investigating the Airbus tragedy. Garrett's staff wondered aloud about the conflict of interest as they pressed for more information on Lustig that was not all that forthcoming from the CNO's staff. Letters and telephone calls were exchanged. And in the end Garrett wrote back to Nunn that the medal had been awarded and to recall it would cause considerable problems. He did not have the stomach for taking it away from an officer who had already suffered enough over the incident. "Larry is a good and honest guy," Armitage said of Garrett's inability to discipline people, especially the blue-suited officers. "He couldn't make the distinction between the blue-suits and his own. He couldn't fathom that the blue-suits might tell him something that wasn't quite right. It was beyond his ken."

On June 29, 1990, Carlisle Trost stepped onto the front steps of Bancroft Hall at the Naval Academy for the traditional change of command ceremony for the chief of naval operations. Standing by him were Cheney and Garrett and the admiral who was to replace Trost as king of the naval empire—Frank Kelso. Four years earlier, when Trost had replaced Watkins on these same steps, he had been almost defiant as he said, "I become disturbed when I am told that in following a very, very fine naval officer who has helped bring us to this unprecedented level of naval readiness, I am on the top of the hill looking down. As chief of naval operations, I don't intend to preside over a Navy establishment that's headed downhill."[21]

When he turned over the helm to Kelso, Trost had spent four grueling years as CNO, years in which many of the programs begun by John Lehman, a man he despised, had caused the Navy severe hardship. "Today marks completion of the fastest four years of my life," he said, "a period of great challenge, frequent frustration, and tremendous satisfaction." One of his greatest challenges, his associates knew, had been dealing with Lehman, who frequently frustrated him. And the tremendous satisfaction he spoke of came from, among other things, Lehman's departure.

Although Kelso was a member of Lehman's dream team, he harbored no ill feelings toward Trost, who had beaten him out of the job four years before. The two men were both nuclear-trained submarine officers, but that was about as far as their similarity went. Trost was by the book, tough, and determined that the admirals, not the secretary, knew best how to run the Navy. Kelso had been nurtured by Lehman, a man who demanded that the admirals respect civilian control of the fleet, which Kelso did. He had been subservient to Lehman, and he would be the same to Garrett. But that in itself was going to be a problem. Although Garrett would not say so publicly, because of his adoration for the admirals he wanted an independent CNO, an officer willing to take charge. Neither realized that their relationship, which was described by some as a love feast, was doomed to failure.

Before the end of Garrett's tour in office, some two dozen admirals and Marine generals would either run afoul of the Uniform Code of Military Justice or violate Navy regulations to some degree.[22] The NIS and the Navy's inspector general kept track of the offenses, which ran the gamut from minor to serious, as did several civilian and uniformed advisers on the secretary's staff. But it was up to Garrett to punish his brass—which he always tried to avoid if possible. He believed it was punishment enough to tell a senior officer to retire quietly, even if it was with full rank and commensurate benefits and outside the public eye. It was a rare occasion when an admiral or general was sent home prematurely. It was even rarer to demote them in rank. The majority were given verbal warnings or nonpunitive letters of reprimand, which were not placed in their files. Some were even promoted or, like Virgil Hill, allowed to go on to another job.

The list of officers was a closely guarded secret. It was intended to be used not as a disciplinary device, but more as a reference tool when an admiral or general came up for a promotion in rank or for a senior job that required Senate confirmation. The names of candidates up for advancement would go from Garrett's desk up to Cheney for his take on the officers. Cheney would send them to the White House, which in turn forwarded letters of endorsement to the Senate. There were glitches throughout the process when information critical of a candidate was not always included in the file before it began its journey, which ultimately ended on Capitol Hill.

On occasion Garrett's staff blamed the admiral in charge of the Bureau of Personnel, Jeremy "Mike" Boorda, for some nominations that had to be recalled. Boorda was viewed within the Navy as a political chameleon who could cut a political deal without leaving any fingerprints. No taller than a jockey, he would have private, one-on-one meetings with Garrett to go over

the names of admirals up for promotion. Garrett's staff was wary of the
meetings because Boorda would bring a stack of nomination letters for
Garrett to sign on his assurance that the officers had been cleared of any
improper behavior. There would be no aides in the room to check for accuracy. And on several occasions packages were sent up the chain for less than
desirable candidates.[23]

Sometimes Garrett's staff and the brass knew that an admiral or general
was involved in some wrongdoing or unethical behavior but still backed
him. If critical information was sent up the chain on a candidate, it was
mixed in with glowing letters of support and became so watered down that
it was barely visible. And not all admirals or generals had to be cleared by
Cheney or the Senate. There were those, according to his aides, who could
be placed in other jobs at Garrett's discretion.

Garrett did not interpret this process as the fudging of information, but
rather the protection of an individual's right to privacy. Even if he had
decided to take a more proactive stance on questionable cases, the CNO or
Marine commandant, never eager to condemn one of their own, was determined to do anything possible to protect the fraternity. And Garrett was
sometimes helpless to stop them and the institutional corruption that had
existed for so many years.

Even the CNO was not above violating laws. Almost yearly during the
winter, the chief of naval operations held a CinC's conference in Pensacola
on the warm waters of the Gulf of Mexico for the Navy's top three- and
four-star officers. For the men to travel to Florida at government expense
was okay. But what drew warnings from the Navy's lawyers was the free
airfare for the admirals' wives and the government drivers and cars provided
to take the women on sight-seeing and shopping excursions.[24]

The lawyers cautioned Kelso and Garrett that the violations might seem
petty, but, if discovered by the Pentagon's inspector general, they would be
viewed through the dimmest of lenses. Still, neither Garrett nor Kelso offered
much in the way of rectifying the problem. But change eventually did come.
To bring the Pensacola trip into compliance with the rules, the Navy put on
a one-day seminar for the women on the importance of being a Navy wife.
Although the women were now taking part in official Navy business, which
in the admirals' eyes made the trip legitimate, it was still a violation of the
spirit of the law.

On Friday, August 24, Garrett stood on the sun-splashed parade grounds
of the Navy's boot camp in San Diego and watched 438 recruits march to
the beat of drums during a graduation ceremony. Twenty-nine years earlier

Garrett had marched on these same grounds at the Naval Training Center, where he had gone through boot camp.[25] Today, as he viewed the ceremony, his eyes were fixed on one sailor standing at attention: H. Lawrence Garrett IV.

That summer Garrett's son had told him that he and a friend had decided to join the Navy. Garrett felt uneasy about the idea and warned him that as the son of the secretary of the Navy, he might suffer.[26] He knew young Lawrence was not well disciplined and often got into trouble—nothing serious, but enough to frustrate his father. Garrett had repeatedly said he was going to rein him in, but he never did. He offered a small bit of fatherly advice: Why don't you join the Air Force or the Army rather than the Navy?

A few days later Garrett mentioned to Mike Boorda, chief of naval personnel, that his son wanted to join the Navy. He told Boorda about his concerns that his son might be singled out for who he was. Boorda, who like Garrett had begun his career as an enlisted sailor, sensed the secretary's anxiety. He offered to act as a recruiter, spelling out the pros and cons about life in the Navy. On a Sunday Boorda met with Garrett's son. When they had finished talking, Lawrence was still eager to join up and Boorda was more than willing to watch over him during his career. Young Lawrence now had something the majority of the enlisted sailors did not have: a special mentor who wore three stars on his shoulder boards.

Boorda made good on his promise. As Garrett's son made his way through boot camp, the admiral's staff made weekly calls to the recruit command to inquire how Lawrence was doing. The calls caused concern among several of the senior officers at the Naval Training Center, who felt Garrett's son was being afforded special treatment by a three-star admiral that another sailor would not receive.[27] But Boorda felt different and believed he was helping to steer a young man on the right course in life. And his guidance seemed to be paying off. As the reports from San Diego filtered back to him, Boorda told Garrett in their frequent meetings that his son was adapting well to Navy life.[28]

At the graduation ceremony, Garrett beamed with pride at his son. Near the end of the event, Garrett stepped onto the parade grounds to review the troops and hand out awards to the best recruits—including his son. Young Lawrence was made a company honorman, the same award his father had received when he'd graduated into the Navy's enlisted ranks. "It restores an awful lot of memories," he said after watching the ceremony.[29]

Later that day, young Lawrence was given permission to leave San Diego early to fly back to Washington on his father's personal Gulfstream. He was scheduled to return to San Diego for further training. After that, Boorda's Bureau of Personnel had arranged for Lawrence to be assigned to the staff of the top admiral on the West Coast. Among other things, Vice Admiral Edwin Kohn and his staff would now become unofficial baby-sitters.[30]

Major General Royal Moore looked out the window of his EA-6B Prowler and banked a wingtip toward the sandy desert below. It was late afternoon on September 6, 1990, and Moore was strapped into the pilot's seat of the $75 million[31] electronic warfare plane, preparing to land the four-seat aircraft in Bahrain.

He was in the Persian Gulf because of Iraq's invasion of Kuwait a month earlier. Saddam Hussein's aggression had triggered a massive U.S. troop buildup to stop Iraq's army from advancing on Saudi Arabia. As part of the U.S. war effort, which became known as Desert Storm, Moore was selected to command the Marine Corps aircraft sent to the region. During the preparations for a potential war, he frequently flew with various squadrons to assess readiness levels. Today he had been flying with VMAQ-2, a Marine squadron based in Cherry Point, North Carolina.

As the jet descended over the desert, the three other aviators on board were relieved to be finally getting back on the ground. Throughout the flight Moore had made a number of mistakes that put everybody on edge. Even before they went aloft, there was apprehension among the crew. Moore had never taken an emergency procedures test, and he had falsified an aviation safety examination that would certify he was qualified to safely fly the Prowler.[32] The squadron's commanding officer, Lieutenant Colonel Richard Bates, had ordered Captain Steve Nitzschke to take the exam himself, then allow Moore to sign his name, which was illegal.[33]

"I've got a problem with that, it doesn't sit well with me," Nitzschke told Bates.

"I don't care what your fucking problem is. You're going to take it!" Bates yelled back. When Nitzschke completed the test, Bates then took Moore up on a flight and determined he was safe.

Since Moore had arrived in the Middle East, it was not the first time his skills had been questioned by other Marine pilots. Earlier that week, after he had flown an F/A-18 Hornet, some pilots in the squadron described him as inept and dangerous. They had joked that if war broke out, "the first thing we would do would be shoot him down before he could shoot us down."[34] When he was taxiing the Hornet along an airport apron at Sheikh Isa Airfield in Bahrain, Moore somehow lost control of the plane and drove one wing, with an armed Sidewinder missile attached to it, through a guard shack, injuring a sentry inside. He did not think the incident was serious enough to file an accident report, a violation of the Department of the Navy's regulations.[35]

Although Moore was listed on that day's flight logs as the lead pilot, Captain Andrew Engelke, his designated wingman, would actually lead the formation. At midafternoon the aviators climbed into their jets and roared down the runway, taking off in pairs until fourteen warplanes were airborne. The training strike went as planned, which left the pilots enough fuel to practice flying in tactical formations on the way back, a procedure used to evade hostile antiaircraft guns and missiles. Moore repeatedly fouled up the formations, failing to fly the jet at the proper speed and angles required to keep up with Engelke.[36]

As the Prowler approached the airstrip for its landing, Moore pitched one wing toward the ground in a maneuver pilots call a break which among other things helps to slow a plane down. But as the jet came out of the break he forgot to lower the aircraft's flaps. At the same time, the Prowler's air speed was dangerously slow, dropping to about two hundred knots, and the plane was near the point of stalling. By piecing together accident reports, the Navy had learned that the EA-6 and similar aircraft landing with their gear down, their flaps up, and traveling at too low an air speed would flip upside down and plow into the ground. If a pilot was in such a precarious position under one thousand feet, chances were slim that he would recover the aircraft.

Moore was oblivious of the apparent danger. His air speed was way too slow, his flaps were up, and he was approaching one thousand feet in altitude. There was an immediate sense of fear among the flight crew, but nobody wanted to tell the general that he was about to kill everybody in the airplane. When he took no action to correct the situation, Captain Henry Jenik in the plane's backseat started screaming at Moore through his intercom. "Flaps! Flaps! Flaps!" he yelled frantically.

"Oh, I thought I did that," Moore said as he lowered the flaps.[37]

The plane landed safely, but several days later, after another incident in which Moore screwed up while airborne, a number of aviators protested that the general should not be allowed to fly and that if he continued to go aloft, they should not have to fly with him. One officer, Captain Ted "Zoom" Vanasupa, who would later plan and lead some thirty-five strikes during the Iraqi war, felt that if nothing was done, people might die. He had seen such disregard for life before, when his best friend was killed during a Navy training exercise that was poorly planned. The dead pilot's mother had asked him to collect his friend's body from the Arizona desert. For whatever reason, the body had not been properly prepared and was not ready to be moved. Still, Vanasupa loaded the car's trunk full of ice and gently laid his friend's remains inside. As he drove back to San Diego with tears streaming down his cheeks, Vanasupa promised himself he would never fly recklessly again—or let anybody else.

In speaking out against Moore, Vanasupa knew he would have to challenge the Marine Corps senior leadership, who would rally to his defense. He was one man against an institution, and he knew he would face dire career consequences. But he felt deeply in his heart that he had to fight this battle out of principle, to correct a wrong, no matter what the personal cost was to him. He was determined to do everything he could to prevent another senseless accident.

On September 22 Vanasupa went to see Captain William Fisher, the officer in charge of ensuring that the squadron's pilots, and Moore, took the required safety examinations and were qualified to fly. "Look what's going on," he said to Fisher, recounting how Moore had almost killed three aviators.

"I know," Fisher replied. "I know it was pencil whipped." Somebody else, Vanasupa remembered Fisher saying, had taken the test. He said he would take the matter up with Bates.

Thirty minutes later Bates had Vanasupa backed up against a wall and was screaming at him. "Lock up your fucking ass and stand at attention," he ordered. He was so angry that the veins on his neck and face were bulging. "Look, you fucking wimp, the general owns these goddamn airplanes, and if he wants to fly them, then he will fly them any fucking time he wants. If you ever speak to anyone regarding his qualifications and the way he got them, I will send you on the next fucking C-141 home and write you a fitness report that will ruin your career for good. Do you understand me?"

Vanasupa stood motionless and at first did not respond, which made Bates even more vocal and irate. He demanded an answer.

"I heard every word that you said, sir," Vanasupa finally replied.

"Get the fuck out of my face!" Bates yelled.[38]

Bates then began an effort to drum Vanasupa out of the Marine Corps. He wrote a negative fitness report that contrasted sharply with earlier evaluations that were full of acclaim.[39] "Capt. Vanasupa is indeed a highly skilled pilot with exceptional abilities in aviation matters who demonstrated courage and endurance under combat conditions," Bates wrote. "Other than his flying abilities, I found him to be generally deficient in leadership, judgment, and maturity. Had I not been critically short of EA-6B pilots, I would have sought to have him reassigned to duties outside my squadron. His negative attitude and schoolboy antics were a drain on the morale of the command. *I do not recommend that he be promoted with his peers, and I also recommend that he not be offered a position in the Marine Corps Reserve* subsequent to his release from active duty."

The poor evaluation, which would end his career if not corrected, sharply contradicted an earlier one Bates had written before Vanasupa reported General Moore's misconduct. "Captain Vanasupa is a capable, intelligent young officer with excellent potential," he had said then. "He also possesses skills which are critical to Marine Corps readiness, and his retention at this time would be in the best interests of the service."

Vanasupa decided to fight back. He wrote a five-page rebuttal in which he described how Moore, with help from Bates, had falsified the safety exam. The rebuttal also gave an account of the near crash in Bahrain and detailed how Marine pilots had been needlessly endangered by the general's poor flying skills. When it landed on the desk of the new Marine Corps commandant, General Carl Mundy, the Marines went into damage control. Mundy had the Marine Corps inspector general, a brigadier general who was junior to Royal Moore in rank, investigate the matter. He telephoned Moore and asked if he had falsified the exam. "No," Moore replied. The IG then closed the case.[40]

But there were still some loose ends that needed to be taken care of to protect Moore and keep his record clean. The Marine Corps headquarters had to correct Vanasupa's negative and inaccurate fitness report written by Bates. If not, there would always be a paper trail that led to Moore. Mundy instructed Major General Chuck Krulak, who was later nominated by President Clinton to be commandant of the Marine Corps, to take care of the evaluation. In a letter, Krulak advised Major General Richard Hearney that it was okay for him to rewrite the fitness report. At the bottom of the letter, Krulak penned a personal note: "Gen. Hearney—You made a great call! Together we can salvage this mess! P.S. Looking forward to seeing you soon."[41] The Marines then promoted Moore to lieutenant general and gave him one of the most important jobs in the corps, commanding general of all Marine forces in the Pacific. His nomination sailed through Cheney's office, the White House, and eventually the Senate—because the Marines concealed the negative information about him.

Meanwhile the Pentagon's inspector general, Derek Vander Schaaf, became aware of the case and had his staff begin a probe. One agent, Mike Suessman, interviewed Moore and asked the general if he had indeed cheated. Again Moore replied no, he had not. Pentagon agents then arrived in Moore's Hawaii headquarters and confiscated his files. Among the documents seized was the falsified test. After further investigation, which included an evaluation of the test by an Army criminal laboratory, the Pentagon inspector general reached a verdict. Moore was guilty. Now Suessman called back. Did you falsify the test? he asked. Moore confessed.

Garrett learned about the case after Moore had been promoted. Neither Mundy nor anyone else in the Marines had volunteered the information. Besides, the generals sided with Moore. It was one of the few times when Garrett got raging mad. He called Mundy in his office and told him to fire

Moore. Take away his job and demote him to two stars. Moore did not deserve to wear the uniform. Mundy pledged to follow Garrett's orders. But days later he wrote a flowery letter requesting that the Senate retire Moore in his current grade with all benefits. That made Garrett even angrier. There was no way he would tolerate such an abuse. And he didn't. Moore was demoted to a two star and forced to retire.

Ted Vanasupa had to leave the Marine Corps. An outstanding aviator with an impeccable flight record, he was turned down for jobs at several commercial airlines. In each case airline officials said he was qualified, but they couldn't tell him why he had been rejected. Vanasupa and his fellow squadron mates suspected it was the long arm of the Marines. He ended up painting boat hulls in North Carolina and working various jobs to help take care of his wife and two children. He later moved to the San Francisco Bay Area and became a manager in a computer store. Although other members of his squadron knew that the senior officers often put themselves above the law, and knew that generals routinely falsified their safety exams, they had now become victims themselves. Their honor had been sullied by the blatant Marine Corps efforts to hide its dirty laundry in order to protect a general. Their faith in an institution that prided itself on fairness was battered and later shattered when Moore was promoted.

The whole episode reminded Engelke of monkeys in a tree. The monkey at the top was Moore, and when he looked down all he could see was the smiling faces of other monkeys climbing up the tree. "When the monkeys at the very bottom looked up, all they could see were assholes," Engelke said.

On January 16, 1991, shortly before 6 P.M., Garrett and several members of his staff were in his office, watching a CNN broadcast being transmitted live from Baghdad. In the five months since the U.S. military buildup had begun in August, the Navy had sent 6 aircraft carriers and 150 other Navy warships to the Persian Gulf region. Among the flotilla was the battleship *Wisconsin* and a number of nuclear-powered submarines that sailed into the shallow gulf. Although the shooting had yet to start, daily reports over the last week had speculated that war was imminent. The last attempts to avoid hostilities, a series of talks between Secretary of State James Baker and Tariq Aziz of Iraq, had faltered. It was now only a matter of time before the attack would begin. The precise moment, however, was known only to a select group of administration officials and world leaders—Garrett included.

CNN had assigned several of its top correspondents to Baghdad. The hope was that they could chronicle the opening moments of the war, which would be a major coup for a news organization. As Garrett and his staff tuned in, CNN correspondents were reporting that Iraqi antiaircraft missiles were shooting at U.S. planes. The war had started, they said. "No, it hasn't," Garrett said matter-of-factly. "The war won't start for another thirty-eight minutes!"

CHAPTER 22

"*Yuk! yuk! no! no! You can't go to Tailhook.*"

There was no way Garrett could avoid seeing the note. Marybel Batjer, one of the few female political advisers on his staff, had scribbled it across a letter from the Tailhook Association inviting Garrett to the 1991 convention to be held in early September. Batjer had heard the stories about the annual bacchanalia in Las Vegas and felt that Garrett's presence would condone the seamy behavior.[1] In her eyes it was not fitting, especially so close to a presidential election year, for the Navy's highest-ranking civilian official and a member of the administration to lower himself to the Sodom and Gomorrah standards so prevalent at the convention. "There is no way Larry should go," she protested to one admiral.

But Batjer's voice of caution was drowned out by the senior uniformed officers advising the secretary. They insisted that this was a celebration of the swift and stunning American victory in the Gulf War. Tailhook '91 was to be one of the biggest and most important conventions in the association's thirty-five-year history. Personally overseeing the planning was Vice Admiral Richard Dunleavy, a big bald man from Boston who was chief of naval aviation. The Airedales had even coined a name for this year's gathering, calling it "the mother of all 'Hooks," a takeoff on Saddam Hussein's threat that the United States would find itself in the "mother of all wars" if it chose to fight in the gulf. Seventy-one active duty and retired admirals and another five thousand officers were coming to Las Vegas.[2] There would be 172 defense contractors, some with displays, others offering hospitality suites.[3] And on Friday, September 6, three of the eight Navy and Marine pilots shot down and captured by Iraq would describe their travails as POWs.

Patting the aviators on the back for a job well done would be an important morale boost for the troops, but it was not the primary reason Garrett's uniformed advisers were urging him, as well as Frank Kelso, to fly to Las Vegas that summer. The Navy's two most senior leaders had to quell a budding insurrection in the aviation community. Maybe, just maybe, they could calm the Airedales who were in an uproar about the Navy's much heralded $128 billion aviation program, which was in shambles. They had to convince the fliers that the brass knew there were problems, but that nothing was insurmountable. It was an almost impossible task. The Persian Gulf War had dramatically revealed that the Navy's spending frenzy of the 1980s by no means fulfilled all of what it had promised. In its rush to rebuild the fleet with an overly optimistic aviation plan, *Nimitz*-class carriers, Aegis-equipped cruisers, and nuclear-powered submarines, John Lehman and the admirals had bought the nation an armada for doing battle with the Soviet navy on the high seas. But it was not well designed to fight an all-out war in a Third World country.[4]

Only a small fraction of the eighty aircraft on a carrier offered any of the combat needs required in the Persian Gulf War. About half of the aircraft were for fleet defense or antisubmarine warfare. But since Iraq had no real navy, the costly American aircraft had no mission. And the warplanes that did take part in the war, such as the controversial F/A-18 Hornet, failed to perform up to their expectations.[5] Because of the Hornet's short-range problem, the Navy had to break its golden rule and move its big-deck carriers into the Persian Gulf to bring the jets closer to their targets. Even so, the Hornets still chalked up a mediocre record. Their most impressive accomplishment was shooting down two Iraqi jets on the first day of the war, a feat the F-14 Tomcats had been unable to achieve.[6] But other than that, the Hornets did not stand out. On one January raid over Iraq, the jets missed every one of their targets.[7] In public Navy and Pentagon officials pronounced the mission a success, claiming it had forced Iraq to shut down its mobile missile launchers. But a classified report told a much different story. A number of frustrated Hornet pilots who took part in the attack violated mission directives, limiting their time over the target to six minutes, some staying as long as twenty minutes. Still, they could not find the targets because the jets were not equipped with laser targeting devices. After the bombs missed, some pilots even strafed the area with twenty-millimeter cannon without inflicting damage because they could not fly below fifteen thousand feet.[8]

The bomber to be replaced by the Hornet, the A-6 Intruder, also took part in that January raid and destroyed 90 percent of its targets. But because the Intruder was so old, the Navy restricted its operations to three G's, about half of what the aircraft was designed for. And only 60 percent of the Intruder force was available for combat duty because the remainder had been grounded with metal fatigue in the wings.[9] The heavy bomber was used extensively during the war as a tanker, as was the S-3 Viking, an airplane bought originally for finding submarines. Even the Tomcats, the premier fleet-defense fighters, could not be used to their fullest potential. On the first day of the air war, an F-14 Tomcat was zeroing in for a kill on an enemy

MiG when the pilot suddenly heard a loud pop and noticed that the plane was losing power. The pilot quickly surmised that one of his two TF30 engines had stalled, forcing him to retreat and the Tomcat Aviators to miss the chance to claim the first air kill of the war.[10] When Iraq realized its air force was no match for the Americans', Saddam Hussein ordered his jets grounded—a move that left the Tomcats with no mission whatsoever.

None of the admirals had told Garrett how disgruntled the Airedales really were about the war and the messed-up aviation plan. He found out the hard way during a trip to the Oceana Naval Air Station in Virginia, shortly after the war. Several hundred officers, from the rank of ensign to admiral, had filed into the Officers Club to hear Garrett talk. After a short introduction he said, "I want everybody from lieutenant commander and above to leave." [11] He intended to talk with only the most junior officers, the JOs, who were usually the most honest and forthcoming. When the room cleared, the secretary was left with a group of ensigns and lieutenants who could now, with the senior officers gone, vent their spleen. And they did. Afterward, when Garrett was flying back to Washington, he turned to Captain Mike Matton, his kindly executive assistant, who had left the room with the other officers and therefore had no idea what had gone on inside. "I was surprised by the direct nature of a lot of the questions and the concerns of the folks," Garrett said, leaving it at that. He did not mention that he was jarred by the episode.[12] But when he reached the Pentagon and finally retreated to his office, the impact of the jeering aviators began to set in. An aide who walked into his office could see that he seemed shaken. He recounted the trip and said that he "never wanted to be thrown into the jaws like that again." The aide left thinking that "Larry was scared to death of the aviators."

It was obvious to some of the civilian advisers and assistant secretaries that Garrett had trusted the admirals to provide him with truthful information about programs in the Navy, including the aviation plan, and that they had failed to do so. They told him what they wanted him to hear, not what was really going on in the fleet. The admirals had Garrett right where they wanted him, recalled Richard Armitage, the burly ex-SEAL who had helped persuade Cheney to pick Garrett as secretary. "He did anything they wanted, believed what they told him, assumed that they were all on the same boat together with the same objectives in mind, the same degree of patriotism and loyalty to the institution, and he was wrong. He was dead wrong." [13]

One floor below Garrett's Pentagon office in the secretary of defense's suite, Dick Cheney was coming to the same conclusion. He had practically written Garrett off for the way he had handled the *Iowa* debacle, and he was particularly irate over the aviation plan. He wanted deep reductions and told Garrett on a number of occasions to look for ways to carry out his orders.

But then Garrett would caucus with the admirals and come back with some scheme as to why the Navy needed to keep its carriers and its aviation plan intact. Cheney finally grew so frustrated with Garrett that he practically excluded him from decisions for downsizing the Navy and paid little attention to his plans and recommendations. "Cheney was just keeping Larry there to have someone walk the plank at the appropriate moment," Armitage recalled.

Armitage, who felt deeply for Garrett, was saddened by the treatment and had tried to convince him to sacrifice two aircraft carriers in order to ease the Navy's personnel burden and bring down spending and costs. These days he was saying it more and more, but Garrett was not listening. Finally, knowing that Cheney was near the end of his patience, Armitage made one last attempt during a lunch meeting to get Garrett to realize what he was up against. "Larry, if you signed on to this job as secretary of Navy with an expectation of holding the line or increasing the Navy, then you signed on under false pretenses. Your job," he said, "is to steer the Navy down to a smaller, but still sufficient for our security, level. That's your job."

But Garrett still resisted. The admirals had so thoroughly compromised him that he was not willing to do away with anything. "I believe this," he said. "Can you ask me to do something I don't believe in?"

Finally, after much browbeating, Cheney forced Garrett to cancel a multitude of programs.[14] One cut that sent morale plummeting was shutting down the F-14D Tomcat program, which Garrett had repeatedly fought for. Cheney felt it was cheaper to go with a new Super Hornet than to upgrade old Tomcats and build new ones.[15] It was a decision that would have long-term consequences and one that pitted the F-14 aviators against their fellow Hornet pilots in a bitter rivalry that caused immeasurable harm to the Navy. What compounded the F-14 loss was the cancellation of the naval version of the advanced tactical fighter. Without the new ATF or the F-14, the Navy would not have a pure front-line fighter after the turn of the century. Also chopped was the advanced support aircraft, a common air frame that was to replace three types of carrier aircraft that were reaching the end of their life span. Some officers who worked in the Secretariat joked that the cuts were so deep that a trail of blood ran from Garrett's desk to Cheney's office.

Amid all of the uncertainty and anger among aviators that carrier air power was withering away and taking second place to the Air Force came one of the worst setbacks in years for the Navy. On January 7, 1991, just nine days before the Persian Gulf War began, Cheney ordered Garrett to get rid of the A-12 Avenger.

The Navy had invested its future in the $57 billion program, so much so that for the last year Garrett and the officers overseeing the A-12 program had been running a deception campaign, concealing from Cheney and Congress critical information that revealed that the research and development part of the program was nearly $3 billion over budget, that the bomber was behind schedule, and that it was experiencing serious design and technical problems.[16] The ruse had been good enough to fool a number of people, including Cheney, who was so confident that the program was on track that he had even testified on the Hill with the good news. When he found out that he had inadvertently lied to the lawmakers because of the Navy's false reports, he was furious and shut down the program.

What made matters worse for Garrett was that Derek Vander Schaaf, who was now the Pentagon's deputy inspector general, and the Defense Criminal Investigative Service had begun an investigation into the conspiracy. Among the principal targets was Garrett, who the investigators said had withheld relevant information on the A-12 from Congress, Defense Department officials, and Paul Beach, a Navy official assigned early on to conduct an internal probe into the mess. The Pentagon's criminal investigation, which followed the Beach inquiry, reported that Garrett tried to cover up his knowledge about the A-12's troubles from investigators by removing a page from his personal daily notes that coincided with the date of a key briefing on the airplane.[17] Even Armitage, who believed Garrett was an honest man who would not lie, went ballistic about the failures of the Navy's leaders. "By God, the naval aviation leadership owes a great debt," he often grumbled to his Pentagon colleagues. "We're going to be paying their bill for a long time, and we don't have a goddamn airplane."[18]

Although Garrett was not entirely to blame for the aviation debacle that had begun under John Lehman, it was up to him to turn around the growing despair among the aviators in the fleet about the way he and the admirals were now running the Navy. The Tailhook convention, where thousands of naval officers would gather, would be the perfect place to carry the message that, contrary to popular opinion, Garrett and Frank Kelso had things under control.

But Garrett was not too keen on attending the rowdy convention. He had gone the year before, not to party as Lehman had done, but to support the aviators then leaving for the Gulf War. He'd attended the symposiums on naval aviation during the day and the dinners at night. Afterward he mingled with aviators on the infamous third floor, dropping into several of the hospitality suites and spending time on the patio outside the rooms. In one suite that he walked into, a woman was lying on a bed with her skirt hiked up while an admiral rubbed her stomach and another officer shaved her legs.[19] The sight neither startled him nor appalled him, recalled a friend walking with Garrett. One thing he didn't like, however, was a thick blue cocktail he drank in one of the rooms that nearly made him vomit.

The shenanigans that Garrett was exposed to at the 1990 convention were little different from those of past.years. One base newspaper in Texas called *The Flying K* ran a telling blurb after the party. ''The 1990 Tailhook Symposium is over. The good news is that all the Redhawks returned home relatively unharmed and none were convicted of any crimes, felonies, that is.'' [20] It went on to say the days were filled with interesting lectures and demonstrations concerning naval aviation, ''while the nights were characterized by celebration, joviality, and debauchery.'' People who visited the Redhawks' suite in 1990 drank 40 kegs of beer, 450 gallons of margaritas containing 315 liters of tequila, and 15 cases of liquor in that room alone. They also got to watch the aviators throw everything but the squadron commanding officer out the window, including a couch. ''The couch failed its initial spin evaluation and suffered complete strike damage. The garbage cans proved, to the dismay of the 'engineers,' to be more aerodynamic than the couch.'' [21]

By 1990 sexual assaults on women entering the third floor of the Las Vegas Hilton, particularly in the crowded hallway, had become more common since Roxanne Baxter had slammed an aviator against a wall in 1986 for grabbing her crotch. More recently, women had walked willingly down the hallway and let the naval officers ''zap'' squadron stickers, about the size of a coffee saucer, on their bosoms, crotches, or rear ends. Some women went topless as they strolled through the ranks of men and enjoyed the sensation of having their bodies fondled by the crowd.

The Airedales still called the third-floor hallway the Gauntlet and carried out their attacks on unsuspecting women in a deliberate and methodical way. A naval officer was posted to watch for women coming off the elevator to the third floor. If they were attractive, the officer would send a signal to the men standing in the corridor to be ready. As the women entered the line of men, several officers would fall in behind them to prevent their escape. An innocent stroll down that narrow hotel hallway then became a journey through hell. The men tried to disrobe many of the women. Others had their breasts and vaginas fondled. Many women fought back out of fear they were going to be gang raped. They scratched and kicked, screamed, bit, and lashed out with their fists. The officers cheered as each piece of clothing was removed and showered the women with alcohol. When Susan Hallett, a small woman from San Diego, slugged two men in the face while she fought her way out of the Gauntlet in 1989, the naval officers started pointing at her and chanting in unison: ''Bring the bitch back, bring the bitch back.'' Hallett was still shaken when she recalled the incident two years later. ''They were grabbing my breast, my butt, and my crotch,'' she said, adding that several men had exposed themselves to her; one of them had painted a smiley face on the tip of his penis. ''I kept thinking, My tax money is going to support these people. I have very little respect for them.'' [22]

The stories about the goings-on at Tailhook had been making the rounds in the Secretariat for years, especially anecdotes about Lehman's antics such as fondling a hooker or starting a food fight during a major banquet.[23] Now Garrett had seen the unorthodox gathering firsthand, too. When he recounted his three days in Las Vegas to some close aides in 1990, they were appalled that the Navy still sanctioned the convention and amused by the thought of Garrett in the middle of such ribaldry. "He was like a fish out of water," recalled one member of his staff.

It was Garrett's recollection of his last visit to Tailhook that spurred Batjer to scribble her plea across the letter inviting the secretary to the 1991 event. Even one of Garrett's military aides, Marine Colonel Wayman Bishop, protested that Garrett should stay home. After much bickering over the invitation, in which Batjer was made out to be the heavy, Garrett agreed that it was important to attend the convention. He decided to fly to Las Vegas late Saturday afternoon and deliver a dinner speech on the final night of the event. Once the decision had been reached, the officers on his staff, such as Rear Admiral Norman W. Ray, a longtime friend of Garrett's, and Commander Neil Golightly, a speech writer, had a rather large task before them. Garrett, who was not known as a charismatic speaker, would have to deliver a spellbinder if he was to put the leadership crisis to rest.

Golightly, who was generally considered one of the Navy's better wordsmiths, began working on a draft with the help of Ray. It would have to be an eloquent speech in which Garrett paid tribute to the bravery and personal sacrifices made by the Navy and Marines during the Gulf War. He had to inspire yet at the same time warn the cocksure aviators at Tailhook that he was in charge, not they. It would be, Golightly mused, one of the toughest speeches he had ever written.[24] The meeting with the pilots in Oceana had been a wake-up call about the widespread discontent bubbling just below the surface. Golightly was trained as an aviator, and he knew how the junior officers felt. Now Garrett was walking into an even more out-of-control crowd at Tailhook. The aviators preparing to gather in Las Vegas were angry over their mediocre record in the gulf, angry at the defunct aviation plan, angry at the fact that Navy women, who had flown transport aircraft and performed other support roles in the Gulf War without problem, were now competing for many of the same jobs as the men, and angry at Garrett and his admirals, whom they blamed for the hopelessness they felt about their future and the future of the Navy. Garrett sensed their turmoil. He also began to sense that in visiting Las Vegas, he would be like Daniel walking into the lion's den.

• • •

Throughout the spring and into the summer of 1991, problems from the Persian Gulf War continued to haunt Garrett and the Navy. Although public acclaim for the American troops was still high, within the Navy a sniping campaign was under way to fix blame for its poor showing in the war compared to the Army and Air Force. Many faulted Rear Admiral Brent Baker, the chief of public affairs, for being too complacent while the Air Force and Army had aggressively captured much of the media's attention. The brass wrongly feared that the nightly television broadcasts and daily newspaper stories coming out of the gulf might give the two other services a leg up on the Navy when Congress began slicing up the defense budget.

In Baker's defense, not all of the problems were related to press coverage. The Navy could fault itself only for the parochial "go it alone" attitude that shunned the new military jointness pushed by Richard Cheney and others. This was illustrated clearly every day when the war's air-tasking order had to be flown out to Navy carriers because its communications equipment was not in synch with the Air Force's. From the beginning of the conflict, the Navy was at a sizable disadvantage because the Persian Gulf War was a land-based battle. Saudi Arabia and other allies in the gulf had provided an abundance of modern air fields and ground bases for the Air Force and Army. The American general in charge, Norman Schwarzkopf, was an imposing Army officer who knew how to manipulate a fawning press. And Air Force General Chuck Horner was in charge of air operations for both services. The Navy was out at sea, boarding more than 1,200 ships as part of the U.N.-mandated blockade of Iraq. It was an important contribution to the war effort, but reporters wanted to be where the action was—and that was on land with the troops.

The Navy did have its high points in the war. The carriers *Independence* and *Eisenhower* were the first forces on the scene, arriving the day after Iraq's August 6, 1990, invasion. Before the outbreak of fighting on January 16, 1991, 2 battleships, 6 aircraft carriers, 115 surface ships, and an unknown number of submarines had sailed for the war.[25] Navy prepositioned supply vessels and fast sealift ships delivered more than 90 percent of the matériel for the early months of the buildup.[26] And although the Air Force and Army won the lion's share of the press coverage, Navy weapons of war produced some spectacular images. John McCutchen's mesmerizing photograph of a Tomahawk cruise missile lifting off from the battleship *Wisconsin* became a symbol of a bloodless, high-tech war and appeared on magazine covers throughout the United States.[27] The Tomahawks were a smashing success, hitting their targets about 85 percent of the time.[28] One missile was filmed by a CNN team as it cruised eerily over Baghdad. And the Marines were nearly unstoppable as they overwhelmed their opponents in a blitzkrieg toward Kuwait City. The Navy's SEALs also carried out a number of successful covert operations, which included fooling the Iraqis into believing that the thousands of Marines off the Kuwaiti coast were launching an amphibious assault. The diversion kept several Iraqi divisions preoccupied on the coast while Army ground troops began their famous "left hook" assault toward Kuwait. But there were also some spectacular gaffes and embarrassments, some of which became public, others of which the Navy had managed to keep secret.

On April 22, *Acadia*, a giant destroyer tender and one of the first major Navy ships that deployed to sea with women aboard, returned home to San Diego from the Middle East. Although tenders are not combat vessels and are to be kept out of harm's way, in an era of modern missiles the ships and their crews have become vulnerable to attack. About 360 of the 1,250 crew members on *Acadia* were women. They worked in the machine shop and in the fire detail and helped to transfer Tomahawk missiles to combat vessels. They also manned machine-gun posts while the ship was at general quarters, experiencing firsthand the fears of war that had long been the purview of men. At one point *Acadia* was in an area that turned out to be salted with Iraqi mines, one of which later exploded and nearly sank the billion-dollar *Princeton*, an Aegis-equipped cruiser.

But the heroic accomplishments of the women who served on *Acadia* were overshadowed by the human failings of the crew. When the ship finally tied up on Friday morning and its sailors and officers fell into the arms of husbands and wives waiting on the dock, thirty-six woman were missing from its ranks. They had been taken off the ship because they had become pregnant.

What was to be a public relations bonanza for the Navy—the showcasing of women carrying out important jobs on a naval vessel at war—turned into embarrassing revelations that *Acadia* was more party ship than warship.[29] Female sailors recounted to a reporter for the *San Diego Union-Tribune* that partying and having sex in the ship's fo'c's'le was so prevalent that it had become almost second nature. The newspaper played the story straight in its morning editions with a headline that read simply NAVY WOMEN REPORT GOOD, BAD. But it didn't take long before the East Coast papers picked up the report and began calling *Acadia* "the love boat." And one editorial cartoonist for the *Union-Tribune* drew thirty-six pregnant women lined up in white sailor suits, saluting *Acadia*, which was flying a Playboy bunny flag at half-mast. The punch line read "In honor of the 36 rabbits that died in the line of duty." Within a matter of days the controversial debate about women serving in combat, particularly for long periods in the close confines of a Navy ship, was spiraling out of control. As much as the Navy tried to put into perspective the role of women on ships, *Acadia* had become a negative symbol that would not sail away. The best they could do was say that men got sick too and missed work.

About a month later, on June 4, the Navy vessel *Austin* was tied up in a Turkish port after a deployment in the Persian Gulf. On board was a secret detachment of Navy SEALs, whose commander was the son of Jonathan T. Howe, the admiral in charge of U.S. naval forces in Europe. Admiral Howe was a legend in the Navy for being a workaholic. He had a doctorate in international relations from Tufts University and had made a name for himself as a deputy to Alexander Haig in the Nixon White House, where he had played a major role in the plans to mine Haiphong harbor in 1972. Later he had put together the background intelligence reports for Kissinger's secret trips to China.

At his headquarters in London, he was a relentless taskmaster, pushing his staff to their limits. One day he was conducting an all-day staff meeting that went well into the night when an aide politely reminded him of the time. "Admiral, sir, it's nearing ten o'clock. Maybe we should stop for the night." Howe nodded in agreement and said, "Let's meet at eight A.M. tomorrow."

But, Admiral, sir, it's Christmas," the aide pleaded.

"Okay, make it twelve o'clock," Howe said.

When *Austin* pulled into Turkey, the ship and its crew, including his son, were in Howe's command jurisdiction. That mattered little until June 4, when tragedy struck. Several members of the SEAL platoon went into town and got drunk. When they came back on board they continued to party, breaking out a bottle of liquor in their spaces on the ship. Then they broke into the weapons locker, where the SEALs kept their guns, and took out a high-powered hand gun to play Russian roulette. The game did not end well for one SEAL, whose head was accidentally blown off. Howe's son, the platoon leader, was not disciplined for letting his troops get out of hand, which led to the perception that he was protected by his father's clout. Many felt it made a mockery of the Navy's time-honored tradition that a captain always goes down with his ship, especially because the deputy platoon leader was reprimanded and another SEAL was court-martialed.[30]

The Navy was able to cover up that incident and an unrelated one in Coronado, California, the SEALs' headquarters, when a commando stationed there beat a woman nearly to death in McPee's, an Irish bar. The SEAL was quickly transferred to Little Creek, and the Navy avoided any embarrassing publicity.[31]

About one hundred miles up the Southern California coast from Top Gun, Lieutenant Colonel Mike Fagan and four Marine aviators were eating pizza and drinking Coke on a warm August day. All of the men had recently belonged to an elite unit called Marine Tactical Reconnaissance Squadron Three, based at the Marine air station in El Toro. As reconnaissance pilots they had been trained to fly low and slow over a target, which was one of the most dangerous jobs in combat, while snapping off hundreds of photographs for analysts back at the Pentagon or the CIA. But their skills had become somewhat outdated with the advent of satellites, and the Pentagon had decided to disband the squadron before the Gulf War began. The decision left the fliers bitter because they had missed the war and, for the most part, would ultimately be forced to retire from the Marines.

"Okay, okay, what are we going to do about the rhino?" Fagan asked the other men. "There's no way that we can get it back in time for Tailhook. So what are we going to do?" The rhino, which was the squadron's mascot, was six feet long and five feet high, just the right size to fit in the back of a pickup truck so it could be carted around town. Its hide was fabricated from papier-mâché. It had Ping-Pong balls for eyes, and it had a very large, two-foot-long penis, which was used to serve alcohol, that swung back and forth whenever the truck and rhino traveled together down the road. The rhino was three thousand miles away at Trader Jon's, a bar in Pensacola, Florida. At the end of the 1990 convention, some members of the squadron had thrown it on a trash heap in a fit of desperation over the orders to disband the unit. Some other aviators had picked it up and taken it on an airplane to Pensacola, then donated it to the bar.[32]

"Okay, you guys, what are we going to do?" Fagan asked again. He was not the usual bone-crunching, muscular type of Marine. He was tall and gangly and spoke with a twang and stutter like Jimmy Stewart, but in short bursts like Humphrey Bogart. If first impressions counted, he seemed more like the kid in science class with a calculator strapped to his belt than a forty-two-year-old Marine officer.

"Do we even need one?" asked somebody at the table.

"Should we even go to Tailhook as a squadron and set up a suite?" another officer wanted to know. After all, they were no longer officially a Marine Corps squadron.

They reasoned that a large number of Navy and Marine Corps aviators would attend the party. The Persian Gulf War had ended in February. And by the summer just about every Navy and Marine Corps male aviator in the country was talking about Las Vegas as if it were the only place to be come September. Pilots who flew the A-6 Intruder were printing up invitations to hand out to local colleges and hotel patrons in Las Vegas. On the invitation were the words

A-6 Tailhookers All-Weather Attack *"We stay up Longer . . . and deliver Bigger Loads."* *Please join the Intruders for an evening of imbibing, chicanery, & debauchery.* Las Vegas Hilton, Suite 307.

Another Intruder squadron, VA-128 from Whidbey Island in Washington State, had made baseball hats with an in-flight refueling probe that resembled a penis attached to the front of the cap. A variety of T-shirts were being made, too. One depicted a hung-over aviator with the slogan "I survived the third floor." Other shirts had antiwoman themes. "Women Are Property" and "He-Man Woman Hater Club" were but a few. Buttons emblazoned with a red line through the word "women" were ready to be dispensed. And one infamous E-2 Hawkeye pilot, Lieutenant Rolando "Ghandi" Diaz, otherwise known as the Barber of Seville, was returning to Las Vegas to set up a suite that featured leg and pubic hair shaves for women visitors. Diaz's hobby was among the most popular at Tailhook.

In past years Fagan knew that the rhino and the squadron's hospitality suite had been a big hit at the party. Women who ventured into the Rhino Room would be encouraged to kiss the rhino's nose and yank its organ. If done in the proper way, the Marines would let out a deep, gut-wrenching wail: oohrah, oohrah. The bartender would then push a foot pedal and a round of rhino spunk, usually Bailey's Irish Cream, would spurt out of the phallus and into a glass.

"Can we build another one?" Fagan asked Captain Dave Prudhomme, who had constructed the original rhino in 1989 out of wood and chicken wire.

"No way, it's too hard," Prudhomme said. "I'm not going through that again. I already did it once. There is no way, we don't have enough time."

"Why don't we just get a picture of a rhinoceros and stick a dildo through that?" asked Fagan. Drill a hole in the dildo, he said, and use it as the drink dispenser.

"That will look stupid," Prudhomme replied. "I don't think we should do that. Let's figure something else out."

"No, it will work, watch." Fagan then began to sketch the dimensions of the rhino and a dildo on a yellow legal pad. "What do you think?"

By this time everyone figured that was about all they were going to be able to come up with. So Fagan said, "Okay, get a dildo."

Prudhomme and another officer at the table, Captain Scott Bolcik, were tasked to make a new rhino and bring it to Las Vegas. When they left for Tailhook on Thursday, September 5, Prudhomme waited with the rest of the fliers at El Toro preparing to board a Navy C-9 transport plane. The two men carried onto the government plane an eight-foot-by-five-foot mural of a muscular rhino foraging in a field, with a rather unique drink dispenser. Then the C-9 taxied down the runway and lifted off into the brown Southern California sky. The rhino would be at Tailhook one hour later.

On Wednesday, September 4, 1991, daylight was slipping away from the desolate Mojave Desert. It had been an oppressively hot day—one hundred and four degrees in the shade. The darkness brought a cool stillness to the Mojave. For just the shortest of moments, the desert was black and quiet. Then the popping began. Pop! the neon lights flickered on at the Sahara Hotel. Pop! went Caesar's. Pop! the Hilton was aglow. Las Vegas, a city founded by Mormons eighty-six years ago, had begun another night of vice.

Above the explosion of lights on the Las Vegas skyline, Captain Frederick "Wigs" Ludwig was relaxing in the Tailhook Association's suite, which had been set up as a command center at the Hilton. Less than three months ago Ludwig had taken the job as president of Tailhook, which was thankless in many respects and, among other things, required that he be an intermediary between the association and Vice Admiral Richard Dunleavy, chief of naval aviation. Ludwig and Dunleavy had worked throughout the summer organizing the convention. Now it was the night before the arrival of the admirals and generals and more than one-third of all the fixed-wing carrier aviators in the fleet. That week Ludwig and Ron Thomas, the association's anemic-looking, chain-smoking executive director, had spent practically every waking moment in the Tailhook suite, working on scheduling and other last-minute details. They made sure there was enough room in the exhibit hall for the defense contractors and their aerospace displays. And they ordered 1,500 gallons of beer, 16,000 cups in all, for the Navy and Marine Corps officers who planned to attend the morning seminars.

Some aviators had already begun to trickle into the Las Vegas Hilton. Ludwig had watched them arrive—men half his age who cheated death every time they went aloft in a high-performance jet. They were arrogant and self-confident and certainly not afraid to die for their country. Ludwig looked at the men not with contempt, but with nostalgia. In these young bucks he saw himself as he had been years earlier: a hard-charging, hard-drinking naval aviator, someone not to be trifled with. They were all unusually handsome, firm-bodied men who, like Ludwig, pumped weights to develop muscular chests and powerful arms. Although an athletic physique helped to reduce the crushing G-forces, the reason for their muscular torsos was vanity more than anything else. They were men all cut from the same cloth. They looked the same. They talked the same. And they walked the same: a ramrod-straight back, chest puffed out, jaw pointed slightly upward, and more times than not a gait with a swagger to it. Above their left breast pockets they proudly wore gold aviator's wings.

The mold had been cast years earlier by Navy instructor pilots at Pensacola, Florida, and at the two training bases in Kingsville and Beeville, Texas. The instructors would take these young men entering flight school and strip them of their individuality, their sense of who and what they were as human beings in a civilian world. They would tear them down, then build them back up in the likeness of a warrior. Although they were all naval aviators, there was a distinctive caste system that identified the best pilots. At the top were the fighter jocks who defended the fleet from enemy airplanes. Then came the attack pilots, followed by the S-3 pilots, who sometimes flew their jets just feet above the water in search of hostile submarines. Next down the line came the pilots of electronic jamming planes, then the tankers, then the propeller jobs like the E-2 Hawkeye early warning aircraft. At the bottom of the strata came the CODs, which hauled mail and VIPs, then the helos, both of which performed important functions, but whose pilots received little respect within the macho world of naval aviation.

Ludwig was a fighter pilot, which placed him at the top of the pecking order. He would squeeze his body, which looked more like that of a heavyweight prizefighter than a pilot, into a cylinder called an airplane, a narrow tube with little wings hanging from it, and throttle the jet up to Mach 2. Then he would make it do remarkable things. He could stall it. Spin it. Depart it. And live to talk about it. He had been doing it for some twenty-five years, flying jets and enduring G-forces thousands of times. It was a familiar sensation: his eyesight would dim, his vision would narrow, and the force of gravity would actually shrink his body several inches in height during high-speed turns. "Wigs" had accumulated thousands of flight hours and had landed Navy jets on the pitching deck of a carrier—too many times to remember. In Vietnam he'd flown combat missions from the decks of *Kitty Hawk*. And he had punched holes in the sky with jets so powerful, they would rattle the windows of houses thousands of feet below.

But things were different now. Although Ludwig still felt a sense of comradeship with Navy pilots, he had made up his mind not to tolerate any gross misbehavior from these young bucks at Tailhook. Since 1986, when he had taken command of Top Gun, the year after Randy Cunningham had complained of misconduct and lurid sexual acts, not much had changed. But for the 1991 convention, Ludwig had mailed out a letter to the association's membership that spelled out guidelines for proper behavior. In particular he warned squadron commanders to guard against what he termed "late night gang mentality," a phrase that investigators would later say was a veiled reference to the Gauntlet. It went without saying that ball walking was out; so was streaking or mooning or, for that matter, anything to do with nakedness in public.

To prevent such antics, Tailhook officials would wear colored shirts identifying themselves as security officers and roam the halls. And they would be helped by a security team from the hotel. There would be three round-the-clock shifts, with each shift manned by twenty-three Hilton employees wearing distinctive dark blue uniforms. The best planning in the past, however, had caught only the worst offenders. By and large, the party, pranks, and drunkenness had gone on with little interruption regardless of what the security teams did. In fact, the Hilton's security detail had rarely followed up on abuses during prior conventions. Barron Hilton was more interested in the aviators having a good time than he was in clamping down on the licentious atmosphere. Even past reports of women being assaulted in the Gauntlet had not been investigated. One of the few orders issued by the hotel was to protect female security guards by restricting them from working on the third floor during the convention.[33]

Now all was in readiness for Tailhook '91. And Ludwig had decided he had done about as much as he could to ensure that the convention would be orderly.

Lieutenant Paula Coughlin tucked a denim skirt and blue tank top with thin shoulder straps into her travel bag. Nothing splashy, but just enough to show her femininity. It would be hot in Las Vegas at the Tailhook party. Besides, she had been at the 1985 convention on the third floor of the Hilton, the party deck, and seen firsthand the sea of sweaty, sticky flesh moving in every direction. She would be more comfortable in the light attire.

A short, compact woman, Coughlin worked hard at keeping herself fit. With broad shoulders and a thin waist, she had the athletic physique of a swimmer. And she had a crop of blond hair, cut short on the sides but long and shaggy on the top. It was her eyes that were most revealing, large and protruding with bags and deep wrinkles that were the result of two tours flying a Navy helicopter at sea.

The Navy had been her life since she was a child. Her father had joined at seventeen as an enlisted man, then gone through Officers Candidate School two years later. After being commissioned, he'd gone to flight school, become a naval aviator in 1954, then spent the next seven years mostly at sea. After that he'd had a prolonged tour on shore. Of the four Coughlin children, Paula was the closest to her father. "Paula was the first child he had time to spend time with," recalled her mother, Rena Coughlin.[34] "He took her with him everywhere he went," she said. "She was always up on his shoulders and off to the hardware store or something. They were very close."

As Paula grew older, her father would tell her stories about "the good old days," flying jets off carriers. His daughter listened intently to the heroic tales about her dad's experiences as an aviator. She had great affection for her father and wanted to follow his example and become an aviator in the Navy. Ambitious and wanting always to succeed despite the odds, she swam, became a cheerleader, and was a good student. And she was brave. Her family's house in Norfolk, Virginia, was near a marshland. One day a neighbor's child waded into the marsh, and soon the water was over his shoulders. He couldn't get out and began yelling for help. But there were no adults around. Paula, who was nearby, waded into the marshy water and the nest of tangled weeds to pull the boy to safety. She was ten years old.

As a sophomore at Old Dominion University, Coughlin enrolled in the ROTC program, graduating in 1984 and entering the Navy as a commissioned officer. By this time she had developed a hard edge and was determined not to take any guff from anybody. During her summer months home from college, she got a job as the first female lifeguard ever hired in Virginia Beach. When her supervisor said it would cost her a blow job if she wanted to break for lunch, Coughlin shot back: "Sorry, pal, I'm on a diet." And when another lifeguard called her a slut, "I clocked him." [35]

Coughlin's can-do personality enabled her to finish at the top of her helicopter class in 1987. She later did two six-month back-to-back tours in the Pacific, as a helicopter pilot assigned to a research ship charting the ocean bed. But she was ambitious and wanted more out of the Navy. She yearned to put her career on a fast track, to be close to the movers and shakers in Washington. So she applied to be an aide to Donald Boecker, the rear admiral in charge of Pax River, Maryland. After getting the job, she became close to Boecker, an attack pilot "who without a doubt was the finest officer and gentleman I have ever met in my life," she later said. "I worked my ass off for the admiral twelve hours a day, writing his schedule, getting him wherever he was going on time, making him look good, watching the nuances that count." [36]

The most distinguishing mark of an aide was the gold loop aiguillette, which signaled that the wearer had a place of importance in the Navy. Coughlin wore hers like a badge of honor. It was prestigious. And she was now a cut above her peers. More important, she was in close proximity to senior people, admirals and the like, who would notice her abilities to get the job done. A good flag aide could ride an admiral's coattails a long way in the Navy. And one who performed "properly," always showing sincerity and deference to the admiral, would be remembered when the best jobs came around. Access was always granted to the aide, even after the admiral moved up the chain of command to some other post.

But nine months after becoming Boecker's aide, Coughlin sensed that her career had hit a setback. Boecker, her ticket to advancement, the man she nearly gave up dating for so she could give him 110 percent of her time and effort, was now leaving. His replacement was Jack Snyder, the former head of Tailhook who had recently been selected for promotion to the rank of rear admiral. Coughlin was beside herself. She told her mother and other close confidants that she was troubled about Snyder. He was a fighter jock, a new admiral, and not a man to rely on a woman to be his aide.

Coughlin described Snyder as a man who "came from an environment where you did everything yourself. The concept of having a staff to do things for him, along with a hard-charging female telling him what to do, challenged our relationship." After a month working with Snyder, Coughlin, a young lieutenant with less than seven years' experience, told her mother that she found it difficult "breaking him in as an admiral." [37]

At Pax River several colleagues advised Snyder to select a male flag aide, that it was not a good idea for a young admiral to have a female aide. Snyder, however, rejected the recommendation. He had had a fairly good track record for promoting women in the Navy and decided that Coughlin should stay.

That summer of 1991 Coughlin made arrangements for her and Snyder to attend Tailhook. They would first fly to the Lemoore Naval Air Station, a major training base for Hornet pilots located forty miles east of Fresno in California's central valley. The schedule Coughlin had helped to plan called for her and Snyder to spend a little more than two days at the California base, talking to the fliers about naval aviation issues. On Thursday, September 5, they would catch a Navy transport plane to Las Vegas, where Coughlin had reserved a room for Snyder at the Hilton. She would stay at the Paddle Wheel three blocks away.

Larry Garrett almost didn't make it to Tailhook. On Saturday morning, September 7, his personal Navy Gulfstream broke down in Washington with a blown wheel bearing. Fortunately three Marine reservists happened to be flying into Washington that day on a T-39 and offered to take the secretary and his entourage to Nevada.

By midafternoon Garrett had landed at Nellis Air Force Base and was driven over to the Las Vegas Hilton, where his personal aide, Lieutenant Mike "Trusty" Steed, helped check him in. After escorting him up to his suite, Steed went back to his own room to begin organizing Garrett's personal papers and other belongings. Among the items was a copy of the Golightly speech, which Steed had hand-carried to Las Vegas. He knew Garrett was anxious about it and wanted to go over it one more time. So he called his room about 5:30 to ask if his boss wanted the speech. Come right up, Garrett said. When Steed knocked on the door, Garrett, who was dressed in his underwear, stepped out of his suite and into the hallway. Then the door accidentally slammed behind them, locking Garrett out of his room. "So I had to get hotel security to come up and open the door," Steed said, "and they actually wanted to check his ID." Garrett's wallet was in the room, so Steed said, "Here's my ID. This is the secretary of the Navy. Please let him in." [38]

Steed said that Garrett "was already mad at me. I've got him out in the hallway in his underwear. It was about an hour and a half prior to the banquet, and he needed to shower and review the speech, get ready for his evening speaking engagement, and it was really rushed." [39]

Shortly before 7 P.M., Garrett, in formal attire, headed down to the banquet room on the first floor of the Hilton to eat dinner and deliver his speech. He had gone over the text and penciled in a few changes. Other than that he felt it was right on the mark. The banquet room was packed. Kelso and Dunleavy were there, sitting at the head table. Jack Snyder was at another table, talking with friends. Paula Coughlin was also in the audience with about eight hundred officers who had come to hear what the secretary had to say about naval aviation. Steed went over to say hello to Coughlin and arranged to meet her at the end of the speech. As the aviators were finishing their meals, Rick Ludwig made some remarks about the association, then read a letter from George Bush, himself an honorary member of Tailhook, congratulating the naval aviators for a job well done in the Persian Gulf War.[40] Then he introduced the secretary of the Navy. Garrett rose from his chair and walked to the lectern. The room fell silent as he began to speak.

Garrett told the group that "accepting an invitation to speak here wasn't a little ill advised, like Gorby taking leave in the Crimea. For all I know, the boys at Strike U have already formed their committee of eight, John Lehman could be back in Washington announcing that my health has failed, and the F-14s might be taxiing up to the mall entrance of the Pentagon." Then, after the crowd relaxed, he addressed the Navy's problems head on. "I'm here in the lion's den because I think every single one of us needs to know and fully understand that we are in the middle of a fight for the future of U.S. carrier aviation—and the stakes are much greater than merely what air frames we'll buy or which systems we'll replace.

"I've heard in the corridors, and read in the gossip rags, a lot about how naval aviation is in disarray,'' he said. ''I've heard that we have no plan, that our junior officers are in revolt, that our thinking is hopelessly parochial, that the United States should replace its carriers with B-2s and Tomahawks, and that the Navy was an also-ran in the air war with Iraq. In short, I've heard and read a lot of baloney.''

Then Garrett played up to the junior officers who had flown in the Gulf War but issued a warning to the young aviators at Tailhook who had ''passionate ideas about how best to do their jobs, and my job, too, for that matter. I don't want aviators out there who are strapping tactical aircraft to their rear ends to be thinking first about the challenges of balancing a decreasing budget, or worrying about what we can afford and what we can't. It's not their chore to navigate the political and fiscal shoal waters of Washington. . . . That is my chore. And I want you to understand tonight, and as you return to your squadrons, what the future of naval aviation is really up against. I'm here to tell you that it won't take any more A-12 development debacles, or intramural squabbles over Tomcats, or who-needs-the-Air-Force rhetoric to jeopardize the support of those who have backed us faithfully in the past. I think we've got a pretty good hand, and this secretary's not going to fold 'em, we're going to play 'em.''

When the speech was over, Garrett left the clear impression that he was in charge of the Navy. He had rallied the troops, encouraged them to give up their petty rivalries and get behind the Navy's leadership. And if the ovation he received was a measure of success, he had accomplished what he and his advisers had hoped for.

As the aviators filed slowly out of the room and headed for the hospitality suites and the pool patio deck, Garrett asked Kelso if he was going up to the third floor to ''mingle with the troops.''[41] Dunleavy had encouraged both Kelso and Garrett, as well as the other admirals in attendance, to make a concerted effort to talk to the junior officers and explain what the Navy was doing to correct the problems with the aviation plan. It was one of the main reasons for the brass to go to Tailhook in the first place. And Kelso had been eager to do that, especially to gauge the reaction that the male aviators had to opening up the combat squadrons to female fliers.[42] He knew this was going to be a big problem for naval aviation. But now he was tired and told Garrett that he had a flight back to Washington scheduled for later that night. He said he was going to his room to pack and prepare to leave. Besides, he had been on the third floor and gone through the hospitality suites the night before.[43] It was an experience he did not care to repeat.

That evening he went out onto the pool patio area and struck up a conversation with Captain Robert Beck, a reserve aviator and commercial airplane pilot. As the two men spoke, a nearby crowd of men and a few women had surrounded a woman and begun chanting, "Tits, tits, tits." After five or six chants, Kelso turned to Beck. "Am I hearing what I think I'm hearing?" [44]

"Well, Admiral," Beck replied, "if you think you are hearing 'tits' shouted, yes, you are absolutely right." About twenty seconds later the crowd erupted into applause as the woman's bathing suit top came off and was hoisted into the air.

"Well, I guess that is the end of that," Kelso said to Beck.

"Well, maybe not, maybe not," Beck responded. A few seconds later the crowd began chanting, "Bush, bush, bush," trying to get the woman to drop her pants.

As Kelso wandered around the pool patio deck that night, the party that had become so infamous over the years was starting to pick up steam. Male officers were streaking and ball walking and consuming large amounts of alcohol. Hookers and strippers were working in some of the hospitality suites. And the Barber of Seville, Lieutenant Rolando "Ghandi" Diaz, had set up his leg and pubic hair shaving chair in room 303. Outside, a fifteen-foot-long banner proclaiming "Free Leg Shaves" hung on the pool patio of the suite, and women had lined up to have Diaz "make them see God." [45] Even Kelso peeked in the window at Diaz. [46]

In another suite, a flier from Australia on an exchange program with the U.S. military was playing a game naval aviators called "butt rodeo," in which they bit a woman's rear end and held on as long as they could, usually while the woman beat them on the back of the head. That Friday night the Aussie had already sunk his teeth into a number of women, some of whom would later require medical attention. Then he zeroed in on Lieutenant Kara Hultgreen. The "Incredible Hulk," as she was known among female aviators, stood nearly six feet tall and had long brown hair and the same "don't fuck with me, I'm bulletproof" attitude that the male aviators had. She was wearing a black leather miniskirt, high heels, and a black blazer, which led some to believe that she was a lady of the night. [47] As the Aussie sank his teeth into Hultgreen's butt, she looked over her shoulder in anger. Then, with all of her strength, she slammed her arm down, striking his head with the back of her elbow. The man fell to the ground, and Hultgreen yelled at him that if he didn't leave her alone, she would kill him. [48]

After more than an hour at the party on Friday night, as Kelso retired for the evening on the twenty-first floor, the officers and gentlemen of the U.S. Navy on the party deck below him were on their way to sexually assaulting some twenty women in the Gauntlet and in several of the hospitality suites. For Kelso, the Southern gentleman, Tailhook was like a bad dream. He didn't drink much, still treated women with chivalry, and thought the aviators needed a good dose of discipline. But that was something nobody was about to do that year at Tailhook—even the chief of naval operations.[49]

Now Garrett was asking him to make the rounds again on Saturday night. Fortunately he had an excuse to decline. But Garrett said he was going to his room to change and would be down in a few minutes. He walked out of the banquet hall with Trusty Steed and Paula Coughlin in tow. Coughlin found it exhilarating to be talking with Garrett, if only for a few minutes as the group rode up in the elevator. After Garrett stepped off the elevator, Steed made arrangements with Coughlin to meet her later on the party floor. She left and went back to her hotel room to change into the blue denim skirt and tank top.

A few minutes later Garrett left his room and headed downstairs. On the third floor he stepped out into a swarm of men. As he walked down the corridor, he stopped by the Top Gun suite and spoke for a few moments with Bob Clement, the F-14 pilot who had shot up the Iranian F-4 Phantom back in 1988.[50] Top Gun, once the rowdiest of all suites at Tailhook, was relatively quiet when Garrett walked in. Most of the officers were sitting around drinking beer or Cubi specials, a cocktail made famous in the Philippines. From Top Gun, Garrett moved into several other suites, then onto the pool patio area, where he chatted with a group of aviators.

Eight floors above him and the crowd, a half-dozen men and women had dropped their pants and were pressing their bare butts against a large window. Suddenly the glass gave way and floated down toward the crowd below. When it hit, the sound of breaking glass shattered the night and sent people running. Three college students from the University of Las Vegas were slightly injured, one suffering a concussion.

Shortly before 10 P.M. Garrett walked into the Rhino Room to get a beer.[51] Since Friday, those partying in the suite had been "lighting their hair on fire," drinking rhino spunk and daring women to bare their chests in return for a squadron T-shirt. On Saturday night a game of deep throat was being played. The Marines had drawn a line on the rhino's dildo and chanted, "Beat the line, beat the line," as a woman would simulate performing oral sex. Some women took part in the contest willingly, others felt as if they were coerced into doing it. At one point one officer removed the dildo and replaced it with his own penis.[52]

Garrett took his beer and stayed only a few minutes inside the suite. Although he would have to have been blind not to see the rhino and its drink-dispensing dildo, he would later claim he had witnessed no untoward behavior. By 11 P.M. Garrett was on his way to bed, tired by the events of the day. And as he fell asleep, Paula Coughlin was on her way back to the Hilton. For her, the night—one that would change her life forever—was just beginning.

• • •

Shortly before midnight, Coughlin entered the third-floor hallway at the Hilton and began searching through the fighter bubbas, looking for Trusty Steed. She made one lap around the floor but couldn't find him. She was now standing at the beginning of the hallway, looking down the dark tunnel at the men lining both sides. They were the clean-cut aviators she had been associated with since she herself became a naval aviator years ago. Although the hallway reeked of booze and sweat, Coughlin stepped forward. About halfway into the corridor, she attempted to squeeze past two men standing in the center. One of the men bumped her hard with his right hip. It was enough of a jolt to make her stop in her tracks. She turned around and said, "Excuse me." She looked at the man, sizing him up. He appeared to be six two, either black or Hispanic, and had big white teeth. He stuck out his chest and smiled at her. She turned around and moved a few steps forward, then heard someone shouting, "Admiral's aide, admiral's aide." She looked at a blond man who was yelling it. She didn't know him, but he knew her.[53]

The shouts turned into a chant, "Admiral's aide, admiral's aide," getting louder and louder. Suddenly she felt herself being lifted off the ground by the large dark man, who had hold of both her buttocks. She broke free and turned around, angry at the man. "What the fuck do you think you're doing?" she screamed. From behind came another blow from a man who was grabbing her butt. She wheeled around to see who it was, yelling again, "What the fuck do you think you are doing?"

Now the hands came from all directions as the men in the Gauntlet began grabbing at her, trying to tear off her clothes. With each pair of hands Coughlin fought back. But she was starting to feel helpless, overpowered, as if she was at the mercy of these naval officers. The large dark man was behind her, his body on hers, pushing her with his hips down the Gauntlet as men on both sides took their best shots. He reached over her shoulders with his arms and put his hands under her bra, squeezing her bare breasts. Coughlin dropped to one knee and attempted to wriggle free, which caught the man by surprise. Then she turned her head to the left and sank her teeth into his forearm, long enough and hard enough until she tasted what she thought was blood or sweat. In pain, he jerked his arm back. Then Coughlin bit his right hand, and the man retreated.

She sensed she was free now, safe from the madness. But as she tried to stand, another man reached under her skirt and grabbed her panties, tugging at them, trying to find bare skin. Coughlin knocked him away before he could get to her vagina. But the grope convinced her that the men were going to gang rape her. They were chanting, "Admiral's aide, admiral's aide," and grabbing and pawing. She got to her feet, saw an open doorway, and took two steps to reach it. But just as she was about to break inside to safety, two men blocked her entrance and smiled at her. She was now trapped, and the assault continued. Through the faceless men she saw someone in blue jeans and a faded red polo shirt walking away from the Gauntlet. He seemed older, a little more mature. Maybe he would help? She reached out and tapped the man, who was a captain, on the hip. "Help me. Just let me get in front of you," she begged. He stopped, turned to her, and then, reaching out with both hands, placed one on each of her breasts and squeezed. Coughlin broke free and ran past him and into an empty room twenty feet down the corridor. She sat in the dark, in shock, trying to sort out in her mind what had just happened. A few moments later she heard a voice. Standing by her was a young lieutenant she knew vaguely from Pax River. "Are you all right?" he asked. "You've just run the Gauntlet."

After composing herself, Coughlin went to look for Trusty Steed. Still dazed, she walked outside onto the pool patio deck. When she found him, she slugged him on the shoulder.

"What happened to you? Have you been in a car wreck or something?" Steed asked. "What took you so long?"

"You're not going to believe what just happened," she said. After she told him the story, they went searching the hallways for the men who had assaulted her. "Do you recognize anybody?" Steed asked. "Is there anybody you see who had something to do with this? Where did it happen?" Coughlin was still disoriented and couldn't even remember where the assault had taken place. "I need a drink," she said.

"That's the last thing you need right now," Steed said. "Let's go get some coffee."

The next morning, Sunday, September 8, Coughlin telephoned Jack Snyder's room shortly after eight. "I was practically gang banged by a group of fucking F/A-18 pilots," she said to her boss. "But we will talk about that later."

Snyder did not react one way or the other to the news. Besides, he thought that was how Coughlin always talked.

By the time Garrett left Las Vegas Sunday morning, eighty-three women had been assaulted in some fashion since the party began on September 5.[54] One teenage woman who was intoxicated ended up in the Gauntlet, where the aviators lifted her up into the air and passed her down the line, removing her clothes and panties. At the end of the line the men threw her into a corner, where she lay half naked and semiconscious. Hilton security guards finally came to help her, covering her with a coat.

That weekend a young woman and her mother walked down the third-floor corridor. The daughter was dressed in a formal cocktail dress and as she stepped into the hallway was hoisted into the air by two men. They lifted her skirt above her waist and pushed their hands between her legs to get inside her panties. The woman's mother and a friend of her mother were also assaulted.[55]

The airmen began to clear out on Sunday to return to their home bases. By all accounts Tailhook '91 had been a smashing success.

CHAPTER 23

At 12:30 on October 25, 1991, I sat down to lunch with a Navy commander at a popular restaurant on the shore of San Diego Bay.[1] That morning the officer had telephoned, saying, "Boy, do I have a story for you," and we had agreed to meet at the Fish Market. We were now sitting less than a stone's throw from the big North Island Naval Air Station, where many of the officers who had attended Tailhook were stationed.

"What's going on?" I asked.

"Something happened at the Tailhook convention," he said, "something about a gauntlet and naval aviators assaulting two civilian women and one female officer. The officer was an admiral's aide stationed at Pax River." Then he gave me a yellow piece of paper with Jack Snyder's name and a telephone number on it. "Oh, there's another thing," he said with a look of horror on his face. "SecNav and the CNO were there, too."[2]

It was nearly 2 P.M. when I made it back to the *San Diego Union-Tribune* to start digging into the story for the next day's paper. It was too late to call my contacts in the Pentagon who might know if an investigation was under way. But I knew that the best information would come from naval officers stationed nearby. The Tailhook Association had sprung up in California, its headquarters was at Miramar, and a sizable number of its members were scattered at Navy and Marine bases up and down the West Coast. Even a local vice admiral stationed at North Island called Air-Pac, an acronym for the commander of the Naval Air Forces Pacific, had for years been the unofficial head of the organization. My first telephone call went to Bob Lawson, a retired Navy chief who had begun the association's magazine, *The Hook,* one of the better journals on naval aviation in the country. Lawson confirmed that something bad had happened at the convention, but he wouldn't talk. He said only that "the Navy should have stopped that fucking party years ago."

More calls went out to civilian and military contacts at Miramar and other Navy and Marine bases. Slowly I began to piece together a sordid account of what had taken place over three days at the Las Vegas Hilton. As I worked the telephones, I found out more about the victims. The two civilians were

Marie Weston and Lisa Reagan, both from Northern California. Then I heard about a third, a teenager who had been stripped and manhandled. Soon I had Coughlin's name. It was late in the afternoon, but I called Pax River anyway, looking for her. When I got through, a female petty officer said Coughlin had been reassigned but took my number and said she would pass it on. A short time later Coughlin called. We spoke for about thirty minutes, but she was nervous and afraid to tell her story in detail. Before hanging up, however, she acknowledged that she had been assaulted in the Gauntlet.

By the end of the day I had enough to write a story, but the editors at the newspaper were reluctant, at least at that point, to report the charges. San Diego was a big Navy-Marine town, the largest in the nation, and the admirals and Marine generals had considerable clout, especially with the newspaper's senior editors, all conservative Republicans and several of whom had served in the Nixon administration. It went without saying that if a reporter was going to take on the Department of the Navy, he better have his facts right. It was decided all around to delay publication until more information could be obtained. I concurred.

On Monday afternoon, October 28, 1991, I drove out to Miramar and met with a source on the base who was wired into the Tailhook Association. I had gotten wind that this person had a copy of a letter, called a "debrief," that Rick Ludwig had sent out on October 11 to every aviation squadron commander in the Navy, summing up the convention. Now I was sitting in a dank office at Miramar, reading Ludwig's letter. When I finished I looked up and shook my head in disbelief, surprised at the candor of Ludwig's words. It was the proverbial smoking gun.

"Dear Skipper," the letter began. "Without a doubt, this was the biggest and most successful Tailhook we have ever had. We said it would be the 'mother of all 'Hooks,' and it was. . . . Our very senior leadership, including the Secretary and the CNO, were thoroughly impressed and immensely enjoyed their time at Tailhook." But then the letter went on to detail "just a few specifics to show how far across the line of responsible behavior we went . . . definitely the most serious was 'the Gauntlet' on the third floor. I have five separate reports of young ladies, several of whom had nothing to do with Tailhook, who were verbally abused, had drinks thrown on them, were physically abused, and were sexually molested. Most distressing was the fact an underage young lady was severely intoxicated and had her clothing removed by members of the Gauntlet.

"Tailhook cannot and will not condone the blatant and total disregard of individual rights and public/private property! I as your president will do damage control work at regaining our rapport with the Las Vegas Hilton and attempt to lock-in Tailhook '92. . . . We in Naval Aviation and the Tailhook

Association are bigger than this." Ludwig signed the letter, "Warm Regards."

It was the confirmation I needed, and I hurried back to the newsroom to write what I believed was going to be an important story. As I was typing it up, Coughlin called again. I told her that I had gotten hold of Ludwig's letter, which she already knew about. She was furious at the comment about doing damage control, viewing it as a clumsy attempt to cover up the assaults. We spoke for a while, and finally Coughlin began to tell me what had happened to her. She did not want her name used, so I said I would describe her only as an "admiral's aide." As we neared the end of our conversation, Coughlin said that when she did go public, which she planned to do, she would do it in the *Union-Tribune*. That was fine, I said, not giving it much thought. Otherwise I would respect her right to privacy. Anyway, the big news was the Ludwig letter. Here was a Navy captain admitting that the officers and gentlemen of the U.S. Navy had criminally assaulted at least five women at a convention attended by the brass. It was an on-the-record confirmation—something the Navy could not deny.

Before I filed my story I called Garrett's public affairs officer, Captain Jeff Zakem, for an official Navy response. "Jeff, I need a comment on some assaults that took place at Tailhook. Does Garrett know anything about them? He was there, you know."

"I don't know," he said. "What else do you know about it?"

"Well, I've got a letter from the president of Tailhook, a captain named Fred Ludwig, describing a gauntlet."

"Can you send me a copy of it?" Zakem asked.

"Let me think about it." I needed a response, and Zakem said Garrett needed more information to give out an accurate statement. So I faxed a copy. After it arrived, some officers on the staff started calling it the "ho-ly shit" letter. A sizable portion of the American people had already been appalled that summer about Anita Hill's graphic allegations that Supreme Court nominee Clarence Thomas had sexually harassed her. He denied it, and that case came down to her word versus his. But in the case of Tailhook, the proof was in a letter written by the president of a Navy-supported organization. Hill's accusations had broken open the door on the seamy subject of sexual harassment. Now Tailhook was about to blow it off the hinges.

Although Ludwig's letter had gone out two weeks earlier and the Navy's top aviation admiral, Richard Dunleavy, had helped to write it, it had been kept from Garrett, who had no inkling that things had gotten *that out of control* at Tailhook '91. He had been there the year before and seen firsthand the licentious atmosphere, but he had viewed it as behavior between consenting adults. He had no idea the Gauntlet existed. Dunleavy, on the other hand, knew a great deal more about the history of the convention. He had been instrumental in planning it. And, in fact, he had one of his aides taking notes at the 1991 gathering, which included references to the debauchery. He had even witnessed the Gauntlet himself and heard some officers yelling "Show us your tits" in the hallway. But he thought the women were taking part willingly and that there was little he could do to control the crowd. "It was my impression from what I saw," Dunleavy later said, "that no one was upset, and I felt that they wouldn't have gone down the hall if they didn't like it." [3] Indeed, for every one woman who resisted, there were many more who couldn't wait to walk down the Gauntlet and be manhandled.

Mike Matton, Garrett's executive assistant, was later incredulous when he heard that Dunleavy had not sent the letter up the chain of command and had failed to get approval before mailing it. [4] Had he done so, Garrett and the Navy would not be in the mess they were in now. When the letter finally did come into the Secretariat late Monday afternoon, Matton took it in to the boss. Garrett was thunderstruck. He had known about only one case, Coughlin's, which he had been told was an isolated incident. He had learned about it from his aide, Trusty Steed, who said it was being handled through the chain of command. Although the NIS had begun an investigation on October 11, the day Ludwig wrote his letter, the case was going nowhere, partly because it was just one of many complaints from women in the Navy about being sexually abused and partly because it was competing with more serious crimes like rape and murder. [5]

Now a large metropolitan newspaper was about to tell the nation how an unknown number of drunken naval officers had forced women down the Gauntlet at a party the top brass had attended. It would be a public relations nightmare for the Navy. What was worse, nobody at the upper reaches of the Navy had ever done anything to thoroughly investigate the activities at Tailhook, despite the convention's notorious reputation. Someone on Garrett's staff wondered out loud if they could get the *Union-Tribune* to hold the story. It was a long shot, but it was worth a try. On Monday evening Zakem called me and asked if I would hold the story. "I'll ask, but I doubt it," I replied. After checking with my editors, I called Zakem back to say the piece was running in the morning edition. Zakem said okay, but then added that Garrett couldn't comment. The case, he said, was now under investigation.

At the end of the day Garrett packed up Ludwig's letter with his other papers. He planned to mull it over at home that night. As he walked out the door, he turned to Matton and said, "Mike, we have to do something about this." [6]

• • •

On Tuesday afternoon an angry John McCain stepped into the well on the floor of the United States Senate. The son and grandson of admirals, McCain had grown up with the Navy. He would himself become a naval aviator and see combat in Vietnam, where he had been shot down and captured by the north. Later, after his release, he entered politics in Arizona and was elected to the U.S. House of Representatives. Eventually he won a seat in the Senate and on the Armed Services Committee, where he had a reputation as an expert on national security issues. His intimate knowledge of the Navy gave him a better insight into the brass than most other senators'. It also made him a feared man on the Pentagon's fourth floor, where Garrett and the admirals were afraid of McCain when he got angry.

Now the stocky, white-haired Republican was ready for a fight. He had read the *Union-Tribune* story, which had been picked up by the Associated Press, and was startled that something like this could happen in today's Navy. He called Garrett and Cheney and told them he was going on the Senate floor that afternoon to demand "a full and immediate convening of a high-ranking panel of civilian and military members in order to investigate this incident."[7] As he stood before his Senate colleagues, he did more than that. "Mr. President," he said, "in the last couple of days—remember that this convention took place well over a month ago—information has surfaced of some very despicable behavior taking place as far as sexual harassment is concerned at this convention."

McCain mentioned Ludwig's letter, of which he now had a copy, and asked that it be printed in the *Congressional Record*. He said the Navy should temporarily suspend its "official or unofficial participation in the so-called Tailhook reunion" until an investigation identified those responsible for the assaults. "Mr. President, there is no time in the history of this country that something like this is more inappropriate, and we cannot allow it. It is unconscionable. And we in the military, who pride ourselves on the equal opportunity that is extended to everyone in the military, should be ashamed and embarrassed—ashamed and embarrassed that this kind of activity went on. And there is no excuse for it." Then, as he neared the end of his remarks, McCain took a shot at Garrett. "The first question that I have of the secretary of the Navy is, if this has been known now for over a month, why has action not been initiated until such time as this became known in media?"

Across the Potomac River, pandemonium reigned in the Secretariat as Garrett and his aides tried to figure out what to do. Garrett had come to work that morning determined to do something about the Ludwig letter. "I have to view the president's letter as not just allegations," he told Matton. "This is something other than allegations." [8] But now McCain had taken the lead and was forcing the issue.

Some officers on Garrett's staff, like Jeff Zakem, were surprised by McCain's ambush and stricken by the irony that he would have the nerve to speak out on Tailhook.[9] Several of the older aviators were aware of McCain's past reputation. "He would fuck a pile of rocks if he thought a snake was in it," said one former Vietnam POW who had served in the Navy with McCain. How true the sea stories were mattered little now. McCain had the upper hand, and he wanted action.

Garrett wanted action, too, but he insisted that whatever steps the Navy took to deal with this scandal be as judicious as possible. It was clear to him that political pressure to do something was clashing with the due process rights of the officers who might be involved. Garrett, the overly cautious lawyer, wanted to go slowly and carefully. The *Iowa* investigation was now beginning to look like a red herring, and the last thing he needed was another foul-up. But he could not afford to procrastinate, so he asked Dan Howard, the undersecretary who was Cheney's spy, to begin work on a plan. Howard then summoned Rear Admiral Ted Gordon, who was now the judge advocate general and therefore the Navy's top legal officer, to his office to figure out what types of investigations could be undertaken. Gordon brought down the JAG manual and rattled off the differences between a court of inquiry, a formal investigation, and an informal investigation. "I explained to him that the most serious investigation would be a court of inquiry and the lowest level would be an IG [inspector general] investigation," Gordon recalled. "He decided that he would do an IG investigation." [10]

But by Tuesday afternoon Garrett was being pressured to do more. Marybel Batjer and a few other civilian aides wanted him to exert strong leadership and establish a special panel, as McCain had called for, or to do something that showed the Navy was taking Tailhook seriously. If it was going to blossom into a major political scandal for the Navy, which many believed it would, then Garrett should take charge now. With any luck he could at least act rather than react. But Gordon and Rear Admiral Mac Williams, who had been Lehman's personal lawyer and was now director of the NIS, strongly disagreed. They believed Garrett was politically vulnerable to criticism because he had been at Tailhook. Take a backseat, they said.

Late on Tuesday the various competing forces had come to an agreement on how to manage the affair. The NIS was directed to use as many agents as necessary to interview Navy and Marine officers around the world to identify the men who had criminally assaulted Coughlin and the four women in the

Gauntlet. The Navy's inspector general, Rear Admiral George Davis, was to look into the noncriminal aspects of the convention that nonetheless violated Navy regulations. And the Navy would break its ties with the Tailhook Association, a decision Garrett had arrived at on Monday night while studying Ludwig's letter. He then directed that the association's few employees and its board of directors—which was split about evenly between active duty officers and military retirees—vacate its offices at Miramar.

Privately Dan Howard would lead a Tailhook task force composed of Barbara Pope, a former Goldwater aide and now assistant secretary of the Navy; Ted Gordon; Mac Williams; George Davis; Commander Peter Fagan, who was the secretary's personal lawyer; and the head of congressional relations, Rear Admiral William J. Flannagan. Excluded from the group was Rear Admiral Brent Baker, chief of public affairs. Baker, many felt, talked too much. As the NIS and the IG investigated, they would hold weekly meetings to, among other things, handle the political fallout from the scandal.

When it came to public pronouncements, Garrett would carry the Navy's water. And that afternoon the secretary's media team started a public relations campaign to win over the press. At 5:46 P.M. in Washington, they began faxing to the media a copy of a scathing letter Garrett had written to Ludwig. "I am writing to you, and through you to your organization, to express my absolute outrage over the conduct reported to have taken place at the Tailhook Association symposium in September as expressed in your letter of 11 October, a copy of which was provided me yesterday," he wrote. "No man who holds a commission in this Navy will ever subject a woman to the kind of abuse in evidence at Tailhook '91 with impunity. And no organization which makes possible this behavior is in any way worthy of a naval leadership or advisory role." [11]

Ludwig was aboard the aircraft carrier *Kitty Hawk,* which was on its way around the tip of South America, when the letter arrived. For him the whole affair was devastating. He had done the right thing by revealing the abuses rather than trying to cover them up and circle the wagons, as the Navy had a history of doing. Yet now the secretary of the Navy had singled him out. If the Navy followed its celebrated tradition of the captain always being responsible for his ship, then Garrett should accept the blame. He had been the senior official present, the captain of the ship. He had been to two Tailhooks and was warned about the behavior. But Garrett was having none of that. He was shifting the blame from himself and the admirals to a Navy captain. And there wasn't anything Ludwig could do about it. To speak out publicly would be suicide. He was depressed, angry, and confused.

A short while later, as the carrier sailed from the Atlantic to the Pacific

Ocean, a team of NIS agents were flown aboard *Kitty Hawk*. The first person they wanted to interrogate was Ludwig.

Within a week of the first news accounts about Tailhook, the brass was looking for a way to placate Congress and the media. To do that, the Navy had to prove to its critics that it was taking serious action about rampaging naval officers. And there was no better way to demonstrate that than the public sacrifice of one of its admirals.

On November 4 Vice Admiral Jeremy Boorda, the chief of naval personnel, called Jack Snyder into his office.[12] Almost from the outset the meeting was tense, even confrontational. Boorda, who sometimes bragged that he could drive a ship better than anyone in the Navy, accused Snyder of being a poor naval officer. How could he, Boorda wanted to know, take no action when his aide told him she was "practically gang banged by a group of fucking F/A-18 pilots"? Boorda said he was going to recommend that Garrett ask President Bush to remove Snyder's name from the flag selection list, thus kicking him back to four stripes as a captain.[13] Kelso was also planning to fire Snyder from his post as commander of the prestigious Pax River test center—all this because Coughlin said Snyder ignored her when she tried to tell him about being assaulted.

Snyder was furious and heartsick that the Navy was prepared to cashier him. The record showed that he did not know until September 19—twelve days after Coughlin was assaulted—the full story surrounding the attack. She had started to tell him on Sunday, the morning after she had run the Gauntlet, but perhaps did not spell it out clearly enough for him to comprehend the magnitude of her assault. According to Snyder, the first he knew there was a problem was when his deputy at Pax River, Captain Robert Parkinson, a helicopter pilot, telephoned him late Wednesday, September 18. Since the Tailhook convention, Snyder had been gone from Pax River. He had seen Coughlin only a handful of times and had no idea that her anger against him had been building. "Paula and I need to talk to you," Parkinson said. He told Snyder that Coughlin had been sexually assaulted at Tailhook and that she had not been able to make him understand what had happened. They ended the call by agreeing that the three of them would meet the following day.[14]

On Thursday Parkinson and Coughlin walked into Snyder's office. "We all need to listen to Paula's story in detail and then plan a course of action," Parkinson said. And as Coughlin relayed her account of the Gauntlet, Parkinson glanced over at Snyder. "I purposely watched Admiral Snyder to get an understanding of his reaction as Paula was talking to him," he later told investigators. "As she started to describe the physical contact that had been made with her by several men, Admiral Snyder's facial expressions and body language demonstrated to me that this was the first time he understood what had happened to her. His face blanched, his mouth opened, his eyes rolled up, and he sat back slightly in his chair." [15]

When Coughlin finished her story, Snyder said he had had no idea about her plight and they had to do something. They spoke for a few moments about how the assault could hurt Coughlin's career if it was not handled right, something she was well aware of. She said she wanted to use the chain of command, and make sure that this could never happen again to another woman in the Navy. Snyder agreed and said that Dunleavy, as head of naval aviation, should handle her complaint. He said he would call Ludwig, Dunleavy, and his direct boss, Vice Admiral William Bowes, immediately. Then he and Coughlin would write letters to Dunleavy, asking for an investigation. "He asked us, Paula and I, if this was agreeable," Parkinson later said, "and we both said yes."

It took nearly two weeks for Snyder to get the letters to Dunleavy, which Boorda later seized upon as further evidence that he was not concerned about his aide's well-being. Coughlin, who was not fond of Snyder in the first place, took his delay in the worst light and grew even more angry about him. Although she had agreed not to go outside the chain, she gave a copy of her letter—which outlined her frightening assault in simple but powerful prose—to a female friend who worked on women's issues for Boorda's Bureau of Personnel. The female officer then gave it to her boss, Rear Admiral Frank S. Gallo, and ultimately to Boorda. Had Boorda seen Snyder's letter, which described Coughlin in glowing terms—"a warrior, a veteran of two cruises, a terrific officer, loves flying helicopters, and is as staunch of a professional naval aviator as you will find"—he might not have prejudged the situation.[16] But having only Coughlin's side of the story, he arranged for her to leave her post as Snyder's aide and come work for Gallo. Then he began a secret investigation, separate from the two now under way into Tailhook, to determine Snyder's culpability.

For Boorda, it came down to Snyder's word against Coughlin's. Yet he put more weight on Coughlin's version of events than on the unbiased statements of Parkinson and others, despite the fact that she mentioned nothing about Snyder's neglect in her first two interviews with the NIS and that, after the story became public, her recollection of events became more dramatic.[17] In at least one interview with investigators, she blamed Snyder for talking to the press but kept secret that she had been cooperating with the *Union-Tribune* since October 26, 1991.[18]

Regardless of the evidence, Snyder had not acted quickly enough to satisfy the Navy's demands for political accountability. And even if the Navy brass wanted to exonerate him, the "women in combat" issue had become so controversial that they would find the public outcry more painful than the loss of one rear admiral. For Kelso, who had come to maturity as a naval officer under John Lehman, a man who moved admirals around like pawns on a chess board, the decision to fire Snyder was not surprising. On November 4 the Navy released a press statement saying Kelso was removing Snyder from command because of his "lack of timely action to investigate an important aspect of this case."

The move, however, would turn out to have the opposite effect from that Kelso and Garrett had intended. It would serve only to exacerbate questions about their own involvement in Las Vegas.

That fall, as Tailhook began to take up an enormous amount of the Navy's time, Garrett and Kelso became embroiled in another, long-running controversy: *Iowa*. After the first investigation flopped because of insufficient evidence and complaints that the Navy had framed a dead sailor, which angered Congress and greatly embarrassed the brass, the Navy began a second probe that relied on an independent laboratory to determine if Clayton Hartwig, the so-called suicidal sailor on *Iowa*, could have ignited a device that caused the devastating explosion in the gun turret. The results of this second investigation sent the brass into a tailspin. There was no clear proof to support the Navy's earlier charge that Hartwig had "most probably" caused the blast.

Brent Baker, the chief of public affairs, took it upon himself to draft a letter from Kelso to the Hartwig family, apologizing for the Navy's rush to judgment. Baker was not held in high regard by the majority of Garrett's staff. His view of dealing with the press, Ted Gordon recalled, was that "you got over these public affairs problems much quicker when you just acknowledged everything you did, and apologized and got done with it." [19] In the secretive Navy, that philosophy was anathema.

When Gordon heard of Baker's plan, he was furious. He was not about to let Kelso sign a formal letter apologizing for screwing up. Admitting guilt would leave the Navy open to a lawsuit. "That's tantamount to giving up a case," he said. "I was protecting my client." Garrett and Kelso agreed that for legal reasons, an apology was out of the question. But they knew it was essential to respond to the latest findings and to do it in a way that would win back the confidence of Congress and the American people. It was especially important now, as Tailhook was again calling the Navy's credibility into question. After much debate, Kelso, with Garrett's approval, went before the press with the results of the second investigation, saying the Navy had erred in blaming Hartwig. Nobody, however, apologized to the Hartwigs for the pain and public humiliation the Navy had caused them.

On April 28, 1992, six months after the Tailhook convention, Dan Howard was deeply worried that some journalists either had a copy of the two-thousand-page NIS report on the scandal or knew enough about its contents to publish a story that would preempt the Navy's official release of it. The Navy had worked for more than five months on the investigation. More than $1 million had been spent to question Navy and Marine officers around the globe. Howard's Tailhook task force, which had met twenty-one times since last November 8, had gone over every aspect of the investigation. Mac Williams and the NIS agents had run down every lead. George Davis, the inspector general, who had run a much smaller probe, had also finished his investigation. There was nothing else left to do. Now was the time to get it out, he told Garrett. But Garrett resisted. Howard argued that any further delay would give an enterprising reporter time to pilfer a copy of the report —which read like an X-rated novel. He pointed to a *Union-Tribune* story published that day that reported key elements of the investigation. And he knew that David Martin, the well-connected CBS Pentagon correspondent, was preparing a report with even more information on Tailhook. Garrett still wouldn't budge. The last thing he wanted was to be forced by the media into doing something. Besides, he was madder than hell over the *Union-Tribune* story, which questioned his own story about Tailhook. NAVY BRASS ACCUSED OF IGNORING MOLESTATION REPORTS, read the headline. Quoting investigators, the story said the number of victims sexually assaulted at Tailhook had risen from the five that had been previously reported into the twenties. But the Navy had only one suspect, a Marine pilot. There was one other suspect, the Australian butt biter who had sunk his teeth into Kara Hultgreen's rear end, but he was not mentioned in the article.

Garrett was irritated by the leaks, but he was even more angry that a group of active duty and retired officers, led by the Big Cooley, Rear Admiral Jack Christiansen, was attacking him in the newspaper for using a double standard. They claimed that Garrett and Dunleavy knew within twenty-four hours about the assaults at the Hilton but did nothing to initiate an investigation.[20] Yet the brass had fired Snyder for the same offense. The Airedales were rallying around Snyder and had decided to go after the secretary of the Navy. Their public vitriol was unprecedented. "Those senior Navy officials who thought that the quick sacrifice of a junior admiral would cause the hounds to be called off should likewise be identified and dealt with as severely as policies permit," said one of the group, Norm Gandia, a retired Blue Angel.[21]

The *Union-Tribune* story also reported something else that caused alarm. Garrett had not been interviewed by either the NIS or the Navy IG. In fact, although some 1,500 officers were questioned, Garrett and the admirals who had attended the convention had somehow been excluded. George Davis, the inspector general, had wanted to question them, but he had been called off by Dan Howard, who felt the effort was not needed.[22] Some advisers to the secretary wondered if the truth about Tailhook would ever come out. In their eyes it appeared as if the Navy had again bungled another important investigation. For the first time they started to mumble the word "cover-up."

Later that day Garrett met with Kelso and the Tailhook task force to discuss the status of the NIS and IG investigations. Garrett was leaving the next morning for a two-week trip to Australia to represent the United States at a celebration marking the anniversary of the Battle of Coral Sea. It was only the third time in six months that he had been involved directly with the Tailhook investigation.[23] Although he did not attend the weekly gatherings, Howard frequently updated him and Kelso. Today's meeting, however, would be the most important. Mac Williams was giving an overview of the evidence and who the suspects were.

The seven people who filed into the conference room that day were agitated by the mounting pressure over the investigation and concerned about leaks to the media. Barbara Pope was the most angry. For the past several months she had taken it at face value that the Navy was doing its best to get to the bottom of the affair. She had supported the approach of the NIS's and IG's investigations and listened patiently to them explain the results of their interviews at the weekly meetings. She could even be comical about some of the findings. When she heard about the Australian playing butt rodeo, she laughed and said, "We used to call that 'chomping' when I was in college." But in the later stages of the investigation she grew impatient and became almost intolerant of the other task force members. Five thousand people had been at Tailhook and twenty-six women were known to have been assaulted, yet the Navy had only two primary suspects. What was worse, it looked as though prosecuting them might be impossible. The Australian was a foreign exchange pilot. The other officer was Captain Greg Bonam, who Coughlin claimed was the large dark man who had assaulted her.

The case against Bonam, Williams told Garrett, Kelso, and the others in the conference room, had been difficult and could go either way. At times investigators didn't even know if they could positively say that he was their guy. They began their search for him with a sketch from a police artist that was startling in its likeness. But it still took time to track him down. He was now an instructor pilot in Meridian, Mississippi, but before that he had belonged to Marine Tactical Reconnaissance Squadron Three, the sponsors of the Rhino Room. Williams was certain the NIS had the right suspect, but he and Ted Gordon were concerned about winning a conviction because of Coughlin's credibility. When she was asked to pick him out of a photo line-up, she identified the wrong man, a stand-in whom investigators had put in as a dupe. Later, with some hesitation, she fingered Bonam in a physical line-up held at the Marine base in Quantico, Virginia. She had also picked the wrong officer out of a photo line-up as the man who had yelled "Admiral's aide" when she was attacked in the Gauntlet. And there were no witnesses to support her story. She thought she had drawn blood when she bit Bonam, meaning hard enough to leave a scar, but there was no sign of any bite marks. She said he had been wearing a burnt-orange shirt, but a picture taken that night showed him wearing a green shirt. Privately both Williams and Gordon began to believe that Coughlin was embellishing her story, that she had probably been assaulted, but not in the dramatic fashion she was now claiming. Even Dan Howard started to think she might have her own agenda.

There were good reasons for all of these errors, from Coughlin's emotional distress to simple problems that affect all witnesses and victims, such as memory lapses. Still, Williams told the meeting that a good defense lawyer could undermine the whole case. Williams had been pessimistic all along about finding suspects, saying in one of the Tailhook task force meetings that "we don't have a fart's chance in a whirlwind of solving this case." [24] Gordon even predicted that Bonam would walk free.

When word began to circulate among Bonam's comrades that he was in trouble, they were shocked. Bonam was a Christian who regularly attended church, and he had a reputation as a shy, all-around nice guy who never got into trouble. His father had flown with the Tuskegee Airmen, the all-black Air Force squadron in World War II. But there were characteristics that conflicted with his saintly image. For one, the Clint Eastwood–type message on his telephone answering machine, that of a tough guy, didn't seem to fit. "Okay, punk, I bet you're looking for Greg. Well, he's out ridding the world of scum like you. So if you feel lucky today, leave a message." [25] His call sign was "Boner." And perhaps most convincing, he had failed an NIS polygraph examination in which he was asked if he had ever touched Paula Coughlin on the breast or the rear end.[26] Regardless of the evidence either way, there was a chance that Bonam might never stand trial. He had been diagnosed with cancer.

As Williams continued his brief, Kelso was becoming uneasy. And when

Williams said a good portion of the aviators refused to cooperate with investigators and had either selective memories or chose to hire an attorney and say nothing, Kelso got angry. "Mac, is it true that these people have a right to remain silent?"

"Yes," Williams replied, "it's their constitutional right. As a lawyer, I'm not bothered by that."

"Well, I am," Kelso said, almost yelling.

Williams felt that Kelso's anger was staged to placate Barbara Pope, who was equally upset. Finding only two suspects begged the question, Was the Navy covering up? The aviators were stonewalling and refusing to identify their buddies. "I don't think it is accidental that this is who we got," she said. "They are closing ranks and not cooperating. People are lying, and we're doing nothing about it. We're sitting here." [27]

Pope wanted the investigators to go back and interview the several dozen commanding officers whose squadrons had taken part in organizing the hospitality suites. They were commanders and captains and, in the case of one suite, a rear admiral. Something had to be done to make them cooperate, she said, and she threw out ideas like grounding them or docking their flight pay. Hold a board of inquiry or a blue ribbon panel. If necessary, use your secretarial right, she said to Garrett, to remove them from their jobs. "I'm not saying you fire them, I'm saying you remove them for lack of confidence. I don't know about you, but I don't have confidence in these people's leadership abilities."

Pope also wanted Garrett to write to the female Navy officers who had been assaulted and, on behalf of the Navy, apologize. "If you can't do that, then I want to," she told him. "These women deserve an apology."

Gordon and Williams were appalled at all of those notions. And so was Garrett.

Pope was on the verge of losing all faith in the Navy's ability to investigate itself. She began to believe that the admirals did not want to broaden the investigation because they intended to protect the flag officers who attended Tailhook. If they pulled the string too hard, it would go all the way back to John Lehman. Pope knew Williams and Gordon were loyal Lehman men. "They didn't want Lehman's name involved," she would later say.

Although Pope was outmaneuvered, Garrett was sensitive to her complaints that the Navy was not holding people accountable. And he and his advisers were smart enough to realize that the *Union-Tribune* story would encourage the press to zero in on him for the same thing. So before leaving for Australia, he had a memorandum he wrote that day, April 28, leaked to the media that would appease both the press and Pope. "I am appalled by the unacceptable behavior and attitudes reported in [the NIS and IG] investigations," he wrote, and went on to say that the findings "indicated a lack of responsibility, absence of moral judgment, and inadequate standards of integrity on the part of Navy and Marine Corps officers who could have asserted positive leadership but failed to do so. It is simply not good enough to abstain from unacceptable conduct, we must demand much more from our officers; society expects no less."

One of his final instructions was to Dan Howard. Don't release the NIS report until it was ready, he said. "I don't want another *Iowa*."

Two days later Howard was champing at the bit. He had already prepared a redacted version of the report so the press didn't have to file under the Freedom of Information Act to get it. The printer was lined up. The flaks were ready. And a media plan was in place to spin the story away from accountability at the top. Brent Baker and his public affairs team would blame the junior officers for obstructing the investigation and preventing the Navy from finding more suspects. Although Baker publicly ridiculed reporters for using unnamed sources, he had already begun giving interviews to selected journalists on a not-for-attribution basis.[28] He said widespread criminal charges were unlikely because investigators could not pierce a "conspiracy of silence" among the Airedales.

Just before Howard was ready to make his move and release the report, Garrett's longtime friend, Norm Ray, poked his head into his office. "I just talked to the secretary," he said, who at this point was in Hawaii. "He thinks that you probably ought to send it to the commandant and the CNO and give them thirty days to respond."

"Norm, I can't do that," Howard said. "We've got the damn thing printed, it's leaking all over the place. I absolutely have to release it. I'm the guy who has to release it. Larry was there. Larry is wooden on camera, like a deer caught in the headlights. He gets angry. He's a former naval aviator. I need to go out and take the beating on this one."

"I agree," Ray said, "but you better call him."

"Norm, if I call him and I get a direct order, we're really in the shit. I've got to release the report."[29]

On April 30 Howard told the press that both the NIS and George Davis's IG reports were available. The two-thousand-page NIS report was not only bulky, it was done in the standard way that the Navy's police force chronicled the results of its investigations. There was no table of contents or index to guide the inexperienced through a morass of complaints, interviews, and sworn statements. The IG report was short, more of a narrative, and easier to follow for those unfamiliar with the Navy's investigative practices.

Still, with its lurid details, like one account of an officer sneaking up behind a woman and wrapping his penis in her waist-length hair, the NIS report got the expected bounce in the media. It was an easy story for the press to trumpet: drunken military men sexually assaulting innocent female victims. The networks, CNN, and the major newspaper dailies easily latched on to that theme and avoided the more complex issues of women as aggressors and men as victims. There were several cases of women grabbing men's crotches in a "package check" or other male officers having their pants pulled down by women. Incidents like these were, in a sense, trivial compared to the Gauntlet and easy to gloss over. By and large the media played it safe and quoted findings from both reports that the convention was a tax-supported sex-and-alcohol binge tacitly approved by the Navy's top brass. "This mentality," the report stated, "led attendees to believe they could get away with 'manhandling' selected women in the gauntlet to the point of assault." And it went on to say that "the victims . . . feared that anything could happen to them and they were helpless to prevent it."

On Capitol Hill, Senator McCain said publicly that "the situation in Las Vegas was as serious as I feared when I first asked the Navy to investigate." But there was more, much more, to the story that McCain didn't know about.

When Garrett arrived back in Washington, he walked into a feeding frenzy. The press and Congress had caught on to Barbara Pope's warning that nobody at the top of the Navy was being held accountable for Tailhook.

Barbara Boxer, the California Democrat who was then running for the Senate, demanded congressional hearings in which Garrett would have to testify.[30] Pat Schroeder, the Colorado Democrat who served on the House Armed Services Committee, jumped into the fray two days later after some officers in the Navy and Marines sent out a worldwide message asking commanding officers to identify aviators eligible for "the prestigious Tailhook Award . . . to pay tribute to an individual whose efforts or unique accomplishments have caused a significant advancement in contemporary carrier aviation within the last two years."[31] Schroeder seethed over the message. She had been pleased that Garrett had broken ties with the Tailhook Association back in October, but now she said that was "nothing but a PR thing to fend off the press and the public. I took them at face value that they really had broken off all ties."[32] She repeated Boxer's call for hearings.

The Navy was paralyzed over the thought of what politicians might do with something as volatile as Tailhook in a presidential election year. If there were two issues that every candidate either feared or was talking about, they were sexual harassment and lifting the ban that restricted women from combat. Tailhook had combined those two into one extremely powerful mega-issue. Advocates for lifting the ban claimed that until the Navy—

indeed all of the services—gave women the same jobs that men had, the sexual harassment and abuse so prevalent at Tailhook would continue. Congressional hearings would give credence to this line of thought, and it would continue to tarnish the Navy's image.

Something had to be done to stop it. Admiral Jerry Johnson, the vice chief of naval operations, visited the offices of key lawmakers to tell them that the Navy was capable of policing its ranks to prevent abuses against female troops. When he approached Schroeder, she turned the Navy down cold. "She thinks it's just hand-holding," said Dan Buck, her veteran spokesman.[33]

It was Sam Nunn, the Georgia Democrat, who really brought things in the Navy to a grinding halt. As his compatriots in the House prepared to hold hearings on Tailhook, Nunn and his Republican colleague on the Armed Services Committee, John Warner, a former secretary of the Navy from Virginia in the 1970s, had a more ominous plan. That May they wrote a letter to Defense Secretary Dick Cheney, informing him the committee was going to hold up the promotions of nearly five thousand naval officers.[34] The freeze was within Nunn's purview, and there wasn't much Garrett or anybody else could do about it. Nunn wanted to ensure that none of the officers up for promotion had been involved with Tailhook. Garrett was furious and believed the Senate was holding five thousand people hostage for political reasons. He wanted to talk with Nunn and Warner personally to get them to change their minds. But Cheney ordered him not to, stating that his only role was to figure out a procedure for responding to the committee. Garrett was so angry about Cheney's lack of support that he thought about quitting.

If the troubles on Capitol Hill weren't bad enough, Barbara Pope was threatening to resign. She did not trust the men running the investigation and was finally fed up. "I'm now at the point where I can't stay here," she said to Garrett as the two of them sat in his office. When she had signed on at the beginning of the Bush administration, her loyalty to Garrett was unquestioned. She had told him then that if she could not support his leadership, she would leave. Now she felt she had to do so. "I'm concerned about leadership," she said. "I'm concerned about this report. It's half-assed. You as the secretary of the Navy can't accept this report. And you can't accept it and do nothing."[35]

Pope gave Garrett a list of things that needed to be done if the investigation was to be put back on track. She again brought up the idea of hitting the squadron commanders hard. "I understand that this is tough for you. You need to decide what it is you can do and want to do. And then I have to decide if I can live with that."

"How much time do I have?" Garrett asked.

"I don't know. I'm not going on the Hill to testify, that's for sure. I want to give you time."

Garrett was tormented by the prospect of Pope's resignation. If he thought he had problems now, having his female assistant secretary quit because she felt the men running the Tailhook investigation were covering up would be a disaster on Capitol Hill. He had already tried once to appease her. On May 14 he asked Gordon to see if any of the squadron commanding officers had obstructed the Tailhook investigation.[36] In the tasking memorandum to Gordon, Garrett said he was concerned that the Navy had only a few suspects, and he wanted more—all the better if they were senior people in positions of authority.[37] Gordon reviewed the cases and found no reason to charge the commanding officers. Overall, the NIS had 383 cases in which officers could be charged under the Uniform Code of Military Justice for making false statements, conduct unbecoming an officer, indecent assault, indecent exposure, or obstruction of justice.[38] Of these, Gordon recommended that seventy people be disciplined.[39] Letters identifying the suspects were then sent to the admirals in charge of the commands, asking them to carry out whatever discipline they deemed appropriate. All except one suspect were junior officers.

But that was not enough for Pope, who rightly saw Tailhook as a failure of leadership. She could not stomach that the men running the Navy were doing little to investigate Tailhook or to address the scandal as a widespread cultural problem. She had become a constant source of consternation to Garrett and his blue-suited advisers, especially Williams and Gordon. They were intent on running the investigation within the narrow confines of the military justice system, and they didn't want the politicians interfering with it and tainting cases that would later be thrown out of court for command influence.

Williams and Gordon accused Pope and Dan Howard of wanting to suspend the due process of individuals to satisfy almost overwhelming political pressures. They were angry and privately told the media and whoever else would listen that Pope was a feminist with an agenda who was out of her league. "She is one of these 'gee whiz wow' people," Gordon said, writing Pope off as a political lightweight. They didn't dare take the same tack with her friend Marybel Batjer, because of Batjer's connections to powerful Republicans and to General Colin Powell. But to Pope they were merciless.

Finally Pope played her best card. She turned to her friends in the Pentagon: Rich Armitage, Dick Cheney, and his influential aide, David Addington. When Pope told Addington that she was quitting because she and Garrett couldn't reconcile their differences over Tailhook, she could see that he was angry. Garrett and Howard had been assuring him all along that everything was under control. Now the scandal was about to get another bump in the TV ratings. "You're not going anywhere," he said to Pope. "Let me find out what's going on. If anybody goes, it's Garrett." [40]

Addington wanted the squadron commanding officers interviewed, and not just by naval officers. Like Pope, he didn't trust the naval investigators. He instructed Craig King, the Navy's civilian general council and a political appointee, to play a lead role in the questioning. If Garrett failed to carry out this order, both he and Frank Kelso would be fired.

On June 1 Garrett sat in his office on the Pentagon's fourth floor, a desperate man. It seemed as if his Navy was unraveling like a cheap sweater and there was nothing he could do to stop it. He was the consummate lawyer who wanted to protect the legal rights of individuals. He could not fathom the idea of firing officers just for the sake of satisfying the political whims of Congress. They were his men, from his Navy family. He had to protect them. But Cheney had had enough. He wanted this mess settled once and for all.

Sitting with Garrett were his old buddy Norm Ray, Ted Gordon, and some other staffers. Gordon had heard about Addington's plans and advised Garrett not to follow them. To allow a political appointee to take part in the questioning would make a mockery of the military's judicial system. Once the politicians ran things, he explained, there was no way to prevent the cases from being tainted by command influence. The Navy would lose everyone in a court of law, he said.

Even so, Garrett said he was going to comply with Addington and that he was going to issue a memorandum instructing the CinCs to cooperate with the general counsel to determine the culpability of the squadron commanding officers who attended Tailhook. He was also establishing a standing committee on women to be headed by Barbara Pope.[41]

Gordon jumped to his feet in a fit of anger. "This whole thing is about saving your job!" he yelled at Garrett.

Garrett stood up and faced Gordon. "You don't understand," he shouted back. "This is not about my job. This is about solving a political problem."

"Goddammit, you're just trying to save your job!" Gordon screamed back. He was so mad, he was shaking. "I have spent my entire time keeping this in perspective, and you're throwing it away." [42]

"Mr. Secretary, I don't know who to believe anymore," a disillusioned Frank Kelso said on June 10 as he plopped down on a chair in Garrett's office.[43] Kelso had just learned the most alarming news. A key interview placing Garrett in the raucous Rhino Room on the final night of the Tailhook convention had somehow been excluded from the two-thousand-page NIS report that the Navy had provided to Congress and the American public. Since Tailhook first broke in October, the Navy brass had stood by Garrett's claim that he had not gone into the suites or seen any misbehavior. That position had been passed on privately to reporters on a not-for-attribution basis to build a case in the media to shield Garrett from any blame. Then, on June 9, assured that Garrett was telling the truth, the secretary's flaks went public with that statement.[44]

Kelso had also sided with Garrett. He had been personally assured by Mac Williams, after the NIS investigation was completed in March, that Garrett's whereabouts at Tailhook were not a problem. "Is there anything in your investigation," Kelso asked Williams, "that's going to place the secretary on the third floor at Tailhook?"

"I've taken the pulse of all the agents in the field," Williams replied, "and there's nothing out there that's going to implicate the secretary."[45]

What Williams didn't tell Kelso was that the statement, taken from Marine Captain Raymond Allen, who said Garrett had visited the Rhino Room, had arrived at NIS headquarters in Washington on February 20, 1992. Williams had placed a copy of the document in his safe, a charge he denies.[46]

When Kelso learned about the Allen statement, which would support allegations that the Navy was covering up to protect the brass, he telephoned Williams and demanded to know what was going on. Williams said the statement was irrelevant because it had nothing to do with the criminal aspect of the NIS investigation. Kelso was so incensed at Williams that he went in to see Garrett to demand that he be fired. But Garrett, who did not know that the Allen statement had been under lock and key for four months, refused, saying he had full trust in Williams's integrity. It was the second time he said no to a plea from Kelso to fire an admiral because of Tailhook. Kelso, George Davis, and Dan Howard wanted to sack Richard Dunleavy for a multitude of gaffes and lack of honesty over Tailhook. But Garrett refused.

Now he was boxed in. *The New York Times,* the *Union-Tribune,* and *The Washington Post* were preparing stories on the missing fifty-five pages, which included Allen's statement. It was only a matter of time before it came out and caused a sensation and a new round of finger pointing. The last thing the Navy needed was more bad press. On June 16, after queries from the newspapers, Garrett's office released a statement that contradicted the one given just a week earlier. "The closest he came to any of the suites, to the best of his recollection, was on one occasion," the statement read, "shortly after he had arrived in the patio area, when we walked over to the poolside entrance to one of the suites which bordered on the patio area to get something to drink."

The story broke big the next day. Not only were there reports about the missing fifty-five pages, but it came out that Garrett had visited the suites on numerous occasions while spending three days in Las Vegas at the 1990 convention. The logical question was this: If he had gone into the suites then, why wouldn't he do it in 1991?

Garrett decided that his only recourse was to ask the Defense Department's inspector general to investigate why the Allen statement had not been included in the initial report. Howard, Gordon, and Williams felt as if they were selling their souls to the devil by going to Derek Vander Schaaf. They commonly referred to the deputy inspector general and his investigators as "Derek and his cutthroat band of Nazis." But Garrett was determined to stop the press mill from speculating that the Navy was covering up. On June 18 he formally asked Vander Schaaf in a memorandum to investigate the matter.[47] For the first time there was a sizable dent in Garrett's reputation as the most honest man in Washington. It appeared to some that the straitlaced Garrett was not so straight after all.

At the White House, General Brent Scowcroft, the President's national security adviser, was taken back by the reports. He had been watching the Tailhook scandal build and was sickened by the daily drumbeat of stories about the debauchery and the failure of Navy leadership. "I think it's a disgrace," he said. "There ought to be some high-level people held responsible."[48] He started thinking that it was time for Garrett to go.

Derek Vander Schaaf felt the same way about holding high-level people accountable. He decided it was long overdue to examine how much the brass really knew about Tailhook. He had three months to come up with the goods.

June 24 was a bad day for Larry Garrett and the Navy. That morning Paula Coughlin's picture and an account of her assault appeared in *The Washington Post*. Written by John Lancaster, the story had tremendous impact. For the first time the public was allowed to see the "admiral's aide" who had become Tailhook's most celebrated victim. "I'm coming forward, and I'm putting a name and a face to this," she told Lancaster.[49] "I've been in the Navy almost eight years, and I've worked my ass off to be one of the guys, to be the best naval officer I can and prove that women can do it. And I was treated like trash." That evening she was slated to be interviewed in a two-part series with Peter Jennings of ABC News. In just a few hours her face and voice would be beamed to millions of homes across the nation.

While Coughlin's coming-out was an important part of the Tailhook story, Larry Garrett was more concerned and personally pained about another newspaper story that ran that day and was making the rounds in Washington. The *Union-Tribune* reported that his son Lawrence, who had joined the

Navy over his father's objections, had been disciplined in an illegal credit card scam that had netted about $15,000. While the group's ringleader would ultimately be sentenced to two years in jail and given a bad conduct discharge, Garrett's son was restricted to base for thirty days and fined $880.[50]

The light discipline angered some officers in the Navy, who believed Garrett's son should have gone to a court-martial hearing after admitting to marijuana use, credit card fraud, and lying under oath. Traditionally that would have been the route for a normal sailor. But this case was far from normal. After young Lawrence graduated from boot camp in San Diego, he got orders to Air-Pac, where the vice admiral in charge, Edwin Kohn, could watch over him. After his assignment there, Jeremy Boorda, the chief of personnel who had recruited Lawrence into the Navy, made weekly telephone calls to Kohn, inquiring how the secretary's son was doing.[51] Boorda also gave Garrett regular updates on Lawrence's life in the Navy. And when Lawrence got into trouble, Boorda's office had him transferred to his staff in Washington before his tour of duty in San Diego was finished. According to Garrett's executive assistant, when Boorda was reassigned to Europe with a promotion to full admiral, he asked Garrett's son if he wanted to come with him as part of his staff.[52] Lawrence declined because he planned to leave the Navy.

Garrett had purposefully avoided any involvement in his son's career. But when Mac Williams tipped him off that agents from the NIS were en route to his home in Oakton, Virginia, to search Lawrence's room, the secretary hurried there. He was so embarrassed as well as emotionally troubled by Lawrence's behavior that he told his aides he was considering resigning. He also told Dick Cheney about the case because of the potential for adverse media attention.

Indeed, the case would drag on for another three years. Before it was over, the Navy–Marine Corps Court of Military Review would rule that Lawrence Garrett had received special treatment solely because he was the secretary's son. "Not only is it uncommon, but it is extraordinary that a sailor could be found to have used marijuana repeatedly, to have stolen property using credit cards taken from a Navy mail room, to have received stolen property stolen by using these cards," a panel of three judges wrote, "and to have lied to NIS agents under oath and then be retained on active duty without being processed for discharge. Based on our experience, we state with confidence that, absent extraordinary circumstances, any other sailor in the U.S. Navy who faced such charges would have been tried by court-martial." The military court blamed Williams and two other lower-ranking captains who were later exonerated. But it stopped short of implicating Boorda, who had watched over Lawrence ever since he had joined the Navy.

Boorda said nothing about the fiasco and let his staff do the talking. At first they said Boorda had never made any inquiries about Garrett's son. Then, as naval officers came forward to corroborate the calls, his staff admitted that, well, yes, he had called Kohn on a regular basis. But Commander John Carmen, Boorda's spokesman, said it was not unusual for the admiral to watch out for an enlisted sailor. That he was the son of the secretary of the Navy mattered little, Carmen said. He would have done it for anybody. Boorda himself refused to talk.

That Wednesday night President Bush turned on the television in the White House. There, looking splendid in her Navy whites, was Paula Coughlin being interviewed by Peter Jennings, the anchor of *World News Tonight*. "I love the Navy," she told Jennings. "I was attacked by naval officers and Marine Corps officers who knew who I was. And it was a sport for them. It was a good time."

After watching Coughlin tell her story, Bush, the former naval aviator, made two decisions. Garrett had to go. And he wanted Paula Coughlin to come to the White House and visit with him and Mrs. Bush.

On Friday afternoon Paul Beach climbed up one flight of stairs from Cheney's office to the fourth floor of the Pentagon. As he paced briskly down the E-Ring, he could see the secretary of the Navy's office dead ahead. It was close to 3 P.M., and Beach was on a private mission for his boss, Dick Cheney. After walking into Garrett's office, he closed the door.

Almost immediately one of Garrett's aides looked through a peephole in his door to see what was going on. There had been rumors for weeks that Bush and Cheney were tired of the scandal and wanted to fire Garrett. The presidential election was just months away, and the administration, headed by a former naval aviator who was an honorary member of the Tailhook Association, wanted to bury the sexual harassment issue in a hurry. Now Beach was standing over Garrett, who was sitting at his desk, writing out what appeared to be his letter of resignation. Twenty minutes later the two men walked out the door and headed for Cheney's office, where Garrett would formally resign.

Just after 5 P.M. that afternoon the Navy released Garrett's resignation letter to President Bush. Until the end he denied knowing about the ribald behavior at Tailhook. "I want you to know," he wrote Bush, "contrary to what has been so maliciously suggested in the media, that in fulfilling what I saw as my responsibility to naval aviation by addressing the 1991 Tailhook convention, I neither saw nor engaged in any offensive conduct." Finally, eight months after he had first read Rick Ludwig's letter, he shouldered the blame for the Navy's failures to put Tailhook behind it. "I further accept responsibility, and hold myself accountable to you," he told Bush, "and all of the innocent men and women in the Department of the Navy for the leadership failure which allowed the egregious conduct at Tailhook to occur in the first place."

His critics, like Barbara Pope, and even his most ardent admirers, like Richard Armitage, suggested that if Garrett had said that in the beginning, Tailhook would never have become the Navy's worst disaster since Pearl Harbor. Instead Garrett had hunkered down, and as each day of the scandal went by, the odds of putting it to rest grew against him. In the end, his integrity, which was considered his most rock-solid quality, had been shattered by his own friends, who told investigators he was lying. When the Pentagon's assistant inspector general, Michael E. Suessman, offered Garrett a chance to vindicate himself by taking a polygraph examination, Garrett refused, saying he stood by his statements given under oath. In his letter to Suessman he wrote, "I want to make sure you understand why I have concluded as I have. As I told you, I have served my country, honestly and faithfully for over thirty years, both in and out of uniform. I have never, during that period of service, knowingly violated my oath of office. You have raised an issue that to me is one of honor and principle, and it is on those grounds that I decline your invitation, not on the practical grounds which I believe motivated you to extend it. My word is my bond, always has been and always will be, and I am deeply offended by the suggestion that a polygraph examination is required to somehow corroborate that I have told the truth, as I know it." [53]

At the end of his letter Garrett took his little ruler and signed his signature as precisely and straight along the bottom edge as he ever had before.

At the end of the day Bush's own statement on Garrett's resignation was handed out to the press. It was a terse, three-paragraph blurb that said nothing about Garrett's service to the nation. Even those angry with Garrett said he deserved more. And that Friday night Bush and his wife, Barbara, had tea with Paula Coughlin in the White House. He assured her that justice would be done and the culprits who assaulted her and the other women at Tailhook would be punished.

With her appearance on ABC and her visit to the White House, Coughlin was now the poster girl for ending sexual harassment and abuse of women in the military. With that title came a flurry of bitter and vicious attacks on her from all over the nation. Naval aviators took out their anger by spreading rumors about her promiscuity, about her being a second-rate naval officer, and about her willingly taking part in the activities at Tailhook. Coughlin did not run from the attacks. And she told her media handlers, who at first tried to persuade her from going public, not to paint her as a lily-white virgin, which she said she was not.[54] If there were doubters, a member of Frank Kelso's public affairs staff had passed on a report from her boyfriend, who flew helicopters with Coughlin. According to the report, she had showed up at a Navy dining-in party wearing black fishnet panty hose, high heels, a short black miniskirt, and a black tuxedo jacket and carrying a large rubber dildo. But all of the mudslinging was irrelevant and only hurt the Airedales' image, which continued to drop among the American public. What kind of personal life Coughlin enjoyed, whether she was a party girl or not, did not justify the criminal sexual assault on her or the other victims.

It was ironic, and largely due to the press, that Coughlin was labeled as the person who blew the whistle on Tailhook. In reality she had little, if anything, to do with exposing the scandal yet would have to pay a horrific emotional price for having the courage to try to end the demeaning attitudes toward women in the Navy. If not for Rick Ludwig's "Dear Skipper" letter, the drunkenness and lurid sexual gymnastics at Tailhook would have continued in much the same fashion as they had since John Lehman's infamous visits to the third deck at the Las Vegas Hilton.

After Garrett's fall, Dan Howard found himself in the unenviable spot of picking up the pieces and putting the Navy back together again. He had been named acting secretary until Bush could find someone to run the department, and he wasted no time in doing something he had wanted to do all along: shake things up.

On July 1, four days after he took over the helm of the Navy, Howard sat some three hundred senior officers down in the Pentagon's auditorium and held what he called a "Come to Jesus" truth meeting. "I think it's important to underline the fact that what happened at Tailhook was not just a problem with the integration of men and women in our ranks," he told the admirals and generals, who felt as if they were being lectured. "It was just as much a problem with the toleration of stone age attitudes about warriors returning from the sea, about Navy and Marine Corps people who think the rules of civility and common decency can be suspended at will, and most of all, about alcohol as an excuse for disgraceful behavior."

By now, many in the audience were sitting straight up on their chairs, listening intently to their new boss. Howard was not speaking like the usual bureaucrat, with words cloaked in caution. He was aiming direct hits at the flags. He blamed them for turning "a blind or bemused eye to the crude, alcohol-inspired antics of a few idiots in our ranks. The hard-drinking, skirt-chasing, 'anything goes' philosophy that led to the crimes and disgraces of Tailhook," Howard said, "has to go."

Then he laid out a six-point plan, which included a day when the entire Navy would "stand down," stop what it was doing, and take lessons on how to identify and deal with sexual harassment. He also said he was asking the secretary of defense to make sexual harassment a crime. Sexual harassment in the armed forces would no longer be "a fuzzy legal concept."

For all of Howard's good intentions, he had one of the shortest reigns as secretary in the history of the Navy. On July 7 Bush nominated Sean O'Keefe, the Pentagon's thirty-eight-year-old bean counter and protégé of Dick Cheney, for the job. With his droopy mustache and brooding eyes, O'Keefe was commonly referred to as Inspector Clouseau. He was anything but a bumbling detective, having a sharp political sense about what had to be done to put the Navy back on track. And for those who questioned if O'Keefe was capable of sparring with the fraternity of admirals, his actions on July 17 left no doubts that he was up to the job.

That day he pulled back the promotions of two popular admirals: Jerry Tuttle, who was nominated to be the Navy's top aviator, and Joe Prueher, who was slated to get three stars and command of the Third Fleet in San Diego. Tuttle had signed off on a newsletter that his staff put out on electronic warfare that contained an innocuous joke comparing beer and women. He apologized for this insensitivity, but it was too late. A short while later, the man who had been the brains behind some of the most unorthodox naval operations during the Lehman era retired.

For Prueher, the Gwen Dreyer case at the Naval Academy continued to haunt him. The Senate was not yet in the mood to forgive him for his harsh treatment of the Dreyer family. Many in the Navy, including Dan Howard, defended Prueher and supported his side of the story that he had never threatened to release pictures of Dreyer having fun while chained to a urinal. Prueher had become a popular officer, and the Navy was not yet ready to force him to retire. The brass decided to bench him until the heat blew over.

O'Keefe did not want to put the two officers before the Senate. The lawmakers would use them as whipping boys. He also refused to let Dick Dunleavy retire as a three-star vice admiral. He was bucked down to rear admiral and forced to leave the Navy in disgrace. There was no retirement ceremony on an aircraft carrier, no flyby, and no Distinguished Service Medal, all of which are traditional good-byes for the head of naval aviation.

But the biggest assault on the flags was yet to come.

• • •

"I need to emphasize a very important message—we get it," Sean O'Keefe said before a throng of television cameras and journalists who packed the Pentagon's newsroom on September 24 to be briefed on the Defense Department's first report on Tailhook. "Sexual harassment will not be tolerated," O'Keefe said, "and those who don't get that message will be driven from our ranks."

As he spoke, strobes flashed, catching an image of O'Keefe pointing his finger and thumb like a gun, as if he were shooting at the Navy. In a sense he was. Before the press conference ended, O'Keefe told the crowded room that Mac Williams and Ted Gordon were resigning effective immediately. And George Davis was being reassigned to another job. Heads were rolling, just as Congress wanted, and O'Keefe was the hatchet man. He had no choice but to make a big splash. He had to convince the Navy's detractors on the Hill, in the White House, and at the Pentagon—and, most important, the American public—that he was cleaning house.

Derek Vander Schaaf's first report, which zeroed in on the failure of the NIS and IG to properly investigate the Navy, gave him the ammunition to do it. "The deficiencies in the investigations," Vander Schaaf wrote O'Keefe, "were the result of an attempt to limit the exposure of the Navy and senior Navy officials to criticism." The report suggested that Garrett had perjured himself, accused Williams of making sexist statements, and claimed that cronyism among the top brass precluded a thorough investigation. Now that Vander Schaaf had finished his first report on the brass, his agents were busy compiling a final report on the Tailhook party itself.

Williams and Gordon had barely had time to review the first report, to correct any inaccuracies, or to defend themselves before O'Keefe went public with it. It would have mattered little if they had protested. O'Keefe had made up his mind to leave a clear message that he was in charge. Dan Howard had wanted to do the same thing, but he had been a part of the Navy system too long. But O'Keefe came in as an outsider with no allegiance to the blue-suited officers corps. He had no problem turning the Navy on its ear.

Gordon was the most incensed. He complained that he was scheduled to retire anyway on November 1 and that O'Keefe was just using him as political fodder. He had even reminded O'Keefe before the announcement that he was leaving. Still, O'Keefe lumped Gordon's retirement with Williams's resignation to leave the impression that he was being fired.

In the following week the three disciplined admirals wrote hundreds of pages of reports defending their actions in how they had managed the Tailhook affair and criticizing Vander Schaaf as overzealous. But O'Keefe held firm, saying their written comments "are not sufficient to absolve them of some measure of responsibility for this failure." [55] But so much attention was focused on the fact that some admirals had been hammered that nobody noticed the obvious. Two more of Lehman's dream team had now left the Navy under less than honorable conditions. And Joe Prueher had barely survived O'Keefe's hatchet.

CHAPTER 24

Cᴀᴘᴛᴀɪɴ Rᴏʙᴇʀᴛ McLᴀɴᴇ, commanding officer of the prestigious Top
Gun Fighter Weapons School, could not believe what he was reading. There,
on the back of a bathroom door in the Top Gun hangar, was a threat to kill
the next President of the United States:[1]

Clinton targeted for assassination 12-24-92.

McLane called the NIS, and when agents showed up to investigate they
pried the door from its hinges and carted it away as evidence. That may have
offered some comic relief to critics of the NIS, but there was nothing funny
about the public thrashing the Navy would take if this got out. Nor was there
anything humorous about a member of the U.S. Navy, a person sworn to
protect the commander in chief and defend the Constitution, doing something so heinous. McLane thought it was serious enough to send a message
to Frank Kelso, using the "Immediate" classification code that required it
to be placed on the CNO's desk within fifteen minutes. Fortunately for the
Navy, it stayed there, buried away with the thousands of other messages to
Kelso, never to be seen again.

Frank Kelso was about as popular at Miramar as was the president-elect.
Throughout the summer and into the fall and winter of 1992, the Top Gun
base had become a hotbed of resentment against him and most other authority figures running the Pentagon. Those months were perhaps the most
critical time of the entire Tailhook scandal because the Airedales' faith in
the Navy's leadership, the core of any military organization, was breaking
down under the strain. To a man, they felt as if they were rogues under
siege, as if the media had painted the entire community as perverted women
haters. Although some male officers were indeed hostile toward women, the
news coverage lumped the good men with the bad. What stung even more,
the brass was going along with the headlines and coming down hard on the
aviators for anything that smacked of sexism. The intensity of the public
ridicule and the propensity for the brass to blame those in the lower ranks, a
rebuke described as "ready, fire, aim," would have long-term consequences.

As the events of that summer rocked the Navy's boat, Commander David Tyler, a squadron commander at Miramar whose reputation for honesty and integrity did indeed epitomize the words "officer and a gentleman," said, "We were willing to fly into combat against insurmountable odds. Even if the pilots knew there was no helicopter to rescue them when they were shot down, they would do it with a cheery 'Aye, aye, yes sir.' Right now, if their admiral asks them to do the same mission, they would say, 'Why? You lead the way, Admiral.' "[2]

The daily drumbeat of negative news, and the brass's implementation of new rules to help end a culture grounded in sexism, only increased the anxiety among men at Miramar and at other bases around the nation. Many of the men held strong, conservative views about duty, honor, country—and embraced moral values instilled in them to protect the women and children of America. Now, even to discuss their fundamental beliefs could cost them their jobs if they were misconstrued as antiwoman. In the post-Tailhook period, women throughout the Navy were filing sexual harassment complaints in record numbers.[3] Some were legitimate, some were bogus. But it got to the point where male aviators did not want to talk with their female counterparts, let alone instruct them how to fly fighters at the Replacement Air Group (RAG) at Miramar.[4] Although a large percentage of women in the Navy were grateful that Tailhook had blown up, thus exposing their daily plight in a world dominated by men, they were also angered that it kept dragging on.[5] In the end, the backlash of male anger in all three fiefdoms of the Navy—surface, submarine, and aviation—was hurting almost as much as Tailhook had helped.

The fliers had at first taken out their rage on Garrett for breaking ties with the Tailhook Association. They came forward and accused the former secretary of lying about his whereabouts at the convention—an unheard-of act that violated every unwritten rule in the Navy. Next they aimed their wrath at the agents from the NIS. Then, when Derek Vander Schaaf's investigators followed the NIS onto the base to search for suspects, it was as if the enemy had arrived. Many described their interviews as interrogations in which the Pentagon gumshoes inquired about their sex lives and asked them if they masturbated. "Sure, three times a day," became a standard answer. If they balked at the questions, they were threatened with discipline and even told they could be thrown out of the Navy. Some were ordered to take lie detector tests. There were unsubstantiated reports at the El Toro Marine base of officers being roughed up and even threats of an IRS tax audit if they didn't cooperate. As the aviators swapped stories, the grapevine hummed, and soon the bull sessions took on the light of a "Can you top this story?"[6]

That summer the aviators at Miramar began wearing "Tailhook '91—I wasn't there" patches on their flight jackets.[7] The brightly colored patches depicted television cartoon character Bart Simpson dressed in a Navy flight suit, holding a can of beer and saying, "I didn't do it! Nobody saw me do it —you can't prove a thing." Kelso ordered the fliers to remove them, which only stirred even stronger resentment of the CNO. Soon more patches popped up. There was one called the NIS Olympics. Another had a topless woman running the Gauntlet.

Kelso traveled to Miramar in August, not to lay down the law with stern warnings, but to extend an olive branch and explain why the Navy was taking the steps it was to deal with the Tailhook crisis. His sincerity only won him scorn. The aviators began calling him "three-knot Kelso," a reference to his brain working in slow motion. After he left Miramar, a T-shirt began circulating on the base that had a sinister-looking Frank Kelso burning an aviator at the stake. The caption read "I survived the Tailhook '91 Witch Hunt."

The more the admirals laid down the law, the more defiant and hot-tempered the fliers became. In July, less than a week after Garrett was fired, the men at Miramar had put the Navy back in the national headlines. Again the story was sex, women, and booze. This time, however, the main victim was Pat Schroeder, the Democrat member of Congress.

At first blush the Tomcat Follies was just another male tradition among the F-14 fighter jocks at Miramar. Similar to Tailhook, the Follies was a week-long party that ended with the Tomcat Ball, a black-tie affair held at one of the big hotels downtown. During the week the F-14 aviators played golf, drank merrily, barbecued, and met one night for an evening of salty skits at the Miramar Officers Club. "Historically, it's been just the guys, and they tape the windows shut and do all sorts of pornographic stuff," said Petty Officer Bobbie Carleton, a longtime aviation watcher who headed up Miramar's public affairs detachment on the base. "It's really a no-holds-barred kind of thing."[8]

Over the past twenty years the skits had included the "butt brothers," a rendition of the talking bare rear ends that Roxanne Baxter encountered back on *Constellation* when the aviators had lampooned her. And Jack Ready, the past Top Gun commander who had gone on to become a vice admiral, often performed his inverted pitch hangup—otherwise known as drinking a beer while standing on his head. Each skit was judged by a panel of aviators who gave a "dicks-up" or "dicks-down" verdict. Traditionally, the fighter bubbas had always tried to outdo themselves by putting on the best—usually the most raunchy—skit. But in the wake of Tailhook, orders went out from the squadron commanding officers to the JOs to keep it tame. Some of the officers even demanded that the skits be reviewed prior to the performance.

When the show began that night, the aviators from the Screaming Eagles of Fighter Squadron 51, David Tyler's unit, had rigged a contraption that used a bowling ball to trip levers that in turn caused words to pop up. After the ball had gone through all of its wickets, the complete message caused a loud roar from the assembled Tomcat fliers: "Hickory, dickory, dock, Pat Schroeder can suck my c——k." A second skit by Fighter Squadron 111 had the message "Pat, don't be a ——" at which point the fliers flashed a picture of Dick Cheney.

Although Frank Kelso personally told Schroeder about the event and offered her an official Navy apology, she later laughed it off and said she had faced more hostile behavior in her Colorado district.[9] She did not want anyone to lose his job over the performance. And she took it in stride when the aviators later came up with a crude T-shirt saying "Pat Schroeder Couldn't Get Laid at Tailhook So She's Been Screwing the Navy Ever Since." Even when a Marine officer faxed her pornographic pictures, Schroeder took the high road and refused to lower her own standards by personally attacking the Airedales. She did speak out, however, saying that the Tomcat Follies sent "a message to women in the Navy that Tailhook did not change things, that it is going to be business as usual."[10]

The Follies episode, which included other questionable skits besides those that made fun of Schroeder, would have died quickly had it not been for one man, Admiral Robert Kelly, the bullish commander of the Pacific Fleet. By the time Kelly had risen in rank to take command of the mighty fleet, he had become an object of ridicule. In fact, the mockery began when he was a lieutenant and his fellow aviators gave him the call sign "Barney." For years thereafter Kelly had tried to distance himself from the name because it conjured up images he did not wish to remember. "We had somebody break into our home when I was a young lieutenant junior grade," Kelly recalled. "I had a gun. We had a confrontation in the bedroom and I pulled the gun out. As he was running down the hallway, I fired at him, the bullet hit the side wall, hit the refrigerator in the kitchen, and came back and broke the window behind my head." At the time, *The Andy Griffith Show,* with its bumbling deputy, Barney Fife, was a big hit, so the nickname stuck.[11]

As a child, Kelly's life had been a difficult one. His father was a musician who left a teaching job to join the Army Air Corps during World War II. Three months after he left his wife and son, Robert, in Pennsylvania, he was killed on a bombing mission. Afterward the Kellys bounced around with relatives in Philadelphia. As a first-grader Robert had visited the Philadelphia Naval Shipyard, where he saw an aircraft carrier. From that point on he wanted to fly from the decks of the grand ships. Years later, in 1959, he walked out of Bancroft Hall as a graduate of the U.S. Naval Academy. He went on to fly A-7s and spend seventeen years of his career at sea.

But nothing could have prepared him for what happened twenty-four years after leaving Annapolis. On April 23, 1983, Captain Robert Kelly stood on the bridge of the aircraft carrier *Enterprise* as it sailed under the Golden Gate Bridge en route to its homeport in Alameda. Kelly had taken the giant flattop into San Francisco Bay, despite the fact that one of the ship's propellers was not working. Less than a mile from its pier, the ship shuddered, lurched forward, then began listing to one side. The massive *Enterprise* had gone off course and was stuck in the muck of the bay. On the pier in Alameda, about three thousand wives and well-wishers who had come out to watch the carrier come home after eight months at sea stood motionless, wondering why the ship had stopped.

On *Enterprise,* Kelly had developed a "very deep feeling in the pit" of his stomach. For six hours he stayed on the bridge until the tide shifted. When the ship floated free and the magnitude of the grounding set in, a catastrophe that he felt would end his career, Kelly went down into his cabin and threw up. He had recently been selected for rear admiral, and some of the Navy brass said he should be removed from the list and sent home. But John Lehman disagreed. He liked the fact that Kelly had accepted blame for the incident.

Despite the good fortune bestowed on him then, in later years Kelly found it difficult, if not impossible, to show mercy on those below him who had similar hard luck or who had run afoul of Navy traditions, regulations, or the law. By the time he placed his fourth star on his shoulder boards, he had turned into a type A personality who treated those around him "like pieces of shit," recalled one officer on his staff. Each day his stewards would prepare his lunch, then walk it over to Kelly's office on a silver tray. One time a sailor accidentally spilled soup on a sandwich, which made the bread soggy and caused Kelly to fly into a rage. On another occasion Kelly saw a sailor speeding on base. He gave chase in his Volkswagen Beetle and pulled the man over, holding him there until police arrived.

But while Kelly was enforcing his strict code of conduct on those below him, he did not always live by the same rules. His lawyers and public affairs officers had warned him on several occasions to back off of legal cases involving officers under his jurisdiction because he was exerting command influence, the unlawful interference in an individual's legal rights. After a group of aviators on *Nimitz* were caught drinking alcohol, Kelly ordered replacement pilots sent to the carrier before the officers had their day in court aboard the ship. And when he heard that Rear Admiral Bob Hickey, the battle fleet commander, had yet to conduct disciplinary hearings for the men, Kelly personally telephoned the ship, saying he wanted the fliers punished immediately.[12] Despite Kelly's success at ensuring that the aviators were found guilty at a captain's mast, some were later cleared during a second review.

By the time the Tomcat Follies boiled over into the press, Kelly had a long list of his own abuses that Navy lawyers in the Secretariat believed were unethical, if not outright violations of the Uniform Code of Military Justice. Individually they seemed minor, like his constant golf outings abroad or accepting an invitation valued at $34,000 for him and some other brass to attend the California Ball, a dinner party hosted by top officials in the defense industry and Los Angeles community leaders. But when the abuses were added up, they painted a dim picture of an admiral who skirted the line.[13] Kelly argued that he wasn't doing anything out of the ordinary for a flag officer and that these perquisites had, over the years, become institutional and therefore condoned by the Pentagon's leaders.

When it came time to hold the squadron commanding officers at Miramar accountable for the skits about Schroeder, Kelly insisted on the harshest punishment. With the approval of Kelso, he directed Edwin Kohn, the admiral in charge of the Pacific Fleet's air forces, to fire five senior officers and discipline eighteen others. One of the men fired was Commander Robert Clement, head of Fighter Squadron 111, who had shot up an Iranian F-4 years before over the Persian Gulf. Later, Kelly reinstated two officers. But Clement, the least culpable because he was on leave when the skits were being planned, was not one of them.[14]

Acting on impulse and principle, Clement took his case public, attacking Kelly personally in the media. If Kelly was going to fire the "Miramar Five," Clement maintained, then he should himself be fired for not stopping the rambunctious behavior at Tailhook, where he was the senior aviator present. Kelly had always admitted being at Tailhook and going into two hospitality suites, including one run by defense contractors, which was against Navy regulations. But he adamantly denied seeing any misbehavior and staunchly said he would not step down. "I am not trying to duck responsibility," he explained. "I am going to stick around and try to fix the problem."[15]

"The hypocrisy in this organization runs a mile deep. That is the major reason I am so bitter," wrote David Tyler, the Screaming Eagles skipper who had been removed from his job.[16] It was odd that Tyler was fired because he was one of the Navy's finest, with a good track record concerning women. He was a top-notch flier who was in the running to be commanding officer of the Blue Angels. And he was a man whose troops were willing to put their lives on the line in combat. "There is a complete double standard that blatantly exists in enforcing the Navy's politically, publicity-motivated actions against certain individuals such as myself," Tyler wrote in response to his demotion. He reminded the brass about the hard-core pornography sold at Navy exchanges and the fact that base newspapers printed advertisements for dancing girl shows, live nudes, and massage parlors. Lest Admiral Kohn forget, Tyler pointed out that a "Hanoi Jane Urinal Sticker" was in the bathroom at his headquarters. And last, how could the Navy turn a blind eye to the bars and whorehouses in overseas liberty ports like the Philippines? "Is this not entirely inappropriate behavior, significantly more detrimental than a comedy skit?" Tyler asked.

For Kelly, fixing the problem meant cutting out the cancer—puckish officers like Tyler and Clement, who were following Barbara Pope's lead and demanding accountability of the admirals. Clement said Kelly believed that Clement had no right to question his authority. At one point he stuck his four stars in Clement's face and said, "Do you always disobey the orders of a four star?"

Several months later the scales of justice had the opportunity to tip against Kelly. During a staff meeting that included three women, he told a joke about "a guy changing a tire on his way home from his fifty-fifth birthday party. A frog jumps up on his lap and says, 'Hi, I'm a talking frog.' And the guy says, 'My goodness, I've never seen a talking frog. What do you do?' The frog says, 'I'm a genie. I'll tell you what. If you let me go, I'll make your penis grow by two inches.' So the guy puts him in his pocket, and the frog jumps out and says, 'Hey, let me go.' And the guy looks in his pocket and says, "At my age I'd rather have a talking frog.' " [17]

After the punch line, the room fell so silent that those assembled could hear a pin drop. Here was the commander of the Pacific Fleet, the man responsible for setting the tone of the new Navy, telling a silly but questionable joke in mixed company. Kelly sensed immediately that he had violated his own orders clamping down on inappropriate behavior toward women and said, "Oh, I guess I will hear about it in the newspaper." He knew that some members on his staff were gunning for him to take a fall. And he was right; several felt this might be the issue that would force him to retire. But Kelso, after reading about Kelly's behavior in the *Union-Tribune* and talking with Kelly, was not about to sacrifice a four-star admiral, even though he had supported the firing of Jerry Tuttle for an even lamer joke.

The event only intensified the rift between Kelso and his admirals and those in the lower ranks, especially the men caught up in the Tailhook scandal and the Tomcat Follies. One thing was clear to them. When it came to holding people accountable for their actions in the Navy, Frank Kelso had two sets of books, one for himself and the fraternity of admirals and one for the rest of the Navy.

On *Kitty Hawk,* which was steaming on the other side of the world in the Indian Ocean, Rick Ludwig was doing his best to cope with the aftermath of Tailhook. Since writing his infamous "Dear Skipper" letter the previous October, his life had turned upside down. Although he had done the right thing in exposing the Gauntlet, it had won him no friends. The junior officers castigated him. His peers ostracized him. But what was worse, the brass had never congratulated him for having the courage to blow the whistle on his fellow aviators. Rather, they were trying to court-martial him.

The charge was ironic. As the president of Tailhook he was responsible for everything that had gone wrong at the convention—the drinking, the public sex, the Gauntlet—everything. He should have known better, the admirals said, and put a stop to the debauchery. But Ludwig was not the only captain of the Tailhook ship that weekend. There was a whole flock of admirals at the convention, men in attendance senior to him, who had gone into the suites and had a long, corporate memory of the shenanigans at Tailhook. If military justice was indeed blind to rank, the three reserve flags and all thirty active duty admirals who attended the convention should also face court-martial charges for not putting a stop to things. Rick Ludwig just happened to be a convenient scapegoat. It was the Navy way: protect the admirals and sacrifice an innocent soul to fend off the attackers.

If one thing had seemed certain before Tailhook, it was that Ludwig would soon be an admiral. He had paid his dues. After Vietnam he made a decision to make the Navy a career, partly because he loved flying and serving his country, but also because he needed the free medical care provided by the Navy. His son Eric had been born with a brittle-bone disease and been confined for most of his life to a wheelchair. Ludwig could have gone the way of other pilots, to the airlines, where the money was good and the hours even better. But he'd decided to stay and work his way up through the system to flag rank.

His promotion to admiral would never come. That fall the Navy took Ludwig off *Kitty Hawk* and placed him in a psychiatric ward in a Singapore hospital under twenty-four-hour guard. He was coming apart at the seams. Ludwig had had the moral courage to do the right thing. His letter, which was the single most important piece of evidence in exposing the Tailhook scandal, had changed history. But it had also turned the Navy, its leadership, and his fellow aviators against him, causing his emotional breakdown.

• • •

As the Bush administration prepared to leave office, Sean O'Keefe was busy looking for a job. In his pursuit he had a pair of overzealous accomplices: Rear Admiral Kendell Pease, who had replaced Brent Baker as head of Navy public affairs, and Commander William Harlow, the secretary's personal flak. Pease was known as the "minister of disinformation," a man who had the reputation for wrapping the truth around a tree. Even his own public affairs officers said he was guilty of telling lies, half-truths, and bogus stories. They called him and his assistants in Washington the "brownshirts" and the "news desk Nazis." A former football player at the Naval Academy, Pease had graduated with Oliver North. But he never went on to serve in any of the war-fighting communities as his peers did. Instead he became a professional public affairs officer and a master at putting the Navy's spin on a story.

Pease and Harlow knew their boss was looking for work and thought it would be nice if the secretary landed the position of baseball commissioner. It was a prestigious, high-profile job with a nice salary that would bring O'Keefe good exposure. There was only one problem. The baseball owners didn't have a clue who O'Keefe was. That was a minor detail for two experienced media flaks who knew how to promote a story. Using their positions as senior public affairs officers in the Navy, the two men began calling reporters around the country and planting false stories that O'Keefe was in the running for the job.[18] They were practicing an old public affairs trick—if a story is told often enough, people start to think it is true even if it's not. When O'Keefe found out about the trickery at a morning staff meeting, he shook his head and rolled his eyes. Here were two senior naval officers who worked for the taxpayers, whose jobs were to represent the Navy, trying to get a job for an outgoing member of the administration. In the end, O'Keefe went to the University of Pennsylvania to become a professor.

He would be remembered by the non-Navy types as a man thrown into a storm with only his moral compass to guide him as he cleaned up the sea service. But on the fourth floor of the Pentagon, the Navy floor, he was viewed as a political hack. The brass, which had cringed every time O'Keefe's hatchet came down on another admiral's head, breathed a sigh of relief when he left. Some still had bitter memories of the treatment afforded Vice Admiral John Fetterman, truly one of the Navy's more distinguished officers. Kelso had recommended that Fetterman retire and be booted down to rear admiral for trying to thwart an investigation of his speech writer, a longtime family friend who was homosexual. When the news leaked out that

O'Keefe had endorsed the recommendation, the Navy was besieged with thousands of letters and phone calls from around the nation, all supporting Fetterman. Everywhere O'Keefe went he was harangued. In San Diego Congressman Randy Cunningham cornered him and demanded that the secretary change his mind. O'Keefe said it was out of his hands, that Fetterman's case had been caught up in the hysteria over Tailhook. Fetterman's retirement problems, he said, were due to the Senate's holding up the nominations of 4,900 officers. There was nothing he could do until Sam Nunn cleared all those up for promotion and retirement. It was a convenient story that O'Keefe used to fend off Cunningham. Fetterman's case was about gays in the military and had little to do with Tailhook.

O'Keefe had played politics with Paula Coughlin, too. The Navy's judge advocate general had advised him that she had violated a law known as the Hatch Act, which prohibited military personnel from endorsing political candidates.[19] John McCain had asked her to support his Senate campaign, which she did by providing a written statement. The Navy's congressional liaison, who acted as an intermediary between Coughlin and McCain, knew she would be in violation of the law but did not warn her. It was more important to placate McCain. Coughlin sensed she might get into trouble.[20] But she was willing to take the risk. Besides, she had become an untouchable. Nobody at the upper reaches of the Navy would dare say or do anything that might offend her. And she was right. O'Keefe said he was not going to punish her for something he believed was a trivial violation of federal law.

When President Bill Clinton took occupancy of the White House, an eerie quiet descended over the Navy. Clinton had already signaled his displeasure over the behavior in Las Vegas. And now Tailhook watchers in the Pentagon, on Capitol Hill, and at naval bases across the country had but one question. When was he going to drop, as the cliché went, the other shoe? Derek Vander Schaaf's "Tailhook Part 2" investigation was done, dripping with salacious detail and ready for the President to release.

But Clinton's focus was elsewhere. For him, Tailhook paled in comparison with another issue that was fast turning out to be the administration's first big gaffe: the debate about gays in the military. In his campaign, Clinton had declared that he was in favor of gays serving openly in the military. But once in office, his White House staff had underestimated the antigay fervor of those in uniform all the way up to the Joint Chiefs of Staff. As a result, the President's plan to allow homosexuals to serve openly backfired, and he looked and acted as if he were inept. As he struggled with the gay issue, Tailhook was put on the back burner, but not forgotten.

Clinton had before him two of the most extreme examples of how hostile the military could be when dealing with social change. One was Tailhook. The other was the brutal murder of Allen Schindler, a gay sailor stomped to death by his shipmates on a cold concrete floor in a Japanese bathroom thousands of miles from his home in San Diego. The October 27, 1992, assault on Schindler, a radioman on *Belleau Wood,* was so vicious that the Navy's forensic pathologist, who had performed more than one thousand autopsies, testified that he had suffered at least four fatal injuries to the head, chest, and abdomen. He likened the attack to a person being crushed to death by a horse, a high-speed auto crash, or a low-speed aircraft accident. Schindler had eight broken ribs, fractures in the back of his skull and in the bones around his eyes, a broken nose, and a broken upper jaw, and the whole middle portion of his face was detached and floating loosely.[21]

The Navy tried to keep secret the fact that the murder appeared to be a gay-bashing hate crime by refusing to let the media cover the first court-martial in the case. But gradually it came out. Schindler became what *Esquire* magazine called the "accidental martyr." And the Navy became the target of charges that it was once again, like so many times in the past when big scandals hit, covering up.

As Clinton compromised over the ban on gays in the military—the "don't ask, don't tell" policy—the bipartisan Congressional Caucus on Women's Issues was determined not to let the President slide on Tailhook. On Monday, February 22, the group sent a fiery letter to Clinton's new defense secretary, Les Aspin, saying that "delaying the release of the final report sends a message to the nation that sexual assault and harassment of women are not sufficiently important to warrant immediate discipline."[22] This was not some radical group with no support in the hinterlands that the President could ignore. The price of peace was the release of Vander Schaaf's report. Without that, the unsaid warning was gridlock from the women lawmakers for Clinton's agenda on Capitol Hill.

The simple reason for the delay was that Clinton and Aspin wanted to wait until the President picked a new secretary of the Navy who could oversee the disciplinary process and handle the expected political fallout. Finding someone willing to take on the job, however, with the Navy dead in the water, was becoming a challenge. Some potential candidates had even turned down the offer.

But a more telling explanation for the delay lay hidden in the thirty-three investigative files that Derek Vander Schaaf's agents had compiled on the admirals who had attended the Tailhook convention. Among the flag files, which were now being guarded by Aspin, was one on Frank Kelso. And it appeared that the chief of naval operations was in big trouble. On April 15,

1993, Pentagon investigator Mike Suessman had advised Kelso of his rights as a suspect and told him that he was in violation for making a false official statement and for lying under oath about his activities at Tailhook on Saturday night, September 7, the evening when most of the assaults took place.[23] Kelso had maintained that he had not gone to the third deck that night, that he had been gambling in the casino on the hotel's first floor. But more than a dozen witnesses, including a Navy judge who was at the convention with her husband, stated that they had seen him.

If Aspin allowed Kelso to handle the flag files, as well as to oversee the discipline of those identified in the Tailhook report, the double standard would be glaring. When O'Keefe left, Kelso had assumed the job of secretary while also maintaining his position as chief of naval operations. He was all powerful, making decisions as the CNO, then rubber stamping them as secretary. If Kelso was himself guilty, or even appeared to be in the wrong, how could he pass judgment on others? That question apparently never dawned on Kelso, who had already picked two officers to oversee the expected disciplinary cases stemming from the Pentagon's investigation: Vice Admiral Paul Reason and Major General Chuck Krulak, who would go on to be the commandant of the Marine Corps.

On Wednesday, April 21, Clinton came one step closer to releasing the report. That day he announced that John H. Dalton, a former Naval Academy graduate, submarine officer, and past Carter administration official, would be the next secretary of the Navy. Of the three service secretaries nominated by Clinton, Dalton was the only one who was not Aspin's first choice. Dalton's reputation was for raising money, first for Carter, then later for Clinton. It was his work for the President as a fund-raiser during a tough bout against George Bush that helped land him the job.

The morning after the nomination, Kelso awoke with a new boss but still no idea when the Tailhook report would be released. By now the Navy was in a state of high anxiety, and there was widespread anticipation that it would soon break. Reporters were making constant queries. And the Pentagon gossip mill was abuzz. There had been the same hysteria before when the report was rumored to be near release, and it had fizzled. But this time it seemed certain that something was amiss. That Thursday night, as he sat in his fourth-floor Pentagon office, Kelso was told that the day of reckoning had arrived. Aspin then gave him Vander Schaaf's report to review—but he kept the thirty-three flag files. Even though they were Kelso's admirals, Aspin was not about to cause a political uproar by letting the CNO choose which flags should be disciplined. He would hand the files to Dalton after he was confirmed by the Senate. It was also important that the other cases be handled independently by Reason and Krulak with no guidance whatsoever from Kelso. His marching orders were to lead the charge for change, to put an end to the culture that had thrived during the military buildup that Kelso and other members of John Lehman's dream team had launched.

Now it was time to drop the other shoe.

"We cannot undo the past, but we sure can influence the future, and we are," Kelso told a packed Pentagon pressroom on Friday afternoon. "Something like Tailhook is not going to happen again," he said. "Tailhook also brought to light the fact that we had an institutional problem in how we treated women. In that regard it was a watershed event that has brought about institutional change."

As he spoke, reporters thumbed through the several-hundred-page Pentagon report, complete with graphic pictures of strippers and the rhino with its phallic drink dispenser, as well as a special pull-out section that showed in which suites and what part of the Gauntlet the assaults had taken place. Nothing quite like it had ever been printed by the Pentagon before. The table of contents alone sent the journalists giggling for the editorial liberty they could take. Chapter headings included "Streaking," "Mooning," "Ball Walking," "Leg Shaving," "Belly/Navel Shots," "Butt Biting," "Zapping," and "Public and Paid Sex."

For all the head shaking about the frat house stuff, there was a much more serious aspect to the report that few in the room failed to notice. The Pentagon inspector general had identified ninety victims of indecent assault, eighty-three of whom were women, some of whom had been forced to go down the Gauntlet against their will. Many were civilians, but twenty-one were naval officers, one was from the Air Force, six were spouses of military officers, and six were government officials. The investigators had identified 140 suspects, 23 of whom had taken part in the Gauntlet.

And while Dunleavy was the only admiral singled out for a rebuke, there was a special section on flag officers. "Some of the Navy's most senior officers were knowledgeable as to the excesses practiced at Tailhook '91 and, by their inaction, those officers served to condone and even encourage the type of behavior that occurred there," the report stated. Unlike the NIS and the Navy inspector general, Don Mancuso, the hard-bitten cop who had run the investigation for Vander Schaaf, pulled no punches about the admirals. "To say that you were a flag officer in aviation and had previously been a commander and had maybe even hosted a suite one year and had been to ten different Tailhooks, to say that you know nothing, didn't even know there were strippers, never heard of an assault, never saw public sex, is absolutely absurd."[24]

At the White House, Clinton even chimed in, saying the conduct displayed in Las Vegas "has no place in the armed services." But he added that the results of the report "should not be taken as a general indictment of the U.S. Navy or of all the fine people who serve there."

With Tailhook behind him Clinton could now move on to the debate about allowing women to serve in combat. On Wednesday, less than a week after the Tailhook report was released, Aspin made an announcement that had long been expected and surprised few people. Women, he said, could now fly combat jets. He added that the Navy was also working out details to open all ships to female sailors, not just tenders and other noncombat vessels. That meant that women would soon be flying jets from the decks of aircraft carriers.

Kelso had been somewhat of a reluctant supporter in removing the ban on women serving in combat. As the Sixth Fleet CinC, he had led the way in pushing the Navy to put women on noncombat ships. But he had always been opposed to the idea of women bleeding and dying for their country, and he had testified on Capitol Hill just before Tailhook that it would be a mistake to let women serve on combat ships or fly warplanes in squadrons assigned to aircraft carriers. But then came Tailhook, and the political dynamics shifted in favor of the forces aligned with Clinton, who were determined to see women achieve equality in the ranks. The writing was on the wall for Kelso, a man who had studied under the master politician in the Navy, John Lehman. Kelso wasted no time changing course to sign on with the supporters of women serving in combat.

With the floodgates now open, the Navy began selecting female aviators capable of piloting attack aircraft and the complicated F-14 Tomcat fighter. Two carriers were chosen to accommodate the women, *Abraham Lincoln* on the West Coast and *Eisenhower* on the East Coast. Both ships soon became known as the Babe and Dyke. There was no turning back now, but the road ahead was uncertain. By picking the two flattops, Kelso had boxed the Navy into a corner. The *Eisenhower* was slated to leave Norfolk in October 1994, with the *Lincoln* leaving in the spring of 1995. And if there was one thing the Navy frowned on, it was missing a deployment date. In the submarine world, for example, captains would take broken ships to sea rather than be late getting out of port.[25] For the two carriers to sail on time, the female candidates had to meet performance and training goals on schedule, no easy task, for fear of delaying the whole process. To save time and reduce the odds for Murphy's law to foul things up, Kelso issued an order to send the female flyers to the head of the training pipeline. Men who had been waiting up to eighteen months to begin F-14 training at Miramar now were told they had to wait for the next class. Male aviators angrily viewed the decision as purely politics, which it was. But to the women—like Kara Hultgreen, who had been picked to train in the F-14 Tomcat at Miramar—it was long overdue.

The Navy would ensure that the women pilots got through the training program regardless of their capabilities. At times Kara Hultgreen's deficiencies had been so poor that under normal conditions she would have washed out. Aviators going through training receive downs or pink sheets when they fail properly to carry out an exercise such as a carrier landing. Two downs had in the past been enough to disqualify a pilot from flying the F-14. Hultgreen had four, two of which were recorded as risking "safety of flight," the most serious safety violations.[26] The Navy defended Hultgreen's record and repeatedly said that she was meeting training requirements and that she was not receiving preferential training. It turned out that the Navy was covering up, that it had again lied to the public. Two years after Hultgreen had begun her training, she was killed when attempting to land on *Abraham Lincoln* on a clear, calm Southern California day.

On July 22 John Dalton had his private swearing-in as the nation's sixty-seventh secretary of the Navy. The most immediate task before him was to salvage the Navy's reputation and work to fuse the rift between the junior officers and the brass. To that end, Dalton promised a prompt and thorough review of the flag files, beginning with the most important name on the list —Frank Kelso. During his confirmation hearings that month, Dalton had recalled John Paul Jones's declaration that in addition to being a capable mariner, a naval officer must be a gentleman with the highest sense of personal honor.[27] And in his first message dispersed to the fleet, the new secretary said above all else, "I place the highest value on honesty, moral integrity, and the consideration of others."

On the surface Dalton seemed squeaky clean. Underneath his Southern charm, however, there was another story that might have ended his hopes of becoming Navy secretary had it been known by the entire membership of the Senate Armed Services Committee. But only a handful of senators, meeting in a secret executive session, were aware that Dalton had a checkered past. When he had run the Seguin Savings Association, the Texas savings and loan had engaged in risky real estate deals, many handled by unqualified managers who failed to obtain proper collateral, appraisals, and loan documentation.[28] Under Dalton's tenure, Seguin's holdings soared from $45 million when he took over in 1984 to $145 million before it finally collapsed in 1988. The federal bailout cost taxpayers at least $100 million. The agency charged with overseeing the savings and loan industry, the Federal Deposit Insurance Corporation, asserted that the rapid growth of the federally insured institution had violated government rules.[29] Nor was it widely known by those judging his nomination whether Dalton had the integrity to take control of the Navy during this critical juncture in its history. In a $3.8 million settlement of possible civil charges against him, government regulators claimed he had violated federal laws and committed gross negligence as Seguin's president, chief executive officer, and chairman of the loan committee and board of directors.[30] When all of this surfaced later in *The New York Times,* Dalton defended his actions and said that he had told the administration about his role in the failed savings and loan.

Even so, he was now sitting in judgment on Frank Kelso, thirty-two other admirals, and two Marine generals. Since his arrival in late July he had spent two months poring over the flag files and had personally interviewed a number of the admirals who had gone into the hospitality suites at the Tailhook convention. And by Friday, October 1, he had made up his mind to ask Aspin to fire Kelso for a failure of leadership to curb the atmosphere of debauchery that had taken place in Las Vegas.

There was, of course, more to the case then just the failure of leadership. There was Mike Suessman's contention that Kelso had lied to investigators under oath. And there was something else that only Dalton and few other people knew about Kelso: his role in yet another Navy cover-up.

After his nomination, Dalton was given an office in the Secretariat so he could begin preparing for his new post, once he was confirmed. By law he could make no decisions, but he was entitled to be briefed on key events, one of which was a big scandal brewing that spring. A number of midshipmen at the Naval Academy had cheated on the December 1992 electrical engineering exam, the same test that had caused a stir back when Joe Prueher was commandant. The academy had done an internal investigation and identified twenty-eight people who had taken part in the cheating. But after several rounds of reviews, only six midshipmen were recommended for dismissal to the secretary of the Navy, who was then Kelso.

When the academy's investigation ended up in the Secretariat, the staff reviewed it and saw that the six people recommended for dismissal were the least guilty. The other students initially cleared, most of whom were football players, were not being punished. The academy's superintendent, Rear Admiral Thomas C. Lynch, one of John Lehman's protégés, who had been a star football player as a midshipmen and former captain of the team, had personally reviewed the list and sent it to Kelso's office. Kelso went along with Lynch and signed off on the recommendations that the six least guilty people be expelled.

When Dalton's staff saw the document, they advised the secretary in waiting that it appeared as if the academy had not done a thorough review and that some officers were protecting the football players. Dalton wanted the Navy inspector general to begin an investigation, which later determined that some of those in charge of the academy were indeed covering up. Ultimately 133 people were found to have taken part in the cheating, including many of the seniors on the football team.[31] It was the biggest cheating episode in the history of the school.

It was obvious to Dalton that he had to do something to shore up the academy's image. When he became secretary, he turned to Admiral Charles Larson, the former head of the Pacific Fleet, and requested that he become the institution's superintendent. Larson had run a close race to replace Colin Powell as chairman of the Joint Chiefs of Staff and lost to an Army general. The only option left for him was to retire, which he did. Dalton made a special arrangement that enabled him to return to active duty and take charge of the academy.

But once again there was another side to the story. While the brass applauded the move, they kept under wraps Larson's poor judgment in a politically charged rape of a female sailor based in San Diego, an investigation Larson had tried to frustrate. The woman had been raped by one or more sailors from the Soviet Union while she visited their ship as a tourist during its much publicized trip to San Diego.

When the Soviets arrived in San Diego on July 31, 1990, as part of a military-to-military exchange program, the opening ceremonies went off without a hitch. The next day, while the admirals celebrated, the female sailor, wearing civilian clothes, had gone to view the warships *Admiral Vinogradov* and *Boyevoy* with thousands of other Americans. She soon became separated from other people and ended up in the hands of one or more Soviet sailors on *Vinogradov,* who physically assaulted and raped her, leaving bruises and contusions. Emotionally and physically shaken, she found her way off the ship and went to a non-Navy rape crisis center in search of help. She was comforted by the wife of a naval officer who worked there and who notified the NIS about the assault. Before the Soviet ships left, the NIS was able to come up with enough information to identify several suspects.

Dennis Usrey, the top NIS official on the West Coast, took this information to Larson the day before the ships were set to sail. "Admiral Larson, we believe this is a very legitimate case," Usrey said, telling him that the NIS had statements and photographs to support the woman's story. William Branniff, the U.S. attorney in San Diego, was also involved and wanted the investigation completed. If a suspect was indeed identified, he wanted to prosecute—regardless of the initiative by the Navy and others to sweep the case under the diplomatic rug.[32] But after Usrey laid out the facts of the case to Larson, he became defensive and refused to believe the woman's story. "I talked about this to my wife, and she doesn't believe this happened, and neither do I. I talked to the Soviets, and they said it couldn't happen," Usrey recalled Larson telling him.

Usrey was dismayed and angered that Larson kept trying to discredit the NIS and thwart the investigation. "A member of his command was assaulted, and that didn't seem to be a concern," Usrey said. The overriding concern was not marring the Soviet visit or Larson's career. "The past four days have been a tremendous success. It's been the high point of my career," Larson said at an elaborate departure ceremony for the Soviets on October 5. Of the woman who was violated, Larson said, "It's important to note at the present time this is just an allegation. The Soviets and the Americans will move swiftly to determine the facts." The Soviets sailed off, and the case was closed.

Kelso's role in the academy cheating scandal never came to light, other than the fact that he was the Navy's top admiral, forced to rule over another embarrassing scandal, especially at the academy, where truth and honor are supposed to be drilled into the midshipmen. Nevertheless, there was clear evidence of his lack of leadership during Tailhook. But before Dalton could advise Kelso that he was going to be fired, CBS's Pentagon correspondent David Martin went on the air Friday night with a report about the impending disgrace for the CNO. Kelso had been tipped off by Navy public affairs to watch the nightly news because something big was coming. But when he tuned in, he had no idea he was going to hear reports about his own firing.[33] Enraged, he demanded to see Les Aspin on Saturday morning. He was not about to resign unless Aspin asked him to. After their meeting, Kelso still had his job. And Aspin was placed in the awkward position of having to support his Navy secretary or Kelso, a man he had known for years and admired. He told Kelso he would review the file over the weekend and make a decision early in the week.

On Monday Aspin ruled in favor of Kelso, telling Dalton that the information and criteria did not warrant that he be forced to retire early. "I understand his reasoning, respect his views, and support his decision," Dalton said. Still, he felt that senior leadership should be held accountable for Tailhook. "I believe the damage done to the Navy's reputation by the incidents at Tailhook," he said, "could have been prevented or minimized by aggressive leadership and foresight by senior Navy officials."

Kelso did receive, however, a nonpunitive letter from Dalton, issued to most of the admirals who had attended the convention. But the letters did not go into their files. Only Dunleavy and one other admiral received letters of censure, which would have forced them to leave the service had they not previously retired.

Kelso left work on Monday buoyed by his victory. But it was only the first battle in a war aimed at stripping away his honor.

By December 1993, more than two years after the Tailhook convention and after the Navy and the Department of Defense conducted at least seven investigations at a cost of more than $3 million, the legal trials against the suspects charged with misbehavior, assault, and other violations of the military law were finally coming to an end—not with a bang, but with a whimper.

Twenty of these military officers were Marines, who had at various stages of the judicial process stood before Lieutenant General Charles Krulak, who was assigned by Marine headquarters to pass judgment on those involved. Krulak listened like a patient father and often referred to the Bible he kept on his desk as he heard the cases. In the end, none of the Leathernecks was court-martialed. Krulak dismissed some of the cases for lack of evidence, six Marines were cleared, and the rest were given nonjudicial punishment. For some the process did not even interfere with their careers. Lieutenant Colonel Mike Fagan, the commanding officer of the rhino men, was promoted to full colonel. Others, however, never recovered. One was Gregory Bonam. He met his accuser, Paula Coughlin, face-to-face in the courtroom and said he was sorry, but she was mistaken, that it was not he who had pawed her in the Gauntlet. And just as Ted Gordon had predicted, Bonam beat the charge of sexual assault. But he would forever be remembered as the man who got off. Despite promises to the contrary, his career was over.

Of the 120 cases brought before Vice Admiral Paul Reason, the black naval officer assigned to judge those aviators found guilty, more than half were thrown out for lack of evidence. Forty-three officers went to admiral's mast, in which Reason handed out the appropriate punishment—which in most cases were letters of caution and forfeiture of pay. Five officers, however, decided to take on the Navy. They refused nonjudicial punishment and asked for a full airing of their cases in a full-blown court-martial.

For three of these men, Commanders Thomas R. Miller, Gregory E. Tritt, and Lieutenant Dave Samples, their behavior at Tailhook was not the issue. The issue they put before Captain William T. Vest Jr., the Navy judge picked to hear their court-martial cases, was the accountability of Frank Kelso and the other admirals who attended the Tailhook convention. Attorneys for the three officers filed a combined motion that called into question Kelso's role in the whole Tailhook affair, from start to finish. The chief of naval operations, the motion argued, was guilty of the same crimes that the three officers stood accused of—namely, witnessing inappropriate behavior and doing nothing to stop it. Further, the motion argued that in picking Reason, an officer junior to him to oversee the disciplinary process, Kelso had shielded himself from prosecution. In Navy jargon, Kelso was accused of unlawful command influence.

It was now the four stars of the chief of naval operations against the four stripes of Captain Vest. Hanging in the balance was Kelso's thirty-eight-year naval career, the Navy's badly bruised reputation, and the integrity of the military's judicial system. The question of the day was simple: Could the nation's top admiral be held accountable?

On Tuesday, February 8, 1994, Judge Vest's Courtroom E in Norfolk, Virginia, came to order. Vest had spent weeks culling the thousands of pages of testimonies and other investigative files that had accumulated in the Tailhook affair. It was difficult reading, and much of the evidence was based on conflicting testimonies of the several thousands of interviews and courtroom appearances of victims, witnesses, and suspects. He had somehow to crunch all of this information into one ruling that, regardless of which way he decided, would have a dramatic impact on the Navy and its officers. There would be no winners, he knew. Even the legal system and his own integrity and intelligence would be called into question.

"This has been a very difficult motion for this court," Vest told an overflowing audience of naval officers who had come to hear the momentous ruling he was about to make. "I read everything," he said. "I took nothing lightly. And that will be demonstrated in my central findings." Then he released 111 pages of judicial prose that, among many other damaging rulings, repeatedly said Frank Kelso had lied under oath. "This court finds that Admiral Kelso manipulated the initial investigative process," Vest wrote, "in a manner designed to shield his own personal involvement in Tailhook '91. This manipulation of the process by Admiral Kelso and others was for their own personal ends."

It was an unprecedented indictment of Kelso and the admirals who had followed in the traditions of past scandals and tried to cover up injustices and wrongdoing rather than come clean at the expense of tarnishing the institution that had allowed them to reach remarkable heights of power. "This court has found that Admiral Kelso was present on the third-floor patio on both Friday and Saturday evenings, near the location where the alleged assaults on female attendees occurred. This court has also found that Admiral Kelso witnessed improper conduct being committed by junior officers. Many other senior naval officers witnessed similar activity. It is clear from the record that no one attempted to intervene to end the lewd and improper sexually oriented behavior. Conduct which began as being merely in bad taste quickly escalated and finally ended in physical assaults. If proper leadership had been shown, the subsequent assaults and other inappropriate conduct might have been prevented.

"These circumstances can only be viewed as a personal embarrassment for all senior naval officers who could have acted but did not. The opportunity to spare the Navy and the Marine Corps the chagrin and humiliation that has been heaped on it was lost." The person most responsible, Vest wrote, was Kelso.

Kelso was thunderstruck when word of the verdict reached him. His honesty had now been cut to threads in a military court of law. It would be useless to fight Vest's ruling, which also had the effect of ending the remaining cases the Navy had against Miller, Tritt, and Samples, as well as others still assigned to go before Reason to receive nonjudicial punishment. He had been wounded by his bout with Dalton, humiliated by the Airedales at Miramar, and ridiculed in the press. And now the system in which he had spent thirty-eight years of his life, a system he had sworn to uphold, had in Frank Kelso's eyes failed him. There was nothing else to do but retire two months early. But it would not be in disgrace, not if he had anything to do about it. He demanded and received statements from Dalton and Clinton's second secretary of defense, William Perry, heaping praise on him for his honor and integrity and for keeping the best interests of the Navy at heart.

The following Tuesday Kelso called the press to his office on the Pentagon's fourth floor. There, standing before a bank of microphones and television cameras, he spoke in his slow Tennessee drawl the words that many said had been too long in coming. "As chief of naval operations, I had a responsibility to lead the Navy through the process of changing the climate which allowed this incident to occur. Having done so, it is my intention to submit my request for retirement as of 30 April 1994. I became the lightning rod for Tailhook," he told the sympathetic reporters, adding that he had decided to retire in order to put the scandal finally to rest. "I think this is the end of Tailhook."

Kelso may have believed that, but it was not the end of his pain and suffering.

As Kelso's professional life as a naval officer crumbled, the Six Hundred Ship Navy he had helped to build with John Lehman in the 1980s had, by most standards, collapsed, too—both physically and spiritually. Lehman and his dream team had repeatedly been warned by their critics that the nation could not afford the massive naval buildup they had embarked on. Even their own internal classified studies concluded that by the 1990s the bills would come due, but there would be no money to pay them. The Extended Planning Annex, the secret study that Lehman had quashed, had been remarkably accurate in predicting the future. If the Navy was to modernize, the EPA said, all it could afford was 450 ships and 12 aircraft carriers. But even those figures had been charitable. For the last several years the Navy had been decommissioning a ship every week, a trend that would chop away at the fleet until only some 320 ships and 12 carriers were left. The mighty *New Jersey,* whose reactivation had marked the symbolic beginning of the Six Hundred Ship Navy, finished its sea days by being towed backward out of Long Beach Harbor.

And with the drawdown in ships came deep reductions in Lehman's Strategic Homeporting plan to modernize and build new naval bases around the nation at a cost of billions of dollars. New and expensive ports like Staten Island were closed down, never having been used by the fleet. For some cities like San Francisco, which had bought the Navy's promise for economic prosperity if they allowed new ships to be stationed along their shores, the balloon had popped. San Francisco's shipping industry, which was relying on the Navy's new business, had withered away when the Navy abandoned its plans for the city. And for cities that did enjoy the benefits of new facilities or new ships, the President's Base Closing and Realignment Commission was shutting down naval installations in record numbers. Cities whose economies had depended on the Navy's cash cow were now facing dire times. Had the Navy not gone forward with Strategic Homeporting to build new bases along the East and West Coasts, and along the Gulf of Mexico, the economic hardship would have been much less widespread. But there would have been no glory in restricting the Navy to only a handful of ports on each coast.

The rallying cry for building the fleet had been the Soviet bogeyman. No one could have predicted the fall of communism, Lehman and those who had defended Reagan's rearming America were saying. That was true. But the Navy had known all along that the Soviet fleet was defensive in nature and not a threat to the United States. All along, the Navy's own experts and its intelligence officers had told Lehman that the Soviets were no match for the U.S. Navy. Even the CIA's classified national intelligence estimate on the Soviet fleet had come to the same conclusion. But Lehman had refused to believe it and squashed factions within the Navy that continued to talk such blasphemy. It was full steam ahead for the Six Hundred Ship Navy and for the controversial Maritime Strategy, which sent ships into Soviet waters, looking to pick a fight.

Of all of Lehman's protégés, Frank Kelso had gone the farthest, rising to become chief of naval operations. But now Kelso, like many of the other Lehman team members who found themselves in the middle of an unprecedented number of Navy cover-ups and scandals, was leaving under less than honorable circumstances.

But even he would not have the final say on his departure. On September 19, 1994, the full Senate began debate on whether he should be allowed to retire as a four-star officer. It was scheduled to be a routine procedure, as Sam Nunn's Armed Services Committee had already voted in favor of Kelso. But then things began to turn against him. Before the debate began, Pat Schroeder and a number of female lawmakers from the House had walked to the Senate to join in support with Barbara Boxer and a handful of female senators who wanted Kelso bucked down to a two-star rear admiral. What was supposed to be a mild protest turned into a bitter floor fight by the entire Senate that lasted for hours. It was not just Kelso the senators were arguing about. It was the Navy's repeated failures to end a culture so demeaning to women. The sexual harassment and abuse of women had been rampant during Kelso's watch. As captain of the Navy ship, he was responsible and should pay the price, his detractors said.

It was the ultimate insult to Kelso, who watched the proceedings in his office, at times growing angry, even despondent. If there was a time when Kelso could have cried, it was then, his supporters said. At the end of the day the effort to demote him had fallen short by the slimmest of margins: 54–43.

He could go home now.

Several months later Frank Kelso lay near death in a hospital bed at the Bethesda Medical Center, with blood clots in his lungs and his legs crippled by a blood disorder that rendered his muscles useless. It was touch-and-go whether he would survive. He did, but he would be restricted to a wheelchair and, later, a walker. Like the Navy he so loved, he had fallen from glory.

CHAPTER 25

WITH FRANK KELSO forced to retire early because of Tailhook, John Dalton prepared a short list of names for the CNO's job. One admiral stood above the others: Mike Boorda, all five feet four inches of him. The other candidates were qualified, of course, such as the aristocratic Charles Larson, a favorite of Dalton's. And Lehman's protégé P. D. Miller was in the running too, though he was a long shot. But Bill Clinton, fond of Horatio Alger stories, was moved by Boorda's own life story, and had set his sights on this diminutive man known in the Navy as a "Mustang." It was a nickname given to all enlisted men who become officers. But the term seemed more appropriate for Boorda, known for his unprecedented bucks against the system. That he had reached the high rank of admiral was even more impressive to the President, considering how difficult life had been for Boorda.

The Boorda family moved around when Mike was young, but eventually settled in Momence, a small farming community fifty miles south of Chicago. The Boordas were a troubled family—a dysfunctional one. Mike was the second of Herman and Gertrude Boorda's three offspring. His parents, who spent most of their time running the only dress shop in Momence, had little time for rearing the children. As a result, young Mike never received the emotional nourishment that helps children develop strong self-esteem. This pained him. But he rarely spoke of it or his troubled youth. There were few outward signs of his inner turmoil, with the exception, perhaps, of his sad, weepy eyes. His life lacked direction. He had given up on high school, rarely showing up for class. And he was drinking heavily, sometimes a six-pack of beer a day. His parents' marriage, never that good, was falling apart, making life even more painful. They would divorce, but not before Boorda's father had been diagnosed with paranoid schizophrenia. When Boorda was thirteen, his father had tried but failed to kill himself by jumping off a bridge.

"Reducing the amount of pain you suffered every day was important to me," Boorda told Tom Philpot, the thoughtful journalist and former editor of *Navy Times*. "I wanted to get away from it." [1] He escaped by dropping out of high school, then lied about his age and enlisted in the Navy at sixteen.

(He would later reconcile with his parents, proudly telling his mom how the President picked him to be the CNO.) Early on, Boorda wanted to give up and drop out of boot camp. Soon, however, he found a role model, and a short while later he graduated first in his class from personnelman school. Boorda then married Bettie Moran, and at nineteen the young couple had their first child, a son they named David. More children would follow. But none were like David. He was born with only one eye and other physical deformities that would require seventeen operations by his fourth birthday. Told that Goltz Syndrome had stricken David and that he might be blind, the doctor recommended that the Boordas place the child in a special home. "I took the baby and said 'No.' And I took Bettie home and we did the best we could," Boorda later said.

Boorda gave his all to the Navy. He worked his way up through the enlisted ranks and was encouraged to join the "seaman to admiral" program and become an officer. At first he was hesitant to leave the secure community where one took orders, not gave them. He felt he had another big strike against him too: he didn't have a college degree, a requirement to get into Officer Candidate School (OCS). The Navy waived this rule for Boorda and after coaxing from his mentor, a petty officer named George Everding, Boorda left in 1961 to be trained as an officer. At OCS, he was shy and quiet. "He was self-contained, kept to himself, was very organized, very neat and very orderly," recalled Lee Van Boven, one of Boorda's roommates. "He wasn't part of the crowd; he was reserved." He was also supremely secure about himself, sometimes even cocky about his abilities, said Van Boven.

As he made his way to flag rank, Boorda never forgot his roots. He knew the Navy could be a jungle for young kids who joined for many of the same reasons he had. And he made it a point to look out for them. Frequently, as the Chief of Naval Personnel, he reached out to people in trouble. Well before Paula Coughlin became a news celebrity after her appearance on *World News Tonight* with Peter Jennings, Boorda had her transferred to his staff so he could watch over her. He also gave former Navy Secretary Garrett's son a job on his staff after he got into trouble for helping to steal credit cards from a base mailroom.

The troops took to calling Boorda "a sailor's sailor." Almost everyone in the enlisted ranks knew Boorda had begun his naval career as a seaman, the bottom rung in an often cruel caste system, that like them, he had performed the most menial of jobs. Boorda knew the officers often treated the enlisted ranks poorly, because he had been there and seen it firsthand. The sailors took solace in knowing that he would somehow keep the officer corps in check. And he did, often to the icy response of senior commanders. Tom Philpot captured this side of Boorda better than most journalists. He wrote in the *Washingtonian* magazine how Boorda's compassion led him to transfer on the spot sailors who had hardship cases. His sincerity grated on their commanders, who felt Boorda was meddling, even abusing the chain of command. If the letter of the law was applied to Boorda's actions, he was breaking ranks and undermining the authority of his commanding officers. Under normal conditions, if a sailor wanted a hardship discharge he would have to work the chain of command, not start at the top with the CNO. But Boorda's reputation preceded him. He received more than the normal number of pleas for help from the enlisted ranks. In the majority of these, Boorda wrote back a personal letter explaining that the sailor had to use the chain of command. But when he visited the fleet, he could not resist reaching out to a sailor in trouble, even though he knew it greatly angered his subordinate commanding officers.

Philpot recounted a scene in Norfolk in which Boorda was taking questions from 2,000 sailors in a base theater. A chief machinist's mate named Frank Salabarria, his knees shaking, began speaking into a floor microphone. "Good afternoon, Admiral. Less than a year ago I was forced to take my ten-year-old and two-year-old daughters from Guantanamo Bay to spend the next three months watching my wife slowly and brutally die of metastatic cervical cancer. She was a master chief." Salabarria wanted to retire early but fell short by about six months. If he reenlisted to meet the requirements, he told Boorda, "I'm slated for sea duty, which will take me away from my children."

"You want to retire next June?" Boorda asked, his voice soft and caring.

"Yes, sir."

"When did your wife pass away?" Boorda asked.

"January first."

"Okay. Your request is approved. We'll work it out."

Boorda had moved the crowd to tears and a thunderclap of applause. "Mike Boorda had saved another sailor," Philpot wrote, "just as the Navy once saved him."

Boorda's critics saw this as pure showmanship. Although he had deep-seated passion for the less fortunate, the criticism was partially valid. He loved being on stage. He loved attention. And he loved the press corps, granting them access and filling them with sea stories—not a few about his panache. He had a boundless regard for his own abilities, more than once calling himself the best ship driver ever. "I am, modestly, the best ship handler in the Navy, still to this very day. There are some people who are very good. But nobody's close."[2] He also had an optimist's view of his power to right the slowly sinking Navy ship. For him, the glass was always half full, never half empty. "There are some who would expect me to start out by talking about what is wrong, but I'm not going to do that," he wrote in his first letter as CNO to the fleet. "We have a lot that is right with our Navy." Not all, of course, shared his optimism. To most Navy watchers in the media and on Capitol Hill, the multitude of scandals since 1981—from *Vincennes* and *Iowa* to Tailhook and the Naval Academy cheating mess, to name but a few—had drained the glass. There was a view among many that despite Boorda's qualities, the demands placed on him were too much for one man to bear.

There was indeed an intense pressure on Boorda to shake up a system that had gone sour. He was not a graduate of the Naval Academy and therefore not obligated by tradition to promote the ring-knockers of Annapolis to the best jobs in the Navy. Because of this, there were great expectations among those in the Navy and elsewhere that the new CNO was going to end the institutional corruption that had racked the service for so many years, and reshape the stereotypical macho culture that had proved to be so demeaning to women. Boorda had always been an honest believer in allowing women to serve on combat ships. When he became CNO, he pledged to place women on submarines, despite the cramped quarters in which sailors must "hot rack," sharing bunks at different times. But when faced with overwhelming hostility from the submarine admirals, Boorda had to retreat and settle for putting women on surface ships and aircraft carriers.

It was a good lesson. Boorda understood the power of the flag community. He understood that he could push his fellow admirals only so far. Individually they would be no match for his administrative power. But if they united against him, he stood little chance in carrying out his reforms. He had won over a considerable number of admirals when he was the Chief of Naval Personnel. There, his most important assignment was shepherding officers picked for flag rank and promoting admirals up the chain and into top jobs. Inevitably, he had some sharp critics. One was Rear Admiral Jack Snyder, whom Boorda offered little due process before recommending his firing as Tailhook's first scapegoat. But many admirals were beholden to him and Boorda would later call in his chits when need be. "He was too political," recalled retired Vice Admiral William Mack, a former Naval Academy superintendent.[3] That was a common complaint. Indeed, he was not above ingratiating himself to his bosses or his many supporters in Congress with expectations of personal benefit. His eagerness in this regard could have cost him his coveted dream of becoming CNO.

During his confirmation hearings, the Senate failed to seriously question Boorda about his zealousness in helping the son of former Navy Secretary H. Lawrence Garrett III. At the time, Boorda was bucking for a fourth star, the highest rank in the peacetime Navy. Going out of his way for the secretary's son could only help sweeten his chances. It was not unusual for Boorda to direct his staff to watch over a young sailor; he had done it before. But in this instance, his personal interest and favoritism, not just the appearance of it, was obvious, and to some of those involved in the endeavor, well over the line.

Although Boorda did not directly lie to a military court, he withheld key information in a sworn affidavit about his personal knowledge and actions in trying to help the younger Garrett. Had a proper investigation been conducted in public, either by Congress or a military board of inquiry, in which all of Secretary Garrett's aides had been called to testify under oath, Boorda's actions would have shown him to be more culpable than his sworn statement suggested. But the Navy bureaucracy went to great lengths to shield its next CNO from any blame, even to the extent of having its media-affairs office leak damaging information to the press about two other officers involved in the case while stating that Boorda had been cleared of any wrongdoing by a former military judge called in to review the matter. The judge, who was supposed to be independent and free of any influence from the brass or civilian officials, was in contact with the Navy's leadership throughout key portions of his probe—thus giving the appearance that he was not a completely impartial investigator.

The Navy was not alone in its desire to protect the new CNO. The Senate Armed Services Committee, then led by Sam Nunn, had no intention of convening hearings that would get to the entire truth either. Boorda got the same softball questions from the senators that John Dalton had received when he became the secretary of the Navy. To question Boorda's honesty when the Navy was rebounding from Kelso's problematic reign would have continued to put the sea service in the middle of controversy, something that the committee members apparently concluded was not in the nation's best interest. It was the same conclusion they made for Dalton. "The adverse information in their background," Senator Charles Grassley said of Boorda and Dalton, "should have been exposed to public scrutiny and debated. But that did not happen. We were sleeping at the switch when they were slipped quietly through the Senate confirmation net."[4]

Grassley believed "these troublesome facts lay buried in Government files somewhere."[5] And he was right. Had he and other senators known about the preferential treatment that Boorda's own officer son, Robert, had received, they might have probed deeper into the new CNO's background. While Boorda refused to discuss the matter, through his aides he claimed that no regulations or laws were violated regarding his son's eligibility for the Law Education Program, which allows commissioned officers to attend law school at the government's expense while drawing a regular Navy salary. The Navy acknowledged that Robert Boorda was allowed to enter law school in the summer semester, well ahead of his freshman peers, who began in the fall. But it insisted that no sweetheart deal was arranged with the university. Boorda, who then headed up the Bureau of Personnel which oversaw the program, said he had recused himself from all dealings regarding the selection of his son. Had Boorda's son not started in the summer, however, he would have been ineligible for the program.[6] So the Navy allowed him to attend ahead of schedule, an arrangement that naval officers say would not have been done for other officers. And once he graduated and returned to the fleet as a Navy lawyer, Boorda's son received orders to a prime job in London that had originally been given to another officer. After a hot-line complaint to Pentagon investigators, and fears that the new CNO would get caught up in the case, Boorda's son received new orders to another London job. "Would that happen for your son, or my son?" a Navy lawyer asked. "Heck no!"

Letting his child's naval career benefit because of his position and providing extra favors for Garrett's son were minor sins in the bigger scheme of the Navy's problems. To be sure, those negatively affected by the admiral's gratuitous goodwill saw it differently. For them, Boorda's much-heralded integrity had failed this small but important litmus test. What would he do when an even bigger test of his character confronted him? The answer, to one harsh critic, was never in doubt. He would, Jim Webb would later say in a dogmatic speech at the Naval Academy, lack "moral courage," choosing instead to curry favor with politicians rather than support the service.[7]

By the time Boorda had become the fleet's top admiral in April 1994, Lieutenant Rebecca Hansen had all but given up on the Navy. Hansen, a handsome woman with dark hair and sharp features, had been going through the grueling training to become a helicopter pilot. Under normal conditions, flight school requires rigorous discipline. For female officers it can be much more demanding—not physically but psychologically, because of the unspoken traditional bias against women who want to pilot naval aircraft. As Hansen struggled with her peers to overcome the first obstacle, she became a victim of the second: one of her instructors found it necessary to harass her sexually. During a preflight check Hansen said a friction control knob was stuck. Her instructor, Lieutenant Larry Meyer, responded by saying, "Isn't that just like a woman to complain about friction?" Meyer suggested that Hansen should dye her hair, don an orange bikini, and wear blue contact lenses because she would look good with blue eyes. Meyer ended a flight by saying, "Come on, wench." She had reported Meyer to her superiors, which spurred an investigation that resulted in his being disciplined and subsequently discharged. But the matter did not die there. As so often was the case in issues where females appeared to benefit from perceived political correctness, a crude form of anger against Hansen followed. Meyer made it clear to another officer that Hansen would pay for singling him out, that she would have to fly with his friends, who would be grading her as she advanced through pilot training. The implication was that the network of male aviators would see to it that she did not succeed in winning her wings and becoming a pilot. These remarks were reported up the chain. Hansen then moved on to the next stage of her training—and to her dismay, she was dropped from the program. She asked for a second investigation, requesting the Navy to determine if her former instructor had somehow influenced her being washed out from pilot training. Although she kept the matter within the Navy, following procedures required by the chain of command, Hansen, like so many others in the fleet, had little confidence in the system. After all, the Navy had failed to investigate itself adequately in numerous past scandals, including Tailhook—the one watershed event that led to new regulations designed to prevent the predicament Hansen now found herself in. She truly wanted to find out if she was dropped because of merit, or if her past instructor had made good on his threat. So she made the decision to go outside the system. She placed a call to the office of David Durenberger, the Republican senator from Minnesota.

Durenberger had little connection to the Navy. Compared to most other states, Minnesota generated little revenues from the fleet. It was not a Navy state; thus, the brass was not overly preoccupied with it or its elected officials. Most noticeably, Durenberger was not on the important Armed Services Committee, the primary legislative vehicle for overseeing the Pentagon. Still, he was a U.S. senator. And that in itself gave him a pulpit from which to bully. The Navy brass might not have taken him seriously, but they respected the power of his office.

Durenberger asked the Navy why his constituent was dropped from pilot training. That she was dismissed after such a bare threat from a former instructor seemed a relevant issue to him. The Navy sent its inspector general over to Capitol Hill to speak with Durenberger and assure him that Hansen failed to make the cut solely because she lacked the necessary skills and nothing more. Indeed, Hansen had a litany of problems, both in her attitude and in the cockpit. She failed to grasp the situational awareness needed to become a good pilot and frequently bantered with instructors who tried to help her. In short, she was a problem student.

Durenberger asked for a copy of the investigative report, but the Navy refused to hand it over. Rather, the brass gave it to the Armed Services

Committee. The report contained privileged information, and despite his requests, he was unable to obtain it from the committee. "I was unable to determine whether the Navy had really investigated the incident or whether they were just sweeping it under the rug," he recalled.[8] The Navy did, however, inform Durenberger that Admiral Stanley Arthur, the vice chief of naval operations, would review the matter further. Arthur was a decorated flier from the Vietnam War who was widely thought of as an honest naval officer. Despite his being a company man, which he was, he was a person who could be evenhanded. Arthur made the trek from his fourth-floor office at the Pentagon, across the Potomac and up to the Senate side of the Capitol to Durenberger's suite. Durenberger was courteous while he repeated his questions that, to him, had yet to be fully answered. Was Hansen's dismissal the result of retaliation, and did the harassment itself contribute to the lack of her success? Arthur promised a full and, most important, a fair accounting and left.

Several weeks later, he wrote a letter to Durenberger reporting that the Navy's decision to drop the woman was justifiable. Arthur personally reviewed the case and, based on his years as one of the Navy's best pilots, had reached the conclusion that Hansen did not have the necessary skills to pilot a naval aircraft. "I then asked him to explain to me the basis upon which he reached this conclusion," Durenberger said. "Admiral Arthur and the Navy, for reasons I have never understood, declined to answer my question."[9] Not to be put off, Durenberger decided to use the power of his office. Arthur had recently been selected to command all U.S. forces in the Pacific, a major promotion, and his nomination was pending before the Senate. Members of the Armed Services Committee staff advised Durenberger's aides that the senator could place a hold on the nomination, thus forcing Boorda and the brass to respond fully to his concerns.

To do this was not an uncommon procedure. But in the wake of the Navy's problems, especially Sam Nunn's freezing the promotions of thousands of officers because of Tailhook, Arthur's dilemma presented a serious problem for Boorda, and one that weighed heavily on him. Nobody had predicted that the Senate would come so embarrassingly close to rejecting Frank Kelso's bid to retire with four stars. Kelso ultimately won, but the Navy lost in the realm of public opinion. Arthur's handling of the Hansen case most likely would be a repeat of that painful episode and expose the Navy to continued public anger and criticism. And, while the case dragged on, an important war-fighting job in the Pacific would be vacant. There was also a bureaucratic reason why Boorda worried. The Air Force sought to capitalize on the Navy's vulnerability and began lobbying to put one of its own officers in the job—a position always before filled by an admiral. What compounded

Boorda's anxiety was the media's fixation on the story. It would not die and continued to bounce because it had all the necessary elements of a good-guy-versus-bad-guy story. As it continued to reverberate, the pressure mounted. It had come down to a decorated Vietnam War aviator versus Durenberger and his concern about a woman who might or might not be qualified to wear gold Navy wings. The conservative pundits railed at Durenberger, unfairly so. "At all times my hold was conditioned only on the Navy answering some simple questions about the investigation," Durenberger wrote in a letter to the *Wall Street Journal* editorial page, which never missed a shot to carve up those its editors disagreed with. "The Navy was specifically told that I did not even have to like the answer to the question in order for the hold to be lifted. They just had to answer the questions." [10] The rest of the media, by and large, reported the story straight.

With the showdown impending, Boorda gave up on Arthur's nomination. Arthur's supporters were flummoxed. Boorda had chosen to support Hansen, a woman who wanted to fly but clearly did not have the skills, against Arthur, a legendary pilot who had repeatedly laid his life on the line during the Vietnam War. Worse, Boorda had offered to bring Hansen aboard his staff in an attempt to appease her. It was clear that Boorda was willing to sacrifice Arthur in favor of currying support from critics on Capitol Hill and in the media who wanted women to succeed in the Navy no matter the cost. The traditionalists who supported Arthur were now suspicious of Boorda. Up to that point, Boorda's efforts to reshape the Navy had been accepted by the traditionalists as a necessary evil. Boorda had been a member of this old guard, a cadre of active-duty and retired admirals. It was clear now that the old guard could no longer back their CNO.

Jim Webb, perhaps the most inflexible of the traditionalists, was particularly embittered by the decision. Webb was a man firm in his convictions, a true believer, a soldier who never retreated, a bureaucrat who never backed down. To him, the Navy leadership had lost its way, caved in to what he believed was a climate of political correctness. He was not alone. Not just the traditionalists but most of the flag community that Boorda had so earnestly courted had begun to turn against him. Even the retired community of admirals, in itself a powerful lobby that quite frequently influenced decisions made by the Navy in Washington, was beside itself. A short while after the decision to deny Arthur perhaps his most important job, one that could have led to his one day becoming chairman of the Joint Chiefs of Staff, Boorda traveled to San Diego and met with both retired and active-duty admirals at a party in Coronado. There, he was constantly harangued, so much so that Boorda went back to Washington realizing he had made a first-class blunder in not supporting a four-star admiral. "If there's one thing I would have done differently, this is it," he told Philpot the journalist. "I should have fought this to the end. [Instead] I helped screw it up and don't feel good about it." [11]

Boorda would not make the mistake again. In the next few months he would fight to save the careers of five senior officers: three rear admiral selectees, one four-star and one two-star, all of whom were charged with sexual harassment or inappropriate sexual behavior. But before he could do that, he would be faced with another politically explosive issue concerning sexual politics: the death of Lieutenant Kara Hultgreen.

The only normal thing about Kara Hultgreen's death was the mistake she made approaching the carrier *Abraham Lincoln,* an error common among aviators without a great deal of experience flying at sea. Weather conditions that day, October 25, 1994, were perfect for flight operations: calm seas that kept *Lincoln*'s stern from bobbing erratically up and down in the blue Pacific; a bright blue sky that allowed Hultgreen to see for miles; and a slight sea breeze with no gusts that she would have to fight while landing. Her training flight had been routine and she was now going through a checklist while preparing to bring the F-14 Tomcat aboard—a plane known for being difficult to land. She flew the jet parallel to the ship then went into a turn that would place the carrier directly in front of her. All of this was according to procedures for approaching the ship. Her problems began when she came out of her turn. Hultgreen had accidentally overshot the center line, an imaginary line that extends from the flattop out to sea that pilots must align with for a proper landing. Rather than veer off and come around for another try, as more experienced pilots normally would do, Hultgreen tried to correct her approach. As she did so, she accidentally began to put the aircraft *in extremis.* The large Tomcat began to lose altitude and fall quickly toward the sea. At the same time, its air speed dropped and became dangerously slow. Dead ahead was *Lincoln*'s stern. Normal procedures required that Hultgreen point the aircraft's nose down toward the water to pick up air speed. But the natural human response is to pull the nose up, away from the sea and the ship. This she did, a mistake that stalled the jet. The landing signals officer, directing her approach by radio from a platform near the ship's stern, had previously waved her off a few seconds earlier when she had overshot the centerline. Now he was shouting frantically, "Eject! eject! eject!" Just below him the plane was moving through the air with its left wingtip pointing down toward the water, which was perilously close. The aviator in the back seat quickly punched out. About three seconds later, Hultgreen's front seat automatically followed. But by this time the aircraft had rolled upside down and the ejection shot her straight into the ocean, killing her instantly, the Navy determined, upon impact.

The news that the Navy's first female pilot to fly in a combat squadron had crashed and died at sea rocketed through naval aviation squadrons nationwide. There was remorse among some aviators at the loss of a comrade. There was, however, also a morbid celebration among others, particularly aviators at Miramar, who felt vindicated by her death. These men had warned of such an outcome. In their righteousness, they had neglected Hultgreen's attributes while pointing out every one of her shortcomings as she went through Miramar's training program for F-14 pilots returning to combat squadrons and sea duty. These aviators were convinced that the brass had intentionally overlooked Hultgreen's failings because of political pressure. A male lieutenant and radar intercept officer on the Tomcat was so incensed that he approached an admiral during a night of drinking at the Miramar officers club, telling him that the female pilots were dangerous and that he refused to fly with them. "Put it in writing and we'll take a look at it," the admiral had replied. Few, if any, did so. Rather, they bitterly complained among themselves that the Navy had allowed Hultgreen and another female pilot named Caroy Dunai Lorenz to pass through the program despite serious deficiencies in their flying. Both female pilots did receive preferential treatment, particularly being moved ahead of others waiting to fly the F-14. But they were not the dangerous pilots that the aviators were making them out to be. Hultgreen and Dunai Lorenz were average, better than some men and well below the skill level of others.

Even if the men had protested the special treatment given to the women, the vice admiral in charge of the Pacific Fleet's Air Forces, Robert "Rocky" Spane, would be hard-pressed to investigate any allegations unless forced to do so. The demise of Stan Arthur, simply for supporting a decision made by a subordinate that grounded Rebecca Hansen, had a clear political message —one not missed by many admirals. It was not written anywhere, but it didn't have to be. Any politically sensitive officer understood, rightly or wrongly, that women were to succeed as pilots—period. Spane had in fact, recently ruled against a safety panel's recommendation and allowed another female helicopter pilot to keep her wings. The woman had been assigned to be an instructor at the training squadron in Coronado, just across the San Diego Bay at the big North Island Naval Air Station. But when she arrived she had failed to pass a routine safety test. A performance review followed and found that the woman had panicked on numerous occasions while airborne with passengers aboard. One time, her copilot had to land the aircraft because the woman had become incapacitated. On the ground, medics had to revive her with oxygen and take her away on a stretcher. In the wake of

Arthur, when a decision made against the wishes of the brass in Washington could cost one his career, Spane simply transferred the woman to an air-traffic-control unit. After Spane had retired, she would be allowed to return to the cockpit. This further exacerbated the anger felt among male aviators at the brass for not having the spine to stand up and do what they, the aviators, believed was the right thing—take the woman's wings away. The case of this particular female pilot supported the notion that the Navy was playing politics on issues of gender. But it was closely held even within the Navy, and Spane refused to discuss publicly the safety panel's findings or how the investigation had been conducted. Now, with Kara Hultgreen's body and her aircraft at the bottom of the Pacific Ocean, Spane would be the point man in an investigation that the public would closely scrutinize.

How thorough it would be was not certain. While Spane would be the man in charge, at least publicly, those truly running the show would be Boorda and his admirals in Washington. After Hultgreen's death, Boorda had told several admirals that he did not want another *Iowa* on his hands. The Navy had erroneously blamed a dead sailor for the explosion aboard the battleship. The political repercussions for that injustice still lingered, and Boorda was not about to make such a dire mistake by publicly stating Hultgreen was guilty of pilot error. The common perception was that the Navy had been dragged into placing women aviators in combat squadrons because of the Tailhook scandal. There was a great deal of truth to that. To now accuse Hultgreen of screwing up would be politically untenable—despite the fact that she was a good pilot who happened to make a mistake in an unforgiving business where errors can kill you. Previously in her career, she had kept her wits in an emergency and safely landed a crippled A-6 Intruder. These were the types of attributes that Boorda and his admirals would champion while deliberately clouding the circumstances that led to her death. Indeed, almost immediately, the Navy began raising the specter of mechanical failure with the infamous TF30 engines that were on Hultgreen's Tomcat.

The charade began on the day after the accident. The Navy had organized a press conference at Miramar in which Captain Mark "Gus" Grissom, a senior aviator at the base, would brief reporters and try to beat back the allegations that Hultgreen was incapable of flying a high-performance jet at sea aboard a carrier. These charges, which also included revelations that Hultgreen had received several downs during her training cycle, violations that normally led to pilots' being washed out, had now reached the press corps. Some of these could be supported by facts. But most others were totally fabricated and would soon escalate into the absurd. Before long, some aviators took to calling reporters and radio shock jocks in San Diego and

Washington with wild stories about Hultgreen and Dunai Lorenz. (Dunai Lorenz would later bring a libel suit against several news organizations.) Even Hultgreen's training file, which had been obtained by a naval officer and doctored to make it appear as if her record were extremely poor, had been given to a major West Coast daily newspaper.[12] And an anonymous letter, written by an aviator and full of inaccuracies about the crash, was surreptitiously sent to the press accusing the Navy of changing standards for women. Grissom told the reporters, who had been assembled in an area in which a gleaming white F-14 Tomcat was displayed for a prop, that Hultgreen had received no preferential treatment and that she had qualified to fly the Tomcat in the same way a male pilot did. There was little else he could tell the reporters other than that a complete Judge Advocate General investigation was under way. It would perhaps take months and it might not find the true cause of the crash.

Rocky Spane repeatedly said that as the investigation played out. But, while doing so, he kept pushing the notion that engine failure had caused Hultgreen's jet to plunge into the ocean. The Navy wanted desperately to prove this. They even raised the aircraft, at a cost of about $1 million, so investigators could examine the engines in the hope of finding a mechanical malfunction. Test results, however, revealed that both engines were working fine, with the exception of a partially closed bleed air valve on one. The valve had been corroded shut for some time. This only showed, however, that the airplane had had no previous problems flying and landing aboard ship in this condition. In fact, such a valve problem is considered a minor "fix-it" and not reason enough for maintenance crews to ground an airplane. It certainly was not enough in itself to cause the jet to stall.

The JAG report in its entirety would, if a reader was careful to look for it, note problems with Hultgreen's flying skills on the day of her death. But the way it was to be presented to the media at an orchestrated press conference suggested quite the contrary. A slimmed-down version of the JAG report had been prepared with covering letters from three admirals stressing mechanical problems. If a reporter wanted the complete JAG report, the Navy said a request under the Freedom of Information Act would have to be made. Officers who were to speak to reporters at the press conference were ordered to wear their dress blues. They looked sharp and official when they went on camera that day, which was the Navy's intent. The story they unveiled for the networks, one the media unflinchingly hooked on to, was a manipulation of the facts: mechanical failure, not pilot error on Hultgreen's part, was the primary cause of the crash. The Navy supported this position by pointing out that the bleed air valve had failed.

The Navy hoped that the JAG report would put the case to rest. But

Boorda and Spane both knew that the contents of a second, much more thorough but secret report, could leak to the press. This Mishap Investigation Report spelled out in clear and direct language Hultgreen's many mistakes that led to her death. The bluntness of the findings was in direct contrast to the shortened version of the JAG report handed out to reporters by the Navy at the press conference. Some officers in the chain of command at Spane's headquarters in San Diego had warned Washington of this and said if it leaked the Navy would appear to be covering up. They had one hope that it would not happen: it was a crime, punishable by time in jail, for anyone in the Navy to unofficially release it.

The first news organization to report its contents was *Newsweek,* followed by the *Los Angeles Times.* Robert Caldwell, who served in Vietnam and was now a columnist for the *San Diego Union-Tribune,* was perhaps the most dogged. He wrote a series of thorough but controversial columns on how the Navy had obfuscated the facts. As the Mishap Investigation Report began circulating (it would eventually be placed on the Internet), Rear Admiral Kendell Pease, the head of Navy public affairs, immediately put his staff to work trying to discredit these news accounts. He released a memorandum for correspondents saying: "If you or your organization have received such a document and are inclined to report on it, please allow Navy public affairs an opportunity to help avoid the errors of fact evident in some recent news reports." The next part of the Navy's strategy to defuse the story was to switch the focus away from the report's damaging findings to the alleged heinous act of a naval officer leaking such an important investigation. "I'm angry. I'm disappointed. I'm concerned. I'm talking about the recent unauthorized release of a Mishap Investigation Report," Rear Admiral J. S. Mobley, the commander of the Naval Safety Center, wrote in a message distributed to the press. Boorda weighed in too. "Unauthorized disclosures really damage the system," he said. In the end, Pease was successful in keeping most major news organizations from writing about the second report.[13]

The statement that Grissom had made on the day after the crash, that Hultgreen had received the same treatment that male aviators did was, at face value, true, but one that neither he nor his superiors in the Navy felt obliged to put into the proper context. Had the Navy been more forthcoming, they would have revealed that male naval aviators receive just as many, if not more, breaks overall in their training and flight careers as Hultgreen had. In fairness to the Navy, flight instructors realize that the government has a sizable investment of time and money in the naval aviators—both male and female—who reach the stage of their flying careers similar to Hultgreen's. There is an unwritten rule to help all potential pilots through the training syllabus if the instructor feels in the long term the aviator will meet the minimum safety requirements.

The result of this practice, however, is that the Navy keeps a number of mediocre and poor male pilots, many of whom are far less qualified than Hultgreen was. But the Navy could not say this after Hultgreen's death, lest it reveal the truth that naval aviation, while demanding and dangerous, does not have one exact standard that all pilots must meet. In fact, the standards are very fluid and often applied on a case-by-case basis. On several occasions the preferential treatment afforded to male aviators has led to crashes similar to Hultgreen's and, unfortunately, to the deaths of the flight crews. One accident involved Lieutenant Commander Jimbo Boyles, a naval aviator assigned to VF-126, a squadron at Top Gun. According to a Mishap Investigation Report conducted by the Navy, Boyles had been grounded during the Persian Gulf War for unsafe flying, had been fired from his job as a maintenance officer for poor performance, was passed over for promotion, was under investigation for his activities at Tailhook, had an alcohol problem, had at one point in his career been reported to have suicidal tendencies, and was going through a divorce while his new girlfriend was nine months pregnant. These problems should have kept him from flying a multimillion-dollar military jet. But little of this record was entered in his official Navy file. And as some pilots had predicted, Boyles died on December 16, 1992, in Idaho, after performing an unorthodox takeoff that the Navy restricted to air shows.

The Navy never released the complete details of Boyles's accident or those of other unsafe pilots who, over the years, had killed themselves while flying a Navy jet. These pilots were allowed to keep flying despite serious deficiencies because the network of naval aviators closed ranks and refused to ground them. None of the individuals who faulted Hultgreen for the apparent favoritism that had been bestowed on her ever mentioned that they themselves were guilty of the same sins. It would become obvious to Boorda over the next year, as a rash of F-14 Tomcat crashes struck the fleet, that the Navy's pilot standards were in need of review and strengthening. What made this clear to him was the fatal crash of an F-14 Tomcat (from Hultgreen's squadron) in Nashville, Tennessee, on January 29, 1996.

Lieutenant Commander John Stacy Bates was piloting the jet when it left the runway under full military power with its nose pointed practically straight up, a maneuver similar to the one that had proved fatal to Jimbo Boyles in Idaho. Bates lost control of the aircraft while in the clouds. He tried to recover the Tomcat as it plummeted to earth, but failed, and the jet crashed in a residential neighborhood, falling through the living room of one home. The crash killed the pilot and four other individuals and set a number of homes ablaze. Bates had left Miramar on a cross-country hop to gain flight hours while visiting his family in Tennessee. Such long-distance flights are not out of the ordinary and offer some training value. But they are frequently abused.[14]

The cross-country flight that Bates was on had been scheduled with his squadron as a routine training mission. But his performance leaving the airfield in Nashville was anything but routine. A Navy investigation later determined that he had violated a number of safety regulations, such as the air-show takeoff and going into a low cloud cover while nearly vertical, mistakes that caused the crash. Pictures of the devastation played prominently on the networks' evening news shows, which added to the Navy's troubles. But what further cast the Navy in a bad light were the strong statements made by some officials right after the crash adamantly claiming that Bates's takeoff was routine. "It is not unusual," and "it is not more risky," Rear Admiral Skip Dirren had said. Dirren's statement would later be repudiated by the facts. And *The New York Times*'s Eric Schmitt soon reported that Bates had lost a jet over the Pacific Ocean the previous April. It later turned out that naval investigators erred in letting Bates return to flight status after that accident. They based their decision on his "community reputation" as a good guy, a flyboy "who walked the walk and talked the talk" of the naval aviator, said one squadron commander, rather than on his flight skills—which were lacking. In fact, prior to his crash in Nashville, Bates had experienced recurring problems landing on carriers and had come close to a midair collision with another Navy jet during a practice bombing mission.

Boorda eventually acknowledged that Bates should not have been flying the jet that fateful day. "He gave it his best every day. But he was having some trouble flying the airplane," Boorda told reporters who attended a press conference in the Pentagon's briefing theater on April 15, 1996.[15] The media had come to hear the results of the Navy's investigation into the Nashville crash. That Boorda was briefing made it a more important news story. He would not disappoint the gathered journalists. If anything, the CNO had learned from the Hultgreen inquiry to play it straight on such high-profile investigations. He admitted that there were serious problems with the system in which senior commanders overlooked pilot deficiencies. He was changing that, he said, changing the way pilots with flight problems are reviewed so cases like Bates (and Boyles) would not happen again. "I want to know that every pilot who is flying an airplane, who has difficulty . . . was evaluated fairly on the ability to fly the airplane safely," he told the gaggle of reporters.[16]

Boorda's changes, though seemingly subtle to a public that had little understanding of the Navy's convoluted bureaucracy, were a warning to the naval aviation community to clean up its act. The new CNO was a baron of the surface warfare community, a community long the butt of jokes among the aviators who saw the black shoes as the lowest class in the Navy. For the aviators, the tables had turned. Boorda was now the Navy's top admiral. Although he represented all three fiefdoms, his heart lay with his ship-driving colleagues—not the flyboys. The once glorious naval aviation community was, if anything, Boorda's biggest headache, and one that would plague him throughout his tenure. The Nashville accident was just the latest of some thirty F-14s that had crashed since 1991—nearly $1 billion in lost aircraft, let alone lost lives. Hultgreen's squadron had lost four in less than a year.

Questionable personnel procedures that allowed unsafe pilots like Bates to go aloft were just one of many pains to confront Boorda. One of the Navy's deepest wounds, but one the press would pay scant attention to, was a federal judge's ruling on the futuristic A-12 bomber that never flew and left taxpayers with a multibillion-dollar debt. McDonnell Douglas and General Dynamics, the aircraft's two builders, had filed suit against the Navy for its impromptu decision to cancel the program. The judge ruled in favor of the contractors. The verdict meant the Navy might have to pay as much as $2 billion to the plaintiffs. The Navy planned to appeal.

This was only one procurement headache. In March 1996 the General Accounting Office released a lengthy report chastising the Navy for its decision to build the controversial F/A-18E/F, otherwise known as the Super Hornet, a jet highly touted by the brass as the end to the Navy's aircraft predicament. The Navy opted to build the new jet from scratch rather than the F-14D Super Tomcat, whose production lines were already up and running. The GAO concluded that the Super Hornet offered only marginal improvements over the existing version of the Hornet, and recommended that the Secretary of Defense cancel the $81 billion program—the Pentagon's most expensive.[17] The GAO reported that the Navy had understated costs and overrated the aircraft's proposed stealth capabilities to Congress.

The aviation admirals always had ready answers for the mess they and their civilian leaders had gotten themselves into. But there was little they could do to influence Boorda on a new weapons program that, if implemented, could reduce the Navy's dependence on carrier aviation in the years ahead. The concept was to build a giant floating barge, load it with missiles, man it with a very small crew, and park it off the coast of a North Korea or the former Yugoslavia or some other world hot spot where U.S. interests were at stake. Tomahawk missiles had proved to be more accurate in the Persian Gulf War than bombs dropped by piloted aircraft. And though they carried less of a payload than an A-6, for example, they were cheaper. This fact threatened such costly programs as the Super Hornet as well as naval aviation itself: missiles could hit targets that aircraft most likely would be shot down trying to reach. The Navy named this program the Arsenal Ship. And just as the aircraft carrier had proved the battleship to be an ineffective way of waging war in World War II, the Arsenal Ship had the potential to render the $5 billion flattops obsolete. That battle was years away. But Boorda had thrown his full weight behind it. In the meantime, carriers continued to have the day. They were still the best show of American resolve. Bill Clinton knew that when he sent two of the giant ships to sit near China and Taiwan when the two countries were feuding. Boorda saw the crisis as a benefit. He would use it and other similar threats around the world to the Navy's benefit in the Pentagon's budget wars.

One of Mike Boorda's most explicit goals when he became CNO was to keep the Navy from shrinking below 346 ships. With the end of the Cold War and the cutbacks in defense dollars that followed, his predecessor Frank Kelso had begun a recapitalization program to retire hundreds of ships, close ports, end programs—all in the name of building a better, albeit smaller, Navy for the future. It would be a far cry from the glory days of the 600-ship Navy. The end of the Cold War was only part of the reason, however, for the recapitalization program. As was predicted, the Navy had grown too big —too many costly ships and too much infrastructure—in the 1980s and could not sustain itself. The expected cuts in defense only exacerbated this problem. Boorda was determined to stop Kelso's plan while simultaneously increasing the Navy's fleet by slowing the retirement of ships. He would justify this by inflating requirements—ratcheting up the Navy's role in crises like Taiwan and China, Bosnia, Haiti, and in housing Cubans at a Navy base after they fled their country. The endgame, Boorda told a group of surface warfare admirals, was to justify getting a bigger share of the Pentagon's dwindling defense dollars.[18] Using his political skills, Boorda was successful in keeping a good many ships from mothballs.

But these accomplishments were constantly overshadowed by the misdeeds of the Navy's most senior officers. In 1995, five prominent officers, including the four-star commander of the Pacific, Richard Macke, had made headlines for problems related to sex and women. Three of those charged with violating Navy regulations had been selected by Boorda for the rank of rear admiral. Each was ultimately taken off the promotion list. One had worked in the Clinton White House as a military aide and was dismissed for making inappropriate comments about the anatomies of female staffers. Two were charged with adultery; one of them had to be confined to quarters for thirty days after he was accused of stalking a subordinate who cut off their affair. And Macke had caused an international incident between Washington and Tokyo. He had said publicly that the two Marines and one Navy corpsman who had kidnapped and brutally raped a young Japanese schoolgirl on Okinawa should instead have hired a prostitute to satisfy themselves.

His blunder exacerbated the rage among Japanese, who launched sizable demonstrations and who demanded that the U.S. military vacate its bases on Okinawa. President Clinton promised that "we are not turning a blind eye to this." And Defense Secretary William Perry traveled to Tokyo carrying a message of contrition for his angered Japanese hosts: "On behalf of all members of the armed forces, I want to express my deep sorrow and anger for this terrible act." The men were convicted, and Washington closed some minor American bases. Macke had not intended to sound so callous. Indeed, had the case not been so politically charged, his comments might have been passed over as nothing more than insensitive. But Macke had another problem. The use of his military jet to visit his girlfriend had also become an issue. This was strictly against the rules. It was this that eventually led to his demise.

Perhaps the most embarrassing case, and one that would linger in the press for months, was that of Everett L. Greene, a quiet, articulate black man who had turned down Princeton in favor of the Naval Academy. He was the first African American to become an officer in the SEALs, rising to the rank of captain. Boorda had known and liked him from his days running the Bureau of Personnel, where Greene had headed the Navy's equal opportunities program. Among his duties there, Greene had an almost impossible task: to oversee the office that dealt with sexual harassment claims and enforcement policies. Boorda was impressed with his performance and selected him for flag rank. It was, at its least, a political promotion. The SEALs already had their allotment of rear admirals and did not need another one. But Boorda and Dalton were strong supporters of affirmative action and had promised to place more blacks into the ranks of the admiralty. Boorda didn't stop there. He made Greene, who was junior to many other commandos, the head of the Navy's Special Operations Command—the top SEAL. From a military perspective, it was a brazen act in that Greene had not held the high-caliber jobs normally required for a position of such stature. A good many of his colleagues in his year group had gone to Vietnam—but not Greene. He had commanded one of the barges used in the secret war that Ace Lyons was running against Iran. But he had later missed the Persian Gulf War. Most of his assignments in the SEAL community, Greene acknowledged, were second and third tier. "I always had to wait until other individual career concerns were taken into consideration before someone gave me an assignment and it was normally what was left over," Greene said.[19] Still, Boorda backed him for the job.

But in October, Greene became the highest-ranking naval officer since World War II to face a court-martial. The Navy accused him of fraternization and sexually harassing two white female subordinates while in charge of the office supposed to prevent sexual harassment. A jury of admirals and captains ultimately acquitted him in a courtroom drama played out in the staid old Washington Navy yard (where Tom Cruise pulled a legal miracle in the movie A Few Good Men). But despite a verdict of innocent, Dalton canceled Greene's promotion to the rank of rear admiral. Greene was convinced that the sexual harassment and fraternization case against him cloaked a hidden agenda: revenge by the fraternity of admirals. While he ran the equal opportunities program, he had investigated several senior admirals for racial insensitivity. In many of these cases, he believed that blacks were being singled out by the admirals for discipline disproportionately when compared to whites involved in similar crimes. What was more, a number of the black defendants were accused of sexual misconduct with white women—just as Greene was. Greene had turned a number of his cases over to the Navy's inspector general with the recommendation that he expand on Greene's findings. But few of these requests were complied with. Those that did go forward were routinely dismissed.

As Greene saw it, he was championing the rights of minorities against a system with a long history of institutional prejudices. But he knew that in the process, he had done nothing more than create some very powerful enemies. If that wasn't enough to anger the brass, Greene's attorney, Lieutenant Commander William Little, was a feisty black litigator with an unfailing reputation for winning cases that embarrassed the Navy. It was Little who had written the motion that led to a Navy judge's finding that Frank Kelso had been less than truthful under oath. Now he was defending Greene, who wanted very much to expose the prejudices of the brass.

There were a number of oddities in the Navy's case against Greene, a good many of which supported Greene's notion that some type of hidden agenda existed. Perhaps most compelling was how the case was first handled. When the two women's sexual harassment claims initially came to light in the spring of 1993, officials in the Bureau of Personnel informally resolved them. This had become the preferred way after Tailhook to handle the less egregious complaints of harassment. In fact, the Navy privately fretted that Greene's case did not meet the legal criteria of harassment or fraternization. Greene had taken to sending poems (construed as love notes by Navy officials) of support to one of the women who worked for him. They were unduly personal: "What you offered to do with me was very special, very precious. I wanted you just as much, if not more, than you wanted me." But both women acknowledged that Greene had never touched them or asked for sexual favors in return for a promotion. And both women told officials they did not wish to file formal complaints in the matter. Still, they felt Greene was overbearing and too personal. Greene maintained his innocence throughout. He and his supporters said his "attachment," as the two women put it, was his way of helping those with low self-esteem. Even so, he agreed to the terms of the informal settlement, not out of guilt, but to ensure that his goal of becoming an admiral would not be derailed. With the case resolved on June 12, 1994, Greene's selection for the rank of rear admiral went forward.[20]

Nevertheless, some nine months later the case was resurrected. Stan Arthur, who was still the vice chief of naval operations after losing the Pacific Command job, was concerned about rumors that one of the women, Lieutenant Mary Felix, was threatening to go to the media after Greene's promotion became public. Arthur asked Rear Admiral Harold Grant, the Judge Advocate General of the Navy, to provide a senior lawyer to conduct a low-key investigation of the entire matter, despite the earlier resolution.[21] At the same time, the case was referred to the Navy's inspector general. As the two probes continued, it became obvious to Arthur and others that there were numerous discrepancies in the stories of the two women.[22] And another critical discrepancy surfaced: Felix had never intended to go public and had made that clear to Navy officials.[23]

When completed, both investigations recommended against formal charges. But the inspector general wrote in a memorandum marked "SENSITIVE—HOLD CLOSE" that Greene had used "extremely poor judgment."[24] With these findings and the problems with the women's stories, Arthur could have simply dropped the case and allowed Greene's promotion to go forward. The Navy desperately needed black flag officers: only 5 out of 266 admirals at the time were African American. But Arthur believed Greene was guilty of poor judgment and for that reason he should face an admiral's mast, otherwise known as nonjudicial punishment, where the accused has little choice but to accept the admiral's verdict. Greene mulled it over, as well as his feelings about Arthur. Little counseled Greene that he could not get a fair hearing in an admiral's mast with Arthur. So Greene turned it down. He wanted to clear his name formally in a formal court-martial proceeding. Arthur then decided to go forward with an Article 32, or pretrial investigation similar to a grand jury that paves the way for a court-martial hearing. In the end, Greene won the legal battle. But ultimately he lost. Greene lost his promotion, and found it difficult to convince the media that his case was as much about vendettas and racism as it was about sexual harassment.

Boorda had stood up for Greene and the four other senior officers privately before John Dalton. He had remembered the fallout over Arthur, and he was determined to get back in the good graces of the flag community. Dalton's ethics may have been in question over his business dealings, but he was not shy about weighing in on sins of moral turpitude. He said publicly he would not tolerate such misbehavior as that shown by the admirals he had dismissed. And he would not yield under Boorda's relentless defense of his admirals. Boorda was not fond of Dalton, even going so far as to criticize him at gatherings with former Reagan and Bush administration officials. Boorda saw Dalton as dimwitted, a slow, dry Texan with little charm or charisma. He did not think that Dalton shared his commitment to the Navy. It was an unfair charge, in that Dalton had every incentive to fix the Navy— but not at the expense of supporting men his CNO wished to protect. Dalton was smart enough to realize that a great deal of the Navy's problems stemmed from selective discipline, of holding lesser-ranking officers accountable but letting the flags avoid punishment. His recommendation to dismiss all five men was a humiliation that would have been unheard of in previous years.

Dalton and Boorda did agree, however, when it came to supporting two dicey promotions for Vice Admiral Joe Prueher—first as a replacement for Arthur; then, when Macke fell, Prueher was picked to become CinCPac. The first promotion in the spring of 1995 went smoothly; the Navy's fears that the Gwen Dreyer incident at the Naval Academy would reappear did not happen. The Navy had made the case privately with several important female senators, who might otherwise have blocked the nomination because of Dreyer, that it desperately needed Prueher. The brass had wanted to promote him in the past but held off out of fear a Democratic Senate would make the effort politically unbearable. But now the Republicans controlled both houses of Congress. And the sexual harassment/women in the military issue had fallen to the back burner. Powerful proponents such as Pat Schroeder, Barbara Boxer, Carol Moseley-Braun, and Patty Murray, had halted their crusade. Sensing the political winds had shifted, the Navy dusted off Prueher's file and nominated him for Arthur's job. There was also an important practical reason for pulling Prueher out of mothballs: few of his fellow flag officers had his experience. He was easily confirmed.

Prueher's second promotion in February 1996, however, was much more rocky. Sam Donaldson, ABC's dogged correspondent, had resurrected Prueher's role in the Dreyer affair. This time the Senate balked. With Donaldson sitting in the front row during the confirmation hearing, Senator

Edward Kennedy placed a courtesy hold on the nomination until more information about the case could be reviewed. But Prueher, to his credit, told the
senators that he had learned from the Dreyer case. He was older and wiser
now. If given the opportunity, he said, he would no doubt handle the entire
case differently. Kennedy removed the hold and Prueher was confirmed the
following day by voice vote.

Prueher's departure from Washington to Hawaii could not have come at a
more opportune time. He was leaving behind a Navy that appeared to be
even more adrift and under constant scrutiny by the media than when Boorda
had taken over. The Navy brass and its supporters felt besieged by the
constant news coverage, primarily by the national media, as if the sins of the
sea service were being capitalized on while those of the other armed forces
were being ignored. There was truth in this. But it was not as if the media
were creating the stories. The constant gaffes by the Navy and its personnel
had given the press plenty to write about. And it just wasn't the flag officers
who seemed incapable of behaving themselves. An intoxicated chief petty
officer made headlines when he repeatedly molested a female sailor sitting
next to him on an airliner. A court-martial was set for the summer to hear
charges that a lieutenant commander raped and impregnated a civilian co-
worker, then threatened to fire her if she went public. Another trial, that of
two Navy SEALs who were arrested in Virginia Beach for the rape and
murder of a young woman, was already playing out. The Navy went after
another SEAL, Matt Napiltonia, when he refused to go along with an attempt
by his command to cover up the illegal shipment and handling of explosives.
Three other SEALs would die mysteriously, two believed to be suicides. In a
predawn raid, agents from the Naval Criminal Investigative Service arrested
twenty-one sailors and an officer for smuggling cocaine and heroin from
Turkey into Italy for a Nigerian drug ring. A number of ship's captains were
removed for reasons ostensibly pertaining to sexual harassment. And in
Guam, two male officers assigned to the flagship of the Seventh Fleet had
sex with a female member of the crew in full view of people visiting a public
beach. And these were the cases that the public knew about.

The countless number of such episodes, of fraternization and sexual harassment, of rape and assault, and the breakdown in discipline, indicated that
the Navy's efforts to change its old culture were still in their infancy. To be
fair to the Navy, such change would not come overnight; it would take
years. Indeed, some of the first statistics after Tailhook, from 1992 to 1995,
compiled by the Naval Criminal Investigative Service and the Department
of Defense were not promising: some 1,000 new harassment complaints and

3,500 charges of indecent assault, from groping to rape, were reported. There was some good news for the Navy Department in these figures—not all the cases had merit. But perhaps more important to the Navy, the Army and the Air Force had similar numbers. By 1996, the numbers were still high, but there was a slight decline in all the services over past findings. A Pentagon survey found that 55 percent of the women in the military had experienced some form of sexual harassment in the previous year. But most of the women who were polled reported that harassment seemed to be on the decline.

What was not on the decline, however, and what caught the attention of the country, was a rash of new embarrassments at the Naval Academy. The Navy's leaders had hoped that Charles Larson would put the academy back on track after the 1992 cheating scandal, the Dreyer affair, and the other problems with women, such as continued harassment in their dorms. Although naval investigators determined that Larson's predecessor, Rear Admiral Tom Lynch, had tried to protect football players involved in the stealing of the electrical engineering exam, Boorda still planned to promote him to a third star. Congress balked at that, and Lynch, a well-liked, gregarious man who was cocaptain of the 1963 football team, was given a job helping to reshape the Navy's war-fighting plan. He then retired with two stars. Larson brought in a new program that stressed ethics. He required midshipmen to read Plato and Aristotle and to visit the National Holocaust Museum. Classes in leadership, once known as "leadersleep," were reformed to stress integrity instead of management techniques. Despite the four-star admiral's view that his reforms were working, by the spring of 1996 and beyond, the Naval Academy had a new reputation as a school for scandal. Some two dozen midshipmen were implicated for selling or using drugs, including LSD, on campus. One was caught buying 200 doses of the hallucinogenic. Police busted a stolen-car ring being run by midshipmen and former students who had washed out of the academy. A midshipman was arrested for molesting a child. Two seniors got caught sneaking into the house of the former state superintendent of police at 2 A.M. in order to see his teenage daughter. And one of the academy's two senior brigade commanders in charge of 2,000 midshipmen would be placed in the brig at Quantico, Virginia, for having "non-consensual sex with one or more women."[25] The academy reacted to this by expelling the midshipman—who professed his innocence by claiming the women were willing partners—and allowing women to lock their doors, two moves that garnered more headlines.

Larson would call these "isolated, unrelated incidents."[26] The superintendent would tell the media that under his tenure the academy had a good story to tell. "I've made significant changes in the last 20 months, and midshipmen say that we're moving in the right direction."[27] What else could a midshipman say to a four-star admiral? Larson's boasting seemed bizarre to a number of the academy's civilian faculty members, particularly to an ethics instructor by the name of James F. Barry. He had taken to collecting letters and anecdotes from his students that he said showed Larson's rosy picture to be a culture of hypocrisy. In an emotionally laden Op-Ed in *The Washington Post*, Barry accused the academy's leadership of papering over cracks in the school's moral foundation and described the school as an "ethically corrupting system—so powerful that, by the end of their second year, most [mids] are confirmed cynics who routinely violate regulations about clothing, driving, alcohol and sex, plus any other rules they feel are superfluous." [28] Many of his complaints had previously been addressed by Richard Armitage, who chaired a panel that reviewed the school's honor code. Armitage's report was equally damning, and it led to a number of important changes. But it did not receive the publicity of Barry's article. Larson was livid at this civilian teacher who had served in Vietnam during the war. He told the midshipmen that he felt betrayed by Barry and removed him from his teaching post. Outraged students and faculty complained that Larson was killing the messenger and seeking revenge for personal reasons. Reluctantly, he reinstated Barry.

Larson weathered the storm and the battered Barry resigned. But the problems that Larson said were ebbing did not end. There would be a number of expulsions, complaints of sexual harassment, and a variety of other flaps that made their way into the headlines or the rumor mill. One student would sue John Dalton for forcing him out of the academy allegedly for political reasons. [29] In the fall, the mysterious death of a female midshipman in her dorm would confound school officials and raise still more questions about the plight of women. Another female plebe would be charged with murder in connection with a love triangle. A midshipman would resign for not telling authorities about the murder. And a chaplain would expose himself.

For those watching the chain of events from afar, the happenings at the academy appeared to be a microcosm of the Navy at large. Inside the Navy, however, the admirals at the top were in denial, blind to the spiritual and moral decay eating away at the sea service's very core. To be sure, it was still the most powerful Navy afloat. Officers and enlisted men and women were still reporting for duty each day, ships were still sailing, and aircraft were still flying. But the very core of the service, faith in the leadership and the discipline this loyalty inspires, was breaking down. Somebody needed to sound the alarm. That somebody would be Jim Webb.

Thursday, April 25, 1996, would be Jim Webb's day. He was to speak at the Naval Academy, invited to Annapolis by the Naval Institute as a guest speaker for its 122nd annual meeting. In the wake of Tailhook, Webb had increasingly become an angry man. He did not hide his ire toward the Navy's leadership, and had written an Op-Ed piece in *The New York Times* that questioned Boorda's fitness to be the CNO. It got the expected response from Webb's followers, who were as much outraged at Boorda and the Navy's leadership as Webb was. Signs of discontent throughout the fleet were frequently published in articles, editorials, and letters by *Navy Times,* which had become a sharp critic of the brass. The privately owned newspaper had a broad following among the troops outside of Washington and occasionally published anonymous letters to protect those who wished to take on the Navy's leaders. One letter that appeared in May 1996 called on Boorda to resign. "Adm. Boorda has not only lost the respect of his admirals; every officer from four star to the newest midshipman at the academy has no respect for the man at the top of their organization. Behind his back, admirals often refer to the CNO as 'Little Mikey Boorda.' "[30]

Boorda would not acknowledge the attacks in public, but privately the anger in Webb's rebuke and the nastiness of the *Navy Times* letter stung him and shook his confidence. Webb no doubt meant it to. In his nostalgia, the Navy of his youth, in which he served heroically in Vietnam as a Marine, was but a relic in today's world where Webb sensed nobody had the courage to stand up for their beliefs. He would tell Peter Boyer of *The New Yorker* that he was aghast at how the country believed Olympian Kerri Strug was a hero because she performed with an injured ankle. In Vietnam, Webb said, John Paul Bobo "won the Medal of Honor because he got his leg blown off and he stuck his stump into the ground and fought until he died. You know, that's a hero. And in this country, the majority of it can't even relate to that anymore. Doesn't even comprehend what it takes to do it. It's lost not only its respect but its ability to form a respect for it."[31]

Webb would have one believe that integrity and bravery could only come to those baptized by the brutality of combat. He would speak of such themes at the Naval Academy in which he would ridicule those he felt lacked courage. He had called a few reporters before he was to give the speech, telling them he had a major address planned. He was worried, however, that Boorda would somehow upstage him. He had heard that the CNO had rearranged his schedule to deliver his own speech at Annapolis on the same day as Webb was to appear. Webb feared that Boorda would make some announcement designed to diminish the contents of his own speech.[32] Webb's information was wrong, however. Boorda had never changed his speech date, according to officials at the Naval Institute.

When Webb took to the podium, the upper decks of the auditorium were filled with midshipmen. Below them were retired and active-duty officers. Various reporters were sprinkled throughout the room. Though the former

Navy secretary had graduated from the school in 1968, he still had a following among the students at the academy, who relished his books and his
old-fashioned stand on honor. He began by reciting his memories at Annapolis, with its historic monuments and buildings that he said had become a
constant in his life. Slowly his talk built as he recounted the lore of past
naval battles, of the admirals who fought the greatest sea battles in history.
The creed of these men, he said, was simple: "where principle is involved,
be deaf to expediency." He went on to say, "there is no substitute for an
insistence on ethics, loyalty, accountability and moral courage. And yet
today I am sadly astounded to see our Navy struggle for its soul, too often
unanchored from those simple yet demanding notions, many of whose leaders have advanced themselves through a blatant repudiation of those very
ideals. Some are guilty of the ultimate disloyalty: to save or advance their
careers, they abandoned the very ideals of their profession in order to curry
favor with politicians." [33]

For a man who puts such stock in moral courage, Webb did not name
Boorda, or Dalton, or Frank Kelso in his diatribe, but they were clearly the
objects of his scorn. Rather, he named Stan Arthur and Jack Snyder, saying
that nobody stood up for them when their careers were on the line. He said
few were prepared to tell the truth about pregnancies at sea. And he quoted
statistics saying 53 percent of the post-command commanders in naval aviation were leaving the Navy; "they saw how the Navy is being led and they
walked." Because of Webb's stature and position in the establishment, his
words and opinions carried considerable influence. It was indeed a powerful
speech. Webb had sounded the klaxon loudly with important points that
needed to be made. And the press dutifully reported his remarks and his
allegations but without checking on their veracity. Webb did not mention,
however, how Boorda stood up to Dalton in defense of Macke, Greene, and
the three other admirals removed from their positions because of misconduct
related to women. And his comments that Snyder never had a chance to
defend himself and that few officers came to his aid were falsehoods. Snyder
spoke to his superiors on at least three occasions over several weeks, and he
wrote lengthy memoranda in support of his position. Many put their careers
on the line to help him, including his former boss at Pax River, Vice Admiral
William Bowes. Several other officers did so in written statements to the
chief of naval personnel. Webb was also mistaken in his comments about
pilots leaving the service on principle. Some no doubt did. But not in the
high numbers that he suggested. The Pentagon's deputy secretary of defense
soon stated the real figure: about 26 percent, or twenty-seven individuals.
Despite these errors of fact, Webb's speech had its intended effect: Boorda
and the leadership were shaken. In the days following the speech they

remained defensive and critical. Webb had insisted that military leaders stand up to Congress and fight for what they believed in; that in their unity and righteousness they would remain pure of a political process which this cadre found so retching. There was one caveat, many defense officials noticed, that Webb seemed to overlook. Had he forgotten about the Constitution? About civilian control of the armed forces? It was one thing to resign in protest over principle. But a servicewide resistance to authority was another matter altogether. At the height of Tailhook, a half-dozen admirals under scrutiny wanted to meet in secret to design a plan to fight back against certain leaders in the Navy and the Congress. They were warned by Rear Admiral Ted Gordon, who happened to be a lawyer, that this would, in the strictest sense, be considered a mutiny.

While the Webb speech and the letter in *Navy Times* weighed heavily on Boorda, there were other problems troubling the CNO. Although he was nearly two years into his term, he was unable to end the misery of the Navy, which was in a downward spiral. He had tried to steer the Navy back on course. But every effort seemed to be met by the traditionalists who suspected Boorda of being too liberal on issues of gender and too willing to please the politicians. The Navy's old guard longed for the romantic past when ships were made of wood and men of iron. Boorda certainly was not viewed as having an iron spine. And he took it personally. He even had made a decision to resign. His mentor, George Everding, who had seen to it that Boorda applied to officer candidate school, noticed a mood change in his friend. On May 10, 1996, six days before Boorda would kill himself, Everding saw Boorda in Pensacola at the annual convention of the Association of Naval Aviation. "When I saw him," Everding said, "he didn't appear to be his usual cheerful self. But he's had a heavy weight on his shoulders." [34] On Thursday, May 16, the weight got a lot heavier.

Several weeks earlier, David Hackworth, a retired Army colonel and part-time contributing editor at *Newsweek,* had approached the magazine's editors in New York with a story about the medals for valor Boorda wore on his chest. Hackworth's friend Roger Charles, a former Marine and close friend of Webb's, had picked up a tip in his capacity as a reporter for the tiny National Security News Service that Boorda was wearing two awards from Vietnam that he had not earned. Charles had passed it on to Hackworth, and "Hack," as he is known, had arranged to interview Boorda. To Hackworth, wearing undeserved medals was a matter of grave concern, "the worst thing you can do." [35] At one point, Hackworth said if Boorda's sin was known, the CNO ". . . might just put a gun to his head." On the day of the scheduled interview, however, Hackworth could not make the trip to Washington. So Evan Thomas, *Newsweek*'s Washington bureau chief, had little choice but to go in his place. But before the interview, Thomas wanted to hear the evidence. He was wary of Charles, who he thought was conspiratorial by nature. Although Thomas respected Hackworth's military background, he did not consider him an investigative reporter. Still, Thomas thought this could be a big story—with one considerable drawback. He had serious concerns about accusing the CNO, a member of the Joint Chiefs of Staff, of fraudulently wearing two awards. He asked John Barry, a *Newsweek* correspondent, and myself to review Charles's evidence.

Just after 9 A.M. on Thursday, May 16, 1996, Charles briefed Thomas, Barry, and me on his reporting, which included documents obtained under the Freedom of Information Act. He said that Boorda was wearing two combat "Vs," small pins worn on top of two ribbons which signify personal valor in combat. He had begun wearing them, Charles said, not as a junior officer, but when he made rear admiral. Indeed, Charles had photographs to prove his point. His reporting was solid and appeared to be on the mark. After the meeting, Thomas asked Barry and me to do some independent reporting to confirm what Charles was alleging. Then he made sure that Kendell Pease knew that he was coming to ask questions about Boorda's medals. Pease and Boorda understood the significance of *Newsweek*'s interest: a call was placed to the Washington Navy Yard where the division that handled the awarding of medals was located. The staff there was instructed to immediately research the history of the CNO's medals. And there was one other order: do not talk to the media.

As it turned out, the medals division had reviewed Boorda's file nearly ten years earlier, when Jim Webb was Navy Secretary. Webb was a stickler for medals. When each of the Navy's flag officers came up for promotion, Webb made it a point to check the status of their medals. One of the first things he did in this process, recalled his public affairs officer, Captain Mark Neuhart, was to review the service photograph of the officer up for promotion. Then he would scrutinize the medals, Neuhart said. As each case came up, the medals division had to review the files. The admiral in charge finally decided to review the medals history of the entire flag community. It would be more efficient this way. In the process, the staff reviewed Boorda's file. They found nothing that authorized Boorda to wear the two combat Vs. Calls were made to several admirals' staffs advising them of the findings. Years later, when Boorda was CNO, the issue popped up again. A staff member in the medals division who had worked on Boorda's file years ago now told the CNO's lawyer that the admiral was not entitled to wear the combat Vs. At approximately the same time, Roger Charles had filed his

Freedom of Information request for Boorda's records. Boorda's lawyer told Boorda he was not eligible to wear the two tiny Vs. The CNO then took them off.

Before Thomas left for the Pentagon, he was apprised of this information. Meanwhile, at the Pentagon, Pease and Boorda spoke about the impending visit from *Newsweek*'s two reporters. The initial appointment had been set for around 1 P.M. Then it was moved to 2:30, just before Boorda was to meet with President Clinton at the White House. Boorda asked Pease for his advice. "What should we do?" But before his chief of public affairs could answer, Boorda said, "We will tell them the truth." He had planned to eat lunch in his office. But then, he abruptly decided to go home to the Washington Navy Yard for lunch. He would drive himself, he said. Boorda did not appear to Pease or others around him to be too upset about *Newsweek*'s inquiries. Few really knew, however, how nonplussed he was.

By the time Evan Thomas and John Barry had arrived at the Pentagon, Boorda had gone home and written two notes. One was to "my sailors," the other to his wife. He wrote that his wearing the medals was an honest mistake. But he did not think the media would believe him, that the press would pounce on the story. After all, Boorda had repeatedly stressed how important it was for his troops to believe in the Navy's core values, that honesty was indeed the best policy. No doubt the troops would now see the CNO as a hypocrite.

> What I am about to do is not very smart but it is right for me. You see, I have asked you to do the right thing, to care for and take care of each other and to stand up for what is good and correct. All of these things require honor, courage and commitment . . . our core values.
>
> I am about to be accused of wearing combat devices on two ribbons I earned during sea tours in Viet Nam. It turns out I didn't really rate them. When I found out I was wrong I immediately took them off but it was really too late. I don't expect any reporters to believe I could make an honest mistake and you may or may not believe it yourselves. That is up to you and isn't all that important now anyway. I've made it not matter in the big scheme of things because I love our Navy so much, and you who are the heart and soul of our Navy, that I couldn't bear to bring dishonor to you.
>
> If you care to do so, you can do something for me. That is take care of each other. Be honorable. Do what is right. Forgive when it makes sense, punish when you must but always work to make the latter unnecessary by working to help people be all they really can and should be. . . .
>
> I will soon be forgotten. You, our great Navy people, will live on. I am proud of you. I am proud to have led you if only for a short time. I wish I had done it better.
>
> J. M. Boorda

With the notes complete, Boorda walked to a far corner of the garden. There he took a .38-caliber pistol, placed the barrel near the medals on his chest, and squeezed the trigger.

≣ EPILOGUE ≣

ON THE TUESDAY after Mike Boorda shot himself, Washington's military cognoscenti arrived at the National Cathedral to pay tribute to, as the President put it, "this small man with a big heart, large vision, and great courage." Joining Commander in Chief Bill Clinton were Boorda's contemporaries on the Joint Chiefs of Staff and a large showing of his fellow admirals. Even the flag officers who had disdained Boorda for the direction in which he had taken the Navy were among those offering a final blessing. All wore their dress uniforms, adorned with medals and ribbons. Sitting nearby, in a cordoned-off section of wooden pews, was a sizable contingent of Boorda's greatest admirers: the men and women of the enlisted ranks, the ordinary sailors whom Boorda most identified with. As the Navy choir sang softly, the majestic house of worship overflowed with a standing-room-only crowd. Though Boorda had been buried for almost three days, laid to rest the previous weekend in a private service at the Arlington National Cemetery, four thousand people showed up at the cathedral. For those who could not come, CNN's television cameras beamed the event live to Navy bases, homes, and offices around the country.

None of the speakers on this warm spring day tried to answer the pervading question: "What killed Mike Boorda?" Running the scandal-plagued Navy, many naval insiders believed, was a terrible emotional burden, perhaps even a killer. Indeed it was my intent in writing this book to determine why the Navy, more than the Air Force and the Army, always found itself mired in such embarrassments. The common thread that ties the Navy's otherwise disconnected scandals together, countless officers told me, is a willingness, especially by the brass and the civilian leaders, to make loyalty to the Navy, not to the truth, a litmus test for the officer corps.

Boorda's memorial service, of course, was not the appropriate time to point out the Navy's failings. Bill Clinton and William Perry, the quiet but determined Secretary of Defense, were content to let the entire matter pass quietly away. In an eloquent eulogy, Perry used the words of the Greek poet and dramatist Aeschylus to remind the gathering that suffering can bring redemption. "In our sleep, pain that cannot forget falls drop by drop upon

the heart until in our despair, against our will, comes wisdom through the
awful grace of God.'' Perry truly believed that the Navy had suffered enough
under the scrutiny of the righteous on Capitol Hill and in the media, and that
now was the time to forgive its sins, bury the past, and seek unity for the
future.

Perry's plea, however, fell on the deaf ears of those intent on using
Boorda's death as a pulpit for vitriol and partisan politics. In the days
following the suicide, many began to lay the blame for Boorda's death on
the media. The most influential person speaking out with attack-dog vi-
ciousness was John Lehman. Lehman's presence on the national scene had
dimmed somewhat since he left his job as Navy secretary. To be sure, he
was still firmly thought of as a public figure—his book *Command of the
Seas* had sold well, keeping his name in the forefront of naval issues. And
he occasionally wrote a column for *The Wall Street Journal* on defense
matters. His contemporary reputation, however, was as a successful entrepre-
neur with a stellar record of turning his business ventures into very profitable
companies. Negative media accounts of him in 1996 did little to interrupt
his business triumphs—by his own admission, John Lehman had become a
wealthy man. Upon Boorda's death, Lehman's stature made him a constant
in the media. There he was, on CNN's *Crossfire,* face flushed with rage,
saying that *"Newsweek . . .* has hired full-time gutter journalists'' and ''de-
serves the blame,'' for ending Boorda's life. There he was on a morning Fox
show, again bashing and slashing. There he was on *This Week with David
Brinkley,* edgy and confrontational as Sam Donaldson and Cokie Roberts
cornered him about his Tailhook frolics. And there he was in the safe and
familiar broadsheet of *The Wall Street Journal*'s Op-Ed page, accusing
almost everyone of having it in for the Navy. The media, he said time and
again, the left-wing, yellow journalists, had a vendetta against the Navy.
''What I'm saying is, the Navy has been subjected for the last five years to
the most unprecedented, an unbelievable witch hunt and lynch mob, I think
in this century,'' he said on *Crossfire.* And of course, Bill Clinton was near
the top of Lehman's bad-guy list. It was Clinton, Lehman said, who
''brought in an administration staffed by former war protesters who largely
shared the prejudices of those in the anti-Navy lunch mob.''

Lehman's themes had all the resonance of a fox trying to steer the hounds
in the wrong direction. His claims of a journalism lynch mob, egged on by
what he described as ''the Navy's enemies'' in the White House were, in
the winter of 1996, more ludicrous than ever. If anything, the press had gone
easy on the Navy, reporting the daily news but not digging deeper in search
of new scandal. Lehman, of course, had a stake in finding a villain or villains
to blame the Navy's problems on. The Navy that Bill Clinton inherited in

the 1990s had been planned and built on Lehman's watch, under his own standards and carried out by his hand-picked team of managers—more than a few who left under a cloud. Though Lehman was not about to accept the notion that a wholesale failure of the Navy's political and military leaders resulted from the policies implemented in the 1980s buildup, it was no secret to a good portion of the officer corps. "Lehman elevated patronage, cronyism, a spoils system for 'Friends of John,' and flagrant bending of rules and regulations to an art form," wrote Ronald "Mugs" McKeown in an essay in the *San Diego Union-Tribune*. A Naval Academy graduate who retired in 1983 during Lehman's first term in office, McKeown was a decorated fighter pilot who flew four hundred combat missions in Vietnam and later became Top Gun's first commanding officer. His words therefore were spoken from experience. "The ultimate test of right and wrong," during Lehman's tenure, "was, 'what's the party line?' . . . The Lehman Legacy," he wrote, left the Navy with questionable ethical standards in the 1990s. "There can be no doubt that his policies abetted and accelerated the climate of behavior that finally erupted in 1991. The most egregious aspect of Tailhook '91, is that it was only the tip of the iceberg and harbinger of more serious and deep-rooted embarrassments to the Navy."

While Lehman reigned over the Navy, he perhaps had won more acclaim, not to mention the acceleration of money for the fleet, than any other secretary in history, with the possible exception of James Forrestal. The thirty-eight-year-old would-be aviator had become something of a cult figure in squadron ready-rooms. And fleetwide, he was revered as the father of the modern Navy. It was easy, therefore, if not a requirement, for ambitious officers wishing to rise in the system, to identify with Lehman's brashness and can-do attitude—dynamic personality traits that helped to rekindle a powerful zeal and pride in the Navy. Hollywood's big-screen fiction accounts of aviators in *Top Gun* and submariners in *The Hunt for Red October* bolstered Lehman's cause.

Not surprisingly, esprit de corps soared. However, commensurate with this *élan* was the rise of arrogance. And it was this arrogance that resulted in, as Mugs McKeown put it, the "flagrant bending of rules and regulations to an art form." It is not surprising, then too, that a byproduct of this attitude was the breakdown of honesty and integrity within the officer ranks, especially at the more senior levels. Intentionally ignoring misdeeds and rule-bending became almost as ingrained as the morning reveille. In the starkest terms, moral corruption had taken hold in the system. It was barely noticeable to outside observers, however, cloaked by the renewed patriotism that swept the country under Ronald Reagan. But it was felt deeply within the system by officers like McKeown.

It is clearer, in hindsight, to see how misguided ethics gave birth to an institutional deceit. Nowhere was this more evident than in the selling of John Lehman's Navy to the American people. The Navy's own experts warned internally in classified reports and in verbal briefings that the buildup would lead to an infrastructure so large and bloated that it would be near impossible to support financially by the 1990s. Did the Navy's leaders ever tell Congress or the American public that its analysts had come to this conclusion? Apparently not; at least not in clear enough terms to jeopardize support for the buildup. When the analysts' warnings proved true, the drawdown came, as the newspaper *Navy Times* pointed out, on the backs of thousands of sailors and officers forced prematurely to leave the Navy. Did the Navy's leaders ever give a full accounting of how its intelligence officers believed the Soviet Navy was a defensive fighting force, one that was no match for the U.S. fleet? Hardly. If they did, Congress might have been more fervent in questioning the need for such a grandiose naval rearmament program. How often did the Navy acknowledge the sins of its senior officer corps, even when they violated regulations or broke federal law? Were the Navy's leaders entirely honest and up front about the A-12 fiasco? Or *Iowa?* Or the rash of improprieties at the Naval Academy? Or Tailhook? Or a myriad of other scandals?

Tailhook, of course, was the Navy's worst failure of leadership. It stayed culturally cemented in the public mind because the sex assaults and perversion were so appalling. But the scandal was merely a symptom of the much larger fundamental problem at hand: institutional deceit. Again, the Navy's leaders displayed the uncanny ability to disregard obvious truths by ignoring the service's fairly clear and historically salacious record on the mistreatment of women. Indeed, misogynistic attitudes did not miraculously appear one weekend at the 1991 Tailhook convention. They had been slowly building over the past decades, passed down as lore in the seamy ports of call in Subic Bay or Thailand. Navy leaders chose to refer to these as rest and relaxation spots, not as the pits of female exploitation that they were. And what of past Tailhook conventions in the 1980s? Were these any better affairs than the notorious 1991 gathering? Indeed not.

Critics like James Webb and John Lehman were dismissive of the whole Tailhook flap. They often opined that the story deserved no more than a week's news play. Considering that they were both occasional pundits with more than a smattering of press understanding, this was, at best, a terrifically naive assumption. There were too many elements crashing together—sex, the issue of women in combat, agendas by women on both sides of the political spectrum, macho Top Gun flyboys, and not least, the involvement of senior Navy officers—that gave this news story legs for five years and made Tailhook almost as recognizable a code word as Watergate or Teapot Dome. There was also a major cover-up and, perhaps the most ignored but important nuance, the disciplinary double standard between the junior officer corps and the admirals. As the Navy sought to put the entire blame for Tailhook on the younger commanders and lieutenants (in many cases rightly so), the admirals and civilian leaders who attended the convention were not even questioned. Only when it became obvious that a cover-up was taking place and the junior officers were beginning to speak out was the brass involved held accountable by the Pentagon's senior leadership.

Perhaps one of the most perplexing paradoxes exposed by Tailhook is this: Why is it that some military men who take an oath based on upholding truth, seem to be the worst offenders against the truth? Thomas Powers, a senior official with the Naval Criminal Investigative Service who retired after investigating Tailhook, has perhaps the best answer: "It's as if they take an oath to the Navy and not the nation." Not all officers, of course, are unethical. There are indeed scores of senior officers who refuse to compromise their principles. Among them are admirals like Bill Cockell and Stasser Holcomb. For their honesty, however, they are pushed aside, their promising careers ended by the cronyism among the Navy's top echelons. Other good and honorable men simply are forced by their allegiance to the system to do the dishonorable—lest they lose their careers.

This was perhaps the fundamental problem that Boorda was trying to wrestle with. He understood the ingrained dishonesty that existed in the upper ranks of the Navy and often referred to it by stressing how important it was to tell the truth. He believed that in the end honesty was more in line with the Navy's true core values. The media, especially those institutions that probed Boorda's death, never seemed to understand this deeper psychology. Rather, its focus was superficial in that it rested its pen and camera on the easy target of the gender wars as the root cause of the Navy's problems.

For all we know, Boorda may have inherited the genes that drove his father to try to end his own life. Mike Boorda's death is tragic in many regards: for his loved ones, for his troops, and in a much bigger sense, for the nation—for Boorda was trying to build a Navy in which all Americans could proudly serve. He was on the right track of returning the Navy to its glory days. Whether the torch is carried is up to the men and women he left behind.

NOTES

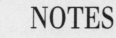

PROLOGUE

1. Pete Stoll, interview with the author, March 28, 1994. Bob Lawson, founder of *Hook* magazine, the journal of the Tailhook Association, also confirmed this in an interview with the author. Both Lawson and Stoll were eyewitnesses. See also the Department of Defense Inspector General's *Tailhook 1991 Report*, Part 2, which mentions a senior Navy official taking part in lurid activity. In interviews with Pentagon investigators, they also confirmed that this official was John Lehman. In addition, this scene was recounted to the author by more than half a dozen active duty officers, including a rear admiral.
2. Charles Moskos, in an interview with the author.

CHAPTER 1

1. Group Research, a Washington, D.C.–based liberal organization that keeps track of conservative groups.
2. John Lehman, in *The Hawk*, November 15, 1962.
3. See *The Prospects for Arms Control*, a book that Lehman edited with James E. Dougherty, a professor of political science at St. Joseph's College, Philadelphia, and an associate at the Foreign Policy Research Institute at the University of Pennsylvania. The book was a compilation of the speeches given at the Philadelphia Collegiate Disarmament Conference, which Lehman helped organize.
4. Peter Rodman interview with the author, April 15, 1994. Rodman was a close aide to Henry Kissinger and viewed Lehman as a friend and a talented individual.
5. George Will interview with the author, April 15, 1994. Richard Perle interview with the author, April 22, 1994.
6. *Command of the Seas: Building the 600 Ship Navy,* by John Lehman.
7. Admiral Ron Hays interview with the author, March 3, 1995. Hays was a vice chief of naval operations, the number two Navy job, and retired as the commander in chief of all U.S. forces in the Pacific, known as CinCPac. The author interviewed Hays several times, beginning in 1993.
8. Admiral James "Ace" Lyons interview with the author, June 15, 1994. The author interviewed Lyons more than a dozen times in 1994 and 1995.

9. Vice Admiral Stasser Holcomb interview with the author, April 15, 1994; see also *Naval Renaissance* by Frederick H. Hartmann, Naval Institute Press, 1990. Holcomb, who attended the meeting, was Hayward's chief planner. The author interviewed Holcomb several times.

10. This version of events comes from Holcomb. John Lehman, in a June 22, 1994, interview with the author, said he did not remember this specific meeting but did recall forcing the admirals to decide whether to follow him or Hayward. The author interviewed Lehman many times over a period of one year.

11. Holcomb interviews.

12. Lehman interviews.

13. Rear Admiral Ted Gordon interviews with the author, the first of which began in 1992. The most recent was March 27, 1995. Gordon held the job of Lehman's personal lawyer, his liaison to Congress, director of the Naval Investigative Service, and, finally, judge advocate general of the Navy.

14. Lehman interviews.

15. "Scratch One Flattop?" *Proceedings,* September 1994. *Proceedings* is the journal of the Naval Institute, a quasi-official organization whose president is the chief of naval operations.

16. *Command of the Seas.*

17. *The Power Game,* by Hedrick Smith. See also *Command of the Seas.*

18. The Navy's office of public affairs uses this figure as a rule of thumb.

19. Some admirals and other senior officers, on the other hand, received preferential treatment if they had mental or emotional problems. One senior officer on an aircraft carrier was having emotional problems on board that required hospitalization. When the admiral in charge of the battle fleet asked the psychiatrist what to do, the doctor replied, "Medicate him, and he'll be okay." The captain stayed and continued to perform vital duties on the ship, although he was incapacitated for several days. Legislation introduced by Barbara Boxer, then a representative and now senator, prohibited all military services from using psychiatric examinations or hospitalization as a way of silencing discontents or whistle-blowers. See, for example, an excellent series on the abuses of military authority by Ed Timms and Steve McGonigle in the *Dallas Morning News,* beginning on November 24, 1991. In one article the journalists report how the Navy tried to silence Michael Tufariello by placing him in a psychiatric hospital. Tufariello, who was voted Sailor of the Year in 1982, blew the whistle on alleged payroll abuses at the Dallas Naval Air Station.

20. This agency used to be called the Naval Investigative Service and was headed by a rear admiral and a civilian bureaucrat. In a reorganization brought on by the Tailhook scandal, the Navy changed the name to the Naval Criminal Investigative Service, and it is now headed by only a civilian.

21. Gordon interviews.

22. This number has varied over the years.

23. When one officer made the rank of captain, the admiral pinning on his four stripes said, "Congratulations. From now on, it's who you know, not what you

know.'' The author interviewed officers from the rank of lieutenant to admiral, all of whom confirmed that the promotion process, especially for that of admiral, was based primarily on politics and not merit, and that the admirals often broke federal laws pertaining to selection boards by discussing candidates with the secretary of the Navy or the chief of naval operations.

24. According to officers who served on the staff of Admiral Robert Kelly, commander in chief of the Pacific Fleet, it took sixty people to support Kelly personally. Assuming each one earned on average about $25,000 per year, that added up to about $1.5 million in personal support, plus additional expenses such as those for his aircraft.

25. Memorandum for the secretary of defense, March 27, 1985, from the Department of Defense's inspector general. The year in question was 1983.

26. Ibid. The Navy bought the china and crystal for a good price: $900.

27. When calculating the cost for Admiral Robert Kelly's airplane, for example, the Navy said only that it cost taxpayers $1,454 per hour to operate. What it didn't reveal was that forty people were assigned to take care of it at the executive flight department at Barbers Point Naval Air Station, Hawaii. These included pilots, mechanics, and in-flight stewards. Kelly flew on average about 450 hours a year in his P-3, which cost about $654,000 annually, according to a statement from Kelly's public affairs office provided to the author on October 16, 1992. However, when the personnel costs were added, the figure exceeds $1 million, according to Kelly's own staff. For an idea of what went into operating Kelly's airplane, see, for example, "VP-3A, BUNO 149675 Celebrates 30th Anniversary in the Navy," *The Barbers Pointer,* July 10, 1992.

28. Kelly and Admiral Charles Larson, the commander in chief of the Pacific who flew in a DC-9, both arrived in San Diego at approximately the same time from Hawaii for a conference. When the conference was over, they both departed the same day for the return trip to Hawaii. But because the admirals were rivals and liked the status of their own airplanes, they preferred not to fly together.

29. Memorandum, September 29, 1992. This twelve-page memo was put together by Kelly's public affairs staff in response to questions from the author. According to Kelly's personal calendar, copies of which were provided to the author, he played golf eleven days in one month. Kelly was also a workaholic and did business, according to his aides, while golfing with other naval officers or visiting dignitaries.

30. Kelly acknowledged that one of his stewards misplaced his clubs but said he did not fire him. Kelly's staff, in interviews with the author on September 29, 1992, disagreed.

31. *The Washington Post,* October 16, 1993.

32. This according to a confidential list kept in the secretary of the Navy's office.

33. The exception to this was James Forrestal in the Truman administration.

34. The literature on naval history is vast. But some of the more recent books include *History of the U.S. Navy* by Robert W. Love; *This People's Navy* by Kenneth J. Hagan; *Shield of the Republic* by Michael T. Isenberg; *Naval*

Renaissance by Frederick H. Hartmann; and *High Seas* by Admiral William A. Owens. Other naval authors, such as Norman Polmar, have provided detailed histories of ships and weapons programs. To say the least, the open literature, that which the Navy releases willingly, is quite extensive.

35. Admiral James Holloway interview with the author, May 5, 1994. Holloway became a Lehman advocate during the fight to derail Kissinger's negotiating strategy on SALT.

CHAPTER 2

1. Jim Patton interview with the author, September 24, 1994. Patton was Hayward's chief of war plans and later headed up the CNO's executive panel.
2. Ibid.
3. Ibid.
4. Woolsey would resign in 1995 over a scandal at the CIA concerning Aldrich Ames, a Soviet mole in the agency.
5. Interviews with Holcomb, Lehman, and naval intelligence officers.
6. Patton interviews.
7. Admiral Tom Hayward interview with the author, August 23, 1994.
8. Lehman kept a copy of West's study, called Sea Plan 2000, in his personal files.
9. NIE 11-15-82/D, "National Intelligence Estimate on Soviet Naval Strategy and Programs through the 1990s," obtained under the Freedom of Information Act by the author from the Central Intelligence Agency. The document was declassified in December 1994.
10. Patton interview.
11. Admiral Stansfield Turner, interview with the author, April 11, 1994.

CHAPTER 3

1. This anecdote is based on interviews with U.S. Navy intelligence officers who worked with the satellite photography. Because the subject is so sensitive, they asked not to be identified.
2. *Guide to the Soviet Navy,* fifth edition, by Norman Polmar. Rear Admiral Sumner Shapiro, who was reticent about discussing overhead reconnaissance capabilities, nonetheless confirmed on March 20, 1994, during an interview at the San Diego Marriott that the satellite had taken pictures of Nikolayev.
3. The author interviewed several naval intelligence officers who worked in the Naval Intelligence Support Center. All asked not to be identified because of the repercussions they felt would come for talking to a journalist.
4. Sumner Shapiro, February 26, 1981, testimony before the House Armed Services Subcommittee on Seapower.
5. The Navy learned that the Soviets had built a titanium sub after the ship had

been towed back to the yard when its nuclear reactor had a meltdown. The Soviets cut the hull in half and left it lying in the open, where a U.S. reconnaissance satellite took its picture. A year later another satellite took the same photograph. When photo analysts compared pictures, they realized that the sub hull had not rusted, which obviously meant it was titanium. The Navy thought the sub was cut in half because it was a failure. However, the Soviets built half a dozen more, improved boats.

6. "National Intelligence Estimate 11-15-82/D" on the Soviet navy prepared by the CIA with the help of the U.S. Navy. It reported that the Soviet navy was a defensive force.

7. Shapiro interview.

8. Shapiro testimony before Seapower Subcommittee, February 1981; the Strategic Arms Limitation Talks, SALT I, limited submarine launch tubes to 950.

9. Lyons interview, June 15, 1994. Not everyone in the Navy held this optimistic view.

10. There were two versions, according to Jim Patton and Peter Swartz, a Lehman confidant, one that was classified and one that was cleansed of secret data and released publicly in the Naval Institute journal *Proceedings* under Hayward's name.

11. Interview with officers who attended the meeting. Shapiro confirmed the meeting during an interview in San Diego on March 20, 1994.

12. Description of Haver comes from *Breaking the Ring* by John Barron. Barron is a former naval intelligence officer.

13. This entire section on Robert Herrick was based on interviews with Herrick, the last one on October 18, 1994, as well as with U.S. naval intelligence officers who sided with Herrick and believed the Navy was grossly embellishing the Soviet naval threat.

14. After the war a midshipman had to serve seven years, according to the Naval Academy. See regulations governing the admission of candidates into the United States Naval Academy as midshipmen and sample examination papers, June 1944.

15. *Soviet Naval Strategy: Fifty Years of Theory and Practice,* United States Naval Institute Press, 1968. Herrick's work was based primarily on open sources gleaned during his travels in the Soviet Union. In May 1978 Lieutenant Commander James T. Westwood wrote in the May issue of *Proceedings,* "Now with ten years behind us, it is time to see if Soviet naval trends and developments substantiate, modify, or refute Herrick's findings." His conclusion, which caused even more controversy, was that Herrick was right.

16. The Ironbark documents were released to the author under the Freedom of Information Act. The documents were long-running articles, written by a half-dozen or so admirals, which appeared in the Soviets' top secret journal *Military Thought.*

17. *Military Thought,* documents declassified by the CIA. Even in the 1980s the Soviet Union stressed the importance of nuclear weapons. While Western na-

vies think less about nuclear weapons, the Soviets "do so as a first order of business, and everything else stems from that," said Rear Admiral William O. Studeman, former head of naval intelligence, in *The Soviet and Other Communist Navies,* edited by James L. George, Naval Institute Press, 1986.

18. Although this was the strategy in the 1960s, it evolved into something quite opposite by 1985.

19. *Military Thought* and Studeman. But Studeman did not reveal this until 1985, well after it was safe to say publicly what the dismal state of the Soviet fleet was. Having said that, however, Studeman warned that there were still "things to be alert to."

20. *Military Thought.* This was known as early as 1962, and their capabilities improved poorly thereafter, even into the late 1980s.

21. Ibid. Also, Holloway interview. He was Hayward's predecessor as CNO.

22. Ibid.

23. William Colby interview with the author, August 23, 1994.

24. Interviews with U.S. intelligence officers.

25. Colby interviews as well as interviews with half a dozen U.S. intelligence officers. A similar figure is given in *The Threat* by Andrew Cockburn, Random House, 1983.

26. Andy Marshall interview with the author, November 21, 1994.

27. Holcomb interview; Harold Brown interview with the author, January 1, 1994; and interviews with U.S. intelligence officers at the CIA and Navy.

28. Interview with a Navy captain who was an intelligence officer, October 24, 1991.

29. Interview with several naval attachés.

30. Holcomb interview.

31. By the late 1980s the Soviets had acquired the technology to substantially quiet their subs, although the U.S. Navy said it could still find them with its advanced sonar.

32. Captain Peter Huchtausen, a retired U.S. intelligence officer who served in Moscow, *Proceedings,* May 1993.

33. Author interviews with Soviet naval officers in Vladivostok, September 1990. This is also based on interviews with U.S. intelligence officers at the CIA and Navy and Josh Handler's valuable work for Greenpeace; Greenpeace visit to Moscow and Russian Far East, July–November 1992.

34. Russian nuclear submarine designs are divided into three generations. The first generation, introduced in 1958–1960, included the *Hotel, Echo,* and *November* classes. The second generation, introduced in 1967–1968, eventually included the *Charlie, Victor, Yankee, Delta, Papa,* and *Alfa* classes. The third generation included the *Typhoon, Delta IV, Oscar, Akula,* and *Sierra* classes. *Proceedings,* May 1993.

35. Greenpeace also reported this accident but differed with naval intelligence. A Greenpeace report said the sub had been deeply submerged and a fire had broken out on the ship. Although not able to confirm a radiation leak, Greenpeace speculated that a nuclear incident had taken place.

36. Author visit to the Soviet Far East, September 10–13, 1990. Interviews with naval intelligence officers and the Greenpeace report. Interview with Greenpeace officials on November 1, 1994.

37. Author interviews with Soviet naval officers and local citizens of Vladivostok, September 10–13, 1990.

38. Holcomb interview.

39. NIE 11-15-82/D.

40. Ken Kennedy interview, May 16, 1994. Kennedy is a civilian intelligence officer with the Navy.

41. Interviews with CIA intelligence analysts.

42. Turner interview.

43. Brown interview. According to Ken Kennedy, now with the Naval Doctrine Command, less than 10 percent of the Soviet navy, or about sixty ships, were true blue-water ships, capable of steaming for long distances on the high seas. Kennedy interview.

44. One of the first naval analysts to describe the bastion theory, in which the boomers would not deploy off the East and West Coasts of the United States but be kept in local waters, was James McConnell, an analyst at the Center for Naval Analyses. It was a controversial theory for years until about 1982, when a number of indicators, including a top secret CIA national intelligence estimate, "Soviet Capabilities for Strategic Nuclear Conflict, 1982–92," NIE 11-3/8-82, declassified June 27, 1994, proved McConnell correct. One thing was certain, however: Everybody in naval intelligence knew that the boomer boats were in their bastions, not lurking off American coasts, as naval leaders often said in public. The Navy knew exactly where the boomers operated off the U.S. coasts, describing the area they visited as the "Yankee Box."

45. NIE 11-3/8-82. There are other references in open literature to the bastion theory, notably *The Soviet and Other Communist Navies*.

46. NIE 11-15-82/D. The Soviets were able to improve targeting by the mid-1980s; interviews with intelligence officers.

47. NIE 11-15-82/D.

48. The *Kiev* made its first operational deployment to the Mediterranean in July 1976. In July the ship was transferred to the Northern Fleet for a year before returning to the Mediterranean area. The ship's homeport is in Murmansk on the Kola Peninsula.

49. Interviews with U.S. naval aviators who witnessed the Forgers in operation.

50. This meeting is based on interviews with those in attendance.

CHAPTER 4

1. Lehman said in one of many interviews, "I had no doubt there was a half-life to the increases I needed. But I believed that if we could get the major capital investment in, we were safe from the readiness cuts of the 1970s because nobody would ever do that again, it was such a consensus to keep flying hours

and steaming days high. Once we got the major capital commitments for ships and aircraft, the rest would take care of itself. I knew I had to get it done by 1984."

2. When the long-term Extended Planning Annex was included, the Navy's overall budget requests neared $1 trillion.

3. Lehman told Peter Swartz, who worked on the development of the Maritime Strategy, that he had to keep this under wraps if he wanted to sell his Navy. Peter Swartz interview with the author, November 21, 1994.

4. Swartz interview.

5. *Human Events,* March 6, 1982.

6. Military posture statement, May 5, 1981, House Armed Services Committee, p. 1344.

7. Seth Cropsey interview with the author, May 23, 1994. Cropsey, who was deputy undersecretary of the Navy in the Lehman administration, found the photograph of Roosevelt. Because of Lehman's fondness for Roosevelt, Cropsey gave him the picture.

8. Gordon interviews.

9. Other stories circulated by naval officers about Lehman compared him to Winston Churchill. The Marines called Lehman "Young Winston." Many newspaper accounts mentioned both Roosevelt and Churchill when the development of the modern-day Navy was discussed.

10. *The Great White Fleet* by Robert A. Hart.

11. *U.S. News & World Report,* August 4, 1986.

12. Donald Rumsfeld interview with the author, April 7, 1994. Jim Wade interview with the author, April 8, 1994. Pete Aldridge interview with the author, April 11, 1984. Wade and Aldridge, both high-ranking Defense Department officials, wrote the study and briefed President Gerald Ford on it. Admiral James Holloway also took part in preparing the report.

13. Lehman interviews.

14. George Sawyer interview with the author, June 21, 1994. Sawyer was an assistant secretary of the Navy for shipbuilding.

15. Peter Tarpgaard interview with the author, July 22, 1994. See also *Policy Review,* Summer 1983. For more views on the role of the Congressional Budget Office regarding the Six Hundred Ship Navy, see "Building a 600 Ship Navy: Costs, Training, and Alternative Approaches," March 1982; "Cost of Expanding and Modernizing the Navy's Carrier-based Air Forces," May 1982; "Manpower for a 600 Ship Navy: Costs and Policy Alternatives," August 1983. For a more current view, see "Future Budget Requirements for the 600 Ship Navy," September 1985; CBO staff memorandum, "The costs of the administration's plan for the Navy through the year 2010," December 1991; and CBO papers, "Options for reconfiguring service roles and missions," March 1994 (all CBO documents, available from the Government Printing Office).

16. Philip Geyelin, "Top Man Pitches for Power," *The Washington Post,* October 2, 1981; John Lehman interview with the *San Diego Union* editorial board,

October 25, 1981. The Congressional Budget Office said the Navy would need an additional 66,000 active duty personnel, on top of the existing 560,000 troops, to man the new seagoing forces. By 1989 its personnel reached 592,000, but still the Navy did not have enough qualified people to run the fleet, according to Carlisle Trost. See *Naval Renaissance* by Frederick Hartmann. Also, author interviews with Trost's staff.

17. Congressional Budget Office, "Manpower for a 600 Ship Navy: Costs and Policy Alternatives," August 1983.
18. Holcomb interviews.
19. "Administration Selling Increased Navy Budget as Heart of Military Strategy," by Richard Halloran, *The New York Times,* April 10, 1982. This figure is in 1983 dollars and does not account for inflation. See also "A-12 Advanced Tactical Aircraft (ATA) Program Weapons Facts," by Bert H. Cooper Jr. of the Congressional Research Service, August 1991.
20. Richard Armitage interview with the author, November 30, 1993.
21. Hayward's written testimony for the record during his appearance before the Seapower Subcommittee.
22. Senate confirmation hearings on Lehman for secretary of the Navy.

CHAPTER 5

1. Dick Allen and John Lehman interviews with the author. The author also interviewed other participants in the meeting. The meeting was arranged by Rear Admiral Sumner Shapiro and Admiral James Watkins, who approached Allen with the message that the President had to sign off on what the Navy was doing. Lehman's calendars also mark the meeting.
2. This was Mitch Snyder.
3. Lehman acknowledged the meeting and losing his chair.
4. Confidential source.
5. Confidential source.
6. Lehman interviews.
7. Watkins switched from UC Berkeley to the Naval Academy. He wanted first to be an aviator, then later changed to submarines. Naval Academy Year Book.
8. Author interview with defense official involved in the project, November 14, 1994.
9. Michael Deaver interview with the author, November 25, 1993. Deaver said the polling material he looked at showed there was a fear that Reagan would get the country into a nuclear war with the Soviet Union.
10. NIE 11-15-82/D.
11. Confidential source.
12. Lehman interviews.

CHAPTER 6

1. Marine Captain Andrew Engelke, who was there and was then a young first lieutenant waiting to go through flight school, said it was a rambunctious gathering, but one where everyone felt proud to be with Lehman. Lehman acknowledged the meeting but did not remember being hoisted onto any shoulders.
2. Gary Gault interview with the author, October 5, 1994. Gault is a historian with the National Guard Bureau in the Pentagon. National Guardsmen were prohibited by law from doing their annual two-week training in Vietnam, according to Gault. They could, however, volunteer for active duty service, which many Guardsmen did. During the *Pueblo* crisis of 1968, when North Korea seized the intelligence-gathering ship, 12,234 Army Guardsmen and 10,511 Air Guardsmen were activated for about a year from seventeen states. John Lehman's home state was not among those that participated in the Army call-up. Pennsylvania's Air National Guard sent 107 officers and 565 airmen.
3. Chief of Army Reserve, interview with Major Hill, October 5, 1994. Hill said that it would take too long to do the paperwork and also that if a reservist went on active duty, it would be for at least thirteen months, not two weeks.
4. *A Bright Shining Lie,* by Neil Sheehan.
5. Jim Webb interview with the author, March 25, 1994.
6. Pendleton James interview with the author, March 30, 1994.
7. Ibid.
8. Ibid.
9. Deaver denied doing this. Allen sided with Lehman. Admiral James Holloway remembered the flight status being a major problem.
10. The leak to Deaver was never identified. But Ace Lyons and others suspected Hayward and Cockell were behind it, an accusation both men denied. Other Lehman confidants blamed a retired Navy captain working on Capitol Hill.
11. *Command of the Seas.*
12. Vince Lesh interview with the author, March 2, 1994.
13. Rear Admiral Jack Christiansen interview with the author, December 4, 1993.
14. Admiral James Holloway interview with the author, May 4, 1994.
15. Christiansen interview.
16. Ibid.
17. Ibid.
18. *Command of the Seas.*
19. Christiansen interview.
20. Ibid.
21. Holloway interview.
22. Ibid.
23. Interviews with a member of Holloway's staff, March 25, 1995.
24. Christiansen interview.
25. Ibid.

26. Holloway interview.
27. Ibid.
28. Ibid.
29. Orr also was being considered for secretary of the Navy.
30. James interview.
31. *Command of the Seas.*
32. James interview.
33. *Command of the Seas.*

CHAPTER 7

1. Gordon interviews.
2. Lyons interviews.
3. Patton interviews. Patton took the two Coast Guard officers to see Lyons.
4. Holcomb interviews.
5. Lyons interviews.
6. John Hattendorf, "The Evolution of the Maritime Strategy, 1977 to 1987," *Naval War College Review,* Summer 1988.
7. The meeting between Lyons and Hayward comes from interviews with Holcomb, Lyons, and others members of Hayward's staff.
8. Holcomb interviews. See also Hartmann's *Naval Renaissance.*
9. Gordon and Lehman interviews.
10. Gordon interviews.
11. Rear Admiral John Jenkins interview with the author, June 24, 1994.
12. Ibid.
13. Lehman interviews.
14. Gordon interviews.
15. Brown interview.
16. Lehman interviews.
17. Gordon interviews.
18. Gordon interviews.
19. *U.S. News & World Report,* July 4, 1988. Boeing disputed this amount.
20. *U.S. News & World Report,* July 4, 1988.
21. Don Price interview with the author, September 16, 1994.
22. Price interview.
23. Ibid.
24. Ibid.
25. Paul David Miller interview.
26. Author interviews with an admiral on Hayward's staff.
27. Gordon interviews.

CHAPTER 8

1. The section on the selection of Ace Lyons comes from interviews with Lehman, Lyons, and Hayward and their staff officers involved with the nomination of Lyons to take over Second Fleet.
2. Hayward acknowledged going down to Weinberger's office and that he not only was opposed to the Lyons nomination, but bitterly fought Lehman to try to derail it.
3. Hayward confirmed the conversation but said that he placed the call to Lehman in Hawaii to tell him that he did not support Lyons.
4. *Command of the Seas.*
5. Swartz interview.
6. Hayward said calling ahead to see if Lehman was available was his normal operating style. He said he had so many meetings with Lehman over the Maritime Strategy that he cannot pinpoint the first one, although he acknowledges asking Cockell what to do about bringing Lehman up to speed.
7. Lehman interviews.
8. Lehman interviews. Hayward said that he wanted to talk to Lehman about the nomination then, not when the secretary was back in Washington.
9. "The U.S. State in Naval Arms Control," the Henry L. Stimson Center.
10. Interviews with intelligence officers.
11. Interviews with confidential intelligence sources.
12. *Human Events,* March 6, 1982.
13. Interviews with Ace Lyons and Commander Pat Roll, his operations planner.
14. Lyons interview.
15. The CIA released this after the author filed a Freedom of Information Act request.

CHAPTER 9

1. Associated Press, July 28, 1981.
2. Sawyer interview.
3. *Congressional Quarterly,* 1981.
4. Military Posture Statement, Committee on Armed Services, House of Representatives, May 5, 1981.
5. This is in 1983 dollars.
6. National Defense Budget Estimates for FY 1995, Office of the Comptroller of the Department of Defense, March 1994.
7. Though Lehman took credit for building five aircraft carriers on his watch, only four were funded when he was secretary.
8. Sawyer interviews.
9. Ibid.

10. Lehman interviews.
11. Sawyer interviews. Ed Campbell interview with the author, August 1, 1994.
12. Gordon interviews.
13. *The New York Times*, February 19, 1967; see also *Covert Action*, no. 29, Winter 1988; *Facts on File*, 1967; *The Reader's Guide to Intelligence Periodicals.*
14. *The Reader's Guide to Intelligence Periodicals.*
15. *Who's Who.*
16. See *The Dissenting Academy*, edited by Theodore Roszak, Pantheon Books, New York, 1967.
17. Gordon interviews.
18. Sawyer interviews.
19. Vice Admiral Jerry Tuttle interview with the author, June 22, 1994.
20. Ibid.
21. Hays interviews.

CHAPTER 10

1. The profile on Hank Kleeman comes from interviews with aviators who knew him, including Jack Ensch and Jack Snyder, as well as from interviews on December 1, 1994, with his widow, Carol, and his mother, who lives in Clinton, Illinois.
2. Details about the dogfight come from a Pentagon transcript following the shoot-down. See also *Best Laid Plans* by David C. Martin and John Walcott, which gives a blow-by-blow account of the air action.
3. Hank Kleeman told his wife he was thinking this.
4. Hays interview.
5. Ibid.
6. Carol Kleeman interview.
7. Deaver interview.

CHAPTER 11

1. Nick Johnson interview with the author, November 30, 1994. Johnson is an expert on the Soviet Union's space program.
2. Tuttle interview.
3. Roll interview.
4. Tuttle interview.
5. Lyons and Tuttle interviews. Lehman also confirmed that the raid took place.
6. Tuttle interview.
7. The range for the F-14 varies. This figure comes from *The Pentagon Paradox*, by Jim Stevenson, Naval Institute Press, 1994.

8. Lyons interview.
9. Lyons, Tuttle, and Lehman interviews.
10. Confidential interview with officer who heard the remark.
11. There are several good books on Forrestal; one of the more recent is *Driven Patriot: The Life and Times of James Forrestal* by Townsend Hoopes and Douglas Brinkley, which is an exhaustive history of Forrestal's service in the Pentagon.
12. Lehman interview.
13. Lyons and interviews with members of Hayward's staff. John Lehman also confirmed this in interviews with the author, as did Admiral Harry D. Train in an interview on November 17, 1994.
14. Train interview.
15. Ibid.
16. Ibid.
17. Patton interview.
18. Ibid.
19. Nick Criss interview with the author, January 5, 1994.
20. Rear Admiral Jay Yakely interview with the author, December 23, 1994. Jay and Robert, who retired this year as a captain, are brothers.
21. Lehman interviews.

CHAPTER 12

1. Private files of John Lehman, obtained by the author under the Freedom of Information Act. The Naval Historical Center tried to keep the documents closed. Navy Secretary John Dalton's staff reviewed the author's request and authorized the release of the files.
2. Interviews with a Navy submarine captain, now retired and living in Florida, and a defense industry official in San Diego who works closely with the Navy's submarine community. Because both are defense contractors, they asked not to be identified.
3. Edward Hidalgo interview with the author, July 22, 1994.
4. The meeting with David Lewis is based on interviews with Lehman, Sawyer, and officials from General Dynamics. For background, see *Running Critical* by Patrick Tyler, which offers a good perspective of the problems between General Dynamics and the Navy.
5. Lehman interviews.
6. Sawyer interviews.
7. Ibid.
8. Ibid.
9. The private files of John Lehman.
10. Associated Press, May 22, 1985.
11. White House meeting based on *Command of the Seas* and White House documents briefing the President on Rickover's accomplishments. Also a close con-

fidant of Rickover's, who spoke with Rickover after the meeting, confirmed Lehman's account.

12. Verne Orr interview with the author, March 30, 1994.

13. Lehman's personal files.

14. Orr interview. Orr was always suspect of Lehman's flight records. Also, interviews with James Webb, who reviewed the file when he later became secretary of the Navy; a public affairs officer on Admiral Carlisle Trost's staff who burned one of the last remaining copies of the probe; Navy lawyers who took part in the investigation; and agents with the Naval Investigative Service, including Dennis Usrey. Mac Williams, Lehman's attorney, disputes this and said Lehman completed the course. Williams would later head the NIS.

15. Aldridge interview. Also, Wade interview. Rumsfeld interview.

16. Aldridge interview. Lehman confirmed the bet but said he did not remember welshing on the deal.

17. Private files of John Lehman.

18. Don Price, Lehman's close friend and aide, said that Lehman belonged to the Knights, saying he saw Lehman wearing a Knights of Malta pin on his lapel. P. D. Miller also thought Lehman was a member. Lehman denied belonging to the Knights.

19. Richard Allen's résumé. For more on the Knights of Malta, see also Martin A. Lee's "Their Will Be Done," in *Mother Jones*, July 1983; *Inside the League* by Scott Anderson and Jon Lee Anderson, p. 183; and *People of God* by Penny Lernoux.

20. Michael Schwartz interview with the author, December 15, 1994.

21. Lehman's private files.

22. Harvey Sicherman, a close Lehman friend, wrote speeches and op-eds critical of the bishops for the secretary. A good number of these were contained in the private files of John Lehman.

CHAPTER 13

1. Bill Manthorpe interview with the author, November 22, 1994.

2. Letter to Vice President George Bush, April 14, 1986, contained in the private files of John Lehman.

3. Ibid.

4. Mike Staehle interviews with the author, December 13, 1994. Staehle was in the Flag Plot when the accident happened.

5. Manthorpe interview.

6. NIS agent interview with the author.

7. John Nieroski interview with the author, December 15, 1994.

8. Ibid.

9. The EPA was declassified in its entirety in 1994 and obtained by the author through the Freedom of Information Act.

10. Harlan Ullman interview with the author, November 29, 1994.

11. Ibid.
12. In constant fiscal year 1995 dollars. National Defense Budget Estimates for FY 1995.
13. Ullman interview.
14. Steve Woodall interview with the author, July 29, 1994. The EPA said that the Navy would need 8 percent real growth into the 1990s to support Lehman's buildup. Between 1983 and 1995 there were only two years when this occurred: 1983 at 13.7 percent and 1988 at 3.5 percent. In each of these two years the Navy got about $8 billion to build two new carriers. In 1985 the Navy also had 15.7 percent real growth. This budget spike came from the Navy taking control of its own retirement money, which had previously been handled by the Department of Defense. In each of the remaining years real growth fell into the negative column, dipping to −14.6 percent in FY 1992. Rolf Clark, a professor at George Washington who worked on the EPA as a consultant, said the Navy could not sustain the buildup because it was getting too much money. Clark said that the bulk of the money would have to go to research and development and procurement and that contractors could not build ships, warplanes, and weapons quickly enough to keep up. Therefore they would drive up the unit price tremendously, which is what happened. The EPA was correct in that by 1994 the Navy was down to about 336 ships, nearly half of what Lehman had called for.
15. Lehman interviews.
16. David Chu interview with the author, May 17, 1994. Chu never thought much of the EPA and never knew that Lehman was so fearful of it.
17. Weinberger editorial, *Forbes*, May 1, 1989.
18. Armitage interview.
19. Ullman interview.
20. Private files of John Lehman.
21. Lawrence Korb interviews with the author, this one on December 20, 1994.
22. Ibid.
23. Robert Garrick interview with the author, March 29, 1994. Garrick was a member of the October Surprise Group during the 1980 presidential election campaign that was established by Bill Casey.
24. Gordon interview. Also, Lehman interview, but Lehman recalled saying "So much for Ted Kennedy."
25. In 1995 dollars the figures would be: to the Pentagon, $350,405 billion, a $93 billion increase; to the Navy, $120 billion; to the Air Force, $106,336 billion; to the Army, $86,725 billion.
26. The remainder went to various other branches in the Department of Defense.
27. Swartz interview. Lehman said this repeatedly to Swartz.
28. Dave Kassing interview with the author, March 21, 1994. See also the *National Journal,* April 2, 1983, vol. 15, no. 14.
29. The letter to Nunn was in the private files of John Lehman.
30. The letter was in the private files of John Lehman.
31. Dov Zakheim interview with the author, June 20, 1994.

32. Paul Thayer interview with the author, March 14, 1994. Also, Paul Thayer oral history with historians from the secretary of defense's office.

33. Ibid.

34. Thayer interview.

35. Committee on Foreign Relations, U.S. Senate, "Nomination of John F. Lehman, Jr. to be Deputy Director, ACDA" February 11 and March 4, 10, and 17, 1975, p. 64; *Reagan's Ruling Class* by Ronald Brownstein and Nina Easton.

36. Committee hearings.

37. Ibid.

38. Ibid. Lehman's denials appear throughout the committee hearing.

39. Ibid.

40. Years later he would offer a more truthful accounting of his feelings about the leaks and the purge in *Command of the Seas*. As to his role in the personnel shake-ups at ACDA, Lehman quipped proudly: "Did I have a role in personnel recommendations . . . right after the '72 election? Sure I did, and I think it really improved the Arms Control Agency." Kissinger, who was traveling in Egypt, cabled the committee from Aswan, which helped sway the committee in support of Lehman. "Dear Mr. Chairman: I understand that the Senate Foreign Relations Committee has asked for my views on the nomination of Mr. John Lehman as Deputy Director of the Arms Control and Disarmament Agency. I should like you to know, and ask that you pass on to your colleagues on the Committee, that I support Mr. Lehman's nomination and hope that the Senate Foreign Relations Committee will soon report that nomination to the whole Senate with a favorable recommendation. I have known John for five and a half years, including a close association with him when he was a member of the National Security Council Staff. He is an intelligent and capable young man who would be a great asset to ACDA and to the country. If confirmed, he would, I know, work closely with you and the other members of your Committee on the whole range of interest shared by the Senate Foreign Relations Committee and the Disarmament Agency. With warm regards, sincerely, Henry A. Kissinger."

41. Private files of John Lehman.

42. Private files of John Lehman.

43. Korb interview. *The Power Game*.

44. Economic breakdown for each port was in the private files of John Lehman.

45. Memorandum for the chief of naval operations, June 20, 1985, subject: "GAO Survey of Strategic Homeporting from Vice Adm. T. A. Hughes," private files of John Lehman.

46. Memorandum for the secretary of the Navy, December 6, 1982, subject: "MIL-CON in Strategic Homeporting Plan," private files of John Lehman.

47. Private files of John Lehman.

48. United Press International, February 22, 1985.

49. NIE 11-15-82/D.

50. Korb interviews. Also, *The Power Game*.

51. Orr interview. See also Thayer's oral history with the historical section of the Department of Defense.

52. Thayer had to resign because he was indicted for insider trading before he took the Pentagon job and had to go to prison.
53. Letter was in the private files of John Lehman.
54. Memoranda were in the private files of John Lehman.
55. Memorandum for the secretary of the Navy, April 24, 1985.
56. Gordon interviews. Lehman also confirmed the meeting in Goldwater's office.
57. Barry Goldwater letter to the author, May 24, 1994.

CHAPTER 14

1. *Newsweek*, August 8, 1988.
2. Memoranda from Sicherman to Lehman contained in the private files of John Lehman.
3. Sicherman is now director of the Foreign Policy Institute at the University of Pennsylvania, where Lehman had worked as a staffer during graduate school.
4. "Current Operations Costs of USS *New Jersey,*" December 1, 1983, memorandum for the deputy assistant secretary of defense, from the Navy's comptroller, contained in the private files of John Lehman.
5. Private files of John Lehman.
6. *Rogue Warrior* by Richard Marcinko and John Weisman. The author also reported this mishap in the *San Diego Union* after interviewing several SEALs in 1990.
7. *The Power Game.*
8. Gordon interviews.
9. Representative Les Aspin floor speech. Remarks prepared for delivery, Tuesday, April 16, 1985. Lehman kept a copy of Aspin's remarks in his private files.
10. Unclassified Navy message from the commander of the supply command in Washington, June 1984.
11. Memo to file, March 8, 1985, from Admiral Steven A. White. Memo was in the private files of John Lehman. White was one of the few admirals who stood up to Lehman.
12. Gordon interviews.
13. April 9, 1985, letter to Goldwater from John Lehman contained in the private files of John Lehman.
14. *Command of the Seas.*
15. This did come about as a result of the Walker case and others.
16. "Prosecuting Espionage under Virginia Law," memorandum for the secretary, June 3, 1985.
17. Documents would be checked out of the custodian library and not returned. They would be lost. And burn bags would not be destroyed. This was still happening in the 1990s. Interviews with naval intelligence officers who admitted to the security lapses.
18. The private files of John Lehman contained information on the Walker spy case.
19. Private files of John Lehman.

20. The Soviets took the opposite view, saying the material supplied by the Walkers was potentially war-winning intelligence for them.
21. This study was in the private files of John Lehman.
22. In a December 20, 1984, letter to Lehman, Kaman said: "You were very nice to call the other day concerning the Chinese and I certainly trust all of our mutual efforts will result in their acquiring some SH-2 Helicopters." Letter was in the private files of John Lehman. Representatives of the U.S. government are forbidden to lobby other nations or companies on behalf of personal friends. It is a conflict of interest. In the case of Kaman, one Navy lawyer asked: "Who was he representing, the United States or his friend?"
23. Memorandum for the secretary of the Navy, January 29, 1987, subject: "New Zealand: Trade and Defense Issues."
24. Lehman letter to Weinberger, February 20, 1987, contained in the private files of John Lehman.
25. This still goes on today.
26. Terry was one of the officers identified in the major sea command review. Private files of John Lehman.
27. Author interviews with officers and sailors who visited Australia.
28. Interview with Navy sailor on an aircraft carrier. The author also interviewed health workers in Australia who confirmed the report that fourteen-year-old girls were legal. They also said that during and after a Navy visit there was an increase in cases of sexual assault, venereal disease, rape, unwanted pregnancies, and a host of other social ills.
29. Defense Department inspector general's memorandum for secretary of defense, March 27, 1985.
30. According to local newspaper accounts.
31. The author interviewed NIS agents assigned to the region, and none of them recalls the accident or was aware of any investigation. In responding to a Freedom of Information Act request from the author, the Navy said there had been no investigation into Graham's death.

CHAPTER 15

1. Two good books on the Hornet are *The Pentagon Paradox* by James P. Stevenson and *Hornet* by Orr Kelly.
2. Carol Kleeman interview with the author.
3. JAG Manual investigation of Kleeman's crash obtained by the author under the Freedom of Information Act.
4. JAG Manual investigation.
5. Ibid.
6. Ibid.
7. Kleeman interview.
8. Obtained by the author under the Freedom of Information Act.
9. Lehman interviews.

10. Some suspect that today this is not the case, that the jet has new structural problems that were not detected in the early 1980s.

11. The landing gear system has since been changed.

12. Commander Randy Clark interview with the author, January 25, 1995. Clark, a former Blue Angel, was the fleet introduction officer for the F-14D Tomcat. Until his retirement in March 1995, he was considered one of the Navy's best pilots.

13. When a component failed, its black box or circuit card was replaced. Still, the old component had to be repaired back at an aviation depot on land. Even so, the quick replacement time allowed the jet to be back on line in minutes.

14. Today, however, as the Hornets get older, or after about 1,200 hours of flight time, they start costing more money. Chuck Spinney interview with the author, February 5, 1995. Spinney works in the Department of Defense's Plans, Analysis, and Evaluation section.

15. *Wings,* February 1992, vol. 22, no. 1.

16. Pilot interviews with the author. See also *Pentagon Paradox.*

17. Spinney interviews.

18. *The New York Times,* April 11, 1982. Internal Navy documents contained in the private files of John Lehman.

19. Vice Admiral Robert Dunn interview with the author, January 1985. A former CNO interview with the author, January 18, 1995. Dunn was the deputy CNO for air warfare, the admiral in charge of the aviation plan. The A-6F program was controversial from the outset. Boeing, Dunn said, at first failed to meet the requirements but finally worked out its problems.

20. Lehman interviews.

21. FY 1975 then year dollars. There are four ways to price a new combat jet. One is the flyaway cost, which includes air frame, engines, and avionics. Second is the weapons system cost, which includes the three previous components plus support and advanced procurement costs. Third is the procurement cost, which includes all of the above plus initial spares. Finally, the most accurate, used by the author, is the program cost, which includes all of the above costs plus research and development and military construction.

22. Lehman preferred to use the flyaway cost. If the program cost was used, the plane would cost as much as $50 million. *Command of the Seas,* p. 230.

23. Spinney interview.

24. Kilcline's accident is based on interviews with accident investigators and others who had heard the voice tape of the crash.

25. When the pilots were thrown forward, the foot of one of the aviators was pinned on the pedal switch that activated the aircraft's microphone. The conversation that took place in the seconds before their deaths was recorded by the Navy. Three aviators who heard the tape recounted it for the author.

26. "Stricken Aircraft by Shop Number," crash record for the F-14 provided by Grumman, the builder of the F-14. Lehman testified that approximately one-third of all Tomcats crashed because of engine problems. The Navy lost about

120 jets overall up to 1995 at a cost of over nearly $2.5 billion. Other aviators believed that as many as half of the crashes were engine–flight system caused, but the Navy usually listed the cause as pilot error. The Navy's own records claim only 14 jets were lost because of a flat spin.

27. Interviews with pilots involved with the F-14 program and pilots involved with investigating crashes.

28. New engines alone cost about $3 million apiece. Each F-14 needed two engines, and approximately five hundred jets required them.

29. Interviews with several dozen aviators who liked flying the jet but knew they had to "fly the engines" rather than the Tomcat, so they wouldn't die. One aviator recounted this quote to me on August 6, 1993, when I was going through two days of water survival training before flying in the Navy's new F-14D Tomcat.

30. For an excellent summation of the F-14 program, see *Wings,* February 1992.

31. *Wings,* February 1992, interviews with aviators.

32. Interviews with Randy Clark and several admirals involved with the development of the F-14 program. John Lehman also confirmed this in an interview. It is difficult, if not impossible, to determine how much money was shifted among accounts because there was so much overlap of the various programs.

33. Bert Cooper of the Congressional Research Service said there were many loopholes to move money around, and even if Congress knew about it, it was fully behind the Hornet.

34. The price for the F-14D has varied from $50 million to $75 million. When two F-14Ds crashed in January 1995 off the San Diego coast, Navy spokesman Doug Sayers listed the jets at $60 million. The four aviators who crashed the jets were screwing around, taking pictures of each other, when they apparently collided in midair. One of the aviators had previously been disciplined for unsafe flying.

35. The airplanes were the F-14, P-3, F/A-18, E-2C, EA-6B, and A-6. Report No. 86-10, Inspector General, Department of Defense, June 17, 1986.

36. Lehman speech to the Naval War College, see also Report No. 86-10, Inspector General.

37. Charlie Murphy interview with the author, February 5, 1995. Murphy was a senior staff assistant to Republican senator Lowell Weicker. Also, Spinney interview.

38. Weicker letter to Sherrick obtained by the author.

39. Lehman admitted that he made a mistake on one aircraft, the P-3, saying that it was more expensive today than in the "bad old years" of the Carter administration.

CHAPTER 16

1. If anyone doubted Lyons's abilities, years after his retirement, the Navy's leadership still consulted him. On February 8, 1995, Vice Chief of Naval Opera-

tions Admiral Stanley Arthur telephoned Lyons to be debriefed on his trip to China at the end of January. Lyons had met with senior members of the Chinese military. At the time, the United States and China were in the throes of an early trade war, and China's leader, Deng, was near death, which was causing rampant speculation in the United States about who would succeed him and whether the military would fill the vacuum.

2. The nuclear war fear was to a certain degree unwarranted. Soviet documents, going back as far as Ironbark, revealed that the Russians always believed the U.S. Navy would try to sink their nuclear missile boats. What they feared more, and what might have triggered a nuclear war, were carrier-based attack planes carrying out strikes on Soviet territory. A skirmish could easily have led to a hot conventional war, which most likely would have gone nuclear, at least at sea, very quickly. For a good overview of the unclassified debate taking place at the time, see "In Harm's Way" by Jack Beatty, *Atlantic*, May 1987.

3. Swartz interview with the author. Many officers helped put together the Maritime Strategy, and Swartz by no means was the single most important person. It was a group effort that included admirals like Bill Small and Bill Pendly and other officers like Captain Roger Barnett.

4. "The Maritime Strategy," *Proceedings*, January 1986.

5. William J. Durtch, "The U.S. Navy: Forces, Doctrines, Missions and Arms Control, in the U.S. Stake in Naval Arms Control," the Stimson Center, October 1990. This is an excellent overview of naval operations vis-à-vis the Soviet Union.

6. Ironbark; Herrick interviews.

7. "The Maritime Strategy," *Proceedings*, January 1986.

8. CinCPac is the commander in chief Pacific. This is a joint job, responsible for the Army, Air Force, Navy, and Marine forces in Asia and the Pacific. The position has always been filled by a Navy admiral. Just below CinCPac is CinCPacFlt—commander in chief of the Pacific Fleet—who from 1985 to 1987 was Lyons. CinCPacFlt controls only Navy and Marine forces in Asia and the Pacific.

9. Captain Kevin Healy, Lyons's executive assistant, interviews with the author throughout February, March, and April of 1995. Healy monitored many of Lyons's telephone calls, including ones with Crowe, and he kept detailed notes on the conversations.

10. Lyons interviews.

11. The following morning Lyons left for Adak, Alaska. During his trip he continued to get message traffic concerning the exercise.

12. Lyons interviews.

13. Ibid.

14. Interview with Lyons and several officers on his staff, as well as aviators who took part in the exercise.

15. Both Lyons and his key aide, Kevin Healy, said the exercises were not carried out in a reckless manner and that the Soviets were clear on this. Both officers said that the A-6 Intruders were not carrying bombs.

16. *Vinson* had returned from a quick transit to the Indian Ocean.
17. Lyons interviews.
18. Healy interviews.
19. Healy participated in an exchange program between the War College and its counterpart in the Soviet Union, where Lyons's name also came up.
20. Several books discuss the capture of the terrorists: Lehman's *Command of the Seas; Best Laid Plans* by David C. Martin and John Walcott; and *Naval Renaissance* by Frederick H. Hartmann. This section is drawn from these, as well as press clippings and interviews with officers involved.
21. It has been widely reported that Israel passed on the information. When news of the Italian help came down to the National Military Command Center, there was a great sense of joy and relief. Interviews with naval intelligence personnel in the NMCC and assigned to a Middle East carrier task force.
22. The CNO must send the nominees to the secretary, who has final approval. But Lehman was trying to pick the officers, which was Watkins's responsibility.
23. John Poindexter interview with the author, February 23, 1995.
24. Ibid.
25. Vice Admiral Don Jones interview with the author, April 25, 1995. The exchange between Miller and Jones comes from Jones.
26. Ibid.
27. Trost had been an Eagle Scout and kept a Boy Scout flag in his office.
28. Poindexter interview.
29. Ibid.
30. Lehman interviews.
31. Poindexter interview.
32. Trost's change of command speech, June 30, 1986, provided to the author by the Naval Academy.
33. Lehman interviews.
34. Gordon interviews.
35. Private papers of John Lehman.
36. This quote and the above information came from a chart Gordon put together to help squelch the criticism of Miller's nomination to a vice admiral. The above names were part of the chart.
37. Gordon interviews.
38. Ibid.
39. Navy public affairs. Ironically, Gordon would have made it the next time around without any help.
40. "Assistance for the Nicaraguan Resistance," National Security Council, December 4, 1984. When the English newspaper *The Observer* publicly revealed Walker as a participant in the contra effort, Lehman kept a copy of the article in his private files. He liked Walker and had invited him on several occasions to the parties he threw on his private barge. One time a photographer took a picture of the two men, which later turned up in public.
41. Memorandum for Captain Joe Prueher, August 26, 1986, from Dave Baker, special assistant intelligence and historical matters. Lehman's private files.

CHAPTER 17

1. Captain Mark Neuhart, Lehman's public affairs officer at the time, said Lehman flew on the DC-9. Lehman had asked Neuhart to go to Tailhook that year, but he had declined.
2. The pilots at Miramar thought the Tom Cruise character was a wimp because he got sick in the cockpit, and they disliked the Kelly McGillis character, calling her a bitch because in their minds she would not have anything to do with them. Captain Robert McLane interview with the author, August 6, 1993. McLane was the commanding officer of Top Gun.
3. Information provided by Paramount Studios.
4. Dunn interview.
5. *Top Gun* movie.
6. Interviews with aviators and women involved as well as a public affairs officer on the base.
7. The $3,000 price is for the F-14 and comes from the Navy's public affairs office at the headquarters for the Air Forces of the Pacific Fleet.
8. Some accounts of this incident have the woman breaking her back. But Ron Thomas, the executive director of the Tailhook Association, said that she only broke her leg. The author interviewed Thomas several times between 1991 and 1994.
9. Stoll interviews.
10. Ibid.
11. Mac Williams interview with the author. Williams would not mention her name, but other members of the JAG Corps did. She did it not for money, but for the fun of it.
12. Obtained by the author. Later, Cunningham's letter also became part of the Pentagon inspector general's report into the 1991 Tailhook Association convention.
13. Norm Gandia interview with the author, April 27, 1992. Gandia, a former Blue Angel and retired Navy captain, said he and Cunningham had been picked up on several occasions for being drunk.
14. Cunningham, through his aide Frank Collins, twice declined to comment about his time in the Navy.
15. Rod McKeown interview with the author, November 12, 1994. McKeown was actually Top Gun's third commanding officer. But his two predecessors, Dan Pedersen and J. C. Smith, had been officers in charge, not commanding officers.
16. Ibid.
17. Ibid.
18. Author interview with Jack Ensch, the executive officer at Top Gun, and interviews with McKeown.
19. October 9, 1985, letter to Martin obtained by the author.
20. *Command of the Seas.*

21. Bonnie Burbidge interview with the author, April 13, 1994.
22. By 1986 Olongapo's mayor, Dick Gordon, had begun a campaign to clean up the city. But the other towns nearby, such as Subic City and Angeles, remained unchanged.
23. The author also interviewed dozens of naval aviators and some of their wives, who confirmed that the Navy knowingly hired prostitutes.
24. Deb Branson interview with the author, February 9, 1994. Branson is a Navy commander.
25. Joanne M. Busby, letter to the author, October 1992. Busby witnessed U.S. military personnel frequently having sex in the water on the local beaches in the Philippines, "bobbing up and down as if a crab had their toes."
26. The author interviewed several members of *Constellation*'s crew. Masher's name was Jim Joyce. He was the radar intercept officer.
27. Roxanne Baxter interview with the author, February 3, 1994.

CHAPTER 18

1. Deaver interview.
2. Report of Investigation, Office of the Inspector General, Department of Defense, April 7, 1987, Case Number S87C00000047; also, interviews with the key players involved in the investigation, including congressional staff, Pentagon investigators, Navy officers, and civilian leaders in the Pentagon.
3. Author interviews with Trost's staff.
4. DeMars did not back down. He resigned his position as chairman of the board instead of giving in to Lehman's demands.
5. The Senate did in fact block the nomination of the two men several months later.
6. The private files of John Lehman.
7. Webb interviews.
8. Reagan would not even mention Lehman in his memoir, *An American Life*.
9. Lehman said, in one of many interviews with the author, that Reagan tried to console him over the Kelso defeat. After playing in an antidrug tennis tournament sponsored by Nancy Reagan at the White House, the President had put his arm around him and said, "I hope you will reconsider and stick around." Administration officials, however, who were close to Reagan discounted this claim, saying that Reagan just didn't act this way and that he had no special feelings for Lehman one way or the other.
10. Lehman interviews.
11. Ibid.
12. Webb interviews.
13. Cox News Service, April 29, 1987; reported in the *San Diego Union*.
14. Memo for the President on ship-counting methods in the private files of John Lehman.

15. *Reconstituting a Production Capability,* Rand, 1993. Under Lehman the Navy built 150 ships but retired 120. In 1990 it had 510 ships. In the 1970s, under Nixon, Ford, and Carter, the Navy built 170 vessels and retired 330.

16. This interview was set up by Rear Admiral Jimmy Finklestein, who was Lehman's chief of public affairs. But Finklestein did not attend the interview, at which he knew Trost was going to blast his old boss.

17. Cox News Service, April 29, 1987.

18. *Command of the Seas.*

19. Captain Steve Clausen interview with the author, August 24, 1995. Clausen was the public affairs officer at the academy when the protest took place.

20. Carol Burke interview with the author, February 8, 1994. Burke was a professor at the Naval Academy. She is now an associate dean at Johns Hopkins University. The references to the jokes at the academy and the songs are based on interviews and on several articles she wrote on the role of women in the military. The author drew extensively from an August 17, 1992, article in *The New Republic* by Burke, as well as interviews with male midshipmen, to establish the hardships of women at the academy.

21. Burke interview.

22. Interviews with two of the pilots in the queues to practice refueling.

23. In naval aviation jargon, a package check was also slang for in-flight refueling between airplanes.

24. Baxter interviews.

25. *The Washington Post,* June 19, 1988.

CHAPTER 19

1. Lyons and Healy interviews with the author. Healy sat in the back of the room. Weinberger was on a trip to Asia and had stopped in Hawaii to be briefed by Lyons on the plan and other naval operations that fell in the bailiwick of CinCPacFlt.

2. Lyons and Healy interviews.

3. Lyons interviews.

4. At the same time, the CNO's executive panel was identifying targets to attack in Iran and had been doing so since late 1984. Panel member interview with the author, March 1, 1995.

5. Lyons appointment calendars, via Kevin Healy.

6. Lyons interviews.

7. Ibid. Healy also gave details of the plan.

8. Lyons interviews.

9. Author interviews with one pilot who flew some of the F-14 missions in the Persian Gulf and who said Navy jets intentionally flew into Iranian air space.

10. Lyons interviews.

11. Jay Coupe, a close friend of Crowe's who served as the admiral's public affairs

officer and later helped him write his memoirs, said there were few if any calls to Lyons from the chairman's office. Healy and Lyons both disagreed staunchly.

12. *Guadalcanal* is an East Coast ship and not normally under the command of the Pacific Fleet. But when Crowe called, it was in an area under Lyons's command.

13. A few months later *Guadalcanal* would publicly take part in the tanker escort mission.

14. Lyons and Healy interviews.

15. Lyons and Healy interviews. Also, Mac Williams, who was the legal adviser to Lehman, Webb, and later H. Lawrence Garrett III, said Lyons was receiving calls from Crowe.

16. Ibid. Much to Healy's chagrin, the Department of Defense division of public affairs drafted a press release saying the ship would sail into the gulf on a certain date, which almost blew the whole operation.

17. Written notes kept by Healy of a conversation between Lyons and Trost in which Lyons passed on details about the C-5 flight and *Guadalcanal*. Admiral Ron Hays interview with the author. Hays, who was the CinCPac at the time, confirmed these secret missions.

18. Ibid. Also, Lyons interviews. It would eventually be made public by the Pentagon, which flew journalists out to the barge to see the operations.

19. Hays interviews.

20. The *Bull's Brigade Song Book* became an issue during the 1991 Tailhook investigation when one aviator caught up in several investigations threatened to reveal it to show that the admirals had long known about the seamy behavior of naval aviators and had taken part in it. After seeing a reference in the *San Diego Union-Tribune* to the fact that it was still being photocopied and passed around at government expense, a Department of Defense investigator called me asking for a copy of the book. I did not provide it.

21. Interview with a naval aviator who sang this song with Bull when they got drunk together in Subic Bay.

22. By the end of the summer, Israeli-made drones were carrying out most of the reconnaissance missions.

23. Lyons interviews. Lyons said the pilots thought they were over Beirut.

24. Lyons was not even certain if the Navy jets downed the Iranian F-4.

25. Lyons interviews.

26. Healy believed the controversy stemmed from Lyons keeping the hospital ship *Mercy* deployed in the Pacific rather than back in the United States. Lyons did indeed do remarkable things with the ship, Healy said, sending it and its medical teams into the Philippines to provide care. Besides the humanitarian benefits, Lyons wanted to do his part to bolster the government of Corazón Aquino. The Navy today has adopted similar physical fitness requirements that Lyons tried to implement.

27. Notes of conversation provided to the author in an interview with Healy.

28. Lyons said that no one ordered him to stand down. He said when he tried to call for permission to launch the attack, Crowe refused to call back.

29. Hays interview. Some in the upper reaches of the Pentagon, attached to the Joint Chiefs organization, found it hard to accept that Hays did not know what was going on in the gulf. Normal procedure was for the chairman to keep in constant contact with his CinCs, especially one as important as CinCPac. But Hays said Crowe probably assumed that Lyons was briefing him and therefore did not feel the need to bring it up with him. Under normal operating conditions, Trost would also have known about both the plan to attack Iran and the other secret operations. The chairman routinely discussed operations in the Tank, the Chiefs' secure briefing room. As a member of the JCS, Trost would have been included in the discussions. Lyons also claimed that he was redirecting messages about his activities to Trost and Hays, including the Iran attack plan, on a regular basis.

30. Hays interviews.

31. Ibid.

32. Lyons admitted refunding money to the government but insisted that he was not shipping antiques for his wife.

33. Rear Admiral Tom Paulsen interview with the author, February 28, 1995.

34. Lehman remembered the phone call, but not the content. Other officers, however, who were privy to the conversation, remember Hardisty's warning to Lehman. Hardisty was later nominated for the best job in the Pacific—CinCPac.

35. Sawyer interviews. See also *Running Critical* by Patrick Tyler. Sawyer later went to work for Lehman, running Sperry Marine, a company Lehman bought in the 1990s.

36. Lehman interviews. *The Commanders* by Woodward, Evans, and Novak.

37. *Storm Center* by Will and Sharon Rogers. See also John Barry and Roger Charles, "Sea of Lies," *Newsweek*, July 13, 1992; also David Evans in *Proceedings*, August 1993.

38. The author repeatedly heard this story during interviews about the change in attitudes among naval officers. This anecdote is also printed in Beatty's "In Harm's Way," *Atlantic*, May 1987.

39. *Newsweek, Proceedings*, and interviews conducted by the author with naval officers familiar with Rogers.

40. Patton interview with the author. Patton said the movie was an accurate depiction of how the system allowed officers like Rogers to advance through the ranks.

41. *Newsweek.*

42. *Storm Center* and *Newsweek.*

43. *Proceedings.*

44. *Proceedings.*

45. *Storm Center.*

46. *Newsweek.*

47. Jay Coupe letter to Allan Ryskind of *Human Events*, March 28, 1989. Coupe served as Admiral Crowe's public affairs officer.

CHAPTER 20

1. Date provided by Captain Bill Harlow, Navy public affairs officer. Garrett would also have another public swearing-in later that year.
2. *The Commanders.*
3. Interviews with four members of Garrett's personal staff.
4. Richard Armitage interviews with the author. Armitage said it was well known in the building that Howard was reporting back to David Addington, who served as Richard Cheney's general counsel.
5. Webb interviews.
6. *Naval Renaissance* by Frederick Hartmann.
7. National Defense Budget Estimates, "The Green Book." Office of the Comptroller of the Department of Defense, March 1994.
8. Armitage interviews. Robin Pierie interview with the author. Pierie today is the assistant secretary of the Navy responsible for military bases. See also the General Accounting Office report "Navy Homeports, Expanded Structure Unnecessary and Costly," June 1991.
9. This section on *Iowa* is based on the Navy's official report into the accident, from *U.S. News & World Report,* April 23, 1990, reported and written by Peter Cary; from interviews with NIS officials, including Ted Gordon, Mac Williams, and Dennis Usrey; and from the August 1991 GAO report "U.S.S. *Iowa* Explosion," Sandia National Laboratories' Final Technical Report, and news clippings.
10. The author interviewed Dennis Usrey several times between 1991 and 1995.
11. Gordon interviews.
12. *U.S. News & World Report.*
13. Smith later retracted this statement, saying he had made it under duress.
14. Armitage interviews.

CHAPTER 21

1. Prueher's curriculum vitae.
2. Prueher was nominated officially as a rear admiral on April 23, 1990.
3. Gwen Dreyer interview with the author, March 17, 1995.
4. These accounts come from Dreyer.
5. Ibid.
6. Ibid.
7. Events based on interviews with Gwen Dreyer, academy officials, the two civilians who recruited her for Annapolis, and news clips. Dreyer insisted on this version of events, but one of the recruiting officers who personally interviewed midshipmen said it was all part of a game and that those who lost would be chained to the urinal.

8. Gwen and Gregory Dreyer interviews.

9. Gwen Dreyer interview.

10. Gwen and Gregory Dreyer interviews.

11. Gregory Dreyer interviews.

12. Scott Harper interview with the author, March 20, 1995.

13. Burke interview. She said there were a number of women in the room, which was filled with 50 percent military and 50 percent civilian. The joke was about FDR inviting Winston Churchill to the White House. During dinner, at which chicken was served, Churchill asked Eleanor Roosevelt to please pass him some more breast. Mrs. Roosevelt responded, "We call it white meat." The next morning before leaving, Churchill had a flower delivered to her room with a note that said "Pin this to your white meat." "It was really quite tame, but totally inappropriate," Burke said.

14. Gregory Dreyer interview.

15. "The Military Reacted to Tailhook, but Was Justice Done?" *San Diego Union-Tribune,* December 26, 1993.

16. Otto Kreisher, Copley News Service, May 24, 1990, the *San Diego Tribune.*

17. Associated Press, *San Diego Union,* June 25, 1990.

18. "Female Midshipmen Face Gender Bias, Reports Say," Marcus Stern, Copley News Service, October 10, 1990.

19. Gordon interviews. Gordon was then judge advocate general of the Navy.

20. Confidential source. Ted Gordon also confirmed the probes into Hill and that Hill was verbally reprimanded.

21. Trost change of command speech, June 30, 1986.

22. As many as fifty flag or general officers had similar alleged violations in the ten years that preceded Garrett, according to a senior member of his staff and others. The number on flag and general officers was compiled from interviews with NIS officers, Defense Department investigators, investigations obtained by the author under the Freedom of Information Act, and interviews with a large number of admirals.

23. Confidential source.

24. Memorandum for the record, February 3, 1993, provided to the author lists the admirals who attended with their wives in 1991 and 1992. In 1991 nine admirals, including Kelso, and five vice admirals all took their wives. In 1992 nine admirals, including Kelso, and four vice admirals attended. All took their wives except Admiral Robert Kelly and Garrett, who also attended that year. Also, according to interviews with investigators and Navy lawyers, including Ted Gordon, the rules say that an admiral's wife may attend an official function at government expense if she takes part in it. But in this case the Navy added a function to make the travel legitimate.

25. *San Diego Union,* August 25, 1990, p. B-7.

26. Declaration of H. Lawrence Garrett III; United States Navy and Marine Corps Court of Military Review, March 31, 1994. Obtained by the author under the Freedom of Information Act.

27. Ensch interviews. Ensch was the commanding officer of the Naval Training Command.
28. Author interviews with civilian and military officials on Garrett's staff.
29. H. Lawrence Garrett III interview with the author, August 24, 1990.
30. Captain Bob Canepa interview with the author, July 13, 1994. Canepa was the chief of staff for Kohn and his predecessor, Vice Admiral Jack Fetterman, who left the job a short time after Garrett's son joined the staff. Fetterman said he remembers Garrett being assigned to his command but didn't pay much attention to it. Fetterman interview with the author, July 19, 1994.
31. Price tag provided by Navy public affairs office, Washington, D.C., March 24, 1995. Some officers in the squadron said the aircraft cost around $60 million.
32. The allegations, which subsequently led to a DoD inspector general investigation and Moore being fired, were contained in a October 28, 1991, memorandum from Captain Ted K. Vanasupa to Marine Corps headquarters. Vanasupa provided the author with a copy. The allegations were also confirmed by Garrett's staff, several Marine fliers interviewed by the author in the VMAQ-2 squadron Moore flew with, and the Pentagon's Inspector General, Derek Vander Schaaf.
33. The only officer to be disciplined, in this case, was Royal Moore.
34. Ted Vanasupa interview with the author; Captain Andrew Engelke interview with the author (both during Christmas 1993). Engelke was part of the training mission, flying another aircraft.
35. Vanasupa memorandum, confirmed by interviews with Engelke. Navy regulations require all mishaps to be investigated regardless of the monetary damages to an airplane.
36. Engelke interview.
37. Ibid. And Vanasupa memorandum.
38. Ibid.
39. The author has reviewed Vanasupa's fitness reports.
40. Author interview with confidential source on Garrett's staff.
41. Krulak letter to Hearney, dated April 10, 1992.

CHAPTER 22

1. Barbara Pope interview with the author, April 4, 1995. Pope, a former aide to Barry Goldwater and an assistant secretary of the Navy under Garrett, said Batjer was one of the few people who really knew Garrett and tried to make him understand that attending the convention was not appropriate. Ted Gordon agreed and confirmed Batjer's opposition to Garrett attending. See also *United States* v. *Commander Thomas R. Miller, Commander Gregory E. Tritt, and Lieutenant David Samples:* Essential Findings and Ruling on Defense Motion to Dismiss, General Court-Martial, United States Navy, Tidewater Judicial Circuit, Norfolk, Virginia. Commonly referred to as the Vest Ruling, this report described how some on Garrett's staff opposed the secretary attending.

2. About four thousand of these were on active duty, many of whom were flown in to Las Vegas at government expense aboard Navy transport planes.

3. McDonnell Douglas sent more than thirty employees, including one of its senior executives, to Tailhook and billed the government about $60,000 for their expenses, including golf outings, tennis tournaments, X-rated movies, and employee salaries. *Los Angeles Times,* October 13, 1993.

4. After Vietnam, the Navy reasoned it would never again fight the type of war in which it parked its carriers and launched deep-penetration strikes. During the war, the Navy operated two types of carriers: attack carriers and antisubmarine warfare carriers. After Vietnam, the Navy reached two conclusions: one, it figured its main enemy was the Soviet navy; and two, it decided to combine the attack and antisub missions into one carrier like *Nimitz.* When it did this, however, it reduced a carrier's strike capabilities because the bombers had to share deck space with antisub aircraft and helos. It also put all of the Navy's focus on high-seas warfare.

5. At the end of the Gulf War, Navy sorties from aircraft carriers numbered nearly 20,000. Navy pilots flew the Hornet on 4,335 sorties; Marine pilots flew the jet on 5,047 sorties. See "The United States Navy in Desert Shield, Desert Storm," Department of the Navy, May 15, 1991. In the plus category, Hornet aircraft were responsible for shooting down two Iraqi MiGs on the first day of the war.

6. *Pentagon Paradox.* The only air kill for the F-14 was an Iraqi helicopter.

7. "Navy's Choice Plane Misses the Target in Combat Ability" by Ed Offley, *Seattle Post Intelligencer,* August 18, 1993. For a detailed account of the Hornet's role in the Persian Gulf War, see *Pentagon Paradox.*

8. Offley.

9. "Navy Carrier Aircraft: Issues and Options," a report by Bert H. Cooper Jr. in the Congressional Research Service, December 16, 1991.

10. Clark interviews. Had the Navy gone ahead with early plans to also use the F-14 as a bomber and fighter, it could have played an important role in the war.

11. Mike Matton interview with the author, December 17, 1993.

12. Ibid.

13. Armitage interviews.

14. "Navy Carrier Aircraft" by Bert H. Cooper Jr. For more detailed reading on the subject, see Cooper's other reports: "A-12 Advanced Tactical Aircraft Program Weapons Facts"; "F/A-18E/F Aircraft Program"; and "AFX Aircraft Program." Cooper has also written extensively on the F-14 Tomcat program.

15. There was a widespread feeling inside the Pentagon that Cheney was scuttling the F-14D program to bail out McDonnell Douglas, the builder of the Hornet, which has been having financial problems. If Cheney canceled the Hornet program, which was now running as high as $60 to $80 billion, the nation's largest defense contractor could be mortally wounded. On the other hand, if Grumman, the maker of the Tomcat, went under, it would not harm the country's industrial base. Grumman eventually merged with Northrop. Vice Admiral Dunleavy, an attack pilot, was pleased with the decision to cancel the F-14D

program. He told Ken Kennedy, a civilian analyst at the CNA, that he didn't like Grumman because it was too arrogant. Ken Kennedy interview with the author, May 16, 1994.

16. Report of Investigation, Department of Defense Inspector General, Defense Criminal Investigative Service, September 20, 1990. Garrett insisted that he did not know about the problems with the A-12.

17. Ibid. On July 7, 1992, a report of investigation that detailed information related to the action of Garrett was referred to the Department of Justice, Public Integrity Section. On September 14, 1993, the Department of Justice closed the investigation, much to the chagrin of the DCIS investigators, who believed Garrett should have been prosecuted.

18. Armitage interviews with the author.

19. Commander John Evans interview with the author, December 20, 1993. Evans, a retired naval aviator, was in the room when Garrett came in. He worked for Al Wise, who owned a small defense firm called Wise Inc. Al Wise was a close friend of Garrett's and in 1991 spent most of the evening with the secretary during his visit to Tailhook '91. See also the Vest Ruling, which stated that Garrett "viewed the female leg shaving to be permissible as conduct between consenting adults." The Vest Ruling said the failure of Navy leadership to stop such antics condoned and contributed to the sexually offensive conduct that later escalated to actual sexual assaults on female attendees.

20. Department of Defense *Tailhook 1991 Report*, Part 2.

21. Ibid.

22. Susan Hallett interview with the author, November 1, 1991.

23. Pope interview.

24. Commander Neil Golightly interview with the author, October 28, 1993.

25. "The United States Navy in Desert Shield, Desert Storm," Department of the Navy, May 15, 1991. While this was the Navy's official record of its role in the Persian Gulf War, it left out critical information that revealed shortcomings in the Navy's massive buildup during the 1980s.

26. The Navy had to purchase eight fast sealift ships from commercial companies and modify them because it had not bought the necessary sealift vessels during its buildup in the 1980s.

27. McCutchen, a photographer with the *San Diego Union-Tribune*, was part of the DoD press pool in the Gulf War. His photo appeared around the world.

28. "The United States Navy in Desert Shield, Desert Storm."

29. Petty Officer Lisa Rodriguez interview with the author, April 26, 1991. Lieutenant Commander Jeff Smallwood, a public affairs officer, confirmed the thirty-six pregnancies on April 26, 1991.

30. This was confirmed by Lieutenant Commander Craig Quigley on August 6, 1991. Howe was not with his men when they went out drinking. But when I called the Navy's public affairs office in Washington, the damage control game began to protect Admiral Howe. Quigley, who was then stationed in Europe, called me in the middle of the night to insist that Admiral Howe did not know

about the incident nor did he have a hand in the discipline that was doled out. This story never made it into the newspaper.

31. This was confirmed by Commander Robert Pritchard, public affairs officer for the Naval Special Warfare Command in Coronado. Still, it never made it into the newspaper.

32. This section on the rhino is based on interviews in 1992 and 1993 with Colonel Mike Fagan, Captain David Prudhomme, Lieutenant Colonel John Bergman, Lieutenant Colonel Cass Howell, and Captain Greg Bonam. All belonged to Marine Tactical Reconnaissance Squadron 3.

33. United States District Court of Nevada, *Paula A. Coughlin*, Plaintiff, v. *Hilton Hotels Corporation*. CV-S-93-44-PMP-RJJ, 1994.

34. Rena Coughlin testimony, September 13, 1994, U.S. District Court of Nevada.

35. *Glamour*, June 1993.

36. Ibid.

37. Unedited transcript of Coughlin's testimony to the Naval Investigative Service.

38. Testimony of Lieutenant Commander Michael Steed, August 15, 1994, for the *Coughlin* v. *Hilton Hotel* lawsuit.

39. Ibid.

40. Thomas interviews.

41. Vest Ruling.

42. Ibid.

43. Kelso denied visiting the hospitality suites at any time during his visit to Tailhook in 1991. The Vest Ruling, however, goes into great detail about how he was in the suites on Friday and Saturday nights. Even so, Kelso argued strenuously that he was not there.

44. Vest Ruling. In a later citation in the ruling, Vest said there were two women who took off their shirts.

45. Diaz had been shaving legs at Tailhook for only two years. Prior to this, a reserve aviator dubbed Dr. Gillette had been doing it for years. He even had a gold-plated razor and a black doctor's bag that he brought to Tailhook, where he would go from room to room, offering his services.

46. Kelso denied seeing any lurid behavior, including leg shaving. However, the Vest Ruling contradicted this.

47. Sally Spears interview with the author, March 25, 1995. Spears was Hultgreen's mother. The author also interviewed Hultgreen at Miramar before she died in October 1994.

48. Ibid.

49. Since Tailhook first broke, Kelso has maintained he saw no licentious behavior or sexual assaults.

50. Bob Clement interview with the author, July 27, 1992.

51. Garrett said in public statements that he could not recall if he went inside or not.

52. Defense Department *Tailhook 1991 Report*, Part 2. Prudhomme said this was impossible, that he had nailed the dildo onto the mural.

53. This section is drawn from unedited transcripts of Coughlin's interviews with the NIS and the Navy inspector general, Coughlin's personal letter to Vice Admiral Dunleavy, and, finally, dozens of interviews with Coughlin in 1991 and 1992.

54. This number has become somewhat controversial and not entirely accurate. The Defense Department inspector general's report said that eighty-three women and seven men had been sexually assaulted in some fashion. But many of the women whom investigators said were victims told them that they did not want to be listed that way. For example, Hultgreen said that she had taken care of the incident and to be listed as a victim would be demeaning. But according to the Uniform Code of Military Justice, it is against the law for an officer to fondle a woman in public, regardless if she consents to it.

55. Tailhook report.

CHAPTER 23

1. At the time, I worked for the *San Diego Union*, which was sister paper of the *Tribune*. Both papers, which are owned by Copley Publishing Co., later merged into the *Union-Tribune*. This Navy captain remains a confidential source.

2. I knew this already because I had written a story on Garrett's powerful speech that was published on September 14, 1991. Garrett's public affairs officer, Commander Jeff Zakem (later promoted to captain), provided a copy of the speech to me. At this point I had no idea that the assaults had taken place or about the wild side of Tailhook. The Navy always pointed out the good side of the convention and left out the seamy details. The two civilian women were Marie Weston and Lisa Reagan. They were the first two women to file a complaint with authorities about the Gauntlet.

3. Vest Ruling.

4. Matton interviews.

5. Pope interview. Also, Ted Gordon, the Navy's judge advocate general, said no extra attention was being given to Coughlin's case. In fact, he said it was so routine that it was being handled out of Pax River and not Washington, where high-profile cases are handled. Also, the NIS routinely advises the secretary and the undersecretary on crimes it thinks are serious. Garrett learned a short while after the fact, which wasn't that unusual, but Howard, who was usually told immediately, learned about the Coughlin complaint only when my story was about to go to press.

6. Matton interviews.

7. *Congressional Record*, October 29, 1991. John McCain interview with the author, October 29, 1991. McCain apparently had been tipped off on Monday about the Ludwig letter and that the media was going to print it on Tuesday.

8. Matton interviews.

9. Captain Jeff Zakem interviews with the author. The author had perhaps hun-

dreds of conversations with Zakem between 1990 and 1992. Other members of Garrett's staff also relayed this story to the author.

10. Gordon interviews.

11. October 29, 1991, letter from Garrett to Ludwig.

12. Although Boorda recommended that Snyder be disciplined, Vice Admiral Ronald J. Zlatoper, who replaced Boorda, carried it out.

13. Snyder memorandum to Boorda, November 15, 1991, subject: "Request for Removal from Fiscal Year 1992 Promotion List to Rear Admiral," lower half.

14. Memorandum for chief of naval personnel, from Captain Robert Parkinson, November 12, 1991. Unedited copy obtained by the author. Parkinson's comments come from this transcript, as well as interviews with members of Snyder's staff, both male and female.

15. Ibid.

16. Snyder letter to Dunleavy, October 2, 1991. The author also has Coughlin's letter to Dunleavy, which did not mention that Snyder was ignoring her.

17. In her first interview with the Naval Investigative Service, on October 11, 1991, Coughlin said she was extremely upset about her assault and reported it to Parkinson and "ultimately to RADM Snyder upon his return to Patuxent River." In this NIS interview, and a second one later that day, Coughlin made no mention of telling Snyder at breakfast what had happened to her. Only after the case became public in the *Union-Tribune* did Coughlin add Snyder to her version of events. On November 1, 1991, she told NIS agent Elizabeth A. Iorio that Snyder had rejected her pleas. "I told Admiral Snyder these guys started grabbing at me and grabbing my rear, they were so out of line, just completely out of line, and they knew I was an admiral's aide. . . . I told him I just walked down the hall and these guys went to town on me . . . it was really bad. I told him again that these guys were completely out of line, I had to kick and fight and bite to get out of there, that I bit the crap out of one guy." Snyder never retreated from his initial statement to the NIS that he first learned about the assault on Thursday, September 19, 1991, upon his return to Pax River. The author obtained all of Coughlin's and Snyder's unedited sworn statements to the NIS and the Navy inspector general. Both Snyder and Coughlin also had witnesses to support their side of the story. Coughlin's friend, Lieutenant Scott Wilson, with whom she stayed in Las Vegas, corroborated her statements. But Commander Daniel Bringle was at the breakfast table, too, and told the author in an interview that "the red flag" would have shot up if he'd heard what Coughlin had allegedly said.

Finally, during an interview in San Diego with the author, Coughlin said, "I guess I didn't tell him enough to make him realize what really happened to me." Coughlin later denied saying this. In the end it comes down to Coughlin's word versus Snyder's. Unfortunately, the truth may never be known.

18. Results of interview between agents with the office of the naval inspector general and Coughlin, November 14, 1991. Unedited transcript obtained by the author.

19. Gordon interviews.

20. Garrett accused me of printing lies in this article and said that I was being used by these officers. Telephone conversation with the author, March 30, 1995. Garrett and Snyder found out about the assaults within about one week of each other. Dunleavy knew about the Gauntlet almost immediately.

21. Norm Gandia interviews, April 27, 1992.

22. Memorandum for the secretary of the Navy: "Response to DODIG Report on Tailhook '91, Part I, October 19, 1992," from Rear Admiral George Davis. Davis claimed he interviewed eight flag officers but added that he did not think it necessary to question all thirty admirals who attended Tailhook.

23. Tailhook meetings, list prepared by Garrett's office on who attended each meeting. The first Tailhook task force met on November 8, 1991. The last was on June 12, 1992. This list was obtained by the author. The first time Garrett was involved was on December 2 with Dunleavy and retired Vice Admiral Dick Houser, to discuss the Navy's future with the Tailhook Association. He met again on January 7, 1992, with the entire task force.

24. Williams interviews.

25. The author called Bonam and got his answering machine.

26. Williams said that Bonam also passed a civilian-administered polygraph examination.

27. Pope interview.

28. Rear Admiral Brent Baker interview with the author, April 29, 1992.

29. Dan Howard interview with the author, April 29, 1995.

30. Barbara Boxer interview with the author, May 11, 1992. Boxer's office provided the author a copy of her letter to Representative Beverly Byron, chairwoman of the Personnel and Compensation Subcommittee.

31. This message, provided to the author by a female Marine, was sent by Marine General Royal Moore, who had not yet been fired. The woman who sent it said: "I felt particularly wounded by the use of the word 'prestigious.' I was under the impression that our guiltless secretary of the Navy had officially disassociated the naval services from the Tailhook Association and its activities. Yet here we find the U.S. Marine Corps, on government time and at government expense, soliciting nominations. Ah, well, life goes on, and nothing much changes."

32. Pat Schroeder interview with the author, May 13, 1992.

33. Dan Buck interview with the author, May 22, 1993.

34. May 28, 1992, letter from Nunn and Warner.

35. Pope interviews. Garrett has also confirmed this.

36. Memorandum for the judge advocate general of the Navy, May 14, 1992. Action for accountability following the Tailhook Association Convention.

37. Gordon interviews.

38. Memorandum for deputy inspector general, May 8, 1992: "Review of Report of Investigation by the Naval Investigative Service in re '1991 Tailhook Symposium.'" Written by Don Mancuso, assistant inspector general for investigations, Department of Defense.

39. Memorandum for the chief of naval operations and commandant of the Marine

Corps, June 2, 1992: "Behavior and Attitudes Towards Women." Written by H. Lawrence Garrett III.

40. Pope interview.
41. June 2 memorandum.
42. Gordon interviews. Also, interviews with Williams and Howard.
43. Garrett statement during the Tailhook disciplinary hearings held in Norfolk, Virginia.
44. Questions to answers asked by the author, provided on June 9, 1992, by the Navy news desk. Although Garrett at first denied going into the suites and seeing any misbehavior, he later said under oath in a military court that "at that time, to the best of my recollection, in 1991, I had not been in that [rhino] suite." Still further, he said he had witnessed leg shaving but did not think it was improper. At first he said he had seen nothing.
45. Vest Ruling.
46. Ibid. Mac Williams denied that he had taken part in keeping the missing pages from senior Navy officials. See "Supplemental Statement of Rear Adm. D. M. Williams Jr. Concerning Department of Defense Inspector General Report of Investigation on Tailhook '91—Part 1."
47. Memorandum for the inspector general of the Department of Defense, June 18, 1992: "Tailhook Investigation."
48. General Brent Scowcroft interview with the author, April 20, 1993.
49. I knew Monday afternoon, June 22, that Coughlin was going public. I got a call from a friend at ABC News. "Paula is going to be interviewed by Peter Jennings on Wednesday for a two-part segment," my friend said.

"Are you sure?"

"Yeah. She has also promised to do an interview with John Lancaster of The Washington Post on Tuesday."

I hung up, then dialed Coughlin at home in Virginia. Knowing of her plans for Tuesday at the Post and Wednesday at ABC News, I pushed the issue. "I think we should do your story now in my paper. Let's do it Tuesday or Tuesday night."

Coughlin said she couldn't because she had to study all day and all night on Tuesday. Wednesday was a big day, she said. It was a day that she planned to take tests to requalify for helicopter duty. She said nothing about Lancaster or Jennings.

Although Coughlin had promised to come out in the Union-Tribune, my editor Todd Merriman and I knew that we could not compete with the Post or ABC News, so we were not that upset over losing an important story. Besides, I had broken the story, and we had led the journalist pack for nearly a year, breaking all of the important stories. I had pages of notes from scores of interviews with Coughlin. We could have easily identified her by name before the Post or ABC did, but we didn't. I had promised not to identify her until she said okay. She may have lied to me, but I was not about to break my word as a journalist.

50. I broke the story in the *Union-Tribune* based on interviews with enlisted sailors who knew Lawrence. Once I had the information, Navy public affairs officers confirmed the story. Later I got the entire file under the Freedom of Information Act.
51. Canepa interview.
52. Matton interviews. Boorda had declined to be interviewed about his involvement in this case. However, through a spokesman he said that he had not made the decision to transfer Lawrence back to Washington. He said, "BUPERS [the Bureau of Personnel, which he commanded] made the decision to transfer him."
53. Garrett letter to Mike Suessman, August 25, 1992.
54. Commander Deborah Burnette interview with the author, March 17, 1995. Burnette was Kelso's main public affairs officer.
55. Memorandum for the deputy inspector general, Department of Defense, October 22, 1992: "Response to Report of Investigation: Tailhook '91—Part 1, Review of the Navy Investigations," written by Sean O'Keefe.

CHAPTER 24

1. December 2, 1992, unclassified message to Frank Kelso, Admiral Robert Kelly, and Vice Admiral Edwin Kohn, obtained by the author.
2. Commander David Tyler interview with the author, August 13, 1992.
3. Clausen interviews.
4. Admiral Robert Kelly interview with the editorial board of the *San Diego Union-Tribune*, published July 26, 1992.
5. Author interviews with female sailors and officers at Miramar, North Island, Oceania, Pax River, and the Pentagon.
6. Author interviews with aviators at Miramar, North Island, El Toro, Lemoore, Cecil Field, Oceania, and the Pentagon.
7. *San Diego Union-Tribune*, August 13, 1992.
8. Bobbie Carleton interview with the author, July 1, 1992. Carleton is now retired from the Navy.
9. Pat Schroeder interview with the author, July 1, 1992. After Kelso informed her what had happened, Schroeder's staff called me with news of the event. I made an inquiry to AirPac, which forced the Navy to release a statement.
10. Ibid.
11. Admiral Robert Kelly interview with the author, August 2, 1994.
12. Author interview with a captain on Kelly's staff, July 28, 1993.
13. Kelly maintained his innocence in dozens of pages of answers to my questions prepared by his public affairs officer, Captain Tom Jurkowsky, on September 29, 1992. The answers basically said two things: one, Kelly was not doing anything out of the ordinary; and two, his stewards, airplane rights, and other perks were permitted by Department of Defense regulations. The answers, when

reviewed by the legal experts in the secretary's office, raised more questions about Kelly's behavior. A story about Kelly's abuses never materialized because Jurkowsky was able to talk me out of writing it. He later said the story was legitimate.

14. Commander Robert Clement letter to chief of naval personnel, August 21, 1992.
15. *San Diego Union-Tribune* editorial board, July 26, 1992.
16. Commander David Tyler letter to Vice Admiral Edwin Kohn, with enclosures, August 25, 1992.
17. Kelly interview with the author.
18. Pease called me with the story, and I almost wrote a piece for the *Union-Tribune* until another source on O'Keefe's staff told me about the ruse.
19. Gordon interviews.
20. Paula Coughlin telephoned me, saying McCain wanted her to write a letter supporting his views on women in the military. She wanted to know if I thought it was okay, because she was concerned that it might cause her trouble with the brass.
21. The Schindler case was widely reported in the media. For perhaps the best summation, see "The Accidental Martyr" by Chip Brown, *Esquire,* December 1993.
22. *San Diego Union-Tribune,* February 24, 1993.
23. Vest Ruling.
24. Don Mancuso interview with the author, April 23, 1993.
25. See a series of stories I wrote in May 1991 for the *Union-Tribune* about the *Guardfish,* a nuclear-powered submarine that left port with a faulty drain pump and nearly sank off the coast of San Diego as a result.
26. There are several documents pertaining to Hultgreen's record: the Navy's JAG Manual investigation; a secret mishap investigation report, which was obtained by the author; and Hultgreen's own flight records, gathered by the Center for Military Readiness, a conservative organization run by Elaine Donnelly, a former member of President Bush's commission that studied whether the ban preventing women from serving in combat should be lifted. For perspective, see a series of articles by Robert Caldwell published in the *Union-Tribune* in March and May of 1995.
27. Otto Kreisher, Copley News Service, July 13, 1993.
28. Jeff Gerth, *The New York Times,* July 22, 1994.
29. Ibid.
30. Ibid.
31. "Report of Investigation, Naval Inspector General," January 20, 1994.
32. Usrey interviews.
33. Admiral Frank Kelso interview with the author, October 1, 1993.

CHAPTER 25

1. "Can Mike Boorda Salvage the Navy?" by Tom Philpot, *The Washingtonian*, February 1995.
2. Ibid.
3. Tom Bowman, *The Baltimore Sun*, May 29, 1996.
4. *Congressional Record*, March 26, 1996, p. S2846.
5. Ibid.
6. Secretary of the Navy Instruction 1520.7E requires eligible candidates to have served at least two years but not more than six years in the Navy. The instruction says these requirements cannot be waived. If Boorda's son had entered with the normal freshman class in the fall, he would have exceeded the six-year requirement.
7. Speech made by Jim Webb, April 25, 1996, at the annual Naval Institute Annual Conference. See also Tom Bowman, *The Baltimore Sun*, April 26, 1996, p. 3A.
8. "The Navy Stonewalled Me," David Durenberger letter to *The Wall Street Journal*, June 16, 1996.
9. Ibid.
10. Ibid.
11. *The Washingtonian*, February 1995.
12. Captain Steve Claussen interviews with the author. Claussen identified the newspaper as *The Los Angeles Times*, which did not use the information.
13. Commander Stephen Pietropaoli, a Navy spokesman, even bragged to H. G. Reza of the *Los Angeles Times* that he had kept the *Boston Globe* and *The Washington Post* from publishing stories. Pietropaoli had himself misled reporters, telling two journalists that he did not have the authority to read the report, while informing two others that he had indeed read it. Pietropaoli adamantly denies saying he had ever read the report.
14. One commanding officer of a squadron at Miramar sent an F-14D across country to fly a friend back to San Diego for a change of command ceremony. Afterward, the F-14D returned the officer to the East Coast, then flew back to Miramar. The Navy tallied up the cost at approximately $64,000. A round-trip commercial airline ticket, at a military rate, would have been under $500. Previous to that, two aviators were competing to be the first to fly the Tomcat more than 2,000 hours. One officer, now a rear admiral, had racked up close to 2,000 hours under normal flight operations. To overcome this lead, the second pilot stayed aloft on a rigorous cross-country schedule that would make him the winner. His reward was a small plaque. The taxpayers won a bill for more than $1 million.
15. Remarks by Admiral Jeremy M. Boorda in a Defense Department briefing, April 12, 1996.
16. Ibid.
17. The first of two GAO reports was a controversial draft titled: "Navy Aviation,

Decision to Procure F/A-18E/F Should Be Reconsidered," March 1996. The second and final report was titled: "Navy Aviation, F/A-18E/F Will Provide Marginal Operational Improvement at High Cost." It was dated June 1996.

18. *Inside the Navy*, Vol. 7, No. 45, November 7, 1994. Boorda denied that he wanted to drive up commitments to boost the Navy budget.

19. Captain Everett Greene, interview with the author.

20. Affidavit of Captain Donald Robert Hess, September 8, 1995, in the Navy's court-martial case against Greene. Hess resolved the case informally.

21. Affidavit of Captain David M. Hardy, September 6, 1995; *United States* v. *Everett L. Greene*, General Court-martial, United States Navy Atlantic Judicial Circuit.

22. Stanley Arthur, interview with the author, July 1996.

23. Hess affidavit.

24. Memorandum for the Vice Chief of Naval Operations, April 6, 1995, from D. M. Bennett, inspector general.

25. Author interview with a defense attorney in the case, April 27, 1996.

26. Admiral Charles Larson on *NBC Today* with Katie Couric, April 18, 1996.

27. Ibid.

28. *The Washington Post*.

29. *Daniel Paul Ensley* v. *Honorable John Dalton* in the United States District Court for the Eastern District of Virginia, Civil Action 96-687-A.

30. The anonymous writer turned out to be Commander John Carey, who five months earlier had been relieved of command of the *Curtis Wilbur*, a guided missile destroyer. See Patrick J. Sloyan, *Newsday*, May 23, 1996.

31. *The New Yorker*, September 16, 1996.

32. Webb called me on September 22, 1996, telling me of his concerns. He asked me if I had heard anything about Boorda and what he might say. I said I would poke around and call him back if I heard anything. I later told him that his information was erroneous.

33. James Webb's speech, Naval Institute Annual Conference, April 25, 1996.

34. "Death Stuns Boorda's Friend Here," *St. Louis Post-Dispatch*, May 17, 1996.

35. Jonathan Alter, "Beneath the Waves," *Newsweek*, May 27, 1996.

INDEX

PHOTO CREDITS